D0215909

An Unofficial Companion to the Novels of Terry Pratchett

An Unofficial Companion to the Novels of Terry Pratchett

Edited by Andrew M. Butler

Greenwood World Publishing
Oxford / Westport, Connecticut
2007

First published in 2007 by Greenwood World Publishing

1 2 3 4 5 6 7 8 9 10

Greenwood World Publishing
Wilkinson House
Jordan Hill
Oxford OX2 8EJ
An imprint of Greenwood Publishing Group, Inc
www.greenwood.com

British Library Cataloguing-in-Publication Data: a catalogue record for this book is available from the British Library

Library of Congress Cataloging-in-Publication Data

An unofficial companion to the novels of Terry Pratchett / edited by Andrew M. Butler.
p. cm.
Includes bibliographical references and index.
ISBN-13: 978-1-84645-001-3 (alk. paper)
1. Pratchett, Terry–Encyclopedias. I. Butler, Andrew M.
PR6066.R34Z93 2008
823'.914–dc22

2007040889

ISBN 978-1-84645-001-3 (hardback)
ISBN 978-1-84645-043-3 (paperback)

Designed by Fraser Muggeridge studio
Typeset by TexTech
Printed and bound by South China Printing Company

Contents

To Andy Sawyer, a Librarian who likes to say 'Oook' (but in a nice way), and in memory of Alice, who was never adulterated.

Acknowledgements

I'd like to take the chance to thank the contributors for their patience through the process of producing this volume and regret the absence of a number of people whose expertise and knowledge is manifest throughout the project but who were unable to contribute directly – in particularly contributors to *Terry Pratchett: Guilty of Literature*. I would like to thank (again) Terry Pratchett and Colin Smythe, without whom there would be nothing to engage with. I have drawn heavily on Colin Smythe's 'A Checklist of Editions of Terry Pratchett's Novels, Shorter Writings and Related Publications' and 'Reviews of Terry Pratchett's Works' (© 2007 Colin Smythe) both for fact checking and adding to the level of detail in this book, especially on publication dates, print runs, editions, reprints, foreign editions and omnibi. It is much richer in detail as a result; any errors are obviously my responsibility. Much gratitude is due to him for his diligence over the years. Andy Sawyer, librarian of the Science Fiction Foundation Collection at the University of Liverpool, has answered a large number of queries for me and has supplied some of the materials I have used. Simon Mason has been an infinitely patient editor at Greenwood. Finally there is my safety net to acknowledge – as always and forever Paul, Mitch, Elizabeth and Colin, but also all my comrades from the Doves, past and present. They know who they are, and sometimes tell me who I am.

List of Entries

Guide to Related Topics

Adaptations

Animation
The Art of Discworld
Audio Books
Briggs, Stephen
Calendars
Comics
Computer Games
Cosgrove Hall
Diaries
The Discworld Almanac
The Discworld Companion
Games
Graphic Novels
Greenslade, Dave
Guards! Guards! (Comic Book Adaptation)
Higgins, Graham
Hogfather (Television Adaptation)
Johnny and the Bomb (Television Adaptation)
Johnny and the Dead (Television Adaptation)
Kidby, Paul
Kirby, Josh
Langford, David
Mort: A Discworld Big Comic
Music
Musicals
Pearson, Bernard
Plays
Quizbooks
Radio
Soul Music From Terry Pratchett's Discworld (Television Adaptation)
Television
Terry Pratchett's The Colour of Magic: The Graphic Novel
Terry Pratchett's The Light Fantastic: The Graphic Novel
Theatre
Troll Bridge (Film Adaptation)
Truckers (Television Adaptation)
The Unseen University Cut-Out Book
Wyrd Sisters From Terry Pratchett's Discworld (Television Adaptation)

The Bromeliad

The Abbot
Arnold Bros (est. 1905)
Audio Books
Diggers
Grimma
Haberdasheri, Angalo de
Icatessen, Dorcas del
Masklin
Nisodemus
Truckers
Truckers (Television Adaptation)
Wings

Characters – Discworld

A'Tuin, The Great
Aching, Tiffany
Archchancellors
Brutha
Celyn, Imp Y
Chriek, Otto
City Watch
Cohen the Barbarian, Genghiz
Coin
Colon, Sergeant Frederick
Cuddy
Cutwell, Igneous
Death
Death of Rats
Detritus
Dibbler, C[ut-]M[y-]O[wn-]T[hroat]
Flitworth, Miss Renata
The Fool, Later King Verence II
Garlick, Magrat
Goodmountain, Mr Gunilla
Greebo
Heroes
The Hogfather
Hollow, Desiderata
Hwel
Igor
Ironfoundersson, Carrot
The Librarian
Lipwig, Moist von
Littlebottom, Cheery
Luggage, The
Lu-Tze
Malich, Albert[o]
Nitt, Agnes
Nobbs, Cecil Wormsborough St. John (Nobby)
Ogg, Nanny Gytha
The Ogg Family
Om
Perks, Polly
Plinge, Walter
Quirm, Leonard of
Ramkin, Lady Sybil
Ridcully, Mustrum
Rincewind the Wizzard

Smith, Esk[arina]
Stibbons, Ponder
Sto Helit, Mort[imer]
Sto Helit, Susan
Sto Helit, Ysabell
Sto Lat, Princess, later Queen Keli of
Thursley, Eric
Tomjon
Trymon, Ymper
Tugelbend, Victor
Twoflower
Überwald, Angua Delphine von
Vampires
Verence I
Verence II
Vetinari, Patrician Havelock
Vimes, His Grace, the Duke of Ankh, Commander Sir Samuel
Vorbis
Weatherwax, Granny Esmerelda
Weatherwax, Lily
Whitlow, Mrs
Witches
Wizards
Worde, William de

Characters – Non-Discworld

The Abbot
Arad, Kin
Crowley, Anthony J.
Culaina
Grimma
Haberdasheri, Angalo de
Heroes
Icatessen, Dorcas del
Kirsty
Masklin
Maxwell, Johnny
Nisodemus
Sabalos, Dom[inickdaniel]
Tachyon, Mrs
The Thing
Yo-Less
Young, Adam

Children's Fiction

Aching, Tiffany
Audio Books
The Amazing Maurice and his Educated Rodents
The Bromeliad
The Carpet People
Children in the Discworld series
Children's Fiction
Diggers
A Hat Full of Sky
Heroes
Johnny and the Bomb
Johnny and the Bomb (Television Adaptation)
Johnny and the Dead
Johnny and the Dead (Television Adaptation)
Johnny Maxwell Trilogy
Kirsty
Masklin
Maxwell, Johnny
Nisodemus
Only You Can Save Mankind
Tachyon, Mrs
The Thing
Truckers
Truckers (Television Adaptation)
'Turntables of the Night'
The Wee Free Men: A Story of Discworld
Where's My Cow?
Wings
Wintersmith
Witches
Yo-Less
Young, Adam

Collaborators

Briggs, Stephen
Cohen, Jack
Cosgrove Hall
Gaiman, Neil
Greenslade, Dave
Hannan, Tina
Higgins, Graham
Langford, David
Pearson, Bernard
Smythe, Colin
Stewart, Ian

Comics and Artists

Comics
Guards! Guards! (Comic Book Adaptation)
Higgins, Graham
Jolliffe, Gray
Kidby, Paul
Kirby, Josh
Mort: A Discworld Big Comic
Player, Stephen
Terry Pratchett's The Colour of Magic: The Graphic Novel
Terry Pratchett's The Light Fantastic: The Graphic Novel
The Unadulterated Cat: A Campaign For Real Cats
The Unseen University Cut-Out Book
Wyatt, David

Discworld Books and Stories

The Amazing Maurice and his Educated Rodents
Carpe Jugulum
'A Collegiate Casting Out of Devilish Devices'
The Colour of Magic
'Death and What Comes Next'
The Discworld Almanac
The Discworld Companion
Equal Rites
Eric
Feet of Clay
The Fifth Elephant
Going Postal
Guards! Guards!
Guards! Guards! (Comic Book Adaptation)
A Hat Full of Sky
Hogfather
Interesting Times
Jingo
Kidby, Paul
Kirby, Josh
Langford, David
The Last Continent
The Last Hero: A Discworld Fable
The Light Fantastic
Lords and Ladies
Maskerade
Men At Arms
Monstrous Regiment
Mort
Mort: A Discworld Big Comic
Moving Pictures
Nanny Ogg's Cookbook
Night Watch
*Once More * With Footnotes*
Pyramids (The Book of Going Forth)
Quizbooks
Reaper Man
The Science of Discworld
The Science of Discworld II: The Globe
The Science of Discworld III: Darwin's Watch
'The Sea and Little Fishes'
Small Gods
Soul Music
Sourcery
Terry Pratchett's The Colour of Magic: The Graphic Novel
Terry Pratchett's The Light Fantastic: The Graphic Novel
'Theatre of Cruelty'
Thief of Time
'Thud – A Historical Perspective'
Thud!
'Troll Bridge'
The Truth
The Unseen University Cut-Out Book
The Wee Free Men: A Story of Discworld
Where's My Cow?
Wintersmith
Witches Abroad
Wyrd Sisters

Fan Culture

Conventions
Fandom, Fans and Fan Clubs
Websites

Genres

Carry-On Films
City Watch
Comedy and Humour
Comics
Detective and Noir Fiction and Films
Fairy Tales
Fantasy
Greek Mythology
Hollywood Comedy
Hollywood Films
Musicals
Narrative
Opera
Parody
Pop Music
Science Fiction

Influences

Adams, Douglas
Carry-On Films
Comedy and Humour
Detective and Noir Fiction and Films
Fairy Tales
Fantasy
Gormenghast
Greek Mythology
Greek Philosophy
Hollywood Comedy
Hollywood Films
Leiber, Fritz
Music Hall
Musicals
Pop Music
Science Fiction
Sellar, W[alter] C[arruthers] and Yeatman, R[obert] J[ulian]
Shakespeare, William
Sheckley, Robert
Tolkien, J[ohn] R[onald] R[euel]
Vampires

Witches
Wizards
Wodehouse, P[elham] G[renville]

Johnny Maxwell Trilogy

Audio Books
Blackbury
Heroes
Johnny and the Bomb
Johnny and the Bomb (Television Adaptation)
Johnny and the Dead
Johnny and the Dead (Television Adaptation)
Johnny Maxwell Trilogy
Kirsty
Maxwell, Johnny
Only You Can Save Mankind
Science Fiction

Locations – Fictional

Agatean Empire
Ankh-Morpork
Arnold Bros (est. 1905)
Bad Ass
Bes Pelargic
Blackbury
The Broken Drum
Counterweight Continent
Death's Domain
Discworld
Djelibeybi
Dungeon Dimensions
Ephebe
Genua
The Hub
Klatch
Lancre
Libraries
Llamedos
L-Space
The Mended Drum
Omnia
Sto Helit
Sto Lat
Tsort
Überwald
Unseen University
Widdershins
XXXX

Locations – Real

Arabic Societies
Australia
China
Egypt
Libraries

Maps

Briggs, Stephen
Death's Domain
The Discworld Mapp
Kidby, Paul
Player, Stephen
The Streets of Ankh-Morpork
A Tourist Guide To Lancre

Merchandising

Audio Books
Briggs, Stephen
Clarecraft
Comics
Computer Games
Death's Domain
Diaries
The Discworld Almanac
The Discworld Mapp
Games
Guards! Guards! (Comic Book Adaptation)
Kirby, Josh
Langford, David
Magazines
Nanny Ogg's Cookbook
Pearson, Bernard
Player, Stephen
Plays
Publishers
Quizbooks
The Science of Discworld
The Science of Discworld II: The Globe
The Science of Discworld III: Darwin's Watch
The Streets of Ankh-Morpork
Terry Pratchett's The Colour of Magic: The Graphic Novel
Terry Pratchett's The Light Fantastic: The Graphic Novel
'Thud – A Historical Perspective'
A Tourist Guide To Lancre
The Unadulterated Cat: A Campaign For Real Cats
Websites

Parodic Sources

Arabic Societies
China
Comedy and Humour
Detective and Noir Fiction and Films
Egypt
Fairy Tales

Fantasy
Games
Gormenghast
Greek Mythology
Heroes
Hollywood Comedy
Hollywood Films
Leiber, Fritz
Music Hall
Musicals
Narrative
Opera
Parody
Politics
Pop Music
Racism
Religion
Science Fiction
Sellar
Shakespeare, William
Sheckley, Robert
Technology
Tolkien, J[ohn] R[onald] R[euel]
Vampires
War
Witches
Wizards

Short Stories

'20p With Envelope and Seasonal Greeting'
'A Collegiate Casting Out of Devilish Devices'
'Death and What Comes Next'
'Final Reward'
'FTB'
'The Hades Business'
'History in the Faking'
'Hollywood Chickens'
'#ifdefDEBUG + "world/enough" + "time"'
'Incubust'
'Night Dweller'
'Once And Future'
'The Sea and Little Fishes'
'Theatre of Cruelty'
'Thud – A Historical Perspective'
'Troll Bridge'
'Turntables of the Night'

Species

Cats
Dogs
Dwarfs
Dragons
Elephants
Elves
Igors
Orangutans
Trolls
Vampires
Werewolves

Themes

Comedy and Humour
Coming of Age
Drink
Feminism
Food
Games
Greek Mythology
Greek Philosophy
Heroes
History
Hollywood Comedy
Hollywood Films
Libraries
Magic
Narrative
Opera
Parody
Politics
Pop Music
Power
Racism
Religion
Sexism
Stratified Societies
Technology
The Trousers of Time
Vampires
War
Witches
Wizards

White Knowledge

Cats
Detective and Noir Fiction and Films
Dogs
Dwarfs
Elves
Greek Mythology
Greek Philosophy
History
Hollywood Comedy
Hollywood Films
Libraries
Music Hall
Musicals
Opera
Orangutans
Shakespeare, William
Trolls
Werewolves

Introduction

Since 1982, Terry Pratchett has been writing novels set on the Discworld, a flat world bathed in magic, resting on the backs of four elephants, themselves stood upon top of a turtle, the Great A'Tuin, which is swimming through space. These novels have brought pleasure to millions. He is now the number two living British novelist in terms of sales, beaten only by J.K. Rowling and her seven novels featuring the child wizard-in-training Harry Potter. This best-selling status has led some reviewers to be rather prejudiced against his work, dismissing it with much of the rest of fantasy, the genre to which most of his novels clearly belong. The fact that the novels are also comedies does not help their critical reputation, as to take them seriously might be to miss or spoil the jokes, and to appear too po-faced.

Terry Pratchett dusting the Great A'Tuin at his home near Salisbury, Wiltshire, UK.

There have been a number of attempts to critique his work, but Pratchett remains ambivalent about reviewers, critics and academic writers, even though in most cases they (we) are dedicated and loyal readers of his work. *Terry Pratchett: Guilty of Literature* (2001, 2004) brought together revised versions of essays by a leading science fiction critic, John Clute, and myself, along with a number of new essays, under the editorship of Edward James, Farah Mendlesohn and I. This was nominated for a Hugo Award for Best Related Work (see the entry on Conventions in the main part of this book). In his forewords to both the editions of *Guilty of Literature*, David Langford describes his attempt to produce a pamphlet about Pratchett for a series of editors for the 'Writers and their Work' series published by the British Council, before the project finally sank without trace. Pratchett was never quite respectable enough. But there have been other articles, including some in academic journals, a section of reprints in *Contemporary Literary Criticism* (2005) and various B.A., M.A. and Ph.D. theses.

Terry Pratchett with dragon in his home office.

The book you are reading is now a companion to his work, not just to the Discworld novels (and stories), but to his other fiction as well. It is intended to appeal both to readers who are relatively new to his works and to his most dedicated readers or fans. It offers entries on each of his books, major and recurring characters, locations, spin-offs and adaptations in various media, sources and influences, collaborators and other areas of interest, which could be broadly thought of as themes. It also contains a certain amount of 'white knowledge', the sort of general knowledge that each of us may pick up on a topic, which we have always known but have not consciously learned, and which Pratchett uses as a springboard for much of his comedy. *Pyramids* (1989), for example, is sort of about Egypt, an Egypt we have pieced together from memories of school lessons and various Hollywood movies featuring mummies and Cleopatra.

A Short Biography of Terry Pratchett

Terence David John Pratchett was born on 28 April 1948 near Beaconsfield, a town between High Wycombe and Gerrards Cross, in Buckinghamshire. He was the only child of David and Eileen Pratchett, an engineer and secretary respectively. He attended Holspur School on Cherry Tree Lane in the outskirts of Beaconsfield, off what is now the M40 corridor. Not particularly happy there, he was put into a stream of pupils thought unlikely to pass the Eleven Plus, an examination which would determine whether he could go onto a grammar school or would have to go to a secondary modern. However, someone gave him a copy of *The Wind in the Willows* (1908) by Kenneth Grahame (1859–1932), which sparked a lifelong love of reading. Joining Beaconsfield County Library, he worked his way through many books, both fiction and non-fiction, for children and adults. In class, his abilities improved, and his marks got better. By the age of ten he was working in the library on Saturdays.

Pratchett did pass the Eleven Plus, but elected not to go to any of the grammar schools in the area – such as the Royal Grammar School, High Wycombe – instead attending High Wycombe Technical School (which is now the John Hampden Grammar School), which offered more practical courses, as well as the more traditional curriculum. Again his interest in formal education dipped, but he did become interested in Greek mythology and history, being taught history by Stan Betteridge, a name shared with a character in *The Last Hero*. A Mr Stibbon taught technology (compare Ponder Stibbons) and Harry Ward was the headmaster and a mathematics teacher – perhaps an inspiration for Evil Harry.

At some point, Pratchett discovered science fiction and began writing it; 'The Hades Business' was written at school when he was thirteen. It was thought to be good enough to be published in the school magazine and he then sold it to *Science Fantasy* 60 (August 1963). A British magazine founded in 1950 and originally edited by Walter Gillings (1912–1979), by then *Science Fantasy* was edited by John Carnell (1912–1972), who also edited the magazine *New Worlds*. Pratchett was still only fifteen. The issue also included an appreciation of Mervyn Peake (1911–1968), author of the Gormenghast books, by writer Michael Moorcock (b.1939) and 'The Dolphin and the Deep' by Thomas Burnett Swann (1928–1976). Pratchett bought a typewriter with his fee, and his mother paid for touch-typing lessons. The story was then reprinted in *The Unfriendly Future* (1965) edited by Tom Boardman (b.1930).

By then, Pratchett had discovered science fiction fandom and started going to conventions. Authors seemed to be relatively normal people, and he thought that it might be possible for him to become one. He wrote a letter to *Vector*, a fanzine published by the British Science Fiction Association, and with Edward James (b.1947) wrote an article, 'The Unconventional Cavalier: An Assessment of Colin Kapp', on British science fiction writer Colin Kapp (b.1928) for the fanzine *Zenith* 6 (September 1965). A second story, 'Night Dweller', was sold, this time to *New Worlds* 156 (November 1965), which was now edited and owned by Michael Moorcock.

Pratchett had met James at a science convention, RePetercon, in Peterborough (Easter 1964), and began exchanging letters with him. Later that year, Pratchett began outlining the world of the Tropnecian Empire, a fantasy world which owed a lot to the Roman Empire. James was more than just a sounding board and contributed to some of the details. Pratchett had gained five O Levels and stayed on to study for A Levels in Art, English and History. However, he decided not to go to university, unlike James who went to Oxford. Pratchett began to send him letters about a society living in a carpet, the first incarnation of *The Carpet People* (1971).

By then, Pratchett had written to a local newspaper, the *Bucks Free Press*, asking for a job at the end of his A Levels, but there was already a vacancy available which he took at once. Pratchett reported on weddings and parish council meetings, but also began writing a weekly serial for children in 300 word segments, and thought about writing a book for children. He took an English A Level and the professional proficiency test for the National Council for the Training of Journalists – coming top for his whole year. One of his assignments was to interview Peter Bander-van Duren about a forthcoming book, *Looking Forward to the Seventies* (1968), to be published by Colin Smythe Ltd, a publisher based in Gerrards Cross, a town between Beaconsfield and London. Pratchett mentioned that he was writing a novel, and, although they did not usually publish new fiction, Colin Smythe took a look at it. In the meantime, Pratchett married Lyn, who is now co-credited as the copyright holder of his books. (Their daughter, Rhianna, was born in 1976, and Pratchett dedicated *Mort* (1987), *Truckers* (1989), *Wings* (1989) and *Only You Can Save Mankind* (1992) to her.) Pratchett moved to Rowberrow in Somerset and started working for the *Western Daily Press* in 1970.

The Carpet People was launched in Heals department store's carpet department on Tottenham Court Road in 1971 and was published in an edition of 500 copies illustrated by Pratchett. There were a few positive reviews, but most copies were sold to libraries. He returned to the *Bucks Free Press* in 1972, as a sub-editor, and in September 1973 joined *The Bath Chronicle*. He drew a number of cartoons about Warlock Hall, an imaginary paranormal research institute, for *Psychic Researcher*, a monthly journal published by Colin Smythe Ltd. In the evenings, he worked on his second novel, eventually publishing *The Dark Side of the Sun* (1976).

In 1980, Pratchett decided to change careers and became a publicity officer for the Central Electricity Generating Board, which gave him responsibility for a number of nuclear power stations. This was in the aftermath of the Three Mile Island Nuclear Generating Power Station meltdown on 28 March 1979 and the release of the film *The China Syndrome* (1979). Still writing part-time, he produced a novel that was partially set on a disc-shaped planet: *Strata* (1981). Like *The Dark Side of the Sun*, this was science fiction, apparently owing a debt to the planet builders of the radio series *The Hitch Hiker's Guide to the Galaxy* (1978) by Douglas Adams (1952–2005). Again, it was published in a small edition by Colin Smythe Ltd, with an under promoted paperback from New English Library.

Pratchett switched his target of parody from science fiction to fantasy, inventing the template for the Discworld series beginning with *The Colour of Magic* (1982). Colin Smythe was able to interest Diane Pearson at Corgi in a paperback edition, and she sold radio adaptation rights to BBC Radio 4. This publicity started the ball rolling, and Pratchett was finally on his way to overnight success; a direct sequel, *The Light Fantastic* (1986) followed. He could soon afford to finally become a full-time novelist. But the Discworld sales were proving too big for Colin Smythe Ltd to handle, so a deal was struck with Gollancz to co-publish further volumes: *Equal Rites* (1987) – now serialised on Woman's Hour – *Mort* (1987) and *Sourcery* (1988). At this point, Smythe moved from being Pratchett's publisher to acting as his agent. Gollancz contracted Pratchett to write six more novels, which he produced at a rate of more than one a year. Sales increased with each new book.

In interviews through the late 1980s, Pratchett kept saying that he could not keep writing the Discworld series indefinitely. The adventures of the wizard Rincewind of the early novels had been set aside for a novel about Eskarina Smith, Granny Weatherwax and the other Wizards, starting a sequence of novels that focused on witches. A novel that featured the recurring cameo character of Death as a central figure – *Mort* – started a sequence about Death and a novel about the City Watch of Ankh-Morpork started another featuring Samuel Vimes and his men. But he also took time away from the series to write the Bromeliad trilogy (1989–1990) for children, *The Unadulterated Cat* with Gray Jolliffe (1989) and *Good Omens* (1990) with Neil Gaiman, the latter being produced to experiment with the modems both had bought for their computers. A second children's sequence – the Johnny Maxwell Trilogy – was published in 1992–1996. More recently, the Tiffany Aching books (2003–) for children have formed a new sequence, and the novel featuring the conman and fraudster Moist von Lipwig, *Going Postal* (2004), is to be followed by his experiences in banking *Making Money* (2007).

Spin offs from the Discworld novels include the *Science of Discworld* books, co-written with Jack Cohen and Ian Stewart, and maps, co-produced with Stephen Briggs. There have also been a number of plays, written mostly by Briggs, conventions, a cookbook, diaries, collections of art by Josh Kirby and Paul Kidby, several comics or graphic novels, a CD of music by Dave Greenslade and several games.

There have been surprisingly few television adaptations: *Truckers* (1991), *Johnny and the Dead* (1995) and *Johnny and the Bomb* (2006) were based on his works for children. The Discworld series has spawned two animated adaptations, *Wyrd Sisters* (1997) and *Soul Music* (1997), and one live action version, *Hogfather* (2006), with *The Colour of Magic* being in pre-production at the time of writing. A short film of 'Troll Bridge' has been made, but remians in post-production at the time of writing. Film rights have been sold and reverted to Pratchett at various points, with *Good Omens* perhaps coming closest so far to production.

Pratchett now seems likely to continue the Discworld series indefinitely. His popularity has grown over the decades, with *Mort, Good Omens, Guards! Guards!*, *Night Watch* (2002) and *The Colour of Magic* placing 65, 68,

69, 73 and 93 respectively in the BBC Big Read top 100 novels in 2003. In 1998, he was awarded an OBE for services to literature.

About this Book

As Pratchett is a working writer, he remains a moving target, with new books scheduled and new projects in the pipeline. During the course of the production of this book, a number of new works appeared and have been taken into account. It covers up to mid-2007, in other words the publication of *Wintersmith* and the Sky adaptation of *Hogfather* (1997), supplemented by a few details of events in Summer 2007. There is no room for more than a mention of *Making Money* (2007), *The Wit and Wisdom of Discworld* (2007, with Stephen Briggs), *The Illustrated Wee Free Men* (2007, artwork by Stephen Player) or *I Shall Wear Midnight* (the projected title for the fourth Tiffany Aching novel). Even in a work of this length, it would be impossible to be completist: minor characters have fallen by the way side, and many locations have been denied entries of their own.

It has been difficult to structure this volume's entries. Some characters are known by their surnames (Granny Weatherwax, Havelock Vetinari), others by their given names (Mort Sto Helit) and still others by one name (Kirsty, Rincewind). This is made more difficult by some characters shifting names through the book. The decision, in deference to the encyclopaedic aspirations of this book, was to use surnames where these are given, although this has sometimes led to some heavy-handedness in the cross-referencing (which is indicated by emboldening when in a sentence, and some silent pluralisation or tweaking for grammar). The index should resolve any areas of confusion.

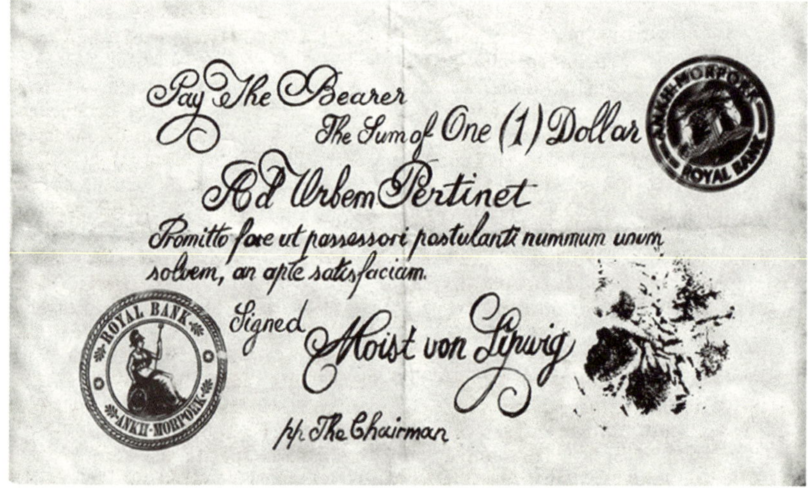

Royal Bank of Ankh-Morpork One Dollar banknote, created for *Making Money* by Discworld Merchandising.

Outside of the introduction, the various volumes by Pratchett and his collaborators have been given by initials, which are listed below. The two versions of *Guilty of Literature* are given as *GOL* and *GOL2* respectively. *The Carpet People* in general is given as *CP*, with *CP71* and *CP92* distinguishing the two editions where necessary. A complete list of abbreviations may be found at the end of this book. Bibliographic details of first editions are given within the entries on the individual books, usually a hardback followed by a paperback with significant later editions (cover changes) noted. A relevant but selected list of further reading is given at the end of many entries, with the full bibliography occurring at the end of the book. Languages into which the novels have been translated are noted in the entry for each book, as are British omnibi. As most of the book have become audio books or plays, these are detailed in the entries for Audio Books and Plays respectively (but see also Radio). The exceptions to this are television and comic book adaptations, which are given their own entries, placed after the book's entry or, in the case of comic versions of *The Colour of Magic* and *The Light Fantastic*, as *Terry Pratchett's The Colour of Magic* and *Terry Pratchett's The Light Fantastic*. Details of American, compact and omnibus editions may be tracked in the entry on Publishers.

Andrew M. Butler

'20p With Envelope and Seasonal Greeting' (OM*WF)

This is probably Pratchett's first published short story under his own byline since '**Night Dweller**', although he did write fiction for a number of the newspapers he worked on. By the time he produced this, he had become a full-time freelance writer. It first appeared in *Time Out* (issue 904/905, December 16–30, 1987), a listings magazine, which also includes features, interviews and reviews; originally published in London in 1968, it has since launched and been franchised in other cities.

One Christmas, Dr Thomas Lunn of Chippenham is disturbed by the appearance of a mad coachman who is apparently the sole survivor of a mail coach which has vanished in a blizzard. Lunn is told of what the man has witnessed on his journey: a giant robin, a curiously two-dimensional street with carol singers, three men from Africa or Asia, giant kittens and a series of slogans and messages. Other people have witnessed similar phenomena.

Pratchett takes his cue from the Dickensian Christmas of snow and good cheer, and clearly the coachman and his passengers have entered into a series of Christmas cards, complete with seasonal greetings. The ending is clearly a subversion of *A Christmas Carol* (1843), and of course the story is set in 1843. *See also* 'FTB'; The Hogfather (Character) *and OM** *WF*.

Andrew M. Butler

A

The Abbot (*T*, *D*, *W*)

The leader of the Stationeri tribe of nomes in **Arnold Bros (est. 1905)**, and thus in effect the leader of the group of nomes living in **Blackbury** (or Grimethorpe, in *T*). In public, at least, the Abbot is very circumspect about what he believes and says, so he holds to the line that there is no Outside, and therefore cannot speak to anyone who claims to have come from there. He is also cautious about who is allowed to learn to read books and access knowledge – it is forbidden for female nomes to learn to read in case their brains explode. In private, he is much more pragmatic, willing to talk to **Masklin**, **Grimma** and The **Thing**, thus learning about the nomes' extraterrestrial origin. Had he not died, he would have tried to lead them to safety. He is worth comparing to Patrician **Vetinari** in terms of how they both deploy **power** and use knowledge to control things.

His successor is Gunner, who travels to Florida with Masklin and Angalo de **Haberdasheri** to meet Grandson Richard 39, but who stays behind on Earth to seek out other nomes. Gunner leaves the nomes in the care of **Nicodemus** during the American trip. *See also* Arnold Bros (est. 1905); The Bromeliad; Children's Fiction; Grimma; Angalo de Haberdasheri; Dorcas del Icatessen; Masklin; Nisodemus; Power; Religion *and* Stratified Societies.

Andrew M. Butler

Aching, Tiffany (*WFM*, *HFOS*, *Wint*)

Tiffany Aching comes from the downlands known as the Chalk and is the granddaughter of Granny Aching, the region's best shepherd, who was perhaps only 'slightly' a witch but who did all the things **witches** do, speaking up for those who did not have voices and making sure by force of personality that people took care of each other. Tiffany first appears in *WFM* aged nine where she is discovered by Miss Tick, whose vocation is to search out promising potential witches and who is surprised to find one in such a geologically unpromising region. A frighteningly precocious child, Tiffany has read all five books of Granny Aching's Library, including the Dictionary (though she is not clear on the pronunciation of many of the words). She is an expert cheese maker and a regular patron of the wandering teachers who bring education to the remote Chalk regions, although she has an irritating habit of correcting their spelling. She possesses First Sight – the imagination that sees the world as it is, rather than how you want it to be. Unlike most people, she has Second Thoughts – the capacity to think about what she is thinking – but also Third Thoughts – she can reflect upon *how* she thinks about what she is thinking. What she wants most is to be a witch, although the Chalk people are distrustful of witches to the point of violence. She wants to stop injustices like the blaming of old Mrs Snapperly for the disappearance of the baron's son, Roland. And, of course, she wants to *know* things.

When her brother Wentworth, a naturally sticky child with a passion for sweets, is threatened by Jenny Green-Teeth (a water-dwelling monster), Tiffany's forthright reaction is to use a heavy frying pan. This is only the start of an incursion of the supernatural. The Nac Mac Feegle, 'Wee Free Men' or 'pictsies', ferocious gnomes who have been thrown out of Fairyland for disorderly conduct, have an interest in Tiffany's potential as a witch or 'hag'. Since Granny Aching's death, the monsters are coming back. Miss Tick goes to fetch help from more powerful witches, but by then it is too late.

Wentworth is kidnapped by the Queen of the **Elves**, who, it turns out, had also kidnapped Roland. With the aid of the Nac Mac Feegle, whose 'kelda' or queen/mother has appointed Tiffany her temporary successor to safeguard the clan until a new kelda arrives, Tiffany enters the realm of the Queen of the Elves. After much peril, she rescues Wentworth and Roland, finding herself at one point in the world of the painting 'The Fairy Feller's Master-Stroke' (1855–1864) by the Victorian artist Richard Dadd (1817–1886), who painted the work after being committed to a lunatic asylum. By the time Miss Tick arrives with Granny **Weatherwax** and Nanny **Ogg**, the Queen is gone. Granny, impressed by Tiffany's stubborn independence as much as her ability, gives her a 'virtual hat' to encourage her in the difficult moments ahead.

In *HFOS*, set two years later, Tiffany joins Miss Level to train as a witch, where she is hurt by local student witches' refusal, led by the appalling Annagramma, to believe in the 'virtual hat' given to her by Granny Weatherwax, and becomes impatient to move away from the domestic drudgery and glorified social work which seems to be a witch's role. She is unable to construct a simple Shambles, or 'magic detector', but she is able to step outside her body and observe it. This makes her vulnerable to a Hiver, a disembodied force, not alive, but seeking out life in the same way as a Hermit **Elephant** seeks a mud hut. The hiver feeds on her discontent and she commits two awful crimes. Once she is rescued by the Nac Mac Feegle, she has to make amends, prove herself, and defeat the hiver once and for all. A key to her victory is the pendant given her by Roland on her departure from the Chalk. It is a figure of the White Horse, carved into the Chalk as a representation, not of a horse, but of what a horse *is*: once more, Tiffany is reminded that there is a great difference between the appearance of a thing or person and its essence, and that witches have to make the hard choices that other people should not have to make.

In *Wint*, another two years later, Tiffany takes part in the Black Morris dance and inadvertently arouses the attentions and desires of wintersmith, the spirit of winter. Meanwhile her latest tutor, Miss Treason, dies and is replaced by Annagramma Hawkin, a witch who needs the assistance of others in performing her duties. Tiffany does not necessarily get what she wants and is discovering that actions have costs and consequences.

Tiffany is also in the process of learning that being a witch is a matter of duties and responsibilities, but above all of knowing when to be a human being *instead* of a witch. She shares Granny Weatherwax's single-mindedness and her own grandmother's destiny to be the soul of the Chalk. Chalk may be soft, but imbedded in it are flints, the hardest of rocks. In the language of the Nac Mac Feegle, Tiffany's name means 'Land under Wave'. It is clear that Granny recognises in her a kindred spirit, perhaps even grooming her to be her successor as leader the witches don't have. *See also* Children in the Discworld Series; Children's Fiction; Coming of Age; Nanny Ogg; Granny Weatherwax *and* Witches.

Further Reading

Baldry, Cherith. 'The Children's Books'. *GOL2.*
Sayer, Karen. 'The Witches'. *GOL2.*

Andy Sawyer

Adams, Douglas (1952–2000)

Douglas Adams and Terry Pratchett are often referred to together by both critics and fans alike. While Adams's work had a definite influence on Pratchett, particularly in the use of word play, and they both use humour in the creation and execution of their respective fictional universes, they are in fact very different writers in terms of subject and productivity. While Terry Pratchett's **Discworld** uses the setting of a pure fantasy world as the setting for his stories, Adams played within the boundaries of the Science Fiction genre.

Douglas Noel Adams was a cult British comic writer for radio, books and television, most notably as the creator of *The Hitch Hiker's Guide to the Galaxy*. Adams's writing career started shortly after his graduation in 1974 from Cambridge University, where he had written several sketches for the influential Footlights comedy revue. This work bought him to the attention of Monty Python's Graham Chapman (1941–1989), and the two formed a brief writing partnership which saw Adams contribute some material to the show along with making two, very brief, on-screen appearances. During the 1970s, Adams continued to work at breaking in as a full-time writer, in the mean time supporting himself with several odd jobs including hospital porter, barn builder, chicken shed cleaner and body guard to a rich Arab family.

In 1977, Adams and radio producer Simon Brett (b.1945) pitched the idea for *The Hitch Hiker's Guide to the Galaxy* to the BBC using an outline for a pilot episode and story outlines for a few further stories in which the world ended. Adams often told the, possibly apocryphal, story that the inspiration for the series occurred to him lying in a field in Innsbruck, Austria, while attempting to travel across Europe accompanied by a book called *The Hitch Hiker's Guide To Europe*.

The first series of *Hitch Hiker's* was broadcast in March–April 1978 on BBC Radio 4 and, despite little promotion and a late night time slot, it received good reviews and positive audience reaction. On the strength of its success, the BBC offered Adams the post of producer on the satirical radio sketch show *Week Ending*. Six months later, Adams left to take up the post of script editor on the seventeenth season of the television science-fiction series, *Doctor Who*. Adams had sent a copy of the script for the pilot of *Hitch Hiker's* to the *Doctor Who* production office and had been commissioned to write an episode for the show. He wrote three scripts for the series: *The Pirate Planet* (1978), *City of Death* (1979, with producer

Graham Williams from an idea by David Fisher, as David Agnew) and *Shada* (1979; only partially filmed, due to industrial disputes).

Writing a Christmas episode of *Hitch Hiker's* and the second series for broadcast in 1980 – alongside duties on *Doctor Who* – soon caused problems for the less than prolific Adams, a problem exacerbated when Adams was approached about turning the radio show into a record and a series of novels. (John Lloyd (b.1951) had already been brought in to cowrite episodes five and six of the original series.) In time, it became a 'trilogy of five books', as well as a television series, a comic book series, a computer game, an on-line encyclopaedia and a feature film. After Adams's death, the last three books were adapted for radio.

Adams was an avid technologist and early adopter of the Apple Mac computer, claiming to be the first person in the UK to have purchased one. He also used or participated in e-mail, hypertext and on-line communities. Adams developed and consulted on several **computer games** such as *Labyrinth*, *Bureaucracy* and *Starship Titanic*, and launched h2g2, the web's first collaborative encyclopaedia project, in 1999.

Douglas Adams in his London studio with a poster for the computer game 'Starship Titanic', April 1998.

Adams was also a talented amateur musician and left-handed guitarist, who often referenced the works of his favourite groups in his writing. He enjoyed a particularly close relationship with members of Pink Floyd and Procol Harum, even appearing on stage with the groups on the odd occasion playing rhythm guitar, and members appeared at his funeral.

Despite the success of *Hitch Hiker's*, the work that bought Adams the most personal satisfaction was *Last Chance To See…*, a radio series (1989) and accompanying non-fiction book that highlighted the plight of endangered species. Adams was an ardent environmentalist and frequent speaker on the subject, just as Pratchett has taken an interest in the plight of **orangutans**.

Adams died of a heart attack aged 49 in California, where he had been overseeing the production of the long in development *Hitch Hiker's* movie. This was eventually released in 2005. Other posthumous projects include the aforementioned final *Hitch Hiker's* radio adaptations, the release of an unfilmed *Doctor Who* script as a CD audio play and the publication of unfinished writings and notes found on his Mac computer under the collective title *The Salmon of Doubt* (2002).

Adams's life and work is celebrated by his fans each year on 25 May with the observance of Towel Day. *See also* Neil Gaiman; Orangutans *and* Science Fiction.

Further Reading

Gaiman, Neil. 1988. *Don't Panic: The Official Hitch-Hikers Guide to the Galaxy Companion.* London: Titan Books.

———, and David K. Dickson. 1993. *Don't Panic: The Official Hitch-Hikers Guide to the Galaxy Companion.* London: Titan Books.

———, David K. Dickson, and M.J. Simpson. 2003. *Don't Panic: The Official Hitch-Hikers Guide to the Galaxy Companion.* London: Titan Books.

———, and M.J. Simpson. 2002. *Don't Panic: The Official Hitch-Hikers Guide to the Galaxy Companion.* London: Titan Books.

Kropf, Carl R. 'Douglas Adams's Hitchhiker Novels as Mock Science Fiction'. *Science Fiction Studies* 15.1 (March 1988). Pp. 61–70.

Simpson, M.J. 2003. *Hitchhiker: A Biography of Douglas Adams.* London: Hodder and Stoughton.

Douglas Adams Official Web Site: http://www.douglasadams.com/

Alan J. Porter

Adaptations *see* Animation, Audio Books, Comics, Computer Games, Cookbook, Diaries, Games, Graphic Novels, Maps, Merchandising, Music, Musicals, Plays, Quizbooks, Television and Theatre.

Agatean Empire (*COM*, *LF*, *M*, *IT*)

The wealthy but isolationist territories that are part of the **Counterweight Continent**, which has limited contact with **Ankh-Morpork** via its single port of **Bes Pelargic**. Its capital is Hung-Hung, and it is surrounded by a big wall. However, it has been conquered at least once, by **Cohen the Barbarian** and his Silver Horde (*IT*), although they seemed to have got bored and wandered off in the direction of The **Hub** (*LH*). There was also a prophecy about a Great Wizzard (in fact **Rincewind**, see *IT*) coming to their aid. Like **Klatch**, it has been in its time a sophisticated **empire**, but is perceived as backwards and feudal.

Agate is a form of silica, often used in the ceramics industry to make china; of course the Agatean Empire is a **parody** of China, and the royal family of China had the jade emperor as a patron deity from the ninth century onwards, jade also being a form of silica. *See also* Bes Pelargic; Cohen the Barbarian; Counterweight Continent *and* Twoflower.

Andrew M. Butler

The Amazing Maurice and his Educated Rodents (2001)

The twenty-eighth Discworld novel, first published in the UK by Doubleday with a cover by David Wyatt; and the first to be explicitly published as **children's fiction**. It also has chapter divisions, each one headed by an extract from *Mr Bunnsie Has an Adventure*. The book is dedicated to D'Niece and an afterword briefly discusses rats. Maurice and his rat friends were twice mentioned in passing in *RM*; in advance catalogues it was announced as *Maurice and his Amazing Disappearing Rats*. The book won the 2001 CLIP Carnegie Medal in 2002. It has been translated into Bulgarian, Chinese (People's Republic and Taiwan), Croatian, Czech, Danish, Dutch, Estonian, Finnish, French, German, Greek, Hebrew, Italian, Japanese, Latvian, Norwegian, Polish, Romanian, Slovak, Spanish, Swedish and Thai. Neil **Gaiman** wrote in a review: 'It demonstrates, if there was any doubt, that [Pratchett] is, unquestionably, a master' (*Weekend FT*, 13–14 July 2002).

A group of rats who have learned to read have passed this onto a talking cat, Maurice. Together with an orphan, Keith, they repeatedly pull a confidence trick: the rats pretend to infest a town and Keith charges for piping them away. On their final job, in Bad Blintz, **Überwald**, they are struck by the puzzling absence of any rat in the area and discover that the local rat catchers have been hoarding the town's food, whilst the people starve. In the meantime, the mayor's daughter, Malicia, has seen through their plan and threatens to expose them unless she can play too. Meanwhile, there is something lurking in the cellar, Spider, an evil presence, ready to manipulate the rats. Maurice gives up one of his nine lives to **Death**, so that the rat Dangerous Beans may live. Keith becomes the official and ceremonial rat catcher of the town.

Cover of *The Amazing Maurice and his Educated Rodents*. Artwork by David Wyatt.

The jumping off point here is 'The Pied Piper of Hamelin' (1849) by Robert Browning (1812–1889) where the unpaid piper took revenge on the people of Hamelin by piping the children away; the poem is quoted in both dialogue and description. This is part of a weave of **narrative** underlying the book – the characters feel they are in a story, the rats read a rather twee children's storybook and Malicia claims that she is related to the Discworld equivalent of **Fairy Tale** collectors, the Grimms here called Agoniza and Eviscera rather than Jacob (1785–1863) and Wilhelm (1786–1859). There are various references to the mayor Dick Livingston, an amalgam of Dick Whittington (*c.*1350–1423), the legendary London mayor who was advised by a cat in the pantomime version of the narrative, and Ken Livingstone (b.1945), who on being elected as mayor of London in 2001 tried to clear Trafalgar Square of pigeons. *See also* Tiffany Aching; Cats; Children's Fiction *and* Fairy Tales.

Further Reading

Butler, Andrew M. 'A Story About Stories: Terry Pratchett's *The Amazing Maurice and His Educated Rodents*'. *Vector: The Critical Journal of the British Science Fiction Association* 227 (January/February 2003). Pp. 10–11.

Andrew M. Butler

Animation

Three of the **Television Adaptations** have been animated, all by **Cosgrove Hall**. *T* was stop motion animation, and the versions of ***Soul Music From Terry Pratchett's Discworld*** and ***Wyrd Sisters From Terry Pratchett's Discworld*** were cel animation with some computer animation.

Andrew M. Butler

Ankh-Morpork

A city-state: the political, administrative, industrial and commercial centre of the **Discworld**. The city is comprised of two cities bisected by the almost solid, silty River Ankh: posh Ankh Turnwise side of the river) and pestilent Morpork (**Widdershins** side). Its location on the edge of the STO PLAINS (the Discworld equivalent of Western Europe) means that the city was built on loam, but, like many ancient cities, Ankh-Morpork is built mainly upon itself, leaving a labyrinth underneath the city streets made primarily of old sewers and flooded streets, which have lately proclaimed as municipal property (*T!*).

Ankh-Morpork Two Pence Stamp created by Discworld Merchandising.

Model of the Assassin's Guild created by Discworld Merchandising.

Model of the Fools' Guild created by Discworld Merchandising.

Pratchett has piled aspects of many large cities into one to make it the quintessential fantasy city. His goal was to create a city that would not stop even if the story did. Bits and pieces of Tallinn, Prague, London, Seattle, Los Angeles, Paris, New York City and more have gone into making Ankh-Morpork a living and resonant city. Not only are there the usual castles, lords, Guilds, monuments and monumental slums (The

Shades) found in most **fantasy** cities, but also factories, workshops, high streets, slaughterhouses and suburbs, all of which are necessary to the running of a large city. Ankh-Morpork is quasi-medieval, Victorian, *film noir* and/or modern as the needs of the novels require.

Model of The Thieves' Guild created by Discworld Merchandising.

Coat of Arms: A shield, supported by two Hippotämes Royales Bâillant – the left enchainé, the right couronné au cou – surmounted by a Morpork Vautré Hululant, bearing an Ankh d'or, ornée a banner with the legend, 'Merus In Pectum Et In Aquam'. The shield bisected by a tower en maçonnerie sans fenêtres and quartered by a fleuve, argent and azure, bend sinister. On the upper right quarter a field, vert, of *brassicae prasinae*; on the lower-left quarter a field, sable. On the upper-left and lower-right quarters, bourses d'or on a field argent. Below the arms a ribbon with the legend 'Quanti Canicula Ille In Fenestra' (*NDC*).

The city mottos are in Latatian (the Old Language of Ankh-Morpork and equivalent to our Dog Latin) and are translated as 'Pure in Mind and Water' (considered to be a good laugh by Ankh-Morporkians) and 'How Much Is The Small Dog In The Window'. Since Ankh-Morpork is commercial in outlook, the latter motto is the one preferred by most citizens.

Ankh-Morpork

Population: 1,000,000, including suburbs and other outlying areas. Chief exports: manufactured goods, processed animal and vegetable produce of the Sto Plains, banking, assassination, wizardry and any other form of squeezing as much money out of the neighbours as possible.

It is common knowledge that the city's oldest building is The Tower of Art, around which the **Unseen University** grew. The city centre is now further downstream, however, as docks and administrative buildings located around the navigable parts of the River Ankh.

There are two legends about the founding of Ankh-Morpork. The first is that two orphaned brothers were found and suckled as babes by a hippopotamus on the River Ankh, which is why the hippopotamus is the royal animal of Ankh (along with the small owl for which Morpork is named). Eight heraldic hippos line the Brass Bridge, and it is said that if enemies ever threaten the city, they will come to life and run away. The other legend says that in ancient times a flood sent by angry gods covered the land, and wise men built a boat and took upon it two of every kind of animal existing upon the Disc. After a time, the manure of the animals began to threaten the stability of the boat, and so the men tipped it all over the rails and called the resulting mound Ankh-Morpork.

Ankh-Morpork is generally a city of fog and drips and rain, although hot weather occasionally strikes in the summer. The bisecting and twisting river, fragments of old city walls, winding streets with funny names and small towns that have grown into one large city inevitably call London to mind, yet Pratchett has said that London was not the biggest influence upon his fictional city.

Often called The Great Wahoonie (a spiky vegetable grown in parts of Howondaland, described as typically twenty feet long, the colour of earwax and smelling worse than an anteater (*NDC*)), Ankh-Morpork's population is highly diverse.

It is the largest dwarfish city on the Discworld, more **trolls** come to the city with every passing day, there is a large population of undead and every barbarian horde which ever attempted to take the city has found itself assimilated quickly into the population (perhaps because they could no longer afford to go back home) after being welcomed with open arms by the city's merchants.

Many of the citizens of Ankh-Morpork belong to groups that have classically warred with, killed and/or eaten at least one of the other groups (trolls/**dwarfs**, humans/trolls, humans/**vampires**, etc.), and it is a credit to the cosmopolitan nature (and love of the AM dollar) of the city that, with some occasional setbacks of both minor and major nature, they more or less rub along together in a peaceful manner, or at least a manner that does not usually result in out-and-out civil war or the fall of the city.

Political structure has changed throughout the history of the city. Monarchy, oligarchy, anarchy and dictatorship have all had a turn. The current form of somewhat benevolent dictatorship (under current Patrician Lord Havelock **Vetinari**) is a rather highly specialised form of democracy: it is One Man, One Vote and Vetinari is the Man and he has the Vote.

However, due to Vetinari's careful leveraging and manipulation of interest groups and the Guilds that he has encouraged to form and thrive, the political structure of the city is one of many interest groups plotting, scheming and conniving to get their way, while Vetinari goes about doing as he sees fit for the health of the city.

It is an open secret that the long-lost rightful heir to the golden throne of Ankh-Morpork (the throne's gold skin hides the fact that there is nothing but worm-eaten wood underneath) walks the streets as the Captain of the **City Watch**, *de facto* second in command to His Grace Sir Samuel **Vimes**, Commander of the Watch. His name is Carrot **Ironfoundersson**, a dwarf by adoption despite his 6′6″ stature. So far, however, the charismatic, scrupulously honest Captain Carrot (as he is usually known) has steadfastly resisted any and all attempts to raise him to the throne or even to acknowledge his Destiny, apparently feeling that his role as a watchman is the best one for the city. This apparently relieves Vetinari to no end, and the two have developed a careful, distant but cordial relationship.

Recent books in the Discworld sequence have given us a closer look at the daily life of citizens of Ankh-Morpork as we follow the actions of the characters through the boroughs and districts of the city, notably in *NW* and *GP*. Pratchett writes that he now obsessively plots and times movement and sightlines throughout the novels on the **maps** (see *SA*, but also *NW*) and models of Ankh-Morpork to get them right, to avoid reader complaints (*AD*).

Ankh-Morpork is also the name of a German Terry Pratchett fan club (*see* **Fandom**). *See also* The Broken Drum; City Watch; Fandom; The Shades; Unseen University; Patrician Vetinari *and* Samuel Vimes.

Further Reading

Pratchett, Terry. 2004. 'The Ankh-Morpork National Anthem'. Pp. 191–192 in *Once More * With Footnotes*. Edited by Priscilla Olson and Sheila M. Perry. Framingham: The NESFA Press.

Zina Lee

Arabic Societies

A label which covers an area of the Middle East, including Saudi Arabia and other states on the Arabian peninsula, which Pratchett transforms into **Klatch** for his **Discworld** novels. The influence of Arab culture and society spread across the north of Africa as far as Spain, before the defeat of the Moors in 1492, and up through the Balkans to the gates of Vienna in 1529 and 1683. Since the life of the Prophet Muhammed, 570–632 CE, the region and culture has been predominately Muslim, although there are also Christian, Jewish and Druze practices and societies.

The medieval period was dominated by the Ottoman Empire, a **Stratified Society** which began with the influx of Turks into Anatolia in the tenth society and became identifiable as a force under the rule of the sultan Mehmed II (1432–1481). The conquest of Constantinople in 1453 led to the collapse of the Byzantine Empire. Much of the army, the janissaries, consisted of slaves and non-Muslims, who had taken a vow of celibacy, and were loyal to the sultan. In return for their military prowess, they would get increased privileges and freedoms; leaders would often be rewarded with land. Ottoman society reached its zenith under Suleiman the Magnificent (1520–1566), but a society could only be as good as its communications systems, and the empire reached a natural limit before stagnating. Despite the increased threat from European power and wealth, thanks to the discovery of the new world, and various military defeats, the empire lasted until the abolition of the role of caliph in 1924.

Arab society is mostly familiar to us through the lens of the west, distorted by centuries of distrust and religious intolerance fostered by the various medieval Crusades. The occupation of Jerusalem and the Holy Land in general was a problem for the Christian church, and Arabs were often depicted as barbarians, with no culture and worse manners. In fact, Arab society both preserved the knowledge gained by Classical Greece and Rome and made advances in architecture, astronomy, chemistry, medicine and mathematics, including the invention of the number zero. The continued existence in English of words like alchemy, alcohol, alembic, algebra, algorithm, alkali and so on, not to mention various star names such as Aldebaran, demonstrates the continued influence of Arab knowledge and science. The society has further been filtered through accounts of the French imperial encounter with north Africa, especially in the French Foreign Legion created in 1831 to wage war in Algeria – this force has been fictionalised in the various versions of the novel *Beau Geste* (1924) by P.C. Wren (1875–1941). A later encounter is in the books of T.E. Lawrence (1888–1935), also known as Lawrence of Arabia, who was involved in the Arab Revolt (1916–1918), persuading the Arabs to help the British in the battle against the Turks. He was the basis of the film *Lawrence of Arabia* (1962), directed by David Lean (1908–1991); this showed the endless desert landscapes crossable only by camels that are part of the popular imagination.

The Palestinian academic Edward Said (1935–2003) appropriated the word 'Orientalism' to refer to the way in which Western or Occidental society misreads other civilisations and blurs them into one for its own ideological ends. Arab and Islamic society was seen by the west as feminine, passive, lazy, libidinous and often as a perverse object of desire; this image justified western foreign policy towards north Africa and the Middle East, and the internalisation of such beliefs by people in the 'Orient' had led to their continued subjugation.

It is this set of images that Pratchett draws upon in his various depictions of Klatch through the Discworld series, most obviously in the confrontation between **Ankh-Morpork** and Klatch in *J.* Samuel **Vimes** is cast in the Lawrence of Arabia role, whilst it is constantly discovered that Klatchians are not as barbaric as usually perceived – although this image of barbarism is used as a weapon back against the Ankh-Morporkians. *See also* Egypt; Klatch *and* Racism.

Further Reading

Findlay, Allan M. 1994. *The Arab World*. London: Routledge.
Mansfield, Peter. 1973. *The Ottoman Empire and its Successors*. London: Macmillan.
Said, Edward. 1978. *Orientalism*. Harmondsworth: Penguin.

Andrew M. Butler

Arad, Kin (*Str*)

The central character of *Strata*, a stand-alone novel that is a distant precursor to the **Discworld** series. Whilst the novel is not written in the first person, she is in most scenes, and it largely focuses through her perceptions of the universe.

A 210-year-old executive of a company which manufactures planets and pays its employees in life extensions, she is contacted by Jago Jalo and enticed to visit a strange alien planet shaped like a disc. Whilst she is dogged by a certain amount of bad luck – crashing into a planet orbiting the disc, say – she is reasonably competent and eventually discovers the truth about the planet and indeed the universe. Her book, *Continuous Creation*, serves to point up a few themes about creating worlds.

Her role and age are clearly intended to recall the 200-year-old Louis Wu of *Ringworld* (1970), by Larry Niven (b.1938), whose life is extended by a mixture of genes and drugs. She does, however, lack the spark of Pratchett's other early protagonists, being more confirmed than changed by her travels. Pratchett was to return more successfully to female protagonists with **Esk** and the **witches**. *See also* Feminism *and* Sexism.

Andrew M. Butler

Archchancellors (*COM*, *LF*, *ER*, *S*, *GG*, *E*, *MP*, *SM*, *IT*, *LC*, *LH*, *SOD*, *SODII*, *SODIII* and 'CCOODD')

Sometimes referred to as Chancellors, these are the leaders of the **Unseen University**, usually promoted by the removal of their predecessor, sometimes with extreme prejudice. Not only are they in charge of the university **wizards**, but they are also notionally in charge of all on the wizards on the **Discworld**, a fair enough notion as long as it is not acted upon. The earliest incumbent of the post was Alberto **Malich**, but the first one to appear on the page was the 304th, Galder Weatherwax, a distant, who was succeeded by the ambitious and bureaucratic Ymper **Trymon** *(LF)*. A later Archchancellor, Cutangle, actually grew up in the next village to Granny **Weatherwax**, and daringly admits a woman, Eskarina **Smith**, to the university, eventually (*ER*). The eighty-year-old Virrid Wayzygoose (*S*) – the name a nod to waysgoose, a printer's picnic – is killed before he assumes the role and is succeeded by **Coin** the Sourcerer (*S*). The Archchancellor in *GG* remains unnamed. Ezrolith Churn is 98 and would have been happy to write his magnum opus on obscure magic instead of taking on the role. He seems dispensable and does not appear a second time (*E*). Mustrum **Ridcully** takes over from *MP* as a safe pair of hands and remains in the role through the rest of the series, against remarkable odds and recent precedent. *See also* Coin; Magic; Malich; Ridcully; Unseen University *and* Wizards.

Further Reading

Hill, Penelope. 'Unseen University'. *GOL, GOL2.*

Andrew M. Butler

Arnold Bros (est. 1905) (*T*)

Inspired by a childhood visit by Pratchett to Gamages on Holborn, London, Arnold Bros was a departmental store which was opened in 1905 in **Blackbury** by Alderman Frank W. Arnold and his brother Arthur Arnold and demolished in the 1990s. Arnold Bros covered an area off the High Street from the Fish Market to Palmer Street, backing onto Disraeli Street, and was situated on five floors. It was subdivided into various sections (departments), such as ironmongery, corsetry, millenary, electrical and domestic appliances, gardening, haberdashery, soft furnishings, furnishing, cloth, a food hall, a delicatessen, young fashions and so on. In the basement is a boiler room that powers the heating of the building, and management and accounts are situated on the top floor. Individual floors are linked by escalators and lifts. Its motto is 'All things under one roof'.

At some point in the twentieth century, the building was occupied by a large number of nomes, four-inch high aliens, who had crash-landed in their ship, *The Swan*, about 15,000 years earlier. The nomes subdivided themselves into clans associated with individual departments, and eventually forgot that they had come from outside of the store, let alone an alien planet. Rivalries between clans led to warfare – the Battle of the Freight Elevator, the Goods Inwards Campaign and so on. Peace was brought to the store by the Stationeri, who set up a theocracy (*see* **Stratified Societies**) based on the idea that Arnold Bros (est. 1905) was a largely benevolent deity who provided for the nomes, assuming they lived peacefully together. There is also a goddess, Bargains Galore, whose name is often taken in vain, whose enemy is the demon Prices Slashed. The Stationeri were led by an **Abbot** and are not a proper department, but rather consist of a group added to with a few boys taken each year from each clan. They are taught to read and therefore have direct access to the nome holy book, *The Book of Nome*. (Females are not allowed to read, for fear their brains may overheat.)

This is a typical **Science Fiction** trope: an enclosed environment whose original nature or purpose has been forgotten by its inhabitants. The classic example is *Orphans of the Sky* (1963, consisting of the stories 'Universe' and 'Commonsense', both 1941) by Robert A. Heinlein (1907–1988), where a spaceship designed to house generations of humans continues on its journey after the officers have died out; no one remembers that it is a spaceship. This is combined with an idea used in **children's fiction**, of beings that exist under the noses of human beings; examples include *The Borrowers* (1952) and its sequels by Mary Norton (1903–1992) and *The Wombles* (1968) and its sequels by Elisabeth Beresford (b.1928).

Rather than the story being one entirely focused on a conceptual breakthrough – the realisation that there is more to the world than first met the eye, rather like frogs discovering that there is more to the world than The **Bromeliad** plant they live in – the catalyst for the store nomes is the arrival of nomes from outside, specifically **Masklin**, **Grimma**, Old Torrit and Granny Morkie. At first, the authorities, both the Duke of Haberdasheri and the Abbot, have to reject the outsiders, the latter because the existence of an outside would suggest that other statements by the Stationeri can be doubted, and the fragile peace would be troubled. The Abbot is a shrewd political operator and meets the outside nomes in private.

Whilst the Abbot is learning that their origin is extraterrestrial, Masklin, Grimma and Dorcas del **Icatessen** discover more cataclysmic news. The old-fashioned store has to compete with other, cheaper, more modern shops in the town centre and has been haemorrhaging customers and losing stock – presumably down to the appropriation of material by the nomes. The holding company for the store, Arnco Group – which has interests in airlines, cinema, recording, television, publishing, petroleum and more – has decided to close and demolish the store, opening a Super-saver Outlet in the nearby Neil Armstrong Shopping Mall and building a leisure centre on the site. This is part of a wider civic redevelopment, as later in the 1990s the Fish Market was redeveloped and the council sold the cemetery for five pence to United Amalagamated [*sic*] Consolidated Holdings (*see JD*).

Arnold Bros

The nomes have three weeks to escape or face the end of the world as they know it. This they do, through the heroism of Angalo de **Haberdasheri**, the intelligence of Dorcas and Grimma and the leadership abilities of Masklin. Arnold Bros is not left behind entirely, as the acting Abbot **Nisodemus** wants the nomes to carry the idea of him in their heads, is sceptical about the demolition and would much rather have a theocracy with him in charge. *See also* The Abbott; The Bromeliad; Children's Fiction; Grimma; Angalo de Haberdasheri; Dorcas del Icatessen; Masklin; Nisodemus *and* Stratified Societies.

Further Reading

Beresford, Elisabeth. 1968. *The Wombles*. London: Benn.
Heinlein, Robert A. 1964. *Orphans of the Sky: A Novel*. New York: Putnam.
Norton, Mary. 1952. *The Borrowers*. London: Dent.
Pratchett, Terry. 2004. 'The Big Store'. Pp. 43–44 in *Once More * With Footnotes*. Edited by Priscilla Olson and Sheila M. Perry. Framingham: The NESFA Press.

Andrew M. Butler

The Art of Discworld see Kidby, Paul

A'Tuin, The Great (*COM*, *LF*, *FE*)

A giant turtle that swims through space with four **elephants** balanced on his (or her) back, on top of which is a large disc that is the **Discworld**. Some people believe that A'Tuin will crawl indefinitely through space and others that (s)he is heading towards a destination where (s)he will mate. This appears to be a partial explanation, as at the end of *LF* eight new baby turtles are born, complete with elephants and discworlds. The existence of A'Tuin was discovered by the people of Krull, who live on the edge of the Discworld and built a scaffold that allowed some of them to be lowered down into space to get a closer look. Later Krullians built a kind of space-going submarine, in order to try and travel far enough to determine her (or his) sex. The followers of **Omnia** deny the existence of the turtle, and its movement.

The image of the world as a disc on the back of elephants on the back of a turtle is part of Hindu mythology, among other cosmologies – the turtle is Chukwa and may support Maha-pudma the elephant. There is an apocryphal story of an eminent scientist being approached by an old lady after a lecture, to be told that the Earth is perched on the back of a turtle. The scientist asked her what supported the turtle, and she responded, 'It's turtles all the way down'.

'A-Tuin the Turtle' is a track on Dave **Greenslade's** *Terry Pratchett's From the Discworld* album. *See also* Discworld; Elephants; Dave Greenslade *and* Omnia.

Andrew M. Butler

A Hindu View of the World. An inspiration for the Discworld.

Audio Books

Most of Pratchett's books have been recorded as Audio Books, some abridged, some unabridged. They have appeared in a number of formats: cassettes and CD initially and now also as MP3s.

The abridged versions were published by Corgi and read by Tony Robinson (b.1946). Robinson played roles in *Discworld* (*see* **Computer Games**) and Vernon Crumley in the television adaptation of *H*, but is most famous for appearing as Baldrick in the *Blackadder* (1983–1991) series and presenting the archaeology programme *Time Team* (1994–). He is a prolific narrator of talking books. His abridged titles are *T, D, W, COM, LF* and *ER* (1993), *M, S* and *WS* (1994), *P, GG, MP, OYCSM* and *J*, (1995), *E, RM, WA, SG, LL, MAA, SM, IT* and *JB* (1996), *FOC, H, J* and *CP92* (1997), *LC, CJ* (1998), *FE* (1999), *TT* (2000), *TOT* and *AMHER* (2001), *NW* (2002), *MR* and *WFM* (2003), *GP* and *HFOS* (2004), *T!* (2005) and *Wint* (2006).

The Isis Audio Books are full versions, initially recorded by Nigel Planer (b.1953) and Celia Imrie (b.1952). Planer performed roles in *Discworld II: Missing, Presumed…!?* and *Discworld Noir* (*see* Computer Games), but is best known for his performance as the hippie Neil Pye in *The Young Ones* (1982–1984) and as Ralph Filthy in *Filthy, Rich and Catflap* (1987). In those sitcoms, he worked alongside Rik Mayall (b.1958) and Adrian Edmondson (b.1957), who he also appeared with in a number of the

Comic Strip Presents films. He was Sideney in ***Hogfather* (Television Adaptation)**. Planer read: *COM*, *LF*, *IT*, *S*, *M*, *RM* and *GG* (1995), *MAA*, *LL*, *WA* and *SM* (1996), *SG*, *MP* and *P* (1997), *LC*, *Msk*, *FOC* and *H* (1999) and *J* and *CJ* (2000). Imrie is a comic actor who frequently appears with Victoria Wood (b.1953), including playing Miss Babs in *Acorn Antiques*, the spoof soap opera and Philippa Moorcroft in the sitcom *dinnerladies* (1998–2000). She had a cameo in *Star Wars I: The Phantom Menace* (1999). She read *ER* (1995) and *WS* (1996).

Subsequent titles have been read by Stephen **Briggs**: *FE* (2000), *TT*, *TOT*, *E* and *AMHER* (2001), *Str* and *NW* (2002), *WFM* and *MR* (2003), *LH*, *HFOS*, *GP* and *T* (2004), *T!*, *D*, *W* (2005), *GO* and *Wint* (2006) and *DSS* (2007). *MR* won the Audie for best **Science Fiction** audio novel in 2004, a prize given by the Audio Publishers Association.

Actor Richard Mitchley has recorded unabridged versions of *OYCSM*, *JD* and *JB* (1997) and *CP92* (1998) for Chiver's Children's Audio Books, aimed at the visually impaired market. The Royal National Institute for the Blind and National Library for the Blind, among other institutions, have talking book and Braille versions, including *COM*, *LF*, *ER*, *M*, *S*, *WS*, *P*, *GG*, *E*, *MP*, *RM*, *WA*, *SG*, *LL*, *MAA*, *SM*, *IT*, *Msk*, *FOC*, *H*, *J*, *LC*, *CJ*, *FE*, *TT*, *TOT*, *LH*, *AMHER*, *NW*, *DC*, *SOD*, *WFM*, *MR*, *HFOS*, *GP*, *T*, *D*, *W*, *OYCSM*, *JD* and *JB*. Large print editions have also been released of some of the novels.

Some different versions have been released in the American market: *TOT* read by Christopher Cazenove and Karesa McElheny (2001, Fantastic Audio) and *NW* read by Stefan Rudnicki, with Gabrielle De Cuir, and Harlan Ellison (2003, Fantastic Audio).

A number of Pratchett's books have been serialised on BBC **Radio** and may be repeated, sometimes being made available for up to a week after the original broadcast on their Listen Again downloading facility.

Pratchett's drabble, **'Incubust'** was written for *The Drabble Project*, which raised money for talking books for the blind. *See also* Stephen Briggs; 'Incubust' *and* Merchandising.

Further Reading

ISIS homepage: http://www.isis-publishing.co.uk/

Unofficial Tony Robinson homepage: http://www.unofficialtonyrobinsonwebsite.co.uk/pages/audio_books/audio_books_pratchett.html

Andrew M. Butler

Australia (*RM*, *LC*, *OYCSM*, *JD*)

XXXX is a **parody** of Australia, a place where Pratchett has visited for conventions and signing tours. Many aspects of Australian culture – as perceived by outsiders particularly through films and songs – are spoofed in *LC*, although there was a mention of a fabled lost continent in *RM*.

Australia was not discovered until 1606, which was probably a surprise to the people who had been living there at least 40,000–50,000 years, who crossed land bridges or had sailed from South East Asia. Australia is an island surrounded by the Indian, Pacific and Southern Ocean and is largely desert or semi-desert, with a richly fertile coastline. Because of its relative isolation from the other land masses of the world, it contains various mammals that are not to be found elsewhere, such as the egg-laying (monotreme) duck-billed platypus and echidna, and marsupials such as kangaroos, koala, wallabies and wombats. There is also the large flightless bird, the emu. A species of **dog**, the Dingo, was introduced by the Aboriginal settlers in prehistoric times. Many other species have become extinct, the vast bulk of these since European settlement. The politics of colonisation by an empire, in which the Aboriginal settlers and their culture were largely displaced by incomers, remains fraught, with many ongoing land rights campaigns and demands for compensation.

With several millennia of experience, the native people had long since learned how to manage the land, and to live off what to European eyes seemed inhospitable. The introduction of camels, **cats**, cattle, foxes, horses and rabbits to Australia in particular was disastrous. In the centre of Australia is Uluru national park, a world heritage site, now largely run by the Pitjantjatjara people. Uluru itself – formerly known as Ayers Rock – is part of a huge underground monolith, which sticks out of the ground for over 300 metres. It is a sacred site.

In the western imagination, there had long been an imagined southern continent, *Terra Australis Incognita* – sometimes even sketched onto maps – and throughout the sixteenth century, explorers must have narrowly missed finding it. The Dutch Willem Janszoon (*c.*1570–1630), sailing from Java, found the west coast, and the Netherlands claimed the territory. British explorers, including Captain James Cook (1728–1778) found and mapped the east coast, and this was claimed as part of the British Empire. In the late eighteenth and early nineteenth century, the land was used as a penal colony, with many being transported there for life for quite trivial crimes.

Much of (European) Australian historical culture seems to come down in the form of ballads. 'Waltzing Matilda' (1895), one of many poems by Banjo Paterson (1864–1941), features a swagman (nomadic worker) who makes himself a drink, then steels a sheep and risks being arrested; he drowns himself in a lake (billabong). Set to music, this is Australia's (unofficial) national anthem. **Rincewind** is in danger of emulating the swagman in *LC*. Paterson also wrote 'The Man from Snowy River' (1890), about the pursuit of an escaped prize-winning racehorse; this inspired two films (1920, 1982) and a television series (1993–1996). Rincewind again recreates these events along with Clancy (a character in the poem) and Old Regret (a variation on Old Remorse, from Paterson). Another folk hero was Ned Kelly (*c.*1855–1880), a bushranger frequently arrested for assault, alleged murders and bank robberies. Kelly and his gang were known for their homemade armour, including helmets. Kelly was eventually arrested and executed. This becomes Tinhead Ned, an XXXX folk hero.

In 1901, Australia became a federation of six colonies, part of the (later) British Commonwealth, with the British monarch as constitutional head. In 1908, Canberra was chosen over the rival cities of Sydney and Melbourne as the country's capital city. In the following century, Australia first became a country stuck in a rut, where people (Peter Carey (b.1943), Germaine Greer (b.1939), Rolf Harris (b.1930), Robert Hughes (b.1938), Barry Humphries (b.1934), Clive James (b.1939), etc.) had to emigrate from to make a mark, and in words attributed to Ave Gardner (but invented by a journalist, Neil Jillett), Melbourne was the perfect place to film the end of the world. But increasingly, the country has thrown off a cultural cringe, with Sydney **Opera** House (Rincewind sees a building which resembles it) and the Sydney Harbour Bridge has some of the most iconic architecture in theworld, and it has become a thriving, bustling, cosmopolitan country – at least in the major cities – a destination of choice for international tourists.

Since the 1970s, a new wave of Australian cinema has challenged **Hollywood films** – the Mad Max trilogy (Rincewind meets a Max, and several scenes parody *Max 2: The Road Warrior* (1981) and *Mad Max 3: Beyond Thunderdome* (1985)). In *Crocodile Dundee* (1986), another representation of a bushranger became an international blockbuster, and this too is parodied in *LC*. Since then, a number of small budget films have had break-out success, most notably *The Adventures of Priscilla, Queen of the Desert* (1994), with depictions of colourful performances from three drag queens travelling from Sydney to Alice in a lavender painted bus; *LC* features Letitia, Darleen and Neilette in a purple cart, Petunia, the Desert Princess. (Subsequent scenes also ape the Sydney Mardi Gras gay parade.)

Australian television has also made an impact on the world and perhaps is most responsible for the way it has been perceived as a country. *Skippy the Bush Kangaroo* (1966–1970) features the adventures of a boy and his kangaroo, solving crimes and rescuing people (Scrappy in *LC*). Even more dominant, in Britain at least, is the sun-kissed suburban utopia of Erinsborough in the soap *Neighbours* (1985–); this becomes the soap *Cobbers* in the **Johnny Maxwell Trilogy**.

L also parodies many more aspects of Australian culture, including beer (*see* XXXX), Vegemite, meat pie floaters, Peach Melba, the band Men at Work, Rolf Harris and much more. It is an affectionate rather than cruel portrait, which is echoed in his fictionalised report of a signing tour, 'No Worries' (*see OM* WF*). *See also* Agatean Empire; Counterweight Continent; Discworld *and* XXXX.

Further Reading
Fiske, John, Bob Hodge, and Graeme Turner. 1987. *Myths of Oz: Reading Australian Popular Culture*. Sydney: Allen and Unwin.
Macintyre, Stuart. 1999. *A Concise History of Australia*. Cambridge: Cambridge University Press.

Andrew M. Butler

Awards

Pratchett has won few awards for one so prolific, even within the **Science Fiction** and **Fantasy** communities which are his core audience. In 1989, *P* won the BSFA Award, given by the British Science Fiction Association and the Eastercon (*see* **Conventions**). Some sources suggest he won the British Fantasy Award given by the British Fantasy Society, but this is probably a confusion of acronyms. Outside the genre, but within **comedy and humour**, Pratchett has twice been shortlisted for the Bollinger Everyman Wodehouse Prize for Comic Writing for *GP* and *T!*

He has been more successful in awards for **children's fiction**. In 1993, he won the Writer's Guild Award for Children for *JD*. Pratchett won the Carnegie Medal for *AMHER* in 2002, having been shortlisted in for *JD* and *JB*. He was on *The Guardian* Children's Fiction Prize shortlists for *OYCSM*, *JD* and *AMHER*. The Nestlé Smarties Book Prize is based on a shortlist drawn up by adults and voted on by children. *JB* won the Silver Award for the 9–11 category in 1996. The W.H. Smith Award for Children's Fiction was jointly won by *AMHER* in 2002. In addition, *WFM* won the W.H. Smith People's Choice Award in 2004. *HFOS* won the *Locus* Young Adult Novel Award and the Mythopoeic Award (Children's Category) in 2005. *Wint* was shortlisted for the British Book Awards Children's Book of the Year in 2007.

Terry Pratchett with his OBE, received from the Prince of Wales at Buckingham Palace, 26 November, 1998.

He was given an OBE – Officer of the Order of the British Empire – in 1998 for services to literature.

Many of his collaborators have won awards – see entries on Stephen **Briggs**, Neil **Gaiman**, David **Langford** and Ian **Stewart**.

Andrew M. Butler

B

Bad Ass (*ER*)

An incredibly small village in **Lancre** in the Ramtops mountains, which is where Granny **Weatherwax** lives, although the name is rarely used in the canon and in the *TGL* the two seem to be relatively far apart. It is also the birthplace of Eskarina **Smith**, the eighth child of an eighth son, and thus mistakenly anointed a potential **Wizard** by Drum Billet. The place is supposedly named after a particularly stubborn donkey who got stuck in the river with the supplies of the settlers and so the village was established there. The name also perhaps suggests a German spa town, but there is also a town called Bad Ass in the Illuminatus! trilogy (1975) by Robert Anton Wilson (1932–2007) and Robert Shea (1933–1994), a centre of red-necked **racism**, but this seems an unlikely source. Of course, 'bad ass' also refers to the mean, tough and stubborn.

Andrew M. Butler

Bes Pelargic (*COM*, *LF*, *IT*)

The major port of the **Agatean Empire** on the **Counterweight Continent**, and perhaps the only area of the empire to have any substantial contact with the rest of the **Discworld** due to its isolationist stance. The Agatean's first tourist – perhaps the Discworld's first tourist – **Twoflower** hails from there, where he is some kind of office worker. There is contact between the empire and **Ankh-Morpork**, as the Patrician **Vetinari** was told to keep an eye on the visitor. Little more is known, although **Rincewind**, **Cohen the Barbarian** and the Silver Horde have presumably passed through there on their way in or out of the empire, causing a bit of a fracas in the process.

In the mythology of **Egypt**, Bes is a dwarf, part human part lion, and the protector of pregnant women and babies, with perhaps a connection to

cats (Besa being Nubian for cat). A bes is also a Roman coin. 'Pelargic' means 'like a stork', a stork being a long-legged wading bird with a long bill, associated with Africa and India, but also resident in Europe and other parts of Asia. Various legends are attached to storks, such as the notion that they deliver babies (which resonates with Bes), that they live for thousands of years or that to kill one is bad luck. A similar word, 'pelagic', related to the deep sea and the ocean, also suggests the port's distance from anywhere else. *See also* Agatean Empire; Counterweight Continent *and* Twoflower.

Andrew M. Butler

Blackbury (*T*, *D*, *W*, *OYCSM*, *JD*, *JB*)

The town which is the setting for The **Bromeliad** and the **Johnny Maxwell Trilogy**, although in *T* it is referred to as Grimethorpe. (Grimethorpe is a former mining village in South Yorkshire in the real world, known for its colliery brass band and as the setting (as Grimley) for the film *Brassed Off* (1996). The existence of a real town may have led to the change of name.)

The precise location of Blackbury is hard to ascertain – it might be imagined to be either near where Pratchett was born (Beaconsfield, Buckinghamshire) or where he lives (Wiltshire, or southwest England more generally). It is close to an airport where Concorde can take off, which might suggest somewhere near Heathrow, such as Reading or Slough. On the other hand, in *JB* it is said that the town is twenty miles from the sea. The television version of *JD* chose a north-western setting, near Mànchester, suggesting somewhere like Blackburn, although that is on the wrong side of the city for the airport. It is a town to be imagined rather than a precise location, and it is not clear that it is precisely the same place in each book (*see* The **Trousers of Time**).

Central to the town was **Arnold Bros (est. 1905)**, a five-storey departmental store on the high street, now sadly demolished as it was not making enough money. The town's industries included the Blackbury Rubber Boot Company (now closed), a motorcycle factory which made the Blackbury Phantom (presumably closed) and Blackbury Preserves (bombed out in the war in March 1941). The town has grown considerably since the war, with the City Council becoming a Municipal Authority. It supports two football clubs, Blackbury Wanderers and Blackbury United. Its newspaper is the *Blackbury Guardian* (or *Echo* in the television version). In an alternate history, Blackbury was centre of a chain of burger bars run by Sir John Seeley, né Stephen Johnson, aka Wobbler.

The high street is now full of identikit shops, the old departmental store being replaced by Arnco Leisure Centre and the Fish Market being redeveloped. This is a no-go area for many people after dark. The Neil

Armstrong Shopping Mall is nearby, complete with fountain, food court and J&J Software, and this was built on the site of the old allotments. The town had not embraced Sunday shopping by the mid-1990s, and it is a deserted waste land on the sabbath.

On the outskirts of the town is a fourteen-storey tower block built in the 1960s, first planned to be named after Sir Alec Douglas-Home (1903–1995, prime minister 1963–1964), then Harold Wilson (1916–1995, prime minister 1964–1970, 1974–1976), then Joshua Che N'Clement, a freedom fighter who became president of his country but went into exile in Switzerland, escaping from embezzlement charges. The block is not a place to go alone, the lifts have not worked since the mid-1960s and naturally it has won architectural awards.

The otherwise insignificant and ordinary town faced notoriety when the council tried to sell the cemetery to United Amalagamated [*sic*] Consolidated Holdings for five pence. The sale was stopped by a campaign started by Johnny Maxwell which led to the establishment of the Blackbury Volunteers, named in honour of the Blackbury Pals, all but one of whom were wiped out in battle in 1916. The last survivor, Tommy Atkins, died in October 1993, during the crisis over the cemetery sale. *See* The Bromeliad *and* The Johnny Maxwell Trilogy.

Andrew M. Butler

Briggs, Stephen (b. 1951)

Playwright, mapper, encyclopedist and producer of **Discworld** merchandising.

A civil servant living in the Oxford area, he began by adapting *WS* for the Studio Theatre Club in 1991. They perform at the Unicorn Theatre in Abingdon, in Oxfordshire. He played the role of Duke Felmet in the original production of *WS*. This was followed by an adaptation of *M* (1992), in which he played **Death**, *GG* (1993), in which he played Patrician **Vetinari**, followed by *MAA* (1994), *Msk* (1995), *CJ* (1996), *JD* (1997), *FE* (1999), *TT* (2000), *IT* (2001), *NW* (2003), *MR* (2003), *J* (2004), *AMHER* (2004), *GP* (2005), *LL* (2006) and *FOC* (2007). The first four of these were published as play scripts, and Briggs controls the amateur performance rights for these. *Msk* and *CJ* were published by Samuel French, and they control the amateur performance rights. *JD* and *AMHER* were published by Oxford University Press, and Briggs controls the rights to these. *FE*, *TT*, *IT*, *MR*, *NW*, *J* and *GP* were published by Methuen, and they control the rights to amateur productions of these. All professional productions need to be dealt with via Pratchett's agent, Colin **Smythe**.

Convinced that **Ankh-Morpork** was a mappable location, in the early 1990s, he began to sketch a street plan from the various textual clues given in the novels, and trying to fit them together. Initially, he used a real town as his framework, but realised that this was not working and so starting from scratch. In consultation with Pratchett and taking into account novels in progress – notable *LL* and *MAA*, the later featuring the **City Watch** and thus much of the city – he worked up a finished product, which was then painted by Stephen **Player**. It was published as *SA* (1993), with an account of how it came about and line drawings by Briggs, and materials by Pratchett. Having worked at the level of the city, Briggs felt able to take on the challenge of fitting the various countries and continents together to produce *The Discworld Mapp* (1995). Again the map came with a booklet including an account of the creation of the map, and how *LC* impacted on its design, as well as line drawings and additional material by Pratchett. The final map that Briggs has been involved with to date is *TGL* (1998), again with line drawings.

Briggs's researches into Discworld, recorded on index cards, enabled him to put together a very useful encyclopaedia-style guide to the series, *The Discworld Companion* (London: Gollancz, 1994), which is co-credited to Pratchett and both draws on his notes and will have some materials written or co-written by him. As well as the entries themselves, it also included line drawings such as various coasts of arms and an interview with Pratchett. Naturally this became outdated, and so a second, paperback, edition was released in 1997. As Discworld novels continued to be produced, so there was the need for a third version, *The New Discworld Companion* (2004). His close working relationship with Pratchett means that a few foreshadowings can be planted, for example the 1997 version includes an entry for William de **Worde**, even though *TT* was yet to appear for a number of years. It is also likely to include details known to Pratchett when writing the novels, but not spelt out in the actual text.

Briggs was also involved in the annual Discworld **diaries** which have been appearing since 1998, beginning with the *Unseen University Diary*. This needed a certain amount of revision to the existing understanding of the Discworld calendar – which has eight days to a week and thirteen months to a year – in order to make it with the existing real-world calendar. It also includes various feast days and festivals.

Briggs's acting experience has meant that he was ideally placed to record the ISIS unabridged **audio book** versions of the Discworld novels and The **Bromeliad**: *FE* (2000), *TT*, *TOT*, *E* and *AMHER* (2001), *NW* (2002), *WFM* and *MR* (2003), *LH*, *HFOS*, *GP* and *T* (2004), *T!*, *D*, *W* (2005) and *Wint* (2006). Some of these, *WFM*, *MR*, *GP*, *HFOS* and *T!* were released by HarperAudio in the USA. *MR* won the Audie for best science fiction audio novel in 2004, a prize given by the Audio Publishers Association.

Briggs has also diversified into merchandising, beginning with his wish for an **Unseen University** scarf, but now offering Unseen University degree certificates, t-shirts, doctorates and badges, a **City Watch** badge and t-shirt, as well as other badges, t-shirts, bookmarks, aprons, pens, tea towels and key rings. He sells his materials under the name C.M.O.T. **Dibbler**. *See also* Audio Books; Diaries; Maps; Merchandising *and* Plays.

Further Reading

For a full list of his published works see the bibliography at the end of this book.
Stephen Briggs's homepage: http://www.cmotdibbler.com/

Andrew M. Butler

The Broken Drum (*Str*, *COM*, *LF*, *M*, *SM*, *T!*)

A public house, perhaps the leading example of its kind, in Ankh-Morpork, on the corner of Filigree Street and Short Street. This is about as far as you can get from a tasteful wine bar – people get hurt in there and in leaving there, perhaps even in trying to enter there if they offend the **trolls** who act as bouncers. Naturally, this is a place that draws **Twoflower** in, like a moth to an oxy-acetylene torch, much to the horror of **Rincewind**. But as always Twoflower is born under a fortunate star, and it is the Drum which burns down, after he has got to observe a genuine pub brawl, with bottles and chairs and everything. After a change of management, if not of clientele, the tavern has reopened as The **Mended Drum**, and that is how it has been referred to ever since.

One of the regular patrons is The **Librarian**, who has surreptitiously slipped out of the grounds of the **Unseen University** in search of company and peanuts. He is thus on hand at the early performances of Imp Y **Celyn** and Music With Rocks In, being recruiting into the group himself – his long arms mean that he is a mean keyboard player (*SM*). As the novel progresses, he is joined by the **wizards** and the latest of the **Archchancellors**, Mustrum **Ridcully**. Towards the end of the novel, the bar is called upon to **parody** the bar where the Terminator gets his leathers in *Terminator 2: Judgment Day* (1991), when **Death** springs into action. Death is a regular visitor, most obviously on business, but also on some of the occasions he has needed to drown his sorrows; Susan **Sto Helit** also visits to see Imp Y Celyn.

The Broken Drum predates *COM*, having had a cameo appearance in *Str*. This glosses the title; the thing about a broken drum is you cannot beat it, and it is thus the best pub in the world. Or at least nothing else must be suggested to the landlord.

The Broken Drum was part of the name of a fanzine, *Tales from the Broken Drum*, published by Octarine: The Science Fiction and Fantasy Humour Appreciation Society, both names indicating an early bias towards Pratchett's works; later issues had variants on the title such as *Tales from the Naked Drum* (*see* **Fandom**). *See also* Ankh-Morpork *and* Drink.

Andrew M. Butler

Model of the Mended Drum created by Discworld Merchandising.

The Bromeliad (*T*, *D* and *W*)

One of the names given to the trilogy consisting of *T*, *D* and *W*. It has also been known as the Truckers or Nomes trilogy. The three books were collected into one volume as *The Bromeliad* (1998) by Doubleday, in a print run of about 10,000 copies; a Corgi paperback followed in 2007. **Cosgrove Hall** did wish to film the trilogy, but the project was lost in development after *T*.

At first glance, the title seems to be an echo of *The Iliad*, the epic poem about the Trojan Wars by Homer (*see* **Greek Mythology**), but in fact it is a reference to a kind of plant. Bromeliads are flowering plants, some of which contain a pool of water inside, and may even include creatures living inside them, 'unaware' of the outside world. This is a metaphor for the consciousness of the nomes. *See also* Abbott; Arnold Bros (est. 1905); Children's Fiction; Grimma; Angalo de Haberdasheri; Dorcas del Icatessen; Masklin; Nisodemus *and* Stratified Societies.

Andrew M. Butler

Brutha (*SG*)

A novice monk with an unfortunate name – Brother Brutha, shades of Major Major Major Major from *Catch-22* (1961) by Joseph Heller (1923–1999) – and with a very strict grandmother who has already drummed many of the precepts of the Church of **Om** into him. At the start of the novel, he is about seventeen and working in the garden when he is chosen to be spoken to by Om, as the last true believer in the god. His photographic memory makes him a useful tool to **Vorbis** who wants to double-cross the ruler of **Ephebe**; he is able to remember his way through the maze that protects Ephebe. After contradicting Vorbis's claims about having been spoken to by Om, Brutha is tortured but rescued by Om. Brutha is declared to be the Eighth Prophet and attempts to bring a more kindly and sympathetic version of religion to the fore.

Brutha echoes Buddha (563 BCE to 483 BCE) – a gentle religious figure – and the song 'He Ain't Heavy, He's My Brother'. His encyclopaedic knowledge of the law and his literalness recalls Carrot **Ironfoundersson**, and his photographic memory and experience of torture echoes Severian in *The Book of the New Sun* (1980–1983) by Gene Wolfe (b.1931). *See* Om; Omnia; Religion *and* Vorbis.

Andrew M. Butler

C

Calendars

The **Discworld** year consists of 800 days and thirteen months, which made the creation of workable **diaries** as **merchandising** difficult. The calendars, both wall and desk versions, stick to the 365/366 day year.

The first *Terry Pratchett's Discworld Collector's Edition 1999* Calendar featured illustrations by Josh **Kirby**, whereas *Terry Pratchett's Discworld Collector's Edition 1999 Day-To-Day Calendar* used art by Paul **Kidby** and extracts from *The Discworld Companion. Terry Pratchett's Discworld Collector's Edition 2000 Day-To-Day Calendar* followed the same format, but with extracts from the novels. *Terry Pratchett's 2000 Discworld Collector's Edition Wall Calendar* used Paul Kidby's art, as did the Terry Pratchett's 2000 Discworld Collector's Edition Calendar Day-To-Day Calendar. *Terry Pratchett's Discworld Collector's Edition 2002 Calendar* returned to Josh Kirby.

Terry Pratchett's Discworld Collector's Edition 2005 Calendar had illustrations by Paul Kidby, Les Edwards, David Frankland, Angela Rinaldi, John Howe (b.1957), Edward Miller, Stuart Williams, Sandy Nightingale, David Wyatt, Jackie Morris and Jon Sullivan.

Terry Pratchett's Discworld Collector's Edition 2006 Calendar featured illustrations by David Frankland, Melvyn Grant (*see WMC?*), Dominic Harman, Paul Kidby, Jackie Morris, Sandy Nightingale, Stephen **Player**, Jon Sullivan and David Wyatt. *Terry Pratchett's Hogfather Discworld Calendar 2007* had photographs by Bill Kaye from *H* **(Television Adaptation)**. *Terry Pratchett's Discworld Collector's Edition 2008 Calendar* used art by Les Edwards, David Frankland, Mel Grant, Dominic Harman, Paul Kidby, Edward Miller, Jackie Morris, Sandy Nightingale, Stephen Player, Jon Sullivan and David Wyatt. *See also* Diaries; Paul Kidby; Josh Kirby *and* Steven Player.

Andrew M. Butler

Carpe Jugulum (1998)

The twenty-third **Discworld** novel, first published in the UK by Doubleday in a first print run of 160,000 copies, and featuring the **Witches**. The title Latin, along the lines of 'Carpe Diem' – 'Seize the Day' – means 'Go for the Jugular'. This is only appropriate for a novel about **vampires**. It has been translated into Bulgarian, Czech, Dutch, Estonian, French, German, Polish, Russian and Spanish. Adam Roberts (b.1965) wrote that 'This novel is one of the brilliant ones' (amazon.co.uk).

Granny **Weatherwax** has to decide between saving the mother or the child at a difficult birth; she chooses the mother. She is depressed as things are changing. Agnes **Nitt** is becoming part of the coven, as the maiden, Magrat **Garlick** is now a mother and so Nanny **Ogg** can become a crone, making Weatherwax superfluous. At the naming ceremony, Magrat's daughter is unfortunately called Margaret Note Spelling. Even more unfortunately, **Verence II** has invited a family of vampires and these can now invade the country, turning everyone into vampires. Making sure that Verence is being protected by the pixy-like Feegles, the witches do battle, but the traditional holy water, garlic and religious iconography seem not to harm them. With the aid of Mightily Oats, an evangelist for OM, the battle is taken to the vampire's castle in **Überwald** and encounter the old Count Magpyr.

The **parody** draws on vampire lore, especially *Dracula* (1931) directed by Tod Browning (1882–1962) for Universal studios with Bela Lugosi (1882–1956), and the Hammer cycle starring Christopher Lee (b.1922) which began with *Dracula* (1958) directed by Terence Fisher (1904–1980). In fact, it draws on the 1930s Universal horror and Hammer House of

Horror films in general – the former gives us the hunchbacked assistant, usually working for a mad scientist such as Frankenstein, and, in the Discworld, **Igor**. Vampires represent an old, aristocratic order that is now passing, but the Magpyr family here is relatively progressive, having seen ways round the traditional methods of stopping the Undead. Weatherwax is perhaps a little set in her ways, and perhaps getting tired of it. The novel hints that she is to be killed off, as potentially superfluous to the witches' three roles. Oats, on the other hand, is curiously flexible for a religious zealot – although post-**Brutha**, the Omnian Church is more humane – and he is willing to admit that perhaps the verse about killing witches in his holy books is a mistranslation. *See also* Hollywood Films; Igor; Agnes Nitt; Nanny Ogg; Überwald; Vampires; Granny Weatherwax *and* Witches.

Further Reading

Sayer, Karen. 'The Witches'. *GOL*, *GOL2*.

Andrew M. Butler

The Carpet People (1971; revised edition 1992)

This was Pratchett's first novel, apparently sketched out in an earlier form in the Children's Circle column in the *Bucks Free Press*. He was also evolving it in letters to (the later medieval historian) Edward James (b.1947). The book was published by Colin **Smythe** Ltd, Gerrards Cross, in a hardback edition of roughly 3,000 copies, after a meeting with Peter Bander-van Duren, Smythe's partner at the publishing company, and launched in the carpet department of Heals Department store, Tottenham Court Road, London. The book was illustrated by Pratchett. It never had a later paperback edition, but remained on lists of Pratchett's work. It did have a German translation. Before he allowed it back into print he heavily rewrote it, claiming that his philosophy had changed from thinking that **war** and kings were central to **Fantasy** to the avoidance of war and doing without kings being important concerns. The enrichment of the text included lines that question **history**, **politics**, the role of the **hero** and leaders. It is written in the tradition of J.R.R. **Tolkien**; it might be argued that between the two editions it shifts from homage to **parody**. Pratchett's illustrations were removed and a cover by Josh **Kirby** added. The revised edition appeared in 1992 from Doubleday and had an initial print run of 18,100 copies. It has been translated into Bulgarian, Czech, Danish, Estonian, French, German, Greek; Hebrew; Italian, Polish, Russian and Slovakian. Rosemary Doyle wrote in *The Irish Times* that 'I feel it's a new dimension in imagination and the prose is beautiful. It is exciting and adventurous'.

Cover of *The Carpet People*. Artwork by David Wyatt.

The Munrungs are a group of tiny people that live in a carpet, in fear of the Fray and footsteps. A census is overdue, and they discover that the nearby city has been destroyed. Glurk the leader, Snibril his brother and Pismire a wise man lead their people towards Ware after their village has been damaged, with the aid of the mysterious Bane, facing the evil mouls along the way. Glurk becomes the leader of Ware and the carpet.

This is a reworking of Tolkien-style fantasy, with the home village of the Munrungs standing in for the Shire, Pismire for Gandalf (although his rationality is a character trait much expanded in the revised version), Bane for Strider and the mouls for the orcs. The issue of scale is one that occurs in other **children's fiction** – say *The Borrowers* – as well as the film *The Incredible Shrinking Man* (1957), the *Doctor Who* serial *Planet of Giants* (1965) and the US television series *Land of the Giants* (1968–1970), and some fun is to be had from the shifts in scale. *See also* Children's Fiction; Culaina; Heroes; History; Politics *and* War.

Further Reading

Baldry, Cherith. 'The Children's Books'. *GOL*, *GOL2*.
Clute, John. 'Coming of Age'. *GOL*, *GOL2*.
James, Edward. 'Weaving the Carpet'. *GOL2*.

Andrew M. Butler

Carry-On Films

Like anyone growing up in the UK during the 1950s and 1960s with a taste for comedy and a sense of the absurd, Terry Pratchett was clearly influenced by the seminal Carry-On film series. His work carries many undertones of the movie franchise, which formed a series of over thirty popular low-budget comedies that were an integral part of British popular culture from the late 1950s to the 1970s. The movies were based on a frantic mix of farce, parody and double extendres and were popularly viewed as classic examples of British comedy. The style of humour used in the Carry-On films was drawn directly from music hall tropes and the peculiarly British tradition of bawdy seaside postcards. The scripts relied heavily on the use of puns in both dialogue and character and location names. Underlying it all was a generally respectful and playful sending up of British institutions and character. Nothing was sacred, with everything from the trade unions to the monarchy; the glories of empire to the absurdities of the British tourist abroad were subject to the Carry-On treatment.

The series began with *Carry On Sergeant* (1958) about a group of raw recruits entering National Service in the army. As the third highest grossing movie of the year, it was considered enough of a success that another movie playing to the same basic formula was given the go-ahead. This time the focus would be the National Health Service and when *Carry On Nurse* became the top grossing movie in the UK in 1959, the future of the series was assured. The next four movies were also straightforward parodies of various British institutions such as the school system, the police, work and holidays.

In 1963, the series entered what is considered to be its classic period. Along with a switch from black and white to colour came an acceptance of the 1960s social revolution. The series became more ambitious in its scope and more open about sexuality, with more explicit references and situations becoming prevalent.

Production moved at an incredible rate at Pinewood Studios with twelve movies made in just six years between 1963 and 1969, using a repertoire company of well-known British comedy actors – especially Kenneth Connor (1916–1993), Charles Hawtrey (1914–1988), Sid James (1913–1976), Joan Sims (1930–2001) and Kenneth Williams (1926–1988) – who would basically play the same character type in each movie. During the mid-1960s, the movies also moved into two new genres: movie parody, perhaps most successfully in *Carry On Cleo* (1964), which even used the standing sets left over from the Elizabeth Taylor/Richard Burton epic *Cleopatra* (1963), and historical settings, such as *Carry On Up The Khyber* (1968), which spoofed British actions in colonial India.

With the dawning of the 1970s, there was a noticeable decline in quality and audiences. Attempts were made to freshen up the series by introducing new actors more familiar to the television audience. The producers also decided to return to the series' roots by parodying some current social and political issues, but times had changed. Social acceptance of explicit sexuality had made the series' reliance on innuendo seem dated. The first eight movies of the 1970s alternated the traditional Carry On formula with the new direction to mixed success. Many consider *Carry On Dick* (1974), a historical spoof on the legend of highwayman Dick Turpin, to be the last true Carry-On, with the last performances of Sid James, Hattie Jacques (1922–1980) and Barbara Windsor (b.1937). The four movies produced between 1974 and 1978 marked a continued decline, with *Carry On England* (1976), featuring almost an entirely new cast, being a flop and pulled from release as early as three days after opening. After twenty years, the series limped to an undignified end with *That's Carry On* (1977), a compilation of clips from previous movies, and *Carry On Emmanuelle* (1978), an attempt to climb on-board the soft-porn band wagon that was already fading as the 1980s approached.

Although the films almost invariably received poor reviews from the film critics, they remained consistently popular with audiences and were frequently shown on television after their first run theatre releases. They also spawned spin-off television programmes, hour-long specials *Carry on Christmas* (1969, 1970, 1972, 1974) and *Carry On Laughing*, thirteen half-hour episodes broadcast in 1975, three stage plays and a number of clip compilations.

An attempt was made to bring the series back in 1992 with *Carry On Columbus*, although this was a commercial and, unsurprisingly, a critical disaster. It was directed by Gerald Thomas (1920–1993) and produced by Peter Rogers (b.1914), who had been responsible for these duties in many of the classic films, and the script was written by Dave Freeman (b.1922), who had worked on *Carry On Behind* (1975) and the television programmes. However, most of the original major actors had died, and others refused to appear. Instead, the movie was largely cast with alternate comedians, with cameos for some of the minor stalwarts of the series. This was too edgy for the core audience and too old fashioned for the new generations of comedy fans. In 2003, plans were once more announced for another attempt at a series relaunch, *Carry On London*, but it remains stuck in pre-production at the time of writing with a 2008 release projected.

Pratchett follows a similar pattern of a repertory style cast, with recurring characters, and a tendency to parody a style of institution or a location – **Arabic Societies**, **Australia**, **China**, **Egypt** and so forth. Whilst he does use puns and double entendre, he usually avoids the level of bawdiness of the later Carry-On films. *See also* Comedy and Humour; Parody *and* Sellar and Yeatman.

Further Reading

Campbell, Mark. 2005. *Carry On Films*. Harpenden: Pocket Essentials.
Webber, Richard. 2003. *The Complete A–Z of Everything Carry On*. London: HarperCollins.
Carry On Line – The Official Carry On homepage: http://www.carryonline.com/
The Whippit Inn – Guide to Carry On films, locations, stars and more, http://www.thewhippitinn.com/

Alan J. Porter

Cats

Terry Pratchett likes cats – *UC*, his book about Real Cats, is dedicated to Oedipuss, one of Pratchett's past Real Cats. The number of cats 'owned' by Pratchett is unknown, but it is known to be large. Some appear to have simply wandered in from wreaking havoc in the Pratchett gardens. Many of his favoured characters are notable for their treatment of cats, and bad characters are sometimes measured by their mistreatment of cats.

The name 'cat' refers to a small, carnivorous feline mammal, often domesticated, sometimes feral, possibly living in packs. Technically, all larger felines such as lions, tigers and cheetahs are also cats. All cats belong to the Felid family and are thought to have evolved around twelve million years ago. The first known domesticated cats were in Cyprus 8,000 years ago and are thought to descend from African wild cats. There is a portrait of a cat wearing a collar in a tomb at Ti dated *c.*2600 BCE. Paintings and effigies of domesticated cats become common around 1600 BCE. Cats have been revered as gods, reviled and tortured as familiars of witches, and have served in roles ranging from working animals to pampered house pets.

Some feline 'white knowledge': cats always land on their feet, can see in the dark, hate water, are finicky eaters and were worshipped in ancient Egypt. In reality, falling cats must have time to realise their situation, relax and re-orient themselves and so, statistically, it is more likely a cat will survive a fifteen-storey fall than a seven-storey one – although it is likely to sustain broken bones and other injuries. There are enthusiastic swimmers among both wild and domestic cats. Most cats prefer strongly scented food and cannot taste sweets.

Cats have been linked to various religions. The Egyptians depicted the goddess Bastet with a cat's head. They first worshipped cats as intermediaries of the goddess, and eventually the cat became a godlet in its own right. The Greeks linked the cat with Artemis the Huntress, and Japanese Buddhists saw cats as intermediaries between themselves and the Buddha.

Granny **Weatherwax** likens cats to **Elves** in terms of their beauty and style, although the Elves in **Discworld** are characterised as cruel (*LL*); in the case of cats, it is an unconscious part of their nature, whereas humans have free will to be evil or not. Discworld's **Death** is famously a cat lover, and he becomes rather angry when he discovers cruelty to cats. While a fast-order cook (*M*), Death fed cats in the kitchen (on some of Harga's best meat), and somehow cats appeared in the kitchen in **Death's Domain** (*H*). Fans have hypothesised that cats, having nine lives, see Death more often than other beings, and so Death has the same sort of friendly relationship with cats that he has with the Abbot of the History Monks, who has been reincarnated many times.

The Discworld novels featuring the **Witches** of **Lancre** usually include **Greebo**, Nanny **Ogg**'s cat, a large, one-eyed tom with what would be mottled grey fur if it was not for all of the scar tissue. He has fathered an enormous incestuous tribe when he is not otherwise busy sleeping, eating or fighting everything from wolves to **vampires**. The after-effects of a spell have left Greebo with a tendency to flip between cat and human form in stressful situations: a tall, dark, rakish man with an interesting accent, a broken nose, and usually dressed in black, who exudes an intense sexuality.

Other Discworld cats include Maurice (*AMHER*), a clever talking con-cat who helps a band of talking rats make enough money to find the place where they can live the peaceful and trapless life of their dreams – taking a significant cut of the profits. Also notable is a talking (with a Sylvester-like lisp) black and white cat who manifests cartoon cat abilities with his mouse partner (*MP*), *á la* Tom & Jerry.

Useful 'white knowledge' includes Schrödinger's Cat, who appears in various Pratchett books, most notably *UC*, *LL* and *SOD*. Erwin Schrödinger (1887–1961), an Austrian theoretical physicist who contributed to the wave theory of matter and other fundamental theories of quantum mechanics, shared the 1933 Nobel Prize for Physics with the British physicist P.A.M. Dirac (1902–1984).

In 1935, Schrödinger, unhappy with the apparent conflict between what quantum theory says about the nature and behaviour of matter and what we observe to be true, proposed a *Gedanken*, or thought experiment. One may easily find the *Gedanken* online or in reference books, but it all ends up with a cat in a box, with some poisonous gas, a particle that is either decaying or not decaying, a particle decay detector as a trigger on the canister of gas and someone observing the whole thing by opening the box. The act of opening the box determines the cat's state: alive or dead. Until the lid is opened, it is in a half-state: half-dead, half-alive. This is of course ridiculous in practical terms, which was Schrödinger's original point, but people have forgotten this and it is rumoured that, near the end of his life, he wished he had never imagined the cat.

Pratchett turns Greebo into a kind of Schrödinger's Cat in *LL*, when Magrat **Garlick** puts him in a box and hands it to an elf. Greebo, in the box, has three possible states: alive, dead or absolutely furious.

It is possible the thoughtful reader has a good idea in which state Greebo emerges even without reading the book. *See also* Elves; Greebo; Nanny Ogg *and* Mrs Tachyon.

Further Reading

Burton, Maurice. 1968. *University Dictionary of Mammals of the World*. New York: Thomas Crowell Company.

The Nobel Foundation. 1965. *Nobel Lectures, Physics 1922–1941*. Amsterdam: Elsevier Publishing Company.

'Schroedinger, Erwin'. *Encyclopaedia Britannica*. http://www.britannica.com/eb/article-9066219.

Quantum Technology Centre, University of Southampton. http://www.qtc.ecs.soton.ac.uk/cat.html.

Zina Lee

Celyn, Imp Y (*SM*)

Musician from **Llamedos** with a slight lisp, who comes to **Ankh-Morpork** to make his fortune. When his harp is broken by his **Troll** friend Lias Bluestone, he goes in search of a new instrument and finds a guitar in a mysterious magical shop. This plays a new kind of music, but he and his friends – Lias on percussion and the **Dwarf** Glod Glodsson on horn – are prevented from legitimate performing as Music With Rocks In by the Guild of Musicians, a Mafia-like institution. The only place they can play is The **Mended Drum**, where they are talent-spotted by C.M.O.T. **Dibbler** who gets them a gig in the Cavern Club, a venue for trolls. By the time of a gig in Hide Park, music is possessing many in **Ankh-Morpork**, including some of the **Wizards**. He is killed in a coach crash, although **Death**, responding to Susan **Sto Helit's** wishes, changes time so that he is now working in a fish shop.

This last detail, together with the fact that everyone is convinced he is a bit Elvish (i.e. Elvis Presley (1935–1977)), is an echo of the 1981 hit 'There's a Guy Works Down the Chip Shop Swears He's Elvis' by Kirsty MacColl (1959–2000). Imp's name is translated as 'Bud of the Holly', a reference to Buddy Holly (i.e. Charles Hardin Holley (1936–1959)), rock and roll guitarist from Lubbock, Texas, who died in a plane crash with musicians J.P. Richardson, the Big Bopper (1930–1959), Ritchie Valens (1941–1959) and the pilot. Their deaths inspired the song 'American Pie' (1971) by Don MacLean (b.1945), also referenced in the novel. *See also* Elves; Llamedos *and* Pop Music.

Andrew M. Butler

Children in the Discworld Series

Many readers came to Terry Pratchett's **Discworld** in their youth. This is not surprising, as many of the early books have children and young adults as their protagonists. As a child, it is comforting and encouraging to read about people one's own age dealing with problems, especially if they are similar to things one also has to deal with. The great secret is that this is no less true as one grows older, because life has a habit of throwing new and interesting problems at you. Children, it turns out, are no small part of that, and Pratchett's books, both for and about adolescents, can be read as guides to childhood – and to dealing with the people going through it.

The definition of the child could be seen as bound by an upper age limit, with physiological, psychological, anatomical and other important changes marking a transition to adolescence or adulthood. *SM*, as Albert **Malich** ponders the sixteen-year-old Susan **Sto Helit**, he recalls the difficulties of the transition between the two states. But in Pratchett's writings, the psychological development takes precedence over the purely physical: childhood is a state of being. It is a period in which important things can (and should) happen, making it a vital concern of those undergoing it and (if the former are lucky) those guiding them through. Children are remarkably open, and this is the prime characteristic of theirs that Pratchett wants us to see. Throughout the Discworld novels, children are shown learning about (although not necessarily being taught) two important subjects: morality and how to look. The first (of course) seeks the Good, the Right, the Proper, the Decent and Correct. The latter means being open to what the Tiffany **Aching** books refer to as First Sight, seeing what is really there rather than what you want to see. Children can do bad things in Pratchett's world and often miss what is in front of them but always come right (and Right) in the end, and always with a bit of help. It should be remarked that many of Pratchett's protagonists, being in some sense ideals, are able to use First Sight, which is explicitly not for everyone, and not for anyone all of the time – Tiffany for one notes how exhausting it can be. It is a skill that comes naturally to children, especially with a little guidance, and one's capacity for it diminishes as one ages, particularly if one stops exercising it.

Since children in the books clearly need guidance, it is interesting that most of them are subject to their parents' benign neglect. **Teppic**, for instance, is have parents too busy and preoccupied to notice him, so that he brings himself up with occasion use of tutors. Eskarina **Smith** has things slightly better in *ER*, with a mother who notices her absence and sends two of her older brothers out to look for her, but the circumstances of her birth – a **wizard** passed his powers to her thinking she would be the eighth son of an eighth son – mean her parents can never quite understand her (who has not felt that in their own, nonmagical life?), and indeed they try not to think about what it means to be a female wizard. Eric **Thursley**'s mother interrupts his initial colloquy with **Rincewind** (*E*), but it is clear she has no idea what he is up to, and Eric's parrot tells Rincewind that Eric's parents spoil him. Susan Sto Helit's parents (Mort and Ysabel) try to hide important facts from her (e.g., tooth fairies exist, her grandfather is **Death**) and die when she is young (*SM*), and she cultivates a talent for becoming inconspicuous to the point of disappearing, which she puts to good and frequent use at her boarding school. When she becomes a governess, her charges' parents are too busy being adults and social climbing to pay enough attention to their children to see that the bogeymen they are scared of actually exist (*H*), and the less said about the previous nanny, who taught the children such charming beliefs as the one that bears would eat them if they stepped on a crack, the better. Mort embarrasses his family, and when an uncle suggests palming him off on someone else, Mort's father jumps at the chance to apprentice him to someone who lives far away. These all sound like fairly sad childhoods, but in fact the child who has it worst is **Coin**, whose father refuses to die and uses his son as a weapon to punish those who made his own life difficult (*S*). Taken together, these books present a clear message that parents should know when to make themselves scarce – and find someone who can be of more use in raising their child.

S also stands out as the Discworld book most obviously aimed at parents rather than children. The perspective stays so far away from Coin for so much of the book that he is not quite a character until the end, when he starts to defy his father. This could be an important message for a child facing their own overbearing parent, but the level of the father's malevolence is hopefully so far away from what anyone reading *S* will ever have to deal with that it is difficult to interpret the book as instructive. Additionally, although Coin knows his father has done (and made him do) great evil, he is only able to come into himself enough to articulate this after Rincewind gives him the opportunity. His agency comes through an external source, which is unusual for a Pratchett character, even a child. He knows his father is wrong, but he does not stand up to him until a stronger, older character does. Perhaps this is because he had never seen how to before that. Afterwards, of course, he has to go away, because he has not learned how to live properly. This is the only time in the Discworld series that it is suggested that a character who has shown positive traits is unfit to stay there. In every other book, Pratchett is at pains to show that when mistakes are made by good people (especially children, who often do not understand the trouble they are getting into), they can be corrected. Esk disobeys Granny **Weatherwax** and nearly loses herself in the mind of an eagle but is found and rescued by the latter and has a quite happy (and, it must be said, final: we never see her again, and there is no reason to think that we might) ending, working with Simon to create a new kind of magic. Eric summons what he thinks is a demon and is nearly sacrificed, turns up in the Discworld equivalent of the Trojan war (*see* **Greek Mythology** *and* **Tsort**), and ends in Hell (although he is on his way out at the close of the book). Tiffany takes the place of Summer in the Dance of the Seasons and attracts the attention of *Wint*'s title elemental, who nearly destroys her world with his cold in a misguided attempt to woo her, but she too is able to put things right and is prevented from repeating her impulsive mistake by Granny Weatherwax at the end of the tale.

The important thing seems to be the kind of influence that is exercised over the child, then. The bond of family and love is not enough. (Nor, obviously, is the bond of family and hatred for the outside world as in *S*.) Children do not raise themselves, so large parts of the books about children are about their education. (Of course, they have to work some things out on their own, even if someone is overseeing their studies. See *WFM*, for example.) Teppic's time at the Guild of Assassins is revealed in telling snapshots; Susan's boarding school gets some time (although not much, which is proper, as she considers it interferes with her education); Mort, Esk and Tiffany are often seen learning the skills of their trades (these turn out to be household chores for the most part in all their cases). The books with Granny Weatherwax especially take the time to show her methods, which aim at instilling knowledge, patience and a sense of duty. The way she teaches these things is a lesson for adults. Children will not pick up these virtues just by reading about them. In fact, the biggest difference between the specifically children's Discworld books and the other books set on that world is that the former show what childhood looks like from the inside (we are always close to Tiffany's perspective, for instance, even when Granny Weatherwax appears in that series), while the latter stay by the adults in the story and often address ways of dealing with children (sending them away, for instance, or taking them in), although they can still also move near the youngsters' perspectives.

The big project of childhood, of course, is **coming of age**. To Pratchett, this is the same as finding one's moral compass, or attuning it correctly. (Thus Samuel **Vimes** may be said to come of age in every novel in which he is the protagonist.) Childhood is the time when this happens for most people, and with the ending of a narrative and thus character development happening when one has decided what kind of person one is going to be (or at least try to be). Additionally, children, having less experience than most adults, are naturally more pliable, but, and here is the fun part, they are often more set in their ways, thinking they know everything and should get what they want. Adults have a more developed sense of right and wrong; children are still testing the boundaries and can be excused for sometimes not knowing which is which. Childhood is the time to find out. But because Pratchett knows what is right and is writing guidebooks of a sort for how to find it, we know these enquiries will lead to the correct place. The really interesting question is whether he could write a coming of age story about an evil or amoral character – C.M.O.T. **Dibbler**, say. One cannot grow up without changing; is the Discworld (or its creator) ready for a story about a good child who grows up to be bad? What is childhood but practice for adulthood? *See also* Tiffany Aching; Children's Fiction; Coin; Coming of Age; Agnes Nitt; Eskarina Smith; Mort Sto Helit; Susan Sto Helit; Ysabell Sto Helit; Teppic *and* Eric Thursley.

Further Reading

Baldry, Cherith. 'The Children's Books'. *GOL*, *GOL2*.
Clute, John. 'Coming of Age'. *GOL*, *GOL2*.

Juliana Froggatt

Children's Fiction

Pratchett's readership has long included child readers, even though the majority of his work has been published for an adult market. This may be because he has predominantly been published as **Fantasy**, a genre of fiction often regarded as 'safe' or even infantile, a notion unfair both to fantasy and to children. He also features child protagonists (*see* **Children**

in the Discworld Series), and a number of the **Discworld** novels are **coming of age** stories, but this need not prove a children's market is being aimed at; *E* for example has a number of references to tantric sex. However, his two trilogies – The **Bromeliad** and the **Johnny Maxwell Trilogy** – *AMHER*, the Tiffany **Aching** books and *WMC* – and, arguably, his first novel, *CP* – are apparently designed for younger readers.

Terry Pratchett with young readers at the British Library, after *The Amazing Maurice and His Educated Rodents* won the 2001 Carnegie Medal.

At the same time, it has been disputed that there is such a thing as 'children's fiction', where the apostrophe misleadingly suggests some sense of ownership of the fiction by children. First, very few of the authors who write for children are themselves children and, second, a legion of editors, publishers, librarians, teachers and parent all police what children are allowed to access and be interested in. Children's tastes are thus simulated and regulated by adults.

Children's fiction is frequently broken down into intended reading age groups, although these are very fuzzy: picture books consist of images and little or no text and are aimed at children from birth to about five or six, to be read either to them or by them, although an examination of the structure of *WMC* (leaving aside its intersection with *T!*) suggests that these volumes demand and reward a fairly sophisticated reading. There are books that have increasing ratios of text to pictures and are aimed at readerships from about seven to eleven, which the child is much more likely to read alone. Finally, there are books which are aimed at a teenaged or Young Adult market, which are unlikely to be illustrated and may contain controversial material. Children of this age are rarely read to, and some may have been abandoned reading fiction altogether – there has been particular concern about the lack of reading done by teenaged boys, who may have gravitated to non-fiction and magazines rather than fiction.

In a sense, the history of children's fiction can only begin with the development of a notion of the child at which the fiction is ostensibly aimed; the child is perhaps an invention of the mid-eighteenth century with the sense that children were not just small adults. A key work is ...*Émile* (1762) by Jean-Jacques Rousseau (1712–1778), which outlines the stages of growing to adulthood for a fictional male and female child. However, there had already been *A Little Pretty Pocket Book* (1744) published by John Newbery (1713–1767), a commercial collection of rhymes linked to letters of the alphabet. From this period on, there was a tension in works aimed at children between the didactic (educating for life in the real world) and entertainment (escaping from the real world).

Broadly speaking, until the late 1960s, children's fiction would contain a strong moral sense, where good would triumph, and evil-doers would be punished, with the difference between the two being clear. Fictional children would lose their parents in one way or another, in other words be absent from the moral protection and nurturing which should keep them safe; characters might be orphans, earning money in exile, sent away to school or find themselves in a different realm – or combinations of the preceding. This would mean that they would be at risk, and that this risk would be resolved through the narrative. In the Chronicles of Narnia (1950–1956) by C.S. Lewis (1898–1963), a number of different children enter at various times into the fantasy land where they work to restore the balance and health of Narnia. Much more recently, the His Dark Materials Trilogy (1995–2000) by Philip Pullman (b.1946) features a supposed orphan Lyra who travels between worlds as part of an attempt to avoid a cosmic disaster against a backdrop of political and religious intrigue. Pratchett's Johnny Maxwell Trilogy belongs in this tradition, given the entry into the virtual (*OYCSM*) or the historical (*JB*); indeed the graveyard the children visit in *JD* offers an alternate world to contemporary **Blackbury**.

Alternatively, the stories could be focused on figures with which children could identify – anthropomorphised animals, soft toys or small (and thus frequently under threat) beings. Such stories include *The Wind in the Willows* (1908) by Kenneth Grahame (1859–1932), *Winnie-the-Pooh* (1926) by A.A. Milne (1882–1956) and *The Wombles* (1968) by Elisabeth Beresford (b.1928) respectively. The interaction between Wombles and humans offers a precursor to the Nomes and humans in The Bromeliad, as does the world of *The Borrowers* (1952) and sequels by Mary Norton (1903–1992). The Wombles scavenge on the detritus of humans dumped on Wimbledon Common, and elsewhere, whilst the Borrowers live in the hidden spaces of the homes of 'human beans'. *CP*, featuring people who are small enough to live in a carpet, may also be thought of as a children's book in this tradition.

One of Pratchett's favourite books as a child was *Mistress Masham's Repose* (1946), by T.H. White (1906–1964), featuring an orphan girl who has a cruel vicar, Mr Hater, as her guardian and the abusive Miss Brown as a governess. Escaping from Miss Brown one day, she discovers a group of Lilliputians are living on an island on the lake in the grounds of her run-down mansion. This narrative combines the two traditions.

Whilst until the late 1960s children's fiction tended to have happy or consoling conclusions – the good rewarded, the family reunited, the adventure completed – there has been a move to more honest or realist – in other words downbeat – endings. In part, this was a response to the impulse to write fiction with a contemporary relevance in the era of a more permissive society, and narratives involving sexuality, pregnancy, abuse, drugs, divorce, violence and so forth would undermine the trust their teen readers placed in them if the authors resolved everything amicably.

The Chocolate War (1974) by Robert Cormier (1925–2000) features Jerry Renault, who is at odds with both his school teachers and his school's fraternity, the Vigils. The teachers and the pupils are complicit in Jerry's downfall, which is not avoided. A number of novels of the period – for example *Z for Zachariah* (1975) by Robert C. O'Brien (1918–1973) and *Brother in the Land* (1984) by Robert Swindells (b.1939) – had very bleak conclusions. This American fiction is echoed in the Young Adult novels of British writers such as Aidan Chambers (b.1934) and Melvin Burgess (b.1954). Whilst it would be a mistake to view these works as immoral, the morality is much more complex than earlier examples, and the good intentions of characters can go awry.

Pratchett is rarely so pessimistic, even in his adult fiction, but he does confront a number of serious issues across his work. The Johnny Maxwell books occupy a recognisable world of urban blight (a minor character is killed whilst joy-riding), racism (the treatment of **Yo-Less**), contemporary family life (Johnny's parents' divorce) and war (*OYCSM* being set against the backdrop of the Gulf War of 1990–1991).

The contemporary world of children's fiction does tend to mix the fantastical with a sense of realism – the best-selling works of Philip Pullman have already been mentioned, but attention must also be drawn to the books of Diana Wynne Jones (b.1934) and Jacqueline Wilson (b.1945). Pratchett's return to writing for children after the two trilogies were completed in the 1990s is in the context of the bestselling and arguably old-fashioned Harry Potter novels (1997–2007) by J.K. Rowling (b.1965) which have at times risked eclipsing other fiction for children.

Children's fiction has a number of awards given to its authors, illustrators and works, usually by adults. The Carnegie Medal has been awarded since 1936 for the best children's book, and Pratchett won it for *AMHER* in 2002, having been shortlisted in 1994 for *JD* and 1997 for *JB*. He was on *The Guardian* Children's Fiction Prize shortlists in 1993 (*OYCSM*), 1997 (*JD*) and 2002 (*AMHER*). The Nestlé Smarties Book Prize is based on a shortlist drawn up by adults and voted on by children. *JB* won the Silver Award for the 9–11 category in 1996. The W.H. Smith Award for Children's Fiction was jointly won by *AMHER* in 2002. In addition, *WFM* won the W.H. Smith People's Choice Award in 2004.

In 1993, he won the Writer's Guild Award for Children for *JD. Wint* was shortlisted for the British Book Awards Children's Book of the Year in 2007.

It seems likely, with the success of the Tiffany Aching books, and the increasingly adult tone of the rest of the Discworld sequence, that Pratchett will continue to produce volumes aimed at a children's audience. Vic Parker's book, *Terry Pratchett* (2006), is a book about his work, aimed at children. *See also* Tiffany Aching; The Bromeliad; Children in the Discworld Series; Coming of Age *and* the Johnny Maxwell Trilogy.

Further Reading

Beresford, Elisabeth. 1968. *The Wombles*. London: Benn.
Chambers, Aidan. 1969. *The Reluctant Reader*. Oxford: Pergamon.
Cormier, Robert. 1974. *The Chocolate War*. New York: Pantheon.
Hunt, Peter, ed. 1990. *Children's Literature: The Development of Criticism*. London: Routledge.
———. 1994. *An Introduction to Children's Literature*. Oxford: Opus.
———. 2001. 'Terry Pratchett'. Pp. 86–121 in Peter Hunt and Millicent Lenz. *Alternative Worlds in Fantasy Fiction*. London: Continuum.
Norton, Mary. 1952. *The Borrowers*. London: Dent.
O'Brien, Robert C. 1975. *Z for Zachariah*. New York: Atheneum.
Swindells, Robert. 1984. *Brother in the Land*. Oxford: Oxford University Press.
White, T.H. 1946. *Mistress Masham's Repose*. London: Cape.
Zipes, Jack. 2002. *Sticks and Stones: The Troublesome Success of Children's Literature from Slovenly Peter to Harry Potter*. New York and London: Routledge.

Andrew M. Butler

China (*IT*)

China is an ancient civilisation and an inspiration for **parody** in Pratchett's works, especially in the representation of the **Agatean Empire**. The word is the English translation of *Zhongguo* (*Chung-kuo*) or the 'Middle Kingdom'. Modern China has now split into the Republic of China (Taiwan – formerly Formosa – Kinman, Matsu and Pengu), established in 1912, and, since 1949, the People's Republic of China (the mainland, and now Hong Kong and Macau). Many inventions – the compass, gunpowder, paper and printing – were developed in China, prior to and independent from Europe (*see* William de **Worde**). It also has one of the oldest systems of writing.

Eastern Asia, specifically China, is one of the places where human civilisation began, roughly 70,000 years ago. In legend, the first set of Chinese rulers were part of the Xia Dynasty 2205 BCE–1766 BCE, with archaeological evidence supporting the existence of a society at that time. The Shang Dynasty ruled, largely along the Yellow River, *c.*1766 BCE–*c.*1050 BCE, but the first unified China was the brief Qin Dynasty, 221 BCE–206 BCE, which was overthrown by the Han Dynasty who ruled until 220 CE. A series of dynasties followed, with China consolidating its position and perhaps turning away from the rest of the world, although links were established with Japan and land was taken in central Asia. In the nineteenth century, some contact was made with the British empire, and opium wars followed. In 1894, Korea declared its independence, leading to war with Japan, and both Korea and Taiwan were lost to Japan.

China needed to reform under a constitution rather than continue under a god-like emperor, and plans were drawn up for this in a context of ongoing civil war and failed uprisings. In 1912, the Republic of China was established, under the provisional rule of Sun Yat-Sen (1866–1925) of the nationalist Kuomintang party. General Yuan Shikai (1869–1916) attempted to oust power and bring China under his rule as emperor, but he died before this happened. In 1920, the Kuomintang brought China together in a single party state, with the lead up to the Second World War and the war itself sidelining the Communist opposition in the name of national until. Civil war started again after 1945, leading to a Communist Party takeover of the country under Mao Zedong (1893–1976, author of the so-called *Little Red Book* (1964)) in 1949. Mainland China remains, despite reforms, a largely closed society with state control of **politics**, and a problematic human rights record. It is viewed as the next great market for the west to open up, although equally the need for resources such as oil and the potential size of the Chinese workforce means that China could easily begin to dominate world economics.

IT parodies a mix of pre- and post-Communist society in its depiction of the largely isolated and isolationist Agatean Empire, which the city of Ankh-Morpork both wants and does not want to do trade with, complete with great wall and Forbidden City, a palace in Beijing. The empire has also had a series of dynasties – the Hongs, the Sungs (960–1279), the Tangs (618–907), the McSweeneys and the Fangs – some of which sound more authentic than others. It has also been under the authoritarian rule of a god-like emperor who controls his people's contact with the outside world.

Chinese culture is represented in the form of foot binding, when Agatean women are perceived to have small feet. More positively, there is Shibo Yangcong-san, the **Discworld** equivalent version of the tile-based Mahjong, although the rules seem to be closer to Cripple Mr Onion (*see* **Games**). The willow pattern used on real-world plates is replicated in Three Solid Frogs's designs. The book *The Art of War* (sixth century BCE) by Sun Tzu is also mentioned, in which military tactics which avoid actual **war** and battles are discussed. Agatean diplomacy is modelled on these ideas, although no one can remember precisely who wrote the book.

The rising led by **Twoflower's** daughters involves a Red Clay army. This is clearly a nod to the red army of the communists, but also to the terracotta army found in 1974 in China which date back to the first Qin emperor, Qin Shi Huang (260 BCE–210 BCE). This was a collection of thousands of life-sized, life-like and apparently individual clay statues, buried with the empire. Here they are somewhat like golem, but controlled in a manner similar to **computer games**. There have been many rebellions in the history of China, most obviously the Communist one – Mao's *Little Red Book* becomes Twoflower's *What I Did On My Holidays* – but also the Taipin (1850–1816) and Boxer (1899–1901) rebellions which Pratchett references. The battles between Lord Hong and Lord Tang's troops echo the ongoing struggle for dynastic control; the intervention of the Silver Horde with **Cohen the Barbarian** echoes the foreign interventions that have tried to take advantage of the political chaos.

The curious thing is that with his grin and his obsessive use of the iconography box, Twoflower always came across as more Japanese than Chinese, but Japanese and Korean culture are also brought in for parody (perhaps dubiously, given they are different cultures). *See also* Agatean Empire; Bes Pelargic; Cohen the Barbarian; Counterweight Continent; Discworld *and* Twoflower.

Further Reading

Ebrey, Patricia Buckley. 1999. *The Cambridge Illustrated History of China*. Cambridge: Cambridge University Press.

McAleavy, Henry. 1967. *The Modern History of China*. London: Weidenfeld and Nicolson.

Andrew M. Butler

Chriek, Otto (*FOC*, *TT*, *MR*, *GP*)

A (reformed) **Vampire** who works for William de **Worde** on the *Ankh-Morpork Times*, **Discworld's** first newspaper. Chriek is a photographer, or at least uses an iconography box. Unfortunately, every time the flash of his salamander goes off, he turns into a pile of dust and has to be revived with a spot of blood. This is a liability in his occupation, but he is good at his job. As an alternative, he has been pioneering the **technology** of dark light, but this is viewed with some superstition. He is an eccentric outsider but at the least tolerated.

His accent and first name are standard issue faux-Germanic. The Chriek is somewhere between 'shriek', a kind of scream, and Max Schreck (1879–1936) who played Graf Orlock, the Count Dracula figure, in *Nosferatu, eine Symphonie des Grauens* (1922) (and the film *Shadow of the Vampire* (2000) implausibly but entertainingly suggests Schreck was actually a vampire). His character as ace (if ghoulish) photographer owes something to Weegee (Arthur Fellig (1899–1968)), a newspaper cameraman who was noted for his stark crime scene pictures of New York, whose nickname (a phonetic version of Ouija) came from his uncanny ability to be in the right place at the right time. *See also* Überwald; Vampires *and* William de Worde.

Andrew M. Butler

City Watch

The City Watch sequence currently consists of the books *GG!*, *MAA*, *FOC*, *J*, *FE*, *NW*, *T!* and the short story 'TOC', though various members of the City Watch appear in several other **Discworld** books. The City Watch books are the detective books of the Discworld and, as the name might suggest, follow the antics of the **Ankh-Morpork** City Watch, and most importantly, the Watch Commander, Samuel **Vimes** (rank in the Watch, from lowest to highest, goes: Lance-Constable, Constable, Corporal, Sergeant, Sergeant-at-Arms, Captain and Commander).

The Night Watch. Artwork by Paul Kidby. (From left to right) Nobby Nobbs, Carrot Ironfoundersson, Samuel Vimes and Frederick Colon. (Back row) Dragon.

When the Watch is first introduced, it is known as the Night Watch. At the time, the Day and Night Watches were separate entities (the Day Watch itself was seen as no better than a common street gang), and the Night Watch was seen as little more than a necessary evil. At the time, the Night Watch only consisted of a then alcoholic Vimes (then Captain of the Night Watch), Fred **Colon** and Nobby **Nobbs**. Their only real job at the time was to wander the streets ringing a bell and claiming that 'all's well'. If things were deemed not well, then they would quickly run away and find some place where all was well.

The introduction of Carrot **Ironfoundersson** (who actually wanted to join, as opposed to being forced like most before him) to the unit soon changed all of this, as his honest and driven nature began to turn the Night Watch into a proper police force. Carrot's single-minded pursuit of justice awoke a need within Captain Vimes to actually act like a Watchman, arrest criminals, and solve crimes. The Night Watch's actions in the incident with the dragon (*see GG*) set their reputation as a unit to be watched (no pun intended), if not feared – yet.

Model of the New Watch House created by Discworld Merchandising.

From here, the Watch began to take their jobs a little more seriously. While Colon and Nobby tried to hold onto their old ways, Vimes and Carrot, along with new recruits **Cuddy**, **Detritus** and Angua von **Überwald**, set about to make Ankh-Morpork a better place to live. In *MAA*, the Night Watch found themselves up against Dr Cruces (the head of the Guild of Assassins) and the Gonne. Again, the members of the Watch became mixed up with serious events and, again, came out on top. As a result of this, the Night and Day Watches were combined into one City Watch with Samuel Vimes, who had retired to marry Sybil **Ramkin**, rehired as City Watch Commander, a post once held by an ancestor of his.

This is where one of the major themes in the City Watch sequence shows up: the increasing influence that Vimes and the Watch has in the political arena. Now officially a proper police force, the City Watch continues to grow and become involved in situations that, at one time, they would have stayed far away from.

For starters, in *J*, Vimes and the Watch (who had officially taken a leave of absence to join Vimes's special forces during the war between Ankh-Morpork and **Klatch**), engage in the pursuit of a potential murderer across Klatchian borders; in the fallout of which, they are even forced to arrest Patrician **Vetinari** for crimes against the state but then reinstate him when no proof of his crime exists. In *FE*, Vimes, as the Duke of Ankh-Morpork, is assigned to be the ambassador to **Überwald** for the Low King's coronation. At the same time, he is asked to investigate the theft of the Scone of Stone from the dwarfen mines there; the process of the investigation brings Vimes up against the old-fashioned political situation in Überwald and against some of their most prominent families (in particular, Angua's family). Finally, in *T!*, the Watch is brought in to investigate the murder (and, again, the political implications deriving from) Grag Hamcrusher, a very influential dwarfen leader; this situation means that the Watch has to deal with the ancient enmity between the **dwarfs** and **trolls** and their integration with the rest of the citizens in Ankh-Morpork. Despite their humble beginnings, the Watch (and Vimes in particular) pulls together and finds the correct solution in each of these situations.

Another major theme that runs through the City Watch sequence of books is that of race (species) relations (*see* **Racism**). Under the rule of Vetinari, the city of Ankh-Morpork increasingly becomes a place where members of any race or nationality can come and make their own future. This increased diversity is mirrored by Vetinari's decision that the Watch should provide equal opportunity employment. While this decision is made, at least in part by Vetinari's desire to keep everybody happy, the cynic might suggest that part of Vetinari's motive was to irritate the then Captain Vimes.

Initially, Vimes was against integration, due to his having irrational racial prejudices (especially against **vampires** – Vimes flat out refused to hire any vampires). Vimes, however, obeys the Patrician and implements this policy, initially hiring the **dwarf** Cuddy, the **troll** Detritus and the **werewolf** Angua. In time, as the Watch expands, every race becomes represented: gnomes, gargoyles, golems, **Igors** and even, eventually, vampires. However, problems always seem to arise whenever new races are introduced, as it may take some people time to accept their new partners. In *MAA*, when people of different races began to be recruited, due to lack of numbers within the Watch, the dwarf, Cuddy, and the troll, Detritus, are forced to be partners. In the Discworld, dwarfs and trolls are natural enemies, and Cuddy and Detritus take an instant dislike to one another.

However, as time goes on, and they are forced to rely on each other to survive, Cuddy and Detritus form a friendship that ignores the boundaries of their respective races. Cuddy even, at one point, makes a special cooling helmet for Detritus to wear so that his brain can operate at colder, and therefore more intelligent, temperatures than he would normally experience. Cuddy's death at the end of *MAA* hits Detritus hard, and in remembrance of Cuddy, it may be the reason that Detritus seems the most willing to look past race when accepting new faces in the Watch (though it could also be that trolls have nothing really to fear from some of the other races since they are immune to attacks like a vampire's bite).

Angua, being a werewolf, has also had a hard time feeling accepted in the Watch, though mostly it is her race's own natural necessities for acceptance and canine conformity that make her feel this way. When first introduced in *MAA*, she keeps her true race a secret from Carrot, who she had fallen in love with, because she was afraid of scaring him off. (Vimes was the only person who officially knew about her, though he told Colon due to his being second in command, and of course, he told Nobby.) When Carrot first saw Angua in her wolf form, he tried to attack her, though this was because he did not realise who it was. When Colon and Nobby inform Carrot of what Angua really is, he accepts her just as readily as he did when he thought she was human.

Angua goes on to have further problems when the dwarf Cheery **Littlebottom** is hired in *FOC*. Cherry, like Angua, comes from Überwald, and she has come to detest werewolves, even going so far as to continually wear a mail vest made from silver to protect her in case of an attack. Again, like with Carrot, Angua hides her race from Cheery, but has to put up with Cheery's continual complaints about werewolves as they (like Cuddy and Detritus) have to patrol together. Despite this, Angua likes Cheery, and they get along well. Angua is forced to reveal her true nature to save Cheery from falling into a vat of molten wax (and proceeds to burn herself on Cheery's silver vest). At this point, Cheery had come to really like Angua, and look up to her as a sort of big sister, and is able to accept this fact about Angua. While she does not necessarily go on to form any love for werewolves as a species, she has accepted one as a friend.

Angua, however, does spend some time on the other side of the fence. In *T!*, Vimes is finally forced to hire a vampire, and Salacia (insert many pages of middle names here) von Humpeding (Sally for short) joins the Watch. Angua, having come from Überwald, has had past dealings with vampires and detests their smug superiority and their ability to seem at ease in every situation. As Angua can attest to, werewolves are naturally subservient. Werewolves are also aware of their precarious position in a society (both canine and human) that does not want them around.

Vampires, on the other hand, can blend in better with society, especially if they are 'black ribboners' (Vampires who have given up human blood). Vampires (in Angua's opinion) have much more class and tend to be better mannered, than werewolves, and therefore receive more sympathy from the more 'normal' races. Werewolves, however, are seen more as an aberration and need to be stamped out.

It is for reasons such as these that Angua has problems with vampires (the fact that she can smell vampire more keenly than other races does not make things any easier). When she is in the presence of a vampire, she automatically feels insecure and submissive. This causes an interesting fight within herself when Sally joins the force, because Sally is just a Lance-Constable, whereas Angua is a Sergeant. However, at times, because of her natural tendencies, she finds herself automatically following Sally's suggestions.

Angua's dispute with Sally is heightened by the fact that Sally finds Carrot to be quite handsome and does not hide this in anyway. While angering Angua, this also worries her because Carrot, being automatically courteous to everybody, is overly respectful of Sally (almost seeming deferential at times), causing jealousy on Angua's part. However, Angua finds herself having to work closely with Sally. While Angua is able to vent her frustrations to Sally, and they are able to come to an understanding of one another, there is no real camaraderie between them.

A good reason why many of the members of the Watch are able to put their differences aside and work together towards a common goal is because of Commander Vimes. As mentioned before, in the beginning, Vimes dislikes the idea of adding non-humans to the Watch, but is forced to go along with it because of Vetinari's authority. Quickly, however, Vimes comes to understand the uses of having 'others' around, as their different abilities can make investigating crimes easier. For example, Angua's fantastic sense of smell allows her to know exactly how events panned out at a crime scene, Detritus is excellent at crowd control (especially once he acquires his crossbow) and gargoyles such Downspout are excellent for stakeouts and observation.

Despite this, though, what makes Vimes accept his new employees is the old Watch standard that Watchmen always stick together. To Vimes, it is important that all Watch members support all Watch members, because nobody else is on the side of the Watch. Therefore, when new races are added, he makes the addendum that in the Watch, there are no races; there is only the Watch. By forcing the other members of the Watch to accept this, he opens the possibilities for people like Detritus and Cuddy, Angua and Cheery, even Vimes and Sally to form, at the very least, working relationships, if not outright friendship.

At this point, the Watch has grown to the point where they can now provide real security for Ankh-Morpork and her citizens. This is not to suggest that the setup of the city has changed in any major fashion, nor does it suggest that the Guilds have lost any of their influence. This just means that the Watch have found its own place within Ankh-Morporkian society and its social structure. *See also* Ankh-Morpork; Frederick Colon; Cuddy; Detective and Noir Fiction; Detritus; Igor; Carrot Ironfoundersson; Cheery Littlebottom; Nobby Nobbs; Racism; Angua van Überwald *and* Samuel Vimes.

Further Reading

James, Edward. 'The City Watch'. *GOL*, *GOL2*.

Mark D. Thomas

Clarecraft

A company which made **Discworld** merchandising, in particular figurines.

The company was established in 1980 in Woolpit Business Park, Clare, Suffolk, by Bernard **Pearson** (b.1946) and his wife Isobel. In 1993, they sold the company to Trish Baker and Sally Couch, who continued to make the merchandising whilst Bernard moved on to other things. In late 2005, they took the decision to close the factory and the company.

Bernard had been reading Pratchett's novels for a number of years before they met in 1990, and the latter drew a sketch of **Rincewind** for him on the back of an envelope. This was turned into a figurine, which went into production in 1991. Further figurines followed, made by self-employed designers and full-time workers, to designs sketched by Pratchett. These included **Death** as the **Hogfather**, Carrot **Ironfoundersson**, Lady Sibyl **Ramkin**, Shawn **Ogg**, Granny **Weatherwax**, Gaspode the Wonder **Dog**, Dr Whiteface (*MAA*) and Lucky Nac Mac Feegle (*WFM*, *HFOS*, *Wint*). They also produced t-shirts, prints, key rings, mouse mats, rings and jigsaws. The company established a fan club (*see* **Fandom**), the Guild of Collectors and, from 1994, organised a number of Discworld **conventions**, which attracted over a thousand attendees. They also produced materials, such as greetings cards, by Graham **Higgins** and Stephen **Player**. Outside of the Discworld, they produced Faerie Realm figures based on designs for fairies by Michael Talbot.

Hand-painted and made in Britain, the figures were clearly a labour of love and the company refused to relocate any of its manufacturing overseas which might have reduced costs (and quality). Clarecraft models already kept their value because they were made in limited editions or retired after a number of years in production (a practical as well as commercial decision), but the closure of the company should ensure the market is kept buoyant by ongoing demand. *See also* Bernard Pearson.

Andrew M. Butler

Cohen, Jack (b. 1933)

A reproductive biologist and honorary professor at the University of Warwick's Mathematics Institute, Jack Cohen has collaborated with mathematician (and sf writer) Ian **Stewart** on a number of popular-science books characterised by a wide-ranging enthusiasm for both science and **Science Fiction**, as well as writing with other partners and on his own. Together, Cohen and Stewart are the collective entity Jack&Ian, whose writings include *The Collapse of Chaos* (1994), *Figments of Reality* (1997), *Evolving the Alien* (2002, also titled *What Does a Martian Look Like?*) and the three *SOD* books in collaboration with Terry Pratchett.

Cohen, Jack

Jack Cohen and aliens.

Individually, Cohen's expertise on the bizarre variant forms life has established on Earth has led him to become a consultant on alien ecologies drawn upon by numerous science fiction writers including Harry Harrison (b.1925), Anne McCaffrey (b.1926) and Larry Niven (b.1938). He is known to the wider public through numerous television appearances and public lectures: variants of one lecture alone on the possibility of life on other planets have been given to schools since the early 1960s. The lecture developed into the book *Evolving the Alien*: an attempt to move speculation about astrobiology (the science of extraterrestrial life – a science which has not yet established that it really does have a subject-matter) from its focus on Earthlike environments. Although there are certain evolutionary 'universals' such as flight or sight, even on Earth they have developed in very different ways. Alien life, contends Cohen, may have developed in even more different ways to have coped with very different environmental challenges, and we should not assume that we would even be able to recognise alien life. Certainly humanoid form may well not be conceived as a 'universal' for intelligent life. In *Evolving the Alien*, Cohen and Stewart develop a scenario where two aliens are exploring the vast array of ecological niches on Earth, engage with the roots of Cohen's 'design work' for authors like Larry Niven and Anne McCaffrey and cite some of the classic imaginings of science fiction to suggest that life elsewhere in the universe could be very different indeed to that on earth.

A reader of science fiction from childhood and active in British science-fiction **fandom** since 1968, he is a frequent and popular guest at science-fiction **conventions**, where his slide-shows are known to illustrate exactly what is meant by the old joke 'How do porcupines make love?' '*Very carefully*'.

'Jack&Ians's' writing examines in a remarkably entertaining fashion the history and philosophy of science, how evolutionary biology can be linked to theories like Complexity and how science is the story of our culture: or one of the stories generated by and forming the conceptual toolkit that makes us human, If the brain's internal capabilities is 'intelligence', they suggest, we may give a similar name to the external influences, cultural or otherwise, which affect the brain and the mind. They call these influences 'extelligence'. Some examples of 'extelligence' are libraries, books and the Internet. In *The Collapse of Chaos* and *Figments of Reality*, we also come across the concept of 'lies-to-children' – the necessarily simplified stories we tell children and students as a foundation for understanding so that eventually they can discover that they are not, in fact, *true*. Science is not a way of discovering an unshakable truth: it is a way of discovering how much there is of the universe that we do not know.

The humour, wide-ranging speculative thought, and wisdom brought to the team's popular-science writing is heightened when Jack&Ian become Jack&Ian&Terry in the *SOD* books.

With Ian Stewart, Jack is co-author of two science fiction novels, *Wheelers* (2000) and *Heaven* (2005). *See also Science of Discworld and* Ian Stewart.

Further Reading

Cohen, Jack, and Ian Stewart. 1994. *The Collapse of Chaos*. London: Viking.
———. 1995. *Figments of Reality*. Cambridge: Cambridge University Press.
———. 2000. *Wheelers*. London: Warner Aspect.
———. 2002. *Evolving the Alien*. London: Ebury.
———. 2005. *Heaven*. London: Warner Aspect.

Andy Sawyer

Cohen the Barbarian, Genghiz (*LF*, 'TB', *IT*, *LH*)

A **parody** of Conan the Barbarian, a character from **Fantasy** stories by Robert E. Howard (1906–1936) (*see* Fritz **Leiber**). The character is a depiction of what **heroes** would be like once they have aged and have been battered around by their adventures – in other words in need of hot water, good dentistry and soft toilet paper. In *LF*, he is already an old man, who still has fighting skills, but who lives in a world where the great fights are all but over. In 'TB', he reminisces about the good old days of heroic **narratives**. In *IT*, he has teamed together with his surviving peers – Boy Willie, Caleb the Ripper, Mad Hamish, Old Vincent, Ronald Saveloy and

Truckle the Uncivil – to form the Silver Horde, the senior citizens' equivalent of the Golden Horde – a state formed out of the Mongol Empire of Genghis Khan (1162–1227). The Horde invade the Agatean Empire as a means of guaranteeing a pension for them all. In *LH*, this appears not to have been enough for them, and the surviving members of the Horde decide to take fire to the gods and attack the Hub. They are defeated by Carrot **Ironfoundersson** and narrative imperative.

Cohen has one known daughter, Conina (*S*). *See also* Heroes; Fritz Leiber *and* Narratives.

Andrew M. Butler

Cohen the Barbarian (central, with eye patch) leading the Silver Horde's attack on the gods; including Mad Hamish (in wheelchair), Boy Willie, Truckle the Uncivil and Caleb the Ripper. Artwork by Paul Kidby from *The Last Hero* (Paperback edition).

Coin (*S*)

The eighth son of an eighth son can become a wizard, and Ipslore the Red is no exception. **Wizards** are forbidden to have sex, possibly because an eighth son would become a sourcerer, able to create magic without spells – rather as Simon seems to have done, although his status as sourcerer is disputable (compare *ER*). Ipslore has been driven away from the **Unseen University** and decides to use his eighth son, Coin, to seek revenge or power or both. Coin is thus a front, a cipher, a coinage, controlled by the staff bequeathed to him and occupied by his father. This explains why he has powers and intelligence beyond his ten years, and why this is not quite a **coming of age** novel like the previous two. In the aftermath of the

Apocralypse, having been rescued by **Rincewind** from the **Dungeon Dimensions**, he is forced to abjure magic – like Prospero in **Shakespeare's** *The Tempest* – but he does create himself a garden in the mountains to retreat to, as did a number of sourcerers before him. *See also* Coming of Age; Children in the Discworld Novels; Dungeon Dimensions *and* Wizards.

Andrew M. Butler

'A Collegiate Casting-Out of Devilish Devices' (13 May 2005)

A satire featuring the **Wizards** of the **Unseen University** which appears in a newspaper aimed at the university market. It deals with the Research Assessment Exercise (RAE), a census of research outputs held roughly every five years to which scores are attached for individual departments, and money from the Higher Education Funding Council for England, the Scottish Further and Higher Education Funding Council, Higher Education Funding Council for Wales and Department for Employment and Learning of Northern Ireland. The process is divisive, in terms of further segmenting the university sector and creating ill feeling between colleagues at specific universities.

A.E. Pessimal (who by *T!* is an accountant induced into the **City Watch**) has been made Inspector of Universities by Patrician **Vetinari** and the Faculty are filled with dread. He wants to know what they do, what their widening participation strategy is and whether they have an ethics committee. They are horrified at this nosing into their business – traditionally they have not paid taxes, say, because traditionally they have not been asked – but reluctantly agree to set up a committee to oversee the issue.

The issues raised in the story are all pertinent to British tertiary education – more so than previous depictions of the university in **Ankh-Morpork** and the reactions of Archchancellor **Ridcully**, the Dean, the Bursar, The **Librarian**, Ponder **Stibbons** and the others are typical of many senior academics – not that they are necessarily wrong to behave this way. *See also* Unseen University *and* Wizards.

Andrew M. Butler

Colon, Sergeant Frederick (*GG*, *MP*, *RM*, 'TOC', *MAA*, *SM*, *FOC*, *J*, *FE*, *TT*, *NW*, *TT*, *T!*)

Colon is a long-time member of the **Ankh-Morpork City Watch** and holds the rank of sergeant. He is past retirement age, but enjoys the perks of his job, so he continues to stay on. Colon is married and has a number of children and grandchildren; the reader, however, has yet to meet any of his family.

Not exactly the smartest of individuals, Colon does appear to be a natural sergeant as he is able to maintain discipline in the lower ranks. Having been around for so long, he also tends to have a good sense about the mood of the populous, and **Vimes** uses Colon to gauge when something is about to go wrong. He is not officer material, as the one time he was promoted to Acting Captain during the absence of both Commander Vimes and Captain Carrot **Ironfounderrson** led to half the Watch quitting and the other half forming a guild to oppose him.

Colon has formed a strong friendship with Corporal Nobby **Nobbs**, and they are usually partnered on beat patrol. Nobby is one of the few people less intelligent than Colon, and Colon is able to use this fact to appear smarter himself. He spends a great deal of time giving Nobby sage (that is, wrong) advice. He is, however, generally friendly to Nobby and most of his co-workers. *See* Ankh-Morpork; City Watch; Detective and Noir Fiction; Nobby Nobbs; racism *and* Samuel Vimes.

Further Reading

James, Edward. 'The City Watch'. *GOL*, *GOL2*.

Mark D. Thomas

The Colour of Magic (1983)

The first of the **Discworld** novels, divided into four, named, sections, the first of which gives the book its title. The colour of magic is Octarine, the eighth colour of the rainbow. The first edition, published by Colin **Smythe** Ltd of Gerrards Cross with a cover by Alan Smith, consisted of 506 copies; Corgi's original paperback run in 1985 was 26,000 copies with a cover by Josh **Kirby**. A second hardback edition of 1033 copies, with an introduction, was published in 1989 by Colin Smythe Ltd with a cover by Josh Kirby. In 1993 Corgi issued the edition with the Vitruvian Turtle cover by Stephen **Player**, in an attempt to widen the market and be filed in with fiction A–Z. Gollancz issued a compact edition of about 20,000 copies in 1995. It was republished with *LF* by Colin Smythe Ltd as *The First Discworld Novels* (1999) and by Gollancz with *LF*, *S* and *E* as *The Rincewind Trilogy* (*sic*, 2001). A commemorative twenty-first anniversary edition was published by Doubleday in association with Colin Smythe Ltd in 2004. From 2005 Corgi have issued a version with a black and gold photographic design. The novel has been translated into over twenty-five languages, including Bulgarian, Chinese, Croatian, Czech, Danish, Dutch, Estonian, Finnish, French, German, Greek, Hebrew, Hungarian, Icelandic, Italian, Japanese, Korean, Lithuanian, Norwegian, Polish, Portuguese, Romanian, Russian, Serbian, Slovakian,

Slovenian, Spanish, Swedish, Turkish and Welsh. It became one of the Discworld **Comics (*see Terry Pratchett's The Colour of Magic*)** and a **computer game**. Sky One are planning an adaptation of the novel for television. Michael Moorcock wrote, in *Wizardry and Wild Romance*, 'Pratchett gives us broad comedy. It is excellent farce – intelligent entertainment'.

Cover of *The Colour of Magic* ('adult' edition). Typical of the sophisticated black and gold photographic covers which have been available in the UK since 2004.

Twoflower has arrived in **Ankh-Morpork** from the **Agatean Empire**, part of the distant Counterweight **Continent**, as a tourist and is keen to see all the delights that such an ancient city has to offer him. The failed Wizard **Rincewind** rescues him from certain death in The **Broken Drum** and becomes his guide through the land – in part because the **Patrician** of the city insists he takes the job. The two find themselves in the realm of the spirit Bel-Shamroth, in a hollowed out mountain which is home to imaginary **Dragons** and their riders, and finally to Krull, an area right on the edge of the Discworld. Along the way, Rincewind has several narrow escapes from death – and encounters with **Death** – and is last seen falling over the edge of the planet.

The first novel in the Discworld sequence is really four novellas, set over a period of months, and without a strong overall story line beyond Twoflower's trip. In the first section, 'The Colour of Magic', the source of Pratchett's parody is largely Fritz **Leiber** and the Gray Mouser stories. The second, 'The Sending of Eight', is inspired by the horror narratives of H.P. Lovecraft (1890–1937), particularly the Cthulhu mythos stories which involve the invocation of evil deities. 'The Lure of the Wyrm', the third section, draws on the dragon novels of Anne McCaffrey (b.1926) which begin with *Dragonflight* (1968) and try to have a certain amount of scientific rationale beneath their fantasy. The final section, 'Close to the Edge', is less difficult to pin to a precise source, but the Chelysphere designed for a space flight to determine the sex of **A'Tuin** has a mock Victorian **Science Fiction** feel to it, although its inventor Dactylos is a variation on the mythical Dedalus, creator of the labyrinth. Some of the imagery may derive from Yes's 1972 album *Close to the Edge*, and its gatefold cover by Roger Dean (b.1944).

Much play is made in novel of the collision between the real and fantasy world – Twoflower is in *in-sewer-ants* (insurance) and speaks of *reflected-sound-of-underground-spirits* (echo-gnomics, that is economics). At one point, Rincewind and Twoflower are even transported onto a TWA airliner. *See also* Great A'Tuin; Audio Books; Discworld; Dragons; The Luggage; Rincewind; Twoflower; Unseen University *and* Wizards.

Further Reading

Clute, John. 'Coming of Age'. *GOL*, *GOL2*.
Langford, David. 2005. '*The Colour of Magic* by Terry Pratchett (1983)'. Pp. 973–975 in *The Greenwood Encyclopedia of Science Fiction and Fantasy: Themes, Works, and Wonders*. Edited by Gary Westfahl. Westport, CT: Greenwood.

Andrew M. Butler

The Colour of Magic (Computer Game) *see* Computer Games

Comedy and Humour

Pratchett's work is very much in the tradition of British comedy, referencing both William **Shakespeare** and **music hall**, and acknowledging such comic forebears as **Sellar and Yeatman**, P.G. **Wodehouse** and the **Carry-On films**. His references to popular culture almost inevitably does include other comedians, such as those in **Hollywood comedies**. Within **Fantasy** and **Science Fiction**, his eventual success was aided by earlier novels by Robert **Sheckley** and Douglas **Adams**. A number of different theorists and philosophers have offered theories of comedy and humour, which this entry will explore as potential ways of understanding how Pratchett's fiction works and suggestive of further possible analyses.

Comedy is a mode of culture which may be found in a range of different media and is a characteristic of Terry Pratchett's writings. The word is thought to derive from the Greek word *komoidia*, amusing spectacle, which in turn comes from *komos* ('revel') and *oidos* ('singer'), with perhaps the sense that it has its origins in singing under the influence of alcohol. An alternate derivation is offered by the Greek philosopher Aristotle (384–322 BCE) in his *Poetics*, from *komai*, or outlying villages, as distinguished from the city. Comedians were thought to wander from village to village, as befitted their lack of seriousness. Comedy is frequently contrasted with other modes, especially tragedy.

Humour derives from the Latin *Umor* ('fluid'), from the medieval theory of bodily liquids which determines the mood of the individual; these were blood (hopefulness), phlegm (apathetic), choler (anger) and melancholy (sadness). By the sixteenth century, humour referred to a state of mind or mood, with the sense of funniness and amusement arriving in the early seventeenth century. Humour refers to a sense of happiness, sometimes in the face of adversity. Again there is a sense of optimism, sometimes despite all the odds, in Pratchett's work.

Both comedy and humour may lead to a reaction of laughter in the audience, but this is not a necessary reaction, nor does the production of laughter necessarily mean that something is comedic or humorous – fear can also produce the same reaction. Laughter is often held to perform three purposes. First, it can be seen as a mark of superiority of the laugher over the butt of the joke, with a corrective function to indicate that the butt has got something wrong. This laughter is perhaps produced by some of Pratchett's more hapless characters, such as **Rincewind** and the **wizards** in general. Second, it marks a sense of relief or release of tension, with comedy as a safety valve. If a situation gets too dark, or too dark, a well-placed joke will refresh the spectator's emotions. Certainly, there are some very dark moments in Pratchett's fiction – from Rincewind's encounters with danger to the fabric of the **Discworld** being put at risk – but Pratchett's jokes rescue the books from being bleak. Finally, laughter is a response to a sense of absurdity, as the mind recognises the similarities between two or more juxtaposed things which on the face of it are very dissimilar. One example of this is the assassins' examination in *P* which resembles a British driving test.

Perhaps because of the easy appeal of comedy to its audience, rather than comedy being something that an audience has to work at, comedy is devalued as a mode and is not taken seriously as the tragic, the epic or even the romance. This is a problem which goes back at least as far as Aristotle's *Poetics*, which was meant to be a description of the workings of both tragedy and comedy, but only the sections on tragedy survive. It is not clear whether the material on comedy was never written, or has been deliberately destroyed in the intervening centuries. However, it is possible to extrapolate a theory of comedy from his notion of tragedy being about a great man with a tragic flaw in his character, leading first to a reversal of fortune for that man, and thus providing a sense of catharsis for the audience. Comedy can equally feature the reversal of fortune of an individual with comic rather than tragic effects, these failures being caused by character flaws such as absent-mindedness, aloofness, obsessive compulsion, jealousy and so forth. The catharsis comes in the form of laughter rather than tears. However, Aristotle writes of comedy as being about the imitation of inferior and ugly people – he does not necessarily recognise a humour which, like some satire, pokes fun at the powers that be.

The need for comedy to be about setbacks means that the comic hero is frequently a failure. The hero wants to become rich, to gain a partner or to communicate with other people, and the success of fulfilling such desires marks the end of the **narrative**. It is no accident that Shakespeare's comedies end with weddings – marriage is the end of laughter and the moment of the renewal of the social order. (Tragedies end with a gesture towards an equivalent rite: funerals.) The narrative thus requires the postponement of successful action, and we might laugh at the protagonist because we feel superior to their lack of achievement, because we are relieved that it is not us in their position, because we recognise their position rather too well or because we empathise with their plight.

One of the reasons that Pratchett moved through a series of adolescent protagonists in the earlier Discworld novels is likely to be the difficulty of restarting a narrative after desires have been achieved. Each protagonist is a substitute for the previous ones, the new characters learn the new lessons. The alternative is to go the route that situation comedy tends to follow, in that whilst the flaws of the characters are exposed through the action of the drama, they nevertheless remain flawed. Here there is a tension between the stand-alone novel and the series – which is perhaps illustrated by the **Johnny Maxwell Trilogy** in which events of one novel are not particularly reflected in another. **Death** seems not to have been able to resolve his existential doubts about his job satisfactorily. Rincewind is perhaps too busy running to learn anything, and the **Wizards** too wrapped up in their own Learning, but the **Witches** and **City Watch** novels offer distinct story arcs. Samuel **Vimes** has battled (and risks recurring) alcoholism, has met and married Lady Sibyl **Ramkin** and now is a father, all the while moving up the aristocratic ladder yet maintaining proletarian roots. At the same time, each of the books is the same pattern, a battle for the leadership and control of Ankh-Morpork, between Lord **Vetinari** and the Law and whatever the latest candidate for king of the city is. Vimes solves each individual case, with no sense that he is improving at his job; he is competent enough.

The social nature of comedy, even comedy which is read in a book, and the licence that is given to comic writers, means that comedians are somewhat akin to shamans or other mystic figures. Somehow they make connections between things that we have never seen before, and yet once they point out the connection it seems as if we knew that all along. They help us to make sense of a frequently hostile and confusing world. At the same time, we often have the sense that we are intimately acquainted with the comedian, whereas we actually only know the persona that they have adopted. Pratchett is no exception to this, and it is a persona that has clearly brought much joy to the world.

The philosopher Henri Bergson (1859–1941) published a book on *Laughter* (1901), which argued that a human being was comic to the extent that they remind us of a machine, generally by repeating certain actions and showing a lack of conscious choices in their behaviour. Laughter was very much seen as a corrective mechanism, but it is also deriving from the absurd juxtaposition of human and machine – characters who behave as if on autopilot, Rincewind's repeated dicing with danger, **Death's** inability to remember Mort **Sto Helit**'s name, Nanny **Ogg**'s tendency to get drunk and so on. Laughter requires the suspension of emotions, especially of empathy, and is something which takes place within the human community. Pratchett's works call this into question, as whilst we are laughing at characters, we do have a sense of concern for them and their plight.

The Austrian psychoanalyst Sigmund Freud (1856–1939) wrote a whole book on jokes, *Jokes and their Relation to the Unconscious* (1905), and an article 'Humour' (1927). Freud argued that jokes were a means of gaining access to the unconscious mind for the analyst, or one way, along with dreams, psychoses, neuroses, tics and art, for the individual to express their desires rather than repressing them. Jokes, especially the sexual or the scatological, are expressions of taboo ideas and desires, and Freud goes into great detail about the way that the language and concepts of jokes work (whilst offering examples that are hardly calculated to cause hysterics). A vulgar Freudian reading of Pratchett's fiction would seem to be a rather impertinent attempt to psychoanalyse him, but Freud's listing of joke mechanisms does offer a useful typology of comedy which might be used to more fruitful ends. Certainly, Nanny Ogg's statements veil or unveil a range of sexual desires, especially when she is inebriated.

Freud's essay 'Humour' is concerned with the superego rather than the unconscious, the superego being part of the human psyche which forbids or (less often) permits the expression of desires. Usually the superego is described in rather negative terms, as a cruel, nay-saying father figure which is a relic of the child's Oedipus complex when the individual yields to the authority of the father due to castration anxieties. Freud sees humour as something which takes place in the face of adversity, the wisecrack on the way to the gallows being a key example. This might be seen as akin to the parent who consoles a child who has had a nightmare; humour is reassurance despite the terrible world. Humorous texts, especially those in which characters survive great adversity (such as Rincewind's entire life story to date) can have the effect of consoling the audience that life is not as bad as they might perceive.

The works of the Russian Mikhail Bakhtin (1895–1975) have also proven useful in the analysis of comedic texts. In *Rabelais and His World* (1965), he analyses the work of the French scholar, monk and doctor, François Rabelais (*c.*1494–1553), especially his book *Gargantua and Pantagruel* (*c.*1532–*c.*1564). The book features grotesque tales, frequently sexual in nature, and a parody of epic voyages such as Jason and the Argonauts. This Bakhtin describes as 'carnivalesque', typical of the various festivals held in the medieval era such as Mardi Gras, Corpus Christi and other Christian holy days. The carnivalesque is a period when the usual rules and conventions are suspended – a king or queen may be crowned for the day – the usual hierarchies of power are reversed. It is associated with excess and debauchery, in contrast with the abstention and cleanliness that would be typical of, say, Lent or a hard winter. It is a collective, democratic endeavour, in a shared time and space, and dogma and authoritarianism are rejected. The carnivalesque is also characterised by repeated rituals – which are echoes of Christian rituals, **parody** and the use of strong language, which is translated as Billingsgate, named for the profane language of the fishmongers of a London market. Pratchett's novels definitely fit into the tradition of the carnivalesque, and his best-seller status, not to mention the activities of **fandom**, ensures that his oeuvre is a collective one. Butler, in particular, has explored how *M* operates within the realm of the carnivalesque.

The grotesque is the name Bakhtin applies to the contortions of the body which occur in the writings of Rabelais and elsewhere. These are the results of sexual activity, the eating of food and the act of defecation. The grotesque female body is often a pregnant one, with legs wide apart, whereas the male equivalent exaggerates his genitalia. By extension, the grotesque has come to be analysed in terms of the comedy of the body, with eating, defecation, sneezing, vomiting, farting and general ugliness being central to the humour. Some critics, such as Frances Gray, have noted the **sexism** that is arguably present in the differing representations of the male and female, which they distinguish from his insight into class and other social issues. They note that a world of sexual excess is a male utopia, but with the dangers of rape and unplanned pregnancy, women may be more circumspect about the carnival. Pratchett has on occasions appeared uncomfortable about dealing with sexual matters, his **coming of age** narratives usually concluding before any relationships develop – although Nanny **Ogg** and **Greebo** offer exceptions to the rule. He also largely avoids the gross-out humour that is typified by, say, the Mr Creosote sequence of *Monty Python's Meaning of Life* (1983). *See also* Douglas Adams; Carry-On Films; Hollywood Comedies; Music Hall; parody; Sellar and Yeatman; William Shakespeare; Robert Sheckley *and* P.G. Wodehouse.

Further Reading

Aristotle, Horace, Longinus. 1965. *Classical Literary Criticism*. Translated by T. S. Dorsch. Harmondsworth, Middlesex: Penguin.

Bakhtin, Mikhail. 1968. *Rabelais and His World.* Translated by Helene Iswolksy. Chicago, Mass. and London: MIT Press.
Bergson, Henri. 1921. *Laughter: An Essay on the Meaning of the Comic.* Translated by Cloudsley Brereton and Fred Roth. London: Macmillan.
Butler, Andrew M. 'Terry Pratchett and the Comedic *Bildungsroman*'. *Foundation* 67 (Summer 1996): Pp. 56–62.
Freud, Sigmund. 1966. *Jokes and their Relation to the Unconscious.* Translated by James Strachey. London: Routledge.
Freud, Sigmund. 1990. 'Humour'. Pp. 425–433 in *Art and Literature.* Translated by James Strachey. Harmondsworth, Middlesex: Penguin.
Gray, Frances. 1994. *Women and Laughter.* London: Macmillan.

Andrew M. Butler

Comics

There have been four **Discworld** comics to date: ***Terry Pratchett's The Colour of Magic: The Graphic Novel, Terry Pratchett's The Light Fantastic: The Graphic Novel, Guards! Guards!* (Comic Book Adaptation)** and ***Mort: A Discworld Big Comic.*** For details, see the individual entries. Pratchett is friends and has collaborated with one of the leading comic writers, Neil **Gaiman**.

Andrew M. Butler

Coming of Age

The coming-of-age story, the tale of the young protagonist going through trials to achieve the transition from adolescence to adulthood, is found in folk stories in most Roundworld cultures and is one of the corner stones of the **Fairy Tale** tradition and by extension **Fantasy** literature, forming the heart of many popular fantasy novels such as J. K. Rowling's Harry Potter series, Ursula Le Guin's Earthsea series and many of the **Discworld** novels, especially the early titles, *AMHER* and the Tiffany **Aching** novels.

This narrative convention is often associated with boys and the rituals of 'becoming a man', and coming-of-age stories about girls are not only far more rare, they do not usually so much deal with the discovery of self in the transition from adolescence to adulthood, as the transition from maidenhood to motherhood. Where the boy in the fairytale is expected to become ambitious and self-sufficient, the girl does not need these qualities because her story is usually simply about finding a husband to take care of her.

Many of the early Discworld books are stories about young men becoming adults through a baptism of fire, but Pratchett has also written several books dealing specifically with girls' coming-of-age. The prevalence of coming-of-age stories in the Discworld canon is hardly surprising as the theme of identity and knowing oneself in general is strongly present in many of the novels in the series, for example in storylines such as the 'liberation' of the dwarfish women in the **City Watch** series or Granny **Weatherwax** recognising her 'true self' among the false mirror images in the end of *WA*. Novels such as *MP*, *TT* and *GP* also have storylines where characters find their place in the world or 'grow up' when they learn to take responsibility for their actions.

The most traditional fairy tale coming-of-age story in the Discworld series is probably the story of Mort **Sto Helit**. He is the humble and clumsy farmer's son who is taken in as the sorcerer's – or in Mort's case Death's – apprentice and learns his trade until he becomes his own master after challenging his mentor and teacher. Similar stories can be found in folk and fairy tales, and in fantasy literature one notable example is Otfried Preußler's classic fantasy novel *The Satanic Mill* (*Krabat*). In the description of Mort's training, *Mort* also parodies some more contemporary coming-of-age stories such as *The Karate Kid* (1984) and *Star Wars* (1977). In the end, Mort does not defeat Death, however, nor take his place or marry the Princess Keli of **Sto Lat** he so passionately tried to save. Instead, the book ends with Mort and Death's daughter Ysabell **Sto Helit** living happily ever after – or at least until the events of *SM* – at Death's mercy, and the moral of the story is in Mort learning that there are consequences to his actions rather than in the actual battle against Death making him a man.

Another rewritten fairy tale coming-of-age story is **Tomjon**'s storyline in *WS* – the long-lost heir-to-the-throne who is brought up by humble adoptive family. From a young age, Tomjon stands out from the people he grew up with, a kind of a positive version of the Ugly Duckling who is clearly destined for greater things than his adoptive family can offer. Where Pratchett differs from the fairy tale narrative, though, is when Tomjon is restored to the throne, but instead of becoming a king, he gives up the crown, choosing to continue his life as an actor, and the role of the secret heir-to-the-throne is instead suddenly thrust at Verence the **Fool**. Pratchett uses a similar storyline with Carrot **Ironfounderrsson**, also a charismatic young man estranged from his family at a young age, who is often hinted to be the lost heir-to-the-throne of **Ankh-Morpork**. Just as Tomjon chooses life in theatre and playing a king rather than being one, similarly Carrot chooses to ignore the attempts to put him to the throne and remains in the Night Watch where he can continue to help people.

The coming-of-age stories Pratchett has written about girls differ from the traditional fairytale coming-of-age stories in that the girls' main motivation is never to find their Prince Charming. *MR* combines two traditional coming-of-age storylines: the girl disguising herself as a boy to enter men's world and the idea of a war making boys into men, with suggestions of the folk tales of a wife setting out to rescue her husband thrown in as well. Girls dressing up as boys, or women dressing up as men, is an age-old story convention (and in *MR* the cross-dressing aspect is played up even more in the book when the boys-who-are-really-girls disguise themselves as washer women), but instead of becoming 'one of the guys' or learning her lesson and realising that her real place is at home, Polly in *MR* discovers that there really is no difference between men's world and women's world, especially if the manliest men are actually women. The soldiers of the regiment Polly joins are stereotypical characters borrowed from war movies and literature, but given a twist when one by one they are revealed to be young girls rather than boys. Shazzer, the quiet religious boy becomes a reborn Joan of Arc, while the story of Lofti, the girl who disguises herself as a boy to stay with her sweetheart Tonker, takes a different turn when it is revealed that Tonker is also a girl.

In *ER*, the most clearly feminist Discworld novel alongside *MR*, Eskarina **Smith**, is born with the magical powers of **wizards** and finds that she cannot use them for witchcraft, women's magic. Her rite of passage is then to be accepted in the **Unseen University** where only men are allowed to study, but also to learn to control the power she was born with. Esk finds her balance between the high academia and powerful magics of the wizards and the everyday magic of the **witches**, but is unfortunately never seen in the Discworld series again. In a way, however, Esk's legacy is continued with the Tiffany Aching series that also detail the of a young girl learning to be a witch and finding her power from within herself, and not by others. When Tiffany defeats the Queen of the Elves, she does this by becoming one with the land and the women who lived on it before her, taking on the legacy of her grandmother, mirroring Magrat **Garlick** being taken over by the spirit of the Queen Ynci without knowing that the power came from Magrat herself, as Queen Ynci had never really existed. Her powers are then born from knowing precisely where, who and what she was. In defeating the Queen, Tiffany becomes a woman as she discovers her identity and takes her place in the line of women before her. The scene reflects the scene in *WA* where Granny **Weatherwax** was able to pick her own reflection (true self) in the hall of mirrors.

Many of Pratchett's coming-of-age stories share the theme of power and how to use it. Both Tomjon and Carrot are offered a position of power, but both decline, seeing that they can be much happier and do more good by remaining who they are. Similarly, when Esk eventually defeats creatures from the **Dungeon Dimensions** that Simon has summoned, she does not do this by using her powers but by realising that the creatures reflect her power, that it is better to give people what they need by non-magical means than what they want by magic. The only way to destroy the creatures is by not using her powers. Tiffany's test is similar. Her fight against the hiver mirrors Esk's fight when she realises that the hiver is not so much possessing people as it is also giving them what they want instead of what they need. She stops fighting the hiver and in doing that, gives it what it needs, an end.

Coming of Age

Magrat's, Esk's and Tiffany's, and to an extent also Tomjon's and Carrot's, coming-of-age stories all share a variation of the same theme – becoming more powerful by possessing powers and not using them. Esk and Tiffany both pass their tests of character by actively not acting, by choosing not to use magic. It is a question of choices: Magrat, even though choosing to settle for the 'second prize', becomes more powerful as a mother and a queen than she was as the maiden and the 'third witch', a role chosen for her by others. By choosing inaction, they take control of their lives and responsibility for their actions – in other words, become adults.

Coming-of-age themes and storylines in Discworld novels:

The **Rincewind** sequence: The universe seems to want to make a man out of Rincewind even though he would prefer to remain a coward.

ER: Both Esk and Simon learn to control their powers, and Esk proves that women can be wizards just as well as men.

M: Mort becomes Death's apprentice and learns much about life when he is forced to take over his master's duties when Death goes missing.

The Lancre witches sequence: The maiden witches Magrat and Agnes grow into women in control of their own lives.

P: **Teppic** is made the king of **Djelibeybi** when his father suddenly dies.

The **City Watch** sequence: – Young Carrot Ironfoundersson joins the watch and is Made a Man.

E: Eric learns that having the power to summon demons does not mean that you should.

SM, *H* and *TOT*: Susan comes to terms with her legacy as Death's granddaughter.

AMHER: The Coming of Age and Becoming a Decent Human Being (or Cat) of the pied piper Keith and Maurice the Cat.

NW: Young Samuel **Vimes** becomes the man he is under the tutelage of old Sam Vimes.

The Tiffany Aching sequence: Tiffany's journey to become a witch.

MR: The girls of the monstrous regiment become men and find out that men are actually women. *See also* Children in the Discworld Series; Children's Fiction; Fairy Tales *and* Narratives.

Further Reading

Butler, Andrew M. 'Terry Pratchett and the Comedic *Bildungsroman*'. *Foundation* 67 (Summer 1996): Pp. 56–62.
Clute, John. 'Coming of Age'. *GOL*, *GOL2*.

Mirka Sillanpaa

Computer Games

The lack of computers (although compare HEX – *see* **Technology**) means there are no computer **games** in the **Discworld** universe, although Leonard of **Quirm** has invented Barbarian Invaders and one of Samuel

Vimes's later Dis-Organisers has games such as Splong on it. Johnny **Maxwell** is the master of computer games, however, playing Only You Can Save Mankind, a Space Invaders game into which he enters (*OYCSM*).

There have been several Discworld computer games. The first was *The Colour of Magic*, released in 1986 for Amstrad/CPC, the Commodore 64 and the ZX Spectrum. This was produced by Delta 4 Productions and released by Macmillan. It was a text-based game which followed the plot of the novel *COM* and can still be played if a Spectrum emulator is loaded onto a computer or if online. Solutions to the problems are also available online. *Discworld* was a 1995 computer game for PC (that is to say on floppy disc), PC-CD Rom and Sony Playstation, as well as the Macintosh, produced by TWG/Perfect 10 and published by Psygnosis Games. Whilst the game was still being developed, it was subtitled 'The Trouble with Dragons', and its plot anticipated *GG*, but with **Rincewind** (voiced by Eric Idle) in the Samuel **Vimes** role. Other voices include Rob Brydon (b.1965), Jon Pertwee (1919–1996), Kate Robbins (b.1958) and Tony Robinson (b.1946, who also read some of the abridged audio books). It is a prequel to *MP*. A sequel, *Discworld II: Missing, Presumed...!?* (also subtitled *Mortality Bytes!*), was published by Psygnosis Games, for PC-CD Rom, Playstation and Macintosh in 1997. This features Rincewind and the **Librarian**, in a narrative that borrows from *MP*, *RM* and *LL*. Pertwee had died and Robinson did not take part, and the cast was joined by Nigel Planer (b.1953), who has since appeared in the **Television** version of *H*. *Discworld Noir* was released in 1999 by GT interactive Software (UK) Ltd, for PC CD-ROM and Playstation. This is an entirely original story which is a **parody** of Film Noir (*see* **Detective and Noir Fiction**) and features a private eye, Lewton. No new elements from this have not yet made it through to the novels, although Pratchett was involved in writing some of the dialogue, and it does feature the **City Watch** and **Unseen University** as it is set in **Ankh-Morpork**. The voice cast is Brydon, Robert Llewellyn (b.1956), Planer and Robbins. *See also* Games *and* Technology.

Andrew M. Butler

Conventions

Many areas of **Science Fiction** and **Fantasy fandom** organise get-togethers or conventions where the fans can meet. Pratchett fandom is no exception to this, with a number of different events in Britain devoted to the man and his works, as well as events in the rest of the world. The first conventions began when letter writers to **magazines** started writing to each other, and a group of them decided to meet up in Leeds in 1937.

A convention is usually an event run by volunteers for fandom, usually managed by an ad hoc committee. (There are also conventions run for profit by companies, often connected to film or television series, where there is a stricter segregation between guests and paying customers. Amateur conventions blur the distinction.) Typically, a convention is held in a hotel over a weekend – sometimes a holiday weekend to allow for an extra day – and consists of a number of simultaneous streams of events. These might include talks, panel discussions, debates, lectures, readings, screenings, singing ('filk singing'), **games** and workshops. Usually, there is a Guest of Honour, who participates in the programme, and socialises with the attendees. In addition, there is a dealers' or hucksters' room, selling books, DVDs, t-shirts and other merchandising. Some, but not all, conventions include a fancy dress parade, the masquerade. Alongside the organised events, and often late into the night, fans socialise with each other; in British conventions, this tends to take place in the bar. A typical convention will produce newsletters in the run-up to and during the convention, as well as a programme book which typically includes articles on and by the Guests of Honour.

Conventions produce a number of newsletters (PRs) in the run up to the event, a Read Me of essentially information given to the convention-goers, a souvenir programme book and newsletters through the event itself. Some of these are likely to become collectors' items, certainly they are ephemeral publications.

Terry Pratchett has been a Guest of Honour at a number of conventions, but also attends as a guest. Pratchett was Guest of Honour at Noreascon 4, the 62nd World Science Fiction Convention, in Boston, Massachusetts from 2 to 6 August 2004 – the first annual World Science Fiction Convention, Nycon, was held in New York in 1939, but this series was interrupted by the Second World War until 1946 and Pacificon I in Los Angeles, which was the first of the annual Worldcons. Whereas the Worldcon attempts to cover all interests in science fiction and fantasy, there are also specialist conventions for individual authors, films or series, for filking, for fanzine writers, for gamers, for costumers and even for con-runners. There have been a number of events devoted to Terry Pratchett.

The first of the Discworld conventions was announced as a minicon-vention, but swelling of numbers led it to become the International Discworld Convention, held at the Britannia Sachas Hotel, Manchester, 28–30 June 1996. A second convention was held at the Adelphi Hotel, Liverpool, 18–21 September 1998, a venue for many of the Eastercons in previous years. Four years later, the convention moved to the Hanover International Hotel, Hinckley, Leicestershire – which had become a frequent choice for science fiction conventions despite poor public transport links and the paucity of nearby restaurants – and took place on 16–19 August 2002. The convention returned to Hinckley 20–23 August 2004, and most recently 18–21 August 2006, although the hotel was renamed Hinckley Island Hotel. Frequent guests at this convention include Stephen **Briggs**, Jack **Cohen**, American science fiction writer Diane Duane (b.1952), Graham **Higgins**, David **Langford**, Northern-Irish-born fantasy writer Peter Morwood (b.1956), Bernard **Pearson**, Colin **Smythe**, Ian **Stewart** and Terry Pratchett himself.

Clarecraft organised events at their workshop in 1997, 1999, 2000, 2001, 2003 and 2005 which were attended by Pratchett and other people from within the franchise, where attendees camped rather than stayed in a hotel. The 2000 event was a replacement for a cancelled Discworld Convention, and led to the idea of an annual outdoor Discworld event for those who wanted to camp or could not afford a hotel-based convention.

Terry Pratchett at the Discworld Jamboree, 2007.

The first of these – named Wadfest – was held in a field in Ambergate, Derbyshire, 28–30 September 2002, the second at Callow Top, near Ashbourne, Derbyshire in 19–21 September 2003 and 17–19 September 2004 (subtitled 'Koom Valley'). The 2005 event, 2–5 September ('Don't Go Near the Castle'), was held in Retford, Nottingham, with Pratchett in attendance. In 2006, it was held on 1–3 September ('XXXX: Dijabringabeeralong?') at Church Laneham, Nottinghamshire. The theme for 2007 was 'The Beggars Guild of Ankh Morpork' (31 August–2 September 2007). Bernard Pearson also organised the First Discworld Jamboree (3–5 August 2007) at Wincanton as a replacement for the Clarecraft Discworld Events. *See also* Clarecraft; Fandom *and* Merchandising.

Andrew M. Butler

Cookbook *see Nanny Ogg's Cookbook*

Cosgrove Hall

A leading British animation company which, like Smallfilms and Woodland Animation, focused on animation for children's television. They produced adaptations of *T* (1992), *M* (1996) and *SM* (1996), each of which has its own entry in this book.

Still from the Cosgrove Hall television adaptation of *Truckers*, 1991. Masklin and Grimma in Arnold Bros.

Brian Cosgrove (b.1934) and Mark Hall (b.1937) studied at the Regional College of Art, Manchester, in the late 1950s, and both worked as graphic designers for Granada, the north-western England franchise of the ITV network. In 1971, Cosgrove formed Stop Frame Animations and, with Hall, made the series *The Magic Ball* (1971–1972) with Eric Thompson (1929–1982) – of *Magic Roundabout* fame – as the narrator, *Captain Noah and His Floating Zoo* (1972) and a version of *Noddy* (1975).

In 1976, with the help of producer John Hambley, they set up Cosgrove-Hall Productions Ltd as a part of Thames Television, which was the weekday franchise of the London region of ITV. They made their animations, both stop-motion animation and two-dimensional cel-based paintings, in a studio in Chorlton-cum-Hardy, a suburb of Manchester, and their first productions included *Chorlton and the Wheelies* (1976) and *Jamie and the Magic Torch* (1976–1979). Their international breakthrough came with *Danger Mouse* (1981–1992), a spoof of *Danger Man* (1964–1966) and the James Bond franchise, with a mouse as the heroic agent, voiced by David Jason (b.1940) – who later went on to play Alberto **Malich** in the television adaptation of *H* and has been cast as **Rincewind** in the television adaptation of *COM*. Much of their material was written, and partially voiced, by Brian Trueman. Other successes included a 1983 adaptation of *The Wind in the Willows* (1908) by Kenneth Grahame (1859–1932) which led to a television series (1984–1988) and *Count Duckula* (1988–1993), a *Danger Mouse* spin-off featuring a vegetarian vampire duck. Much of their material was written, and partially voiced, by Brian Trueman.

T was intended to be the first part of an animated trilogy, but in 1992 the ITV regional franchises were reawarded, and Thames lost its licence, with Carlton Communications taking over on midnight at the start of 1993. The rest of the trilogy was lost in development hell. Cosgrove Hall, meanwhile, set up Cosgrove Hall Films, in association with distributors ITEL who were owned by United News and Media. The latter bought Anglia television, the ITV franchise for the east of England, in 1995. Cosgrove Hall Films continued to make cel and stop-motion animation, branching out into digital and computer animation, working with the BBC, Disney and Gerry Anderson (b.1929). Their adaptations of *M* and *SM* were co-productions with Channel 4, a British, advertisement-funded public service broadcaster. *See also* Animation *and* Television Adaptations.

Further Reading

Cosgrove-Hall Films homepage: http://www.chf.co.uk/

Cosgrove Hall Ate My Brain homepage: http://www.nyanko.pwp.blueyonder.co.uk/ chamb/

Andrew M. Butler

A Cosmic Cornucopia see Kirby, Josh

Counterweight Continent (*IT*, *LC*)

A small continent, but a heavy one because of all of the gold and octiron (an otherwise rare and unstable metal, full of **magic**) which is to be found there. This has given it the name of the Aurient. It performs the useful function of counterbalancing the rest of the disc which is the **Discworld**, presumably so that it does not slide off the backs of the **elephants**. It includes the **Agatean Empire**, Bangbangduc, Nafooi, Slakki and Land of Fog and, now, **XXXX**. The wealth of this area is to their benefit, leading to the first tourist, **Twoflower**, to be perceived as being as rich as Creosote (a seriph of El-Khali, **Klatch** (*S*)) when he arrives in **Ankh-Morpork**. There is a certain amount of trade between the two powers, and **Rincewind** has travelled there on more than one occasion. *See also* Agatean Empire; Counterweight Continent *and* XXXX.

Andrew M. Butler

Crowley, Anthony J. (*GO*)

A demon who had fought in the war in heaven on the losing side, and who has been hanging out on Earth, especially in Britain, ever since. Among his other works of evil, he was responsible for Manchester, Value-Added Tax and Welsh language television and for arranging for the London orbital motorway the M25 to be laid out as a symbol representing great evil. He dresses well, wears sunglasses (to hide his eyes) and drives a 1926 Bentley which transforms any music cassette left in it into Queen's *Greatest Hits* (1981).

His first appearance was as a snake called Crawly in the Garden of Eden; probably he tempted Eve. There he met Aziraphale, an angel with whom he formed a grudging friendship, and with whom he has to cover up the debacle of swapping the Antichrist for Adam **Young** from the prying eyes of their respective masters. Neither of the two particularly welcomes the prospect of Apocalypse. Their New Years Resolutions appear on the HarperCollins website.

His name is a nod to the English mystic and occultist Aleister Crowley (1874–1947), who wrote a mystical text *The Book of the Law* (1904) which takes the mythology of **Egypt** as its starting point. The real Crowley was labelled the wickedest man in the world by *John Bull* magazine. *See also* Neil Gaiman *and* Adam Young.

Further Reading

Gaiman, Neil and Terry Pratchett (n.d.) 'Crowley and Aziraphale's New Year's resolutions', *HarperCollins* Website. http://www.harpercollins.com/author/AuthorExtra.aspx?displayType=essay&authorID=3417.

Andrew M. Butler

Cuddy (*MAA*)

Lance-Constable Cuddy is the first **dwarf** to be hired by the **Ankh-Morpork City Watch**. He appears to look like your standard dwarf (that is: short, long beard, armed to the teeth), with all the normal dwarf prejudices (i.e. he hates **trolls**). He does possess a glass eye.

Cuddy is (much to his chagrin) partnered with **Detritus** the troll for his patrols. However, Cuddy tends to be a little more tolerant than other dwarfs, and he and Detritus actually form a bit of a friendship. It is the first instance in the Watch of positive race relations, and the first example of **Vimes's** insistence that in the Watch, there is no race, only Watchmen (*see* **Racism**).

Cuddy also has the dubious distinction of being the first 'visible' member of the Watch to die in the line of duty. He was killed by Dr Cruces, the head of the Assassin's Guild, who was under the control of the Gonne.

In typical dwarfen belligerent fashion, however, Cuddy refused to follow Death into the beyond due to the fact that he would not be given a proper dwarfen burial. He will, instead, walk the world as a tortured soul. *See also* Ankh-Morpork; City Watch; Detritus; Dwarfs; Racism *and* Samuel Vimes.

Mark D. Thomas

Culaina (*CP92*)

One of the wights encountered by the Munrungs, but a special case. Whereas the wights can remember everything that has happened and will happen, as a Thunorg Culaina can see what may happy – she can look down all the legs of The **Trousers of Time**. This gives her an odd perspective on history, since she can see both the positive and negative outcomes of events. Culaina tells Glurk how to escape the Mouls, and he has to make sure that he returns to tell her how he escaped so that she knows what to tell him. This breaks the usual pact the wights have not to tell the future to non-wights. Culaina is aware that history is something that is made and that anything, however small, can have an impact on what happens next. In most futures, say, the mouls will win, but there is a million to one chance that could be made to happen.

The wights are very distantly inspired by the Barrow wights of **Tolkien's** *The Lord of the Rings* (1954–1955), but are far less sinister and give little more than their name. In *CP71*, Culaina was a wise man named Culain, and it was a much more male world (*see also* **Sexism**).

Further Reading

Baldry, Cherith. 'The Children's Books'. *GOL*, *GOL2*.
James, Edward. 'Weaving the Carpet'. *GOL2*.

Andrew M. Butler

Cutwell, Igneous (*M*)

A wizard with a DM (Unseen) – in other words a Doctor of Magic from the **Unseen University** – and Marster of the Infinit, Illuminartus, Wyzard to Princes, Gardian of the Sacred Portalls, Holder of the Eight Keys and Traveller in the Dungeon Dimensions. His spelling appears to be as bad as his magical abilities, and his facility with fireworks. Since he is twenty, and lacks a beard, his skills and claims need to be questioned. He is a rare example of **Wizards** who are not connected to the University on a day-to-day basis – perhaps this is unsurprising – and he lives on Wolf Street in **Sto Lat**. Princess Keli of **Sto Lat** who wants to be reassured by him that she is still alive, and she awards him the role of Royal Recogniser. There is a suggestion of a romantic connection between the two. Like **Rincewind**, and indeed most of the **Discworld** wizards, he is an antithesis of **Tolkien's** Gandalf. *See also* Wizards.

Andrew M. Butler

D

The Dark Side of the Sun (1976)

Terry Pratchett's second novel was a work of **Science Fiction**. The title may well allude to the popular Pink Floyd album *The Dark Side of the Moon* (1973), but very much with a sense of something being hidden away – perhaps in plain sight. The first printing was either 800 or 921 copies, by Colin **Smythe** Ltd, Gerrards Cross, with a cover by Pratchett. The first paperback was by New English Library (1978) with a Tim White (b.1952) cover. Later paperbacks were issued by Corgi from 1988, with a cover by Josh **Kirby**; a second Kirby cover was used from 1993. In the UK Doubleday produced a hardback in 1994. The novel has been translated into Bulgarian, Croatian, Czech, Dutch, Estonian, French, German, Polish and Russian. The *Western Daily Press* noted: 'I can forecast an excellent future for the author if he can only bring off the difficult feat of curbing ever so slightly the riotous imagination which enables him to write sci-fi in the first place' (21 May 1976).

The Jokers have left behind vast artifacts from giant towers to chains of stars threaded together, and now all of sentient life seems united in supporting or opposing the quest for the Jokers' original world. Dominickdaniel **Sabalos**, who has inherited the Chairmanship of the planet **Widdershins** on the assassination of his father, is predicted to locate this in the near future. As he sets out on his quest, accompanied by his pet-like swamp-ig called Ig, there are various attempts on his life, each of which he survives. Some theories suggest that Jokers' World is home to one of the fifty-two sentient species, the Creepii, others that it is on the dark side of the sun, and therefore on an invisible planet. Dom suspects that the dark side is a state of mind rather than a physical location. In the end, Dom discovers that the various species were created by the incredibly powerful but non-empathic igs, and that the so-called Jokers' artifacts were talking points to engineer reactions.

Cover of *The Dark Side of the Sun*. Artwork by Josh Kirby used on Corgi editions.

Whilst the giant artifacts would belong in Larry Niven's novels, such as *Ringworld* (1970), Pratchett is drawing on the Foundation trilogy (1942–1951) by American science-fiction writer Isaac Asimov (1920–1992). This is a series of linked novellas in which the predictive science of Psychohistory anticipates the collapse of the galactic civilisation, and so a foundation is set up to preserve knowledge through the coming dark ages, along with a second, secret, institution as insurance. Psychohistory in *DSS* becomes p-maths, and just as Psychohistory had its blind spots, so does p-maths in the figures of the Jokers and Dom. Both *DSS* and the Foundation trilogy contain extracts from fictional texts to flesh out their imagined worlds. Dom's robot, the significantly named Isaac, offers a variation on the three laws of robotics explored in Asimov's story collection *I, Robot* (1950), with it being governed by at least eighteen – although inspiration may also have come from Robert **Sheckley**. Alien races are a staple of science fiction, with the Instrumentality of Mankind stories by Cordwainer Smith (1913–1966) being a likely precursor.

The Dark Side of the Sun

This is a picaresque novel, the quest basically a MacGuffin to allow Dom to pass through a variety of bizarre situations. The Jokers become the Spindle Kings in *STR* and mentions of festivals surrounding Small Gods, Hogswatchnight and Soul Cake Friday anticipate the **Discworld** sequence. *See also* Science Fiction; Robert Sheckley; Dominickdaniel Sabalos *and* Widdershins.

Further Reading

Clute, John. 'Coming of Age'. *GOL*, *GOL2*.

Andrew M. Butler

Darwin's Watch see The Science of Discworld

Dead People

Despite Pratchett being a writer of comedies, he does not shy away from dealing with serious issues, one of which is death. Whilst there is never a sustained afterlife in his works – or not one that he describes at length (although see '**The Hades Business**' and *E*) – he does depict people who have died but not yet moved onto wherever they are going.

This perhaps should not be a surprise when one of his most popular characters is **Death**, an anthropomorphic personification which humans have imagined into existence to perform the role of Grim Reaper. Whilst he has been weakened, and temporary replaced – the **Death of Rats** being a side product of this – the character has appeared in each of the **Discworld** novels until *WFM*. Death has an adopted daughter and apprentice, Ysabell and Mort **Sto Lat**, who die at the start of *SM* and who are not heard from again. Death also appears, in a slightly different guise, as one of the four horsemen of the apocalypse in *GO*, although Neil **Gaiman** has also depicted Death in his *Sandman* comics.

Dead people are often mourned – Death goes off the rails in *SM* when his daughter and son-in-law die, wishing that he had been able to intervene, but realising that it was their choice. Samuel **Vimes** is mourning Henry Gaskin at the start of *GG* with copious amounts of alcohol and visits the supposed grave of his mentor, Sergeant-at-Arms John Keel (actually Vimes himself), and other martyrs of the Glorious Revolution in *NW*.

Some characters have died before their time – the murdered King **Verence I** haunts his killers and **Lancre** castle in *WS*, plotting revenge – and others manage to cheat Death and live after their time. Alberto **Malich** is one such person who has come to an arrangement, serving Death as a butler or valet, only occasionally using up his meagre ration of remaining time. Mort also beats death and survives the novel in which he first appears, *M*. In the same volume, Mort resists taking the life of Princess Keli of **Sto Lat**, causing all manner of fluctuations in the space–time continuum.

In 'Death and What Comes Next', a philosopher attempts to reason with Death about the impossibility of dying, but fails to win his case, and the **Wizard** Greyhald Spold builds a box which he hopes is impregnable to Death – but it is not (*LF*). Moist von **Lipwig**'s cheating of death is a faked hanging engineered by Patrician **Vetinari** rather than a genuine escape. The Abbot of the History Monks (*SG*, *TOT*) is a rare example of reincarnation, which is not exactly a triumph over Death but eternal extra time, as is Abbot Lobsang of the Listeners (*M*, *GG*). Equally, Dios (*P*) has a circular life, due to the power of pyramids to manipulate time. (Mrs **Tachyon**, in the **Johnny Maxwell Trilogy**, is even more unstuck in time.)

Most dead people hang around long enough to be surprised by what has befallen them – with the exception of wizards and **Witches** Death's visit is not usually anticipated – and usually those moments are ones of confusion and bewilderment. Some, however, have long afterlives which may be equally productive.

This is the realm of the undead, and in particular **Igors**, **vampires** and zombies. Notable zombies include Baron Saturday, once ruler of **Genua** but murdered by the Duc as party of Lily **Weatherwax's** scheming (*WA*). Another zombie is the **Ankh-Morpork** lawyer, Mr Slant (*TT*). The wizard Windle Poons failed to die because Death was busy at the time (*RM*), and spends some time as a zombie, which he thoroughly enjoyed.

Since there is a place for everything in Ankh-Morpork, there is a support group for zombies and other examples of the undead: the Fresh Start Club run by the zombie Reg Shoe (*RM*). Members include the world's last banshee, Mr Ixolite, who is rather nervous and retiring, a bogeyman, Schleppel, who carries his own door to hide behind, a ghoul, Mrs Drull, two vampires, the Count and Countess Notfaroutoe (Arthur and Doreen Winkings), the wizard Windle Poons and the yennork, Lupine (*see* **Werewolves**). However, Reg has since joined the **City Watch** and has less time for the support group. Reg had died during the Glorious Revolution, but rose again out of a spirit of patriotism (*NW*).

Dead people also play a role in *JD*, as Johnny **Maxwell** visits the cemetery and meets the most significant dead people of **Blackbury**. On discovering that the graveyard is to be sold off for redevelopment, Johnny starts a campaign to save it for the dead, but by the end of the novel, it is clear that cemeteries are more important for the living, to mark where they have come from. The dead, meanwhile, have better things to do. Johnny also witnesses the ghostly march of a dead Pal's Regiment from the First World **War**. *See also* Death *and* Vampires.

Andrew M. Butler

Death (*CM*, *LF*, *ER*, *M*, *S*, *WS*, *P*, *GG*, *E*, *MP*, *RM*, *WA*, *SG*, *LL*, *MAA*, *SM*, *IT*, *Msk*, *LL*, *FOC*, *H*, *J*, *TLC*, *CJ*, *FE*, *TT*, *TOT*, *AMHER*, *LH*, *NW*, *GP*, *T!*, 'DWCN' and *GO*)

The anthropomorphic personification of death, and both servant and an aspect of Azrael, the Death of Universes and one of the Old High Ones. He has major appearances in *M*, *RM*, *SM*, *H* and *TOT*, and cameos in each of the other novels with the exception of the Tiffany **Aching** books.

He rides a pale horse (Binky) and carries a scythe and a sword, which can slice wind, to cut souls from their bodies at death. He can only be seen by children, cats, wizards, witches and other personifications, such as the **Hogfather**. He looks like an animated skeleton in a black cloak, and speaks in capital letters. Death takes his Duty seriously, but because it brings him into the company of time-bound humans, he becomes fascinated with humanity and tries to understand humans by trying human entertainments, working at a series of jobs, celebrating Hogswatch and building his house, Mon Repos, in the timeless dimension of **Death's Domain**. In the end, however, Death is first and foremost a Horseman of the Apocralypse.

In a fit of compassion, he saves Ysabell **Sto Helit**, an orphan, and lets her grow to be sixteen. Thirty-five years later, hoping to marry her off, he takes an apprentice named Mort. But Mort defies the Duty and tries to save the life of Princess Keli of the Sto Plains. While Mort collects souls, and history rearranges itself around Princess Keli's non-death, Death tries fishing, partying at the PATRICIAN's palace and gambling. He achieves satisfaction as a short-order cook at Harga's House of Ribs in **Ankh-Morpork**, surrounded by stray cats. Furious at Mort for intervening with an individual's fate, Death leads Mort to challenge him to a duel, hoping that Mort will win and take on the onerous, lonely Duty. When Mort is about to lose, and shows that he understands Death's endless aloneness, Death rearranges time so that Mort, Ysabell and Princess Keli have a place in the present and future.

When the Auditors of Reality retire him, he finds a job, as Bill Door, bringing in the harvest at the farm of elderly Miss Renata **Flitworth**. Death's duties are taken on by the deaths of every species, including the **Death of Rats**. While a mortal, Bill Door awaits the new Death, gradually understanding how passing time steals life away even during sleep, and becomes determined to fight back. He sharpens Miss Flitworth's scythe on her grindstone, fabric (including her unworn wedding dress), cobwebs and finally the slow-moving Discworld dawn light. When the new Death appears, crowned and eager to rule, they battle, and Miss Flitworth gives Death enough of her lifetime to overcome him. When Death gets his job back and takes back the other deaths, Death of Rats resists and Death lets him retain an independent existence. Back at Mon Repos, between the black orchard and the mountains, Death creates a golden wheat field, billowing in the breeze, to remind him of the human harvest he cares for.

Years later, Death again is dissatisfied and leaves to find the meaning of existence and learn to forget the entirety of past and future. His teenage granddaughter Susan **Sto Helit** takes over the family Duty of collecting souls, but breaks with tradition by trying to protect the young man, Imp 'Buddy' Y **Celyn**, from his doom. Death joins the **Klatch** Foreign Legion and endures being buried in sand for several days without managing to forget. He drinks himself into a comatose state at The **Mended Drum** in Ankh-Morpork without effect. Eventually, he joins the beggars of Ankh-Morpork as Mr Scrub. Finally aware that an ancient music has taken Imp over, he realises that he needs to travel quickly. At **Unseen University**, where the **Librarian** has constructed an archetypal motorcycle, Death borrows a long leather jacket from the Dean, and rides off, with roses in his teeth, in a clear homage by Pratchett to the Grateful Dead and Meat Loaf. He saves Imp, defeats the music and teaches Susan how and why death must be impartial.

When the Auditors of Reality engage the assassin Teatime to delete the Hogfather, Death takes over the Hogfather's duties to hold a space of belief for him to return to. He tricks Susan into helping him, knowing that her humanity and pragmatism are an undefeatable combination for the Auditors. The experience of fulfilling Hogswatch wishes of children and fantasies of adults softens Death's usual hard-line take on human destiny to the point that he rejects the story of the little match girl, choosing justice over faith, saves her life and puts her in the care of Watchman Nobby **Nobbs**. With his guidance, Susan saves the Hogfather from the Auditors and comes to understand the relationship between the human belief in mythical personalities and in such values as mercy, duty and justice. As Death frequently repeats, there is no justice; there is just him.

When the Auditors of Reality again conspire to end the Discworld, Death asks Susan for help while he does what we have not seen him do before: his own job as one of the Horsemen of the Apocralypse. From Pestilence to Famine to War, Death tries to persuade the other Horsemen, now all too human, to ride out. Meeting their ambivalence, he goes to face the Auditors alone, only to be joined by the Horsemen he had, unknown to himself, won over by questioning whose side they were on.

Death is a necessary figure, called into existence by the belief of humanity, and on the whole it is a thankless task. He does not quite understand the humanity he serves, yet is eternally fascinated by them. Like other immortal or long-lived beings in fiction, he faces a choice between the sterility of everything remaining static – his companions and relatives being fixed at a given age – or the grief of them aging whilst he remains the same. The novels focused on him tend to reflect upon the alienation of work – the job is what he is, or what he has become.

A different Death appears in *GO*, again as one of the Four Horsemen, called together by the apocalypse associated with the **coming of age** of the Antichrist Adam **Young**. Death is a visitor to a party in '**Turntables of the**

Night' – although it is presumably different from the Discworld one – and argues philosophy in 'DWCN'.

All these versions draw upon a long tradition of personifying Death as the Grim Reaper, associating death with the harvest and the cycle of crops and life. He is depicted on Tarot cards and in engravings as a skeletal figure, with or without a scythe. In the play *La Morte in vacanza* (*Death Takes a Holiday*, 1924) by Alberto Casella (1891–1957), Death takes time off to visit mortals as Prince Sirki, to see why they fear him; in the meantime people stop dying. This was filmed in 1934 by Mitchell Leisen (1898–1972) with Fredric March (1897–1975) in the main role, with a television remake in 1971 and a new film version was later made, *Meet Joe Black* (1998), with Brad Pitt (b.1963) as Death. Whilst these share plot points with Pratchett – although Death has yet to really fall in love save in a paternal way – the archetypal image is shown in *Det Sjunde Inseglet* (*The Seventh Seal*, 1957) directed by Ingmar Bergman (b.1918). Bengt Ekerot (1920–1971) is Death, with pale skin and a flowing black cloak, playing the knight Antonius (Max von Sydow, b.1929) at a game of chess for the latter's life. In *Bill and Ted's Bogus Journey* (1991), Death (William Sadler, 1951) follows the game of chess with Twister, Cluedo and Battleships. *Love and Death* (1975), directed by Woody Allen (b.1935), offers a more loving homage to Bergman, via depressing Russian narratives. The film climaxes with a Dance of Death, although here Death wears white. Death has also been a recurring character, as a Goth girl, in *The Sandman* comics of Neil **Gaiman**.

Bengt Ekerot and Max Von Sydow play chess in Ingmar Bergman's film *The Seventh Seal*, 1957.

'Death' is a track on Dave **Greenslade**'s *Terry Pratchett's From the Discworld* album, and he has a cameo, tap-dancing, on 'Wyrd Sisters'. *See also* Dead People; Death of Rats; Death's Domain; Neil Gaiman; Dave Greenslade; Alberto Malich; Mort Sto Helit; Susan Sto Helit *and* Ysabell Sto Helit.

Further Reading

Hanes, Stacie. 'Death and the Maiden'. *GOL2.*
Moody, Nickianne. 'Death'. *GOL.*
———. 'Death and Work'. *GOL2.*

Susan Spilecki

'Death and What Comes Next' (*OM*WF*)

This is a **Discworld** short story, originally published as part of an online puzzle website (*TimeHunt*, 2002), and apparently including a cipher which unlocks something in the game. It is not clear what the cipher is, but evidence suggests that it is something to do with Schrödinger's Cat. The online game no longer appears to exist.

Death visits a philosopher who is about to die, who argues that he should be allowed to live. He invokes quantum physics, the many worlds interpretation and Schrödinger's Cat, which is a famous thought experiment in which a cat in a box is both dead and alive until observed (*see UC*). Death points out that he is observing the philosopher.

A slight but amusing story, little more than a vignette. *See also* Cats *and* Death.

Andrew M. Butler

Death of Rats (*RM*, *SM*, *H*, *TOT*, *AMHER*)

Grim Reaper for the souls of rats. A skeletal rat, he wears a black robe and carries a small scythe. Rats call him the Bone Rat. He comes into being after **Death** is fired by the Auditors of Reality, and Death's duties are taken on by several thousand smaller deaths. When Death gets his job back and absorbs all the other personifications, Death of Rats resists. Death lets him retain his independent existence, in part to relieve loneliness, and in part to allow Death to have a part of himself that can do rebellious things. A talking raven named Quoth translates for Death of Rats with humans, particularly with Death's granddaughter, Susan **Sto Helit**. In addition to his reaping duties, Death of Rats makes himself useful to Death by guiding Susan when she does Death's job (*SM*), saves the Hogfather from assassination (*H*) and saves reality by saving the son of

Time (*TOT*). He is also the inventor of a device that, by dropping buttered toast on squares of carpet, measures malignities in reality. Although strictly speaking, he only reaps rat souls, he frequently reaps the souls of rat like humans, such as Mr Clete (*SM*) and Mr Pin (*TT*). *See also* Death; Death's Domain *and* Susan Sto Helit.

Susan Spilecki

Death's Domain (1999)

The last of the Discworld **Maps**, apparently produced without the aid of Stephen **Briggs**. It consists of a tilted perspective of **Death's** Domain – closer to a plan than a map – complete with his mansion, his maze and his garden, and pictures of **Death**, Alberto **Malich** and Susan **Sto Helit** in the corners. It is painted by Paul **Kidby**, who had done the similarly designed *TGL*. It was published in the UK by Corgi, with an edition in Czech.

Cover of *Death's Domain, A Discworld Mapp* by Terry Pratchett and Paul Kidby. Artwork by Paul Kidby.

Like the other maps, it comes with a booklet, which explains who Death is, and describes his Domain. It notes Death's taste, and his confusions about how the real world operates – he cannot for example see what the point of a maze is, since he cannot get lost, or the point of golf, since he can always pot a ball. There is a note on the predominance of black in the palette of the Domain, whether in his **cats** or peacocks. There is a description of his house, Mon Repos, as from W.H.J. Whittleby's *Guide to Impossible Buildings*. It also has a key to the various locations on the map. *See also* Death; Alberto Malich *and* Ysabell Sto Helit.

Andrew M. Butler

de Haberdasheri, Angalo *see* Haberdasheri, Angalo de

del Icatessen, Dorcas see Icatessen, Dorcas del

Desert Island Discs

A BBC Radio 4 programme first broadcast on 29 January 1942 (then on the Home Service). Terry Pratchett was a guest on the 9 February 1997 programme. It was created by Roy Plomley (1914–1985) and has the conceit of interviewing guests about which eight gramophone records they would take with them if they were cast away on a desert island. Over the decades, this has been supplemented with a luxury object and a book (in addition to the assumed Bible and the complete works of William **Shakespeare**). Plomley was the first presenter, replaced by Michael Parkinson (b.1935) when he died. Sue Lawley (b.1948) took over in 1988, and the current presenter (from October 2006) is Kirsty Young (b.1968).

Pratchett chose the following:

Hector Berlioz (1803–1869), *Symphonie Fantastique: Dream of a Witches' Sabbath* (1830) by the London Symphony Orchestra, conducted by Sir Eugene Goossens (1893–1962).

Steeleye Span, *Thomas the Rhymer* (1974).

Bernard Miles (1907–1991), *The Race for the Rheingold Stakes*.

Wolfgang Amadeus Mozart (1756–1791), *The Marriage of Figaro: Voi che sapete* (1786; see **Opera**) Royal Concertgebouw Orchestra, Amsterdam, conducted by Nikolaus Harnoncourt (b.1929).

Meat Loaf (b.1947), 'Bat Out of Hell' (1977) (*see* **pop music** and *SM*).

Kitaro (b.1953), *Silk Road: Theme* (soundtrack recording) (1980).

Icehouse, 'Great Southern Land' (1989).

Antonio Vivaldi (1678–1741), *Four Seasons: Summer* (1723), Israel Philharmonic Orchestra, conducted by Itzhak Perlman (b.1945).

His luxury was the Chrysler Building (1928–1930) in New York, designed by William Van Alen (1883–1953). His book was a practical choice, on edible plants of the South Seas, and of the eight records, he would whittle it down to *Thomas the Rhymer*. *See also* Opera *and* Pop Music.

Andrew M. Butler

Detective and Noir Fiction and Films

Detective and Noir Fiction are branches of the crime fiction genre and are the traditions that Terry Pratchett uses in the **City Watch** sequence of books. The main point of a detective story is that some crime has happened, and somebody has to set about solving the particulars of the crime (who?, where?, why?, how?), usually a murder (murder is usually the crime of choice because the very nature of murder guarantees the greatest reaction out of the reader). A detective story is often related to the mystery novel; however, detective stories tend to have a far greater reliance on a single protagonist (often a reoccurring character in a series) and the particulars of the case. Famous detectives in fiction have included Philip Marlowe (Raymond Chandler (1888–1959)), Lew Archer (Ross MacDonald (1915–1983)), Miss Marple (Agatha Christie (1890–1976)) and (of course) Sherlock Holmes (Sir Arthur Conan Doyle (1859–1930)).

Noir Fiction is a subgenre of Detective Fiction. *Noir* is the French word for black, and as the name suggests, the subject matter in Noir Fiction tends to be a little darker and grittier than in a generic detective story. Noir Fiction will usually have a heavier use of sex and violence (shootouts, rape and beatings) and is characterised by its almost clinical, hard-edged and sometimes even cynical view of these events. In Noir, mood is the key element. Another difference between the two is that Noir has a heavier emphasis on the journey the protagonist takes to get to the conclusion. A Noir protagonist tends to have issues dealing with normal life (in Noir, the protagonist can oftentimes be the criminal him/herself). While the outcome is important, what the protagonist learns about him/herself and life is really more important. Notable works in the Noir genre include *The Postman Always Rings Twice* (1934) by James M. Cain (1892–1977) and *They Shoot Horses, Don't They?* (1937) by Horace McCoy (1897–1955).

Film Noir is the motion picture equivalent of Noir Fiction. The important detail in Film Noir is that of light and setting. Film Noir first appeared in the 1940s, using the cinematic effects seen in 1930s horror movies and German Expressionist films (though Film Noir itself is decidedly American), taking all the elements of a Noir Fiction story and sets them in an insensitive, cynical world full of harsh lighting and deep, angular shadows (high contrast). The dark visuals help to enhance the gritty nature of the story. Chandler's *The Big Sleep* (1939, filmed 1946),

Hammett's *The Maltese Falcon* (1930, filmed 1941) and Billy Wilder's *Sunset Boulevard* (1950) are all classics of the Film Noir genre.

Another subgenre of Detective Fiction is the Police Procedural. In a Police Procedural, the main character/detective is a police officer. While this may not be different from some non-Police Procedural detective stories, the idea behind the Police Procedural is that the protagonist has the controls, whims and needs of his/her police department working with and against his/her attempt to solve the crime. Besides figuring out 'whodunit' (or in some cases where the who is known, figuring out the proof), the detective also has to decide which (if any) department rules should be broken, worry about getting results in a hurry for superior officers, potential political pressure and (if applicable) and media coverage following the case. The Police Procedural also differs from a standard detective story in that many times the detective in a Police Procedural does not do a lot of the ground work (he/she may be the last on the scene of the crime, has forensics experts to assist, has officers to go harass suspects, etc.). Often, the detective's job is just to sit back and look at all the pieces brought to him/her and sort them out. TV shows like *Law & Order* (1990–), *NYPD Blue* (1993–2005) and *Dragnet* (1952–1959) are examples of Police Procedurals. Popular Police Procedural authors are Ed McBain (1926–2005) and J.D. Robb (a pseudonym of Nora Roberts (b.1950)).

The main purpose behind the typical detective fiction is for the reader to follow along with the detective him/herself and learn about the case and pick up clues along with the detective. Typically, the single most important piece of information in a detective story is whodunit. With a whodunit, the detective's main purpose in the story is to figure out who committed the crime and how. A well-built detective story will eliminate all suspects but the correct one for the reader at the same time that the detective has put it all together.

Like most detective fiction, all of the City Watch books centre around, or begin with, a murder or series of murders. When the crime is first discovered, the Watch is always left with more questions than answers; usually there is an obvious lead that turns out to be false, and the original crime always leads the Watch to discover a much bigger situation, whether it is the presence of a long extinct dragon, the question of who is responsible for a golem to be seen as a murderer or what exactly is the secret behind the Battle of Koom Valley. The search for a motive always takes the Watch down strange paths.

The most important piece to the detective novel is that of the detective him/herself. The detective tends to be an archetypal character: usually unmarried, hard-nosed and has a number of bad habits (many times involving alcohol). Noir Fiction and Film tend to take these stereotypes to the extreme. Sometimes the detective has some sort of outside income (possibly they are independently wealthy), but many times (especially in Noir Fiction and Film), the detective is looking for that next payday.

While these stereotypes do not always describe the protagonist, one thing always remains the same for the detective, regardless of his/her circumstances: an almost obsessive desire to solve the crime. For the true detective, nothing will stand in the way of him/her and the answer.

In **Ankh-Morpork**, the detective of choice is the City Watch Commander, Samuel **Vimes**. When Vimes is first introduced in *GG*, he encompasses many of the typical stereotypes of the detective: he is a tough man who has been broken by the system, he is alone, virtually penniless and a drunkard. A man who would like to make a difference, but also one who is too beaten down by life that he has no real will left. In time, with a little bit of luck, Vimes is able raise his station, but the stereotypes remain (or change a little). He marries into money (moving from the broke stereotype to the independently wealthy stereotype), but he is still a streetwise brawler who does not really trust the system. The only stereotype he breaks away from is that he manages to quit drinking, though the temptation is always there.

However, regardless of his other personal qualities, the important detective trait remains: nothing can get between Sam Vimes and solving the crime. He is more than willing to irritate city leaders, bully and threaten people and even cause an international incident if at the end of the day he knows 'whodunit'. Even when Vimes is still the drunken Captain of a virtually non-existent (and wholly unimportant) Night Watch, the urge to discover who has been murdering people in Ankh-Morpork is overwhelming (finding out that the perpetrator was a dragon just fuelled his rage). Bringing the criminal to justice is more important to him than anything else.

Another common element to the detective story is the sidekick. In most cases, the sidekick is a less intelligent person, whose only real purpose is ask the right questions, or remember the key details, at just the right time to light the flicker of inspiration in the head of the detective. Sometimes, the sidekick is more important than this, but usually not. In these cases, the sidekick acts as a foil to the detective: i.e. the person who is the complete opposite to the protagonist that, through contrast, highlights the traits of the protagonist. In the case of Sherlock Holmes, Dr Watson plays the sidekick role perfectly.

Within the City Watch, more often than not, it is Carrot **Ironfoundersson** that plays this role for Vimes (though each member of the Watch can play this role at times – Angua von **Überwald**, Cheery **Littlebottom**, Sally and even **Detritus** have been Vimes's foil). While Carrot is not stupid (he is more innocent/naïve), he does not have the same sort of street smarts that Vimes does. Carrot, therefore, tends to take a more following role to Vimes. He watches and observes Vimes at work. Carrot's good-natured honesty continually plays against Vimes's bad-tempered drive. Carrot, however, does play a more important role than most sidekicks, because many times, he actually puts together (at least) part of the larger puzzle that Vimes is working on, though that part is the important piece that Vimes needs to solve the larger, overall crime.

The City Watch sequence of books embodies many of the elements of standard Detective Fiction and a number of its subgenres. Vimes is a typical detective, though he works both in the traditional sense (doing his own investigating) and as a Police Procedural detective (looking at the clues members of the Watch bring him and sorting them out). The books all start with the crime and numerous different suspects/motives/causes, but slowly, one-by-one, eliminating them all until there is only one answer left. Curiously, though, the City Watch sequence never really settles into a certain subgenre. The stories can get gritty (Noir), though there are enough light-hearted, humorous, or even tender moments that yank them out of the darker genres. They cannot even really be classified as a true Police Procedural, even though it is about a police force, because the Watch does not always act like a proper police force (not to mention Vimes' complete disregard, at times, for other people and their wants/needs). The best that can be said is that these books are detective stories with influences from across the board. *See also* City Watch; Colon; Carrot Ironfoundersson *and* Patrician Vetinari.

Further Reading

Doherty, Brian, ed. 1988. *American Crime Fiction: Studies in the Genre*. London: Macmillan.
Haut, Woody. 1999. *Neon Noir: Contemporary American Crime Fiction*. London: Serpent's Tail.
James, Edward. 'The City Watch'. *GOL*, *GOL2*.

Mark D. Thomas

Detritus (*GG*, *MP*, *MAA*, *SM*, *Msk*, *FOC*, *J*, *FE*, *TT*, *NW*, *T!*)

Detritus is a **troll** from **Überwald**. He is a little short for a standard troll (his knuckles tend to drag on the ground); however, he makes up for it in pure strength. Like most trolls, Detritus's intelligence fluctuates with the temperature: the colder it is, the smarter he is and vice versa. At extremely low temperatures, Detritus is nothing short of a genius; however, at normal temperatures, he tends to be a bit simple, even for a troll. He is married to another troll named Ruby, who apparently keeps him on the straight and narrow.

Detritus first appears as a splatter (i.e. bouncer) at The **Mended Drum**, though gets beaten up in a fight with Carrot **Ironfoundersson**. Soon, however, he joins the **City Watch** and is now a sergeant. He, literally, is **Vimes's** siege engine. Detritus's weapon of choice is a siege crossbow (like a mangonel) that he has converted to a hand crossbow. Initially, he used standard siege bolts, but recently he has switched to bundling crossbow bolts together for ammunition. The sheer pressure of the shot tends to disintegrate most of the bolts, and what gets shot is more of fireball. When breaking down doors, Detritus often takes out the wall behind it as well. Potential Ankh-Morporkian ne'er-do-wells clean up their act in a hurry when Detritus and his bow arrive. *See also* Ankh-Morpork; City Watch; Cuddy; Trolls *and* Samuel Vimes.

Mark D. Thomas

de Worde, William *see* Worde, William de

Diaries

The first **Discworld** diary was produced in 1997, which was an attempt to be both a useful artifact (fitting in with the real world's 365-day, 52 weeks of seven days and change calendar) and a piece of merchandising (800-day rotation with two lots of four seasons, thirteen months and eight day weeks) which was an understandable headache for Stephen **Briggs**. There was also the problem that Gollancz (*see* **Publishers**) were not usually producers of diaries, and so there were problems with agreeing the commission. This meant that the artist, Paul **Kidby**, only had a short time to produce the artwork. The first diary was tied to the **Unseen University**, the second to **Ankh-Morpork City Watch** (1997). After a gap, the 2000 diary was tied to the Assassin's Guild (1999), the 2001 diary to the Fool's Guild (2000), the 2002 to the Thieves' Guild (2001), the 2003 to the (Reformed) Vampyres (2002) (*see* **Vampires**), followed by another gap and then the 2007 diary was the *Post Office Handbook* (*see GP*). In 2007, it was *Lu-Tse's Yearbook of Enlightenment 2008*. There have also been a number of **calendars**, for both the wall and the desk. *See also* Stephen Briggs; Calendars; *Discworld Almanak and* Paul Kirby.

Further Reading

Pratchett, Terry and Stephen Briggs. 1997. *Discworld's Unseen University Diary*. Illustrated by Paul Kidby. London: Victor Gollancz.

———. 1998. *Discworld's Ankh-Morpork City Watch Diary 1999*. Illustrated by Paul Kidby. London: Victor Gollancz.

———. 1999. *Discworld Assassin's Guild Yearbook and Diary 2000*. Illustrated by Paul Kidby. London: Victor Gollancz.

———. 2000. *Discworld Fools' Guild Yearbook and Diary 2001*. Illustrated by Paul Kidby. London: Victor Gollancz.

———. 2001. *Discworld Thieves' Guild Yearbook and Diary 2002*. Illustrated by Paul Kidby. London: Victor Gollancz.

———. 2002. *Discworld (Reformed) Vampyre's Diary 2003 Sponsored by the Überwald League of Temperance*. Illustrated by Paul Kidby. London: Victor Gollancz.

———. 2006. *Ankh-Morpork Post Office Handbook and Discworld Diary 2007*. Illustrated by Paul Kidby. London: Victor Gollancz.

———. 2007. *Lu-Tse's Yearbook of Enlightenment 2008*. Illustrated by Paul Kidby. London: Victor Gollancz.

Andrew M. Butler

Dibbler, C[ut-]M[y-]O[wn-]T[hroat] (*COM, WA, GG, MP, RM, SG, MAA, SM, IT, H, TT, NW*)

The master salesman of the **Discworld** in general and **Ankh-Morpork** in particular, he is renowned (or disliked) for his fast food sales (something – do not enquire too closely what – onnastick or in a pie) and, later, an agent for actors (*MP*) and musicians (*SM*). He also runs a mail order business as Grand Master Lobsang Dibbler (*WA*), a nod to the fraudulent Tibetan monk and guru Lobsang Rampa (actually Cyril Hoskin (1910–1981)). A staple of **Comedy** is the conman who is himself conned and Dibbler is a distant **Fantasy** cousin of Del Trotter in the BBC sitcom *Only Fools and Horses* (1981–2005), with perhaps a debt to characters from *Monty Python's Flying Circus* (1969–1974). Dibbler goes from comparative success to comparative success, never giving up.

Dibbler has a number of cousins or parallel-evolved versions in other times and locations: Disembowel-Myself-Honourably Dibhala (*IT*), Cut-Me-Own-Hand-Off Dibblah (*SG*), Al-Jiblah in (*J*), Fair Go Dibbler, May-I-Never-Achieve-Enlightenment Dhiblang, Dib Diblossonson, May-I-Be-Kicked-In-My-Own-Ice-Hole Dibooki and Swallow-Me-Own-Blowdart Dhlang-Dhlang (*LC*). In the Discworld 2 **Computer Game**, there is the Aborigine Point-Me-Own-Bone Dibjla. Where more than three people are gathered together, someone will try to sell them revolting and overpriced food. In the meantime, Stephen **Briggs** has earned the soubriquet C.M.O.T from his pushing of Discworld merchandise. *See also* Stephen Briggs *and* Merchandising.

Andrew M. Butler

Diggers (1990)

Subtitled *The Second Book of the Nomes*, this is the second book in The **Bromeliad**, Nomes or Truckers trilogy. The first edition was 13,500 copies and published in hardback in the UK by Doubleday; the Corgi paperback was 1991; both editions had a Josh **Kirby** cover. Post-2004 copies have a David **Wyatt** cover. The book has been translated into Bulgarian, Czech, Danish, Finnish, French, German, Greek, Hebrew, Hungarian, Icelandic, Italian, Japanese, Polish, Romanian, Russian, Serbian, Slovakian, Slovenian, Spanish and Swedish. A digger is a petrol-driven vehicle designed to excavate holes; in the novel the digger is a JCB, as originally built by J.C. Bamford (Excavators) Ltd. The novel begins with a recap of *T*, 'In the beginning...', and is divided into chapters, each preceded by an extract from *The Book of Nome*. *The Horn Book Magazine* noted in its review: 'Satire and allegory abound, but so fascinating are the nomes as a microcosm of human society that their trials and emotions are both moving and amusing'.

Diggers

The nomes have settled into a quarry, and a new hierarchy has emerged, those who drove the truck and the passengers. Two new threats face them, the onset of a winter which might see them starve and the reopening of their quarry for blasting. Through a scrap of newspaper, they discover that Richard, the 'grandson' of **Arnold Bros (est. 1905)**, is involved with a space mission in Florida, and through a conversation with The **Thing** discover that they might use this to contact their spaceship. Abbot Gurder, **Masklin** and Angalo de **Haberdasheri** set off for the airport, leaving **Nisodemus** in charge. An accident with a runaway truck and a train nearly kills Dorcas del **Icatessen** and makes some of the nomes sceptical about outside. The humans are beginning to take an interest in the quarry, and Nisodemus is killed by a police car. **Grimma** and Dorcas get Jekub, the JCB, running, and lead the nomes to safety, with Grimma seemingly in charge. They find a spaceship hovering in the air, complete with a Bromeliad plant.

Nisodemus is set up here as a representative of blind belief, who cannot let go of the god-like image of Arnold Bros (est. 1905), and who is not entirely clear that the store has indeed been demolished. When he leads a group of impressionable nomes in an act of passive resistance against the humans, the result is fatal for him. Grimma, who has not sought power but seems to have it thrust upon her after proving she can weigh up information, shows nothing like the same amount of complacency and certainty in her position. *See also* Arnold Bros (est. 1905); The Bromeliad; Children's Fiction; Grimma; Angalo de Haberdasheri; Dorcas del Icatessen; Masklin; Nisodemus *and* The Thing.

Further Reading

Baldry, Cherith. 'The Children's Books'. *GOL*, *GOL2*.

Hunt, Peter. 2001. 'Terry Pratchett'. Pp. 86–121 in Peter Hunt and Millicent Lenz, *Alternative Worlds in Fantasy Fiction*. London: Continuum.

Andrew M. Butler

Discworld

The location and by extension the universe in which a series of novels by Terry Pratchett are set, also the name usually given to refer to the whole enterprise. As well as various formats of novel, there have been **comics**, a **cookbook**, **diaries**, **merchandising**, **plays** and **television adaptations**, as well as a range of **conventions** and **websites** and a subset of **fandom.**

The Discworld is a flat planet, shaped like a disc, which sits on the back of four **elephants** named Berilia, Great T'Phon, Jerakeen and Tubul. A fifth elephant is believed to have existed in an earlier age, but crashed into the surface of the planet, creating the continents (*FE*). The elephants rest on the back of a giant turtle, *Chelys galactica*, known as the Great **A'Tuin**, whose existence was discovered by the rim-dwelling people of Krull. The turtle is swimming towards an unknown point, which may have something to do with the red star seen in *LF*, and the birth of eight new Discworlds.

The Disc is orbited by a small star and a small moon – although reports of their sizes vary – whose eccentric trajectories mean that occasionally an elephant has to lift its leg to allow the body to pass. The whole is bathed in a magical field which appears top slow down light and time. The planetary system results in eight seasons in any one year, and the Discworld calendar has thirteen months and eight day weeks. At the edge of the disc, the water from the oceans pours off into space, to be returned by some as yet unknown mechanism. In some areas, there is the Circumfence, which catches the flotsam and jetsam, and occasionally **wizards** such as **Rincewind**, for use as salvage. The area is also notable for its rimbows, eight coloured arc caused by the passage of light through magic. As the planet is round and flat rather than an oblate spheroid, directions such as north, south, east and west would have little meaning. Instead, the two axes are across the diameter of the disc, rimwards and hubwards, and with the rotation of the Disc, turnwards and **widdershins**.

Moving turnwards from Krull through the Rim and Turnwards Ocean, there are the Brown Islands, Mithos, the Trobi Islands, and the **Counterweight Continent** and the **Agatean Empire**. This area is known as the Aurient, because it is where the gold comes from. The weight of the precious metals – the Agatean Empire is particularly wealthy – counterbalances the unnamed continent which has been explored in much more detail (*M*, *IT*). Continuing turnwards, across the Agatean Sea is Bangbangduc, possibly Nafooi, Slakki and Land of Fog (the geography is hazy in this area), and bathed in the Widdershins Ocean is **XXXX**, also known as EcksEcksEcksEcks or Foureks. It is also referred to as Terror Incognita (fear of the unknown). It is most recently made of the continents, and as such may be unfinished. For millennia, it has been bathed in a magical cloud which prevented it from raining.

Further rimwards lies the unnamed continent, and most inwardly is the town of **Genua**, known for its river, its music and its voodoo culture, and it looks onto the Swamp Sea (*WAA*). Further turnwards again is Brindisi, and the continent of **Klatch**.

Klatch consists of a number of different countries, notably Klatch, Hersheba, Ymitury, Howondaland, Urabewe, Laotan, Elharib, S'Belinde and Syrrit. To the rimwards of Klatch is the Great Nef, where Ysabell's parents died (*LF*, *M*). On the hubwards side, Ell Kinte, **Djelibeybi** (*P*), **Omnia**, Ur, **Ephebe** and **Tsort** nestle for access to the Circle Sea. In the middle of the Circle Sea lies – or rather lay – the lost island of Leshp, fought over by Klatch and **Ankh-Morpork**, although quite what either of them needed it for seems to be lost to history (*J*).

On the hubwards side of the Circle Sea lies the great city of Ankh-Morpork, effectively the cultural capital of the Discworld, although its

Discworld

A Reading Order for the Discworld Novels

The books fall into four interconnected sequences (the City Watch, Death, the Witches (including the Tiffany Aching books) and the Wizards (including the adventures of Rincewind)). A few books fall outside this scheme. Titles entirely within a sequence (ignoring minor cameos of characters such as Death) are given in boxes, those which straddle sequences are given in circles. Krzysztof Kietzman has offered another version at http://www.lspace.org/books/reading-order-guides/. The lack of consistent dates within the novels makes a more detailed order problematic, but a timeline of the Discworld may be found at http://www.lspace.org/books/timeline/dw-timeline-intro.html.

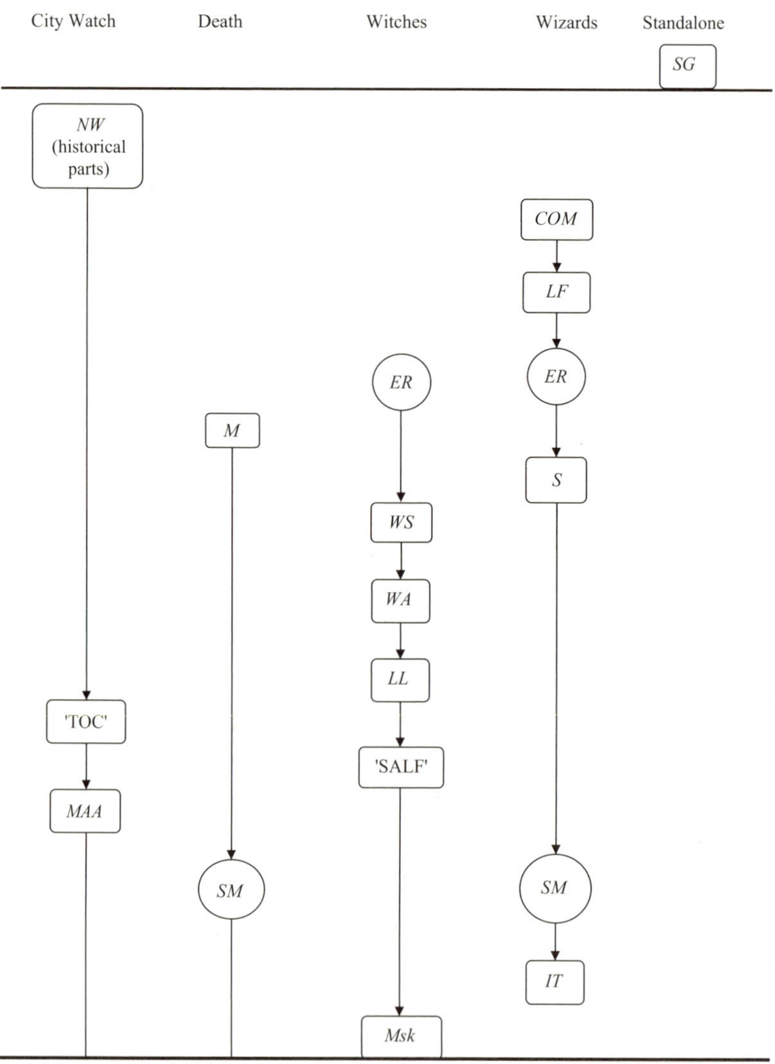

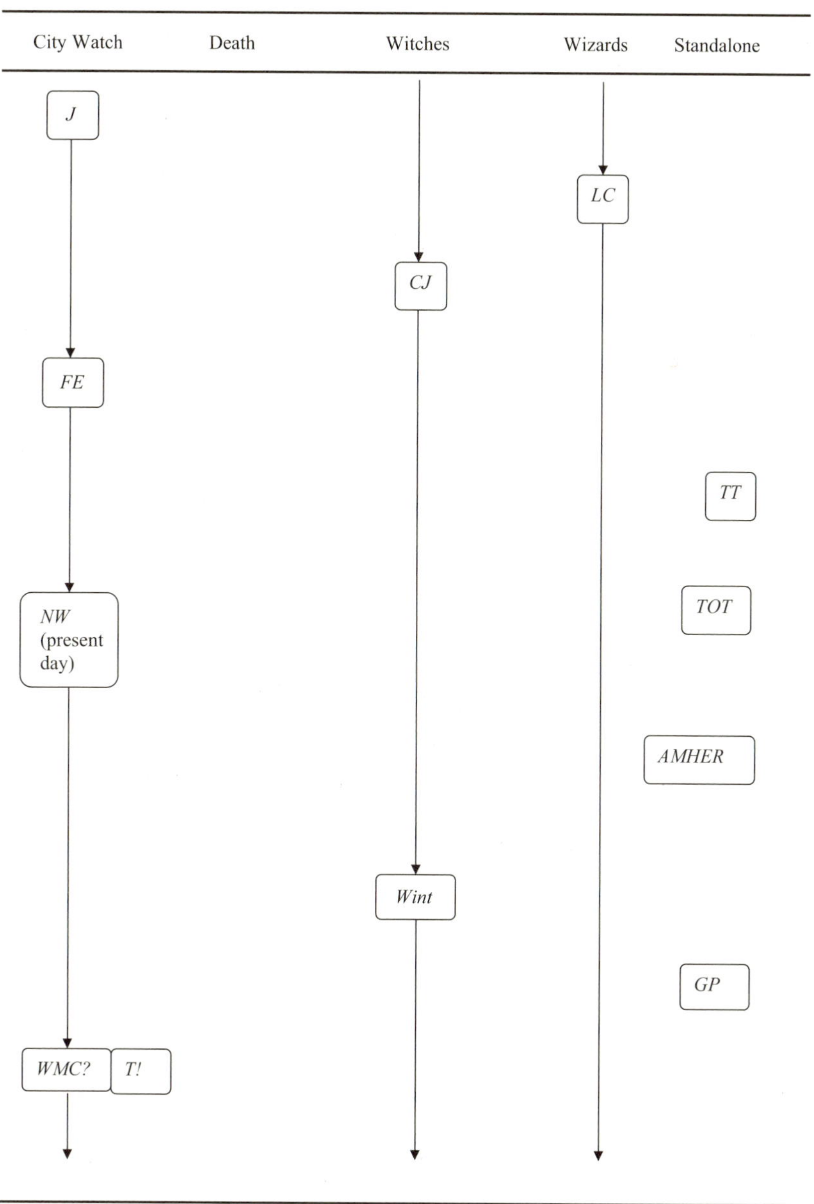
City Watch
Death
Witches
Wizards
Standalone
J
LC
CJ
FE
TT
NW (present day)
TOT
AMHER
Wint
GP
WMC?
T!

LL

wealth does not compare with the Agatean Empire, which tends to keep itself to itself. The city is home to both magic – most obviously in the shape of the **Unseen University**, which acts as the educator for the Disc's wizards – and **technology** – with the printing press and communication devices called Klacks. Order in the great city is maintained by a complicated system of guilds, ultimately masterminded by Patrician **Vetinari**, and the City Watch, run by Samuel **Vimes**.

Immediately hubwards of Ankh-Morpork are the Sto Plains, and **Sto Helit** and **Sto Lat** and then the kingdom of **Lancre**. The plains are largely flat lands, flooded seasonally by the river Ankh, and fertile enough to grow millions of cabbages. Many young people from this area go to seek their fortunes in Ankh-Morpork. In this area is The Chalk, a limestone area which is thought to be free of witchcraft and will not support magic, although in fact witches are merely banned or discouraged (*WFM*, *HFOS*, *Wint*). The various kingdoms and other territories are constantly disputing boundaries, and uniting or splitting lands through marriages.

Rimwards towards the Turnwards Ocean, or turnwards, is the octarine grass country and Wyrmberg, home to imaginary **dragons**, and the small, rain-lashed village of **Llamedos**, which nestles in the Ramtops mountains (*SM*). Widdershins from Lancre are the kingdoms of Borogravia and **Überwald**, the latter having fallen prey to vampires and werewolves, but it is also home to **dwarfs** (*FE*, *CJ*). Borogravia is a territory seemingly locked in constant civil wars.

At the exact centre or hub of the Discworld is a mile-high spike, Cori Celesti, surrounded by the Ramtops Mountains and the Hubland Steppes. The spike acts as the point of references for Discworld compasses, though they hardly make navigation any easier. Cori Celesti is home to the gods, who spend their time playing games, Dunmanisfestin, sometimes gambling with the lives of mortals. This area was invaded by **Cohen the Barbarian** (*LH*).

Because of the magical field in which the Discworld is bathed, belief systems are very important and powerful, so that anything which is believed in strongly enough does exist. This is true of dragons (*COM*), **Death** (especially *RM*), the **Hogfather** (*H*) and a variety of other anthropomorphic manifestations. Some of these practices are monitored by the Auditors of Reality, who are always wanting to intervene and rationalise reality. Time is also rather fluid (*see* The **Trousers of Time**), and it is not definite that we have always seen the same version of Discworld. Discworld has also been the object of attack from outside – in the form of **Hollywood films** (*MP*), **pop music** (*SM*) and various gods from the **Dungeon Dimensions**.

The Discworld as a series has been divided into a number of sequences according to the central characters. The Rincewind novels feature the misadventures of a cowardly wizard and his travels around the Disc

(*CM*, *LF*, *ER*, *S*, *E*, *IT*, *LC*, *LH*), usually with other wizards as well. The **Witches** novels initially just featured Granny **Weatherwax** (*ER*), but she was later joined by Nanny **Ogg** and Magrat **Garlick** (*WS*, *WA*, *LL*, 'SALF' and *CJ*), Magrat's place in the coven being taken in time by Agnes **Nitt**. These stories are often about the struggle for power. Death and his granddaughter take centre stage in a number of books, usually featuring Death stepping aside from his Duties (*M*, *RP*, *SM*, *TOT*). Death has a greater or lesser appearance in each book save for *WFM*. Another sequence is the **City Watch** (or Night Watch, Guards or City Guards) novels, where the force led by Samuel Vimes tries to keep order, and not be a tool of the Machiavellian Patrician Vetinari (*GG*, 'TOC', *MAA*, *J*, *FE*, *NW*, *MR*, *GP*, *T!*). The final sequence to date, featuring Tiffany **Aching**, is another witch-narrative, aimed at children. A number of novels, notably *P*, *SG* and *AMHER*, stand alone to date, although Gollancz published an omnibus of *P*, *SG* and *H* as *The Gods Trilogy* (2000). *TT* centres on William de **Worde** and *GP* on Moist von **Ludwig**, but does feature the City Watch. Ludwig is projected to return in *Making Money*.

The first two Discworld novels were effectively travelogues – a pattern maintained during the Rincewind books – and many of the early to mid-period feature child or child-like protagonists in **coming-of-age narratives**. This is something returned to in the Tiffany Aching books. The Witches and City Watch books centre on more mature figures, and tend to explore darker and more adult themes, although it has to be noted that the Discworld is not at its most confident when dealing with sexual matters.

Pratchett, often compared to P.G. **Wodehouse**, among other writers, uses **parody** of **Fantasy** and **Science Fiction** to drive his plots, but also draws on real-world versions of **Arabic Society**, **Australia**, **China**, Germany, Italy, New Orleans and Norway, among others, to inspire his locations. He had previously used a version of the Discworld cosmology in the sf-tinged *Str*. *See also* Agatean Empire; Ankh-Morpork; Great A'Tuin; Counterweight Continent; *The Discworld Almanak*; Djelibeybi; Ephebe; Genua; Klatch; Lancre; Llamedos; Omnia; Sto Helit; Sto Lat; Tsort; Überwald *and* XXXX.

Andrew M. Butler

The Discworld Almanak: The Year of the Prawn (2004)

Written with Bernard **Pearson**. Illustrations by Pearson, Sheila Watkins and Paul **Kidby**. First published in the UK by Doubleday.

As the volume notes this covers the Scholar's Year 1657, but also the Common Year 2005 – the first full year after publication in the real world.

The Discworld Almanak: The Year of the Prawn

This could just about be used as a **diary**, or a year planner, but this would probably be more trouble than it was worth.

The volume contains predictions for the year, which would have included the Great **A'Tuin** in a roll, and folk wisdom and advice about each of the **Discworld** months. It also includes lucky vegetables for each month, advice on gardening and horticulture, proverbs and lucky foods at various times of the year. It details the feasts and markets of **Ankh-Morpork** and surrounding areas, and offers especial details on the cabbages of the Sto Plains. It runs through the Discworld zodiac, with relevant astrology. It also includes adverts for C-M-O-T **Dibbler** in various guises, the **Überwald** Temperance Movement and many more – as an in-joke it includes adverts for various producers of Discworld **merchandising**, including Pearson, Kidby and Stephen **Briggs**. Like *NOC*, it includes 'pinned in' memoranda between the publisher and the printer, Ronald Goatberger (*see* Gunilla **Goodmountain**) and Thomas Cropper, some of which spare the readers' blushes by obscuring illustrations.

The source for all this is *Old Moore's Almanack*, first published by Francis Moore (1657–1715) in London in 1697 with weather predictions and from 1699 with astrological forecasts. It was originally called *Vox Stellarum Or A Loyal Almanack* and is still published annually. An Irish publication, *Old Moore's Almanac*, dates from about the same period. *See also* Calendars; Diaries *and* Bernard Pearson.

Andrew M. Butler

The Discworld Companion (1994)

Co-written with Stephen **Briggs**, who also provided illustrations, this is the official encyclopaedia of **Discworld** characters, places, species and so forth. It draws upon both canonical evidence – the novels and the short stories – and extratextual material, either information Pratchett knows but has not worked into the books, or material invented for the Companion. Each volume contains Easter Eggs – such as the first appearance of William de **Worde** – so a careful reading is rewarded. The volume also includes an interview with Pratchett.

The first edition of 32,750 copies was published in the UK by Victor Gollancz in 1994. The paperback (1997) was an updated edition of 70,000 copies; *The New Discworld Companion* (2003) updates the material to *We Free Men* [*sic*], with a paperback from Gollancz. The cover shifted to one by Paul **Kidby** in the third version, from those by Josh **Kirby** in the first two. Further editions of this indispensable guide seem likely.

Andrew M. Butler

Discworld (Computer Game) *see* Computer Games

Discworld II: Missing, Presumed...!? see Computer Games

Discworld II: Mortality Bytes! see Computer Games

The Discworld Mapp (1995)

Subtitled *Being the Onlie True & Mostlie Accurate Mappe of the Fantastyk & Magical Dyscworlde*. The credits say that it was devised by Terry Pratchett and Stephen **Briggs**, and the map was drawn by Stephen **Player** who had done *SA*. It was published in the UK by Corgi in an edition of 120,000. There are Czech and Polish translations.

In the epigraph to *S*, Pratchett says that there is no map to the **Discworld**, but readers were free to draw their own. This is a spoof of the tendency of a branch of **Fantasy** to contain a map in the front of the first volume, and to explore the land through the subsequent narrative. J.R.R. **Tolkien's** books contain various maps, and he clearly drew them to help his imagination – and others have since come along and drawn much fuller versions.

Pratchett had been sent various amateur maps of the Discworld by fans, and there were similarities between them, suggesting a coherent geography was emerging. He was also increasingly wary, as the series progressed, that he risked contradicting himself between books as to times of journeys and the location of towns and villages. Briggs produced a first draft of what he thought the world looked like, and then had to move EcksEcksEcksEcks or **XXXX** because of details in *LC* which was already gestating at the time of the map being drawn (*LC* did not appear until 1998).

Like the earlier map, the format is of a short booklet, containing an introduction by Pratchett and an account of the process by Briggs, and a key to some of the places on the fold out map. It also offers a brief account of some of the past Discworld explorers, and an account of theories about the movement of continents. General Sir Ruthven Purdeigh undertook three voyages in search of the lost continent of XXXX and failed to do so through remarkably careless sailing. Note that Ruthven is a reference to fiction representations of poet Lord Byron (1788–1824) in *Glenarvon* (1816) by former lover Caroline Lamb (1785–1828) and as a vampire in *The Vampyre* (1819) by his physician John Polidari (1795–1821). Lars Larsnephew went on various looting and pillaging missions from NoThing, NoThingfjord, and is the Discworld equivalent of a Viking, but more polite. Llamedos Jones may have come from the village of **Llamedos**, but was limited to brief explorations due to his commitment to regular druidic rituals and choir practice. He may have taken the culture of Llamedos to one of the Brown Islands. Lady Alice Venturi travelled in **Klatch** and

Howandaland and is like the archetypal Victorian and early twentieth-century female explorers, who determinedly stick to their own culture and mores in foreign climes. Ponce da Quirm, who has been depicted in *E*, was a seeker for an elixir of youth, which he found at the age of eighty. Finally, Venter Boras was a geologist, who discovered the history of the Discworld could be found in the strata of rocks – Discworld's version of geologist Charles Lyell (1797–1875). *See also* Stephen Briggs; Maps *and* Stephen Player.

Andrew M. Butler

Discworld Noir see Computer Games

The Discworld Portfolio see Kirby, Josh

Djelibeybi (*P*)

A long, narrow kingdom, largely desert with a single river, between enemies **Ephebe** and **Tsort**. In the wet season, much of the land is flooded, and much of the available fertile land is taken up with the pyramids which are monuments to the dead pharaohs who have previously ruled the land. Their possessions, including their servants, are stored with their mummified bodies in pyramids which store time and let it flare off at night, preserving the remains as fresh or allowing a dying pharaoh some extra life.

The real **power** in the land is Dios, who had been assumed to be a number of different people with the same name, but has in fact been priest for seventy centuries and is deeply resistant to any change, including soft furnishings and plumbing. He is particularly hostile to **Teppic** and his new-fangled ways.

The size of the pyramid is such that it distorts the space-time fabric and turns the country ninety degrees through the fourth dimension, rendering one of the builders flat as a pancake, and turning the fiendishly comply Djelibeybian mythology as truth – the dead are brought back to life, dog- and hawk-headed gods walk the streets and a giant scarab beetle pushes the sun around on the Pharaoh's instructions. Another result is that Ephebe and Tsort come to the brink of war. Eventually, the pyramid is brought back under control, and Ptraci takes over as king, thanks to the country's relaxed attitude to incest, nepotism and the absolute power of the pharaoh to do what they want – at least as long as the priest wants it to happen or is not around.

Clearly, Djelibeybi is a version of **Egypt**; in the tradition of **Sellar and Yeatman**, it is a parody of the details that are remembered about Egypt rather than actual Egypt history or religion. The name of the country derives from Jelly Babies, a popular British fruit-flavoured jelly sweet, shaped like a baby and lightly coated in icing sugar. They were originally sold just after the end of the First World War and were then known as Peace Babies; after a hiatus in production during the Second World War, they were relaunched as Jelly Babies in 1953. The cultural specificity of the joke led Pratchett to introduce more confectionary into **Discworld**, namely the kingdom of Hersheba. *See also* Egypt *and* Teppic.

Andrew M. Butler

Dogs

The name 'dog' refers to a small, carnivorous canine mammal, often domesticated, but as often in Pratchett's work, feral. Unlike **cats**, there is not the same level of grudging respect for this animal, nor is the 'owner's' treatment of them necessarily as significant. They are perhaps more likely to be points within the development of the plot. All dogs belong to the Canid family and are thought to have been domesticated from wolves less than one hundred thousand years ago, possibly in **China**. Dogs are thought of a loyal – man's best friend – and intelligent, with a good sense of hearing and an acute sense of smell (*see also* **Werewolves**).

Ankh-Morpork does boast a Dog Guild, which regulates barking, scavenging and howling, and consists of dogs who have run away from their owners. It is run by the Chief Barker. There is a particular kind of big black dogs peculiar to the **Discworld**, the Lipwigzer (*TT*, *GP*).

Gaspode is an intelligent mongrel with the ability to talk, though most people tend not to hear him, and when it suits him he can adopt an innocent look which throws people off. His speech derives from the same **magic** which started the moving picture craze at Holly Wood (*MP*). His first appearance is aiding Victor **Tugelband** to break into movies; his own success is limited as he is passed over in favour of the more photogenic Laddie. He claims to have been named after a Greyfriars Bobby-type dog, who had sat waiting for his master John Gray (d.1858) at his grave in Greyfriars Kirkyard, Edinburgh. Pratchett had intended for Gaspode to die at the end of the novel, but was persuaded against this by early readers of the manuscript. Later Gaspode regains and keeps his powers by his snuffling around the rubbish at the **Unseen University**. His sense of smell is something which worries the closeted werewolf, Angua von **Überwald** (*MAA*). He may have a cameo as a dog who stares into a music box, as a parody of Nipper in the HMV logo (*SM*). Later, Gaspode is called upon to help Carrot **Ironfoundersson** track Angua, using his sense of smell (*FE*). Most recently, he has been involved in the mystery surrounding Patrician **Vetinari** and his dog Wuffles in *TT*. Aware of what has really gone on, he acts as Deep Bone – a Deep Throat figure – to William de **Worde**.

Dogs

Wuffles is an extremely old terrier which is probably the only living creature that he is known to care for despite him lacking most of his teeth and having bad breath. Wuffles first appears in *S*, is mentioned in *GG* and tends to sleep under Vetinari's desk in the Oblong Office. He is significant in the attempt to kidnap the Patrician by Mr Pin and Mr Tulip – he bites the Döppelgänger they had planned to replace Vetinari with. Wuffles's behaviour and the reaction to it is a variation upon the exchange from 'The Adventure of Silver Blaze' between Sherlock Holmes and Inspector Gregory:

> 'Is there any other point to which you would wish to draw my attention?'
> 'To the curious incident of the dog in the night-time'.
> 'The dog did nothing in the night-time'.
> 'That was the curious incident,' remarked Sherlock Holmes.

(These lines were also echoed in *GG*.) As Wuffles cannot speak, it is necessary for Gaspode to act as interpreter.

In *JB*, **Kirsty**, noticing that she is surrounded by three token boys is relieved that they do not also have a dog as a companion, in an ironic reference to Timmy in *The Famous Five* novels (1942–1963) by Enid Blyton (1897–1968) (*see* **Sexism**). A dog, imaginatively called Dog, is part of Adam **Young's** gang in *GO*, and in theory it is a hellhound before Adam tamed it. *See also* Patrician Vetinari *and* Werewolves.

Further Reading

Burton, Maurice. 1968. *University Dictionary of Mammals of the World*. New York: Thomas Crowell Company.
Doyle, Sir Arthur Conan. 1984. *The Penguin Complete Adventures of Sherlock Holmes*. Harmondsworth, Middlesex: Penguin.

Andrew M. Butler

Dragons

Mythical lizards that appear in several forms in the **Discworld** series.

In *COM*, the *Lure of the Wyrm* section is a **parody** of the dragon books by Anne McCaffrey (b.1926), including both the flight of the beats and their telepathic abilities. These dragons are imaginary, and only exist if believed in, an early version of the anthropomorphic personifications in *SG* and especially *H*. Although it is suggested in *COM* that Swamp Dragons (*Draco vulgaris*) are extinct, the species is first seen in *GG*, as cared for by Lady Sybil **Ramkin**. They are small, semi-flightless and liable to explode from the gas inside them. In the same novel, a bigger dragon, *Draco nobilis*, is summoned into **Ankh-Morpork** by **magic** from another dimension and becomes temporary king of the city. In *LH*, there are the silvery Moon Dragons (*Draco lunaris*) who flame from the rear, and Star Voyaging Dragons (*Draco stellaris nauticae*), who exist in open space.

Pratchett draws upon the dragons of folklore and **Fantasy**, most obviously those of McCaffrey, but also Smaug in J.R.R. Tolkien's *The Hobbit* (1937). *See also Fantasy.*

Andrew M. Butler

Drink

There seem to be two kinds of drink in the **Discworld**: things that make you drunk and things that sober you up. As a **Fantasy** world without its own version of Louis Pasteur (1822–1895) or sewer engineer Joseph Bazalgette (1819–1891) and so you probably do not want to drink the water unless it has been distilled or boiled.

One of the most potent brews is Scumble, first seen in *M*, which is made from apples somewhere at the start of the process, and can dissolve metal. It is drunk in thimbles; any more than that will leave the drinker looking like death warmed up – though curiously it takes **Death** quite a few pints of it before it works on him. An authentic version ('Suicider') is made by Nanny **Ogg**, who is well known for having a tipple or three.

Dwarfs brew their own beer, and mixed with Scumble this makes Fluff (*T!*) – rather different from its real-world name of Snakebite, but presumably even more lethal. There are a variety of beers available across the Discworld, including Turbot's Really Odd (*SM*) and Winkle's Old Peculiar (*FOC*, *SOD*), although often it is wiser in taverns, such as The **Broken Drum**, not to enquire too closely into the brand name. Polly **Perks**, who grew up in a pub, points out to one landlord that they are selling them the urine-like beer rather than the proper stuff, and the mistake is rapidly rectified (*MR*).

Given the strength of the beer, spirits are hardly necessary, but Jimkin Bearhugger distils various kinds of whisky, which are more or even more lethal (*GG*). There is also Ghlen Livid (*COM*), the Discworld equivalent of Glenlivet, a Speyside Scottish Single Malt whisky, which is widely distributed in the USA. C.M.O.T. **Dibbler's** Genuine Authentic Soggy Mountain Dew, allegedly 150% proof, and sometimes the downfall of Samuel **Vimes** (*MAA*). Brose is a liqueur of whisky, herbs and other stuff, brewed by the Nac Mac Feegles, which is used to protect **Verence II** from the **vampires** (*CJ*). Cocktails are not exactly common, but one example is the Screaming Orgasm (*T!*).

When re-annual plants (plants that are harvested before they are sown) are fermented to produce an alcoholic beverage which still makes people drunk, but produces a hungunder, like a hangover but occurring several hours before the session – the only solution is to drink large amounts to cure it.

Drink

A number of characters in Discworld attempt to drink to forget – this is true of Death for example, and of Samuel Vimes in *GG*. Vimes is clearly an alcoholic, and has had some lapses (*MAA*) and his love of drink may be used against him. However, the love of a good woman (Lady Sibyl **Ramkin**) and the need to be there for his son, Sam, seems to have kept him on the wagon for a number of books. Nanny Ogg remains a heavy drinker, but she seems to be able to take it in her stride. The existence of Bilious, the O God of Hangovers, should be noted (*H*).

Nothing is likely to sober up a drunk more quickly than coffee, especially coffee from **Klatch**. This is particularly strong, which is why Vimes often had to drink it at Sham Harga's House of Ribs (*GG*, *MAA*) and is able to tell when it has been watered down, when the pots have been cleaned and so forth. Too much coffee will leave the drinker knurd, which is the opposite of drunk; in fact it gives the drinker clarity and insight into the world, stripped of illusion. Its impact may explain why Klatch is such an advanced society in science, astronomy and mathematics. The effects of knurdness can be mitigating by drinking Orakh, a brew of snake venom and cactus sap which is again alcoholic. *See also* The Broken Drum; Food *and* Samuel Vimes.

Andrew M. Butler

Dungeon Dimensions (*COM*, *ER*, *S*, *E*, *MP*)

An infernal series of dimensions outside of the 'real' time and space of the **Discworld**. The barrier between these can be broken down by **magic**, and demonic creatures may attempt to breakthrough to take over the work or the universe.

Rincewind and **Twoflower** visit Bel-Shamharoth, the Sender of the Eight (*COM*), whose name is commemorated in the Young Men's Reformed-Cultists-of-the-Ichor-God-Bel-Shamharoth Association. Simon's sourcery opens up a hole between the dimensions, and is sucked into the dimensions, having to be rescued by Eskarina **Smith** (*ER*). **Coin** is also thrown into the beyond my his meta-magic and has to be the subject of a rescue attempt by Rincewind (*S*). Rincewind is an old hand at the game by *E*, as Eric **Thursley**'s magic moves him around, and beyond, the universe. In *MP*, there is some kind of demonic force which makes people fall for the moving pictures.

The Dungeon Dimensions is a **parody** of the Cthulhu Mythos as described in the stories of H.P. Lovecraft (1890–1937), a realm of demons such as Shub-Niggurath (the black goat) and Yog-Sothoth. Pratchett invokes them to narrative and comic affect, whereas Lovecraft and his followers intended to invoke horror. *See also* Coin; Greek Mythology; The Luggage; Rincewind; Eric Thursley *and* Twoflower.

Andrew M. Butler

Dwarfs

A major race on the **Discworld**, who divide into three groups:

1. the miners of Überwald, ruled by an elected Low King (*FE*) who is anointed leader on the Scone of Stone (a ritual going back B'hrian Bloodaxe, a millennium and a half ago),
2. the miners of Copperhead (*GG*), in the Ramtops mountains, **Lancre,**
3. a sizeable group resident in (or under) cities, notably **Ankh-Morpork**.

The first two groups largely distrust each other, and – unless they are the recipients of money being sent home – are distrustful of the third group.

The dwarfs are an ancient race, steeped in culture and tradition, and desirous above all of gold. Gold forms a major topic of their music. Dwarf sex is an area of some embarrassment, and it is difficult to tell males and females apart, although the coming out of Cheery **Littlebottom** and some comments about Rhys Rhysson, the new Low King (or Queen), have caused a minor sexual revolution.

The dwarfs look back to a creator god, Tak, who wrote the world and created dwarfs, men and **trolls**. Having produced the laws, it seems that he left the world – but it did mean that dwarfs respect the word and to rub out a word is heresy or sacrilege. Another figure in dwarf mythology is the trickster Agi Hammerthief (*FE*) who steals tools. Dwarfs do fear the dark, especially in the form of an ancient demonic being of pure vengeance, the Summoning Dark (*T!*).

Technically, Carrot **Ironfoundersson** is a dwarf, having grown up in Copperhead to be made a man of in the **City Watch** (*GG*). **Cuddy** is the first biological dwarf to sign up (*MAA*), partnered with **Detritus**, a troll. Dwarfs and trolls have a long enmity, traced back to the Battle of Koom Valley, or, rather, battle*s* (*see* **War**, *T!*). It is not clear who started it or who won, but both sides claim ambushes took place.

Other notable dwarfs include writer **Hwel** (*WS*), seducer Giamo Casanunda (*WA* and *LL*), Glod, a victim of a dyslexic curse which meant that everything the Seriph of Al Ybi touched turned to Glod (*WA* and *SM*), Glod Glodsson, a member of Music With Rocks In It (*SM*), delicatessen owner Gimlet Gimlet (*SM*, *MAA* and *RM*), printers Gunilla **Goodmountain** and Bodony (*TT*), and loremaster Bashfull Bashfullsson and murder victim Hamcrusher (*T!*).

Pratchett is drawing on folklore and **Fairy Tales**, especially Norse mythology, but most obviously is offering a **parody** of the Disney *Snow White and the Seven Dwarfs* (1937) and the dwarves (note spelling) of J.R.R. **Tolkien**, who also commented on the apparent scarcity of the female of the species. Dwarfs are a staple of role playing **games**. *See also* Cuddy; Fairy Tales; Gunilla Goodmountain; Hwel; Cheery Littlebottom; *Thud! and* J.R.R. Tolkien.

Andrew M. Butler

E

EckEcksEcksEcks see XXXX

Egypt (*P*)

Egypt, a country bounded by the Mediterranean Sea and Red Sea, also by the Gaza Strip, Israel and Libya, forms the basis for Pratchett's **Djelibeybi**, especially in *P*. Egypt has been a unified country since approximately 3200 BCE. Egypt was ruled by various dynasties of Pharaohs for three millennia and, like Djelibeybi, was a society traditional enough eventually to become dangerously static, and so concerned with ostentatious display of wealth in burials that serious economic consequences ensued. The Persian Empire conquered Egypt in 525 BCE, under the Cambyses II (*c.* 484–521 BCE), one of history's great psychopathic tyrants, at least in the eyes of the Greek historian Herodotus (484–425 BCE). Macedonian Greeks under Alexander the Great conquered Egypt in 332 BCE. (For the record, Cleopatra VII (69 or 70 BCE–30 BCE) was *not an Egyptian*; she was a Greek of the Ptolemy dynasty. She also had four children, including a set of twins.) After the victory of Octavian, later called Augustus (31 BCE–14 CE), the Romans and later Byzantines were the rulers of Egypt until 642 CE, when they were succeeded by the Arab, Mamluk and finally Ottoman rulers, all Islamic (*see* **Arabic Societies**). These in turn fell to France, under the leadership of Napoleon Bonaparte (1769–1821), but France held Egypt for only four years (1798–1802). There followed the dynasty of Mohammed Ali Pasha (1802–1892), which proved to have more staying power than France had. Egypt's last foreign rulers were the British, who took occupied the country in 1882. Egypt became a republic on 18 June 1953; the first President was Mohammad Naguib (1901–1984).

Djelibeybi is strikingly similar to Pharaonic Egypt during the golden age of pyramid building, approximately 2630–1817 BCE. While the Egyptians were building ever-more sophisticated pyramids and temple complexes, the rest of the world was far behind them technologically and artistically. Naturally, **Teppic** at first finds **Ankh-Morpork** and its inhabitants oddly barbaric. Since Djelibeybi is a comic reflection of Egypt, Teppic has grown up with sophisticated art, a highly developed religious system, and the knowledge that he himself is at least potentially a god.

Teppic's divinity is perfectly normal for a Pharaoh; ancient Egyptians did consider kings and kingship sacred. Many of the familiar elements of Egyptian religion show up in Djelibeybi: the reverence shown for cats reflects worship of the cat-goddess Bastet or Bast, while the crowded and often overlapping pantheon of the country is thoroughly Egyptian as well: Egyptian gods went out of fashion, but were never actually discarded.

Pratchett uses well-understood conventions about ancient Egypt, but takes them to their logical conclusions. If mummies are understood, as Hollywood has constructed them, to lurch around and haunt people, then they ought to be designed for this: hessian rather than calico becomes Dil's choice for the late Teppicymon XXVII. Complex symbology was also a feature of Egyptian culture. Hence, Teppic is burdened with the Flail of Justice, the Sheaf of Plenty, the Honeycomb of Increase and the like. Pharaohs frequently married close female relatives; Teppic is urged to marry his aunt.

Egyptology has long had a strong popular appeal: Jews and Christians have always been historically interested in the scenes of Biblical events. (By the way, if you want to stir up ill feelings among archaeologists – always an amusing pastime – innocently ask a group of them which Pharaoh was the one in the Book of Exodus. A fight will almost certainly ensue.) The romantic story of the 1922 finding of the tomb of Tutankhamen by archaeologist Howard Carter (1874–1939), and rumours that the tomb was cursed attracted attention all over the world. The death of Carter's patron, Lord Carnarvon (1866–1923) from pneumonia in Cairo, soon after the opening of the tomb, also contributed to the contemporary interest in things Egyptian.

Alternative researchers maintain that food stored in pyramids does not decay, and that pyramids can sharpen dull razor blades. Pratchett has a field day with New-Age pyramid power theories, for in Djelibeybi, pyramids are genuinely magical, and hence wreck havoc on the ordinary flow of time. No wonder Teppic's ancestors are able to wake and to walk, however clumsily.

The shambling mummies of Hollywood horror films soon became symbols ripe for **parody**: *Abbot and Costello Meet the Mummy* (1955) is once of the first ancient-Egypt comedies. *Carry on, Cleo* (1964) is set in England and in Rome rather than in Egypt, but Cleopatra is very much her Egyptian (Greek) self. Other light treatments of Egypt include two notable spoofs from 1968: *Mad Monster Party* and the not-to-be-missed animated comedy *Astérix et Cléopâtre*. *See also* Carry-On Films; Djelibeybi; Hollywood Films *and* Teppic.

Further Reading

Herodotus of Halicarnassus. 2003. *Histories*. Translated by Aubrey de Selincourt. London: Penguin Classics.

Hornung, Erik. 1996. *Conceptions of God in Ancient Egypt: The One and The Many*. Translated by John Baines. Ithaca: Cornell University Press.

Shaw, Ian, ed. 2000. *Oxford History of Ancient Egypt*. Oxford: Oxford University Press.

Amy Vail

Elephants

The name 'elephant' refers to a large, herbivorous pachyderm mammal, with a long proboscis and large ears. There are three surviving species, the African Bush Elephant (*Loxodonta africana*), the African Forest Elephant

(*Loxodonta cyclotis*) and the Indian Elephant (*Elephas maximus*). The elephants ridden by Hannibal (247 BCE–c.183 BCE) over the Alps are probably an extinct species.

The most significant elephants are clearly the four stood on the back of the Great **A'Tuin**, Berilia, Great T'Phon, Jerakeen and Tubul, on whose backs the **Discworld** rests and rotates. There was a fifth, which millennia ago crashed into the surface of the Disc in **Überwald**, laying down fatty deposits which are mined to this day (*FE*). The elephants have occasionally to cock their legs to allow a sun or moon pass on its orbit.

An elephant is mentioned at the end of *WA*, as seen by the **witches** who had taken the long way home from **Genua**, a reference to Bilbo Baggins who never got to see one in J.R.R. **Tolkien's** *The Hobbit* (1937) or *The Lord of Rings* (1954–1955). A presumably different species, described as the strangest and saddest species, is the hermit elephant which lives in huts in a variety of sizes (*MAA*). Elephants also appear (with a cast of thousands) in *MP*, and in a sacrifice in ***Mort: A Discworld Big Comic***. *See also* Great A'Tuin *and* Discworld.

Further Reading

Burton, Maurice. 1968. *Universal Dictionary of Mammals of the World*. New York: Thomas Crowell Company.

Andrew M. Butler

Elves

Post-**Tolkien**, elves have been portrayed as noble, cultured creatures with the sleekness of **cats**. In Pratchett, in the unambiguous title of an article, he wrote for a convention handbook, 'Elves Were Bastards' (*see OM* WF*). They are at best tricksters, at worse nasty and violent with a penchant for kidnap. Elfland also features in *Thomas the Rhymer* (1974), the Steeleye Span record Pratchett choose on *Desert Island Discs*. This was based on a ballad which can be traced back to the thirteenth century.

They come (return?) from a parallel dimension to the **Discworld** and are able to hypnotise humans with their glamour and music (not for nothing is it suggested that Imp Y **Celyn** is a little Elvish), and only iron can stand against them. They are ruled by a king and queen, and it is the queen who is more aggressive. In *LL*, they attempt to invade **Lancre**, but are defeated by Magrat **Garlick** fighting for her husband, **Verence II**. The invasion is repeated in *WFM*, via dreams and kidnappings, but Tiffany **Aching** and the fairy-like Nac Mac Feegle defeat them. In *SODII*, the Elves attempt to invade Roundworld. *See also* J.R.R. Tolkien.

Andrew M. Butler

Ephebe (*P*, *E*, *SG*, *LH*)

Ephebe is **Discworld's** answer to classical antiquity in general, and to Athens of the fifth century in particular. Both Ephebe and **Tsort** are said to be parts of ancient **Klatch**, and both are also reflections of some of realities of contemporary travel in the Mediterranean. The Tuesday Symposium is more like a meal in a modern Greek restaurant than the symposium described by Plato (*c.* 429–347 BCE). The word 'Ephebe' is an Anglicisation of the word 'ephebos', relating adolescent and often referring to young men being trained together, although Pratchett was no doubt influenced by the sound of Thebes, an important Greek city-state from the sixth- to fourth-century BCE.

Like the Athenians, Ephebians have a unique self-invented political system: **Teppic** thinks it is perhaps called 'mocracy'. Like Athenian democracy, the Ephebian system limits the franchise severely: foreigners, children, madmen, slaves and women have no say in the government.

The Ephebian gods resemble those of the Greek pantheon. Athena, goddess of wisdom, sometimes depicted with wings, finds her reflection in Patina, a female penguin. Like the Romans, however, Ephebians sometimes worship foreign gods: Offler is an import from **Djelibeybi**.

The most prominent Ephebian citizens are philosophers and natural scientists. Among these is Xeno, who is reminiscent of Zeno of Elia (*c.* 490–425 BCE), famous for his paradoxes. Xeno's practical experiments with tortoises and hares prove that his theories simply do not work. Pthagonal the geometrician was probably inspired by the mathematician Pythagoras of Samos (*c.* 560–480 BCE). Ibid, author of *Principals of Ideal Government* and expert on practically everything, is based on Aristotle (384–322 BCE), the greatest political scientist and polymath of his day. The forgetful and tedious Copolymer is a rhapsode, or a professional performer of Homeric epic. (Incidentally, a copolymer is a biggish molecule made up of two or more kinds of smallish molecules.) The blind philosopher Didactylos, who lives in a barrel, is the Discworld avatar of Diogenes the Cynic (*c.* 412–321 BCE).

Ephebe is based on Alexandria as well as on Athens, for it has one of antiquity's largest **Libraries**. Like the Alexandrian Library, burned (for the first, but not the only time) in 41 BCE by Julius Caesar (100–44 BCE), the Library at Ephebe is doomed to go up in flames.

Lavaeolus, who is on the Ephebian side on Tsortean War, is a figure out of Ephebean ancient history: he is close imitation of Odysseus. Eric **Thursley** points out that Lavaeolus is probably an ancestor of **Rincewind**.

See Djelibeybi; Greek Mythology; Greek Philosophy; Libraries *and* Religion.

Further Reading

Kitto, H.D.F. 1991. *The Greeks*. London: Penguin Books.

Martin, Thomas R. 2000. *Ancient Greece: From Prehistoric to Hellenistic Times*. New Haven: Yale University Press.

Amy Vail

Equal Rites (1987)

The third novel in the **Discworld** series, the first not to feature **Rincewind**, although it does include **Wizards**. It was the first to have a major hardback release, thanks in part to advice given to Gollancz by David **Langford** (*see* **Publishers**). It was published in the UK in an edition of 2,850 copies in association with Colin **Smythe** Ltd, with a cover by Josh **Kirby**. The Corgi paperback first appeared in 1987, with an alternative black and gold photographic edition available since 2004. It was published by Gollancz with *WS* and *WA* as *The Witches Trilogy* (1994). A compact edition was published in 1995. It has been translated into Bulgarian, Chinese, Croatian, Czech, Danish, Dutch, Estonian, Finnish, French, German, Greek, Hebrew, Hungarian, Italian, Japanese, Norwegian, Polish, Portuguese, Romanian, Russian, Serbian, Slovakian, Slovenian, Spanish, Swedish and Turkish. The novel is dedicated to Neil **Gaiman**. The title is a pun on 'equal rights', a demand of **Feminism**, but also has the sense of the conflict between the rites performed by wizards and witches – different but equivalent. The novel was serialised on BBC Radio 4's *Woman's Hour* (possibly because Pratchett's unisex name may have been assumed to be that of a woman). *Time Out* described it as 'A great antidote to all those boring sword and sorcery sagas and Tolkien spin-offs'.

The eighth son of an eighth son may become a wizard, and the dying Drum Billet thinks he has found one in the village of Bad **Ass** in the Ramtops mountains. Unfortunately, the child, delivered by Granny **Weatherwax**, is a daughter, Eskarina **Smith**, so is the wrong sex to become one. However, the staff has been passed on to Esk. Granny Weatherwax takes the child under her wing, and begins to teach her some of the ways of witchcraft, but at the age of eight Esk travels to the **Unseen University** in **Ankh-Morpork** in order to enrol. As a female, she is refused entry by **Archchancellor** Cutwell, but Weatherwax finds her a job as a cleaner which allows her to overhear the teaching. When Esk's friend Simon gets lost in a spell and possessed by Things, she tries to follow him with her mind and is also lost. Cutwell and Weatherwax go in search of her lost wizard's staff in an attempt to rescue them and to save Ankh-Morpork. Cutwell makes Esk a wizard and offers Weatherwax a Chair.

In this novel, the **sexism** of many institutions, including Oxbridge-type educational establishments, is satirised. For Weatherwax, **magic** comes out of the ground, but is often psychological – or Headology as she has it – whereas wizard's magic comes from the sky, and is about male power. She does resist Esk's desire to become a wizard, but helps because she detests being told that people cannot do something. *See also* Coming of Age; Feminism; Magic; Sexism; Eskarina Smith; Unseen University; Granny Weatherwax; Witches *and* Wizards.

Andrew M. Butler

~~*Faust*~~ *Eric* (1990)

A **Discworld** book – properly ~~*Faust*~~ *Eric* – not included in the numbering of the Corgi paperbacks, being initially published in hardback and paperback by Gollancz – but it does count to make *TT* the twenty-fifth Discworld novel. The original UK edition of 4,200 hardbacks and 50,500 paperbacks was heavily illustrated by Josh **Kirby**, who got equal billing with Pratchett. It thus needs to be seen as an illustrated novella rather than as a children's book – it contains some swearing and references to tantric sex within the first few pages. It was republished in A format in 1991, without illustrations, and reissued in 1996. It has been collected by Gollancz with *COM*, *LF* and *S* as *The Rincewind Trilogy* (*sic*, 2001). *E* has been translated into Bulgarian, Czech, Dutch, Estonian, Finnish, French, German, Hungarian, Italian, Norwegian, Polish, Russian, Serbian, Spanish and Swedish. This is loosely part of the **Wizards** subsequence, and the scored out title *Faust* indicates the parodic focus; Eric Thursley is the Faust figure. The *Locus* review suggested: 'Artist Kirby outdoes himself (in full colour), and Pratchett continues to turn everything he touches to comedic gold' (October 1990).

The **Unseen University** is being haunted and the wizards summon **Death** to explain – **Rincewind** appears to be the cause. Meanwhile, the failed wizard is summoned by Eric Thursley, a thirteen-year-old demonology hacker who had planned to get a demon but at the crucial time it was otherwise engaged. Eric wants three wishes: to live forever, to rule all the world and meet the most beautiful woman in the world. Rincewind protests that he cannot fulfil these, but with newly gained demon powers he may be wrong. First, they travel to Tezumen, where Eric discovers that ruling might not be all it is cracked up to be, then to **Tsort** where he meets the legendary beautiful Elenor – who has not aged well – and to the beginning of time so he can live forever. In the meantime, the **Luggage** has been following doggedly behind them. Finally, Rincewind and Eric end up in a dimension like hell.

The Faust legend – best known in versions by Christopher Marlowe (1564–1593) and Goethe (1749–1832) – is of a doctor selling his soul to the devil (Mephistophilis) in return for twenty-four years of powers. Faustus in the Marlowe version general wastes these and is dragged to Hell at the end. Pratchett's version sees Eric visit Discworld equivalents of the Aztec civilisation and Troy (*see* **Greek Mythology**), as well as the beginning of time, and a loose version of Hell as seen by Dante (1265–1321) and others. The Rincewind narratives were an early favourite with fans, and this is his biggest role since *S*. *See also* Coming of Age; Death; Dungeon Dimensions; The Luggage; Rincewind; Eric Thursley; Unseen University *and* Wizards.

Andrew M. Butler

F

Fairy Tales

Fairy tales, the extensive body of stories embodying folk-wisdom and wonder handed down from generation to generation, pervade the **Discworld** series. Because of their status as common-stock stories that many readers will remember at least the bones of from childhood, they are particularly important as the source of jokes (because they can be easily and recognisably parodied), as recognisable motifs or allusions and as sources for darker ironies.

Discworld operates by what Terry Pratchett in *WA* calls **narrative** causality. Stories have their own momentum, taking a shape, coiling around the universe, imposing patterns on **history** and shaping events. Pratchett suggests that story can be *parasitic* upon people, or that we can allow ourselves to live in other peoples' stories. One of the most parasitic forms of story is the fairy tale.

Fairy tales (or folk tales, which J.R.R. **Tolkien** says are significantly different but share a number of elements) infuse the modern fantastic through the Victorian passion for fairies and the nineteenth-century rediscovery of folk tales – Jacob Grimm (1785–1863) and Wilhelm Grimm (1786–1859), Joseph Jacobs (1854–1916), Andrew Lang (1844–1912) (the great collectors), Hans Christian Andersen (1805–1875), very much a creative inventor and re-teller, and inventors of original fantasies such as George MacDonald (1824–1905) or Lewis Carroll (1832–1898). In his influential essay 'On Fairy-Stories', Tolkien talks of the 'Cauldron of story' which is forever boiling, a stock from which we can pluck characters, themes and motifs. Indeed, cataloguing of types from folk tales has become a standard way of coming to understand what is happening when we read such stories, as we understand only too wearily when Joseph Campbell's 'monomyth' from *The Hero with a Thousand Faces* (1949) is used yet again to justify stereotypes in bad **Science Fiction** films.

Tolkien himself is at pains to establish that Fairy stories are stories about *Faërie*, the numinous location or mental state, in which Fairies might be said to have their being, and the interaction between 'Fairies' and humans. Following George MacDonald, Tolkien is concerned with the quality of 'arresting strangeness': the distinguishing feature of a sub-creation which imagines something not to be found in our world. Although it is difficult to think of something possessing more 'arresting strangeness' than a Discworld on the backs of four elephants carried on a giant turtle, Pratchett is also engaged with the way humans tend to behave *like* characters in stories. This is a source of both anxiety and humour. **Comedy and humour** of course are based on stereotypes – our feelings of superiority towards those whose behaviour we judge as conforming to a pattern we despise or find amusing – but Pratchett finds his deepest vein of humour (and his darkest morality tales) in the way that stereotype stories become an unthinking excuse to impose roles on others (*everyone knows*, for instance, that old women who live alone in woods are witches).

Fairy tales are often seen as collective folk-wisdom, explaining to young girls, for example, that they must not walk out in the woods alone in case they meet a (sexual) predator. Such cautionary tales may, however, impose stereotypes as much as proffer useful advice. As Tiffany **Aching**, whose mini-Library contains a volume entitled *The Goode Childe's Booke of Faerie Tales*, muses in *WFM*, stories can stop people thinking properly: why *does* a boy stupid enough to sell a cow for a handful of beans have the right to murder a giant? Stories are not real and can be sentimental barriers to understanding the real world. Part of *WA* is its own games with stereotypes. Granny **Weatherwax**, here, and later in *CJ*, is faced with understanding her own 'story' and preventing her role as part of the three witches 'Crone-Mother-Maiden' trope from overcoming her. In her relationship with Lily **Weatherwax**, she has been cast, like it or not, as 'the good one'. Inherent in her is the danger of becoming 'Black Aliss', the wicked witch from the European tradition with the gingerbread cottage and sinister oven. Lily, though, wants people to live according to the narrative 'rules' of fairy stories, and there are echoes of 'Little Red Riding Hood', 'Sleeping Beauty' and 'Cinderella', among others, which weave through the story in a way which is both chilling (the way the 'wolf/grandmother' motifs are used to suggest the uncaring cruelty of the woodcutter and his village) and amusing (the complex series of jokes about pumpkins and Embers/Magrat **Garlick** 'going to the ball'). These are the canon of fairy tales best known to children in the Anglo-American tradition, and because of their very familiarity can be played with, subverted, inverted and twisted to create complex meanings. There are also echoes of the more modern fairy tale *The Wonderful Wizard of Oz* (1900) by L. Frank Baum (1856–1919) with Nanny **Ogg's** clicking of her red boots at the end of the story. Elsewhere, *AMHER* is based on the 'Pied Piper' story collected by the Brothers Grimm and retold by the poet Robert Browning (1812–1889) in 1849.

Although strongly rooted in an oral tradition, a number of our best-known fairy tales owe their popularity to *literary* retellings such as those of Charles Perrault (1628–1703), whose *Stories or Tales from Times Past; or, Tales of Mother Goose* (1697) contains the three stories mentioned above. Towards the end of the eighteenth century, fairy tales became increasingly useful source material for moral tales for children, and the expanding book trade produced numerous cheap chapbook versions, although, according to fairy tale scholar Jack Zipes, there was also, among some early British writers for children, deep suspicion of the un-Christian images to be found there. Later collectors, investigating national 'folk' traditions, rediscovered bawdy and sadistic elements: versions of some of these are hinted at in Granny Weatherwax's refusal to hear anything about the symbolism of maypoles and witch's broomsticks, and in *H*, where the different side of our jovial Father Christmas is suggested. The Grimm brothers revised their collection to attract children and middle-class audiences. This editing for cosiness continues in Disney movie adaptations, but at the same time a long tradition of subversion and playful experimentation includes Lewis Carroll, E. Nesbit (1858–1924), J.M. Barrie (1860–1937) and L. Frank Baum's 'Oz' series. Later in the twentieth century, feminists, such as Angela Carter (1940–1992) in *The Bloody Chamber* (1979), reworked fairy tales for adult readers, while children's writers such as Babette Cole (b.1947) and Catherine Storr (1913–2001) produced amusing versions of classic tales for younger readers suggesting that being married off to Prince Charming or eaten by the Wolf were but two of the *lesser* possibilities open to female characters in fairy tales. The controversial child psychologist Bruno Bettelheim (1903–1990), in *The Uses of Enchantment* (1976), argued that fairy tales carried important messages for the inner life of the child.

Little Red Riding Hood and the wolf.

Pratchett is therefore working in a long tradition of adaptation and satire of fairy tale, both as author and as moralist. Well aware of how even the most complex narratives fall back into fairy tale motifs, he nevertheless keeps them alive as sources for reworkings and retellings. *See also* Tiffany Aching; Fantasy; Heroes *and* Narrative.

Further Reading
Tartar, Maria, ed. 1999. *The Classic Fairy Tales*. New York: Norton.
Tolkien, J.R.R. 1964. 'On Fairy-Stories'. *Tree and Leaf*. London: Unwin.
Zipes, Jack. 1987. *Victorian Fairy Tales*. London: Methuen.

Andy Sawyer

Fandom, Fans and Fan Clubs

Terry Pratchett fandom is a subset of **Science Fiction** (and, later, **Fantasy**) fandom, which can be traced back to the genre magazines of the 1920s. Some of the editors of magazines such as *Amazing Stories* edited by Hugo Gernsback (1884–1967) would print letters of comment on stories from previous issues of the magazines, including the addresses of the letter writers. Some of these people began communicating with each other by mail, and producing their own amateur magazines or fanzines expressing their opinions about science fiction, the world, other fans and other fanzines, and sometimes including their own amateur fiction. Many professional science fiction and fantasy writers – including Pratchett – began as fans.

Discworld fans dressed as the Silver Hoard.

Discworld fans in witches' hats.

The earliest fanzines, such as *The Comet* from 1930 onwards, would be printed on various kinds of lithographic or stencilling machines, with the growing availability of the photocopier improving reproduction standards. In some cases, such as the later fanzines of Bruce Gillespie (b.1947) including *Steam Engine Time*, and the publications of the British Science Fiction Association, professional printers would be used. Fanzines tended to be produced for exchange through the mail with other fanzines, or in return for contributions of material, whether an article, illustration or letter of comment. The death of the fanzine has often been claimed, but the growth of the internet (*see* **Websites**) has offered a relatively low cost means of production and distribution which means there is now more fan writing than ever before, albeit in virtual rather than paper form. Discussions that once took months or even years in paper fandom are now conduct in minutes on Bulletin Boards, on Usenet, in Blogs and other electronic fora. The Pratchett-inspired fanzines have tended to be associated with unofficial societies or fanclubs.

The leading unofficial Terry Pratchett society in the UK is The Guild of Fans and Disciples, founded by Phil Penney and Jacqui Edge in 1994. It publishes a fanzine *Ramtop to Rimfall* three times a year, produces merchandising and offers discounts on some of the spin off materials which are available. In the United States, Joe Schaumburger edits *Wossname*, an electronic newsletter which is primarily aimed at the north and south American market but is available elsewhere. There is a German fanclub, **Ankh-Morpork**.

Octarine is a science fiction and fantasy humour appreciation society, and as the names of the society (Pratchett's invented eighth colour of the spectrum, and the colour of magic) and their fanzine, *Tales from the Broken Drum*, suggest, Pratchett is a major part of this. However, they also cater for fans of Harry Harrison (b.1925), Tom Holt (b.1961), Robert Rankin (b.1949), *Red Dwarf* (1988–1993, 1997, 1999) and others.

Some of the 1930s fans of science fiction arranged to meet face to face, holding the first of many **conventions** in Leeds in 1937. Over the decades, both general, big-tent and specialist conventions have developed, including conventions based around the **Discworld**, which are discussed in the entry on conventions.

Some fans also write their own fiction, some of it based within the universes created by their favourite authors and known as fan fiction. Some authors take a relatively relaxed attitude to such fiction which would technically infringe their copyright, whereas others – especially at the end of the market involved materials where film and television rights are to be protected – will encourage lawyers to send cease and desist letters. A particular subgroup of fan fiction is Kirk/Spock, K/S or, more frequently slash fiction, which began in the mid-1970s with the production of erotic fiction imagining a sexual relationship between Captain Kirk and Spock in *Star Trek*. There is Discworld slash, for example imagining sexual encounters between Patrician **Vetinari** and Samuel **Vimes**. Whilst such fiction is usually homosexual in theme, many of the writers of it are heterosexual women.

Like many hobbies, fandom has evolved its own set of customs and vocabulary, which both identifies particular individuals as being part of the subculture and excludes the rest of the population (sometimes referred to as 'mundanes') from the conversation. Early fandom used to be largely white, male and included people in their teens and twenties; individuals would often be educated up to degree level or higher, and/or an autodidact. They would have a formidable knowledge of the subject of their fandom. Pratchett fandom encompasses people from eight to eighty, and many women are part of the subculture.

Some fans move across the line from amateur to professional. Stephen **Briggs** has been a frequent collaborator with Pratchett on the **maps** and **diaries**, as well as most years writing a play adapting one of the novels for his amateur theatre company. Paul **Kidby** moved from being an interpreter of Pratchett's existing work to becoming the cover artist for the novels after the death of Josh **Kirby**. Bernard **Pearson** carved sculptures of Discworld characters and building for **Clarecraft**, and cowrote *DA* with Pratchett. Whilst some fannish activities fall into the nebulous area of 'fair use', with authors seeing fans as a source of free publicity and viral marketing, there is clearly a sense in which copyright and intellectual property right may be infringed. Whilst a fanzine is unlikely to make money for its editor, a piece of merchandising might, and could, compete with rights to be sold by the copyright holder.

There is no official fan organisation sanctioned by Terry Pratchett or his agent, Colin **Smythe**, although an official one may well miss the point of the way that fans poach other people's works for their own uses. However, Pratchett is a regular attendee of the major conventions and maintains good relations with a number of organisations. His signing sessions, when he spends hours giving autographs, mean that he is certainly accessible to the public in general and fandom in particular, and he does contribute to online discussions. *See also* Stephen Briggs; Clarecraft; Conventions; Fantasy; Paul Kidby; Bernard Pearson; Science Fiction *and* Websites.

Further Reading

Bacon-Smith, Camille. 1999. *Science Fiction Culture.* Philadelphia: University of Pennsylvania Press.
Hills, Matt. 2002. *Fan Cultures.* London: Routledge.
Stableford, Brian. 1987. *The Sociology of Science Fiction.* San Bernadino: Borgo Press.
Tulloch, John, and Henry Jenkins. 1995. *Science Fiction Audiences: Watching Dr Who and Star Trek.* London: Routledge.

Andrew M. Butler

Fantasy

The genre with which Terry Pratchett is most associated (aside from **Comedy and Humour**), and more widely a form of cultural representation, written, visual or oral, which needs to be contrasted with realism. Realism as we understand it today was a genre which emerged in the mid-eighteenth-century novel, and was an attempt to represent the world as it was, with a sense of unity and coherence as a system. At the same time as this emergence of rationality in fiction, there was a renewed celebration of the supernatural – something which had been part of culture since pre-literate times. Supernatural fiction formed one strand of the Gothic novel, typified by *The Monk* (1796) by Matthew Lewis (1775–1818), which featured pacts with the devil, a wandering Jew and ruined locations and consists of an attempt by an author to deliberately represent things which are known not to exist. (The other strand of Gothic was where such phenomena turned out to have a natural explanation, such as the madness or drunkenness of the narrator or the fraudulent actions of others – the rational Gothic is typified by *The Mysteries of Udolpho* (1794) by Ann Radcliffe (1764–1823).)

Whilst many writers who are lauded today for their realist fiction did write works that were fantasies or contained fantastic elements – Charles Dickens (1812–1870), for example – the mode was increasingly dismissed as being escapist or infantile. It was certainly initially excluded from the canon of great works which evolved with the creation of English Literature in universities. In part, fantasy mutated into a form which would become known as **Science Fiction**, with pacts with the devil being replaced with scientific endeavour. But it also existed in pulp magazines which remained largely off the critical radar.

American H[oward] P[hillips] Lovecraft (1890–1937) wrote fantasy which was intended to arouse feelings of horror in the reader, and published in the pulp *Weird Tales*. In the various stories which make up the Cthulu Mythos, he represents a variety of evil gods and demons from other dimensions, which will destroy almost any human with which they have contact. This is the major origin of the **Dungeon Dimensions** in Pratchett's work, although his demons are less destructive in the end. Lovecraft also wrote *Supernatural Horror in Literature* (1927), one of the earliest studies of the form.

His near contemporary, Robert E. Howard (1906–1936), also wrote for *Weird Tales* and is best known today for the Conan the Barbarian sword and sorcery stories, set in an age prior to the ancient civilisations, the Hyborian Age. Conan is a wandering warrior, who encounters a variety of **wizards**, lords, monsters and so forth, which he fights and usually defeats, often gaining power in the process. Conan can be seen in Hrun the Barbarian (*COM*) and **Cohen the Barbarian** (*see* also Fritz **Leiber**).

In Britain, there was arguably a greater acceptance of fantasy as a mode, in that it was possible for novels to be published in hardback from major publishers. Significant authors include E. F. Eddison (1882–1945) – whose *The Worm Ouroboros* (1922) and Zimiamvian Trilogy (1935–1958) were praised by J.R.R. **Tolkien** and C.S. Lewis – Tolkien, Lewis (1898–1963) – especially his Chronicles of Narnia (1950–1955) – and Mervyn Peake (see ***Gormenghast***), most of which are referenced by Pratchett at some point.

The pirated editions of *The Lord of the Rings* from Ace in the 1960s fed a boom in fantasy fiction in America, the apparent retreat from everyday life appearing desirable to the counterculture. **Witches**, **wizards**, **dragons**, **dwarfs**, **elves**, goblins, gnomes, talking trees and **trolls** became clichés of fantasy fiction. Fantasy became identified with the quest of a hero – often someone insignificant – across a landscape which would be depicted in a map at the front of the first of three (or more) volumes. The hero often saved the world at a cost to himself. In the terms advanced by Clute and Grant in *The Encyclopedia of Fantasy* (1993), there is a sense of Wrongness, where things are not operating as they normally should, and this is followed by what they label Thinning, which includes various kinds of disorder and chaos, usually caused by some agent, often some dark lord. The dynamic of the narrative is then to seek for some form of Healing, or recovery of the earlier state of the land, which also involves the recovery of the hero, either in terms of the remembering of who he (less often she) is or in terms of health or status. This pattern occurs to some extent in novels like *S* and *TOT*, where the Discworld is threatened, but often the comic impulse means the structure is subverted.

From the fantasy milieu emerged role-playing **games**, such as *Dungeons & Dragons* (1974), where players using various dice would go on quests set by a 'dungeon master'. Sometimes, these quests would be commercially produced, sometimes they would be the work of amateur players. The growth of the genre was ripe for **parody**; indeed the Harvard Lampoon had already attempted to do so with *Bored of the Rings* (1969). The early **Discworld** novels drew on the clichés of quest or epic fantasy, such as the mock-medieval city (*see* **Ankh-Morpork**), the quest which takes characters to various disparate locations (especially *COM* and *LF*), dragons (especially as depicted by Tolkien in *The Hobbit* (1937) and by Anne McCaffrey (b.1926)) and so forth.

Fantasy is still often seen as an adolescent form of writing, with no redeeming literary merit, and is often characterised as being reactionary or right-wing, with its fear of progress and suspicion of **technology**. It is rarely in the running for literary awards such as the Man Booker Prize, although sales are often healthy without the need for such endorsements. But the best fantasy can be seen to be making commentary on real-world events, perhaps through the use of metaphor or allegory, and inevitably reflects the age in which it is written. There is often more to the morals or ethics than pure good versus evil.

Many of the definitions of fantasy depend on the interaction between what is perceived to be the real world and what is presented as a fantasy realm. The Bulgarian literary theorist Tzvetan Todorov (b.1957) comes to a definition of what he calls the Fantastic by contrasting the marvellous with the uncanny. In a marvellous text – which might be typified by *The Monk* or *Buffy the Vampire Slayer* (1997–2003) – the magical events are real, whereas in the uncanny one – such as *The Mysteries of Udolpho* or *Scooby Doo* (1969–) – they turn out to have a rational explanation. The fantastic text is one in which the reader or characters within the narrative hesitate between marvellous and uncanny explanations for the events. A pure fantast text is rare – Todorov suggests 'The Turn of the Screw' (1898) by Henry James (1843–1916), but *eXistenZ* (1999) directed by David Cronenberg (b.1943) might be a clearer example – but the moments where Pratchett refers to the real world or to writing processes draw attention to the fictionality of the work and so might create a similar form of hesitation.

The British critic Farah Mendlesohn (b.1968) offers a fourfold taxonomy of types of fantasy: the portal, the immersive, the intrusive and the estranged. The portal fantasy is one is which a character from the 'real' world enters into a fantastic realm, most famously the entry into Narnia through the wardrobe in Lewis's *The Lion, the Witch and the Wardrobe* (1950), but also in the Thomas Covenant chronicles (1977–1983, 2004–) by Stephen R. Donaldson (b.1947) where the eponymous leper finds himself in the Land. The fantasy realm is segregated from the real, and may even be dismissed by some as a hallucination. It could be argued that the **Johnny Maxwell Trilogy** fits into this category, although there is more interplay between the real and fantastic realms.

The immersive fantasy is one which is entirely set within an imagined fantasy realm. The reality of this realm is not to be questioned; we share the attitudes and assumptions of the protagonists and identify with them. Broadly speaking, all of the Discworld novels fit into this category, as it is presented as a coherent and entire world. The only quibble with this suggestion is that many of the comic references are dependent upon the reader's recognition of the real world and its culture, and the foregrounding of notions of **narrative**, especially in the middle period of the Discworld series, perhaps call the planet's existence into question.

The intrusive fantasy is supposed to be located in the real world, with fantastical elements invading it and needing to be investigated, comprehended or repelled. This is perhaps exemplified by *JD*, where Johnny **Maxwell** can see the dead themselves, whereas all the other characters can only see their impact – although the voices heard on the radio contradicts this. An intrusive fantasy can also be set within an immersive one – and certain there are various Discworld novels where things come from outside to threaten it.

The final form Mendlesohn describes is the estranged fantasy, for her the rarest and most interesting form. Here there is an apparently real world being described, but with fantastical elements that seem to be taken in their stride by the characters, as if these are part of their everyday life.

Clute and Grant's *Encyclopedia* offers a variety of terms for different subgenre of fantasy, and one that needs to be mentioned is the wainscot, where a society or individuals live in the gaps of society – underground, behind walls, in skirting boards and so on. This is true of the civilisation described in *CP*, where the characters literally live in a carpet, and the nomes in **Arnold Bros** in *T*. Another good example is *Neverwhere* (1996), a television series scripted by Neil **Gaiman**. *See also* Children's Fiction; Coming of Age; Fairy Tales; Fandom; Gormenghast; Fritz Leiber; Neil Gaiman; Science Fiction *and* J.R.R. Tolkien.

Further Reading

Armitt, Lucie. 1996. *Theorizing the Fantastic*. London: Edward Arnold.

Attebery, Brian. 1992. *Strategies of Fantasy*. Bloomington and Indianapolis: Indiana University Press.

Clute, John and John Grant, eds. 1997. *The Encyclopedia of Fantasy*. London: Orbit.

Hume, Kathryn. 1984. *Fantasy and Mimesis: Responses to Reality in Western Literature*. New York and London: Methuen.

Kincaid, Paul. 1995. *A Very British Genre: A Short History of British Fantasy and Science Fiction*. Folkestone: BSFA.

Manlove, Colin. 1999. *The Fantasy Literature of England*. London: Macmillan.

Mendlesohn, Farah. 'Toward a Taxonomy of Fantasy'. *Journal of the Fantastic in the Arts* 13.2 (2004): Pp. 169–183.

Slusser, George E., and Eric S. Rabkin, eds. 1987. *Intersections: Fantasy and Science Fiction*. Carbondale and Edwardsville: Southern Illinois Press.

Todorov, Tzvetan. 1973. *The Fantastic: A Structural Approach to a Literary Genre.* Translated by Richard Howard. Cleveland and London: The Press of Case Western Reserve University.
Wolfe, Gary K. 1986. *Critical Terms for Science Fiction and Fantasy: A Glossary and Guide to Scholarship.* Westport, Ct.: Greenwood.

Andrew M. Butler

~~*Faust*~~ *Eric* see *Eric*

Feet of Clay (1996)

The nineteenth **Discworld** novel, and part of the **City Watch** sequence. The first edition, published by Gollancz, had 85,000 copies, with a cover by Josh **Kirby**. The paperback came out in 1997 from Corgi. Since 2005 an alternate black and gold photographic cover edition has been available from Corgi. In 1999 Gollancz published it, bound with *GG* and *MAA*, as *The City Watch Trilogy*. *FOC* has been translated into Bulgarian, Czech, Dutch, Estonian, Finnish, French, German, Italian, Polish, Russian, Serbian, Spanish and Swedish. The title is a Biblical allusion to Daniel 2, 31–34: 'Thou, O king, sawest, and behold a great image. This great image, whose brightness was excellent, stood before thee; and the form thereof was terrible. This image's head was of fine gold, his breast and his arms of silver, his belly and his thighs of brass. His legs of iron, his feet part of iron and part of clay. Thou sawest till that a stone was cut out without hands, which smote the image upon his feet that were of iron and clay, and brake them to pieces'. Feet of clay are figuratively flaws in a character; here they also refer to parts of a golem. Barbara Davies reviewed it thus: 'I didn't find *Feet of Clay* "screamingly funny", as the back cover blurb suggests, but it did elicit many chortles' (*Vector* 189 (1996)).

Commander Samuel **Vimes** has to visit the Royal College of Heraldry in **Ankh-Morpork** and discovers that, because his ancestor, Stoneface Vimes, executed the last king, his family coat of arms has been withdrawn. He also hears that Nobby **Nobbs** is a descendent of the last Earl of Ankh. There are a series of murders across the city, and **Vetinari** is being poisoned by an unknown method. It looks like golems are behind some of the deaths, and there is a rogue one around town. Vimes eventually works out that Vetinari is being poisoned by the Dragon King of Arms (Vetinari has realised this for some time) and that there was a plot to install a fake and pliable constitutional monarch in the Patrician's place. Vimes admits Dorfl, a golem with freewill, to the Watch. Angua von **Überwald**, uncomfortable with her relationship with Carrot **Ironfoundersson**, thinks about running away.

The golem is a figure from Jewish myth, which can be traced to the Talmud, but comes into its own in the tales of Rabbi Judah Loew of sixteenth-century Prague, who created a golem to protect the ghetto from attack. The golem are made from clay, and animated by the words on (in the novel *in*) their foreheads; they cannot speak or sleep and are killed by the removal of the words. *See also* City Watch; Samuel Vimes *and* Patrician Vetinari.

Further Reading
James, Edward. 'The City Watch'. *GOL, GOL2.*

Andrew M. Butler

Feminism

Terry Pratchett's works have a strong female following due in part to his remarkable female characters; in fact, one of his early **Discworld** novel (*ER*) was featured in BBC Radio 4's programme *Woman's Hour*. Three Pratchett works in particular directly address concerns of First, Second and Third Wave feminists: *ER* explores gender equity in education, *MR* refutes the *de facto* subordination of women in patriarchal societies and the **Johnny Maxwell Trilogy** profiles the self-reliant, no-nonsense attitude of Girl Power.

The title of *ER* refers to the book's two main feminist themes: equal rights for women to access institutions of knowledge, **power** and prestige; and the interrogation of women's work (in this case witchcraft) as being inherently inferior to men's work (wizardry).

The overall idea for *ER* seems to have been inspired by the 1929 essay *A Room of One's Own* by Virginia Woolf (1882–1941), which discusses various institutions that historically refused access to women. At one key point, Woolf imagines what would have been the fate of a woman as talented as William **Shakespeare** during Shakespeare's time: 'Any woman born with a great gift in the sixteenth century would certainly have gone crazed, shot herself, or ended her days in some lonely cottage outside the village, *half witch, half wizard*, feared and mocked at' (my emphasis). *ER*'s Eskarina (Esk) **Smith** is one such 'Shakespeare's Sister', whose destiny to be a wizard is consistently opposed solely on the grounds that she is female, but who nonetheless ends up becoming both witch and wizard. In her quest for self-definition, Esk must struggle against the cultural determinism of the Discworld, expressed in the traditional views of Granny **Weatherwax**, Esk's own prejudices against witchcraft and the institutional sexism of the **Wizards** of **Unseen University**.

Granny Weatherwax is a keeper of tradition. She believes that Esk cannot become a wizard because of biology. For Granny, witchcraft is the proper knowledge for Esk both because of Esk's sex and because she believes that witchcraft is proper use of magic, while wizardry is 'nothing but lights and fire and meddling with power'. Accordingly, Esk's training as a witch does not consist of casting impressive spells, but of learning about the natural world and how to manipulate people's perceptions and convictions (what Granny calls 'headology'), combined with the occasional 'borrowing' of an animal's mind and body. This leads Esk (and the reader) to initially perceive witchcraft as inferior to wizardry.

Like Granny Weatherwax, the Wizards of Unseen University also believe magical ability is based on sex but they, of course, consider only wizardry as 'high magic' and, therefore, exclude Esk (and all women) from their programme of study on the grounds that women's brains 'tend to overheat' when they attempt it (*see* **Sexism**). The belief that witchcraft is not 'high magic', however, proves a misperception when Granny successfully duels the **Archchancellor** of Unseen University.

Pratchett's redemption of witchcraft from a dark art to sensible and helpful magic marks a transgressive acceptance of the female Other and ties his narratives closely to the feminist project of interrogating and reclaiming women's spaces, practices and images. **Witches**, in fact, are some of the most admirable female characters in the Discworld novels. In *WS*, *WA*, *LL*, *Msk* and *CJ*, Granny Weatherwax and the **Lancre** coven invariably fight for what is right (which is not the same as what is nice), sometimes at great personal cost. In *WFM* and *HFOS*, the young witch Tiffany **Aching** can confront great foes partly because of her relationship to her native land, but also because of her connection to her dead grandmother, a witch who always stood for those who could not speak for themselves.

In *ER*, witchcraft plays a crucial role in Esk's development. Though Esk's magical abilities come from her wizard's staff – a symbol of inherited male power – and she internalises its power when she is accepted into Unseen University, her apprenticeship with Granny Weatherwax gives her the advantage of being able to straddle between the practical world of witchcraft and the abstract world of wizardry. Thus, Esk does not become a mere female wizard, a woman in borrowed (men's) robes, but a hybrid being. Most importantly, her 'woman-manly' mind – as Woolf would term Esk's androgynous status by the end of *ER* – allows her to rescue the young wizard Simon from the creatures of the **Dungeon Dimensions** and save the day. As the book closes, Esk and Simon fuse their magical talents to create a new kind of magic beyond anything previously experienced in the Discworld.

The title of *MR* is a take on John Knox's 1558 invective against women in positions of authority, entitled *The First Blast of the Trumpet against The Monstrous Regiment of Women*. It also suggests outrage at the notion of (cross-dressing) female soldiers. Citing Aristotle (384–332 BCE), Tertullian (*c.*155–230), St Paul (*c.* 3–62 CE), St Augustine (354–430) and St. Jerome (*c.* 347–420) among others, *The First Blast of the Trumpet* argues that Biblical scripture as well as history reveals the pre-eminence of man over woman so 'that it is more than a monster in nature that a woman shall reign and have empire above man' and that woman's rule can only bring 'the subversion of good order, of all equity and justice'. *MR* counters these misogynistic arguments by depicting everyday women who, empowered by their military uniforms, become national heroes and bring peace and stability to their homeland.

MR undermines the notions of feminine weakness and inferiority in the duchy of Borogravia by having a regiment of untrained cross-dressing female conscripts take back the nation's command fortress, liberate its army and create the conditions for a much-needed truce. Their leader, legendary and indomitable career military Sergeant Jackrum – also a woman in disguise – has been practising a personal version of 'Don't ask; don't tell' that has resulted in numerous cross-dressing female commanding officers in the Borogravian army. As a consequence of playing the role of men successfully, the women of the regiment feel empowered to go beyond the domestic and subservient roles Borogravian culture reserves for them.

In Pratchett's work, cross-dressing liberates female characters from the constrictions of their respective cultures and ultimately sows the seeds of social change (*see* **Sexism**). In *MR*, Polly Perks's transformation at first seems as harmless and temporary as that of Viola in William Shakespeare's *Twelfth Night*, and her quest to find her brother as properly feminine as that of the romantic heroine of the folk song 'Sweet Polly Oliver'. But the soldier's uniform begins to alter what Polly says and does, particularly after she stuffs her trousers with a pair of socks to mimic a penis at Jackrum's suggestion. Polly's use of the socks to look more physically like a man also has a profound psychological aspect – she begins to feel more empowered – which highlights the performative nature of masculinity: one does not need a real penis to 'be a man'; rather, one needs only a phallus to feel like a man and be treated as such (even a pair of socks will do). Thus, playing the part of a man allows Polly to explore a new side of her personality – Ozzer the soldier – she could not have expressed properly as a woman. Outspoken, courageous, resourceful and a natural leader, Polly as Ozzer invalidates the Borogravian notion that women are weak and need to be under masculine supervision.

The irrationality of misogyny is exposed most directly in the book's instances of double cross-dressing – a girl dressed as a boy dressed as a girl. For instance, the Borogravian soldiers do not mind being rescued as long as they perceive their rescuers to be *men* dressed as washerwomen, but when the rescuers turn out to be actual women, they are thrown in prison and put on trial as Abominations. In all, as long as the women pretend to be men, or as long as they say they were merely aiding a man, or as long as they can be turned into a joke or kept in their place as mascots, the status quo of Borogravia is safe. For admitting that women and men are the same means that feminine qualities are as valuable as masculine ones, and the patriarchal Borogravia would have to change its social structure.

Feminism

In pointed contrast to the normalising ending of *Twelfth Night*, the women's charade does begin social change in Borogravia. By enabling the spirit of the Duchess to speak against the folly of war and command an immediate *coup d'état* against Borogravia's mad god Nuggan, the 'monstrous regiment' again rescues Borogravians from captivity – this time from their own smothering cultural codes. As a New Woman, Polly will continue the struggle to be accepted on her own terms, not as just a soldier, but as a *female* soldier. Most significantly, she will not continue the fight for women's rights alone. Shaped by the lessons of Sergeant Jackrum and supported by her army buddy Maladicta, Polly will be in charge of fashioning future generations of female soldiers, who, thanks to the 'monstrous regiment', now have the chance of serving openly as women.

In the Johnny Maxwell Trilogy, aimed at children, the character of **Kirsty** exemplifies the tenets of the Girl Power movement: since she has not been told there are things she cannot do because she is a girl, she has lived to her full potential, even outdoing boys at what traditionally have been considered boys' activities: shooting rifles, playing videogames and doing karate. As a successful product of Second Wave feminism, Kirsty's hero and role model is the formidable Lt Ripley from the *Alien* film series, and so her chosen nickname is Sigourney (after Sigourney Weaver, the actor that portrays Lt Ripley). Kirsty is also one of Pratchett's many female organisers (*see* **Sexism**).

Pratchett has developed several other female characters that rebel against their inherited abilities, cultural traditions or destiny to create a new identity for themselves: **Grimma**, Peaches the rat, Malicia and the Scree Wee Captain in the children's books; and Ysabell **Sto Helit**, Conina, **Ptraci**, Susan **Sto Helit**, Cheery **Littlebottom**, Angua von **Überwald** and Salacia von Humpeding in the Discworld novels, to name a few. *See also* Magic; Politics; Power; Sexism *and* Witches.

Further Reading

Knox, John. 1967. *The First Blast of the Trumpet against the Monstrous Regiment of Women*. Edited by Edward Arber. New York, AMS Press.
Shakespeare, William. 2003. *Twelfth Night*. Edited by Elizabeth Story Donno. Introduction by Penny Gay. Cambridge: Cambridge University Press.
'Sweet Polly Oliver'. *Wikipedia*. http://en.wikipedia.org/wiki/Sweet_Polly_Oliver
Woolf, Virginia. 1929. *A Room of One's Own*. New York: Hartcourt Brace Jovanovich.

Ximena Gallardo C.

The Fifth Elephant (1999)

The twenty-fourth **Discworld** novel, featuring the **City Watch** and largely set in **Überwald**. The first UK Doubleday edition was 145,198, with a Josh **Kirby** cover and the Corgi edition appeared in 2000. It has been translated into Bulgarian, Czech, Dutch, French, German, Polish, Russian and

Spanish. The Discworld rests on the back of four **elephants**, but legend has it that a fifth crashed into the disc, creating mountains and valleys. Now 'fifth elephant' is another name for *eminence grise*, someone who manipulates events behind the scenes. This could be Patrician **Vetinari**, or the assassin Inigo Skimmer. The title also echoes the **Hollywood film** *The Fifth Element* (1997) directed by Luc Besson (b.1959). Roland Green wrote in *Booklist*: 'Pratchett is now inviting comparison with Kurt Vonnegut, but if he ends up with a reputation equivalent only to that of P.G. **Wodehouse**, the world will be the better for his having written'.

Cover of *The Fifth Elephant*. Artwork by Josh Kirby.

The **dwarfs** are about to crown a new Low King, Rhys Rhysson, from a village near **Llamedos**, and this is a controversial choice. The Patrician decides to send Samuel **Vimes**, Lady Sybil **Ramkin**, **Detritus** the **troll** and Cheery **Littlebottom**, along with Skimmer to observe. Before they leave, two crimes occur; someone attempts to steal the replica Scone of Stone – the real version of which figures in the coronation – and someone has killed Wallace Sonky, a manufacturer of rubber goods. Angua von **Überwald** disappears, and Carrot **Ironfoundersson** goes on her trail with Gaspode the Wonder **Dog**. The Patrician appoints **Colon** as acting captain, but within days the City Watch is decimated and striking. Vimes gets caught up in the politics of Überwald – the possible disintegration of dwarf society after the theft of the real Scone and problems with their rivals, the werewolves. Vimes is arrested after foiling an assassination attempt on the king and is allowed to escape from prison only to be chased by werewolves. He is rescued by Angua and Carrot. After the coronation, Vimes returns to **Ankh-Morpork** with one of the **Igors**.

Once more, Vimes is the ordinary guy caught up in **politics**, determined not to be impressed by the aristocracy. The Patrician continues to use him precisely because he will not be diplomatic – it pleases him to shake things up. To vampires are added the horror staple of werewolves in more detail, as well as a deeper study of dwarf society. The City Watch union offers a parody of shop floor politics. *See also* City Watch; Überwald; Patrician Vetinari *and* Samuel Vimes.

Andrew M. Butler

'Final Reward' (*OM*WF*)

This story was written for *G.M.: The Independent Fantasy Roleplaying Magazine* (*see also* **Games**) and published in October 1988. Pratchett has rewritten it a number of times since first publication, and it also appeared in Peter Haining, ed. *Space Movies: II*. London: Severn House, 1996. Pp. 230–245. Pratchett has considered expanding it to novel length.

Dogger is a **Fantasy** writer, creator of the barbarian hero Erdan, and has just fallen out with his girlfriend, Nicky. In a fit of alcohol-fuelled pique, Dogger decides to kill off his hero in his latest book, *Erdan and the Serpent of the Rim*. But Erdan is made of stronger stuff and appears at his doorway. As Erdan adjusts to the real world, Dogger realises that he really cannot write any more about him, and that the barbarian is likely to steal his girlfriend. Dogger disappears into his own fantasy world, to be written by Erdan.

A number of writers have reported being trapped by their own characters – Sir Arthur Conan Doyle (1859–1939) killed off Sherlock Holmes in 1893, and *Misery* (1987) by Stephen King (b.1947) features the author Paul Sheldon who has just killed off a character in his novels. After a car accident, he is nursed by Annie Wilkes, who is a fan of his work and is distinctly unhappy that the character is dead. She forces him to write a novel resurrecting her. Pratchett has yet to kill off a recurring character – discounting Ysabell **Sto Helit** – apparently preferring to retire them. *See also* Fantasy; Heroes *and* Narrative.

Andrew M. Butler

Flitworth, Miss Renata (*RM*)

A widowed farmer in a village in the Ramtops near Sheepridge where **Death** looks to get a job. Her husband seems to have been killed in an avalanche some years before, and since then she has lived alone. She is happy to employ Death – under his nom de plume of Bill Doors – and pay him six shillings a week, but she feels that it is only proper that he stays in the barn and she in the house. As the weeks progress, she allows him closer to her, and it almost looks as if a romance is developing between the two, and when New Death comes to collect his soul, she gives him some of her life so that he might survive to defeat it. In return, Death reunites her with her husband at the time of his death.

The character resembles the steady, tough but lonely widows who appear in numerous **Hollywood films**, particularly westerns and melodramas – and especially in the 1940s and 1950s – whose husband has been killed, leaving them to cope with the business in a tough, male world. Often, they are aided by a nomadic and alienated single male with whom they form an uneasy bond. *See also* Death.

Andrew M. Butler

Food

The world of Pratchett's **Discworld** is one of unique tastes and flavours that can never be experienced elsewhere. The food which features in the novels works as a kind of verisimilitude, convincing the reader of the reality of the fictional world. It also offers a chance for **parody** of other **Fantasy** writers, notably J.R.R. **Tolkien**.

There is relatively little food in Pratchett's **children's fiction** – traditionally a space where eating almost seems to replace sexuality with sensuality. Johnny **Maxwell** and his friends do eat a fair amount of junk food such as burgers – Wobbler becomes head of a burger chain having been left behind in the 1940s – and fish and chips – Johnny gives his to Mrs **Tachyon** in lieu of grapes.

On the Discworld, one of the premiere purveyors of fast foods is C.M.O.T. **Dibbler**. Wherever there is a crowd, Dibbler will attempt to sell them overpriced food. He specialises who specialises in things on sticks and pies – whose contents are as much a mystery as the original species of meat in some Indian takeaway curries. The best curries come from **Klatch**; the versions available in **Ankh-Morpork** are rather different. **Death** is known to be partial to a good curry (*M*).

For those who prefer something less spicy, there is antipasta, which is presumably made with re-annual wheat, wheat planted after it is harvested. Antipasta needs to be cooked some time after the meal and travels back into the past. The effects on the unwary can be somewhat catastrophic (*RM*). The best ribs are from Harga's House of Ribs, where Death briefly works as a short-order cook, and which is the greasy spoon of choice of Samuel **Vimes**. Sham Harga's cleaning out of some of the pans and changing of the fat in the deep fryers has not improved the flavour for the better though (*MAA*). Burnt Brown Crunchy Bits are their speciality.

There are various goods that may be snacked upon. The Figgin is a small short crust pastry with raisins often eaten with coffee (*GG*), but it also appears to be a euphemism as Patrician **Vetinari's** predecessor, Lord Snapcase, was strung up by his figgin (*IT*). (A figgin is also the name given by David **Langford** and others to a running joke within a Pratchett novel, a reference that is repeated three or more times.) Banged Grains were invented by the Guild of Alchemists and were eaten during the moving pictures despite only tasting of whatever coated the popped corn grains (*MP*).

The area around **Sto Lat**, the Sto Plains, are famed for their cabbage plantations, although no one seems to ever eat them (but see *DA*). The best cheese comes from **Lancre** and Quirm, and Tiffany **Aching's** skills involve cheese making. Ankh-Morpork is famous for Clooty Dumplings, Distressed Pudding, Fikkun Haddock, Jammy Devils, Knuckle Sandwich (made from pig's knuckles), rat and cream cheese (rat is a staple of many diets, whether by design or poor hygiene, and may often be sold on a stick, or possibly in curries) and Slumpie (*MAA*).

Dwarfs do eat rat, rather than any other meat. Dwarf bread is both a staple and a delicacy (not to mention a potential weapon) which lasts indefinitely, if only because no one can eat it. In Ankh-Morpork, some of the older and more significant examples are to be found in the Dwarf Bread Museum on Whirligig Lane (*MAA*, *FOC*, *FE*). This bread is a **parody** of the various waybreads eaten by characters in Tolkien's *The Lord of the Rings* (1954–1955). There are also dwarf cakes and scones – the Low King is traditionally crowned upon the Scone of Stone (*FE*).

Many Discworld recipes have been collected in *NOC*, a volume that was a sequel to her bestselling *The Joye of Snackes*, which was full of recipes which were aphrodisiacs or improved sexual performance. *See also* Drink *and Nanny Ogg's Cookbook.*

Further Reading

Katz, Wendy R. 'Some Uses of Food in Children's Literature'. *Children's Literature in Education* 11.4 (Winter 1980): 192–199.

Andrew M. Butler

The Fool, Later King Verence II (*WS*, *LL*, *CJ*)

In *WS*, the Fool initially slept in the stables in the reign of **Verence I**, but was brought into the palace by the increasingly paranoid Felmet. He is the one sent to fetch the travelling thespians, and at the end of the novel succeeds the throne as Verence II, with Magrat **Garlick** eventually becoming his queen. It seems that he is the illegitimate half-brother of Tomjon, although it is not entirely certain whether this is through Verence I's philandering or his mother's.

The Fool is a traditional court figure, in Britain up to Charles II in 1688, although they are recorded later than that as well. Usually clad in multicoloured clothes and wearing a floppy hat with bells, they speak apparent nonsense and were given licence largely to talk freely by their royal employers. In literature, the Fool is often given wise words to say and is a staple of such plays by William **Shakespeare** as *Antony and Cleopatra* and *King Lear*. Foolish characters who never the less have streaks of good fortune are frequent through comic narratives. *See also* Narrative *and* Power.

Andrew M. Butler

Foureks see XXXX

'FTB' (*OM*WT*)

A short story written for one of the newspapers that Pratchett used to write for – *Western Daily Press* (24 December 1996), p. 31 – also published as 'The Megabyte Drive to Believe in Santa Claus'. It later appeared in the programme book for the 1998 **Discworld Convention**. In revised form, it became part of *H*, which Pratchett was writing at the time. 'FTB' is an abbreviation for 'Fluffy Teddy Bear'.

Father Christmas arrives at an office from which he has received fifty thousand copies of a Christmas letter, which lists what Tom wants, complete with product numbers and their prices. Tom is a computer – Trade and Office Machines – who believes in Father Christmas, unlike far too many children. Having shown Tom some toys, Father Christmas leaves him a teddy bear. Every time someone tries to remove it, it closes down.

This is a rather sweet short story, which develops the importance and power of belief which is central to *H*, and the existence of the various personifications, such as the Tooth Fairy. Belief powers the world. *See also* '20p With Envelope and Seasonal Greeting'; The Hogfather (Character) *and* Technology.

Andrew M. Butler

G

Gaiman, Neil (b. 1960)

The first book promotion interview that Terry Pratchett ever did was in February 1985, following the publication of *COM*, with a young English journalist. The resulting interview was published in the magazine *Space Voyager*, but more importantly a lifelong friendship had been forged. As Pratchett recalls in the additional material to the twentieth anniversary edition of *GO*, they shared a sense of the oddness of the universe and kept in touch ever since. That young journalist was Neil Gaiman, and the result of their friendship would be the novel *GO*, which was initially started as a way of using the modems which both had recently acquired.

Neil Gaiman at the Frankfurt Book Fair.

Neil Richard Gaiman, now one of the world's most prominent fantasy writers, was born on November 10, 1960, in Hampshire England but as of 2005 is resident in Minneapolis, Minnesota, USA.

After leaving school, Gaiman worked as a journalist conducting interviews and book reviews which he credits (in an email to this author) with giving him the chance to see 'bits of the world I hadn't known existed, and talk to people I would otherwise never have encountered'. His first book was a biography of pop band Duran Duran (1984), and he wrote articles for a variety of British magazines, through which he met people like Terry Pratchett and Alan Moore (b.1953). Gaiman wrote a semi-biographical book on Douglas **Adams** and the development of *The Hitch Hiker's Guide to the Galaxy* (1978) entitled *Don't Panic* (1988). This was followed by his collaboration with Pratchett on *GO*.

Gaiman became associated with a group of British-based writers, critics and editors known as the Midnight Rose collective, including Mary Gentle (b.1956), Roz Kaveney (b.1949) and Alex Stewart (b.1958). As well as Kaveney's *Tales from the Forbidden Planet* (1987) and *More Tales from the Forbidden Planet* (in which Gaiman's 'Webs' and Pratchett's '**Hollywood Chickens'** appeared), Gaiman co-edited *Temps Volume 1* (1991) with Stewart and contributed to the creation of *The Weerde: Book 1* (1992) edited by Gentle and Kaveney. *ER* is dedicated to Gaiman, and Gaiman is one of a number of dedicatees of *GG*.

A friendship with comics writer Alan Moore led to Gaiman writing the *Miracle Man* series between 1991 and 1992 after Moore's departure. This brought him to the attention of DC Comics, for whom he created *The Sandman* comic series (1987–1996). This became the flagship title for DC Comics' 'mature readers' imprint Vertigo, ran for eight years and over seventy-five issues. It has also been collected into a series of eleven graphic novels and is widely regarded as one of the most original, sophisticated and artistically ambitious comic book series of the modern age. *The Sandman* chronicles the tales of Morpheus, the anthropomorphic personification of Dream and covered a variety of genres from horror to fantasy, while interweaving many strands of both classical and contemporary mythology. *The Sandman* received many awards, including the World Fantasy Award for Short Fiction for the issue entitled 'A Midsummer Night's Dream' (1991). Gaiman has won a total of fourteen Eisner awards for his comics work. Gaiman returned to comics to produce the critically acclaimed *1602* series (2003–2004) for Marvel and worked on a new version of Jack Kirby's (1917–1994) *Eternals* (2006–2007), also for Marvel comics.

Gaiman co-devised (with British stand-up comedian and actor Lenny Henry (b.1958)) and wrote the dark fantasy TV series *Neverwhere* (1996) for the BBC which he later adapted into a novel (1997) and which was also adapted into comic book format (2005–2006). Gaiman's other notable TV work includes scripting the episode 'Day of the Dead' (1998) for *Babylon 5* (1993–1998). He also wrote the screenplay for the movie *MirrorMask* (2005) as well as cowriting the motion capture movie of *Beowulf*. Several of Gaiman's works have been optioned for movies and are in production including *Death: The High Cost of Living* (collected 1994), *Stardust* (1998) and *Coraline* (2002).

Although he had previously published three other novels, *GO* (with Terry Pratchett), *Stardust* (with Charles Vess), and *Neverwhere* (an adaptation of his TV series) with the publication of *American Gods* (2001), Gaiman became firmly established as a novelist in his own right. This may have been aided by the establishment of a blog in which he documented the later stages of revision on the novel, as well as the marketing of the volume. He has continued to blog on an almost daily basis. *American Gods* is a mix of Americana, fantasy and various shades of ancient and modern mythology and won the Hugo, Nebula and Bram Stoker **Awards** for Best Novel. In 2005, Gaiman published a tangential sequel, *Anansi Boys*, although with a more comedic undertone, in that it primarily deals with the relationship between the two sons of the god Anansi who was a supporting character in *American Gods*. Gaiman has also produced three children's books, *The Day I Swapped My Dad for Two Goldfish* (1997), *Coraline* and *The Wolves in the Wall* (2003). *Coraline* won a Hugo award for Best Novella.

According to a profile published by *The Guardian* newspaper in the UK, Gaiman 'tends to be praised more for his imagination, which is rich, dark and very twisted, than the quality of his writing, which veers towards efficient rather than poetic'. Gaiman readily admits that he does not consider himself a novelist, preferring to call himself a storyteller. *See also* Douglas Adams; Comics; Death; Fantasy; Graphic Novels *and* Science Fiction.

Further Reading

Gaiman, Neil. 1988. *Don't Panic: The Official Hitch-Hikers Guide to the Galaxy Companion*. London: Titan Books.

———. 1990a. *The Sandman*. London: Titan.

———. 1990b. 'Webs'. Pp. 136–144 in *More Tales from the Forbidden Planet*. Edited by Roz Kaveney. London: Titan Books.

———. 1994. *Death: The High Cost of Living*. London: Titan Books.

———. 1997. *Neverwhere*. London: Penguin.

———. 1998. *Stardust: Being a Romance Within the Realms of Faerie*. London: Titan.

———. 2001. *American Gods*. London: Gollancz.

———. 2002. *Coraline*. London: Bloomsbury.

———. 2005. *Anansi Boys*. London: Bloomsbury.

———. Email to AJP June 2006.

———, and Alex Stewart, eds. 1991. *Temps: Volume One*. London: ROC.

Gentle, Mary, and Roz Kaveney, eds. 1992. *The Weerde: Book One*. London: ROC.

The Guardian/Author Profiles, http://books.guardian.co.uk/authors/author/0,,-187,00.html

Pratchett, Terry. 2004. 'Neil Gaiman: Amazing Master Conjurer'. Pp. 171–174 in *Once More * With Footnotes*. Framingham, MA: The NESFA Press.

———. 2006. 'Terry on Neil' additional material *Good Omens Anniversary Edition*. New York: William Morrow.

Neil Gaiman Official Website and Online Journal, http://www.neilgaiman.com/

Alan J. Porter

Games

There are both games played in the **Discworld** (and other novels by Pratchett) and Discworld games.

There are a number of card games played or mentioned through the series. The Four Horsemen have been known to play cards in **Death's**

Domain (*LF*), and the gods are also keen card players, with higher stakes to play with than people (*COM*, *SG*, *IT*, *LH*). Several of the gods, especially fate, have been known to cheat. The **Witches** seem to be particular fans of card games, such as Chase My Neighbour Up the Passage – which echoes Beggar My Neighbour – (*WA*) and Cripple Mr Onion – a version of poker and blackjack (*WS*, *WA*, with an **Agatean** version Shibo Yangcon-san (*IT*)). A real version of this game was devised in 1993 by Andrew Millard and Terence Tao, which is played with a deck with eight suits, a French set (clubs, diamonds, hearts and spades) and a Latin one (cups, coins, staves and swords), which then represent the Minor Arcana of the Discworld caroc (cups, coins, staves, swords, octagrams, crowns, terrapins and elephants). Aces are worth one or eleven, number cards are worth their numeric value, picture cards are ten and tricks can be won through various pair totals and flushes. A Great Onion (five aces and five picture cards) can be beaten (crippled) by a nine card flush; there are other modifications. There is also a game, Aqueduct, likely to be a variant on Bridge (*LF*).

Board games also exist on the Discworld, Exclusive Possessions (*RM*), which is obviously a variation on Monopoly, complete with streets and utilities (although presumably not stations), and Significant Quest (*S*) a variation of Trivial Pursuit, much beloved by the gods. The Assassins' Guild play Stealth Chess, a version of chess with additional red and white squares into which the assassin pieces can move. (The game of chess, incidentally, is rarely played by the gods, and Death seems to seek alternatives.) The Assassins' Guild also play the Wall Game, a three-a-side game for two teams, a complicated wall and a small board. Injuries are frequent.

Thud! the discworld board game. Box artwork by Paul Kidby, similar to that on the novel *Thud!*.

Games

There are two volumes of Discworld material written by Pratchett and Phil Masters for role-playing within the GURPS (Generic Universal Rôle-Playing System) system developed by Steve Jackson Games in 1986: *GURPS Discworld* (1998), which came with a cut-down version of the GURPS rules, and the book contains a lot of information about Discworld overseen if not fully authorised by Pratchett (the subsequent novels may contradict some details). It was re-released as *The Discworld Rôle-Playing Game*. A sequel was *Discworld Also* (2000), with later details from the novels.

The Discworld board game, *Thud*, is a version of the Battle of Koom Valley (*T!*, see **War**) and was developed by Trevor Truran (b.1942). The game is played on an octagonal board, with the two sides being **trolls** and **dwarfs**. It was developed after Truran met Bernard **Pearson**, and early versions were played at Wadfest (*see* **Conventions**) before it was released in 2000. A cut-down version of the game was released in 2005, using the same board and pieces, but with publicly available rules. This version draws on events in *T!* The history of the fictional game is recounted in '**Thud – A Historical Perspective**'. *See also* Computer Games; Conventions; Merchandising *and* Bernard Pearson.

Further Reading

Rules for Cripple Mr Onion: http://cripplemronion.info/
Thud homepage: http://www.thudgame.com/

Andrew M. Butler

Garlick, Magrat (*WS*, *WA*, *LL*, *CJ*)

Magrat Garlick, the youngest original member of Granny **Weatherwax's** coven, is introduced in *WS* as the maiden and the lowest ranking one of the three **Witches**. She is described as a thin young woman with unruly hair. When we first meet her, she is a kind-hearted but clumsy and insecure, more of a healer and a herb woman than a **Fairy Tale** witch with supernatural powers. Pratchett's 'maiden witches', Magrat included, are often shown as practitioners of a parody of modern (commercialised) occultism (see Annagramma Hawkin in the Tiffany **Aching** books, for example). Surface and glamour instead of 'real' witchcraft, which in Pratchett's world appears to be in large part simply life experience. However, Pratchett treats Magrat far more gently than Diamanda Tockley and the coven that Agnes **Nitt** joins in *LL*. Although Magrat in her younger years puts a bit too much trust in crystals, black candles and other romanticised magical paraphernalia, her knowledge of herbs and her interest in researching things eventually make her a better healer than even Granny.

An important part of the **Lancre** witch books is Magrat's journey from the shy young girl to a grown woman and a witch in control of her own life. It begins in *WS* where Magrat, the junior member of the coven and still mainly in charge of making the tea, meets **Verence** the **Fool** who is eventually put to the throne by the witches, and falls in love with him. Their courtship is slowed down by the fact that they are both too shy to make a move until Verence, under Granny's instructions, arranges their marriage while Magrat is away. In an act of defiance against the meddling older witches, Magrat then discards her occult jewellery and other magical accessories in *LL* and chooses the court life over witchcraft.

Life as the future Queen of Lancre is not what Magrat imagined, however, and she is sorely disappointed to find out that her pastimes are limited to tapestry and interior decorating. Magrat is roused from her passivity when the Queen of **Elves** threatens to steal her husband-to-be in order to take over the kingdom and to become the queen herself. When the elves take over the castle, Magrat puts on the armour of the ancient warrior queen Ynci the Short-Tempered and challenges the Elf Queen while believing to be under the possession of the warrior's spirit. Ynci's name, when spelled backwards, resembles the name of the Iceni tribe, suggesting that Magrat believes to be under the influence of the Discworld equivalent of the Roundworld warrior queen Boadicea (d. 60 CE). What Magrat does not know, however, is that Queen Ynci never actually existed, and both she and the armour are simply creations of a king with too much imagination and an interest to make Lancre's history more interesting than it was. The spirit that possesses Magrat is then only she herself.

In marrying the King, Magrat takes on the role of mother, first symbolically as the queen and mother of the kingdom, and some time later a mother of a small daughter (named Esmeralda Note Spelling of Lancre due to an unfortunate misunderstanding at the christening), and leaves behind the role of the maiden. Still, even as a queen and a mother, in the eyes of the other witches she has nevertheless 'settled for the second prize' by choosing a husband over a career in witchcraft. Magrat as a mother comes across as a parody of a modern working mother. She is over-enthusiastic about her daughter's development, already hoarding educational toys when the child is only a few days old, her earlier interest in magic paraphernalia now manifesting in her interest in baby equipment, and after the Magpyr family has taken over the castle, she simply grabs the baby (and the entire contents of the nursery) and returns to her 'job' as a witch.

Magrat's motherhood also disrupts the delicate balance of roles in the coven. Agnes takes Magrat's place as the maiden, and nanny reluctantly assumes the role of the crone, prompting Granny, now without a place, to leave the group. In the end of *CJ*, however, the witches discard the maiden-mother-crone trinity and even though Magrat is a mother now, she in many ways still remains a maiden the same way that Nanny, even as a crone, does not stop being a mother. *See also* Tiffany Aching; Coming of Age; Fairy Tales; the Fool; Lancre; Magic; Nanny Ogg; Granny Weatherwax *and* Witches.

Further Reading
Sayer, Karen. 'The Witches'. *GOL*, *GOL2*.

Mirka Sillanpaa

Genua

The city of Genua is situated at the mouth of the 'Vieux (Old [Masculine]) River'. It is an old, wealthy, city, which taxed the traffic in and out of the estuary and developed a particularly rich cuisine out of the teeming wildlife of its swamps. During the days of the **Ankh-Morpork** Empire, Genua's royalty became so inbred that the courtiers asked Ankh-Morpork for help, and received the famous general Tacticus as Duke. The Duke's first action was to identify and take action against the greatest military threat to Genua (Ankh-Morpork). In *WA*, Genua is depicted as a **parody** of New Orleans, a region whose local witchcraft is described in terms very similar to voodoo: the witch Mrs Gogol has the same first name (Erzulie) as a voodoo goddess, a cockerel, Legba, as her familiar and a zombie consort, Saturday. However, Genua has become a **Fairy Tale** city under the rule of Lily **Weatherwax**, who insists upon all its inhabitants behaving according to their narrative conventions. In stories, all toymakers, for instance, whistle and sing all day long, and Lily's 'People's Guards' make sure that they do.

$1 Genua Stamp created by Discworld Merchandising.

Genua is partly generic 'foreign parts'. It is on the other side of the continent from Ankh-Morpork and to get there the three **witches** have to travel a long way and overcome a number of prejudices about other cultures. Nanny **Ogg**, in particular, is the stereotypical Englishwoman Abroad, firm in the belief that foreigners understand everything so say as long as you shout pidgin-English loudly enough, and taking enthusiastically to exotic drinks. There are, in fact, two cities in Genua, which looks like a white crystal set in the green-brown of the swamp. One is the white-painted city with a multiturreted fairy-tale castle at its centre. This is the city of the imposed fairy-tale world of Lily Weatherwax with its classically European story references such as 'Cinderella'. The other is the old city, the 'city of cooks' (the future can be told by examining gumbo or jambalaya, rather than the more traditional tealeaves), a melting pot and cauldron of cultures, easy-going but, like the swamp inhabited by alligators, not to be underestimated. Uniting (or at least connecting) the two is the carnival/ball, where for once Magrat **Garlick** can be as glamorous as she wants to be and even Granny Weatherwax can dress up in style.

Genua was also the planned destination of the clacks vs. mail competition in *GP* (*see* **Technology**). *See also* Fairy Tales; Magic; Narrative; Granny Weatherwax *and* Lily Weatherwax.

Andy Sawyer

The Globe see Science of Discworld

Going Postal (2004)

The thirty-third **Discworld** novel, published by Doubleday in the UK in 2004 with design work by Bernard **Pearson** on the endpapers. The paperback came out from Corgi in 2005. It has been translated into Bulgarian, Czech, Dutch and German. *GP* is a stand-alone novel, although Moist von **Lipwig** will reappear in *Making Money*. There are cameos from William de **Worde**, Otto **Chriek** and Samuel **Vimes**, and Patrician **Vimes** is definitely pulling the strings. 'Going postal' is the phenomenon of individuals suddenly going mad and shooting lots of people in a public place – in the mid-1980s, a number of such incidents involved US postal workers. The British cover, by Paul **Kidby**, is a **parody** of the *Star Wars* (1977) poster. Unusually for an adult novel by Pratchett, it is divided into chapters, with chapter titles and descriptions of forthcoming events. Waterstone's gave away Discworld First Day Covers and stamps with the first edition. Roz Kaveney suggests: 'it is a book about redemption in which a man who inflicts a fair amount of casual cruelty as a con artist is forced into a new life and becomes the better for it – there's a moral toughness here, which is one of the reasons why Pratchett is never merely frivolous' *Time Out London* (13–20 October 2004).

Bonk One Bizlot Stamp created by Discworld Merchandising.

Ankh-Morpork Halfpenny Stamp created by Discworld Merchandising.

It appears that Moist von Lipwig has been executed for fraud, but this itself is a con, ordered by Patrician Vetinari. Vetinari offers him a choice: take over the running of the **Ankh-Morpork** Post Office, now more or less derelict, or die for real. He chooses the former, and is assigned a golem, Mr Pump, as a parole officer. The post office is a dangerous place – the previous five postmasters had died in the previous few months, and Lipwig sets about reviving its fortune; he invents postage stamps, which become a new craze. He draws the attention of the corrupt Grand Trunk Semaphore Company who are running the clacks system into the ground. Reacher Gilt, their chairman, orders an arson attack on the post office, leading to Lipwig swearing revenge – he also wants to atone to Adora Belle

Dearheart, whose father had invented the clacks and who lost her job due to his earlier frauds. He bets that he can get a message by post to **Genua** faster than by clacks, but in the meantime discovers the corruption in the Grand Trunk Company. He is given control of the clacks by Vetinari, but wants it to be returned to the Dearhearts.

The post office is a source of parody, but more importantly stamp collecting (the officer Stanley Howler named for Stanley Gibbons, a stamp dealer), hacking culture, corrupt business practices and conspiracies. *See also* Ankh-Morpork; Moist von Lipwig; Technology *and* Patrician Vetinari.

Andrew M. Butler

Goodmountain, Mr Gunilla (*TT*)

A **dwarf** who set up a printing press at the sign of the Bucket, Gleam Street, **Ankh-Morpork** – the tavern of choice for the **City Watch**. This prints William de **Worde's** *Ankh-Morpork Times*, although the hostile reaction to this in some quarters led to the destruction of the presses. Goodmountain's name is an Anglicisation of Johannes Gutenberg (1398–1468), the inventor of the moveable type printing press in Europe. He is referred to as 'Mr Goodmountain', but, as with all matters of dwarf sex, no one has inquired too closely as to the accuracy of the honorific. Goodmountain married the second in command in the print room, Boddony.

Model of the Dwarfs' printing press created by Discworld Merchandising.

Goodmountain, Mr Gunilla

Not to be confused with J.H.C. Goatberger (*Msk, NOC*) who is the publisher of *The Joye of Snacks* and the *Ankh-Morpork Almanak*, and who has grown wealthy on Nanny **Ogg's** book. Goatberger is worried about the innuendo and tries to tone it down in a number of memos sent to the head printer, Thomas Cropper (whose name is suspiciously similar to that of the populariser (1838–1910) of the flush lavatory). His nephew has had similar difficulties with the *DA*. *See also* Technology *and* William de Worde.

Andrew M. Butler

Good Omens (1990)

Co-written with Neil **Gaiman**, apparently as a reason to justify the modems they had both recently purchased. Pratchett drafted about 60,000 words, including the Adam **Young** sequences, and Gaiman drafted 45,000 words, but it was all rewritten by both of them. Subtitled: *The Nice and Accurate Prophecies of Agnes Nutter, Witch.* The first UK Gollancz edition was 17,700 copies, with a cover by Chris Moore (b.1947). The US edition, published by Workman with a cover by David Frampton, had some extra material, mostly explanatory footnotes to explain British culture. This then formed the basis for the British 1991 Corgi paperback, with some further revisions and a cover by Graham Ward. Terry Gilliam (b.1940) has the film rights, but has been unable to raise the money to make it. It has been translated into Bulgarian, Chinese, Croatian, Czech, Dutch, Estonian, Finnish, French, German, Hebrew, Hungarian, Italian, Japanese, Korean, Polish, Portuguese, Romanian, Russian, Serbian, Spanish and Swedish. It comes with a caveat, asking kids not to try Armageddon at home, and a dedication to the memory of English Catholic novelist and essayist G. K. Chesterton (1874–1936), perhaps best known for the *Father Brown* stories, but here the influence is likely *The Man Who Was Thursday: A Nightmare* (1908) in which most of the Central Council of Anarchists turn out to be undercover agents. The title is an allusion to *The Omen* (Richard Donner, 1976), a film about the birth of the Antichrist.

At a hospital near a small village in Oxfordshire, the newborn son of the American ambassador is to be switched with the Antichrist. Unfortunately, the wrong baby is taken, and so he grows up in the village as Adam **Young**. Meanwhile, the angel Aziraphale and the demon **Crowley**, smarting over their roles in the cock-up, are called upon to hasten Armageddon, and neither are sure they want the world to end just yet. The Four Horsemen of the Apocalypse – War, Famine, **Death** and Pollution (Pestilence having retired) – assemble, nuclear reactors go missing and all the events go as predicted by the prophecies of the **witch** Agnes Nutter. Unfortunately, Adam, never an obedient son, does not want to rule the world, and averts the apocalypse.

Cover of UK paperback of *Good Omens* by Terry Pratchett and Neil Gaiman. Artwork by Graham Ward.

The major target of satire is *The Omen*, where Gregory Peck played the American ambassador, but there are also hints of other horror films such as *Witchfinder General* (Michael Reeves, 1968) and *The Exorcist* (William Friedkin, 1973), as well as the prophecies of figures like Mother Shipton (1488–1561) and Nostradamus (1503–1566). At the end of the book, a new volume of prophecies is found, leaving the space open for a sequel. The sequences with Adam and his friends invoke the Famous Five books by Enid Blyton (1897–1968). *See also* Anthony J. Crowley; Neil Gaiman *and* Adam Young.

Andrew M. Butler

Gormenghast (*ER*, *WS*)

Influential fantasy series, novel and location, occasionally name checked by Pratchett.

Chinese-born author and artist Mervyn Peake (1911–1968) was educated in Kent from the age of eleven, before attending the Royal Academy art school. In 1934, he moved to Sark in the Channel Islands for three years with a group of artists, then taught art at the Westminster School of Art in

London, publishing and exhibiting. He was conscripted to the army during the Second World War, but was invalided out in 1943 having had a nervous breakdown. Eventually, he became a war artist, and visited Belsen, the liberated concentration camp, in Germany. He had married Maeve Gilmore (d.1983) in 1937, and the family moved to Sark in 1946, returning to Kent in the early 1950s. Ill health dogged him, and there was a further nervous breakdown, and he began to suffer from Parkinson's disease. He died in 1968.

Mervyn Peake, author of the 'Gormenghast' books, sitting amidst a collection of his oil paintings, 1940s.

The first of the sequence *Titus Groan* (1946) featured the birth and early years of Titus, the seventy-seventh earl of Groan in the gothic and decaying castle of Gormenghast. In parallel, Steerpike, a boy in the kitchen, plots his own rise to power. This was followed by *Gormenghast* (1950), in which Titus comes of age and has to face Steerpike's machinations. Titus succeeds to the dukedom, but leaves the castle. In *Titus Alone* (1959), he travels to a futuristic, industrial landscape. Peake was already ill when writing the book, and the English writer and editor Langdon Jones (b.1942) re-edited the manuscript after Peake's death. At least two further books had been projected but not written in what is wrongly viewed as a trilogy. The first two books were adapted for television as *Gormenghast* (2000) by Malcolm McKay for a four-part BBC serial, with Jonathan Rhys Meyers (b.1977) as Steerpike. The cast included Celia Imrie (b.1952) as Lady Gertrude, Christopher Lee (b.1922) as Flay, Ian Richardson (1934–2007) as Lord Groan and Zoë Wanamaker (b.1949) as Clarice Groan; Imrie had read some of the ISIS **Audio Books**, Lee was **Death** in ***Soul Music From Terry Pratchett's Discworld* (1997)** and ***Wyrd Sisters From Terry Pratchett's Discworld* (1997)**, Richardson was in *Hogfather* **(Television Adaptation) and** Wanamaker played Mrs **Tachyon** in *Johnny and the Bomb* **(Television Adaptation)**.

Peake is hailed as a **Fantasy** writer who is the alternative to and superior of J.R.R. **Tolkien**, avoiding what British fantasy writer Michael Moorcock (b.1939) calls 'Epic Pooh' – whimsical talking animals or animated soft toys. He remains an influence upon writers of dark, post-gothic, weird fiction.

There are a number of direct references to Gormenghast within the **Discworld** novels. In *ER*, the vast rooftops of the **Unseen University** and its infestations with birds, frogs and ants are compared to Gormenghast, which is smaller than the building here. On the other hand, in *WS* **Lancre** castle is described as a poor imitation, but it is still fairly gothic. Meanwhile, the Machiavellian rise of Ymper **Trymon** in *LF* seems to echo the rise of Steerpike, and the wizards have more than a hint of the bumbling schoolmasters who tried to teach Titus. Peake's novels have a much darker comedy than Pratchett's. *See also* Fantasy; J.R.R. Tolkien *and* Ymper Trymon.

Further Reading

Gardiner-Scott, Tanya J. 1989. *Mervyn Peake: The Evolution of a Dark Romantic*. New York: Peter Lang.

Moorcock, Michael. 1987. *Wizardry and Wild Romance: A Study of Epic Fantasy*. London: Gollancz.

Peake, Mervyn. 1950. *Gormenghast*. London, Eyre & Spottiswoode.

———. *Titus Alone*. London, Eyre & Spottiswoode, 1959. Revised: New York: Ballantine Books 1968.

———. 1946. *Titus Groan*. London: Eyre & Spottiswoode.

Winnington, G. Peter. 2000. *Vast Alchemies: The Life and Work of Mervyn Peake*. London: Peter Owen.

Andrew M. Butler

Graphic Novels

Alternative name for **Comics**, with the implication of artistic or thematic seriousness. ***Terry Pratchett's The Colour of Magic*** and ***Terry Pratchett's The Light Fantastic*** were published as four individual volumes respectively before being collected in two single volumes. ***Guards! Guards!*** and ***Mort: A Discworld Big Comic*** were both originally published in single volumes. Pratchett is friends with Neil **Gaiman**, one of the leading writers for comics. *See also* Stephen Briggs; Neil Gaiman *and* Graham Higgins.

Andrew M. Butler

Greebo (*WS*, *WA*, *LL*, *Msk*, *CJ*)

Greebo is Nanny **Ogg's** notorious **cat**. He appears in all of the novels in the **Lancre Witches** arc, described by Pratchett as an enormous, nasty, smelly, filthy tomcat with an air of violence. Greebo dominates the Ramtops wildlife by cunning and brute strength, frightening wolves for sport and preying on anything smaller than him. His appearance is given in repellent terms: he has only one eye, his ears have been nearly obliterated in fights, and his fur is more like the inside of a mouldy loaf of bread than the outside of a cat.

Greebo is an example of a minor character whose popularity has resulted in lengthier and more significant use in successive novels; each Lancre Witches novel features some Greebo humour, and in *Msk* he played an important role in the dénouement of the story.

In *WA* and later novels, Greebo sometimes appears as a darkly handsome human man of sinister appearance, possessing catlike grace and an extremely powerful sexual presence. He was first transformed into a man by the witches to help defeat Lily Weatherwax; later, Pratchett uses Greebo's involuntary metamorphoses into human form to comedic effect, playing on his wavering self-assurance as a human being. *See also* Cats *and* Nanny Ogg.

Further Reading

Hanes, Stacie. 'A Pussy in Black Leather: Greebo & the Queer Aesthetic; OR, Someone Had to Do It'. *Vector* 241 (May/June 2005). Pp. 10–13.

Stacie L. Hanes

Greek Mythology

The gods of the **Discworld** are many, and (very) loosely parallel our most influential polytheistic religion: the mythologies of ancient Greece, developed over a roughly five-century period (thirteenth-century BCE to eighth-century BCE) of epic poetry and mythology based around the cultures centred about the Aegean.

'Mythologia' is compounded of the words 'mythos' (meaning 'spoken word' and implies that the narrated events are not normally verifiable, yet have a claim to truth in a more philosophical sense) and 'logos' (which translates as 'word', yet implies a broad philosophical meaning of 'reason' and the ability to grasp and follow that reasoning). The power of mythology for the ancient Greeks should not be underestimated.

The gods of the ancient Greeks were many and varied. Many localities had their own gods in addition to the Olympians. Probably starting with natural gods (gods or personifications of aspects of nature), their pantheon was peopled with demigods, gods and heroes.

Three divisions of mythology are used:

1. Theogonies, or 'birth of gods' myths: explaining creation of the universe, the gods and mankind;
2. Myths of Gods and Men: interactions between gods and men;
3. Heroic Age myths: stories of heroes with limited divine intervention.

(Some researchers regard the Trojan War Cycle as a fourth division.)

Hesiod's *Theogony* (which also explains the almost magical power of the ancient poet) begins with Chaos, a great tumultuous nothingness, from which emerged Gaia (the Earth) – who gave birth to Uranus (the Sky) – and Eros (Love), Tartarus (the Abyss below Hades) and Erebus (Darkness).

Gaia and Uranus produced the Titans, twelve elemental deities (six males and six females), the one-eyed Cyclopes and the Hecatonchires ('hundred-handers'), who Uranus banished to Tartarus, drawing the enmity of Gaia. She persuaded her youngest and 'most terrible' offspring, Cronus (Time – and a name of a character in *TOT*) and his brothers to murder their father. Cronus castrated his father (creating even more deities with the bits and blood) and overthrew him, forcing Uranus to flee. But what goes around, comes around: the offspring of Cronus and his sister-wife Rhea, Zeus and his siblings later challenged the Titans for the kingship of the gods. With the help of the Cyclopes, Zeus and his siblings imprisoned Cronus and the Titans in Tartarus. Other theogonies exist with other versions of these stories.

The Greek gods had corporeal yet ideal bodies unaffected by age or disease, and were born, usually had a childhood, and grew to an immortal adulthood at physical peak. The gods can disguise themselves, become invisible, travel great distances in the blink of an eye or cause humans to behave as they wish. Each has his or her own genealogy, a distinct personality, a different area of expertise (which sometimes changed in different localities) and his or her own agenda. The gods were all part of a huge multigenerational family, with the oldest creating the world and the younger usurping their power.

There are always twelve Olympians, though seventeen gods have been recorded as residing on Mount Olympus, the traditional home of the Greek gods. Six of the gods are siblings (Zeus, Hera, Poseidon, Demeter, Hestia and Hades); all others are usually considered the children of Zeus by different mothers, excepting Athena, who was born of Zeus alone. (Hephaestus is sometimes stated as being born of Hera alone.)

1. Zeus is the ruler of the gods, most powerful, and god of weather and thunder. (Blind Io is his Discworld counterpart.) Zeus would sometimes manifest as a shower of gold, a swan or a bull; Om's attempt at this left him as a tortoise due to lack of belief.
2. Poseidon, along with Hades (who resides in the Underworld), is the next of the most senior of the gods. He rules the sea, rivers, springs, floods and earthquakes.
3. Hera is the sister-wife of Zeus. She is the Queen of the heavens and stars and rules over marriage and fidelity.
4. Demeter holds domain over fertile earth and agriculture.
5. Hestia is goddess of the home and hearth, ruling over families.
6. Artemis is goddess of the hunt, animals, the wilderness and the protectress of young girls.
7. Apollo is god of prophesy, light, music, archery, healing and medicine. (He was often later merged with Helios, god of the sun, whose sisters were the moon, Selene, and the dawn, Eos.)
8. Athena is goddess of wisdom, war, education and crafts.

9. Hephaestus is god of workmanship and weaponry, fire, artisans and craftsmen.
10. Ares is god of war and the slaughter that attends war. War is an anthropomorphic personification, like **Death**, in the Discworld series (*S*, *IT* and *TOT*), and also appears in *GO*.
11. Aphrodite is goddess of love, sex and beauty.
12. Hermes is the god of travellers, commerce, guidance, athletics and oratory. He is the patron of thieves and shepherds. Parts of this are drawn on for Fedecks.

The equivalent of the Olympians are the gods in Dunmanisfestin and include Bibulous, the god of wine (*H*, compare Dionysus in the next paragraph), Blind Io, equivalent to Zeus and Odin from Norse mythology, Destiny, Errata, goddess of misunderstandings, Fate, Fedecks, a version of Hermes, Flatulus, god of the winds, The Lady (*COM*, *LF*, *M* and *LH*), Neoldian, smith to the gods (*LH*), Nuggan, a state god of Borogravia (*MR*), crocodile-headed Offler and the vengeance god Seven-Handed Sek. Many of these gods are depicted in *Discworld Noir* (*see* **Computer Games**) and *LH*.

Discworld fans dressed as Offler the Crocodile God and acolyte.

In Greek mythology, Hades is the Lord of the Underworld and of the dead. He is married to Persephone, queen of the underworld, and, as daughter of Demeter, the goddess of Spring. The story of Persephone is referenced in *E*, as part of Ephebian mythology; it is also a factor in *Wint*. Dionysus is the god of wine, fertility and vegetation, and rules over the theatre. He alternates with Hestia on the ancient lists of the gods of Olympus. Some scholars do not count him as a true god because his mother was mortal. His female worshippers, the Maenads, are mentioned in *H*.

River gods, nymphs of natural features, heroes and heroines, and other localised deities were also venerated, and often the Olympians had local epithets and stories found nowhere else. Some deities or demigods were venerated only at certain festivals during the year, or only in certain locations.

In the age of gods and men, myths featured valuable artifacts (such as fire, knowledge of agriculture, or craft secrets, etc.) being stolen from the gods or being invented, as parodied in *LH* in **Cohen the Barbarian**'s actions. Other popular myths featured the birth of heroes after gods mated with human women or goddesses with human men.

The Heroic Age gave us epic poems describing heroes and events, often linking them by families or other associations. Often, these stories explained a ruling family's curse influencing the fates of nations, or rationalised a ruling house's claim to the throne; Alexander the Great slept with a copy of the Iliad and traced his history back to Achilles.

The best known of the heroes is probably Heracles. Scholars believe that a historical Heracles existed (not unlike Arthur), ruling over the kingdom of Argos. However, Heracles was mythically known as the son of Zeus and Alcmene, granddaughter of Perseus. His labours and adventures made him one of the most popular heroes in not only Greek but also Etruscan and Roman mythologies. The rulers of Mycenae, Sparta, Argos, Lydia and Macedonia all claimed their right to their thrones partly by declaring themselves descendants of Hercules.

Also of note are the adventures of Jason and his Argonauts (most of the famous heroes of the age, including Heracles, were among the Argonauts), set into motion when King Pelias received a prophecy that his nemesis would be a man wearing one sandal. Jason, who lost a sandal in the river on his way to Pelias's court, was sent to bring back the Golden Fleece from the land of Colchis, as impossible quests were apparently popular methods to get rid of inconvenient heroes. The heroic age stories also include the generations chiefly known for their crimes, such as the House of Atreus, and the Theban Cycle.

Of major interest is the Trojan War Cycle, parodied in *E* as the Tsortean Wars. Many epic poems make up this cycle, but the best known are probably the Iliad and the Odyssey, both by Homer. It is almost impossible to give a good short synopsis of the Trojan War Cycle, which culminates in the decade-long conflict between the Greeks and the Trojans. It begins with the personification of Discord, Eris, being snubbed for a wedding invitation. To take revenge for the snub, Eris throws the Golden Apple, engraved 'for the most beautiful one', into the party of Olympians going to the wedding. Paris, the Prince of Troy, is appointed to select between Hera, Athena and Aphrodite as the recipient of the Golden Apple, and dooms his city to destruction by choosing Aphrodite. 'Beautiful-haired' Helen, Queen of Sparta, is 'abducted' for her beauty (the conflict was more likely over trade routes), Iphigenia is sacrificed, Patroclus, Hector, Penthesilia, Memnon and Achilles are killed (along with many others) in various battles, the Trojan Horse is built and, despite the warnings of seers who die for their pains, dragged into Troy, King Priam and his sons are killed and the Trojan women are sent into slavery when the city of Troy is destroyed. It then takes Odysseus, one of the most recurrent characters in Western literature and arts, ten years to return home from the Trojan Wars, having many adventures along the way.

Their mythologies allowed the ancient Greeks – and us today – to examine important things: our relationship to our gods, the meanings of community and the issues of being human: mortality, honour, war, death, how we relate to others. Demonstrating the usefulness of these mythologies, there are modern revivals of Greek polytheism around the globe today. Pratchett's own accounts of the many gods of Discworld go to prove how useful such mythologies remain – and see **Religion** for further details on these gods. See also Ephebe; Greek Philosophy; Narrative; Religion; Tsort and War.

Further Reading

'Greek Mythology'. 2002. *Encyclopaedia Britannica.*
Alexander, Caroline. 'Echoes of the Heroic Age: Ancient Greece Part 1'. *National Geographic* 166.6 (1999): P. 58.
Bulfinch, Thomas. 1971. *Bulfinch's Greek and Roman Mythology.* New York: Collier Books.

Zina Lee

Greek Philosophy (*E*, *P*, *SG*)

The popular idea of the philosopher as an enlightened sage pondering the meaning of life and seeking wisdom is largely derived from the image of the Greek philosophers, and is a subject for **parody** in Pratchett's works. In fact, philosophy – in the sense of 'thinking about life and stuff' – was only a small part of the work of the Greek thinkers, whose work also encompassed mathematics, geometry, physics, cosmology, biology, engineering and political science. Greek philosophy – not really being philosophy – was not wholly Greek either: the 'Greek' world encompassed parts of Italy, Sicily, Asia Minor (modern Turkey) and **Egypt** at one time or another. Nevertheless, the Greeks pretty much set the agenda for Western philosophy that is still followed today, delineating such subjects as epistemology (how do we know things?), logic (what makes an argument valid?), ontology (what things exist?), metaphysics (what things *really* exist?) and ethics (how should we live?).

What marked out the Greek philosophers from earlier thinkers was their rejection of not only religious explanations for phenomena, but also religious modes of thinking. Philosophers discounted myth and tradition in favour of *logos*, i.e. reasoning or logic. Greek philosophy did not deny the existence of gods, but saw them as something that could be subjected to rational enquiry. Democritus (*c.* 460–*c.* 370 BCE), founder of atomism (the theory that everything was made from tiny particles called, unsurprisingly, atoms), believed that there were gods, but that they were as much a part of the natural world as stones and trees. This is an exact equivalent with the gods of the **Discworld** (*see* **Religion**), who although powerful are not separate from the world, nor responsible for its creation.

Ephebe, the Discworld's counterpart of Greece, is a city full of philosophers, and philosophy is the country's chief export. The characterisation of Ephebian philosophy as falling into two broad schools roughly mirrors the major division of Greek philosophy into two camps. The Ephebian Xenoists – for whom the world is 'complex and random' – echo the materialist Democritus and, to a lesser extent, Aristotle (384–322 BCE) who attempted to understand the universe through observation and analysis of phenomena. The Ibidians, who argue that the world is 'basically simple and follows certain fundamental rules' resemble Pythagoras (*fl. c.*530 BCE) and Plato (*c.*427–347 BCE), both of whom posited the existence of a realm beyond the material that – in some obscure sense – governed the world we see. For Plato and his followers, the universe was defined by eternal and unchanging 'Ideas' that existed in this abstract realm.

One of the main themes of *SG* is the Omnians' insistence that the world is round. It was Pythagoras – or one of his followers – who first advanced the theory that the Earth was a sphere, although he did so on rather less logical grounds than we might expect. Just like the Omnians, the Pythagoreans concluded that the world must be round because a sphere was the most perfect shape. However, some centuries later, the astronomer Eratosthenes (276–194 BCE) made a fair stab at calculating the circumference of the Earth by measuring the angle of the sun on Summer solstice at different latitudes. By contrast, on Discworld, the philosopher Didactylos simply takes a trip to the edge of the world and has a peek over the side.

Didactylos, with a barrel for his house and a lantern which is of no use to him, is clearly modelled on Diogenes the Cynic (*c.*412–323 BCE), who lived in a tub and carried a torch with which – it is said – he searched (in daylight) for an honest man.

Pratchett seems to draw a parallel between philosophers and priests in Discworld: both professions are described as attracting people interested in non-physical work (*SG*), and this is in line with his general view of people being basically the same at heart, whether **dwarf** or **troll**, living or undead. Nevertheless, a vital distinction is drawn between them in the characters of **Vorbis**, who embodies absolute certainty and faith, and Didactylos, who doubts everything, even the nature of being a philosopher (*SG*). *See also* Arabic Societies; Egypt; Ephebe; Greek Mythology; Religion *and* Tsort.

Further Reading

Cohen, S. Marc, Patricia Curd, and C. D. C. Reeve, eds. 2005. *Readings in Ancient Greek Philosophy: From Thales to Aristotle*. Indianapolis, IN: Hackett.

Gottlieb, Anthony. 2001. *The Dream of Reason: A History of Western Philosophy*. London: Penguin.

Alex Bussey

Greenslade, Dave (b. 1943)

Musician, composer and keyboarder, who was born in Woking, England, and is a friend of Pratchett who has written an album of music inspired by the **Discworld**. After playing in a number of rhythm and blues bands through the 1960s, he co-founded jazz-rock band Colosseum, who released *Those About to Die Salute You* (1969), *The Valentyne Suite* (1969) and *Daughter of Time* (1970) before splitting up. The second album's title track, some seventeen minutes long, was written by Greenslade. He set up his own progressive rock group, Greenslade, who released four albums, *Greenslade* (1972), *Bedside Manners Are Extra* (1973), *Spyglass Guest* (1974) and *Time and Tide* (1975) before disbanding in 1976; they reformed in 2000. As a solo artist, he has released four albums: *Cactus Choir* (1976), *The Pentateuch of the Cosmogony* (1979), *From the Discworld* (1994) and *Going South* (1999). He has also scored programmes for BBC television.

He can be seen as an exemplar of 1970s progressive rock, a style of music typified by an earnest and serious approach to **pop music**, the wish to say something serious whilst often borrowing from jazz and classical styles. Prog rock stage shows would often feature long instrumental solos, expensive light shows, slides, films and even full orchestras, whilst the albums would be hung around a particular concept or **narrative**. Typical of this genre are Yes, whose album *Close to the Edge* (1972) features a Discworld-like environment painted by Roger Dean (b. 1944). Often, these would draw upon **Fantasy** or **Science Fiction** conventions; the Swede Bo Hansson (b. 1943) recorded *Sagan Om Ringen* in 1969 (*Music inspired by Lord of the Rings*, 1972), inspired by J.R.R. **Tolkien** and, later, *Music Inspired by Watership Down* (1977). Greenslade's *Pentateuch* is an instrumental double album based on a story written and illustrated by Patrick Woodroffe (b. 1940), about humanity in the twenty-fourth century being scattered to ten planets within the solar system after the wrecking of Earth.

Having become friends with Pratchett in the mid-1980s, he asked whether he could make an album of music inspired by the **Discworld**. It would not just be expansions and settings of songs mentioned in the novels – such as 'A Wizard's Staff Has a Knob on its End', Nanny **Ogg's** 'Hedgehog Song' aka 'The Hedgehog Can Never Be Buggered At All' or the various **dwarf** hihos and 'Gold Gold Gold' – nor a soundtrack album for *SM*. Instead, he produced *Terry Pratchett's From the Discworld* (Virgin, 1994; UK: CDV 2738), which includes sleeve notes by Pratchett and artwork by Josh **Kirby**.

1. 'A-Tuin the Turtle': features a voiceover from Tony Robinson (b. 1946), who does the abridged **Audio Book** versions of Pratchett's novels and was to play Vernon Crumley in the television adaptation of *H*, but is most famous for playing Baldrick in

the *Blackadder* (1983–1991) series and presenting the archaeology programme *Time Team* (1994–). The plodding rhythm suggests the Great **A'Tuin**'s gait.

2. 'Octarine The Colour Of Magic': an instrumental track, with lots of synthesised strings and guitars.
3. 'Luggage': again a rhythm to suggest walking (*see* The **Luggage**), another instrumental track, starts with rhythm guitar sounds, but moves through various instruments including a guitar, synthetic strings and saxophone.
4. 'Shades of Ankh Morpork': a song, mostly two lines repeated throughout, inspired by The **Shades**. The synthesisers here sound very 1980s pop funk. The words are sung by Tim Whitnall (later to be a narrator of the BBC children's programme Teletubbies (1997–2001)).
5. 'Wyrd Sisters': an instrumental that begins with a storm, but which also features **Death** tap dancing. At points, it has shades of Antonio Vivaldi (1678–1741) or Edvard Grieg (1843–1907).
6. 'Unseen University/The Librarian': instrumental with a certain amount of synthetic choral vocals; dominated by the organ – which is the instrument of choice of the **Librarian**.
7. 'Death': instrumental with martial undertones. It also has a tolling bell and a synth trumpet solo.
8. 'Wizard's Staff Has A Knob On The End': folk song, although it has a long sub-Bach introduction, based on the song sung drunkenly by various characters, including **Wizards**. Beginning with the phallic double entendre of the title, which forms a much repeated chorus, the lyrics continue on the theme about the wizards' staffs and what they do with them. They are written by Heather Wood who has also done a version of 'The Hedgehog Song'. Vocals by Tim Whitnall.
9. 'Dryads': atmospheric instrumental invocation of the tree spirits encountered in *COM*.
10. 'Pyramids': inspired by one section of *P* which describes Djelebeybi. It is a Parody in parts of the style of music used in Hollywood films, especially sword and sandal epics, but using synthetic strings. It also includes the sound of pyramids flaring.
11. 'Small Gods': instrumental summary of the novel SG, with additional musicians Rhianna Pratchett (keyboards) and Kate Greenslade (flute); it ends with Stephen **Briggs** speaking a line from the novel.
12. 'Stick and Bucket Dance': instrumental morris dance tune for *LL*, with echoes of early Mike Oldfield (b.1953) and his versions of the traditional 'Jubilee' and 'Portsmouth'. Co-written by Pratchett fan Adrian Easlea.
13. 'One Horseman and Three Pedestrians of the Apocralypse': instrumental inspired by a line from *S*.

14. 'Holly Wood Dreams': instrumental invoking various styles of Hollywood film, including crime, film noir and western, before returning to Tony Robinson, who here reads from *MP*. *See also* Stephen Briggs; Parody *and* Pop Music.

Further Reading

Blake, Andrew. 1997. *The Land Without Music: Music, Culture and Society in Twentieth-Century Britain*. Manchester: Manchester University Press.
Stump, Paul. 1977. *The Music's All That Matters: History of Progressive Rock*. London: Quartet.
Woodroffe, Patrick. 1987. *The Second Earth: The Pentateuch Re-told*. London: Paper Tiger.

Andrew M. Butler

Grimma (*T*, *W*)

One of the nomes from Outside, who comes to the store built by **Arnold Bros (est. 1905)**, and a bit of a token female (*see* **Sexism**, **Kirsty**) in the trilogy – although there is also Granny Morkie, whose attitudes owe a little to Granny **Weatherwax**. Whereas the nomes insist that females cannot be allowed to read, because their heads may explode, Grimma teaches herself to read, beginning with *The Highway Code*, and is the one who discovers about The **Bromeliad**, which act as a metaphor for the nomish condition. She is constantly supportive of **Masklin** and helps him through any doubts that he may have – not that she is entirely self-confident herself. She is, however, very good at coming up with ideas, and keeps the nomes alive. In the absence of the **Abbot** Gunner and after the death of **Nicodemus**, she becomes the *de facto* leader of the nomes, despite this apparently being an exclusively male role (*see* **Feminism**). At one point, she even (unknowingly?) paraphrases the 'We'll fight them on the beaches' speech (1940) by Winston Churchill (1874–1965). She is not present in the third volume. *See also* Abbot; Arnold Bros (est. 1905); The Bromeliad; Children's Fiction; Feminism; Angalo de Haberdasheri; Dorcas del Icatessen; Masklin; Nisodemus; Sexism *and* Stratified Societies.

Andrew M. Butler

Guards! Guards! (1989)

The eighth **Discworld** novel and the first to centre on the **City Watch**. The first UK edition was 14,200 copies published by Gollancz with a cover by Josh Kirby. The 1990 Corgi paperback run was 161,000, with an alternative black and gold photographic cover available since 2005. It was printed by Gollancz, bound with *MAA* and *FOC*, as *The City Watch Trilogy* (1999). It has been translated into Bulgarian, Croatian, Czech, Dutch, Estonian, Finnish, French, German, Hebrew, Hungarian, Italian, Norwegian, Polish,

Portuguese, Romanian, Russian, Serbian, Spanish, Swedish and Turkish. *GG* is dedicated to the sort of characters who are usually just present in a narrative to attack the hero one by one and be knocked out or killed – sometimes on the villain's words, 'Guards! Guards!'. The book is an attempt to make us care for such minor roles. It is also dedicated to British science fiction and fantasy writers M. John Harrison (Mike) (b.1945), Mary Gentle (b.1956) and Neil **Gaiman**. The book has been a Radio 4 serial, adapted for the stage by Stephen **Briggs** and by Geoffrey Crush, and as a Big Comic (*see next entry*). *Locus* reviewed it thus: 'Pratchett demonstrates just how great the distance is between one- or two-joke writers and the comic masters whose work will still be read well into the next century'.

Carrot **Ironfoundersson**, a human of possibly royal origin adopted by **dwarfs**, is sent to **Ankh-Morpork** to join the City Watch and takes his duties more seriously than everyone else does (crime is heavily regulated by various Guilds). A secret society, the Brotherhood of the Elucidated Brethren, summon a dragon so that the person who defeats it may be made king. Meanwhile, the frequently drunken Captain **Vimes** begins to investigate a series of strange fires and deaths and suspects that there is a dragon at large. The dragon is too strong to be controlled and takes over the city, with **Vetinari's** secretary, Lupine Wonse, as spokesperson. Vimes has been sacked and thrown in the dungeons with Vetinari, the City Watch seem unable to work out a way of killing the dragon and Lady Sybil **Ramkin** – who trains **dragons** and has given Vimes a small dragon of his own – is set to be sacrificed as a virgin. Vimes is rescued by the **Librarian**, and his dragon first defeats then becomes the mate of the dragon which has been terrorising the city – it turns out to be female. Wonse falls to his death when being arrested.

The novel is stuffed full of references to American **Detective and Noir Fiction**, including the novels of Raymond Chandler (1888–1959), *Dirty Harry* (1971) and *Kojak* (1973–1975), plus *Dixon of Dock Green* (1955–1976). Patrician Vetinari's actions begin to look more Machiavellian than in previous books – he is manipulating the situation. *See also* City Watch; Frederick Colon; Dragons; *Guards! Guards!* (Comic Book Adaptation); Carrot Ironfoundersson; Nobby Nobbs; Lady Sybil Ramkin; Patrician Vetinari *and* Samuel Vimes.

Further Reading

James, Edward. 'The City Watch'. *GOL*, *GOL2*.

Andrew M. Butler

Guards! Guards! (Comic Book Adaptation) (2000)

Adapted from the book *GG* by Stephen **Briggs** – who had also adapted the book as a **play** in 1993 – this was the second **Discworld graphic novel** drawn by Graham **Higgins** after *Mort: A Discworld Big Comic*. It was published by Gollancz in hardback (1,500) and paperback (12,500) in 2000, with Czech, French, German and Italian translations. Pratchett dedicates it to all those 'who died in the making of this Big Comic', suggesting that this was going to be subtitled as a Big Comic as well. Higgins dedicates it to his parents, his teachers Ken Jacobs and Michael Abbott and Mickey Jupp.

Higgins drew the roughs on A3 paper and did the inks on a lighting box. Gavin Lawson, described as offering 'Fonts, balloons and digital support', scanned the pictures and added the various levels of art and speech using Quark and Illustrator. He then sent these back to Higgins, who coloured them in Photoshop with the aid of his son James. His deal with Gollancz got him the G3 Mac computer that Lawson used.

The adaptation stays close to the original storyline, with a certain amount of dove-tailing and tightening up – Lady Sibyl **Ramkin** loses a couple of scenes, and Samuel **Vimes's** alcoholism is given less space. Vimes has a bit of a Clint Eastwood (b.1930) look about him, which is only appropriate as he lifts lines from *Dirty Harry* (1971). When in helmet and silhouette, the character bears a resemblance to Judge Dredd from *2000AD*, a comic that Higgins had worked on, although he did not draw Dredd. As has become traditional, Patrician **Vetinari** looks like Stephen Briggs. Nobby **Nobbs** is a dwarfen figure with a large nose, scraggly beard and bandy legs and looks like a refugee from comic drawn by Hunt Emerson (b.1952) or Gilbert Shelton (b.1940). There is a shift to pastel tones to represent Carrot **Ironfoundersson's** rose spectacled view of the Discworld.

There are some nice minor touches – the **witch** that Carrot's parents consult about the sword and crown found with him is revealed to be Magrat **Garlick**, a detail not in the novel, and their mine is the distinctly Disneyfied High Hough. Carrot and Fred **Colon** eat **Sto Lat** tater chips – although perhaps it would be better for them to be made from cabbage rather than potato. There are some very good panoramas of **Ankh-Morpork**, as well as crowd scenes – there is a revue bar supposedly with **Klatch** erotica, where the Playboy bunny is a hog – and a particularly fine set of depictions of **Death**. The whole is topped and tailed with long shots of the Discworld and Ankh-Morpork, drawing very closely on the source. *See also* Ankh-Morpork; Stephen Briggs; City Watch; Frederick Colon; Comics; Dragons; Food; Magrat Garlick; Graphic Novels; Graham Higgins; Carrot Ironfoundersson; Nobby Nobbs; Lady Sybil Ramkin; Patrician Vetinari *and* Samuel Vimes.

Further Reading

Apple computers page on Graham Higgins: http://www.apple.com/za/creative/digitalimaging/grahamhiggins/index.html

Andrew M. Butler

H

Haberdasheri, Angalo de (*T*, *D*, *W*)

One of the nomes who lives in the store made by **Arnold Bros (est. 1905)**, part of the Haberdasheri clan, who of course live in Haberdashery, a section selling buttons, threads, ribbons and cloth. Of a distinctly sceptical turn of mind, he is the opposite of **Nisodemus**. His interest in science, invention and his obsession with the outside has led him to be estranged from his father, Duke Cido. In fact, he would rather that Arnold Bros did actually exist, so that not believing in him was a deliberate choice rather than merely common sense. It is thus appropriate that he is the one to run into **Masklin**, **Grimma** and the other nomes from Outside. He disappears for a brief period, to travel on a truck, and works out how to use it; he also goes along to America with Grimm and the **Abbot** Gunner, taking a particular interest in the flight deck of the Concorde. His rationality seems to be endorsed by The **Bromeliad**, unlike the religious characters who are either killed off or are left behind by the events of the narrative. He is the author of *A Scientific Encyclopedia for the Enquiring Young Nome*. *See also* The Abbot; Arnold Bros (est. 1905); The Bromeliad; Children's Fiction; Grimma; Dorcas del Icatessen; Masklin; Nisodemus; Religion *and* Technology.

Andrew M. Butler

'The Hades Business' (*OM* WF*)

Pratchett's first published story, written as a piece of class work when he was about thirteen and published in the school magazine. It was then submitted to and published by a British **Science Fiction** magazine, *Science Fantasy*, then edited by John Carnell (1912–1972) and appeared in issue number 60 in 1963 (Pp. 66–76). It was reprinted in *The Unfriendly Future*, edited by Tom Boardman, Jr. (London: NEL, 1965; Pp. 119–130).

Crucible, owner of the Square Deal Advertising Company, is employed by the Devil to promote Hell and exploit its assets, as the infernal realm has seen a drop in the number of admissions. This he does with such great success that the Devil is being driven mad by the crowds. He repents of his evil – which has been Crucible's aim all along.

This story feels very much in the tradition of Robert **Sheckley** and is certainly very competent work for a teenager. It also anticipates *E* and *GO* in its satirical depiction of the afterlife and heaven and hell. *See also* Science Fiction *and* Robert Sheckley.

Andrew M. Butler

Hannan, Tina (b. 1968)

Provider, with Stephen **Briggs**, of the recipes for *NOC*. She was born in Perivale, London, and has trained as an aromatherapist. At the **Clarecraft** event (*see* **Conventions**) in November 1997 (where she was dressed as a member of the **City Watch**), she gave Terry Pratchett dwarf bread, figgins and a sticky toffee rat onnastick – all inspired by his novels – and he invited her to come up with recipes for a future project. The proceeds of this book went to the Orangutan Foundation, as have those of various attendances at later Clarecraft events. She also takes photographs, for example of faded advertisements, painted on walls and balanced toy ducks. *See also* Stephen Briggs; Food *and Nanny Ogg's Cookbook*.

Further Reading

Tina Hannan's homepage: http://web.onetel.com/~wulf1/index.htm

Andrew M. Butler

A Hat Full of Sky (2004)

The thirty-second **Discworld** novel, aimed at children, and the second of the Tiffany **Aching** sequence. It is also a sequel to '**SALF**'. The story is continued in *Wint*. The first UK hardback edition, with a cover by Paul **Kidby**, was published by Doubleday in 2004, the Corgi paperback following in 2005. It has been translated into Catalan, Chinese. Czech, Danish, Dutch, Estonian, Finnish, French, German, Indonesian, Italian, Japanese, Lituanian, Norwegian, Polish, Romanian and Spanish. It won the *Locus* Young Adult Novel Award and the Mythopoeic Award (Children's Category) in 2005. The hat of the title is the **witches'** hat worn by Tiffany at the end of the book, although the whole sky is in fact her hat. It is divided into chapters, begins with a note on the Nac Mac Feegles as by Miss Perspicacia Tick and has an author's afterword about the doctrine of signatures – the idea that plants which resemble human parts in colour or shape can have an impact on that part – white chalk horses and witch trials.

Tiffany, now eleven, is sent to Miss Level, a research witch, for more training. Miss Level has two bodies, which work in unison. Tiffany encounters a coven of teenage witches, who are keen to modernise witching. She is possessed by a Hiver, an ancient undead spirit, and starts throwing her powers of **magic** around. The Nac Mac Feegles come to her rescue, by entering into her mind, but not before half of Miss Level is killed. Granny **Weatherwax** also shows up and helps Tiffany to defeat the Hiver. They go to the witch trials, where the Hiver is finally vanquished. It is a spirit which is terrified because it is aware of everything, and Tiffany leads it to the edge of a desert where it can finally meet **Death**.

In the next spring, she returns the hat that Weatherwax has lent her and makes her own out of the sky as she becomes a witch for her village.

Tiffany is beginning to rival Weatherwax in terms of **power**, but as yet does not have the good sense and wisdom that age and experience can bring. Weatherwax is such a formidable character that it is difficult to envisage a suitable antagonist for her – the last book with the **Lancre** was *CJ* in 1998 – so a maiden who is actually a potential rival presents a new challenge. *See also* Tiffany Aching; Children's Fiction; Coming of Age; Magic; Power; Granny Weatherwax *and* Witches.

Andrew M. Butler

Heroes

Since antiquity, the definition of a hero has been variable and the type of hero a society produces or admires can say a lot about that society. From *COM* onwards, the **Discworld** series has been ambivalent about who the heroes are. It is not Hrun the barbarian or the naïve explorer **Twoflower**, who features as the central protagonist, but rather **Rincewind**, who seems anything but a hero. Thus, from its inception, the Discworld series is peppered with unlikely heroes and challenges to the notion of hero.

Unlikely heroes of the Discworld include the **Orangutan**-shaped **Librarian** who not only saves a number of other characters but also braves the dangers of **L-Space**, a romantic **dwarf**, Casanunda, who proclaims himself to be the world's second greatest lover, **Archchancellor** Mustrum **Ridcully**, who in *LL* is fooled by Granny **Weatherwax** into going back for his crossbow thereby leaving her to face the **elves**, or Mightily Oats, the Omnian priest with bad skin and a handy resistance to **vampires**. All these characters attempt some kind of heroic deed, but are not the protagonists of their narratives. In contrast, Rincewind is the protagonist of a number of **narratives**, but does not generally attempt great heroic deeds or fit into the traditional mould of hero. The hero is brave, Rincewind is a coward. The hero is strong, Rincewind is scrawny. The hero is knowledgeable, Rincewind is a wizard who cannot do magic. The hero is virile, Rincewind prefers potatoes to sex. So rather than offering to be a guide with full intention of doing so, Rincewind would gladly con the innocent tourist Twoflower, but when threatened with certain death if he allows harm to come to the tourist, he soon falls into the role. Where a hero would stand up to threats, Rincewind hides or runs away. So Rincewind is not a heroic character, but he fulfils the role of hero in a number of narratives. He inadvertently saves Twoflower on a number of occasions, he frees slaves and saves the revolution in *IT*, and it is implied in both *LC* and *LH* that he has a hand in saving the world.

Heroes

In contrast to Rincewind, Carrot **Ironfoundersson** is a likely hero; he is the obvious hero who is also oblivious to his heroic status. In *GG*, Carrot, the adopted son of **dwarfs**, is sent to **Ankh-Morpork** to be among his own kind. He has a typically heroic appearance; he is tall, muscular, broad shouldered and apparently good looking. He is honest, amiable and noble. He wants to be a watchman in order to serve the city, not just for the pay cheque. He is a natural leader, people follow his example and are inspired by him to do more than they normally would. Like the mythical heroes of antiquity, there is doubt surrounding his origins, he is adopted, but he has a strange crown-shaped birthmark and he has a sword. Like the ancient heroes, Carrot appears destined for something. However, it is not Carrot who slays the dragon in *GG*. Although the narrative is constructed around the idea that when the city is in peril a hero will come forth to save it, the ending to a Pratchett story is never so simplistic.

As a natural Hero figure, Carrot regularly gets promoted and he gets the girl, in this case, Angua von **Überwald**, a beautiful werewolf also in the **City Watch**. However, by the fifth novel in the watch series, *FE*, Pratchett begins to problematise the impact of a Hero on those around him. For if a guard becomes the Hero, someone else needs to be the disposable minor character. If Carrot will always come out on top, then other people have to lose. At the end of *FE*, Angua's friend Gavin, a noble and honourable wolf, dies. He is not the hero of this particular narrative and is therefore sacrificed in the way that the lowly guards would be in someone else's story.

In *GG*, it is in fact Samuel **Vimes** who best fulfils the narrative function of hero. It is Vimes who rescues the aristocratic Lady Sybil **Ramkin** when she is offered as a sacrifice to the dragon. But he struggles with alcoholism and gets thrown in gaol along the way, he is not a heroic character. Sam Vimes is not a hero who automatically succeeds, he is an anti-hero having more in common with the hard-boiled characters of **Detective and Noir Fiction**, who succeed due to a combination of dogged hard work, not being afraid to get their hands dirty, understanding of human nature and an element of luck.

For a traditional hero, saving the heroine results in a happy ever after scenario, perhaps receiving half the kingdom as well as the hand of the princess. Although Sam Vimes does marry Lady Sybil and thereby gain about half the city, it does not happen automatically. He has to pluck up the courage to actually ask one of the richest women in the city to marry him and then negotiate everything that entails. From his humble origins, he becomes Sir Samuel Vimes and then the Duke of Ankh. Where Carrot never claims the throne of Ankh-Morpork, a status that may be considered rightfully his, choosing instead a simpler way of life, Sam Vimes has status and responsibility thrust on him and is forced to rise to the challenges of those responsibilities. In *J*, his rank entitles him to form an army, and thereby prevent a war. In *FE*, he is appointed ambassador and again prevents a war, this time by solving the crimes surrounding the coronation of the Low King.

Considering the notion that the type of hero it produces reflects the concerns of a society, it is worth noting that Vimes does not aspire to the social mobility of the early 1980s yuppie. He loves his wife despite her status, not because of it. He does not wish to emulate the higher echelons of Ankh-Morpork society, rather he uses his street knowledge and understanding of human nature to negotiate his way through both the social structures of Ankh-Morpork and those of other societies he encounters.

In *T!*, Vimes represent the delicate Life/Work balance which working parents of both sexes struggle with. Alongside the detective story, there is the idea that the responsible parent gets home in time to read their child a bedtime story. Going beyond the 1980s notions of masculinity in crisis, Vimes represents the modern man negotiating his way through the major aspects of life, work, love, marriage and parenthood.

Moist von **Lipwig** is another protagonist who does not fit in with a traditional idea of heroism. Somewhere between Rincewind and Vimes on the anti-hero spectrum, Moist does not wish to be heroic. Saved from the gallows to run Ankh Morpork's failing postal service, Moist's only wish is to run away. However, like Rincewind his attempts at cowardice backfire until he manages to reinvigorate the post office, then to be faced with saving a bank (*GP*).

The Discworld characters depicted as most fitting the traditional concept of hero are the barbarians, they are the professional heroes. Generally found in the taverns of Ankh Morpork such as **The Broken Drum** when they are not working, the job of the barbarian hero involves slaying monsters, saving princess and stealing from gods. But on the Discworld, they are not particularly honourable or noble, heroism is their job and they would not work for less than the going rate. In *GG*, they refuse the job of killing the dragon because **Vetinari** does not offer a princess and half the kingdom as the reward. Interestingly, whereas these types of heroes would be major characters elsewhere, on the Discworld they are only afforded bit parts.

The exception is **Cohen the Barbarian** and his Silver Horde, who appear in *IT* and then take centre stage in *LH*. To an extent, Cohen is just an idea, the idea that old heroes never die. If they do not, what happens to them? The narrative of *LH* addresses this quite seriously even if the notion of these old heroes is simply a play on the idea of boys who never grow up, the hero equivalent of Peter Stringfellow (b.1940), a club-owning entrepreneur who dresses as if forty years younger and claims a string of lovers.

Cohen decides to return to the gods what the first hero stole (fire), but with interest. Effectively launching a terrorist attack on the gods. Cohen and his Silver Horde resent their decrepitude and blame the gods. They see themselves as freedom fighters not realising that their actions will destroy the whole Discworld. They are on the point of victory when confronted by the arrival of Carrot and are forced to reassess who the hero is. Carrot accepts the odds of seven to one and does not expect any more of a reward for saving the discworld, than his normal wages as an Ankh Morpork watch captain.

LH is a prime example of the way Pratchett shifts perspective. Published just over a month after the 9/11 attacks on the World Trade Center in New York and the Pentagon in Washington D.C., this could not be a response to those events, but seen in light of them this notion of who the hero is hero takes on a whole new significance, whether it is the professional hero, the obvious, oblivious hero, or the small man who just wants to run away. After all who really is the last hero? *See also* Cohen the Barbarian; Coming of Age; Fairy Tales; Fantasy; Fritz Leiber; Moist von Lipwig; Johnny Maxwell; Masklin; Narrative; Power; Rincewind *and* Samuel Vimes.

Further Reading

Adams, Rachel, and David Savran. 2002. *The Masculinity Studies Reader*. London: Blackwell.

Carlyle, Thomas. 1966. *On Heroes and Hero-worship and the Heroic in History*. Lincoln, Nebraska: University of Nebraska Press.

Whitman, C.H. 1964. *Aristophanes and the Comic Hero*. Cambridge, MA: Harvard.

Eve Smith

Higgins, Graham (b.1953)

Artist, illustrator, cartoonist and writer, born in Liss, Hampshire, but went to school in Nottingham. He collaborated with Pratchett on ***Mort: A Discworld Big Comic*** and with Stephen **Briggs** on ***Guards! Guards!:* (Comic Book Adaptation)**. Preparatory sketches for *Mort* are on his website, as are drawings for *SM*.

His early comics were published by Arts Lab Press in Birmingham and Knockabout Press. He has been a cartoonist for *Punch*, who ran his noir **Detective** strip 'Luke Carew'. In 1988, he drew the pictures for 'A Short Walk on a Cold Day' written by Roz Kaveney (b.1949) for the comic book anthology *AARGH!* and later published short stories in two collections edited by Kaveney and Mary Gentle (b.1956) – 'Jabberwockish' (*Villains!* (1992)) and 'Sounds and Sweet Airs' (*Weerde: Book 2* (1993)) – and 'The String Man' in *Temps Volume 1* (1991, edited by Neil **Gaiman** and Alex Stewart). For *2000AD*, he drew 'Zippy Couriers' ((1989–1990), created with and written by Hilary Robinson) and 'Tharg's Future Shocks' ((2001), written by Steve Moore). He has also worked for the two major America comic companies, DC and Marvel. For DC, he inked part of *Animal Man* (1993) and the Rachel Pollack (b.1945) incarnation of *Doom Patrol* (1993). For Marvel, he has worked on *X-Men 2009* (1995). From 1993, he worked part-time for Hansi Kiefersauer's Honk!studio, Berlin, on materials based on the character Käpt'n Blaubär (Captain Bluebear) from comics and books by Walter Moers (b.1957) such as *Die 13½ Leben des Käpt'n Blaubär* (*The 131/2 Lives of Captain Bluebear*) (1999).

See also Stephen Briggs; Comics; Neil Gaiman; Graphic Novels *and Mort: A Discworld Big Comic.*

Further Reading

Higgins, Graham. 1991. 'The String Man'. Pp. 189–204 in *Temps Volume 1.* Edited by Neil Gaiman and Alex Stewart. London: Roc.

———. 1992. 'Jabberwockish'. Pp. 251–282 in *Villains!* Edited by Mary Gentle and Roz Kaveney. London: Roc.

———. 1993. 'Sounds and Sweet Airs'. Pp. 151–178 *The Weerde: Book 2.* Edited by Mary Gentle and Roz Kaveney. London: Roc.

Moers, Walter. 2001. *The 13 1/2 Lives of Captain Bluebear: A Novel.* Translated by Alan Brownjohn. London: Vintage.

Graham Higgins website: http://www.pokkettz.demon.co.uk/

Andrew M. Butler

History

History is the **narrative** we tell about time – the series of significant and less significant (but still narratable) events that have led up to now. It is also, according to **Sellar and Yeatman**, what we remember – and for them there were only two truly memorable dates.

Whereas some **Science Fiction** and **Fantasy** stories or series have a mappable history which can be worked out in great detail – the chronology of the Future History stories of Robert A. Heinlein (1907–1988) was plotted out and published before all of them were written, for example – Pratchett's history is somewhat looser. Some dates are given as a way into a joke – Queen Griminir the Impaler (1514–1553, 1553–1557, 1557–1562, 1562–1567, 1568–1573) as a way of indicating a frequently staked **vampire** – any attempt to work out a coherent chronicle would fail. There is the sense of the growth of particular characters – witness the rise of Samuel **Vimes** – but it is difficult to know whether this has taken years or just months, and whether time progresses in **Discworld** novels at a rate equivalent to the real world.

The ambiguity of history is present in the two novels written prior to *COM*: both *DSS* and *Str* look back to artifacts built by races who are no longer around. The fact that the evidence does not quite point where the archaeologists initially thought it did is not the issue. The point is the stories told about the potential abilities of species. A long period of time also separates the world of the Nomes in The **Bromeliad** from their extraterrestrial origins. Only The **Thing** remembers, and the new knowledge opens up a new world, which is frightening to some and gives **power** to others.

History

If *DSS* and *Str* suggest that history can be faked, then other books by Pratchett suggest that it may be rewritten. Johnny **Maxwell** and his friends travel back in time to the Blitz in **Blackbury** and discover how different attitudes were back then. Having inadvertently left Wobbler behind, they return to a rather different present day, and have to go back to the Second World War to make things go back to how they should be (*JB*). This novel – if not the **Johnny Maxwell Trilogy** in total – is a good example of the idea of The **Trousers of Time**, Pratchett's metaphor for alternate histories or alternate worlds. Equally, it is not clear that the three novels are continuous given the lack of reference between them.

In *NW*, Vimes is sent back in time whilst investigating a serial killer. Here he meets the younger version of himself, and metamorphoses into his erstwhile mentor, John Keel. Whilst history is here a little fluid, there is a certain of necessity for Vimes as mature **City Watch** commander to live through experiences he had had as a young man, but from a different perspective. There are still paradoxes, as Vimes has learnt many of his skills from himself, and so he is pulling himself up by his own bootstraps. The narrative of *P* is even more circular, as the villain of the book is sent back in time to live his life over again.

Death has a rather distant perspective on history, given that **Death's Domain**, despite the millions of hourglasses, is out of time proper. He knows when everyone will die; in the case of **wizards**, **witches** and royalty he will go to meet them in person. As early as *M*, he is able to rearrange things so that Mort **Sto Helit** and **Keli** can be spared, despite the bifurcation of history. At the start of *SM*, he does not intervene to save Mort and Ysabell **Sto Helit** as it seems to be their decision to be mortal (Mort's hourglass being turned over presumably gives him less than two decades' more life.), but at the end of the novel he does revise reality so that Imp Y **Celyn** is working in **Ankh-Morpork** rather than dead.

Sometimes history needs to be seen to happen – the History Monks are sometimes sent out from their monastery in a hidden valley in the Ramtops to observe time in action. This was the case when **Lu-Tze** was assigned to observe the case of **Brutha**, **Om** and **Vorbis** (*SG*), a situation where the century that the narrative requires puts it out of sync with the rest of the sequence. Lu-Tze also intervenes in the events of *NW*, advising and confusing the transported Vimes. In *TOT*, we see the monks in their everyday work, stitching and unravelling the threads of time, before it is threatened by the invention of an impossibly accurate clock. The end of the world is nigh, and history may be stopped in its tracks.

The Russian literary theorist Mikhail Bakhtin (1895–1975) contrasts the linear time of history and the life of the individual with the circular time of the **Fairy Tale**, where the sense is the same protagonist, albeit with a different name and face, endures repeated equivalent hardships. The **coming of age** narratives of the earlier Discworld novels are from a period before the linear time of the series came to dominate – but, as the manipulation of time by the witches in *WS* demonstrates – history and time are largely subservient to narrative. *See also* Coming of Age; Fairy Tales; Fantasy; Narrative *and* The Trousers of Time.

Further Reading

Bakhtin, Mikhail. 1986. *Speech Genres and other late essays*. Translated by Verne W. McGee. Edited by Carol Emerson and Michael Holquist. Austin: University of Texas Press.

Andrew M. Butler

'History in the Faking'

A short story in which a television presenter, called The Wogan, interviews a historian about the 1990s and reconstructs a false but amusing history from the artifacts which have survived. It appeared on 2 February 1990 in the 'Weekend Section' of the *Evening Standard* (a London daily newspaper owned by Associated Newspapers, who also publish the British national newspaper *Daily Mail*).

Andrew M. Butler

Hogfather (1997)

The twentieth **Discworld** novel, and one of the novels to focus on **Death**. The first UK edition of the book was 70,000 copies, published by Gollancz in 1996 with a cover by Josh **Kirby**. A Corgi edition of 230,000 appeared in 1997. Since 2006 an alternate black and gold photographic cover has been available and – to tie in with it being filmed for Sky One (2006; *see* ***Hogfather*** **(Television Adaptation)**) – there is a photographic tie-in edition with Susan **Sto Helit** on the cover. In 2000, Gollancz published a hardback with *P*, *SG* and *H* as *The Gods Trilogy*, in a print run of about 11,000 copies. *H* has been translated into Bulgarian, Czech, Dutch, Estonian, Finnish, French, German, Italian, Polish, Russian, Spanish and Swedish. Hogswatchnight has been mentioned at various points through the sequence, as well as in *DSS*, but this is the first time Pratchett has focused on it, aside from a footnote in *RP*. The **Hogfather** (*see* next entry) is the Discworld version of Father Christmas, with perhaps an echo of *The Godfather* films. Dedicated to ppint, the proprietor of Interstellar Master Traders, a **Fantasy**, **Science Fiction** and horror shop in Lancaster, founded in 1985. A section of the novel appeared, in a different form, as '**FTB**'. A.S. Byatt writes: 'Like all great creators of imaginary worlds, he writes like an enthralled and driven reader, he creates a brilliant excess of delectable detail, he respects his own creation and his readers' (*The Sunday Times* 15 December 1996).

Hogfather

The Auditors of Reality continue their attempt to rationalise the universe, but this time have their eyes on the Hogfather. They employ the Guild of Assassins to kill him off, and hence the ruthless Jonathan Teatime is engaged to do the job. Seeing that the Hogfather is missing, **Death** and Alberto **Malich** set out on the round to deliver the presents to all the good girls and boys. In turn, Susan Sto Helit, now a governess, is contacted and needs to be prepared to step into her grandfather's shoes. Death tells her to stay out of the way – guaranteed to get her involved. Meanwhile, the **wizards** discover that there are new personifications associated with phenomena, such as Bilious, the Oh God of Hangovers and the odd sock monster. Teatime has found the castle of the Tooth Fairy, which is made of children's teeth, and through the teeth he is controlling the children's belief in the Hogfather. Without belief, the Hogfather will fade away, and the spare belief is creating the new personifications. Death and Susan have to rescue the Hogfather, to ensure the Sun continues to rise.

Customs and culture surrounding Christmas are here the basis for **parody**, with the illogicalities of Santa Claus's mission being undercut. The new personifications make sense, and do explain where all the odd socks go to. Whilst in *FOC* there was an exploration of how ideas can be put into someone's head, here the theme is the importance – and dangers – of belief: it is necessary to believe the little lies, in order that the big lies of mercy and justice can be believed in. *See also* '20p With Envelope and Seasonal Greeting'; Death; The Hogfather (Character); *Hogfather* (Television Adaptation); Susan Sto Helit; Technology *and* Wizards.

Andrew M. Butler

The Hogfather (Character; *RM*, *SM*, *H*)

A personification on the **Discworld** – like the Tooth Fairy, the Soul Cake Tuesday Duck and **Death**, dependent on continued belief to exist. He is a god of winter renewal (contrast wintersmith in *Wint*), responsible for the rebirth of the Sun. He is fat, bearded, wears red and drives a sleigh pulled by the pigs Gouger, Rooter, Snouter and Tusker. Every Hogswatchnight, he used to deliver pork products to all the good girls and boys, and bones to all the bad ones, but now it is toys. The Auditors of Reality want him dead, and Teatime is the assassin for the job; Death briefly takes his place.

The source is Father Christmas, an amalgam of Norse Mythology and Santa Claus, a corruption of St Nicholas. The Norse Odin would drive his chariot across the sky, pulled by Sleipnir, his eight-legged horse, on a Wild Hunt and people would leave out sock stuffed full of hay to feed it. St Nicholas of Myra used the wealth of his dead parents to pay for anonymous gifts to the poor. But the iconography of Father Christmas derives in part from the poem 'A Visit from St. Nicholas' (1822) attributed to Clement Clarke Moore (1779–1863) – and parodied in *H* – and 1930s advertisements for Coca-Cola. Pratchett depicts Father Christmas in 'FTB' and Christmas in general in **'20p with Envelope and Seasonal Greetings'**. *See also* '20p With Envelope and Seasonal Greeting'; Death; 'FTB'; *Hogfather* (Television Adaptation); Susan Sto Helit; Technology *and* Wizards.

Further Reading

Sievker, Phyllis. 1997. *Santa Claus, Last of the Wild Men: The Origins and Evolution of Saint Nicholas, Spanning 50,000 Years*. Jefferson, N.C.: McFarland.

Andrew M. Butler

Hogfather (Television Adaptation) (2006)

Director: Vadim Jean. Producers: Rod Brown and Ian Sharples. Executive Producers: Robert Halmi Jr, Robert Halmi Sr and Elaine Pyke. Writer: Vadim Jean. Cinematography: Gavin Finney and Jan Pester. Cast: Susan: Michelle Dockery; Albert: David Jason; Teatime: Marc Warren; Death (Voice): Ian Richardson. TV version: 2 × 120 minute episodes, with commercials, broadcast 17–18 December 2006, Sky One. DVD version: 184 minutes; Region 2 20th Century Fox Home Entertainment 1 Disc edition (ASIN: B000MRP3Y4), 2 Disc limited edition (ASIN: B000MRP3YE). Certificate PG.

Sir David Jason (left), the Hogfather and Terry Pratchett attending the world premiere of the *Hogfather* television adaptation, in London, in December 2006.

Hogfather (Television Adaptation)

A live action version of the **Discworld** novel made by the Mob Film Company, RHI Entertainment (part of Hallmark), British Sky Broadcasting (BSkyB) and the Moving Picture Company (MPC) for Sky One. Budgeted at £6,000,000, this was Sky One's most expensive single drama to date, although it was a tight budget compared to a film. After the initial showing over two nights, it was repeated in a HD version.

It remains faithful to the book (*see* entry on H for the plot summary), with some streamlining and cutting down of scenes. The episode break comes with the collapse of the Palace of Bones, home to The **Hogfather**, when Susan **Sto Helit** discovers the comatose body of Bilious, the Oh God of Hangovers. An epilogue shows **Death** visiting the toyshop which Alberto **Malich** had looked at as a child, to buy the toy wooden horse for him that he had always wanted.

Perhaps the reason that this of all the books was adapted was its seasonal nature – there is always a slot at family holidays such as Christmas and Easter for family dramas with a fantastical edge, and the Discworld equivalent to Christmas fits in a tradition that includes *Santa Claus* (Jeannet Szwarc, 1985). *The Nightmare Before Christmas* (Henry Selick, 1993) and *The Santa Clause* (John Pasquin, 1994). However, this is not the first narrative to feature Susan and Death by now has a back story; the new viewer is kept in suspense as to whether Susan is really killing monsters for the children she is nanny to, and it is not immediately clear that she is Death's granddaughter. A certain amount of explanation is felt necessary, although the narration, by an uncredited Ian Richardson, is limited to the opening exposition of each episode, and the fact that this is set on a Discworld is effectively just a way to declare this a fantasy. The pace is perhaps a little slow at times, and the family audience means that the violence is implied rather than always shown. Pratchett had long talks with the producer, Rod Brown, before he sold the rights, to be sure that this could accept their vision of the novel, and was involved in the production, both in script contributions and his cameo as the toyshop salesman. There are certainly references that would make more sense to regular readers – the **Death of Rats**, the appearance of Nobby **Nobbs** and the **wizards** – than to newcomers.

This version of Discworld is the Victorian model, with the upper middle classes living in large mansions with nannies and butlers, the gentlemen wearing top hats and them driving around in horse drawn carriages through the snow; Charles Dickens (1812–1870) is presumably the model here (compare **'20p with Envelope and Seasonal Greetings'**). The **Unseen University** seems to consist of a number of crypts and vaulted rooms. Stephen **Player** was responsible for the storyboarding and has done much work in Discworld before. Most of the action – until the Hogfather's rebirth – takes place at night, and so the production seems very dark and under lit, being closer in tone to *Nightmare* than most other Christmas films. This makes a contrast with the whiteness of the Tooth Fairy's Palace. **Death's Domain** is more or less filmed in monochrome, with the exception of Death's blue eyes; Susan is also in colour in her visit there.

Vadim Jean (b.1963) is best known for his feature film *Leon the Pig Farmer* (1992), which he codirected with Gary Sinyor (b.1962), about a Jewish Londoner who discovers his father is a pig farmer. He also wrote the script, with some input from Pratchett. Producer Rod Brown is part of The Mob Films, with a previous credit being on *Dream Team* (1997–) a Sky One drama about fictional football team Harcester United. Ian Sharples is a producer who had previously worked with Jean on the film *One More Kiss* (1999) and the documentary *Working the Thames* (1999). Sam Halmi (b.1924) and Sam Halmi Jr are father and son producers, who have worked in television, currently for Hallmark. They produced *Merlin* (1998), *Snow White* (2001) and *Dinotopia* (2002), so have a track record in family fantasies. Elaine Pyke had also worked on *Dream Team* and an episode of *Hex* (2005), a supernatural drama for Sky One. Gavin Finney had been director of photography on films such as *Tom's Midnight Garden* (1999) and *Gormenghast* (2000), so is no stranger to filming fantasy locations; he also did second unit work on *Harry Potter and the Sorcerer's Stone* (2001). Jan Pester has previously been a Steadicam operator, including on *Merlin*, and a second unit director of photographer, including on *The Little Vampire* (2000).

Sir David Jason (b.1940) is best known for his roles in two sitcoms, the much put-upon Grenville in *Open All Hours* (1976–1985) and Del Trotter in *Only Fools and Horses* (1981–2003), as well as voicing the **Cosgrove Hall** *Danger Mouse* (1981–1992), and dramas *The Darling Buds of May* (1991–1993) and *A Touch of Frost* (1992–2006). He is one of the most popular actors in Britain and would have guaranteed an audience for the programme; he is announced as playing the role of **Rincewind** in Sky One's planned adaptation of *COM*. Alberto is given standing joke of trying to roll but fail to smoke a cigarette. Ian Richardson (1934–2007) became best known for his role of Machiavellian chief whip Francis Urquhart in *House of Cards* (1990), *To Play the King* (1993) and *The Final Cut* (1995), and his character's catchphrase of 'You might well think that. I couldn't possibly comment', is parodied here. He had also been Lord Groan in the television adaptation *Gormenghast*. As it was one of Richardson's last performances, the DVD was dedicated to him. Michelle Dockery (b.1981) had played Betty in the BBC2 adaptation *Fingersmith* (2005), and this was her biggest role to date. Marc Warren (b.1967) had been the central character of the *Doctor Who* episode 'Love and Monsters' (2006) and a leading character in the BBC1 drama *Hustle* (2004–), as well as playing Albert Blithe in *Band of Brothers* (2001) and the title role in *Dracula*, premiered on BBC1 on 28 December 2006.

It is Warren's performance that seemed to divide people: contact lenses gave him two bizarre, mismatched eyes, and he performed his lines with a squeaky voice and an awkward, forced laugh that is to say the least unnerving but perhaps the wrong kind of comic. He certainly pulled off being uncomfortable to watch – and Teatime is a psychopath. However, the production did show that it is possible to translate Discworld to screen. *See also* The Hogfather (Character); Stephen Player *and* Television Adaptations.

Further Reading

Jean, Vadim, and Terry Pratchett. 2006. *Hogfather: The Illustrated Screenplay*. London: Gollancz.

Andrew M. Butler

Hollow, Desiderata (*WA*)

One of the **witches** and a fairy-godmother, especially to Esmerelda in **Genua**, although living and dying in the Ramtops. She is clearly a good judge of psychology as she knew she needed someone to sort out Esmerelda after her death, and had she asked Nanny **Ogg** and Granny **Weatherwax** straight out, they would have likely refused. By asking Magrat **Garlick** instead, and telling her not to tell the other two, she guaranteed her wishes would be carried out.

The name comes from a famous prose poem 'Desiderata' (1927), written by American lawyer Max Ehrmann (1872–1945), although it is sometimes thought to be words found in a church – Old St. Paul's Church, Baltimore, written in 1692. Ehrmann's legal heirs have protected the copyright of the poem, which is advice about behaving well, getting on well with people, being cautious in business. The title is Latin for 'Desired Things'. It seems that Desiderata has lived by this creed. *See also* Fairy Tales; Magrat Garlick; Genua; Nanny Ogg; Granny Weatherwax *and* Witches.

Andrew M. Butler

'Hollywood Chickens' (*OM* WF*)

A short story supposedly based on a true story related to Pratchett by the American **Fantasy** writer Diane Duane (b.1952). It appeared in *More Tales from the Forbidden Planet*, edited by Roz Kaveney (London: Titan, 1990; Pp. 2–10). Roz Kaveney (b.1949) is best known as a **Science Fiction** critic, but she has also edited anthologies with the Midnight Rose Collective: Neil **Gaiman**, Mary Gentle (b.1956) and Alex Stewart (b.1958). *More Tales* followed *Tales* (1987) and contained original fiction. Forbidden Planet is a specialist comics and science fiction shop in London, originally run by Titan Comic Distributors.

In 1973, a lorry crashed at a freeway interchange, scattering some of the crates of chickens it had been carrying. The chickens survived, and bred, on the verge. Occasionally, scientists would research the health of the birds, and various strange events have been associated with the site – a large flying thing, unexplained fires, purple glows and so on. Seventeen years later, it was discovered that all the chickens had disappeared – but there is a colony on the opposite verge where none were before.

A variant on the chicken crossing the road joke – in this case the how is the key question – where chickens have clearly but inexplicably developed high technology.

Andrew M. Butler

Hollywood Comedy

Comedy and Humour has been a staple of film, including Hollywood film, since the very beginning, and Pratchett occasionally draws upon these precursors.

Charlie Chaplin (1889–1977) was born in England and began his career in **music hall** and vaudeville. After two tours of America with the Fred Karno Troupe, Chaplin was signed up by Mack Sennett (1880–1960) for his Keystone Films in 1913. In the second film for them, *Kid Auto Races at Venice* (1914), he introduced the figure of the perpetually down at heel tramp, with big shoes, a large coat, a hat and a cane. His immediate success enabled him to direct and edit his own films, and on moving to Essanay in 1915 and Mutual Film Corporation in 1916, he acquired more or less complete creative control. The same was true of the films financed by First National 1918–1923, but at the same time Chaplin set up his own studio, United Artists, with Douglas Fairbanks (1883–1939), D.W. Griffiths (1875–1948) and Mary Pickford (1892–1979), along with a lawyer and politician, William Gibbs McAdoo (1863–1941). With Universal Artists, Chaplin moved into making feature films rather than shorts well into the talkie era. Chaplin is one of the figures **Hwel** dreams of in *WS*. Chaplin's most successful silent film was *The Gold Rush* (1925), about a starving gold prospector in the Klondike, and this becomes *The Golde Rushe* in *MP*.

The Keystone Films were best known for the Keystone Cops films, centred on incompetent cops and produced between 1912 and 1917. There are times when the **City Watch** behave or – perhaps more to the point – are perceived to behave like the Keystone Cops; in *J* among other places, although Samuel **Vimes's** use of the word 'keystone' to describe Fred **Colon** and Nobby **Nobbs** is tinged with several layers of irony even without a filmic reference. In fact, the **wizards** in *MP* and elsewhere are closer to the early Hollywood slapstick.

Alongside Chaplin in the Karno Troupe on its American tour in 1912 was Stan Laurel (1890–1965). He left the troupe and went into American theatre and vaudeville, making some films, including *The Lucky Dog* (1918) with Oliver Hardy (1892–1957), his future double act partner. Laurel was under contract to Universal, then Joe Rock Comedies and then worked for Hal Roach Studios from 1926. It was here that he was reunited with Hardy, and their double act survived the transition from silent to synchronised sound film as they added fast dialogue to physical stunts and pratfalls. They are often remembered for various misquotations of 'Well, *here's* another *nice* mess you've gotten me into'. **Rincewind** is struck by the phrase (but here's it's a 'fine mess') as he passes out on one occasion in *COM*, and Hwel tries a variation in a script in *WS*. In *MP*, one moving picture is *Sons of the Dessert*, a variation on Laurel and Hardy's French Foreign Legion, *Sons of the Desert* (1933), potentially an influence upon the depiction of the **Klatch** Foreign Legion in *RM*.

The Marx Brothers are another example of Hollywood comedy alluded to by Pratchett. The classic team consisted of Chico (Leonard, 1887–1961), fast-talking with an Italian accent, Harpo (Arthur, 1888–1964), the silent clown with a coat filled with useful props and Groucho (Julius Henry, 1890–1977), again fast-talking, cigar-chomping and with a grease stick moustache. One other brother, Gummo (Milton, 1892–1977), did not appear in the films, and a final one, Zeppo (Herbert, 1901–1979), tended to act as the straight man and romantic lead, and left to become an agent after *Duck Soup* (1933), their last film for Paramount. The Marx Brothers began in vaudeville, and frequently tested out much of their material in live performances across the United States. After leaving Paramount, they joined MGM in 1935 and were forced to have stronger plotlines, romantic subplots and straight songs. The formula was successful at the box office before retiring from film with *The Big Store* (1941) – although they did two more feature films, released by Universal Artists. Typically, these three figures are imagined by Hwel, as clowns, and the characters of Chico, Harpo and Groucho are easily recognisable. One Marx Brothers film becomes a moving picture: *A Night at the Arena* is *A Night at the Opera* (1935) and *Turkey Legs* might be *Duck Soup*. *Hijinks at the Store* might be *The Big Store,* or the Norman Wisdom (b.1915) film *Trouble in Store* (1953). In *SM*, an eating scene quotes from the famous stateroom full of people sequence from *A Night at the Opera* (and, indeed, disruption of plays in by fast-talking witches in *WS* and the treatment of **opera** in *Msk* may well be inspired by the Brothers' impact on a production of *Il Trovatore* (*The Troubadour*, 1853 by Guiseppe Verdi (1813–1901)). In *LC*, HEX is taught the song, 'Lydia the Tattooed Lady', first sung by Groucho in *A Day at the Races* (1939). Finally in *NW*, the password is 'Swordfish', a reference to the speakeasy password in *Horse Feathers* (1932).

Pratchett also references rather more recent comedies, especially *The Blues Brothers* (1980) directed by John Landis (b.1950), with dialogue lifted from it in *WA* and *SM*. The latter shades into a Marx Brothers reference. *SM* spoofs Elwood Blues's line 'They're not gonna catch us. We're on a mission from God' to good effect, although 'God' becomes the **dwarf** Glod

Glodsson. Equally, *MP* borrows another line from Elwood, 'It's 106 miles to Chicago, we got a full tank of gas, half a pack of cigarettes, it's dark, and we're wearing sunglasses'.

In part, these nuggets are there to please people who can spot the references, although the various visions of Hwel might say something about the nature of inspiration: ideas seem to seek out someone to host them. It may also be a nod to the impossibility of comedy being purely original and allows Pratchett to acknowledge some of his forebears. *See also* Comedy and Humour; Hollywood Film; Music Hall *and* Parody.

Further Reading

King, Geoff. 2002. *Film Comedy*. London: Wallflower Press.
Rickman, Gregg, ed. 2001. *The Film Comedy Reader*. New York: Limelight.
Robb, Brian J. 2001. *Laurel & Hardy*. Harpenden: Pocket Essentials.

Andrew M. Butler

Hollywood Films (*MP*)

Pratchett draws upon a variety of real-world culture as a source for **parody**, and film, specifically Hollywood film, is one such source. There are allusions to other national cinemas – notably **Australia's** in *LC* – but Hollywood dominates the frame of reference. Hollywood is both a label for a certain kind of industrially produced film and a real place – the location for Pratchett's short story, **'Hollywood Chickens'**. Pratchett's own encounters with Hollywood have seen a number of his books optioned, but nothing yet produced for the big screen; *GO* has come closest, largely through the efforts of Neil **Gaiman**. A version of **'TB'** is in postproduction, made by an independent Australian film company, Snowgum Films.

The recording and projection of movement was first achieved in the 1890s; Auguste Marie Louis Nicholas Lumière (1862–1954) and Louis Jean Lumière (1864–1948) private and public screenings in 1895 being taken as the start date. The first films were around a minute in duration – depending on the cranking speed – black and white and silent. Individual entrepreneurs followed, setting up businesses in Australia, Britain, Russia, the United States and elsewhere. In 1910, D.W. Griffiths (1875–1948) went to a small village, Hollywood, California, to make films for the Biograph Company, and he was followed by a number of other companies, in part wanting to take advantage of the west coast climate, in part escaping from the attempts of patent holding inventor Thomas Edison (1847–1931) to control the industry on the east coast. Hollywood transformed film making into an industry based around individual studios: the five majors – Fox Film (1913, Twentieth Century Fox from 1935), Paramount Pictures Corporation (1914), Warner Brothers (1923), Metro-Goldwyn-Mayer (1924, a merger of Metro Pictures (1915),

Goldwyn Pictures Corporation (1916) and Louis B. Mayer (1917)), RKO Radio Pictures Incorporated (1928) – and the three minors – Universal (1912), United Artists Corporation (1919) and Columbia (1924). Many of these studios owned distribution companies and cinema chains, giving control over the product from beginning to end. Each studio had control over a roster of actors and directors, and tended to be associated with specific genres. The coming of synchronised sound in the late 1920s gave bankers more control of Hollywood, which then became the dominant cinema of the world. The studio began to decline after 1948, when studios were forced to sell off their control of distribution companies, and the industry faced competition from television. Today, Hollywood consists of a number of studios linked to a small number of multinational media conglomerates.

In *MP*, Pratchett spoofs the studio system, Century of the Fruitbat is Twentieth Century Fox, Microlithic Pictures is Paramount and Untied Alchemists, United Artists. Fir Wood Studios is Pinewood Studios, a British studio created in 1934 in Iver Heath, Buckinghamshire, close to where Pratchett grew up; many of the **Carry-On films** were filmed there. The starlet Ginger – née Theda Withel, screen name Delores de Syn – has a dream which includes the logos for Columbia, MGM, Paramount and Twentieth Century Fox. (**Detritus** hits a gong at a performance, in a homage in the Rank Organisation logo.) Thomas Silverfish, president of the Alchemist's Guild and a film producer, is a version of MGM mogul Samuel Goldwyn (1882–1974, born Schmuel Gelbfisz which he anglicised to Samuel Goldfish), complete with the original's malapropisms. Silverfish gets to use a variant on Victor **Tugelband** of an alleged RKO Pictures screen test comment on the auditioning Fred Astaire (1899–1987): 'Can't sing. Can't act. Balding. Can dance a little'.

The novel is obviously stuffed full of moving picture titles with real-world parallels and references to Hollywood films. Victor is cast in *Blown Away*, a version of the MGM epic *Gone with the Wind* (1939). C.M.O.T. **Dibbler** re-enacts the dancing in the rain sequence of *Singin' in the Rain* (1952), a film which is itself about Hollywood. *Golde Diggers of 1457* is musical *Gold Diggers of 1933* (1933) and a number of similar titles, *The Golde Rushe* is Chaplin's *The Gold Rush* (1925, *see* **Hollywood Comedy**). *The Third Gnome* is *The Third Man* (1949), although this was made by Lion Pictures rather than at Pinewood. Variations on *The Wizard of Oz* (1939) and the *Tarzan* films are also noted. The climax of the book, in which a fifty-foot woman takes an **orangutan** up the skyscraper that is the Tower of Art at the **Unseen University**, is an inversion of *King Kong* (1933), but also alludes to *Attack of the 50 Foot Woman* (1958).

References to Hollywood are not limited to *MP*. In the later books, there are various echoes of horror characters whose popular images were cemented by films made in the 1930s and 1940s at Universal Studios: Bela Lugosi (1882–1956) as the archetypal vampire *Dracula* (1931), **Igor** as descendent of the servant Fritz in *Frankenstein* (1931) and Ygor in

Son of Frankenstein (1939) and the werewolf lore of *The Wolf Man* (1941). The novels set in or featuring characters from **Überwald** – notably *CJ* and *FE* – draw on the feel of these movies in particular – although there are elements of the British Hammer horror cycles (1955–1972) in there as well.

Contemporary films have also been a source of parody. *Reservoir Dogs* (1992), directed by Quentin Tarantino (b.1963), features a group of criminals who are given colours for false names – Mr White, Mr Orange and so on – and this is echoed in the names given to the Auditors of Reality (*TOT*). The same director's *Pulp Fiction* (1994) is referenced in *TT*: Mr Pin and Mr Tulip are of a type of gangster double act which Jules Winfield and Vincent Vega in the film also reference, but this association is made firmer by Pin's variation on the exchange about what the French call a quarterpounder with cheese. There are other echoes of the film in the dialogue of other characters. *TOT* also references the cyberpunk film *The Matrix* (1999) and especially the line 'There is no spoon'. The Auditor of Reality in human form, Myria LeJean, is renamed Unity by Susan **Sto Helit** at the end of *TOT*, which might be an echo of Trinity in *The Matrix* – LeJean being a reference to 'Legion', a demon, as in 'My name is Legion: for we are many' (Mark 5: 9).

The film references reward the knowledgeable reader or cineaste, for getting the joke, of spotting the real world parallel or inversion – although sometimes, as in *Turkey Legs*, it may have been made up. Films do not seem to have the same **narrative** power of **Fairy Tales** to impose a pattern on characters – although arguably the dwarfs are trying to escape from the Disney mould and, as Andy Sawyer has noted, *MP*'s inclusion of an ape, a starlet and a tall, scaleable building means that only one plot resolution is available. *See also* Australia; Neil Gaiman; Hollywood Comedy; Narrative *and* Parody.

Further Reading

Hayward, Susan. *Key Concepts in Cinema Studies*. London: Routledge, 1996.
Sawyer, Andy. 'The Librarian and his Domain'. *GOL*, *GOL2*.

Andrew M. Butler

The Hub (*COM*, *M*, *SG*, *MAA*, *TOT*, *LH*, *NW*)

The geography of a **Discworld** means that the sense of direction is even more arbitrary than designating a north and south pole on a sphere. But there is a point around which the planet rotates, and this is the hub of Discworld's wheel. (The Rim more or less coincides with oceans and seas, with the Circumfence set up at various points to gather together the flotsam, jetsam and stray tourists.) This means that one of the directions given on Discworld is Hubwards (as opposed to Rimwards;

the other two are Turnwise and Widdershins) and compasses point towards it.

The Hub is a cold and mountainous region, with a density of magic concentrated to it. The centre is the mountain Cori Celesti, and there is Dunmanifestin, the home to many of the gods (*see* **Religion**). When Pratchett cuts away from the action to the gods playing games or betting on mortals, it is likely that they are there. In *LH*, **Cohen the Barbarian** and the Silver Horde decide to take fire to the gods, it is to the Hub that he heads, followed by the *Kite*, designed by Leonard of **Quirm**. The History Monks reside in this general area. *See also* Discworld *and* Greek Mythology.

Andrew M. Butler

Hwel (*WS*)

A **dwarf** who travels with a theatrical troupe and writes their plays. It is clear that he is the **Discworld's** equivalent of William **Shakespeare**, writing speeches and plays that are variations, pastiches or burlesques of Shakespeare's plays and poetry. Titles include *A Wizard of Sorts Or, Please Yourself*, whose subtitle echoes *Twelfth Night, Or What You Will* and *As You Like It*, the later comedy even being parodied in the form of a rewrite of the 'All the world's a stage' monologue by Jacques.

The **play** he is commissioned to write by Felmet is called *A Night of Kings: A Tragedy in Nine Acts*, although a good deal of crossings out have preceded that. His heart is clearly not in it and, like *Macbeth*, which is superstitiously referred to as *The Scottish Play*, it feels cursed. Hwel is usually very inspired, being hit by a whole series of ideas that seem like **Hollywood Comedies** and occasionally by staging that would be more suited to an Andrew Lloyd Webber **Musical**. *See also* Dwarfs; Hollywood Comedies; Musicals; Plays; William Shakespeare; Theatre; Tomjon *and Wyrd Sisters From Terry Pratchett's Discworld.*

Andrew M. Butler

I

Icatessen, Dorcas del (*T*, *D*)

One of the nomes who lives in the store made by **Arnold Bros (est. 1905)**, who is part of the del Icatessen clan – presumably resident in the delicatessen. Like Angalo de **Haberdasheri** he is interested in Outside, and carefully watches how humans behave in order to understand what the place is like. He is also intrigued by electricity and is an inventor. Whilst it is Angalo who works out how to use the truck in which they escape from the store, it is Dorcas who devises the strings and levers that will form a mechanism with which to drive it. The hole in his plan is not remembering to open the garage doors. In the quarry he risks his own life and that of other nomes by accidentally stealing another truck – at first it seems that he has been killed in a collision with a train. He then leads them out of the quarry on Jakeb, the JCB. He also acts as a conversational foil to **Grimma** in the second volume of The **Bromeliad** trilogy. *See also* The Abbot; Arnold Bros (est. 1905); The Bromeliad; Children's Fiction; Grimma; Angalo de Haberdasheri; Masklin *and* Nisodemus.

Andrew M. Butler

'#ifdefDEBUG + "world/enough" + "time"' (*OM*WF*)

A short story written for an anthology of stories written about computers, which first appeared in *Digital Dreams*, edited by David V. Barrett (London: NEL, 1990; Pp. 79–93). Barrett had previously been editor (1985–1989) of *Vector*, the critical journal of the British Science Fiction Association, and has also written on cults, religion and the paranormal. The title of the story mixes computer code with the opening lines of 'To His Coy Mistress' (*c.*1655) by Andrew Marvell (1621–1678) – 'Had we but world enough, and time,/ This coyness, Lady, were no crime' in which the narrator attempts to persuade someone to have sex with him. The imagery of the poem is perhaps more appropriate than the exact subject matter – the lines 'The grave's a fine and private place / But none, I think, do there embrace' are effectively disproved by the action of the story.

Sometime in the future, after the Information Revolution, Darren Thompson is called in to examine an Artificial Reality machine which may have caused the death of its user. The corpse is Dever, a thirty-eight year old computer expert who worked from home for the leading technology firm, Seagem. In the next room is the body of Dever's girlfriend, Susannah, who appears to have died from a complication in her pregnancy some five years earlier. However, Susannah seems to have survived as a virtual presence and Dever may have transformed himself into a computer virus.

This is a darker tale than Pratchett usually writes, with a humanist ending, but **comedy** is provided by the tone of the narration.

Further Reading

Marvell, Andrew. 2005. *The Complete Poems*. Edited by Elizabeth Story Donno. Introduction by Jonathan Bate. London: Penguin.

Andrew M. Butler

Igor (*CJ, FE, TOT, TT, NW, MR, GP, T!*)

Igor is the stereotypical hunchbacked, dwarfen assistant to the mad scientist, although the equivalent character in *Frankenstein* (1931) was called Fritz (Dwight Frye (1899–1943)) in the Universal horror films cycle – and there was Ygor (Bela Lugosi (1882–1956)) in *Son of Frankenstein* (1939) and *The Ghost of Frankenstein* (1942). The **parody** *Young Frankenstein* (1974) directed by Mel Brooks (b.1926) featured Marty Feldman (1933–1982) as Igor, complete with a moveable hunch. There is also an Igor in the **Cosgrove Hall** *Count Duckula* (1988–1993) cartoons, voiced by Jack May (1922–1997), as well as a mention of them in *GO*.

Marty Feldman as Igor in *Young Frankenstein*, 1975.

In **Discworld**, Igors hail from **Überwald**, and are misshapen assemblages of body parts, who exist merely to help and who, on their death, donate what survives of their bodies to others – this being a fairly common occupational hazard. All males are called Igor, and females are called Igorina. Some Igors have banded together to form an agency, We R Igors, to supply assistants where needed. They all have remarkable skills as surgeons, which led Samuel **Vimes** to appoint one to the **City Watch** at the end of *FE*. *See also* City Watch; Cosgrove Hall; Hollywood Films *and* Parody.

Andrew M. Butler

'Incubust' (*OM*WF*)

This first appeared in *The Drabble Project*, edited by Rob Meades and David B. Wake (Birmingham: Beccon Publications, 1988; P. 53). 'Drabbles' are stories 100 words long. Beccon were raising money for the Royal National Institute for the Blind to produce talking books. Other contributors to the volume included Brian Aldiss (b.1925), Isaac Asimov (1920–1992) and David **Langford**. The same editors produced *Drabble II: Double Century* (1990) and Wake with David J. Howe edited a collection of *Doctor Who* themed drabbles in 1993. It is an account of a revenge that fails because an incubus cannot perform on cue. *See also* Audio Books.

Andrew M. Butler

Interesting Times (1994)

The seventeenth novel in the **Discworld** series, first published in the UK in hardback by Gollancz in edition of 43,000 copies with a cover by Josh **Kirby**. The Corgi paperback of 290,000 copies first appeared in 1995, with an alternative black and gold photographic cover available since 2005. It has been translated into Bulgarian, Czech, Dutch, Estonian, Finnish, French, German, Hebrew, Polish, Russian, Serbian, Spanish and Swedish. As an epigraph suggests, the title is inspired by the alleged ancient Chinese curse, 'May you live in interesting times', a saying popularised by its use by Senator Robert F. Kennedy (1925–1968) in an Affirmation Day speech in Cape Town, South Africa, June 7 1966. However, the earliest the phrase has definitely been traced to is the story 'U-Turn', *Astounding Science Fiction* (April 1950), written by British sf writer Eric Frank Russell (1905–1978) under the pseudonym Duncan H. Munro. The phrase is thought to have been used by Swiss psychoanalyst Carl Jung (1875–1961) in an introduction to *The Secret of the Golden Flower* (1931), but it has not been located in the subsequent English translation. *Interesting Times* is part of the **Wizards** sequence and features **Rincewind**. Edward James writes in *The Times Literary Supplement*: 'Pratchett is pro-feminist, pro-pacifist, pro-anarchist, and pro-just being a thoughtful human being without any of that silly heroism which gets people killed' (23 December 1994).

The **Counterweight Continent** wants to be visited by the Great Wizzard, who is assumed to be **Rincewind**. He is magically summoned by the wizards to the **Unseen University** with the aid of their computer, HEX, and blackmailed into going there by **Ridcully**. Once in the Agatean Empire, Rincewind runs into **Cohen the Barbarian** and other elderly heroes, the Silver Horde, who are here to usurp the emperor. The country is in turmoil – for centuries inward looking and static, it is being revolutionised by a *samizdat* tract, *What I Did On My Holidays*. Eventually Rincewind realises this is written by his old companion **Twoflower**. He meets two of Twoflower's daughters at Hunghung, the capital city, and in time Twoflower himself, in prison. They are aided to escape and discover the emperor to be dead and Cohen in his place, but discover that Long Hong is engineering the rising. Rincewind runs away and finds an army of golem-like terracotta warriors – the Red Army – and leads them to battle. Twoflower has a duel with Lord Hung, the latter being killed by the return of the canon earlier swapped for Rincewind when the wizards sent him there; Rincewind ends up in **XXXX** (*see LC*).

This is set in the Discworld's version of **China**, although Twoflower had been carefully established as a Japanese tourist in his appearances in *COM* and *LF*. *See also* Agatean Empire; Bes Pelargic; China; The Luggage; Rincewind; Technology; Twoflower *and* Wizards.

Further Reading

Mendlesohn, Farah. 'Faith and Ethics'. *GOL*, *GOL2*.

Andrew M. Butler

In the Garden of Unearthly Delights see Kirby, Josh

Ironfoundersson, Carrot (*GG*, 'TOC', *MAA*, *FOC*, *J*, *FE*, *TOT*, *NW*, *TT*, *T!*)

Orphaned as a child, Carrot was adopted and raised by **dwarfs** in Copperhead. Because of this, Carrot is accepted as a dwarf, despite really being a human over six feet tall. Carrot has a picturesque physique: tall, red hair, broad shoulders and well-developed muscles. He also has a birthmark in the shape of a crown and carries a decidedly non-magical sword (which does happen to be very sharp).

Between the birthmark and the sword, it is widely believed and accepted (even by Patrician **Vetinari**) that Carrot is actually the long lost king of **Ankh-Morpork**. Carrot, however, has no interest in being royalty and is happy with his job in the **City Watch**, where he is currently the Captain (second in command under Commander **Vimes**). Carrot rose through the ranks of the watch quickly, being promoted to Captain straight from Corporal by Vetinari himself, with whom Carrot seems to have formed a friendship.

Carrot is a very honest, straight-laced young man. Being a dwarf (or sort of one), he has no concept of irony, and instead takes everything anybody says at face value. He also believes that everybody really wants to do the right thing, and if given the chance, will do so. Because of this, he has an almost supernatural ability to get people to do the right thing just by talking to them.

Carrot tends to universally like (and be universally liked by) everybody he meets, purely due to his attitude and positive outlook on life (a rarity in Ankh-Morpork). He has fostered a fierce admiration for Commander Vimes and the way he runs the Watch. He has also fallen in love with Sergeant Angua von **Überwald**. Though there are drawbacks in dating a werewolf, he has fully accepted her situation and sees no problem with their relationship. *See also* Frederick Colon; Coming of Age; Cuddy; Detective and Noir Fiction; Detritus; Dwarfs; Igor; Carrot Ironfoundersson; Cheery Littlebottom; Nobby Nobbs; Racism; Angua von Überwald; Patrician Vetinari and Samuel Vimes.

Further Reading

Brown, James. 'Believing is Seeing'. *GOL2*.
James, Edward. 'The City Watch'. *GOL*, *GOL2*.

Mark D. Thomas

J

Jingo (1997)

The twenty-first **Discworld** novel, the last to be published by Gollancz until *LH* (*see* **Publishers**) and featuring the **City Watch**. The Gollancz edition was 120,000 copies, and featured a Josh **Kirby** cover; the Corgi edition of 308,000 copies appeared in 1998 with an alternative black and gold photographic cover available since 2006. It has been translated into Bulgarian, Czech, Dutch, Estonian, Finnish, French, German, Polish,

Russian, Spanish and Swedish. Jingo relates to jingoism, excessive patriotism, deriving from a 1878 **music hall** song by G.W. Hunt (1834–1904) sung by the Great (Gilbert Hastings) Macdermott (1845–1901): 'We don't want to fight,/But by Jingo if we do,/We've got the ships,/We've got the men,/And got the money too./We've fought the Bear before,/And while we're Britons true,/The Russians shall not have Constantinople'. The lines are alluded to by Lord Selachii in the first few pages, and then reversed by Patrician **Vetinari**. Peter Donaldson writes that: 'Pratchett's invention remains undiminished, his wit as sharp as ever, as he sets war and nationalism firmly in his sights' (*The Bookseller* 19 September 1997).

A lost island, Leshp (last seen in *M*), shows up between **Ankh-Morpork** and Klatch, and becomes a bone of contention between the two powers. It just so happens that Klatchian Prince Khufurah is in town, in a parade led by Samuel **Vimes**. Vimes spots a would-be assassin trying to kill the prince, and begins to investigate the crime. At first it seems to be the work of a lone assassin, Ossie Brunt, who has killed himself, but it is clear that he was not working alone. There was a second bowman, Snowy Slopes, who has also been killed. It seems that the evidence points to the conspiracy being Klatchian, but it is not clear who is planting evidence to make it look that way. Lord Rust usurps the Patrician and takes the city to war. Meanwhile Sam and Carrot **Ironfoundersson**, sacked from the Watch, have gone after 71-Hour Ahmed and find him to be a more civilised person than they had assumed. On the eve of battle, Vetinari surrenders his claim to Leshp, and he is tried for treason; however the island has gone. Vimes is made a duke and a statue is erected to Stoneface.

Klatch is a **parody** version of **Arabic Society**, and the war invokes the first Gulf War (*see OYCSM*), as well as the First World War (white feathers, jingoism and football matches) and the Falklands. The assassination attempt is played like *JFK* (1991), complete with lone gunman, a book depository, a grassy knoll (well, a Snowy Slope), a magic bullet and conspiracies galore. *See also* Arabic Society; City Watch; Klatch; Politics; Leonard de Quirm; Patrician Vetinari; Samuel Vimes *and* War.

Further Reading

James, Edward. 'The City Watch'. *GOL*, *GOL2*.
Mendlesohn, Farah. 'Faith and Ethics'. *GOL*, *GOL2*.

Andrew M. Butler

Johnny and the Bomb (1996)

The third book in the **Johnny Maxwell Trilogy**, set in **Blackbury** during the Second World War and the mid nineties and is a **Science Fiction** novel aimed at children. The first edition was published by Doubleday with a cover by Larry Rostant in an edition of 24,900, and the Corgi paperback (1997) of 105,000 had artwork by John Avon. Post 2004 editions have new artwork attributed to http://www.hen.uk.com. The novel has been translated into Bulgarian, Czech, Danish, Estonian, French, German, Italian, Polish, Romanian, Russian, Serbian, Slovakian, Swedish, Thai and Turkish. It was shortlisted for 1996 Smarties Prize. This novel begins with an acknowledgement to the Meteorological Office, the Royal Mint and Bernard **Pearson** for help with research, and is divided into named chapters. It was filmed by the BBC and broadcast in 2006 (*see next entry*). Norman Stone in the *Sunday Telegraph* called it: 'a brilliant, wonderful book' (31 March 1996).

Blackbury, May 21, 1941, Paradise Street has been bombed, and Mrs **Tachyon** is rooting around in the wreckage. In 1996, Johnny is worried, and having dreams about the Second World War bombing raids; he knows Paradise Street was bombed. He, **Yo-Less**, Wobbler and Big Mac find an injured Mrs Tachyon and phone an ambulance for her. Johnny contacts **Kirsty** – now calling herself Kasandra – and they look at Tachyon's shopping trolley, discovering that it is some kind of time machine. The five of them travel back in time to May 1941, and accidentally leave Wobbler behind. Back in 1996 Johnny meets a man who has been following him in a big, black car; it is a billionaire version of Wobbler who had set up a burger business in 1952 and invested in VCRs and so forth. Their interference in the past has led Wobbler's grandfather to be killed in the bombing raid, so Johnny decides they need to go back in time again and rescue their version of Wobbler. The air raid siren has broken, the motorcycle back-up will not start, but Johnny manages to help his grandfather raise the alarm. Back in the present day, things are subtly different, but no one save Johnny and Kirsty notices the difference. Mrs Tachyon disappears from hospital and travels back to 1903.

Like all the Johnny Maxwell books, this deals with war and its consequences. It also exposes how far attitudes have or have not changed. Yo-less is called Sambo by a shopkeeper, much to his annoyance, and this seems to be a rare experience of **racism** for him. Kirsty, always sensitive to **sexism**, seems to make it worse. Kirsty acknowledges her position as token female, whilst still being supremely competent at activities and now being politically engaged. *See also* Awards; Blackbury; Children's Fiction; Coming of Age; *Johnny and the Bomb* (Television Adaptation); Johnny Maxwell Trilogy; Kirsty; Johnny Maxwell; Racism; Science Fiction; Sexism; Mrs Tachyon; War *and* Yo-Less.

Further Reading

Baldry, Cherith. 'The Children's Books'. *GOL*, *GOL2*.

Hunt, Peter. 2001. 'Terry Pratchett'. Pp. 86–121 in Peter Hunt and Millicent Lenz, *Alternative Worlds in Fantasy Fiction*. London: Continuum.

Andrew M. Butler

Johnny and the Bomb (Television Adaptation) (2006)

Director: Dermot Boyd. Producer: Peter Tabern. Executive Producer: Jon East. Writer: Peter Tabern. Cinematography: Nick Dance. Cast: Mrs. Tachyon: Zoë Wanamaker; Bigmac: Scott Kay; Yo-Less: Lucien Laviscount; Johnny Maxwell: George MacKay; Wobbler: Kyle Herbert; Tom Maxwell: Frank Finlay; Kirsty: Jazmine Franks; Councillor Seeley: John Henshaw; Sergeant Bourke: Paul Copley; Sir Walter: Keith Barron; Young Tom Maxwell: Matthew Beard. TV version: 3 × 45 minute episodes broadcast 15–29 January 2006, BBC1. DVD version: 120 minutes; Region 2 Warner Vision International (ASIN: B000HRLWS0), Certificate PG.

A live action version of the third **Johnny Maxwell Trilogy** novel made by Childsplay for the BBC. Childsplay specialise in drama for children, often with a **Fantasy** or **Science Fiction** element to it and often based on novels. This adaptation is divided into three episodes, 'Mrs Tachyon and the Bags of Time', 'The Butterfly Effect' and 'Deja Voodoo'. The serial is set in **Blackbury**, which is meant to be close to Manchester in the context of the programme, but filming took place in South Wales.

This adaptation largely stays faithful to the original novel but fleshes it out a bit. In the book Tom the grandfather is on his mother's side of the family (the three generations of Maxwells being Arthur, Peter and Johnny, see *JD*), whereas here Tom is on his father's side of the family. Wobbler changes his name to Sir Walter rather than to Sir John, the name in the book presumably intended to fool the reader into thinking that he is actually a version of Johnny **Maxwell**. The Blackbury Phantom motorcycle becomes a bicycle. The scenes set back in 1941 are longer and more involved, and here it is Johnny Maxwell who has not been born rather than Wobbler. He gets to meet his paternal grandmother, Rose – possibly meeting the maternal version would have seemed too oedipal.

In the first episode Johnny tries to have a conversation with his mother about changing history, and asks whether if they could go back in time to the point his parents split up, they could change things. Presumably it is at the back of his mind that he can fix his broken family. However, his mother points out that the failure took much longer than one day, and it would be impossible to change it. Their inadvertent changing of the past – and their initially failing attempts to correct it – mean that nothing has actually changed by the end of the serial, although he and his grandfather are a bit closer.

Johnny attempts to convince the Maxwells that there is going to be a bombing raid by showing them a box of his grandfather's mementos, including a photograph that has not yet been taken, and the photograph of Rose and Mrs **Tachyon**. In the book, it was by Johnny telling the air raid watchmen what the next card to be picked from a deck was. Bigmac gives young Tom the gun from the grandfather's box, and the grandfather had said that it had been given to him, but the gun is visible on the table in the future when Johnny has given the box back to him. Before they depart from 1941, Johnny promises Tom and Rose he will see them again – Rose apparently said that Johnny being born was the promise kept (she died when he was a baby) and Tom sees that Johnny, **Yo-Less**, **Kirsty**, BigMac and Wobbler are in the photograph of the survivors of the bombed-out Paradise Street. In the book there is a more shared sense of the connection between grandfather and grandson.

Dermot Boyd had worked on episodes of soaps *The Bill* and *EastEnders*, as well as the BBC family dramas *Ballykissangel* (1996–2001) and *Two Thousand Acres of Sky* (2001–2003). He had also worked on the adaptation of *Feather Boy* (2004) from the novel by Nicky Singer (b.1956). Peter Tabern was also the adapter and producer of *Feather Boy*, made by Childsplay, which he runs. Other productions include *Children of the New Forest* (1998), *Lifeforce* (2000) and *Stig of the Dump* (2002). Cinematographer Nick Dance had worked on *Children of the New Forest*, *Lifeforce*, *Footballers' Wives* (2002–) and *Bodies* (2004–).

Zöe Wanamaker (b.1949) was born in America but moved to Britain with her blacklisted father, Sam Wanamaker (1919–1993). Best known for her appearance in the BBC sitcom *My Family* (2000–), she also played Clarice Groan in the BBC adaptation of *Gormenghast* (2000), Madame Hooch in *Harry Potter and the Philosopher's Stone* (2001) and Martha in *Five Children and It* (2004). She often plays characters with a slight tinge of madness or mania. Frank Finlay (b.1926) is a British character actor, who worked for many years at the National Theatre in London, including playing Iago to Laurence Olivier's (1907–1989) eponymous *Othello*. He played the title role in *Casanova* (1971) by Dennis Potter (1935–1994) and was Porthos in *The Three Musketeers* (1973), *The Four Musketeers* (1974) and *The Return of the Musketeers* (1989). Keith Barron (b.1936) was born in Yorkshire and has mainly worked in television, coming to prominence in *Stand Up, Nigel Barton* (1965) and *Vote, Vote, Vote for Nigel Barton* (1965) by Dennis Potter. He played Terence Chesterton in ITV LWT sitcom *Holding the Fort* (1980–1982) and starred as David Pearce in the ITV Yorkshire sitcom *Duty Free* (1984–1986). George MacKay (b.1992) previously appeared in *Peter Pan* (2003) as Curly and in *The Thief Lord* (2006) as Riccio, so was used to working with special effects.

The earlier adaptation of a Johnny Maxwell novel, *JD*, was let down by an uncertainty of tone, whereas Childsplay's experience with directing children's drama, particularly in the fantasy genre, allows a more even tone. The book is slightly updated, from 1996 to 2006, which would put the grandfather at about eighty – which is after all Frank Finlay's age – and includes mobile phones and a Harry Potter reference. The only wrong note is perhaps Kirsty's **feminism**, which needed to be handled a little more subtly, although her use of Judo to get them out of tricky circumstances and Johnny's apology for it is a nice running joke. The care of the production is evident from the car in the 1940s crashing into a water trough engraved with the name of Alderman Thomas Bowler, a civic amenity mentioned in the novel of *JD*. *See also* Blackbury; Children's Fiction; Johnny Maxwell Trilogy; Kirsty; Johnny Maxwell; Racism; Sexism; Mrs Tachyon; Television Adaptations; War *and* Yo-Less.

Andrew M. Butler

Johnny and the Dead (1993)

The second book in the **Johnny Maxwell Trilogy** is set in **Blackbury** during October 1993 and is a **Science Fiction** novel aimed at children. The first, Doubleday, edition of 22,400, had cover art by John Avon, and the Corgi edition of 122,500 copies appeared in 1994. In 1995 there was a tie-in cover to mark the **television adaptation** (*see next entry*) and from 2004 the cover has been artwork credited to http://www.hen.uk.com. *JD* has been translated into Bulgarian, Czech, Danish, Dutch, Estonian, French, German, Italian, Japanese, Polish, Russian, Serbian, Slovak, Swedish, Thai, Turkish and Welsh. It was winner of the 1993 Writers' Guild of Great Britain Best Children's Book Award and shortlisted for the 1994 Carnegie Medal. The novel begins with an author's note admitting to bending some of the **history** – and dedicating the book to all the Tommy Atkinses. It is divided into chapters, and was filmed in 1995 (*see next entry*). Martin Taylor labelled it: 'A good story, achingly well written, filled with characters who step off the page and live with you. It also makes you look again at the way we live today' (*Vector* 174 (1993)).

Twelve-year-old Johnny **Maxwell** is now living with his grandfather, and hanging out with his friends **Yo-Less**, Bigmac and Wobbler at the Neil Armstrong Mall and the graveyard in **Blackbury**. One day at the cemetery he begins to see the ghosts of the dead people, including Alderman Thomas Bowler, William Stickers, a revolutionary, and Sylvia Liberty, a suffragette. The graveyard is under threat, having been sold by the council as building land to United Amalagamated [*sic*] Consolidated Holdings for fifteen pence. Johnny decides that he will campaign to save the graveyard for his new dead friends. Meanwhile he has to visit his grandmother in Sunshine Acres, a care home, and discovers that Tommy Atkins, sole survivor of the Blackbury Pals regiment from the First World War, has died. The ghosts of the other pals collect him from the cremation, where Johnny meets Ronald Atterbury from the British Legion. Atterbury agrees to attend the open public meeting held by United Amalagamated and the council, to protest the sale of the cemetery. The cemetery is saved, but the ghosts abandon it, having discovered they are not tied down to this location.

The cemetery sale is inspired by the sale of Hanwell, Finchley and Mill Hill graveyards for fifteen pence by the council in Westminster during the 1980s. The Pals Battalions were attempts, before conscription, to sign up whole communities of men to fight in the First World War on the principle that putting friends together in the trenches would boost morale. When communities were decimated in battle, it had the reverse effect. The war theme is picked up in *JB*. In the end, the cemetery is a place for the living to remember the dead, as the dead have left the place behind by the time Johnny has saved it. *See also* Awards; Blackbury; Children's Fiction; Coming of Age; Dead People; *Johnny and the Dead* (Television Adaptation); Johnny Maxwell Trilogy; Johnny Maxwell; Science Fiction; Mrs Tachyon; War *and* Yo-Less.

Further Reading

Baldry, Cherith. 'The Children's Books'. *GOL*, *GOL2*.
Hunt, Peter. 2001. 'Terry Pratchett'. Pp. 86–121 in Peter Hunt and Millicent Lenz, *Alternative Worlds in Fantasy Fiction*. London: Continuum.

Andrew M. Butler

Johnny and the Dead (Television Adaptation) (1995)

Director: Gerald Fox. Producers: Gerald Fox and Peter Pearson. Executive Producer: Melvyn Bragg. Writers: Gerald Fox, Terry Pratchett and Lindsey Jenkins. Cast: Johnny Maxwell: Andrew Falvey; Alderman Bowler: George Baker; William Stickers: Brian Blessed; Mrs. Sylvia Liberty/Miss Liberty: Jane Lapotaire; Yo-Less: Jotham Annan; Bigmac: Paul Child; Mr. Antonio Vicenti: John Grillo; Mr Soloman Einstein: Harry Landis; Stanley 'Wrong Way' Roundway: Neil Morphew; Wobbler: Charlie Watts; James Bowler: Ray Lonnen; Eric Grimm: Barrie Houghton; Fletcher: Geoffrey Whitehead. TV version: 4 × 30 minute episodes broadcast 4 April-25 April 1995, ITV. Video version: Warner Vision International, 94 minutes (ASIN: B00004CQNX). Certificate U.

A live action version of *JD*, which remains fairly faithful to the original narrative. It was produced by London Weekend Television, which was responsible for weekend broadcasting for the London franchise of the British commercial-driven channel ITV from August 2, 1968 to October 27, 2002, when merging of franchises meant the channel as a whole was to be subsumed into one unit as ITV1. LWT was also a production company, though, as *JD* was broadcast on Tuesdays during the children's programming slot.

The major differences between the original and the adaptation are the building up of the roles of the developer, a councillor with a conscience and the corrupt and hypocritical council leader, Miss Liberty. With the doubled casting of Jane Lapotaire, there is the suggestion that Miss Liberty is a descendent of Mrs Liberty, the suffragette, which perhaps offers a critique of **feminism** as the portrait of the councillor is hardly flattering. The naming of the developer (who is here part of United Amalgamated Consolidated Holdings) as James Bowler suggests a rather less public-minded descendent for the Alderman. We see more of the scenes of the planning of the development, taking us away from Johnny **Maxwell** and the various **dead people**. At the end of the narrative, after the dead have departed – Stickers with **Death**, singing the Internationale, Einstein and Fletcher on a homemade device, Vicenti in a cloud of dove feathers and Bowler and Liberty in a reborn car – Johnny goes back to the graveyard for one last time, only to find that the dead have missed him, and have returned. This rather undercuts what had been the message of the book, about the need for the living to remember and the dead to forget.

George Baker (left) and Andrew Falvey in the television adaptation of *Johnny and the Dead*, 1994.

There is also a difference in tone. Whilst the book is able to balance the everyday life of Johnny with the fantasy of the dead, here there is a sense of the uncomfortable whimsical potential of **Fantasy**. There is the sense that some of the adult actors are not as comfortable as they might be in interacting with the children, and whilst the tone is more even where it is just the dead, there is a sense of something being held in check. The appearance of the dead is frequently heralded by the horror cliché of dry ice. The Alderman is taught to break-dance by Johnny, to the character's embarrassment, although he is keen to teach it to the other dead. This leads to a choreographed dance of the dead, and this is turn is echoed in the Halloween dance. The numerous policemen and the two developer-hired thugs are comic relief. The book is able to maintain an ambiguity as to whether the dead have been seen by Johnny – although it is clear in the end he has– here it is clear he has.

Johnny himself is fine, but then he is the cipher around which the action takes place, even though he is the narrator for the series. However, Wobbler and BigMac are undeveloped; Wobbler is simply fat and cowardly, and BigMac's skinhead tendencies are not mentioned. Most developed is **Yo-Less**, who is usually seen in a smart suit at odds with the un-uniformed appearance of the other school children. His guise of Baron Samedi for Halloween is declared to be not racist, as it was his idea (*see* **Racism**).

The children are played by previously unknown actors, with Andrew Falvey and the others largely just going on to play a few bit parts in television series. Most of the adult roles were played by much more established stars. George Baker (b.1931) has appeared in films since the early 1950s, as well as in many television programmes, and is best known now for the role of Detective Chief Inspector Reg Wexford in the adaptations (1988–) of novels by Ruth Rendell (b.1930). Brian Blessed (b.1937) is a large, loud, usually bearded character actor, mostly playing boisterous roles and perfectly cast as Prince Vultan in *Flash Gordon* (1980) and as Richard IV in *The Blackadder* (1983). Whilst he does have the chance to shine as the quasi-Marxist activist, his performance is comparatively subdued and held in check.

Director Gerald Fox has largely worked in the medium of documentary, most notably in the LWT arts strand *The South Bank Show* (1978–), edited by arts commentator and novelist Melvyn Bragg (b.1939) who was also executive producer of *JD*. Peter Pearson had been a location manager, production manager and producer on the arts show. This documentary background may explain the uneven tone of the production. Lindsey Jenkins has also worked as a journalist and a script reader. The adaptation of another volume in the **Johnny Maxwell Trilogy**, *JB*, was a much more satisfying experience. *See also* Blackbury; Children's Fiction; Coming of Age; Johnny Maxwell Trilogy; Johnny Maxwell; Racism; Sexism; War *and* Yo-Less.

Andrew M. Butler

Johnny Maxwell Trilogy (*OYCSM*, *JD*, *JB*)

A non-**Discworld** trilogy, aimed at the **children's fiction** market, featuring the adventures of Johnny **Maxwell** and his friends. Each of the books confronts ethical issues, and explores the theme of **war** in differing ways. Doubleday issued an omnibus of all three titles in 1999 with a cover by John Avon, and there was a slipcase of paperbacks in 2005. *See also* Blackbury; Children's Fiction; Coming of Age; *Johnny and the Bomb*

(Television Adaptation); *Johnny and the Dead* (Television Adaptation); Kirsty; Johnny Maxwell; Racism; Science Fiction; Sexism; Mrs Tachyon; War *and* Yo-Less.

Andrew M. Butler

Jolliffe, Gray

Cartoonist and illustrator of Pratchett's *UC*.

Jolliffe is most famed for his *Wicked Willie* series of cartoons that were written by Peter Mayle (better known for *A Year in Provence* (1989) and its sequels). Wicked Willie was a cartoon penis, with an eye, a mouth, a nose and arms, which enabled Jolliffe and Mayle to make jokes about sex, sometimes but not always at the expense of men. Besides various books – including *Man's Best Friend* (1984), *Wicked Willie's Low-Down on Men: The Essential Guide to Male Misbehaviour* (1987) and *Willie's Away!* (1988) – he has appeared on t-shirts, mugs, cards and, of course, boxer shorts. Jolliffe also worked for children, illustrating books such as *Trevor Trunk* (1989), *Willie Woof* (1989) and *Charlie Oink* (1989), all with Roger Hargreaves (1935–1988) who wrote the Mr Men books, and writing the script for *Stainless Steel and the Star Spies* (1981), a one-off comedy for children with Deryck Guyler (1914–1999). He also provided the cartoons of suspects doodled by Eddie Shoestring in the television series *Shoestring* (1979–1980). Perhaps most significantly Jolliffe was the illustrator of *How to Be a Happy Cat* (1987) by Charles Platt (b.1945).

Jolliffe's style is of a basic black ink line with a fairly simple block of colour within it. There is no sense of any attempt at photorealism. The lettering for the captions tends to be Letraset. *See also* Cats.

Further Reading

Jolliffe, Gray (Text by Peter Mayle). 1984. *Man's Best Friend Introducing Wicked Willie in the Title Role*. London: Pan.

———. 1987. *Wicked Willie's Low-Down on Men: The Essential Guide to Male Misbehaviour*. London: Pan.

———. 1998. *Willie's Away!* London: Pan.

Mayle, Peter. 1989. *A Year in Provence*. London: Hamish Hamilton.

Platt, Charles. 1986. *How to be a Happy Cat*. London: Gollancz.

Andrew M. Butler

The Josh Kirby Discworld Portfolio see Kirby, Josh

The Josh Kirby Poster Book see Kirby, Josh

K

Kidby, Paul (b. 1964)

The artist who took over doing the covers of the **Discworld** novels after the death of Josh **Kirby** and who had also illustrated *LH* and two of the Discworld **maps**.

Kidby was born in Middlesex, England and started drawing at a very early age, going freelance in 1986. His influences include Dutch painters such as Rembrandt Harmenszoon van Rijn (*c.* 1606–1669) and Johannes Vermeer (1632–1675), and the Pre-Raphaelites of the nineteenth century and twentieth-century fantasy artists who designed books and album covers, such as Roger Dean (b. 1944), Rodney Matthews (b. 1945) and Patrick Woodroffe (b. 1940). Kidby worked for various magazines, such as *Gamesmaster*, *Total!* and *Computer Format*, as well as producing artwork for **Computer Games**.

Photo of Paul Kidby working on a picture of Maurice, complete with educated rodents.

Kidby discovered the Discworld in 1993, and started producing portraits of many of the characters contained within the novels. These were gathered together in *The Pratchett Portfolio* (1996), with text by Pratchett. He worked on the various Discworld **Diaries** with Stephen **Briggs**, beginning with the 1998 *Unseen University Diary*. Because of the nature of the project, which did not quite fit the profile of the publisher, Kidby was only given a brief period of time in which to produce the artwork.

He was then commissioned to illustrate *TGL* (1998), producing the fold-out picture of **Lancre**, although not the line drawings, which were produced by Stephen Briggs. He also produced the black and white artwork and fold-out map for *DD* (1999), for which Pratchett wrote the text. He produced the covers for the *SOD* books, the first (1999) featuring a **parody** of An Experiment on a Bird in an Air Pump (1768) by the English artist Joseph Wright (1734–1797), known for his use of unusual artificial lighting conditions and landscapes. He also produced the covers for *SODII* (2002) and *SODIII* (2005). In this period he illustrated *NOC* (1999).

He became the artist of choice for the Discworld fable *LH* (2001), which, like *E* (1990), was an illustrated story. It included full page illustrations and double page spreads, as well as smaller pictures in the text. Unlike *E*, which dropped the pictures when going to mass market paperback, this added sixteen additional pages of illustrations and had a large format paperback (2002). The new cover features **Rincewind** aping the positioning of the figure in *The Scream* (1893) by Edvard Munch (1863–1944), although it should be noted that in the original the figure is blocking his ears from the scream, rather than producing it – in Kidby's version it is definitely Rincewind screaming.

By then he was the successor to Josh Kirby on the Discworld novels proper, beginning with *NW* (2002). This was a double cover, with his illustration on the front, and Rembrandt's *Night Watch* (1642) on the back, of which it is a parody. *MR* (2003) also offered a parody, this time of the photograph *Raising the Flag on Iwo Jima* (1945) taken by Joe Rosenthal (1911–2006). Kirby's covers were busy, full of grotesque figures and suggesting action, whereas Kidby's are either much quieter depictions of a smaller group of characters, or, as has been noted, parodies of existing pictures. They are no more realistic than Kirby's were, but perhaps are more straight-forwardly in the British **fantasy** painting tradition, and are less manic. His work has also appeared in Discworld *calendars* and a second collection, *The Art of Discworld* (2004). Prints, Christmas cards and other **merchandising**, including the diaries, are available from his Website and mail order business, PJSM Prints. *See also* Stephen Briggs; Calendars; Computer Games; Diaries; *The Discworld Almanak*; Josh Kirby; Maps; Merchandising *and Nanny Ogg's Cookbook.*

Further Reading

Pratchett, Terry. 1996. Illustrated by Paul Kidby. *The Pratchett Portfolio*. London: Gollancz.
Pratchett, Terry. 2005. Illustrated by Paul Kidby. *The Art of Discworld*. London: Gollancz.
Paul Kidby's official homepage: http://www.paulkidby.com/
Paul Kidby's personal homepage: http://www.paulkidby.net/

Andrew M. Butler

Kirby, Josh (1928–2001)

Josh Kirby's distinctive covers for the paperback *COM* and *LF* established him as *the* artist of **Discworld**. He went on to paint jacket art for most 'main sequence' Discworld novels and numerous spin-offs, until his death on 23 October 2001.

TT was the last Pratchett novel for which Kirby painted the cover. His last completed cover appeared on a spin-off **quiz book**, David **Langford**'s *The Wyrdest Link* (2002). Additionally, his artwork appeared on The **Bromeliad** trilogy, on Discworld-era reissues of *CP*, *DSS* and *Str*, and on both original and revised editions of *DC*. Some paperbacks differ from the hardbacks: Kirby added an **Ankh-Morpork** city background to the original *MAA*, and produced new interpretations for *IT* and *LL*.

His artwork also appeared on non-literary spin-offs, including three Discworld computer **Games**, the 1994 *From the Discworld* music CD (*see* Dave **Greenslade**), the 1995 poster *Rincewind and the Luggage* and Discworld **calendars** for 1999 and 2001.

To evoke the comic chaos of Discworld, Kirby used lavishly rich colours and crowded compositions reminiscent of the artists whom he regarded as major influences: Hieronymus Bosch (*c.*1450–1516), whose famous *Garden of Earthly Delights* was echoed in Kirby's art collection *In the Garden of Unearthly Delights*; Pieter Bruegel the Elder (*c.*1525–1569), whose depiction of the Tower of Babel inspired Kirby's monumental movie poster for Monty Python's *Life of Brian* (1979); and the muralist Frank Brangwyn (1867–1956).

The cover of *COM*, set in that low dive **The Broken Drum**, is more realistic than the exuberant interpretations that followed. One oddity is that **Twoflower** the archetypal tourist appears with four literal eyes: Pratchett described him as 'four-eyed', intending this as schoolboy slang for 'wearing glasses'.

Later Discworld covers were usually constructed as what Kirby called an action tableau. A central image loosely suggested by the novel – preferably a headlong chase – is surrounded by further characters, props, and fragments of scenery that caught the artist's fancy. Thus the original *LF* painting shows Rincewind and other characters clinging to the Luggage as it careers through a swirling cloudscape, with the Four Horsemen of the Apocalypse in distant pursuit. Outraged birds, axe-wielding **trolls** and architectural whimsies frame this energetic action. No such tableau appears in *LF*: 'I like to bring small scenes together if I can't find a single incident that represents the whole book,' said Kirby in *A Cosmic Cornucopia* (13).

His comic-fantasy stereotypes, or Platonic ideals, sometimes clashed with Pratchett's twisting of cliché. Women tend to be more voluptuous and scantily clad than their prose descriptions. Redoubtable witch Granny Weatherwax, specifically described as uncronelike and wart-free, has a hook nose and warts on the *ER* cover. Her appearance was adjusted for *WS*.

The space/time travelogue in the short novel *E* was devised as an opportunity for Kirby to produce sumptuous colour spreads of Discworld itself, its creation, its equivalents of Aztecs and the Trojan War, its demon-infested Hell and the artist's favourite character **Death**. Without this riot of artistic energy, the later unillustrated paperback seems sadly thin.

Occasionally Kirby was asked to redo Discworld covers. His fondness for the action tableau made a careering wheelchair laden with **wizards** the centrepiece of his initial *MP* painting; at Pratchett's request, the final version emphasised movie elements and marginalised that wheelchair. An interior view of the unexpected submarine in *J* was rejected for giving away this plot element. 'Lost' covers are collected in *A Cosmic Cornucopia*.

The popularity of these Discworld paintings made Kirby, to some extent, a victim of his own success. By publishing tradition he received a one-off fee for each cover. Most books which continue to sell well are regularly repackaged, but Kirby's covers were reckoned to be definitive (although later printing of the early Discworld novels now have new covers). Fortunately, his Discworld notoriety generated further commissions, and he painted covers for a variety of comic fantasies by Esther Friesner (b.1951), Craig Shaw Gardner (b.1949), Tom Holt (b.1961), Dan McGirt (b.1967), Christopher Moore (b.1957) and Robert Rankin (b.1949).

As Ronald Kirby, his birth name, he studied from 1943 to 1949 at the Liverpool City School of Art. There he acquired the nickname Josh – supposedly, he painted like Sir Joshua Reynolds (1723–1792). After a period of producing film posters, he began his long freelance career as a cover artist with a painting for the minor **Science Fiction** novel *Cee-Tee Man* (1955) by Dan Morgan (b.1925). Better remembered is his artwork for the first UK paperback of *Moonraker* (1956) by Ian Fleming (1908–1964).

Kirby worked slowly and meticulously, usually with oil paint. From the outset he had a strong taste for the fantastic and surreal. His own official checklist of his paintings omits almost all realistic work. But he loved to paint Science Fiction scenes with bulging, almost organic domes and spaceships, like his 1969 Corgi cover for *The City and the Stars* by Arthur C. Clarke (b.1917), or swashbuckling swordsmen like John Carter of Barsoom created by Edgar Rice Burroughs (1875–1950), or images both witty and macabre, such as his many comic-sinister jackets for horror and suspense anthologies edited by (in fact, ghost-edited for) Alfred Hitchcock (1899–1980).

After Discworld, Kirby's favourite cover assignments were for Robert Silverberg's 'Majipoor' science fantasies, set against a vast planetary backdrop which Kirby rendered impressionistically. Dreamy pastels predominate, though some compositions vibrate with an energy surprisingly different from his Discworld extravaganzas.

Another of Kirby's variant styles was influenced by Guiseppe Arcimboldo (1527–1593), who constructed surreal human faces from mosaics of animals or vegetables. Kirby's cover for *The Illustrated Man* (Corgi, 1963) by Ray Bradbury (b.1920) shows the title character glowing with tattooed scenes from the stories he tells. In similar vein, Kirby assembled Alfred Hitchcock's face from images of horror and filled Terry Pratchett's with ghostly Discworld characters – as seen on the first edition of Terry Pratchett: *Guilty of Literature*.

An exhibition, 'Out of this World: The Art of Josh Kirby' was held at the Walker Gallery, Liverpool, UK, June 15 to September 30, 2007. No catalogue was produced for this, but reprint collections were available for sale. *See also* Calendars *and* Paul Kidby.

Further Reading

Kirby, Josh. 1990. *The Josh Kirby Poster Book*. London: Corgi.

———. 1991. *In the Garden of Unearthly Delights*. Text by Nigel Suckling. Limpsfield, Surrey, UK: Paper Tiger.

———. 1993. *The Josh Kirby Discworld Portfolio*. Limpsfield, Surrey, UK: Paper Tiger.

———. 1999. *A Cosmic Cornucopia*. Text by David Langford. London: Paper Tiger.

Langford, David. 'Book Covers by Josh Kirby'. [checklist prepared with Kirby]: http://ansible.co.uk/misc/joshlist.html

David Langford

Kirsty (*OYCSM*, *JB*)

Thirteen-year-old Kirsty would rather be known as Sigourney, after Sigourney Weaver (b.1949) who is best known for her appearances as Ellen Ripley in *Alien* (1979) and its sequels. She later experiments with other names, such as Kimberly, Klytemnestra and Kasandra, some of which she has abandoned because they made her sound like a hairdresser. At no point is her surname given. She lives in a nice area of **Blackbury**, Tyne Crescent, and is first seen by Johnny **Maxwell** in J&J Software in the Neil Armstrong Mall. She is good at everything she tries, including chess, rifle shooting and various sports, and she has a bedroom full of trophies, ribbons and certificates. At first it is hard to convince her that she must not kill the aliens – she plays to win. She does not seem to be around during the encounter with the dead, having in the mean time gotten into political causes. However, she travels back in time with the gang and witnesses **racism** against **Yo-Less**, and is unwittingly racist herself. She has learnt how to use **sexism** to her advantage, though. At first it appears that she has forgotten the time travelling, but her memory is jogged when she finds a pickled onion in her pocket from the factory that was destroyed in the Blackbury Blitz. *See also* Blackbury; Children's Fiction; Coming of

Kirsty

Age; Feminism; *Johnny and the Bomb* (Television Adaptation); Johnny Maxwell Trilogy; Racism *and* Sexism.

Further Reading

Baldry, Cherith. 'The Children's Books'. *GOL*, *GOL2*.
Hunt, Peter. 2001. 'Terry Pratchett'. Pp. 86–121 in Peter Hunt and Millicent Lenz, *Alternative Worlds in Fantasy Fiction*. London: Continuum.

Andrew M. Butler

Klatch

The name of both a country and a continent on the **Discworld**. The continent consists of **Djelibeybi**, **Ephebe**, Hersheba (*SG*), Howondaland (*RM*), Klatch, **Omnia**, the Tezuman Empire (*E*) and **Tsort**. It is separated from the Sto Plains by the Circle Sea.

The country of Klatch has its capital at Al Khali, which stands on the river Tsort, and is ruled by a Seriph – at the time of *S* it was Creosote; in *J* the Princes Cadram and Khufurah visit **Ankh-Morpork**. The society of Klatch is very advanced in terms of culture, science and **technology**, though they are viewed by the rest of the world as savage and backward – curse words are often followed by the expression, 'Pardon my Klatchian'. There is an obvious rivalry between Klatch and Ankh-Morpork, their closest trading partner – their principle export is coffee (*see* **Drink**). This relationship nearly boiled over in the struggle over the ownership of the island of Leshp (*J*). They have their own version of the **City Watch**, run by 71-Hour Ahmed, and an army, the Klatchian Foreign Legion (*RM*).

The culture of Klatch and the reaction of characters to it allow Pratchett to parody representations of **Arabic Societies**, especially the Ottoman Empire. *See also* Arabic Societies; Djelibeybi; Ephebe; Omnia *and* Tsort.

Andrew M. Butler

L

Lancre

Kingdom of Lancre is on the **Sto Lat** side of the vertiginous Ramtop Mountains, five hundred miles from the city-state of **Ankh-Morpork**. Lancre (pronounced 'lank-er') is one of the best known kingdoms in the Ramtops. It is a major earthing point for the magical fields of **Discworld**, so rains of fish or frogs, walking trees, standing stones that hide from people, 'gnarly ground' (terrain that contains more land than appears to be there on first glance), and ghosts are the norm. Lancre has given the Discworld some of its most powerful **witches** and **wizards**.

Lancre has a nominal border about 100 miles long, but its geography and topography makes it difficult to know the exact acreage. It occupies what is basically a ledge 40 × 100 miles up against the Ramtops near Copperhead Mountain (*see TGL*).

Pratchett says Lancre is based on his childhood home in South Buckinghamshire, with added magic, mountains and a deep river gorge. Peaceful, sleepy Lancre is meant to be what people imagine rural England was like before television told them about vitamins, and boiling their vegetables until white. People matter-of-factly believe all the old tales in Lancre, and because 'belief=reality' on the Discworld, the tales are in fact true.

Even with all this **magic** around – the King and Queen of the **Elves** both have gateways to their homes there – the people are pragmatic and practical, as country folk usually are. Witches cure livestock and people, can't be overawed, and see saving the world from elves and vampires as just another daily task. The people are monarchists to a man, though any monarch who oversteps the mark will know about it soon enough.

The only things that seem to unnerve Lancrastians are direct attacks by elves (*LL*), a lack of the normal thaumaturgical chaos – such as the man who walked across the moors one night without seeing a single phenomenon and had to be taken into a tavern and given a drink (*WS*) – and Nanny **Ogg**'s annual bath, as her ablutive singing has been known to paralyse goats and shatter flowerpots.

Most human habitations are in tiny Lancre Town, hard by Lancre Castle, a cut-rate **Gormenghast** that is checked every morning to see what has fallen into the river gorge overnight. There are also the villages of Mad Stoat, Bad Ass, Slippery Hollow, Razorback and Slice. **Dwarfs** and **trolls** usually live beside or on Copperhead Mountain.

Many young Lancrastians leave to find fortune, mostly in Ankh-Morpork. Agnes **Nitt** joined the Ankh-Morpork **Opera** (*Msk*), Carrot **Ironfoundersson** has become a captain (the only captain) in

Ankh-Morpork's **City Watch** (*GG*) and Eskarina **Smith** became **Unseen University**'s first female wizard (and, insofar as is known, the last) (*ER*).

Model of Lancre Castle created by Discworld Merchandising.

Some features of interest include the Long Man, three overgrown barrows (one long and two round), which contain both an entrance to the Hall of the King of the Elves and the entrance to Lancre Caves, which folklore says contains many things, including sleeping kings with their warriors, the Minotaur...and yourself coming back the other way, if you walk far enough.

The Dancers are eight standing stones guarding the entrance to the kingdom of the Queen of the Elves, a winter land where spring has never come. The stones are magnetic, attracting iron to them, surprising for a world ruled not by magnetism, but by magic. No catalogue of Lancre's sights is complete without a mention of the Place Where the Sun Does Not Shine, near Slice. It is a small rocky overhang between a Rock and a Hard Place.

Lancre is technically a constitutional monarchy. Recently a Parliament was established; the population seems to feel this is the king's way of avoiding work, and they aren't having it. They prefer their kings to get on with the hand waving, posing for coins, and acting like a king should, while they go on doing what they've always done for thousands of years.

The current king is **Verence II**, a former **Fool**, the illegitimate son of **Verence I**, or possibly of his wife. He is married to Magrat **Garlick**, a village witch who demoted herself to Queen to marry Verence. They have a daughter, Princess Esmerelda Margaret Note Spelling. The King and Queen have instituted many social, agricultural and educational improvements for the well-being of their subjects, who generally ignore these efforts as politely as they can, as per above.

Known monarchs of Lancre include: King Verence II (*WS*, *LL*, *CJ*), King Tomjon (*WS*), King Leonal Felmet (*WS*), King Verence I (*WS*), King Thargum (*WS*), King Gruneweld (*WS*), King Lully (*LL*), Queen Grimnir the Impaler (1514–1553, 1553–1557, 1557–1562, 1562–1567, 1568–1573) (a **vampire**) (*WS*), King Champot (ruled 1000 years prior to present, had Lancre Castle built, his ghost appears in *WS*), King Gruneberry the Good (906–967) (*WS*), King Murune (709–745) (*WS*), Queen Bemery (670–722) (*WS*), King My God He's Heavy I (*CJ*), and Queen Ynci, the spiky-armour-clad warrior queen of Lancre, who didn't actually exist but was invented by King Lully, as he felt that Lancre's history was not romantic enough (*LL*).

There is no state **religion**, but Lancrastians practice a sort of religion of tradition, with ceremonies to mark births, deaths and weddings that are not dedicated particularly to any one of the many gods available. There is an annual harvest festival to give thanks, but not to anyone specifically.

One of Lancre's interesting traditions is the naming of infants. Named at midnight, so the child starts a day with a new name, the child's name is exactly as the priest says it during the ceremony. Hence there are children with names like Magrat Garlick, Esmerelda Margaret Note Spelling (which was Queen Magrat's attempt to keep her daughter from having the same trouble with her name as the Queen did), King My God He's Heavy I, and James What the Hell's That Cow Doing in Here Poorchick. *See also* The Fool; Magrat Garlick; Carrot Ironfoundersson; Magic; Maps; Agnes Nitt; Nanny Ogg; Religion; Eskarina Smith; *A Tourist Guide to Lancre*; Unseen University; Verence I; Granny Weatherwax; Witches *and* Wizards.

Zina Lee

Langford, David (b.1953)

David Langford has been associated with the **Discworld** sequence since its early days, first as a reviewer and subsequently as **publisher**'s reader, editorial consultant, literary authority and the compiler of two official Discworld **quizbooks**.

His 'Critical Mass' **Science Fiction/Fantasy** review column (*White Dwarf* magazine 1983–1988, continuing in GM 1988–1990 and GMI 1990–1991) discussed several early Discworld titles, beginning with the paperback COM. All 101 columns were later collected as *The Complete Critical Assembly* (2001). Langford's longer essays on Pratchett and Discworld appear in his *Up Through an Empty House of Stars* (2003).

Langford, David

David Langford.

When Gollancz considered adding Discworld to their hardback SF/fantasy line in 1986, Langford was asked for a reader's report on the typescript of *ER*. The report was favourable, and *ER* became the first Pratchett title to appear from Gollancz.

Pratchett later requested detailed editorial feedback on the more ambitiously complicated plot of *M*, and Langford was again called in by Gollancz. This led to the tradition of 'Langfordisation', in which Langford reads early drafts and reports to Pratchett on issues of continuity, plot logic and comic devices. The tradition applies only to full-length Discworld novels – not novella-length work, such as *E* or the *SOD* fictional strands, or shorter novels for younger readers.

This extensive study of Discworld was put to devious use in Langford's *The Unseen University Challenge* (1996), which not only featured straightforward questions about the series but tested the reader's understanding of Pratchett's more esoteric real-world allusions. A second quizbook, loosely themed around Discworld's many guilds and societies, was *The Wyrdest Link* (2002). Each quizbook contains a slightly bemused introduction by Pratchett.

Langford has frequently been commissioned to write about Pratchett and Discworld for encyclopaedias and other reference works. Examples include *St James Guide to Fantasy Writers* (1996), Editor David Pringle; *The Encyclopedia of Fantasy* (1997), Editors John Clute and John Grant; *The Ultimate Encyclopedia of Fantasy* (1998), Editor, David Pringle; *Supernatural Fiction Writers: Contemporary Fantasy and Horror* (second edition, 2003), Editor Richard Bleiler and *The Greenwood Encyclopedia of Science Fiction and Fantasy: Themes, Works and Wonders* (2005), Editor Gary Westfahl. Additionally, he contributed a Foreword to *Terry Pratchett: Guilty of Literature* (2000), Editors Andrew M. Butler, Edward James and Farah Mendlesohn, and expanded this into an introduction for the revised edition of 2004.

He worked closely with Discworld artist Josh **Kirby** on the coffee-table art book *A Cosmic Cornucopia* (1999), containing numerous Kirby paintings with text commentary by Langford. Two of the six chapters present and discuss an assortment of Discworld artwork.

Langford himself has a background in science, having graduated from Brasenose College, Oxford, with a 1974 honours degree in physics. His first full-time employment was as a UK Ministry of Defence physicist at what was then the Atomic Weapons Research Establishment. He has been a freelance author and critic since 1980. Langford edits the British science fiction newsletter *Ansible* (1979-current) and has received numerous SF honours including no fewer than twenty-eight Hugo awards (as of late 2007). Perhaps his most popular work of fiction is the satirical novel *The Leaky Establishment* (1984), set in a dysfunctional nuclear research centre. Pratchett, having his own quirky memories of the nuclear industry, contributed an appreciative foreword when *Leaky* was reissued in 2001. The three Pratchett introductions to Langford books are collected in *OM*WF*. *See also* Josh Kirby; Publishers *and* Quizbooks.

Further Reading

Langford, David. 1996. *The Unseen University Challenge: Terry Pratchett's Discworld Quizbook*. London: Gollancz/Vista.

———. 1999. *A Cosmic Cornucopia*. Art by Josh Kirby. London: Paper Tiger.

———. 2001. *The Complete Critical Assembly*. Gillette, NJ: Cosmos Books.

———. 2002. *The Wyrdest Link: The Second Discworld Quizbook*. London: Gollancz.

———. 2003. *Up Through an Empty House of Stars: Reviews and Essays 1980–2002*. Holicong, PA: Cosmos Books.

David Langford

The Last Continent (1998)

The twenty-second **Discworld** novel and the first to have a hardback original by Doubleday (see **Publishers**), a print run of 93,500 copies, with cover art by Josh **Kirby**. The 1999 Corgi paperback came in two batches 77,500 and 272,000, because the Australian market was being targeted. An alternative black and gold photographic cover has been available since 2006. *LC* has been translated into Bulgarian, Czech, Dutch, Estonian, French, German, Polish, Russian and Spanish. *The Last Continent* features **Rincewind** and the **Wizards**. It is partly set in **XXXX**, the last continent to be made and considered unfinished. The title also alludes to the idea of lost continents – such as perhaps Atlantis or Lemuria. An epigraph insists that this is not a book about **Australia**. Kay Douglas grumbles; 'while it may not be Pratchett's best Discworld novel, it's still an enjoyable one' (*Washington Post Book World* 29 (9 May 1999)).

The **Librarian** of the **Unseen University** is ill and changes shape every time he sneezes. The wizards figure he needs to be turned back into a human for him to be cured, and they need to know his name for that to be possible. The only person they can think who might know this is Rincewind, last seen in XXXX at the end of *IT*. Rincewind, meanwhile, has problems of his own. He has been found by Scrappy the Kangaroo, and is resisting being used for some purpose or other. Moving through the landscape, he meets various tribes that he offends by talking about weather (this land only has sunny spells) and is accused of stealing a sheep and is sentenced to be hung. His escape is aided by an unseen Tinhead Ned. The wizards, in search of ways of getting Rincewind back, open a window into another part of the disc, a beautiful tropical island, and get stuck there with Mrs **Whitlow**. They discover that they are thousands of years in the past, and that the island is run by a God of Evolution. Rincewind reaches his destination – another university for wizards, and meets Bill Rincewind who wants him to help it rain. The wizards arrive as it starts to rain, and they head off home.

Cover of *The Last Continent* ('adult' edition). Typical of the sophisticated black and gold photographic covers which have been available in the UK since 2004.

Despite the epigraph, XXXX is the Discworld version of Australia, stuffed with mentions of everything that is memorable about the country – the thought that this is the last continent inverts the idea that Australia contains very old civilisations and mammals low down on the evolutionary scale. As always, the Rincewind books are about keeping one step ahead of death (and **Death**), and running through odd landscapes. *See also* Australia; Counterweight Continent; Publishers; Rincewind; Mrs Whitlow; Wizards *and* XXXX.

Andrew M. Butler

The Last Hero: A Discworld Fable (2001)

The twenty-seventh **Discworld** novel, in a large format, illustrated by Paul **Kidby**, was published by Gollancz in a print run of 175,000 copies. The Gollancz paperback (2002) has sixteen extra pages of illustrations – eight double page spreads – and adds a **Rincewind** 'Scream' cover, although the **elephant** which is the source of the terror is not visible. *LH* has been translated into Bulgarian, Czech, French, Polish and Russian. Kidby dedicates the work to his family, and Pratchett, presumably, to Old Vince. The title refers to **Cohen the Barbarian**. Faren Miller, in her *Locus* review, notes: 'Pratchett's takes on human creativity and layered systems of myths evoke some grandeur between the guffaws, as he works toward what may be the most difficult question of all: what it means to be a genuine hero, rather than just a bully with a big sword' (December 2001).

Ankh-Morpork receives news from the **Agatean Empire** that the emperor Genghiz Cohen the Barbarian is leading his Silver Horde on a mission to Cori Celesti, the home of the gods, to return fire to them, potentially ripping a hole in the planet. Patrician **Vetinari** puts together a mission consisting of Leonard of **Quirm**, Rincewind and Carrot **Ironfoundersson**. They will travel in a ship designed by Leonard to fly under the Disc and land at its Hub. What they do not at first realise is that the **Librarian** has stowed away on the ship, the *Kite*. The Silver Horde arrive at the **Hub** where Cohen plays a **game** against Fate – and wins. The *Kite* crashes into Cori Celesti, and the Horde prepare to fight a solo Carrot. However, they realise that it would be seven against one, and thus unfavourable odds for them to beat him. They leave, as their device explodes, creating a valley and a volcano. Leonard is forced to paint a picture of the whole world on a chapel ceiling within ten years or Ankh-Morpork will be destroyed.

This novel is a return to the more straightforward **parody** of **fantasy** tropes, continuing the joke about what happens to **heroes** when they get old, and reflecting on the stories told about them (*see also* **'TB'**). The *Kite* allows Pratchett to play with the space missions of NASA, including the ill-fated Apollo 13. The illustrations include portraits of major characters that appear within the book, as well as various pages from Leonard's notebooks – although of course, his real-world source Leonardo da Vinci wrote in mirror writing. It also includes an annotated picture of **dragons**, as published by Lady Sybil **Ramkin**, and a **map** of Discworld. *See also* Cohen the Barbarian; Dragons; Fantasy; Games; Greek Mythology; Heroes; Carrot Ironfoundersson; Paul Kidby; Narratives; Leonard of Quirm; Religion; Rincewind; Ponder Stibbons *and* Technology.

Andrew M. Butler

Leiber, Fritz (1910–1992)

Fritz Leiber was a key figure in the evolution of the 'sword and sorcery' (S&S) genre – also known as heroic fantasy – and there are several echoes of his witty fantasies in **Discworld**. This is especially true of *COM*.

In *COM*, Leiber's classic S&S duo Fafhrd and the Gray Mouser are homaged as minor characters: Bravd, an intelligent barbarian like Fahrd, and the 'cat-like' Weasel. Lankhmar, the teeming, sleazy, functional city at the heart of Leiber's world Nehwon (No-when), both resembles and sounds like Ankh-Morpork – although Pratchett observes that this was less intentional. Both cities have an established Thieves' Guild, and some similar names: Lankhmar's Street of the Gods, Plaza of Dark Desires, and Silver Eel tavern are echoed by **Ankh-Morpork**'s Small Gods, Plaza of Broken Moons and Crimson Leech.

One sequence in *The Swords of Lankhmar* (1968) sees Fafhrd racing across the Sinking Land. This sea-island of Nehwon is lifted by accumulated volcanic gases and floats until instability sets in, the gas 'belches' away and the Land sinks again. Compare the coming and going of Leshp in *J*. The same Leiber novel features a plague of highly intelligent, talking rats who are much better organised than in *AMHER*.

Nehwon is not flat but, according to its philosophers, inside-out with continents floating on the inner surface of a huge bubble in the universe-filling ocean. One crazed Overlord of Lankhmar attempts to explore other worlds via a leaden capsule slid into the sea – not unlike the Krull space programme in *COM*, with its launch off the edge of Discworld.

Fritz Leiber was a notable author of **Science Fiction** as well as **Fantasy**. He coined the term 'sword and sorcery' in response to Michael Moorcock's 1961 request for a label to describe this subgenre. The basic template for S&S had emerged in Robert E. Howard's crudely vigorous stories of the barbarian hero Conan (also parodied by Pratchett). Lacking any magic power, Conan relies on physical strength and determination to overcome an unending succession of warlords, sorcerers, and monsters both natural and supernatural.

Leiber's first published story, 'Two Sought Adventure' (*Unknown* magazine, 1939), introduced his much-loved S&S team. Fafhrd is a huge northern barbarian, but also intelligent; the Gray Mouser, small and dextrous, is a quintessential thief. Both characters were suggested in correspondence by Leiber's friend Harry Otto Fischer, who also wrote part of one story. They were loosely based on the friends themselves: Leiber was very tall, Fischer small and nimble.

Their adventures appeared until 1988, collected in a sequence of books whose titles led to this being also called the Swords series – *see* Further Reading below. By internal chronology *Swords and Deviltry* (1970) comes first, since it describes the heroes' childhoods and first encounter. The latter story, 'Ill Met in Lankhmar', won a Hugo award.

Some apparent Leiber 'influences' on Discworld are matters of common fantasy tradition. Magic shops which sell weird merchandise and are likely to disappear without warning appear in *LF*, *SM*, and Leiber's earlier 'Bazaar of the Bizarre' (1963, included in *Swords Against Death*) – but this much-exploited theme can be traced back to H.G. Wells's 'The Magic Shop' (1903). The notion of **Death** being a hard-working character with a duty to perform, as in both Nehwon and Discworld, is also far from new. *See also* Fantasy; Heroes *and* Science Fiction.

Further Reading

Leiber, Fritz. 1968a. *Swords Against Wizardry*. New York: Ace.
———. 1968b. *Swords in the Mist*. New York: Ace.
———. 1968c. *The Swords of Lankhmar*. New York: Ace.
———. 1970a. *Swords and Deviltry*. New York: Ace.
———. 1970b. *Swords Against Death*. New York: Ace.
———.1977. *Swords & Ice Magic*. New York: Ace.
———. 1988. *The Knight and Knave of Swords*. New York: Morrow.

David Langford

The Librarian (*LF*, *ER*, *M*, *S*, *GG*, *MP*, *SG*, *LL*, *MAA*, *SM*, *IT*, *Msk*, *H*, *LC*, *LH*, *T!*)

Originally a human (named, according to *AD*, Horace Worblehat, B.Thau, DM), the University Librarian of **Unseen University** was transformed into a small, sad **orangutan** by a burst of magic in *LF* and has refused any attempts to turn him back, partly because with three hundred pounds of muscle, huge yellow fangs, a strong territorial imperative and a hair-trigger temper, 'budget cuts' have become something that happen to other people and overseeing committees are extremely polite. ('Small' here is obviously by orangutan, not human standards.) His form also enables him to search the higher shelves and, if necessary, deal with some of the physical manifestations of the dangers of **L-Space**. He thus resists any attempts to return him to his human form. From a 'bit part' he has become a major character and one of the **Discworld** series' most popular characters, especially among human librarians – despite the fact that he is a caricature of them.

Although he encourages Eskarina **Smith** in *ER*, he is not good at liberal ideals of 'social inclusion': he refuses entry to Windle Poons in *RM* because Poons is, in fact, dead. He encourages reading, but (like Adso in Umberto Eco's novel *The Name of the Rose* (1980)) feels that readers tend to wear the books out by reading them. He believes that library books should remain on the shelves where nature intended them to be (*MAA*) and that theft of a book is worse than murder (*GG*).

Nevertheless, he is an embodiment of the adage 'the right book for the right reader'. He fetches books for his readers even if he has to traverse the space–time continuum to do so. When, for instance, asked by **Vimes** for a book on **Klatch**, when **Ankh-Morpork** goes to war with the rival nation over a tiny and useless island, the Librarian supplies the autobiography of General Tacticus, whose shrewdness, understanding of the nature of power and preference for victories that do not involve the glorious deaths of everyone except the people who wanted war in the first place reinforces Vimes's own. The Librarian's colleagues respect him (even if partly because they do not understand his expertise and are intimidated by his whipcord muscles and huge fangs). He has an active social life (sometimes involving Patrician **Vetinari**'s menagerie), and is a regular drinker at the **Mended Drum** and an expert player of B.S. Johnson's organ (we learn in *SM* that he played keyboards in the Discworld's first rock band). Despite an unfortunate attitude to the Vitally Challenged, he otherwise does not take prejudice and insults lightly, especially if it involves confusion between 'monkey' and 'ape'.

Only once, in the series so far, does he become a purely slapstick figure, although a parody of Hollywood that includes an ape and a starlet among its dramatis personae, and has the possibility of a huge climbable building already built-into the scenario, can only end one way (*MP*).

Like most librarians, he is paid peanuts, but given his species that is an advantage. He has a healthy scepticism for the capabilities of his academic colleagues because unlike them, he can not only understand L-Space but he can also travel in it. Only he can control the books: his illness in *LC* results in chaos among the volumes as the contents of the books leak and interact.

The Librarian is a central figure for three main reasons. First, he is practical: a foil to the **wizards** of Unseen University and a reminder of how much academics needs librarians. Like **Death**, Gaspode and other such non-human characters, he shows us how ridiculous human beings are when we are behaving naturally. Second, he illustrates the importance of knowledge – or of the right kind of knowledge. The Librarian's job is to communicate: to allow chaotic material to find its way to its users – without, preferably, allowing them to stray, metaphorically or literally, into domains like the Lost Reading Room. The irony of the fact that he communicates through sign language and the single word 'ook' that means anything he chooses is not lost upon the reader, or his fellow-characters. His skill, however, is to mediate between the knowledge-seeker and sought knowledge. The complexities of L-Space reduce, in the end, to the simple matter of the right piece of information arriving to the right person at the right time.

Third, he follows the fashion for reclaiming an image by emphasising or distorting the received version of it. He embodies many of the jokes made about librarians, and as a result is popular among librarians themselves.

The Librarian is also the University Archivist, a useful doubling of roles when it becomes necessary to destroy all records that mention his name so he cannot be turned back into a human. *See also* Death; Libraries; L-Space; Magic; Orangutans; Unseen University *and* Wizards.

Further Reading

Sawyer, Andy. 'The Librarian and his Domain'. *GOL*, *GOL2*.

Andy Sawyer

Libraries

Libraries, as repositories of knowledge, and books, as a medium by which knowledge is propagated, are important on the **Discworld** and elsewhere in Pratchett's fiction. The Library of **Unseen University** is not the only major library on the Discworld. The second largest – until its destruction – was the library of **Ephebe** in *SG* whose books were the work of philosophers and their purpose was to establish the academic credentials of their authors rather than to be read. Unseen University requires a library because, as **Archchancellor Ridcully** says (*LC*), it adds *tone*, but also because books are powerful. Unseen University Library holds the largest collection of magical texts on Discworld. Said to have a circumference of a few hundred yards but an apparently infinite radius, it contains unwritten books on distant shelves. Shelving problems are minimised by topological distortions: the floor seems to become the wall in the distance, while the wall tends to turn into the ceiling. Unseen University Library is described in *LF* as having 'Mobius shelves'. The presence of so many books on magic pressed so closely together is, perhaps, one of the reasons for the existence of **L-Space**, but any sufficiently large collection of books. Even mundane books are dangerous, but in Discworld, magic can leak out of the more occult books to form a 'critical Black Mass'. Some books have to be chained to the shelves, not to protect the books, but to stop the readers getting too absorbed in them. Books contain *stories* – and it is through story, whether it is fiction or the interpretive stories that we call 'non-fiction', that we make sense of the world (*see* **Narrative**).

The library's stock includes *The Necrotelicomnicon, Maleficio's Discouverie of Demonologie, The True Art of Levitatione* and *The Summoning of Dragons*. Books such as Ge Fordge's *Compenydyum of Sex Majick* and other such titles for the more discerning **wizard** are kept under ice. The melting of the ice creates a cool area in which the **Librarian** can relax on a hot day. The University Librarian, for reasons described elsewhere, is an **orangutan**, but this has probably made him better at his job – certainly he can wield four date-stamps at once and budget committees are generally polite to a 300 lb angry ape. In the earlier novels, he is aided by **Rincewind** as honorary assistant librarian (*S*), partly because basic indexing and banana-fetching is about Rincewind's level of expertise. The most important book in the Library is the *Octavo*, kept in a room in the cellars of the University, which was left behind by the Creator of the Universe. The *Octavo* contains eight spells, one of which escaped into the mind of Rincewind when he opened up the book for a bet (*COM* and *LF*).

The library is a perilous place. There are tales about books that go out of control (*ER*), lost tribes of research students (*GG*) and perilous domains such as the Lost Reading Room (*LC*). Magic crackles and has to be earthed in copper rails fixed to every shelf. At night, one can hear the sound of the books talking to each other. Students searching for books are reputed to tell their friends before they go and leave chalk marks on the shelves. All libraries contain variants of the three basic rules of the Librarians of Space and Time: (1) Silence, (2) books must be returned no later than the last date shown and (3) do not interfere with the nature of causality. A fourth rule for Unseen University Library would involve learning the classification of the primate family tree.

It is not surprising that books and 'book-learning' are sometimes regarded with suspicion. A book stolen from the Library (*GG*) almost brings disaster to **Ankh-Morpork**. Managerial types like Astfgl – the demon lord in *E* – and Archchancellor Ridcully drive their colleagues frantic by applying the platitudes of management textbooks. **Verence**, the former **Fool** who becomes King of **Lancre** and marries Magrat **Garlick**, is gently mocked for trying to teach himself 'kinging' out of books. Nijel the Destroyer in *S*, learning how to be a **hero** from a manual allegedly written by **Cohen the Barbarian**, is also a figure of fun, but significantly it is **Coin**, whose response to a library of ninety thousand volumes is to order its destruction, who is *S*'s villain. A little knowledge may be dangerous, but wilful ignorance is sinful. Books are dangerous, but tyrants have always known that. The Omnian tyranny in *SG* arises from taking a text too literally. In *SG*, **Brutha** rescues the Library by memorising it: he 'reads' but does not understand, saving knowledge and opinions but remaining uncontaminated by their pretensions. The result of the revolution brought about by Brutha is that Mightily Oats, in *CJ*, is brought up to believe that the *Book of Om* is Holy Writ, but nevertheless is capable of sacrificing it to keep Granny **Weatherwax** alive. In The **Bromeliad**, women are forbidden to read because it might make their heads explode (or give them ideas above their station). In *T* (the first book of The **Bromeliad**), **Masklin** begins the nomes' exodus from the Store by insisting that everyone who wants (including women) is taught to read because whatever they need to do, there will be a book that tells them how. Tiffany **Aching** has read the dictionary and corrects her teachers' spellings, but her knowledge is based upon experience as well as upon book-learning. A general rule (**Vimes**'s use of Tacticus's *Veni Vidi Vici: A Soldier's Life* in *J* is possibly an exception) might be that reliance on a single book is dubious, but a library, however small, offers choice and the capacity to explore alternatives.

If magic is action at a distance, then books, which literally do change the world, are inherently magical; those who care for and establish the relationship between books are necessarily wizards, and there is very little difference between Unseen University Library and any other. *See also* Tiffany Aching; The Bromeliad; Brutha; Heroes; The Librarian; L-Space; Magic; Narrative; Om; Unseen University; *The Unseen University Cut-Out Book and* Wizards.

Further Reading

Sawyer, Andy. 'The Librarian and his Domain'. *GOL*, *GOL2*.

Andy Sawyer

The Light Fantastic (1986)

The second book in the **Discworld** series and a direct sequel to *COM*. The first edition was 1034 copies, published by Colin **Smythe** Ltd of Gerrards Cross in 1986. Corgi issued a print run of 34,100 in 1986, with a Josh **Kirby** cover. In 1995 Gollancz issued a compact edition. It was republished with *COM* by Colin Smythe Ltd as *The First Discworld Novels* (1999) and by Gollancz with *COM*, *S* and *E* as *The Rincewind Trilogy* (*sic*, 2001). Since 2004 an alternative black and gold photographic cover has been available from Corgi. *LF* has been translated into over twenty-five languages, including Bulgarian, Chinese,Croatian, Czech, Danish, Dutch, Estonian, Finnish, French, German, Greek, Hebrew, Hungarian, Italian, Korean, Norwegian, Polish, Portuguese, Romanian, Russian, Serbian, Slovakian, Slovenian, Spanish, Swedish, and Turkish. The title is an allusion to *L'Allegro* (1645) by John Milton (1608–1674): 'Come, and trip it, as you go,/On the light fantastic toe', a reference to nimble dancing. *LF* has been adapted into one of the Discworld **Comics** (*see* ***Terry Pratchett's The Light Fantastic***). Neil **Gaiman,** under the pseudonym W.C. Gull, wrote: 'it does for the worlds of fantasy, magic and adventure what Douglas Adams did for science fiction and what pigeons do to Nelson's Column . . . . go out and buy this book. Right now. I mean it's *funny*' (*Knave*).

The Light Fantastic

Rincewind finds himself miraculously saved from falling into space off the edge of the Discworld and is reunited with **Twoflower**, last seen on the chelysphere. Meanwhile, back at the **Unseen University** in **Ankh-Morpork**, the **Wizards** are worried. Great **A'Tuin** is swimming towards a strange red star. The wizards perform the Rite of AshkEnte to summon **Death**, who tells them that the world will be destroyed unless they speak the eight great spells of the Octavo. Unfortunately one of these spells has escaped, and is currently residing in Rincewind's head. **Trymon** decides that he wants the spell back, and will stop at nothing to become head of the wizards. Rincewind and Twoflower are blissfully unaware of the coming crisis, and meet up with **Cohen the Barbarian**, facing their own dangers and bounty hunters along their way, including a visit to **Death's Domain**. They return to Ankh-Morpork for a showdown with Trymon, who, having read several of the spells, has been possessed by demons from the **Dungeon Dimensions**. The crisis point is reached: the red sun has been incubating eight more discworlds. Rincewind considers re-enrolling at the University, whilst Twoflower decides it is time to go home and leaves him the **Luggage**.

For the first time Pratchett sustains a novel-length narrative set on the Discworld, although he cannot quite yet control the counterpoint of the parallel narrative threads; Trymon and the rest of the wizards are offstage for much of the book. This is also the close-up look we get of the Unseen University, with the wizards dominating over any other academic faculties. The wizards have the feel of the schoolmasters in ***Gormenghast*** (1950) by Mervyn Peake (1911–1968). The fantasy lightly parodies the Conan the Barbarian stories by Robert E. Howard (1906–1936), and **Fairy Tales** including 'Hansel and Gretel' and 'Goldilocks and the Three Bears'. *See also* Ankh-Morpork; the Great A'Tuin; Cohen the Barbarian; Death; Fairy Tales; The Luggage; Rincewind; Twoflower; Unseen University *and* Wizards.

Further Reading

Hill, Penelope. 'Unseen University'. *GOL, GOL2*.

Andrew M. Butler

Lipwig, Moist von (*GP*, *T!*)

Lipwig is a twenty-six year-old fraudster from **Überwald**, whose previous frauds included the passing of faked cheques at a bank in Sto Lat, leading to the sacking of Adora Belle Dearheart. In **Ankh-Morpork** he is sentenced to death and is apparently executed by Patrician **Vetinari**. This turns out to be a front for the Patrician's dirty work – he offers Lipwig the opportunity to take over the Post Office or die, in the full knowledge that a successful mail service will threaten the corrupt semaphore system of clacks (*see* **Technology**). Naturally von Lipwig tries to escape, but he is brought back by his golem parole officer, Mr Pump. Von Lipwig thinks big, knows the power of showmanship, and with the invention of stamps and good PR, turns the company around so that it draws the ire of the General Trunk Semaphore Company. In the mean time he sets about befriending Dearheart, the only person seemingly not taken in by him, and daughter of the inventor of the clacks. In part in revenge for attempts on his life, in part to atone for his earlier acts, he sets about bringing the GTSC down, and is rewarded by being given control of it. He is mentioned in passing in *T!* (relating to stamps) and returns in *Making Money* (2007). *See also* Technology; Überwald *and* Patrician Vetinari.

Ten Pence Stamp created by Discworld Merchandising.

Andrew M. Butler

Littlebottom, Cheery (*FOC*, *J*, *FE*, *NW*, *T!*)

Cheery Littlebottom is a **Dwarf** from **Überwald**; she is also the first openly acknowledged female dwarf in the **Ankh-Morpork City Watch**. As time goes on, due to the influence of Angua von **Überwald**, she becomes more open with her sex and is not afraid to wear a dress or makeup. She also decides that her name should be pronounced 'Cheri' and does keep her beard.

Littlebottom, Cheery

Before joining the Watch, Cheery was an alchemist, and has been hired by Commander **Vimes** to be the Watch's official coroner and forensics expert (though she has recently given up the coroner's job to **Igor**); she does not patrol like the rest of the Watch. Due to the speciality of her job, she was automatically given the rank of corporal and has since risen to sergeant. When not working on a case, she helps **Colon** on the desk.

Like many, Cheery has an extreme distaste for werewolves and initially took to wearing a silver vest. However, she became friends with Angua before learning the Sergeant's secret, and the two continue to be friends to this day. She looks at Angua as a bit of a big sister, because Cheery can be a bit naïve, and Angua is always around to set her straight. Cheery is still wary of werewolves but is mindful of Angua's feelings and has even quit wearing her vest out of friendship. Her brother, Snorey, was blown up in the line of duty in Borogravia (*FE*).

Between January 2003 and October 2006, 200 hundred issues of an unofficial weekly comic strip *The Adventures of Cheery Littlebottom* were published online. *See also* City Watch; Frederick Colon; Dwarfs; Feminism; Carrot Ironfoundersson; Nobby Nobbs; Racism; Sexism; Angua van Überwald *and* Samuel Vimes.

Further Reading

The Adventures of Cheery Littlebottom. Online at http://www.cheerycomic.co.uk/.

Mark D. Thomas

Llamedos (*SM*, *FE*)

Llamedos is a small village in the Ramtops, full of rain, bards, Eisteddfods and music, and the home of Imp Y **Celyn**. This location is the **Discworld** equivalent of Wales, and features only very briefly. Rain is its dominant industry, although most of the druids work in stone circles. The village's name is 'Sodemall' reversed, a mild curse. This is a reference to the play *Under Milk Wood* (1953) by Dylan Thomas (1914–1953), first broadcast in January 1954 with Richard Burton narrating. This work, drawing on Thomas's experiences of Laugharne, Carmarthenshire and New Quay, Ceredigion, both in Wales, is an account of a day in a seaside village, Llareggub – which against his wishes was to be rendered Llaregyb in some printed versions, as his village is 'Buggerall' reversed. Thomas drew a map of Llareggub in the 1940s to help him plot the play; this is now in the National Library of Wales. *See also* Imp Y Celyn *and* Dwarfs.

Further Reading

Thomas, Dylan. 1954. *Under Milk Wood. A Play for Voices*. London: J.M. Dent.

Andrew M. Butler

Lords and Ladies (1992)

The fourteenth **Discworld** novel and part of the **Witches** sequence – the book contains an author's note advising the reader to read *ER*, *WS* and *WA* first. The first edition, from Gollancz, was 30,000 copies with a cover by Josh **Kirby**. The Corgi edition of 242,000 copies appeared in 1993, with an alternative black and gold photographic cover available since 2005. *LL* has been translated into Bulgarian, Czech, Dutch, Estonian, Finnish, French, German, Hebrew, Norwegian, Polish, Russian, Serbian, Spanish, Swedish and Turkish. The lords and ladies of the title are the fairies or **elves**; in *A Midsummer's Night Dream* by William **Shakespeare** and elsewhere fairies are named after flowers, and the title is also a name for the cuckoo pint or wild arum (*Arum maculatum*). John Clute, in his review in *Interzone* 67, wrote that *LL*; 'lies deep within the Discworld tessitura: funny and fluent, loving but swift, sane and paradisal' (January 1993).

The three witches are returning from **Genua** (*see WA*) after being away for eight months and things have been sliding in the mean time – a group of young girls, including Agnes **Nitt**, are trying to be witches and are dancing around the standing stones outside the village. The fabric between realities is thinning there, and the elves are trying to break through. When Magrat **Garlick** returns, she finds that **Verence** is well advanced with plans for their marriage, and a group of locals including Jason **Ogg** are rehearsing a play for the celebrations. Archchancellor **Ridcully**, the Bursar, Ponder Stibbons and the **Librarian** accept invitations to the wedding and have an eventful journey to **Lancre**. Having shown their superiority over the girl witches, Granny **Weatherwax** and Nanny **Ogg** will have to face the elves, but in the mean time are distracted by romantic interludes with Ridcully and Casunanda, respectively. Magrat, having fought elves with iron, has to retrieve her kidnapped groom.

The novel is an appropriation of materials from *A Midsummer's Night Dream* in which the marriage of Theseus of Athens and Hippolyta of the Amazons leads to the performance of a play by 'Rude Mechanicals'. Before the wedding can take place, the tangled love lives of Demetrius, Helena, Hermia and Lysander have to be straightened out, despite the interference of the fairies. Here the fairies/elves have the menace that underlies the Shakespeare play, and the book does end with a sense of the three witches being in relationships, even in love. There is also a threat to the maiden, mother and crone trinity, as Magrat will presumably soon stop being a maiden, and Weatherwax is feeling her age. *See also* Elves; The Fool; Magrat Garlick; Genua; Lancre; The Librarian; Magic; Agnes Nitt; Nanny Ogg; Religion; William Shakespeare; Verence; Granny Weatherwax; Witches *and* Wizards.

Further Reading

Sayer, Karen. 'The Witches'. *GOL*, *GOL2*.

Andrew M. Butler

L-Space

Reading a book takes us to different worlds. The idea of phase-space was conceived by the nineteenth century French mathematician Henri Poincaré (1854–1912) as an imaginary space plotting all possible states of a system. 'Possible' does not necessarily mean 'existing'. Books, especially fiction (and especially that series of branches known as science fiction) are imaginative spaces of 'what if?'. If knowledge is power, then power is energy that (according to Einstein's famous equation) is mass. Therefore, a sufficiently large collection of books will distort space. By travelling through the 'bookwormholes' thus created, the **Librarian** is able to retrieve books which, like *The Summoning of Dragons* in *GG* have gone missing from the **Unseen University Library**, do not even exist on Discworld, or even, like Darwin's *Theology of Species* in *SODIII* do not exist at all. All libraries, everywhere, are connected through L-Space.

In 'real' library systems, this is a virtual linkage, a metaphysical/metaphorical connection between areas of knowledge imposed by classification schemes from shelf order to the Colon Classification (nothing to do with Sergeant **Colon** of the **Ankh-Morpork City Watch**), and, increasingly, hypertext links via the Web. But in Pratchett's **Discworld**, where personification becomes actuality, this connection is far more than metaphorical and the secret of L-Space is one of the Mysteries of librarianship. Travel through L-Space is restricted to senior members of the library profession, for it is dangerous and can result in interference with causality. L-Space even has its own specialised ecology, such as the kickstool crabs, the monstrous thesaurus, and the Critters that feed on the contents of other books and leave behind them piles of literary criticism.

It is by travelling through L-Space that the Librarian can rescue some of the philosophical scrolls in the Library of **Ephebe** when it is set on fire by the Omnians. Theoretically, libraries are the putting into action of the axiom 'Every reader his book: Every book its reader'. Through inter-library loan systems, on-line catalogues, and digitalisation projects, we may track down the locations of even the most obscure book and (sometimes) ensure that it is available for a reader. L-space is what libraries in the 'real' world aspire to be. On Discworld, however, things are simpler. *See also* Ephebe; The Librarian; Libraries; Magic; Science of Discworld *and* Unseen University.

Andy Sawyer

The Luggage (*COM*, *LF*, *S*, *E*, *IT*, *LC*, *LH*)

A trunk made from sapient pearwood, with an inter-dimensional interior second only to TARDISes for size, and having lots of little legs. It is fiercely loyal to its current owner and just fierce to everyone else. It arrives in **Ankh-Morpork** with **Twoflower** (*COM*) and contains his clothes, his iconograph and his money. It doggedly follows Twoflower wherever he goes, across continents, into other dimensions, including **Death's Domain** and over the edge of the planet. When Twoflower returns to **Bes Pelargic** he gifts the Luggage to **Rincewind**, which leads to a whole new set of travels, including a return to its origin (*IT*). The Luggage appears to follow Rincewind with the sort of ambivalent devotion that Gollum showed to Frodo in J.R.R. **Tolkien**'s *The Lord of the Rings* (1954–1955).

Pratchett says in the dedication to *S* that he once saw an American tourist in Bath with a very large tartan suitcase on lots of wheels, which seemed to have a mind of its own. In *AD* he notes that he created the Luggage in a role-playing **game** he had designed – the two explanations are not necessarily mutually exclusive.

'Luggage' is a track on Dave **Greenslade**'s *Terry Pratchett's From the Discworld* album. *See also* Dave Greenslade; Rincewind *and* Twoflower.

Andrew M. Butler

Lu-Tze (*SG, TOT, NW*)

One of the History Monks, who go to observe events to make sure that they have historical significance – and they are not above intervening to change the way the world is going. In *SG* he travels to observe Brutha's rise to Eighth Prophet, and is mostly seen sweeping inscrutably. In *TOT* he is forced to take on an apprentice, Lobsang Ludd, who had been raised by the Ankh-Morpork Thieves' Guild and now plays a role in preventing the creation of a clock that will help the Auditors of Reality rationalis the universe. Finally, to date, he appears at various points in *NW*, ensuring Samuel Vimes's travels between past and present.

The character's name echoes Lao Tze (sixth century BCE), the purported author of the Taoist book *Tao Te Ching*, and also a character in the fables of Chuang Tze and others who debates with and bests Confucius. His behaviour with a broom recalls Chief Bromden in *One Flew Over the Cuckoo's Nest* (1962) by Ken Kesey (1935–2001), but his speech sounds like the stereotypical Chinese monk of *Monkey* or Doctor Fu Mancu. *See also* Brutha; History; Religion *and* Samuel Vimes.

Andrew M. Butler

M

Magazines

There has been one Terry Pratchett magazine, *SFX Presents The Authorised Terry Pratchett's Discworld Magazine*, a special publication by *SFX* magazine published in May 1997 to coincide with the **Cosgrove Hall** adaptations of *SM* and *WS*. *SFX* is a professional magazine devoted to **Science Fiction** across various media, published from 1995 by Future Publishing who specialise in computer magazines. Regular contributors to *SFX* include M.J. Simpson, an expert in Douglas **Adams**, and David **Langford**. Simpson edited the one-off issue, as 'Publyshed by Dibbler Press, **Ankh-Morpork**'. It included a poster of the **Discworld**, stapled in the magazine. Thirty-five thousand copies were printed.

There have been various fan magazines – fanzines – published by **fandom**, with a greater or lesser amount of attention paid to Pratchett. At least thirty issues of the newsletter of Octarine, a Science Fiction and **Fantasy** humour appreciation society, *Tales from the Broken Drum*, appeared from 1989. The first editor was M.J. Simpson, then Bob Summons. *The Horrible Knuckles* (a quote from *LF*) had two issues in 1990. *The Wizard's Knob* was a fanzine initially edited by John Penney and David Baxter for its first two issues in 1993; Penney was solo editor to issue 5 (Spring 1996), after which Steven Dean took over until it ceased publication in 2000. The Guild of Fans and Disciples publish *Ramtop to Rimfall*, edited by Phil Penney from December 1994 to August 2000 (issue 26), thereafter Elizabeth Alway has edited it. There is also *Discworld Monthly*, online (*see* **Websites**). *See also* Douglas Adams; The Broken Drum; Comedy and Humour; Cosgrove Hall; Fandom; David Langford; Merchandising; *Soul Music From Terry Pratchett's Discworld and Wyrd Sisters From Terry Pratchett's Discworld.*

Andrew M. Butler

Magic

According to ***NDC***, there are three types of magic in the **Discworld**: intrinsic, residual and induced.

Intrinsic magic

Intrinsic magic is what the Discworld is made of. Magic consists of elementary particulate fragments, in much the same way that energy is in quantum physics. The basic unit of magic is the thaum. A thaum consists of particles known as 'resons' (literally, 'thingies') that have five 'flavours': *up*, *down*, *sideways*, *sex appeal* and *peppermint*. (Our quarks, on the other hand, have six flavours: *up*, *down*, *top* or *truth*, *bottom* or *beauty*, *strange* and *charm*.)

Wizards and **witches** store and channel intrinsic magic. It is subject to laws similar to our own conservation of energy, so it is very difficult for, say, a wizard to create something new out of nothing. He can lift himself off the ground (levitate or fly) by using the energy of a falling object that is of equal mass to himself, but, without that falling object, must be able to physically lift his weight to the required height. Essentially and practically, a wizard cannot achieve a result beyond his own physical powers.

The only wizards able to use pure creative force are sourcerers. Sourcerers, who engaged in magical wars that have left areas of the Disc crawling with strange species, potent magical artefacts, and reservoirs of residual magic, have been fortunately few recently, because of the enforced practice of celibacy by wizards, as sourcerers must be the eighth son of a wizard (*see S, but see also ER*).

Residual Magic

Residual magic is a very powerful and unpredictable force. Left mainly by the sourcerers' wars across the Disc, it can be exploited by wizards and witches, but the results can be very difficult to control, i.e. fatal.

Induced Magic

According to *SOD*, what runs Discworld is *narrative imperative*, the power of story. **Narrative** imperative in the Discworld universe shows up as narrativium, which is in every atom. On Discworld, words and belief have a real actual power, and their magical potential is great.

For example, the armour of Queen Ynci of **Lancre** enabled Magrat **Garlick** to defeat the Queen of the **Elves** (*LL*). When Magrat wore Ynci's armour, she felt that Ynci's bravery and strength transferred to her. The fact the warrior Queen was completely fictional does not matter; Magrat's belief alone gave her Ynci's warrior strength.

Another example is the Scone of Stone, believed by **dwarfs** to burn hot at the sound of a lie, and upon which their Low Kings are crowned. In *FE*, the Low King uses the Scone to expose a murderer by forcing him to touch it while lying. The Scone burns his hands, even though he knows the Scone is a fake plaster copy made in **Ankh-Morpork**.

Then of course there is Granny **Weatherwax**, who has never bothered to physically turn anyone into a frog. She prefers to persuade them that they are a frog but leave their body as it is. This, Granny believes, is easier, slightly less cruel and also affords much innocent entertainment for passers-by (*WA*).

Magic

Conjurers

Conjurers have their own Guild House near **Unseen University**. They tend to be fat, jolly entertainers, who do not actually perform magic. Everything is trickery and sleight-of-hand. They are very popular in Ankh-Morpork, where magic is seen as humdrum. This annoys the wizards no end.

Thaumaturgists

Thaumaturgists have no magical training, and are usually sent to get supplies for spells and clean up around the workshop.

Magicians

Mostly students who failed exams at Unseen University, magicians assist wizards in the workshop with tasks that need rudimentary magical training.

Witches (see also main entry on Witches*)*

Witches tend to be solitary and matrilinear, enrolling in no schools and following no formal set of regulations. They are generally trained by another experienced witch, and then take over when their teacher dies or otherwise leaves a gap in coverage for any area.

The rural witch (and most witches are rural, with some exceptions) serves her folk through midwifery, attending to the dead and through folk medicine. They stand at the edge of life and death, making the decisions others cannot, will not or are unaware of the need to make. For many villagers, the first and last person they see in life is the village witch.

Most witches occupy their predecessor's cottage, and tend to follow similar career paths. A cottage may accommodate research witches, specialists in herbal medicine, etc. Villagers must look after their caregiver; witches tend to live in cast-off clothing and be fed by food that appears on their doorsteps or is given to them on their rounds.

Covens are not common among Discworld witches, who tend to get together irregularly and infrequently to gossip, exchange news or discuss local issues. The Lancre coven was largely initiated by Magrat **Garlick** and included Nanny **Ogg** and Granny **Weatherwax**. After Magrat became a mother, she was replaced by Agnes **Nitt**. Another exception to the solitude is the annual Ramtops Mountains Witch Trials ('SALF' and *HFOS*) at which witches show their powers, which in no way constitutes any kind of competition whatsoever, of course. Granny Weatherwax is the undisputed champion of the competitions that aren't held at the Witch Trials.

The three Lancre witches we know best are Esmerelda 'Granny' **Weatherwax**, Gytha 'Nanny' **Ogg**, and Magrat Garlick (now officially retired since she became the queen of **Verence** II of **Lancre**). They represent the classic crone, mother and maiden trio; since Magrat's ascension to the throne of Lancre, Agnes **Nitt** has moved into Magrat's cottage and taken the maiden role.

There are no truly black or white witches on Discworld, as there is no black or white magic. There are only magic users choosing how to use it.

***Wizards (see also main entry on* Wizards)**

There are many schools of wizardry, but most wizards we know from the series matriculate at Unseen University in Ankh-Morpork. There are eight grades of eight orders of wizardry associated with Unseen University. (The number eight has great power in Discworld. Wizards are careful not to say the number aloud outside well-protected areas, lest the Dungeon Dimension creatures break through into Discworld.) Like all magic workers, wizards try to use magic sparingly. They store magical power in their staffs, which are charged daily with rituals for use as required. Senior wizards at UU tend to spend their time sleeping, eating four very large meals per day, and giving virtual lectures in non-existent lecture halls as they nap. Their general somnolence, overall impression of a small mountain range and argumentative, querulous ways might suggest they are less than powerful or intelligent, but one does not become a senior wizard without being both, even if some are also mad as hatters.

Wizards, unlike witches, place great store in books. The Unseen University **Library** contains enough magic to destroy the universe twice over. Energy of various sorts can be stored in books and released through a spell. Over time, books can become somewhat sentient in their own right. Certainly, individual spells of great power can become sentient (*COM*). Wizardry, if you take away the illusions, fireballs and coloured lights, largely consists of persuading the universe to do everything your way.

Sourcerers

A sourcerer is the eighth son of a wizard, who himself has to be the eighth son of an eighth son (although *see ER*). A sourcerer is a natural channel through which magic flows into the universe. They cannot work with other magic workers or indeed live comfortably with other people, as their every thought controls everything around them. Their wars have created some of the most magic-polluted sites on the Disc. Received wisdom says that only a sourcerer can beat another sourcerer in any magical duel, but **Rincewind** has discovered that a well-aimed half brick in a sock will suffice (*S*). *See also* Coin; Dwarfs; Magrat Garlick; Libraries; Narrative; Agnes Nitt; Nanny Ogg; Power; Rincewind; Unseen University; Granny Weatherwax; Witches *and* Wizards.

Zina Lee

Malich, Albert[o] (*M*, *RM*, *SM*, *H*, *TOT*)

Servant to **Death**. As Alberto Malich, he was one of the greatest **Wizards** on the Disc and the founder of **Unseen University**, where a statue in his honour stood. His career in magic ended when he blew himself up in his attempt to perform the Rite of AshkEnte backwards to achieve

immortality. In return for service, he has lived in Death's land – where there is no time – for a thousand years, only aging when he returns to the world, and usually staying at the Young Men's Reformed-Cultists-of-the-Ichor-God-Bel-Shamharoth Association. On the last such visit, while attempting to bring a distracted Death back to do his duty, Albert was struck and his Lifetimer broken. All but the last thirty-four seconds leaked out and are now safely kept in a beer bottle. During this trip, he also destroyed his statue; the wizards of Unseen University, who thought that the statue had turned into him, proposed to rebuild the statue in the dungeons under UU, where they would be safe if it happened again.
The name Malich may come from the Hebrew name for the Phoenician demon/god Moloch, another name for Ba'al. He was played by David Jason (b.1940) in the Sky One version of ***Hogfather* (Television Adaptation)**. *See also* Archchancellors; Death; Death's Domain; *Hogfather* (Television Adaptation); Mort Sto Helit, Susan Sto Helit; Ysabella Sto Helit *and* Unseen University.

Susan Spilecki

Maps, *see The Discworld Mapp, The Streets of Ankh-Morpork, A Tourist Guide to Lancre* and *Death's Domain*

Maskerade (1995)

The eighteenth novel in the **Discworld** sequence and features the **Witches**. The first edition, published by Gollancz with a Josh **Kirby** cover, was 55,000 copies. The Corgi paperback was 295,000 copies in 1996; since 2005 an alternative black and gold photographic cover has been available. *Msk* has been translated into Bulgarian, Czech, Dutch, Estonian, Finnish, French, German, Polish, Portuguese, Russian, Serbian, Spanish and Swedish. The title is a variation on Masquerade, a group of people in disguise, or, as a verb, to pass oneself off as something; it is also a song in the second act of Andrew Lloyd Webber's *The Phantom of the Opera* **musical** (1986). The book is dedicated to people who attempted to get Terry Pratchett to appreciate **opera**. The *SFX* reviewer noted: 'What is remarkable is that while it lampoons opera for the ridiculous, elitist, over-priced, over-hyped and pretentious rubbish that it is, it also simultaneously celebrates opera for the glorious elitist, over-priced, over-hyped, pretentious splendour that it is!' (November 1995).

Agnes **Nitt** has run away from **Lancre** to **Ankh-Morpork** to join the opera; however, she is considered too fat to be a leading soprano, despite having a great voice. Meanwhile the coven is down to two, and Nanny **Ogg** is worried that Granny **Weatherwax** is not at her best without a maiden to boss around; she knows that Agnes would make a potential third witch, but she's in Ankh-Morpork. When Weatherwax discovers that Ogg has been cheated out of royalties for her cookery book they head to the city, and happen to call in on the opera. There a series of people are being murdered, apparently by a ghost, and the evidence seems to point to Walter **Plinge**, the strange janitor. However, whilst he is undeniably creepy, the real criminal is the musical director, Salzella, who is stealing money. Plinge becomes musical director, and the witches return to Lancre, with Agnes as a new recruit.

The story rewrites the musical *Phantom of the Opera*, where the diva Carlotta quits, and Christine, part of the ballet, is drafted in to sing. The Phantom falls in love with her, and takes her to his underground lair. Rivalry between Carlotta and Christine flairs up, with demands from the opera ghost for who sings what and with a body being discovered on stage. Christine meanwhile has fallen in love with and gets engaged to Raoul, to the jealousy of the Phantom. The Phantom forces her to choose between them, warning her that Raoul will be killed, but in the end he lets them both go. Almost every character in the novel seems to have a double identity – as if everyone is wearing a mask. *See also* Ankh-Morpork; Fairy Tales; Musicals; Lancre; Agnes Nitt; Opera; Nanny Ogg; Walter Plinge *and* Granny Weatherwax.

Further Reading

Brown, James. 'Believing is Seeing'. *GOL2*.
Sayer, Karen. 'The Witches'. *GOL*, *GOL2*.

Andrew M. Butler

Masklin (*T*, *D*, *W*)

A nome from Outside, who comes to the store **Arnold Bros (est. 1905)** with **Grimma**, Old Torrit, Granny Morkie and other nomes. He is resourceful and a good leader, being cast into that role in the plan to help the nomes leave the store for safety when it is due to be demolished. He does not relish leadership, however, and is plagued with doubts, which Grimma helps him through. In fact he realises that it may be that honest doubts may be better than the self-deluding certainties – of, for example, blind faith in the existence of Arnold Bros, a position he cannot comprehend. Through being thrown into a new society, he realises the gender imbalances of his thinking and his old ways, and how females had been given domestic roles – his name may be an echo of 'masculine', the binary opposite of 'feminine'. Unlike the Stationeri nomes, he insists that female nomes should be taught to read as well as the male, and trusts lessons learned from books. It is he who suggests that they try to find Grandson Richard 39 and their lost spaceship in Florida, so he is absent for the majority of *D*, and he returns to **Blackbury** with the ship via South

America so he can bring back a **Bromeliad** so he can show Grimma he has been listening. He leaves Earth with most of the nomes. *See also* Arnold Bros (est. 1905); Blackbury; The Bromeliad; Children's Fiction; Grimma *and* Heroes.

Andrew M. Butler

Maxwell, Johnny (*OYCSM*, *JD*, *JB*)

The eponymous hero of the **Johnny Maxwell Trilogy**, he is twelve in the first two books, and thirteen in the third, despite the fact that they are set in 1992, 1993 and 1996 respectively. As the third volume explains about The **Trousers of Time**, which is to say alternate realties, a staple of **Science Fiction**, the Johnnies need not be the same person, and there is little reference to earlier events in later books.

His family has long been residing in **Blackbury**, his maternal grandfather Tom being an air-raid warden during the war and his paternal grandfather Arthur worked at the boot factory that dominates the town. His grandmother is now a resident at Sunshine Acres, a retirement home. His father, Peter, and his mother have a stormy relationship, which Johnny refers to as Trying Times. These have led to him being neglected, with laundry going unwashed and food not being bought for proper meals. For a period he had to live with his granddad, Tom, and his father has now left.

Johnny is part of a gang, whose nicknames he has provided. Simon Wrigley, known as Bigmac, is white, has LOVE and HAT written on his hands in Biro and, along with Bazza and Skazz, is one of only three skinheads in Blackbury. He is asthmatic and slightly criminal, but a genius at maths. Stephen Johnson, white, known as Wobbler because of his weight, is a computer genius who briefly became a billionaire when left behind in 1940s Britain (*see JB*). **Yo-Less** is black but does not conform to stereotypical ideas of what black British culture is. On the edge of the gang is **Kirsty**, who initially preferred to be called Sigourney, and who is not entirely trusted by the rest of them. Johnny has a rarely used nickname, Rubber, which presumably refers to slang for condoms, Rubber Johnnies. The gang hangs around various locations in Blackbury, including the parts of the Neil Armstrong Shopping Mall that Wobbler is not barred from, the cemetery and the local cinema, where their taste runs to anything with laser beams and explosions.

Johnny frequently escapes from his family troubles by playing **computer games**, and it is one of these which is at the heart of *OYCSM*: the female captain of the ScreeWee surrenders to him and expects him to take responsibility for their safe transportation to the border of the war game. As he is forced to confront the realness of the war game he is playing – in which he might be resurrected, but the aliens die for real – the Gulf War (1991) is playing out on television like a video game, with impressive laser displays. Whilst he has to learn not to shoot the alien fleet, he does have to shoot the male gunnery officer, as the only solution to the situation he is in.

He also helps the dead in *JD*, by giving them newspapers, a radio and, finally, televisions. He is sensitive to the dead, and is the only person to see them, although they may be heard through electricity and thus can appear on phones or radio programmes. He is determined that he will save the cemetery, and stands up to those in authority.

In *JB* he ensures that Mrs **Tachyon** gets medical attention, and when Wobbler is left behind in the past he is determined to go back and rescue him, and change history back. Here he reveals a sensitivity to time, being able to predict cards and travel through time without the aid of Mrs Tachyon's shopping trolley.

His surname may derive from James Clerk Maxwell (1831–1879), the Scottish physicist, who worked on electromagnetism. *See also* Blackbury; Children's Fiction; Coming of Age; Computers; Dead People; Games; *Johnny and the Bomb* (Television Adaptation); *Johnny and the Dead* (Television Adaptation); Johnny Maxwell Trilogy; Kirsty; Racism; Science Fiction; Sexism; Mrs Tachyon; The Trousers of Time; War *and* Yo-Less.

Further Reading

Baldry, Cherith. 'The Children's Books'. *GOL, GOL2.*

Butler, Andrew M. April 2004. ' "We has found the enemy and they is us": Virtual War and Empathy in Four Children's Science Fiction Novels'. *Lion and the Unicorn* 28.2: 171–185.

Andrew M. Butler

Men At Arms (1993)

The fifteenth novel in the **Discworld** sequence, and one which focuses on the **City Watch**, following on from *GG*, although there have been cameos from Watch characters in intervening books. The first edition, with Gollancz with a Josh **Kirby** cover, had a print run of 40,000. The Corgi paperback appeared in 1994, with a 250,000 print run; an alternative, black and gold photographic cover, edition appeared from 2005. Gollancz published *MAA* bound with *GG* and *FOC* as *The City Watch Trilogy* (1999). *MAA* has been translated into Bulgarian, Czech, Dutch, Estonian, Finnish, French, German, Hebrew, Italian, Polish, Russian, Serbian, Spanish, Swedish and Turkish. The title is a translation of Gendarmerie, a branch of the French police force, although the term also dates back to a Middle Ages term for a professional soldier who is not of noble birth. *MAA* (1952) is also the first novel in the Sword of Honour trilogy by British comic novelist Evelyn Waugh (1903–1966), where minor aristocrat Guy

Crouchback's sense of heroism and traditional English values is at odds with the real world. Colin Greenland (b.1954) wrote in his review: 'there is sex in *Men at Arms*. It is conscientiously veiled, but unequivocally sex, quite delightful and really very romantic. It is happy sex. The book later permits a well-known character to be killed; and if that is not acknowledging evil, evil is here, too; for Pratchett it is still a hot potato, to be shuffled quickly from one character to another until it can safely be attributed to an object and allowed to lurk, rumbling malignly through the plot' (*The Sunday Times*).

Edward d'Eath is determined that **Ankh-Morpork** needs a king to rule it, and settles on Carrot **Ironfoundersson** as the suitable candidate. In the meantime he hopes to cause disturbance and civil strife by committing a number of murders and crimes, including an explosion at and the theft of a weapon from the Assassin's Guild. Captain Samuel **Vimes** is preparing for his wedding to Lady Sybil **Ramkin**, and is facing retirement from the City Watch after twenty-five years. This is just as well, as the Watch is changing with the addition of **trolls** and a **werewolf** (*see* Angua von **Überwald** *and* **Racism**) to the ranks in the name of ethnic relations. Vimes and Carrot continue to investigate the crimes even after Patrician **Vetinari**'s explicit order not to do so, and they eventually unravel the conspiracy which leads to the head of the Assassin's Guild, in the process setting up a militia force. Vimes is married, and Carrot made Captain of the Watch, but only on the understanding that the Night Watch is upgraded and that Vimes is made its commander.

The parodic references are to **Detective and Noir Fiction**, including *Columbo* (1968–2003), *Hill Street Blues* (1981–1987) and *Twin Peaks* (1990–1991), with parts of the climax, in the sewers of Ankh-Morpork, owing much to *The Third Man* (1949). Carrot continues to refuse explicit **power**, although is beginning to learn how to manipulate other people, such as arch-Machiavellian Vetinari. *See also* Ankh-Morpork; City Watch; Detective and Noir Fiction; Carrot Ironfoundersson; Power; Racism; Lady Sybil Ramkin; Trolls; Angua von Überwald; Patrician Vetinari; Samuel Vimes *and* Werewolves.

Further Reading

Brown, James. 'Believing is Seeing'. *GOL2*.
James, Edward. 'The City Watch'. *GOL*, *GOL2*.

Andrew M. Butler

The Mended Drum

A hostelry in **Ankh-Morpork**, known as The **Broken Drum** prior to the refit.

Andrew M. Butler

Model of The Mended Drum created by Discworld Merchandising.

Merchandising *see* Audio Books, Stephen Briggs, Clarecraft, Comics, Computer Games, Cookbook, Diaries, Games, Graphic Novels, Tina Hannan, Maps, Music, Musicals, Bernard Pearson, Plays, Quizbooks, Television and Theatre

Monstrous Regiment (2003)

The thirty-first **Discworld** novel, which largely stands alone but features cameos from Samuel **Vimes**, Angua von **Überwald** and William de **Worde**. The first edition was published by Doubleday, with a cover by Paul **Kidby**; the paperback appeared from Corgi in 2004. It has been translated into Bulgarian, Czech, Dutch, French and German. The title comes from a pamphlet by Scottish protestant reformer John Knox (1514–1572), *The First Blast of the Trumpet against the Monstrous Regiment of Women* (1558), which attacked the hideous and ungodly rule of women such as Mary I (1542–1587), Queen of Scotland (1542–1567) and Mary I (1516–1558), Queen of England (1553–1558). The succession to the English throne of a protestant woman, Elizabeth I (1533–1603, queen from 1558), hardly did his cause any good. The cover of the British editions is a **parody** of the photograph *Raising the Flag on Iwo Jima* (1945) taken by Joe Rosenthal (1911–2006) of US Marines raising their flag when taking Mount Suribachi during a battle for the island against the Japanese. The frontispiece is a parody of a nineteenth century cartoon. Sara Ludovise complained in an online review that the novel 'lacks in the warmth and development that gives so many others [*sic*] Pratchett novels their soul. Clearly it is not the author's talent that is lacking here, but rather the convoluted story and poor choice of subject matter that make the novel seem so stale' (*The Tufts Daily* (November 2003)).

Cover of *Monstrous Regiment*. Artwork by Paul Kidby. A tribute to a famous photograph.

Polly **Perks** disguises herself as Oliver to join the Borogravian army to go in search of her brother. Borogravia is a country with a strict puritanical religion which is against pretty well everything, and they are locked in a losing battle with the Zlobenians. Perks seems to be led towards certain death in battle, under an aging craggy but wise sergeant, Jackrum, and an idiot officer, Blouse. She soon discovers that someone is trying to help her hide her sex, and that she is not the only disguised woman in the regiment. Disguised as men disguised as washerwomen, they take control of a key stronghold, and manage to negotiate peace, whilst facing some kind of trial for being women in war. It transpires that not only is virtually the whole regiment female, but much of the hierarchy is too. Perks returns home, but goes off to war again.

Here Pratchett confronts war directly, but it seems not something caused by the pettiness of men but the silliness of women pretending to be men (*see* **Sexism**). The Napoleonic Wars (1805–1815) seem to be the model, with a nod to the 1980s and 1990s conflicts in the Balkans. *See also* Feminism; Polly Perks; Sexism; Angua Von Überwald; Samuel Vimes; War and William de Worde.

Further Reading

Knox, John. 1967. *The First Blast of the Trumpet against the Monstrous Regiment of Women.* Edited by Edward Arber. New York, AMS Press.

Andrew M. Butler

Mort (1987)

The fourth book in the **Discworld** series is dedicated to Rhianna, Pratchett's daughter. The first edition was published by Victor Gollancz in association with Colin **Smythe** Ltd in a print run of 3,950 copies, with a cover by Josh **Kirby**. The Corgi paperback appeared in a print run of 111,500 in 1988; since 2004 an alternative cover with a black and gold photograph has also been available. In 1995 Gollancz published a compact edition in a run of about 20,000, and bound it with *RM* and *SM* as *The Death Trilogy* (1998). Translations include Bulgarian, Chinese, Croatian, Czech, Danish, Dutch, Estonian, Finnish, French, German, Greek, Hebrew, Hungarian, Italian, Japanese, Norwegian, Polish, Portuguese, Romanian, Russian, Serbian, Slovakian, Slovenian, Spanish, Swedish and Turkish. *M* is another **Coming of Age** narrative, featuring Mort Sto **Helit**, **Death**'s apprentice. The title refers both to the character's name (and Death's name is Mort in *LF*) and to the French word for death. There is very much a sense that the cultural references are widening beyond fantasy. It has been adapted into a comic book (*see* ***Mort: A Discworld Big Comic***). Jon Wallace wrote in *Vector* 142: 'Terry Pratchett has been called the Douglas Adams of fantasy, and in the sense that both satirise aspects of SF, this is true, but Pratchett's books are fresher than Adams's, they have more plot, and the jokes are funnier...' (February 1988).

In a village in the Ramtops, the young Mort is apprenticed to Death, and lives with him in **Death's Domain**, along with Alberto **Malich** and Death's adopted daughter, Ysabell. Death goes fishing whilst Mort goes out on his first solo round, and Mort refuses to allow Princess Kelirihenna of **Sto Lat** to be assassinated. This opens up a fissure in time, as the rest of the universe wants to carry on as if she were dead. Death meanwhile turns to **drink** in the **Mended Drum** and then gets a job as a short-order cook. Mort and Ysabell enlist the help of Alberto to try and save the situation, before Mort, slowly being subsumed into the Death personality, has to fight with Death. Mort and Ysabell marry and become the Duke and Duchess of **Sto Helit**, and Death visits them at the wedding feast.

The novel draws on various earlier representations of Death, such as the play *Death Takes a Holiday* (1924) by Alberto Casella (1891–1957) for Death taking time off and *The Seventh Seal* (1957) directed by Ingmar Bergman (1918–2007) where a medieval knight, Antonius Block, plays Death at chess for his life. Another comedic version of Death can be seen in *Love and Death* (1975) directed by Woody Allen (b.1935). This novel also makes references to **Fairy Tales** and the plays of William **Shakespeare**. *See also* Coming of Age; Death; Death's Domain; Drink; Fairy Tales; The Mended Drum; *Mort: A Discworld Big Comic*; William Shakespeare; Mort Sto Helit, Susan Sto Helit; Ysabella Sto Helit; Sto Lat *and* Keli of Sto Lat.

Further Reading

Butler, Andrew M. 'Terry Pratchett and the Comedic *Bildungsroman*'. *Foundation* 67 (Summer 1996): Pp. 56–62.
Butler, Andrew M. 'Theories of Comedy'. *GOL, GOL2.*

Andrew M. Butler

Mort: A Discworld Big Comic (1994)

Adapted from the book *M* by Terry Pratchett, this was the first **Discworld** graphic novel, as opposed to ***Terry Pratchett's The Colour of Magic*** and ***Terry Pratchett's The Light Fantastic*** which had been released as individual comics and then collected. The artwork is by Graham **Higgins**, with colouring by Carol Bennett and lettering by Euan Smith. Initially it had been planned to do both colour and black and white versions, so it was necessary for the artwork to work without the use of colour. Higgins did about two pages every day he worked on it, drawing onto A3 size paper. Gollancz issued it in hardback (1,750 copies) and paperback (33,500). Pratchett dedicated it to his daughter, Rhianna, and Higgins to his sons, Matthew and James.

Perhaps because of the involvement of Pratchett in the adaptation, it does stay close to the original story-line, although it is perhaps slightly confusing in some of the shifts between focus – **Death**, Mort **Sto Herit** and Keli of **Sto Lat**'s intertwining strands switch in midpage rather than between pages. There is some sense of counterpoint, but it is Mort's story that dominates whilst Death's adventures in the mortal world seem only glimpsed. **Ankh-Morpork** is richly imagined as a teeming city out of Pieter Bruegel the Elder (*c.*1525–1569) and Gustave Doré (1832–1883), full of detail. Some of the Breughel imagery makes its way into the depiction of **Death's Domain**, especially the hanging poles from *The Triumph of Death* (*c.*1562). In the battle between Death and Mort towards the end of the book, there are visual echoes of Michelangelo (1475–1564).

One added element is the use of the **Librarian**, in **orangutan** guise, as an explanatory device, particularly in regard to the explanation about the change to reality caused by Mort's saving of Keli's life. The Librarian is depicted with a blackboard scrawled with a large number of (fake) mathematical equations. The text refers to The **Trousers of Time**, a concept not yet developed in the Discworld novels when *M* was published; *LL* is the earliest mention. *M* only has a sense of history being stretched out of shape. Mort's line to Keli, 'Come with me if you want to live', is an echo of Kyle Reese to Sarah Connor in *The Terminator* and T100 to John Connor in *Terminator 2: Judgment Day* (1991).

As characters in comics tend to speak in capital letters, and by tradition Death does in the Discworld oeuvre, Death has to have a more gothic font for his speech bubbles, to distinguish his voice. Wherein the book Mort sometimes gets Death's voice, here he never quite identifies enough to share the typeface.

This is a solid adaptation, with some neat touches, but the novel is both funnier and more richly detailed. *See also* Ankh-Morpork; Comics; Coming of Age; Death; Death's Domain; Fairy Tales; Graphic Novels; Graham Higgins; Hollywood Films; The Librarian; The Mended Drum; Orangutans; Mort Sto Helit, Susan Sto Helit; Ysabella Sto Helit; Sto Lat; Keli of Sto Lat *and* The Trousers of Time.

Andrew M. Butler

Moving Pictures (1990)

The ninth (or tenth, see *E*) in the **Discworld** series, and part of the **Wizards** sequence. The first edition was 18,200 copies, published by Gollancz with a Josh **Kirby** cover. The Corgi paperback was 150,000 in 1991, with an alternative black and gold photographic cover available since 2005. It has been translated into Bulgarian, Czech, Dutch, Estonian, Finnish, French, German, Hebrew, Hungarian, Italian, Norwegian, Polish, Portuguese, Russian, Serbian, Spanish, Swedish and Turkish. The title comes from the novel's exploration of the Discworld version of the movies. The book's dedication is in the form of a thank-you speech. Brendan Wignall wrote in a review: '*Moving Pictures* may be wobbly by Pratchett's extraordinarily high standards but it is still the funniest book I have read for some time' (*The Oxford Times*).

Up in distant Holy Wood, the last Keeper of the Door has died and something begins to stir. The alchemists have discovered a variation on the camera where an imp paints a picture: they can now produce moving pictures which can be projected with the careful use of a Salamander. A new industry is waiting to be born. At the **Unseen University** there is a new **Archchancellor** after a period of instability, Mustrum **Ridcully**, who has been absent from the University for a number of years and so is not mired in **Wizard** politics. One of their students, Victor **Tugelbend**, runs away to Holy Wood, called by powers beyond his comprehension. He is joined by many others, from across the Disc, including potential actress Theda Withel, the troll **Detritus** and the ever avaricious Cut-My-Own-Throat **Dibbler**. Whilst Victor and Theda become film stars in versions of the great Hollywood epics, including *Blown Away* (that is, *Gone With the Wind* (1939)), Dibbler becomes a Holy Wood mogul, pushing for huge effects, thousands of **elephants**, and opportunities to sell popcorn and sausages in buns. Victor is aided by Gaspode, a talking **dog**, who acts as an agent and who is able to help him in his growing conviction that something is going on. Alarm bells are also ringing at the Unseen University – something is coming through from the **Dungeon Dimensions**. Chaos engulfs the **Ankh-Morpork** premiere of *Blown Away*, before the thing causing it moves into a different location, and the Holy Wood business collapses.

This novel is stuffed full with references to **Hollywood Films** in the same way that *SM* was to include jokes about popular music. Besides particular films, it references studios (Century of the Fruitbat, Firwood Studios, Microlithic Pictures and Untied Alchemists), actors and producers. *See also* Ankh-Morpork; Archchancellors; Detritus; C.M.O.T. Dibbler; Dogs; Dungeon Dimensions; Elephants; Hollywood Films; Politics; Mustrum Ridcully; Trolls; Victor Tugelbend; Unseen University *and* Wizards.

Further Reading

Hill, Penelope. 'Unseen University'. *GOL, GOL2.*

Andrew M. Butler

Music

Dave **Greenslade** has produced a CD of music inspired by **Discworld**, and there was a soundtrack CD for ***Soul Music From Terry Pratchett's Discworld***. Music is also a source for **parody** within the novels – see **Musicals**, **Opera** and **Pop Music**.

Andrew M. Butler

Musicals

In 2003, a musical version of ***OYCSM*** was performed at the Soho Laundry Workshop and it then premiered at the Pleasance Courtyard, Edinburgh Festival (4–30 August 2004). The composer was Leighton James House (b.1980) and the lyrics were written by Shaun McKenna, who has since co-written the book and lyrics for *The Lord of the Rings* musical (2006).

Pratchett makes a number of references to musicals in his fiction, as he does to **Hollywood films**, **music hall**, **opera** and other forms of popular culture. Much culture is so engrained that many people tend to use musical theatre clichés and situations without thinking consciously where these ideas came from. This seems to hold true on the **Discworld**; the constant onslaught of creative impulse sleeting through the multiverse apparently inspires characters to make familiar references to delight Pratchett's readers, especially in *WS*, *MP*, *SM*, *Msk* and *NW*. The reader who recognises the references is free to feel superior about their knowledge of the world.

Cast of *Les Miserables* from the performance in Singapore, February 1994. Note resemblance to *Night Watch* depictions of the City Watch.

There are basically two types of modern musical:

A theatrical, film or television production which involves the use of music, singing, dancing, acting and/or speciality acts to tell a story (also known as a 'book musical');

A theatrical, film or television production which highlights the performances of writers, composers and/or performers, with no real story involved (more properly known as a 'revue'), usually within a specific genre.

The modern musical has its roots in many different places: music hall, opera, theatrical spectacles, the ballet and more. (Though musicologists may argue in favour of their own pet theories about where musicals may or may not have their roots, in reality development of the musical was doubtless less clear-cut than many would prefer.)

The history of musical theatre – theatrical productions that include music, dancing and singing – spans from the ancient Greeks, medieval pageantry and mystery plays, the development of the grand opera,

opera *buffo* and *comique*, to the ballad operas of the 1700s, through the burlesques, pantomimes and operettas of the 1800s, music hall, vaudeville and variety, the revues of the early 1900s and on to the productions (theatrical, film and concept album) we all think of as 'musicals': *No No Nanette* (1925), *The Wizard of Oz* (1939), *Oklahoma!* (1943), *Singin' in the Rain* (1952), *My Fair Lady* (1956), *West Side Story* (1957), *The Music Man* (1957), *Chicago* (1975), *Evita* (1976), *All That Jazz* (1979), *Cats* (1981) and, of course, many more.

There are certain conventions of musical theatre that have passed into the area of what Terry Pratchett has called 'white knowledge' (which is to general knowledge what 'white noise' is to sound).

These include music swelling-up under dialogue until the actor bursts into song, dance or both (as **Detritus** and Ruby nearly do at the end of *MP*); a character wanders city streets, bursts into song and dance while various citizens also manifest musical and dancing talent (as described in *MAA*); and even the familiar story of an understudy who is forced to sing behind the scenes as a star mouths the words (as Agnes **Nitt** does in *Msk* – although usually in a musical the star's deception is unmasked, as in *Singin' in the Rain*).

In *LF* there's a reference by **Rincewind** to 'Summertime' (the first line is 'Summertime, and the living is easy'), from *Porgy and Bess* (1935) by George Gershwin (1898–1937). Old Man Trouble, as mentioned in 'I Got Rhythm' in the musical *Girl Crazy* (1930) is a character in *FOC* and *H*.

The Discworld's version of William **Shakespeare**, the dwarf **Hwel**, has been writing a sort of über-**play**, which (in *WS*) we see references plays such as *Waiting for Godot* (1953/1955), actors such as the Marx Brothers and Laurel and Hardy, and also the Andrew Lloyd Webber musicals *Cats*, *Starlight Express* (1984) and *The Phantom of the Opera* (1986). Death also quotes from the song 'There's No Business Like Show Business' from *Annie Get Your Gun* (1946).

The Ramtops are described as mountains where 'no one ran up them wearing dirndls and singing' (*WA*). This refers to the opening scene of the movie version of *The Sound of Music* (1965), wherein an aerial shot skims through the Alps and finds Julie Andrews as the novice nun turned housekeeper/nanny running up a grassy bluff, where she bursts into the title song of the musical. Even people who hate this musical, or perhaps especially people who hate this musical, seem to have an iconic picture of this scene tattooed indelibly into their consciousness. *The Sound of Music* is also referenced in *RM*, when the Ramtops are compared to the mountains in the song 'The Lonely Goatherd', and also in *LL*, when Magrat **Garlick** is described as having a soft spot for raindrops and roses and whiskers on kittens' (from 'My Favorite Things').

SM contains more references to rock 'n' roll and pop music than it does to musical theatre, but there is a reference made to the dwarf songwriters Gorlick and Hammerjug, the Discworld equivalents of Rogers and Hammerstein. (Richard Rogers (1902–1979) and Oscar Hammerstein II

(1895–1960) wrote nine musicals together: *Oklahoma!*, *Carousel* (1945), *South Pacific* (1949), *The King and I* (1951) and *The Sound of Music* were probably their best-known hits.)

In ***H***, Susan **Sto Helit** refuses to countenance the thought of dancing on rooftops with chimney sweeps, which refers to the musical *Mary Poppins* (1964), in which Julie Andrews dances across the rooftops of London with a troupe of sweeps led by Dick Van Dyke, who sports an atrocious cockney accent.

Samuel **Vimes** remembers the bad business of 'the barber in Gleam Street', Sweeney Jones (*J*). This refers to Sweeney Todd, The Demon Barber of Fleet Street, who was immortalised in one guise or another from the early nineteenth century on. (He murdered his customers and, in the Sondheim version (1979), gave the bodies to his neighbour to make into meat pies.) *J* also gives us a thief called The Artful Nudger, a reference to The Artful Dodger in *Oliver Twist* (1838; musical *Oliver!* (1960)).

The Wizard of Oz has numerous references ('lions and tigers and bears, oh my!' turns into 'generals and majors and captains, oh my' in *MR*, for instance) and there are many references to Disney's *Snow White and the Seven Dwarfs* (1937) in the books featuring dwarfs. These include the tendency of Pratchett's dwarfs when happy to break into something he calls 'The HiHo Song' (also known as 'that song') and a description of the name Cheery **Littlebottom** being part of 'the old naming traditions' (that we can probably safely assume include Doc, Grumpy, Bashful, Happy, Sleepy, Sneezy and Dopey).

The two books that most heavily reference musicals, however, are *Msk* and *NW*.

Msk closely parodies Lloyd Webber's *The Phantom of the Opera*. In *Phantom*, which takes place in an opera house, a beautiful young opera singer named Christine is taken under the tutelage of a mysterious masked man known as The Phantom. Christine is reluctant to take her rightful place in the opera, not in small part because of Carlotta, the jealous diva with an ageing voice. The Phantom wishes to have Christine's talent presented by the opera, but the owners fear Carlotta's jealous rage, and Christine eventually struggles to get out from under The Phantom's despotic wing.

Msk takes place in **Ankh-Morpork**'s Opera House. Christine is not talented, but is beautiful, and so the owners put her up front and put Agnes, who has a beautiful voice but unfortunately has 'good hair', behind her to sing the actual arias. The Phantom trains Agnes thinking she is Christine (the girls switch rooms). There are chase scenes and chandeliers with dramatic possibilities in both *Msk* and *The Phantom of the Opera*.

Msk also makes reference to some of Walter **Plinge**'s musicals, which show us that Walter is the Discworld's musical **Hwel**. Some of his musicals are *Guys and Trolls* (*Guys and Dolls* (1952)), *Hubwards Side Story* (*West Side Story*), *Miserable Les* (*Les Miserables* (1980)), *Seven Dwarfs for Seven Other*

Dwarfs (*Seven Brides for Seven Brothers* (1954)), and it's quite clear that one of the musicals is a version of *Cats*.

NW, on the other hand, is not so much a **parody** of *Les Miserables* (and in fact Pratchett's inspiration may not have been *Les Miserables*, as many of the themes involved are universal to revolution and uprising) as it mainly contains a number of mirrored, Discworld versions of characters and themes. However, given the strong themes of legalism, grace, justice, mercy and redemption that are always attendant in any book that features Sam **Vimes**, *Les Miserables* (the musical version is often referred to as simply *Les Mis*) would be an ideal story to reference.

In *Les Mis*, Jalvert the policeman is the apparent antagonist and the ex-convict Valjean is our protagonist. Jalvert is concerned only with justice and believes that the guilty must be punished. Jalvert joins the rebels on the barricades in order to spy on and defeat them. Valjean's original crime was to steal bread for his starving family, and Jalvert pursues Valjean over distance (and over a long period of time) when Valjean breaks his parole. Valjean tries to save a prostitute. The street urchin Gavroche keeps company with the whores and beggars of the capital and is later killed on the barricades.

In *NW*, Vimes the policeman is our protagonist, and psychopathic murderer Carcer is our antagonist. Vimes is concerned only with justice and believes the innocent must be protected. Vimes leads the rebels on the barricades in order to protect the citizens of Ankh Morpork, and Carcer becomes part of the corrupt **City Watch**. Carcer claims that his original crime was stealing a loaf of bread. Vimes pursues Carcer through Ankh Morpork and then back in time after Carcer murders a policeman. Vimes is saved by a prostitute. Street urchin Nobby **Nobbs** keeps company with the watchmen, and survives the attack on the barricades. It has been pointed out that both *Les Mis* and *NW* are peopled with passionate revolutionaries in frilly shirts who make impassioned speeches while taking a long time to die. *See also* City Watch; Detritus; Magrat Garlick; Hollywood Films; Hwel; Cheery Littlebottom; Music Hall; Agnes Nitt; Nobby Nobbs; Opera; Parody; Plays; Walter Plinge; Pop Music; Rincewind; Susan Sto Helit; Theatre *and* Samuel Vimes.

Zina Lee

Music Hall

Music Hall had an incalculable influence on British society. There are many references in the **Discworld** books to classic jokes from Music Hall. In the United States, Music Hall is closely related to Variety and Vaudeville. It was from Music Hall, Variety and Vaudeville that stand up and sketch comedy emerged, and from that emerged possibilities for situation comedy.

Throughout the 1700s, pubs and inns held 'sing-songs' of folk and popular songs in back rooms. Popular theatre was often presented at travelling fairs. Song and Supper Rooms were essentially public clubs where men could enjoy a night out on the town. Outdoor musical 'pleasure gardens', beer gardens and gin palaces flourished.

By the early 1800s, many pubs and inns had rooms specifically for saloon entertainment. The audience felt free to participate, offering encouragement (or discouragement), singing along and interacting with performers. Gradually, a variety of acts began to be offered in one evening: jugglers, animal acts, acrobats, dancers – opera, ballet, monologues and other high-minded acts were often offered as well.

By the second half of the 1800s, as Music Hall grew in respectability, some landlords had moved their entertainments to purpose-built halls; London had about three music halls around 1870. A chairman would introduce the acts as the audience ate, drank, sang along and heckled the performers. In 1878, there were major licensing changes, and the smaller music halls began to decline in numbers as people began to flock to the large theatres.

Music Hall songs were often unabashedly aimed at lower-class audiences. There were sentimental 'bawlers' (such as Nellie Dean mentioned in *GG*), songs detailing the love affairs of milkmen and parlour maids, ditties about moonlight flits to avoid the rent collector, lampoons of all the classes from rich to poor, and silly songs for simple amusement.

Music Hall composers and performers rallied public support for the First World War. Songs like 'Keep the Home Fires Burning', 'Pack up Your Troubles', 'It's a Long Way to Tipperary', and 'We Don't Want to Lose You (But We Think You Ought To Go)', were sung, whistled and hummed by everyone. Singers sang lyrics like 'I didn't like you much before you joined the army, John, but I do like yer, cockie, now you've got your khaki on'. After the First World War, film and other forms of theatre replaced Music Hall as the popular entertainment, though some performers successfully brought Music Hall to film.

There were many popular performers, including Dan Leno, Little Tich, Gus Elen, Vesta Tilley, Harry Lauder, and George Formby, both Sr. and Jr. (in *LC*, **Rincewind** says, 'Turned out nice again', the catchphrase of George Formby Jr., usually said a split-second before he started running away from trouble), and comedy teams such as Weber and Fields, Flanagan and Allen and Wilson, Kepple and Betty (in *J*, **Vetinari, Colon** and **Nobbs** form a troupe reminiscent of these acts).

Perhaps the best-loved performer of all was Marie Lloyd (1870–1922), and a look at her life and act speaks volumes about Music Hall; to many, Marie Lloyd was Music Hall. A genuine Cockney, born Matilda Victoria Wood in 1870 in Hoxton, Marie (pronounced to rhyme with 'starry') was famous for her saucy wink, risqué lyrics and gestures. There is a widespread but apocryphal story that Marie sang a song beginning, 'I sits among my cabbages and peas'; the Lord Chamberlain was supposedly appalled by these lyrics and so Marie temporarily changed the lyrics to 'I sits among my cabbages and leeks'. It is easy to imagine Nanny **Ogg** singing these songs.

What Marie definitely did do was appear before the Vigilance Committee after Mrs. Ormiston Chant of the Purity Party made a public protest against Marie from the stalls of the Empire. Marie proceeded to sing all of her songs with nary a wink or gesture; including 'Oh Mr. Porter', which proclaimed, 'I've never 'ad me ticket punched before'. The songs sounded completely innocent and the Committee had to let her off. Marie, incensed by such censorship, then sang the blameless ballad, 'Come Into the Garden, Maude' with such gestures and knowing looks that the song became quite obscene. Despite being widely proclaimed the Queen of the Music Hall by an adoring public on both sides of the Atlantic, Marie was not invited to perform at the first Royal Command Performance of Music Hall performers in 1912 because of the bawdiness of her act. Deeply hurt and mortified, she rented the London Pavilion on the same night, playing to a sold out house, with posters proclaiming, 'Every Performance by Marie Lloyd is a Command Performance' and 'By Order of the British Public'.

Marie's personal life was scandalous and tragic, with three unsuccessful marriages; there was abuse, alcoholism, and charges of moral turpitude. Still, she remained generous to others in her profession, helping the smaller artists in the Music Hall Strike, and was instrumental in forming the Variety Artists' Association, later to become part of Equity, the actor's union.

In October 1922, the audience in Edmonton laughed delightedly as Marie literally staggered, mortally ill, through her famous song 'It's a Bit of a Ruin That Cromwell Knocked About A Bit', portraying an upright lady who gets tipsy. Three days later, she was dead, and many felt that the true Music Hall days died with her.

In *The Dial* magazine, T.S. Eliot wrote about Marie's death:

> '...no other comedian succeeded so well in giving expression to the life of that audience, in raising it to a kind of art. It was, I think, this capacity for expressing the soul of the people that made Marie Lloyd unique and that made her audiences, even when they joined in the chorus, not so much hilarious as happy.'

One of Marie's best known hits, 'A Little of What You Fancy Does You Good', could be Nanny Ogg's theme song. *See also* Frederick Colon; Nobby Nobbs; Nanny Ogg; Rincewind *and* Patrician Vetinari.

Further Reading

Eliot, T.S. 'London Letter'. *The Dial* 73.6. (December 1922): 659–663.
The English Music Hall. http://www.amaranthdesign.ca/musichall/past/lloyd.htm
Hackney Empire. http://www.hackneyempire.co.uk/
Hinckley, Paul. *A Dictionary of Great War Slang*. http://sir.cyivs.cy.edu.tw/~hchung/warslang.htm
Windyridge CDs. Music Hall and Variety Songs on CD. http://www.musichallcds.com/index.html

Zina Lee

N

Nanny Ogg's Cookbook (1999)

Subtitled: *Including Recipes, Items of Antiquarian Lore, Improving Observations of Life, Good Advice for Young People on the Threshold of the Adventure That is Marriage, Notes on Etiquette & Many Other Helpful Observations that will Not Offend the Most Delicate Sensibilities.*

By Terry Pratchett, Stephen **Briggs** and Tina **Hannan**. Illustrated by Paul **Kidby**. The first edition was published by Doubleday in hardback, with a paperback from Corgi in 2001. It has been translated into Bulgarian, Czech and German. Basically a book featuring recipes collected by Nanny **Ogg**, some of which are supplied by characters from the **Discworld**, such as Patrician **Vetinari**, Mustrum **Ridcully** and **Verence II**. Some of the recipes are versions of **food** mentioned in the sequence, and some of the recipes are actually practical. In line with its **parody** of Mrs Beeton-style household advice, the book deals with the philosophy of food, how to deal with **dwarfs**, **trolls**, **witches** and **wizards**, eating etiquette and courtship and marital relations. It is intercut with memos between J.H.C. Goatberger (compare Gunilla **Goodmountain**) and his chief printer, Thomas Cropper, worrying about the innuendo and doubles entendres that seem to be part of Nanny Ogg's style. The chapter on 'Etiquette in the Bedroom' is particularly dogged with notes.

Cover of *Nanny Ogg's Cookbook*. Artwork by Paul Kidby.

Nanny Ogg's Cookbook

Proceeds from the sales of this book went to the **Orangutan** Foundation. *See also* Stephen Briggs; Drink; Food; Tina Hannan; Paul Kidby; Merchandising; Nanny Ogg *and* Orangutans.

Andrew M. Butler

Narrative

In the *SOD* series, Terry Pratchett, Jack **Cohen** and Ian **Stewart** argue that rather than being called *Homo sapiens*, humans should be described as *Pan narrans*, the story-telling ape. Whether the case for this is made or not, Terry Pratchett's own concern with narrative has come to be one of the principle ethical concerns of the **Discworld** books (and to a lesser extent the **Johnny Maxwell Trilogy**).

Pratchett's interest is in the power of narrative expectation. In the earliest Discworld books, *COM* and *LF*, this was the power behind a loosely linked set of jokes and a whole world in which the power of narrative expectation as tied to **Science Fiction** and **Fantasy** clichés was exploited. At this stage, the humour rested in the absurdity of clichés taken to their inevitable conclusions such as running literally off the edge of a flat earth, or of clichés punctured such as the realisation that eventually heroes grow old and lose their teeth. By *ER*, however, a new use for narrative was beginning to emerge.

In both *ER* and *M*, Pratchett took common narratives – the girl wanting to do a boy's job, the apprentice taking over the master – and considered what really happens. Both these books show very strong resemblances to the revisionist 'feminist **Fairy Tales**' of the 1970s and 1980s. Like these tales, once having subverted the narrative expectation of gender (*see* **Sexism** *and* **Feminism**) or of class, the stories lose their impetus.

The first strong use of narrative as the subject of the story is in *WS*. As a very obvious riff on *Macbeth*, the story follows the general narrative structure of that play but is told from the point of view of the **witches** who want to work with the classic story of tyrant overthrown by true heir. To achieve this, however, they have to play with time so that the heir grows up before the tyrant secures his hold on the kingdom. Running alongside this are some very unsubtle metaphors about the theatre and the role of performativity in real life. This is where things get interesting.

At the end of *WS* when the heir to the throne arrives with his troupe of players, they stage a performance intended to secure the usurper Felmet on the throne. The witches realise that they are being rewritten on stage, turned into hags who are somehow less frightening than they know themselves to be. They interrupt the play and take it over, imposing truth on the narrative. The conclusion of the story – in which the heir's brother (the **Fool**) takes the throne rather than **Tomjon** – is a throwback to

Pratchett's more traditional subversion of narrative; the Fool and the Actor are related through the Fool's father and not the King. It is the moment when the witches take over the play that is important. From this moment on, Granny **Weatherwax**, the senior witch, is going to be fascinated by the power of narrative causality, and will become its life-long enemy.

In *SODII*, Pratchett, Cohen and Stewart write that it is possible to resist the power of story and take control of the narrative like Granny Weatherwax does. She and Johnny **Maxwell** are both the embodiment of this attitude, but for the Granny it is a head on fight to the death, for Johnny, it is passive resistance.

Granny Weatherwax's fight against narrative causality begins at the end of *WS*, and continues through *WA*, *LL* and *CJ*. Granny Weatherwax hates two things about stories; first, that they stop people thinking, and second that they have lives of their own. If people tell themselves stories about witchcraft they will believe that water can cure all ills (as opposed to carefully applied chiropraxy). If people tell themselves stories about **elves** and **vampires**, they will be seduced by glamour, their power to resist undermined by narrative inevitability. It is therefore the witch's duty to insert the sharp axe edge of refusal into the tale as the witch Agnes **Nitt** does in *CJ*. Stories can be so powerful that they will oil the assembly line of atrocity, and people will stand by for blood donations to vampires and the martyrdom of the innocent, personal stories of niceness and good parenting can wipe out the wider narrative of torture inflicted (see *SG*).

But much, much worse, in Granny Weatherwax's worldview, is the sense that stories or narrative causality feed on humans. In *WA*, Granny's sister Lilith (aka Lily **Weatherwax**) has discovered the recursive nature of stories: as a story works its way through it acquires the power of inevitability, it spawns more stories which structure the narratives people are capable of conceiving, so that the beautiful princess will marry the prince and will fall in love, because to ask awkward questions about character and bad breath would be to spoil the narrative structure. And here again is where it gets interesting: Granny Weatherwax destroys narrative by destroying linearity. This is an element that has been present in Pratchett's novels from the first: little asides, footnotes, small riffs, all destroyed the smooth impermeability of the characteristic mass market fantasy (what John Clute memorably called Extruded Fantasy Product, or EFP). EFP depends on the willingness of the audience to suspend judgement, depends absolutely on the main character's willingness to accept everything the mage figure tells him/her about the world. Pratchett and Granny Weatherwax (and also Samuel **Vimes**) drive a coach and rats through this model of fantasy. In place of the footnotes and asides we have Granny's sarcastic comments, and her companions' well meaning interference. Nanny **Ogg**'s ability to say something embarrassing on any given occasion is one of the most powerful weapons Granny can wield. Magrat **Garlick**'s well-meaning empathy for story is not far behind, because it can render any romance trite. The result is that the linear narrative which Lilith wants to promote in *WA* is continually punctuated by discord as Granny asks all the awkward questions missing from the fairy tales of Charles Perrault (1628–1703).

However, this is not all about punctuating niceness. The Grimms' fairy tales are just as compelling (and mind-numbing), just as capable of removing the power of thought and action. For these Granny Weatherwax offers **theatre**, the use of story to undermine the power of story: what we see, watch and throw eggs at, can have no power to hurt us. In *LL* and later in *SODII*, Pratchett demonstrates the most powerful skill of the story-telling ape, the power to rewrite and rework the narrative, to use narrative in fact as a large poker with which to challenge the stories of the world. (See Susan **Sto Helit** in *H* – not believing in Bogeymen is a good start, but believing in them and carrying a poker is a better ending.)

Stories give people comfort: Pratchett, Cohen and Stewart talk about this a great deal in *SOD* series. The story-telling ape prefers a good story about Creation, than the somewhat more complex and fragmented narrative about evolution. As story tellers we like to be at the centre of the narrative (the earth around which the sun moves), although frequently the margins are both more realistic and more comfortable places to be. Granny Weatherwax is one of the rare people who fiercely preserves her marginality (while also insisting on her importance of course – she is a witch!), she is always and ever the interferer in other people's stories. It is Johnny, however, who demonstrates the human power to rework stories and hence change narrative.

In *OYCSM*, Johnny finds himself in a **computer game** of space invaders aiding the 'aliens' to get away from human game space. His perennial cry is 'why me?'. The answer emerges when he introduces **Kirsty** to game space to help him release the Captain of the ship after a coup. The ship gets darker, shadows creep around corners. The 'aliens' develop sharper teeth and longer jaws. Kirsty's world-narrative is both more threatening and binary than Johnny's. It does not include the ordinary things in life, such as the squeaky trolley and missing teeth of the alien tea lady. Later Johnny will contemplate the construction of the narrative of the other in the free plastic aliens which fall out of the cereal box: somehow there is no place in the world-narrative for a plastic alien with hedge-clippers.

Yet where Granny Weatherwax is deeply suspicious of narrative imperative, in the two later books Johnny learns to harness it. In *JD*, narrative imperative keeps the graveyard open, as Johnny offers 10p for a graveyard bought by a developer for 5p. Later he will explain how constructed narratives of the past are essential to enable humans to construct narratives of the present (ironic in a series which speaks sneeringly of 'empathy essays' for history homework). And in *JB*, Johnny draws attention to the importance that individuals construct their own narratives, as he gives the hospitalised Mrs **Tachyon** hot fish and chips instead of grapes. In the end **Coming of Age** and finding control or agency is truly about finding your own personal narrative, rather than remaining subject to someone else's. *See also* Coming of Age; Fairy Tales; Fantasy; Heroes; Magic; Johnny Maxwell Trilogy; Johnny Maxwell *and* Witches.

Farah Mendlesohn

The New Discworld Companion see The Discworld Companion

'Night Dweller'

Pratchett's second story, published in the British **Science Fiction** magazine *New Worlds* (issue156, November 1965; Pp. 83–88), which was edited by Michael Moorcock (b.1939). It has never been reprinted and is quite different in tone to his other works.

An unnamed narrator is on a spaceship heading out beyond the orbit of Pluto in search of a mysterious entity. The crew includes the narrator and Jasson, who would have been facing a court-martial and execution on Earth, Donovan with a terminal disease and a Christian, Brewer. They have with them the words of a civilisation destroyed by the howling entity, and the suicide mission is to seek it out and destroy it with nuclear material. The radiation from the warhead is leaking and will kill them, but they will die anyway when they set it off. The story ends as they head towards the entity.

This is a slight science fiction story, uncharacteristically devoid of humour, and probably the straightest fiction that Pratchett has ever written. It is perhaps a little over-written, and is rather descriptive instead of being dramatic. *See also* Science Fiction.

Andrew M. Butler

Night Watch (2002)

The twenty-ninth **Discworld** novel, featuring Samuel **Vimes** and the **City Watch**. The first edition was published by Doubleday, with a cover done by Paul **Kidby**, the first of the novels to be published after the death of Josh **Kirby**. The paperback from Corgi followed in 2003. *NW* has been translated into Bulgarian, Czech, Dutch, French and German. The novel is a pastiche of *The Company of Frans Banning Cocq and Willem van Ruytenburch* (1642), more commonly known as *Night Watch*, by Rembrandt Harmenszoon van Rijn (*c.*1606–1669). The night watch is an alternate name for the city watch or guards. John Newsinger wrote that: *NW* 'is probably Pratchett's greatest joke ever: a revolution that is carried out by the police! This is obviously the only safe sort of revolution, because the police will be able to protect private property. None of this left-wing socialism rubbish in Ankh-Morpork' (*Vector* 232 (2003)).

On the thirtieth anniversary of the Glorious 25 May, Vimes plans to visit the grave of his mentor, John Keel, but is waylaid by the news that serial killer Carcer has been spotted. Vimes and Carcer are struck by a magical discharge – a side effect of a lightning strike from *TOT* – and are sent back in time thirty years. Having failed to get help from the **wizards**, and being confused by **Lu-Tze**, Vimes becomes Keel and joins the City Watch as a sergeant. His style of policing is at odds with the more corrupt and blind-eye tactics of the old watch, and he begins to be a mentor to a younger version of himself. A revolution is brewing, and the Pseudopolis Yard watch benefits from his tactics. Someone, meanwhile, is taking an interest in his progress: the enigmatic Lady Roberta Meserole, who has engaged her nephew (the future) Patrician **Vetinari** to protect Vimes and assassinate the Patrician Winder. As the revolution comes, Vimes barricades the streets around the watchhouse to keep out the cavalry, and his men push them back to encompass a third of **Ankh-Morpork**. The new patrician, Snapcase, grants the revolutionaries an amnesty, but wants Vimes/Keel killed. Vimes and Carcer square off, but return to the present where Lady Sybil **Ramkin** gives birth to Samuel's son. Vimes arrests Carcer at the grave of Keel, and Vetinari reveals that he thought Keel and Vimes were the same person.

Cover of *Night Watch*. Artwork by Paul Kidby. A tribute to Rembrandt.

A parody of revolutionary tales and histories, including Les Miserables (1862) by Victor Hugo (1802–1885) – the musical by Claude-Michel Schönberg (b.1944) and Alain Boublil (b.1941), opened in Paris in 1980 and London in 1985 (*see* **Musicals**) – *A Tale of Two Cities* (1859) by Charles Dickens (1812–1870) and the Peterloo Massacre in Manchester (1819). It also reveals Vimes's youth, prior to his alcoholism, and confirms that Vetinari is an ex-assassin.

See Ankh-Morpork; City Watch; History; Paul Kidby; Lu-Tze; Musicals; Politics; Patrician Vetinari and Samuel Vimes.

Further Reading

James, Edward. 'The City Watch'. *GOL2*.
Newsinger, John. 2003. 'The People's Republic of Treacle Mine Road Betrayed: Terry Pratchett's *Night Watch*'. *Vector: The Critical Journal of the British Science Fiction Association* 232 (November/December). Pp. 15–16.

Andrew M. Butler

Nisodemus (*D*)

Nisodemus is one of the nomes who lives in the store **Arnold Bros (est. 1905)** and is part of the Stationeri tribe, thus able to read. He is left in charge when **Abbot** Gurder decides to go to Florida with **Masklin** and Angalo de **Haberdasheri**, and is not presented as a particularly good leader, in part because he likes **power** so much. Pratchett's works are littered with rightful rulers who refuse to rule (*see* Carrot **Ironfoundersson**) and at best ambiguous leaders who have agreed to rule. A firm believer in the existence of Arnold Bros, Nisodemus does not want the nomes to leave him behind with the store, preferring to maintain a theocracy, and he is still sceptical that the store has been destroyed. He is equally sceptical about the danger facing the quarry of human intervention, and resists the plans to move on a second time. He leads a delegation out to face down the humans, and is last seen being run over by a police car, his body never being found. His name may be derived from Nicodemus, a Pharisee and leader of the Jews mentioned in the Gospel of St. John. *See also* Arnold Bros (est. 1905); the Bromeliad; Children's Fiction; Grimma; Angalo de Haberdasheri; Dorcas del Icatessen; Masklin; Power; Religion *and* Stratified Societies.

Andrew M. Butler

Nitt, Agnes (*LL*, 'SALF', *Msk*, *CJ*)

Agnes Nitt is first introduced in *LL* where she is a member of a coven of young **witches** led by Diamanda Tockley. Diamanda had been given magical powers by the Queen of the **Elves**, and is trying to prove herself as a greater witch than Granny **Weatherwax** and to challenge the 'old ways' of witches like Granny Weatherwax and Nanny **Ogg** who believe in power that comes from herbs, headology and plain words rather than 'real' magic. With Diamanda's coven, Pratchett is commenting on people who see occultism (or other subcultures) as a fashion statement, and Agnes, like the other young witches, wears all black clothing with lace and occult jewellery and is inspired to call herself Perdita X. Dream.

The pale make-up and romanticised ideas about witchcraft are not a natural fit for Agnes, however. Nanny calls her a fine figure of typical young **Lancre** womanhood and she is described to be large and not particularly pretty. She is the kind of girl who gets compliments on her great hair and great personality, and her practical nature makes her suspect Diamanda's ideas even when she is still in the coven. Unlike Diamanda and the others, Agnes also has real potential to become a witch and both Granny and Nanny take notice of this, deciding to take her into their coven when Magrat becomes a queen.

Agnes, like Magrat before her, does not, however, take kindly to being told what to do by the older witches. In *Msk* she then tries to escape her destiny as a witch to **Ankh-Morpork** where she fulfils her life-long dream and joins the Opera. Although Agnes is a talented singer – her magical skills manifesting in her magnificent singing voice and her ability to project her voice and sing harmonies with herself – she is not pretty enough to be a star, and becomes the 'understudy' for the Opera's star, the beautiful yet talentless and dim-witted Christine. The whole book is a parody of the Andrew Lloyd Webber musical The Phantom of the Opera where the phantom is enamoured by the beautiful young Christine who has talent but needs training, while the older and more talented diva Carlotta is pushed to the side (*see* **Musicals**). In Pratchett's version, however, Agnes is not driven by jealousy, and truly would deserve the attention Christine receives, and although *Msk* too ends with Christine getting both the man and the fame, this only prompts Agnes to realise that she is too practical to the shallow world of the opera and to return to Lancre to take her place as the junior witch in Granny's coven.

Perdita, the exotic sounding name Agnes made up for herself when she was a member of Diamanda's coven and which she also used during her stay at the Ankh-Morpork Opera house, is not simply a name but a whole alternative personality. Perdita is the thin (and somewhat mean) girl inside Agnes, waiting to be let out, and all the feelings and thoughts that Agnes represses because of her sunny disposition. Perdita is the unruliness Agnes tries to suppress, but which – when set loose – allows her to rebel against the part of her personality that insists that she must comply to society's rules and expectations. Her personalities are in constant battle, Agnes disliking the selfish and vicious Perdita, and Perdita hating the weak-willed and insecure Agnes. Most of the time Perdita is satisfied with simply offering cynical commentary on Agnes's life, but she can also takeover if needed. Being in two minds about everything is then not only

Agnes's curse, but also a talent as it makes her resistant to the vampire's mind control in *CJ* – every time one of her personalities falls under the thrall, the other one takes over.

Agnes, the fourth witch, whose arrival – together with Magrat **Garlick**'s motherhood – shook the maiden-mother-crone form of the coven, combines qualities from all three old witches. She holds Magrat's slightly romanticised view of magic and her interest in practicing witchcraft by finding things out rather than just making them up, and despite her occasional shyness, has Nanny's openness and people skills. With Perdita as her companion, Agnes also has Granny's constant vigilance over herself – according to Nanny, Granny Weatherwax always has Granny Weatherwax looking over her shoulder, and similarly Agnes always has Perdita looking over her shoulder, and Perdita has Agnes – and with her practical nature and natural talent in magic, she has the makings of becoming a very powerful (yet sensible) witch. *See also* Feminism; Magrat Garlick; Lancre; Magic; Nanny Ogg; Granny Weatherwax *and* Witches.

Further Reading

Sayer, Karen. 'The Witches'. *GOL*, *GOL2*.

Mirka Sillanpaa

Nobbs, Cecil Wormsborough St. John (Nobby) (*GG*, 'TOC', *MP*, *MAA*, *SM*, *Msk*, *FOC*, *H*, *J*, *FE*, *TT*, *NW*, *T!*)

Nobby Nobbs is the third longest tenured member of the **City Watch** after Fred **Colon** and Samuel **Vimes**. However, he has yet to ascend past the rank of corporal. Nobby is a much better follower than a leader. While most people agree that Nobby is probably *technically* human, his size and features are so indiscriminate that nobody can really be sure what race he is. He is frequently described as a bit of a monkey.

Before joining the Watch, Nobby was a scavenger on battlefields, a profession that he continues to this day. Pilfering, larceny and thievery are not beneath Nobby. He even steals from the Watch's petty cash, though Vimes lets him get away with it. There are times that Vimes uses Nobby's penchant for stealing to his advantage, like when the Commander is trying to find the dwarfen cube at Koom Valley before the Low King.

For a man of virtually no character, Nobby has a few odd hobbies. He is a member of the **Ankh-Morpork** Historical Society and is an avid dancer. Also, he has an affinity for dressing up in women's clothing after being forced to dress like one for a ruse designed by Patrician **Vetinari** on the island of Leshp. Despite having no real sense of class, Nobby believes that he is at the height of it. *See also* Ankh-Morpork; Frederick Colon; Detective and Noir Fiction; Carrot Ironfoundersson; Cheery Littlebottom *and* Samuel Vimes.

Nobbs, Cecil Wormsborough St. John (Nobby)

Further Reading

James, Edward. 'The City Watch'. *GOL*, *GOL2*.
Mendlesohn, Farah. 'Faith and Ethics'. *GOL*, *GOL2*.

Mark D. Thomas

Nobby Nobbs *see* Nobbs, Cecil Wormsborough St. John

O

Ogg, Nanny Gytha (*WS*, *WA*, *LL*, *Msk*, *CJ*, *TOT*, *WFM*, *Wint*)

Gytha Ogg, usually known only as 'Nanny', forms one third of Granny **Weatherwax**'s coven of **Witches** in **Lancre**. She is Granny's best friend, occasional conscience and a frequent source of annoyance. Nanny has a face like a raisin, a bosom that can be used as an assault weapon and a singing voice that makes both people and animals flee to the mountains at the first note of 'The Hedgehog Song'.

Nanny is introduced in *WS* where she is captured by Lord Felmet when she follows her beloved **cat Greebo** to the Lancre castle, and ends up smuggling the ghost of late King **Verence** out of the castle by allowing him to haunt her apron. The largest role Nanny has in the novels is in *Msk* where Granny finds out that she has published a popular erotic cookbook under the name of 'A Lancre Witch' and the two of them head to **Ankh-Morpork** to set straight the mistaken identity concerning the Lancre Witch (a title which, according to Granny, does not belong to Nanny) and to collect the money the publishers owe Nanny (the same publishers later produced *NOC*).

Nanny is then different from Pratchett's other main witches in the respect that she is more of a supportive character than the protagonist and does not really have major storylines of her own. She is mainly a comic relief character whose contribution to the story is her unruliness, be it walking into the strictly forbidden for women and suspiciously phallic burial mound of the Elf Queen's husband in *LL* (the disrespect for 'men's places' appears to be hereditary because, according to Nanny, the reason why she knows of the place is because her great-grandmother used to sneak there to watch the Ogg men (*see* **The Ogg Family**) perform secret rituals) or having a dalliance with Casanunda in *WA* and *LL*. Everything in Nanny is larger than life: she laughs, eats and talks in excess, and refuses to fade into the background and adjust to the rules of the society.

According to Nanny herself, she – like the Ogg family in general – has a natural talent for magic, but her love of life keeps her from dedicating herself to harvesting that talent to the fullest. She may then not be as powerful a witch as Granny magic-wise, but she nevertheless holds formidable power over the people of Lancre – mainly by being related to most them. Unlike Granny, she is one of the people, friendly and out-going, not only respected but also liked, and one of her greatest powers is her ability to connect with people, to make them open up to her and let her learn to know them very quickly.

Nanny's open-mindedness is then a quality that separates her from Granny. Even though well past her prime, she refuses to become genderless and asexual and while Granny – the virgin crone – insists that she is not naked underneath her clothes, not with the three vests she has on, Nanny is openly sexual, flirting with Casanunda, and, much to Granny's chagrin, freely talking about her sexual exploits. And although Casanunda is described to be 'world's second greatest lover' and has few centuries' worth of experience under his belt, even he is often overwhelmed by Nanny's overt sexuality and lack of modesty.

Nanny Ogg has been married three times, outliving all of her husbands, and is the unrivalled matriarch of the Ogg clan, ruling over fifteen surviving children and a flock of grandchildren, son-in-laws and daughter-in-laws like a benevolent dictator. She dotes on her sons and grandchildren, and sees her daughters and daughters-in-law as a useful way to get the housework done. When the king threatens to put a tax on liquor exports or a family of vampires has taken over the castle, Nanny can organise a mob faster than anyone, and in *LL* she does not hesitate to use her sweet-toothed grand-son as a distraction to help Granny win her magical duel against Diamanda Tockley.

Nanny is then first and foremost a mother, not only of her family, but also a 'mother of the country' through her role in the coven and her friendliness with the people of Lancre Town. Her powers are related to birth and life and she is the best midwife on Discworld, so good that Time herself wanted her as a midwife when giving birth (*see TOT*). This makes her the opposite of Granny who, as the crone, is usually called by the people at the event of a death than birth. According to Agnes **Nitt**, you could cut Nanny in half and find the word 'Ma' all the way through, and Nanny herself seems to be most comfortable with this role as well, becoming very distraught when in *CJ* Magrat **Garlick** becomes a mother and Nanny suddenly finds herself forced into the role of the crone.

In Discworld, witches' magic, or women's magic, is tied to earth as opposed to the wizard magic which according to Granny is 'of the sky', and while Granny's connection to the land is spiritual (through her ability to borrow the minds of animals), Nanny's connection is more concrete. The Oggs have deep roots in the Lancre soil, and her role as the 'people's witch' connects her to the people living on the land far more than Granny ever could – when the land becomes ill under Lord and Lady Felmet's rule in *WS*, the spirit of the forest goes to Granny for help while the people come to Nanny. *See also* Feminism; Magrat Garlick; Lancre; Magic; Agnes Nitt; Granny Weatherwax *and* Witches.

Mirka Sillanpää

Further Reading

Sayer, Karen. 'The Witches'. *GOL*, *GOL2*.

The Ogg Family

The Oggs have deep roots in **Lancre**, and form a large part of the village populace. Nanny **Ogg** is the unrivalled matriarch of the family with fifteen children (named in *WS* as Jason, Grame, Tracie, Shirl, Daff, Dreen, Nev, Trev, Kev, Wane, Sharleen, Darron, Karen, Reet and Shawn) and more grandchildren than she can count. However, only two of Nanny's children have had major roles in the books.

Jason Ogg, the village blacksmith, is the eldest of Nanny's children. According to Nanny, the Oggs have natural talent in magic and in Jason this manifests in his ability to shoe anything that is brought before him. His skill comes with an obligation that he in return must shoe every animal that is brought before him. He shoes **Death**'s horse, Binky, has put silver shoes on a unicorn and has even shod an ant.

Jason's youngest brother is Shawn, who is barely in his twenties even though his father Sobriety Ogg (presumably Nanny's last husband) has been dead some thirty years, suggesting that things are done slightly differently (and more often, as **Ridcully** notes) in the Ramtops. Shawn makes his mother proud by working at the Lancre castle where his duties include acting as the royal trumpeter, privy cleaner, mail man and customs officer. He also forms Lancre's entire standing army.

The only one of Nanny's grandchildren to get more than mention in the novels is Pewsey, the four-year-old with a sweet tooth and a permanently runny nose who is seen in *LL*. *See also* Lancre *and* Nanny Ogg.

Mirka Sillanpää

Om (*SG*)

A god who gives his name to **Omnia** and thus the Church of Omnia. Om has been a largely distracted god, despite his omniscience, omnipotence and omnipresence, leading to the **religion** being a very intolerant, monotheistic one. This is because of the way the Omnians have interpreted his words, and their evolution of the Quisition to torture, punish or kill any nonbelievers – for example anyone who claims that the world is flat, a neat inversion of the real world's Inquisition's charge against the astronomer Galileo Galilei (1564–1642). In fact this has led to a decline in true believers, and any god who is not sufficiently believed in becomes extinct. Om appears to **Brutha** in the form of a tortoise, and at first is quite abusive, learning through the course of the novel to be more humble. He even battles with the other gods to save Omnia from invasion, and rescues Brutha. Post-Brutha, his religion is less dogmatic about monotheism and has to take its chances in the marketplace.

The tortoise is of course a mainstay of paradoxes (*see* **Greek Philosophy**), but the tortoise being dropped on someone's head by an eagle refers to the very unlikely death of the Greek playwright Aeschylus (sixth century BCE). *See also* Brutha; Greek Philosophy; Omnia; Religion *and* Vorbis.

Andrew M. Butler

Omnia (*SG*)

Omnia is a coastal country between **Klatch** and Howondaland, the capital city of which is Kom. For centuries the country was dominated by the Church of **Om**, or, more accurately, by the priest of the Church of Om, who were bloody in their application of the strict letter of the law. Their internal secret police was the Quisition, who frequently destroyed bodies to save souls. Equally, the country was aggressive to its neighbours in its efforts to bring them the good new of Om. This was ironic because their god was not as such intolerant, but indifferent. The appearance of **Brutha** in *SG* as a prophet changed all this, more or less overnight, and instead the Church is much softer in its approaches. It does produce a large number of evangelists who travel from door to door across the **Discworld** – Visit-the-Infidel-with-Explanatory-Pamphlets (*FOC*, *J*, *H*, *FE* and *T!*) works for the **Ankh-Morpork City Watch** but distributes literature with Smite-the-Unbeliever-with-Cunning-Arguments when off duty.

Omnia is in part a **parody** of Crusades era Jerusalem and Inquisition period Vatican City, standing in for a distrust of organised religions. *See also* Brutha; Discworld; Klatch; Om; Religion *and* Vorbis.

Andrew M. Butler

'Once and Future' (*OM*WF*)

A short story which was part of a collection of stories on Arthurian themes – *Camelot*, edited by Jane Yolen (New York: Philomel, 1995;

Pp. 41–60) – including contributions from **Fantasy** writers Anne McCaffrey (b.1926) and Nancy Springer (b.1948). Yolen (b.1939) had previously written the introduction to *After the King* (1992) which featured 'TB'. 'Once and Future' refers to the lines supposedly on King Arthur's grave and the title of the series of books (collected 1958) by T.H. White (1906–1964). Pratchett notes that he is tempted to expand it into a novel.

Mervin is a time traveller lost in time, having come from the future. He finds himself in a strange version of 500 CE, in which the architecture is eleventh century Norman and the armour looks like fifteenth century, when he had planned to observe the crowning of Charlemagne. He is aided in his survival by Nimue, a girl of fifteen, as he starts to build a device that will enable him to anoint someone as King Arthur: a sword in a stone that only the right person (with his help) can remove. Nimue tells him of a child who is the hidden offspring of the true king, and he allows this person to pull at the stone; he is bemused to discover the child is Ursula.

This is a neat subversion of the Arthurian mythos with Mervin (aka Merlin) being not quite as smart as he thinks he is, and not as smart as Nimue. *See also* Fantasy *and* Science Fiction.

Further Reading

White, T.H. 1958. *The Once and Future King*. London: Methuen.

Andrew M. Butler

*Once More * With Footnotes* (2004)

A collection of fiction, articles, poems and so forth, edited (like the second edition of *Guilty of Literature*) for the 2004 World **Convention** (Noreascon 4) where Pratchett was Guest of Honour. The cover was by Omar Rayyan, who as well as being an artist was a concept artist on the film *The Chronicles of Narnia: The Lion, The Witch and the Wardrobe* (2005). The introduction, 'Terry Pratchett: The Man, The Myth, The Legend, The Beverage', pp. 13–14, was by Esther Friesner (b.1951), an American author of comic **Science Fiction** and **Fantasy**, often with punning titles. The afterword, 'The Titles That Got Away', pp. 279–280, is by Priscilla Olson, who has co-edited a number of author collections for NESFA. It should be noted that it is not a complete collection of Pratchett's short fiction (*see* '**Night Dweller**'), journalism, introductions or non-fiction.

The contents are:

'Apology'. Pp. 15–16. Introduction to the volume by Pratchett.

'**Hollywood Chickens**'. Pp. 19–25. Short story reprinted from *More Tales from the Forbidden Planet*. Edited by Roz Kaveney. London: Titan, 1990. Pp. 2–10.

'Doctor Who?' Pp. 27–29. A transcript of Pratchett's speech accepting an honorary Doctor of Letters from University of Portsmouth (2001).

'The Hades Business'. Pp. 31–41. Short story reprinted from *Science Fantasy* 60 (1963). Pp. 66–76.
'The Big Store'. Pp. 43–44. An article revealing the inspiration for *T* in a shop Pratchett visited as a child, first published as part of the programme for a touring stage production in 2002.
'20p With Envelope and Seasonal Greeting'. Pp. 45–51. Short story reprinted from *Time Out* (16–30 December 1987).
'Paperback Writer'. Pp. 53–55. Article reprinted from *The Guardian* (6 December 2003) on getting ideas about writing; it has a nod towards the plot of *FE*. Online at
http://books.guardian.co.uk/review/story/0,12084,1100081,00.html
'Incubust'. P. 57. A drabble reprinted from *The Drabble Project*. Edited by Rob Meades and David B. Wake. Birmingham: Beccon Publications, 1988. P. 53.
'Final Reward'. Pp. 59–69. Short story reprinted from *GM: The Independent Fantasy Roleplaying Magazine* (October 1988).
'And Mind the Monoliths'. Pp. 71–73. Humorous article reprinted from *Bath & West Evening Chronicle* (3 April 1983), on media representations of history.
'FTB'. Pp. 75–78. Short story reprinted from *Western Daily Press* (24 December 1996).
'Theatre of Cruelty'. Pp. 79–82. Short story reprinted from a shorter version in the W.H. Smith magazine, *Bookcase* 45 (July/August 1993). Pp. 10–11.
'Introduction: *The Unseen University Challenge*'. Pp. 83–84. Introduction to the **quizbook** written by David **Langford**. London: Gollancz, 1996. Pp. 5–7.
'2001: The Vision and the Reality'. Pp. 85–88. Article reprinted from *The Sunday Times* [London] (24 December 2000). Pp. 5, 17. It compares the vision of the Stanley Kubrick film, *2001, A Space Odyssey* (1968), with the reality of his present, noting the lack of computers visible in the film and the odd ways in which they were used.
'High Tech, Why Tech?'. Pp. 89–91. Article reprinted from *The Electronic Author* (Summer 1993): P. 2, focusing on Word Processing and software written for him by Ansible Information.
'Roots of Fantasy'. Pp. 93–96. Article reprinted from 'Roots'. *The Roots of Fantasy*. Edited by Shelley Dutton Berry. Seattle: 15th World Fantasy Convention, October 1989. Pp. 73–75.
'Introduction: *The Wyrdest Link*'. Pp. 97–98. Introduction to the second quizbook by David Langford. London: Gollancz, 2002.
'Thought Progress'. Pp. 99–101. Article reprinted from *20/20* (May 1989): 143, about prevaricating on writing, and thinking about tortoises. Pratchett clearly has **Om** and the novel *SG* in mind.
'The Sea and Little Fishes'. Pp. 103–137. A **Discworld** novella, reprinted from *Legends*. Edited by Robert Silverberg. New York: Tor, 1998. Pp. 63–97.

'Once and Future'

'Introduction: *The Leaky Establishment*'. Pp. 139–141. Introduction to a novel by David Langford (Abingdon, Oxon: Big Engine, 2001), Pp. vii-viii. Pratchett was a press officer for British Nuclear Fuels, so knew how much this novel about the nuclear industry rang true.
'Let There Be Dragons'. Pp. 143–147. Speech about the importance of fantasy as Guest of Honour at the Booksellers Association Conference (1993) held in Torquay, Devon, reprinted from *The Bookseller* (11 June 1993). Pp. 60, 62.
'#ifdefDEBUG + "world/enough" + "time"'. Pp. 149–159. Short story reprinted from *Digital Dreams*. Edited by David V. Barrett. London: NEL, 1990. Pp. 79–93.
'Foreword: *Brewer's Dictionary of Phrase and Fable*'. Pp. 161–162. Foreword to an edition of the reference work. Edited by Adrian Room. London: Cassell, 1999. P. vii.
'**Thud – A Historical Perspective**'. Pp. 163–165. Fictional history reprinted from *Thud! The Discworld Boardgame*, Millennia Marketing, 2003 relating to one of the Discworld **games**, Thud
(see *T!*).
'**Death and What Comes Next**'. Pp. 167–169. Short story reprinted from the online puzzle *TimeHunt*, 2002.
'Neil **Gaiman**: Amazing Master Conjurer'. Pp. 171–174. Article reprinted from a *Programme Book*. Boston: Boskone 39, 2002.
'Introduction: *The Ultimate Encyclopedia of Fantasy*'. Pp. 175–176. From a volume edited by David Pringle. London: Carlton, 1998.
P. 6.
'**Elves** Were Bastards'. Pp. 177–1979. Article reprinted from the *Programme Book*. Rotterdam, Holland: Hillcon III (Beneluxcon 18), 27–29 November 1992.
'Medical Notes'. Pp. 181–183. Reprinted from 'Nac Mac'. *Programme Book*. Hinckley: Discworld Convention, 16–19 August 2002.
Pp. 16–17.
'Sheer Delight'. Pp. 185. Obituary letter on Northern Irish science fiction writer Bob Shaw (1931–1996). *SFX Magazine* (April 1996).
P. 31.
'The **Orangutans** are Dying'. Pp. 187–190. Article about an endangered species. Reprinted from *The Mail on Sunday Review* (19 February 2000).
P. 63.
'The **Ankh-Morpork** National Anthem'. Pp. 191–192. Details about and the words to an imaginary anthem, first broadcast on BBC Radio 4 (15 January 1999) and set to music by Carl Davis (b.1936).
'Alien Christmas'. Pp. 193–197. After dinner speech from the convention Beccon 87 (17–20 August 1987). Reprinted from David Langford's fanzine, *Ansible* 50 (August/September 1987).
'**Turntables of the Night**'. Pp. 199–207. Short story reprinted from *Hidden Turnings*. Edited by Diana Wynne Jones. London: Methuen, 1989. Pp. 169–180.

'Cult Classic'. Pp. 209–213. Article on J.R.R. **Tolkien**, reprinted from *Meditations on Middle-Earth*. Edited by Karen Haber. New York: St Martin's Press, 2001. Pp. 78–80, 82–83.
'The Choice Word'. Pp. 215. Article reprinted from *The Book of Favourite Words*. Edited by Gordon Kerr. London: Bloomsbury, 2001. The word was 'susurration'.
'Whose Fantasy Are You?'. Pp. 217–218. Article on fantasy reprinted from the W.H. Smiths magazine, *Bookcase* (17 September 1991). p. 19.
'No Worries'. Pp. 219–226. Article about a signing tour of **Australia**, reprinted from *SFX Magazine* (June 1998). Pp. 64–68.
'**Troll Bridge**'. Pp. 227–235. A Discworld short story reprinted from *After the King*. Edited by Martin H. Greenberg. New York: Tor, 1992. Pp. 46–56.
'Faces of Fantasy/On Writing'. Pp. 237–238. Article about the fun of writing, reprinted from 'On Writing'. Pp. *The Faces of Fantasy: Photographs by Patti Perret*. New York: Tor, 1996. P. 126. Photo of Pratchett on P. 127.
'Imaginary Worlds, Real Stories'. Pp. 239–251. The 18th Katherine Briggs Memorial Lecture to the British Folklore Society (1999), on real and made up folklore. Reprinted from *Folklore* (October 2000). Pp. 159–168.
'**The Secret Book of the Dead**'. Pp. 253–254. Poem from *Now We Are Sick*. Edited by Neil Gaiman and Stephen Jones. Minneapolis, Minnesota: DreamHaven, 1991. Pp. 29–30.
'Magic Kingdoms'. Pp. 255–259. On the British writing of fantasy. From 'Fantasy Kingdom'. *The Sunday Times Review* [London] (4 July 1999). P. 4.
'**Once and Future**'. Pp. 261–273. Short story reprinted from *Camelot*. Edited by Jane Yolen. New York: Philomel, 1995. Pp. 41–60.
'A Word About Hats'. Pp. 275–277. Article on Pratchett's hats, reprinted from *Sunday Telegraph Review* [London] (8 July 2001). P. 4.

See also Ankh-Morpork; Conventions; Elves; Fandom; Neil Gaiman; David Langford; Merchandising; Orangutans; Quizbooks and J.R.R. Tolkien.

Andrew M. Butler

Only You Can Save Mankind (1992)

The first book in the **Johnny Maxwell Trilogy**, set in **Blackbury** during 1991 and is a **Science Fiction** novel aimed at children. The first edition, published by Doubleday, was 16,700 copies with a cover by David Scutt. The paperback appeared in 122,000 copies from Corgi in 1993. From the thirteen printing (1999), it had a cover by John Avon, then from 2004 had cover art attributed to http://www.hen.uk.com. Due to a line of text being missing from the back cover of the 2004 mass market edition – there was also a slightly larger B format paperback – almost all of the first printing were destroyed. A limited edition of 1,000 copies of the novel with a tie-in cover was produced for a run of a **musical** version of the novel which was premiered at the Pleasance Courtyard, Edinburgh Festival (4–30 August 2004), composed by Leighton James House (b.1980) with lyrics by Shaun McKenna, who has since co-written the book and lyrics for *The Lord of the Rings* musical (2006). A concert version had been held at the Soho Laundry Workshop in 2003. *OYCSM* has been translated into Bulgarian, Czech, Dutch, Estonian, French, German, Italian, Korean, Lithuanian, Polish, Romanian, Russian, Slovakian, Spanish, Swedish, Thai and Turkish. It is dedicated to Pratchett's daughter, Rhianna. This novel has an advert for the (fictional) game *Only You Can Save Mankind* and is divided into named chapters. It is the only book of the trilogy yet to be filmed for television. It was shortlisted for the 1992 *Guardian* Children's Fiction Award. The review in *School Librarian* notes: 'This book demonstrates that Terry Pratchett is a serious humorist, carrying as it does the thought-provoking message that games of destruction can really hurt people'.

Cover of *Only You Can Save Mankind* Artwork by http://www.hen.uk.com.

The twelve-year-old Johnny **Maxwell** is living in Trying Times – not only does he have to cope with school and being a teenager, but his parents are arguing all the time and neglecting him. Meanwhile the Gulf **War** unfolds on television. He has some escapism in the form of a computer game, Only

You Can Save Mankind, but one evening when he is playing it, the aliens inexplicably surrender to him and demand that he gives them safe passage out of game space. At first he does not believe this, but in all the other copies of the game played in Blackbury the alien ships have disappeared, just leaving a star field. Johnny tries to enlist the help of a girl he has only seen in the computer game shop in the Neil Armstrong Mall, but is distracted by his friend Bigmac's near-miss with a joyriding accident and collapses in exhaustion. Eventually he finds **Kirsty**, who wants to be known as Sigourney, and together they try to help the aliens or ScreeWee. This is threatened by a mutiny led by the male gunnery officer against the female captain, but Johnny succeeds in rescuing the ScreeWee fleet.

The virtual reality war of the 1991 Gulf War forms a counterpart to the computer game war, with it being difficult to know which is the more real – the French postmodern philosopher Jean Baudrillard (1929–2007) has written about the Gulf War as a simulation of a real war. It is rare for Pratchett to depict war, usually stepping back from the brink of it (see *P*, *J*, *NW*, but compare *MR*), and here the message is a pacifist one. The message is also that there is more to people than meets the eye – **Yo-Less** is not a stereotypical black Briton, Bigmac is smarter than he lets on and so on. *See also* Blackbury; Children's Fiction; Coming of Age; Computer Games; Johnny Maxwell Trilogy; Kirsty; Johnny Maxwell; Racism; Science Fiction; Sexism; War *and* Yo-Less.

Further Reading

Baldry, Cherith. 'The Children's Books'. *GOL*, *GOL2*.

Butler, Andrew M. April 2004. ' "We has found the enemy and they is us": Virtual War and Empathy in Four Children's Science Fiction Novels'. *Lion and the Unicorn* 28.2. Pp. 171–185.

Andrew M. Butler

Opera

Whilst most of the targets of Pratchett's **parody** are from popular culture, he does also allude to high culture such as the plays of William **Shakespeare** and opera. On one occasion there is a reference to a building that looks like Sydney Opera House (*LC* and see **Australia**) and characters sometimes quote operas (and **Musicals**) in passing – such as the line 'On with the motley' from *Pagliacci* (1892) by Ruggiero Leoncavallo (1857–1919). In *FE* Lady Sybil **Ramkin**'s rendition of Ironhammer's Ransom aria gains Samuel **Vimes** access to the High King. The greatest number of references to opera, however, is embedding in the narrative, dialogue and incidental details of *Msk*, and some background and knowledge of opera is helpful to understand and enjoy many of the jokes in *Msk*. In part, though, grand opera is referenced through its parody of

The Phantom of the Opera (1986), a musical about a grand opera company (*see also* Walter **Plinge**).

Opera's roots lie in the lyric theatre of the ancient Greeks and in medieval dramatic presentations (the pageants presented by the church were sometimes remarkably secular in nature). In the sixteenth century, musical entertainments were popular in the courts of Europe; in 1598, the first true opera was written for the Medici court in Florence.

This began a long history of Italian grand opera, giving opera an association with royal patronage and the upper class (which opera has been trying to live down ever since). The first public opera house opened in Venice in 1637, which gave the public (albeit only that portion of the public which could afford such expensive entertainment) the chance to see and hear opera. Castrati (boy singers who were castrated before puberty in order to retain their soprano voices) were wildly popular and often fêted much as pop stars are today.

By the eighteenth century, several forms of opera had developed:

Opera Seria featured stories based on myth and history. The castrati usually sang the important roles. *Da capo* solos showcased soloists' skills at variations and ornaments, and breathless contemporary accounts of an evening's arias are still available.

Opera Buffo had comic plots that involved ordinary people. Storylines featured impersonations, mistaken identities and disguises. Leading roles were generally sung by basses and tenors. Classic opera buffo includes *Le Nozze di Figaro* (*The Marriage of Figaro*, 1786, part of which Pratchett chose for ***Desert Island Discs***) and *Cosi Fan Tutte* (*All Women are Like That*, 1790) by Wolfgang Amadeus Mozart (1756–1791).

Singspiel (German), *Opéra Comique* (French), and ballad operas (English) featured spoken dialogue and, in the case of singspiel and ballad operas, featured popular music set with new lyrics.

Opéra comique, despite the name, was often quite serious; *Carmen* (1875) by Georges Bizet (1838–1875) is classified as opéra comique. *The Beggar's Opera* (1728) by John Gay (1685–1732) is one of the best-known ballad operas, and *Fidelio* (1805) by Ludwig van Beethoven (1770–1827) is written as a *Singspiel* (but usually classified as a 'rescue opera' by musicologists). Mozart's *Die Zauberflote* (*The Magic Flute*, 1791) is written as a *Singspiel*, but also has *opera seria* music for solos and *opera buffo* ensemble pieces.

Bel Canto ('beautiful singing') developed from *opera seria*, with the same virtuosic expectations of soloists, but with tenors singing the lead roles.

Grand Opera was largely a French style and is the kind of over-the-top opera featured in The Phantom of the Opera and *Msk*, generally including a ballet (with full corps of dancers), enormous casts, dramatic lighting, scenery effects, hideously expensive costumes, often unlikely plots and full orchestra.

Verismo ('realism') rose in the late nineteenth century and generally featured criminal characters and violent crimes of passion – much as television shows do now.

Opera was so popular in the nineteenth century that presentations of opera music were often given on music hall stages and it was not uncommon to hear someone on the street whistling a tune from an opera or to hear operatic music coming from street organs.

Other styles of opera include the Romantic operas of Germany (out of which Richard Wagner (1813–1883) developed his particular brand of opera), operettas, lyric operas and the various national operas (such as **China**, Russia and Turkey).

Twentieth century opera has a divergent and fragmented approach. Composers such as Kurt Weill (1900–1950) incorporated jazz and popular music into opera (Die Dreigroschenoper (*The Threepenny Opera*, 1928) is his best known), and hybrids of musical theatre and opera appeared, such as *Porgy and Bess* (1935), by George Gershwin (1898–1937), to which **Rincewind** alludes in *LF*.

The most popular operas today are probably those of Mozart, Wagner, Guiseppe Verdi (1813–1901) and Giacomo Puccini (1858–1924), with *Messiah* (1741), by 1685–1759 enjoying most popular status at the Christmas holidays. Puccini in particular has enjoyed many modern stagings of his operas, especially on American stages.

The owner of the Opera House, Seldom Bucket, mentions that the stereotype of an armoured, spear-carrying, horn-wearing soprano – the mythical fat lady – belongs to the past. There are many divas who do not fit the stereotype, although the habit of performers going out after a performance and having a late meal and drinks can contribute to it coming true.

Opera goers are somewhat used to the suspension of disbelief in operas such as *La Bohéme* (1896), where a consumptive Mimi often outweighs her Rudolf by quite a bit, or *La Traviata* (1853), with an equally tubercular Violetta often coughing her way to death with a wonderful personality and good hair, but have their limits. (The opening night of *La Traviata* was widely considered a disaster and the opera did not catch on until Verdi hired a slimmer soprano.) 'Ghosting' the role of an incapacitated singer is, while not common, considered something of an option in emergencies, as Agnes **Nitt** discovers.

The conversation between Bucket and musical director Salzella (a nod to Antonio Salieri (1750–1825), Mozart's rival and alleged murderer) in regards to using the murders to attract ticket sales is very similar to a conversation in the stage version of Phantom. As young Henry Lawsy is informed, knowing the libretto (the script and story) of an opera is often essential to full enjoyment, and, indeed, discovering what it's all about while actually watching the entertainment can be a rather dicey proposition. Even if one is fluent in the language the opera is presented in (Italian, German, and French are the most usual, although English language performances are now offered by many companies, and quite a few now offer subtitles projected onto screens during the performance), the language is sometimes archaic or opaque, and the plot lines are often somewhat confusing and illogical in any language.

Opera

All of the parody operas mentioned in *Msk* are fairly easy to identify with their originals.

Cosi fan Hita is *Cosi Fan Tutte*, *opera buffo* by Mozart featuring lots of disguises as everyone encourages two girls to cheat upon their military beloveds (and then becomes indignant when they do).

Il Trovatore (*The Troubadour*, 1853; Verdi): accused witches, love triangles, hidden identities, the heroine and hero die, the rival discovers too late that the hero was his brother. (Pratchett's *Il Truccatore* is subtitled *The Man with a Thousand Faces*, the epithet of Lon Chaney (1883–1930), who was in the original film *Phantom of the Opera* (1925). The mentions of being beaten to death and thrown in the river refer to how the original Phantom dies.) *La Triviata* is *La Traviata* (*The Wayward One*, Verdi): a consumptive prostitute, her true love for whom she gives up her sinful life, the protective father who causes her to give up her lover for the sake of the social reputation of his family, her death.

Die Meistersinger von Scrote is *Die Meistersinger von Nürnberg* (*The Mastersingers of Nuremberg*, 1868; Wagner): a cobbler and Mastersinger named Hans Sachs brings together two young lovers through a singing contest, despite his own love for the girl. *The Ring of the Nibelungingung* is *Der Ring des Nibelüngen* (*The Ring of the Nibelüngen*, 1848–1874; Wagner, a four-part opera cycle): Alberich the **Dwarf** makes a magic ring, which is stolen by Wotan. Alberich curses the ring, which causes the downfall of Wotan's son, grandson, daughter Brunnhilde the Walkyrie and Hagen the Dwarf (Alberich's own son) and causes the end of the Age of the Gods. *Lohenshaak* is Wagner's *Lohengrin* (1850). A duke's daughter is accused of the murder of her missing brother. A miraculous knight becomes her champion and marries her, on the condition that she never asks his identity. She is tricked into doing so, to discover that he is Prince Lohengrin, a knight of the Holy Grail. Lohengrin brings back her brother and goes sorrowfully back to the Castle of the Holy Grail.

Die Flederleiv is *Die Fledermaus* (*The Bat*, 1874; Johann Strauss II (1825–1899)), a comic operetta that includes the operatic plot-device that Agnes derides (of spouses successfully disguising themselves from each other with a skimpy mask or hood).

Genua's La Scalda is Milan's La Scala (*Teatro alla Scala*), one of the most famous opera houses in the world.

Lyrics of arias generally make a bit more situational sense than the translation given for the 'Departure Aria' in *La Triviata*. Violetta's '*Addio, del passato*' in *La Traviata* is not nearly so nonsensical. But even the most beautiful arias can have rather silly lyrics when translated into English; one of the most beautiful arias ever written is Lauretta's aria '*O mio babbino caro*' (from Puccini's *Gianni Schicchi* (1918)), which translates out more or less as:

> Oh my dear daddy,
> I like him, he is beautiful, beautiful;
> I want to go to Porta Rossa and buy the ring!

Yes, yes! I want to go!
And if my love is in vain,
I'll go on the Ponte Vecchio, I will jump into the River Arno!
My longing and my torment!
Oh God, I want to die!
Daddy, have pity! Have pity!

But as André of the Watch tells Agnes, the feeling is what is important, not the meaning of the words. That sums up opera perfectly. *See also* Desert Island Discs; Genua; Musicals; Agnes Nitt; Parody; Pop Music *and* Walter Plinge.

Further Reading

Grout, Donald J. and Hermine Williams Weigel. 2003. *A Short History of Opera*. 4th ed. New York: Columbia University Press.

Zina Lee

Orangutans

Two endangered species for which Pratchett has had a soft spot since for the purposes of a joke he turned the **Librarian** of the **Unseen University** into one.

These great apes have two distinct species, the Bornean Orangutan (*Pongo pygmaeus*) and Sumatran Orangutan (*Pongo abelii*), although they once lived throughout much of south-east Asia, including **China**. They are largely solitary and tree dwelling, and vegetarian. Normally they are gentle, but can be angered. They are highly intelligent and have been known to use tools. Both species are rare, due in large part to the destruction of their habitat and Pratchett is a trustee of the Orangutan Foundation UK which works to save them. Fees from the performances of the **plays** and the proceeds of ***NOC***, as well as some **conventions** go to the charity. He wrote an article about the apes for the *Mail on Sunday* and made a television documentary in the *Jungle Quest* series for Channel 4, broadcast 12 June 1995.

Orangutans also appear in the comedy films *Every Which Way But Loose* (1978) directed by James Fargo (b.1938) and *Any Which Way You Can* (1980) directed by Buddy Van Horn (b.1929). *See also* Conventions; Fandom; The Librarian *and* Nanny Ogg's Cookbook.

Andrew M. Butler

P

Parody

Just as Terry Pratchett is one of England's most popular living writers, so he is recognised as one of the leading parodists working today. Parody is intrinsic to the **Discworld** books, at the more complex end of a literary spectrum that extends from simple, light entertainment featuring continual cheap gags to literature involving an intricate pastiche of genres and human issues. Parody is the imitation of another, usually serious, composition; it is intended to poke fun at a particular author, work, or style. Parody often exaggerates the characteristics of the original, usually to comic effect. Sometimes parody is affectionate homage, sometimes ferocious ridicule.

In his Carnegie Medal acceptance speech, Pratchett said 'Recent Discworld novels have spun on such concerns as the nature of belief, **politics** and even journalistic freedom. But put in one lousy **dragon** and they call you a fantasy writer'. The **Fantasy** label, in particular, has not traditionally mixed well with the literary one, carrying the connotation that anything bearing it ought not to be taken too seriously – even if the works in question demand knowledge of history, literature, and numerous other fields for full comprehension. Calling the same works parody only complicates matters.

In simplest terms, the Discworld is a parody of Larry Niven's *Ringworld* (1970). The first Discworld novel, *COM*, was almost entirely a simple parody of genre fantasy, but the baffling and wonderful thing about the Discworld novels is that they did not remain simply fantasy, parody, or anything else. In fact, 'simple' is an astonishingly bad description of the Discworld novels: they are nothing less than a survey of humanism, in which each novel nonetheless stands out as legitimate fantasy, with questions of parody, satire, and literary form thrust completely aside. The level of parody has decreased steadily since the beginning of the series, but existing parodic elements have been carried forward. As Andrew M. Butler writes, they are critiques of the genre but they also play fair: they work as fantasy novels (10). In the past, parody has allowed authors to engage sensitive subjects 'in a covert manner, where direct criticism might bring down censorship (or a libel suit) onto the parodist' (Rose 22).

The most sophisticated kind of parody does more than distort the original; it 'involves the audiences and tradition of the literary work' (Rose 53). In other words, it is intriguing to the reader for its own sake as an example of the kind of literature being parodied. It is fiction and metafiction at the same time. As parody and satire, the Discworld novels all function in more or less the same ways as each other; as fiction there are a few differences, although many elements remain the same. The distinct story arcs deal with different groups of characters: the **Lancre Witches**, the **Ankh-Morpork City Watch**, **Death**, and the **Wizards** of the

Unseen University. Pratchett admits that the Unseen University (including **Rincewind**'s appearances) novels are pure larks, while the other three groups tackle larger issues. The Lancre Witches novels contain large elements of mythology, folklore, and **narrative** theory; the City Watch novels stand out as a complex pageant of political and social satire; the Death novels approach humanity from the outside. At the end of the day, even Rincewind has something to say about the way fiction works.

All of them deal with humanity, our common heritage and our future – society as it has been, as it is and as it perhaps ought to be.

As Pratchett would likely insist, the world is not a story. It is impossible to live well in the world, treating it as a story – if for no other reason than the other characters' stubborn refusal to learn their lines properly. The hackneyed phrase 'not on the same page' takes on new meaning when one realises that other inhabitants of the world are not, perhaps, even in the same play as oneself. Every Discworld novel methodically destroys clichéd expectations of what other people should be like and how they should behave.

Pratchett parodies and satirises (sometimes simultaneously, sometimes by turns – it is particularly difficult, and perhaps impossible, to separate parody from satire when dealing with the Discworld novels) much of the popular 'sword and sorcery' (see Fritz **Leiber**) fantasy published since J.R.R. **Tolkien**'s *The Lord of the Rings* (1954–1955). Nor does he spare Tolkien; but the satire aimed at fantasy novels, excepting the truly dreadful ones, is of the gentle, reflective Horatian type in which readers are urged to laugh quietly at the less logical aspects of their favourite novels, as well as at themselves.

In addition, the novels are structured so that the entire world is both a parody of a fantasy world and an engaging world in its own right; each novel reads as a parody of the fantasy genre as a whole. Within the Discworld, the characters in each novel serve as components of the Horatian commentary on fantasy, while also being complex and sympathetic people about whom readers often come to care deeply. The main character in each book always has some sharply insightful, yet hilarious, observations about the situation presented in the novel.

The backdrop against which all of Pratchett's characters move is a thorough parody of contemporary fantasy fiction, in all of its somewhat repetitive glory. It is important to note that parody and satire are not necessarily harsh or demeaning. Though Tolkien is satirised and parodied throughout, the tone is affectionate rather than hostile.

Pratchett's parody becomes more caustic in reaction to the derivative fantasy that emerged in the late 1970s and early 1980s, after some of Tolkien's fans, toddlers when *The Lord of the Rings* was published, had grown old enough to write their own books; the genre grew, but few apprentices possessed the genius of the master. Though Pratchett says that he began the series for the fun of parodying bad fantasy, he maintains that good fantasy may still be parodied.

Parody

Humankind has been searching for truth for a very long time, as if it either were something we possessed once and lost, or exists in some place we have not yet discovered. But for all of our searching, we seem curiously resistant to anything offered as truth, perhaps because truth often challenges our comfort. Our ability to create concepts like justice and mercy by believing that they exist is not a completely safe power; we can also construct for ourselves comfortable worlds that are at variance with the cold equations of the world we inhabit. We react with caution to new information that appears to run contrary to what we already believe because the revelations we receive sometimes hurt or shock us – even new information that does not distress us in some way often requires re-evaluation of everything we believed we knew about the world. We are primed to meet direct challenges to our perceptions not with invitation, but with suspicion.

Satire and parody are sly truths, the trickster gods of literature; by invoking them in his Discworld novels, Pratchett is a part of a great literary tradition; the startling part is that he illuminates and challenges readers while also being funny enough make its audience laugh aloud.

The cardinal sin of the main body of popular culture is that it asks so little of its acolytes. The cardinal virtue of good popular culture is that it affords such great scope for the exercise of more than minimal mental effort. Although it is possible to read a Discworld novel simply as an adventure story, much of the humour requires some familiarity with history, culture, and literature. Pratchett writes like Charles Dickens (1812–1870) or Miguel de Cervantes (1547–1616), placing a level of expectation on the reader that we are unaccustomed to seeing very often, and preserving aspects of literary heritage, history and folklore that might otherwise be lost. Every book is dense with allusions; just getting them all on the page while maintaining legitimacy as a narrative and satire is a rare feat. Pratchett's characters are multifaceted and dynamic; the world on which they live may be flat, but they are not.

This juxtaposition of the sublime and the ludicrous only casts the aptness of the Discworld as an extended metaphor for the real world into relief so sharp that it cuts. *See also* City Watch; Comedy and Humour; Death; Hollywood Comedy; Music Hall; Sellar and Yeatman; Witches and Wizards.

Further Reading

Butler, Andrew M. 'Theories of Comedy'. *GOL GOL2.*

Dentith, Simon. 2000. *Parody.* London: Routledge.

Pratchett, Terry. 2001. Carnegie Medal Acceptance Speech, http://www.carnegiegreenaway.org.uk/press/pres_terspeach.htm

Rose, Margaret A. 1993. *Parody: Ancient, Modern, and Post-Modern.* Cambridge: Cambridge University Press.

Silver, Steven H. 'A Conversation with Terry Pratchett – Part 1'. *SF Site.* http://www.sfsite.com/04b/tp79.htm

Stacie L. Hanes

Pearson, Bernard (b. 1941)

Founder, with his wife Isobel, of **Clarecraft** in 1980, and since 1991 a producer of **Discworld merchandising**.

Pearson had run a series of pottery companies since 1967, supporting himself through a series of part-time jobs – not full-time if only because he spent much of his time with his kiln. In 1990 he met Pratchett, who had made a sketch of **Rincewind** on the back of an envelope which Bernard then made into a figurine. This was first sold in 1991, and further figurines followed. He soon acquired the nickname of Most Cunning Artificer, from the Street of Cunning Artificers, **Ankh-Morpork**. On leaving the company he started sculptures of various Discworld buildings, including the **Unseen University**, several guildhalls, the **Unseen University** Organ, the **Mended Drum**, the music shop (*SM*) and the Vampyr Castle (*CJ*). He has now given up sculpture to focus on engraving, going on to produce stamps (for the endpapers and merchandising of *GP*, indeed Pearson was an influence upon the designs mentioned throughout the volume) and now money (for the projected *Making Money*). He has collaborated on ***The Discworld Almanak*** (2004) with Terry Pratchett and **The Unseen University Cut-Out Book** (2006) with Pratchett and Alan Batley.

Twinning ceremony, Wincanton, 7 December 2002. Wincanton is twinned with Ankh-Morpork (the only town in the UK to be twinned with a fictional location).

He now runs a shop, The Cunning Artificer, with his wife in Wincanton, Somerset (a town twinned with Ankh-Morpork), selling his own merchandising, along with materials produced by Paul **Kidby**, Stephen **Briggs** and others. He has organised the First Discworld Jamboree (3–5 August 2007) at Wincanton as a replacement for the Clarecraft Discworld Events. *See also* Ankh-Morpork; Stephen Briggs; Conventions; Paul Kidby *and* Merchandising.

Pearson, Bernard

Further Reading

Pratchett, Terry, Alan Batley and Bernard Pearson. 2006. *The Unseen University Cut-Out Book*. London: Doubleday.
Pratchett, Terry and Bernard Pearson. 2004. *The Discworld Almanak*. London: Doubleday.
Bernard Pearson's homepage: http://www.artificer.co.uk/

Andrew M. Butler

Perks, Polly (*MR*)

The nineteen-year-old daughter of a publican, she joins the army in order to track down her brother Peter. As her country, Borogravia, is under the puritanical rule of the Duchess (and their god, Nuggan, is apparently insane), she has to disguise herself as a man, teaching herself to behave like a boy. Early on, someone – later revealed to be Sergeant Jackram, herself a woman disguised as a man – gives her a pair of socks to act as a fake genital bulge, and Polly slowly realises virtually the whole regiment is female. The socks make her much braver, and able to defend herself in the **war**. Later in the novel she has to cross-dress as a washerwoman to get into a fortress, and no one is convinced she is a woman; lest anyone not note that this has an antecedent in some of William **Shakespeare**'s comedies where all the female parts would be played by men who are then required to masquerade as women disguised as men, it is described as 'much ado about nothing' (although ironically, unlike *As You Like It* and *Twelfth Night*, cross-dressing is not part of that play's plot, although disguise is). At the end of the novel she rejoins the army. Her nom du guerre, Oliver, comes from the (English) folksong 'Sweet Polly Oliver'. Not to be confused with the deceased first wife of Sid Perks, the publican in the BBC Radio 4 soap opera *The Archers*. *See also* Feminism; Religion; Sexism *and* War.

Andrew M. Butler

Player, Stephen (b.1965)

Player is an artist best known for his work on the **Discworld Maps**, the alternative Corgi 1993 edition 'Vitruvian Turtle' cover of *COM* and covers of some of the **plays** (*WS*, *M*, *GG* and *MAA* (all 1996) *Msk* and *CJ* (both 1998) and *LL* (2001)) by Stephen **Briggs**.

He grew up in Hertford and studied art at Saint Albans School of Art, 1983–1984 and Camberwell School of Arts and Crafts, London, 1984–1987. He has done book covers for novelists such as Clive Barker (b.1952), Kim Newman (b.1959), Mervyn Peake (1911–1968) and Ruth Rendell (b.1930).

For children he has done covers for books by Joan Aiken (1924–2004), John Christopher (b.1922) and Geraldine McCaughrean (b.1951). He has done production design for Sky One's adaptation of *H* and for a projected adaptation of *COM*, and is working on an illustrated version of *WFM* (2007). He has also had his designs on cards and t-shirts, which were distributed by **Clarecraft** and Bernard **Pearson**. He has also contributed to **calendars**, **games** books and the design of money for **conventions**. Since 2000 he has lived in the United States. *See also* Stephen Briggs; Calendars; Clarecraft; Conventions; Games; *Hogfather* (Television Adaptation); Maps *and* Bernard Pearson.

Further Reading

Briggs, Stephen and Terry Pratchett. 1993. *The Streets of Ankh-Morpork*. Painted by Stephen Player. London: Corgi.
Pratchett, Terry and Stephen Briggs. 1995. *The Discworld Mapp*. Painted by Stephen Player. London: Corgi.
Stephen Player's website: http://www.playergallery.com

Andrew M. Butler

Plays

Most of the **Discworld** novels have now been adapted for the stage, which is remarkable given that they are works of **Fantasy**. Plays have also occurred within the novels, most notably in *WS* and '**Theatre of Cruelty**'. Performance is also a factor in *MP*, *SM* and *Msk* but **Hollywood Films**, **Pop Music** and **Opera** are the respective targets of the **parody**. Moist von **Lipwig** has an element of performance in his character, as part of his conman routines, as does the Patrician **Vetinari**.

The narrative of *WS* fuses together elements from several plays by William **Shakespeare**, most notably Macbeth, with its regicide and three **witches**, and Hamlet where the ghost of a murdered king haunts the castle and a play is used to flush out the guilty party. The supposed long-lost heir to **Verence**, **Tomjon**, has been placed with the travelling theatrical troupe of Olwyn Vitoller, and has grown up to be a great actor. On their return to **Lancre**, the guilt wracked Lord Felmet commissions them – and their bard-like **dwarf Hwel** – to write a play that will expose how evil witches are. The witches, Granny **Weatherwax**, Nanny **Ogg** and Magrat **Garlick**, no strangers to theatrical gestures themselves, appear confused about what is reality and what is an act in the play – although this may of course be feigned.

'**TOC**' is a short story presented as a murder mystery, in which the Discworld equivalent of a punch and judy man has apparently been murdered – but his death is deserved because of the cruelty that he has displayed to his cast of gnomes who have been performing as if they were puppets.

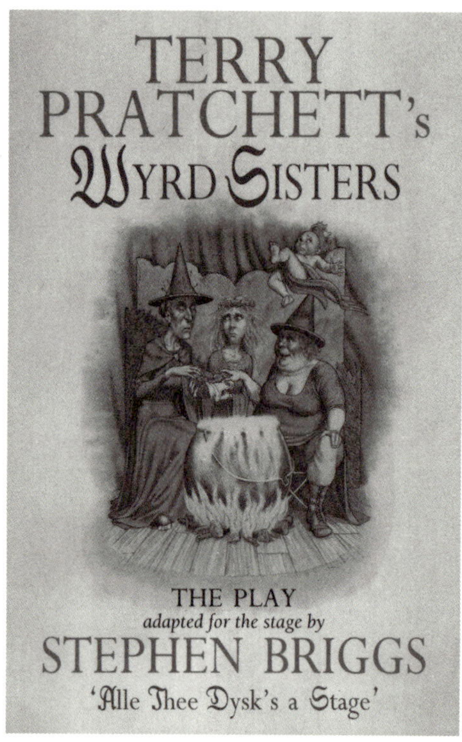

Cover of *Terry Pratchett's Wyrd Sisters, The Play* by Stephen Briggs. Artwork by Stephen Player.

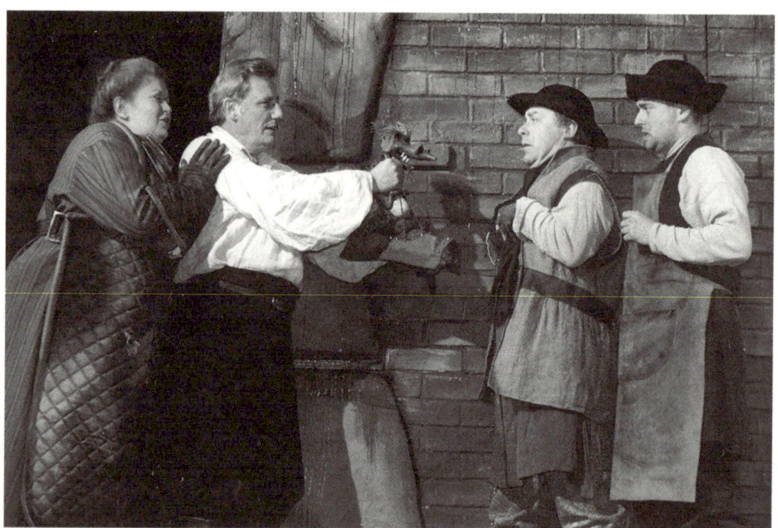

(From left to right) Roz McCutcheon, Paul Darrow, Rob Swinton and Nick Conway in the first professional stage presentation of *Guards! Guards!*, Hackney Empire, London, March 1998.

Cover of *Terry Pratchett's Mort, The Play* by Stephen Briggs. Artwork by Stephen Player.

Perhaps because it is about theatre, *WS* was the first of the novels to be adapted by Oxford-based civil servant, Stephen **Briggs**. His first amateur performances were held in 1991, at the Unicorn Theatre in Abingdon, in Oxfordshire; he played the role of Lord Felmet. The following year, he was **Death** in a production of *M*, and in *GG* played Vetinari for the first of many occasions in 1993. Subsequent plays were *MAA* (1994), *Msk* (1995), *CJ* (1996), *JD* (1997), *FE* (1999), *TT* (2000), *IT* (2001), *NW* (2003), *MR* (2003), *J* (2004), *AMHER* (2004), *GP* (2005), *LL* (2006) and *FOC* (2007). Briggs controls the amateur rights for most of the plays, some of which have been published by Corgi, Samuel French and Methuen.

LL had been adapted a number of times before Briggs produced his version. D. Paul Griggs adapted it for the University of Essex in Colchester in March 1997. Two years later Jonathan Petherbridge, artistic director of The London Bubble Theatre Company, toured his outdoor production around London. In 2002 Irana Brown wrote a version for the Unseen Theatre Company (who had previously performed Briggs's scripts and director Pamela Munt's adaptation of short stories 'TOC', '**TB**', '**Hollywood Chickens**' and '**Turntables of the Night**') at the Bakehouse Theatre, Adelaide, Australia. This is the version performed around the world, before Briggs finally adapted it in 2006. The Unseen Theatre Company performed *P* in May 2007, in a script by actor and director Danny Sag, which was then adapted by Pamela Munt.

There have been a number of professional productions of adaptations of Pratchett's work by other hands. Tours of Geoffrey Crush's adaptation of *GG* in 1998 and 1999 starred Paul Darrow (b.1941) – best known as Avon in *Blake's 7* (1978–1981) – as **Vimes**. In 2002 a professional tour of *T*, adapted by Bob Eaton, Artistic Director of the Belgrade Theatre, Coventry, 1996–2003, was premiered at Harrogate Theatre, where its director Rob Swain was artistic director. The play had a third theatre involved in its production, the Theatre Royal, Bury St Edmunds. Pratchett's programme note for the play, 'The Big Store', is included in *OM*WF*. An open air production of *E* was performed in Clifford's Tower, York, in July 2003, before going on tour in 2004. The adaptation was by Scott Harrison and Lee Harris for The Dreaming Theatre Company. *See also* Stephen Briggs; Hwel; Musicals; Music Hall; Opera; Walter Plinge; William Shakespeare; Theatre *and* Tomjon.

Andrew M. Butler

Plinge, Walter (*Msk*)

Janitor at **Ankh-Morpork Opera** House with a secret identity as the building's sophisticated phantom and trainer of singers. He succeeds Salzella as musical director.

One of a whole series of doubles in the novel, Plinge is the sort of potentially sinister figure which was a mainstay of the *Scooby Doo* cartoons (1969–), but his awkwardness recalls superhero real-world identities such as Clark Kent/Superman. Granny **Weatherwax** realises that Plinge wears a mask under his skin, rather than over it, and that invisible mask is who he can become – a situation which echoes Agnes **Nitt**'s transformation into Perdita. Plinge's beret refers to the accident-prone Frank Spencer of the British sitcom, *Some Mothers Do 'Ave 'Em* (1973–1978), played by Michael Crawford who later starred in Andrew Lloyd Webber's musical *The Phantom of the Opera* (1986) (*see* **Musicals** *and* **Opera**).

The name Walter Plinge is derived from British and American theatrical tradition, where if an actor's name cannot be listed because the part has not yet been cast, the actor is doubled in two roles or for some reason they want their name removed from the credits, Walter Plinge is used. The name may be taken from a London publican. *See* Musicals; Agnes Nitt *and* Opera.

Andrew M. Butler

Politics

Whilst Pratchett operates in the genres of **Comedy and Humour**, he explores themes in his fiction which are broadly speaking political. Politics is a series of mechanisms about some people holding on to **power** or by which that power may be passed onto someone else; it also refers to the observations made about the situation of those who lack power. This might be due to an individual's or group's sex, race or nationality. Clearly Pratchett is writing within the context of a British constitutional monarchy and parliamentary democracy, with three major political parties, the right of centre Conservatives and the left of centre Labour party, with a third, the Liberal Democrats, occupying the middle ground – although this spatial metaphor is no longer useful in the shift of political positions to gain votes. There are also various nationalist, far left, anti-European and ecological parties. It is not clear from the evidence of his writing how Pratchett votes; comedy can often be a conservative genre when it criticises change, but can equally be revolutionary and radical in its attack on those people unwilling to face change.

The quasi-medieval version of the **Discworld** has yet to develop political parties, although there are at the least various factions in the form of Lords and Guilds, which might yet turn into Tories and Whigs of the seventeenth to nineteenth centuries. Certainly the two factions are jockeying for power, and both have looked to individuals such as Carrot **Ironfoundersson** to be a puppet king to represent their interests. In the mean time, the real power is held by the Patrician Havelock **Vetinari**, a firm believer in the one man, one vote principle; as long as it is his vote.

These factions tend to be held in check by Vetinari's favoured branch of the repressive state apparatus, namely the **City Watch** and its frequently promoted leader, Samuel **Vimes**. It is he who stands against the biggest crime of all, **war**, and who attempts to arrest armies for breaches of the peace. According to the critic and academic John Newsinger, as Pratchett himself has become older and more fêted, so his interest has shifted from the outsider **Rincewind** to the quasi-aristocratic Vimes, now Duke of Ankh and weighted down with honours. Newsinger points to the rebellion of Treacle Mine Road in *NW* with scorn, as the oxymoron of a police-led revolution. The cruel Lord Winder, the patrician of thirty years previous, is overthrown, only to be replaced by Lord Snapcase, who is little better. Life goes on, the powers that be are, and the common people remain common. Newsinger suggests that Pratchett here displays contempt for the common people, and too much insecurity about private property.

Certainly many of Pratchett's novels do involve the re-establishment of a destabilised social order, and end with marriages – such has long been true of comedies, and of **narratives** about the **Coming of Age** of individuals. Pratchett tends to display interest in individuals – although he seems to have lost interest in many of his earlier protagonists – rather than in social movements and classes of people. His books invoke the great man of history vision of the world, where the actions of an individual can change everything – this is key in *CP92* – rather than is wider movements. But then people who go along with masses tend to get derided – but there is a distinction to be made between a herd mentality and collectivism and collegiality.

There is certainly a sense that Pratchett is against war, and the stupidity which it inculcates in people in the form of blind patriotism. This is clear in *J*, which as a squabble over an island may be read as a **parody** of the Falklands/Malvinas war (1982) – hardly a contemporary target. Even thinking of it in terms of the Gulf War of 1991 is not satire being drawn from immediate headlines. The ongoing rivalry between the **dwarfs** and **trolls** which is about to boil over in *T!* may be read in terms of more recent conflicts, although it was written too late to be a response to the London bombings of 7 July 2005. The entrenched opinions of the deep down dwarfs and their dislike of those who have become more humanised may be a critique of a variety of 'fundamentalist' or religious positions – equally it can be read in terms of the ongoing battle over Ireland, with the battle of Koom Valley standing in for the Battle of the Boyne (1690).

Curiously it is in the **Children's Fiction** that he is more open about political attitudes, especially the **Johnny Maxwell Trilogy**, which invokes Norman Schwarzkopf (b.1934) and the idiocies of the Gulf War, as well as dubious practices of the Conservative councils and their connections with big business – on the other hand he also attacks the social utopian architectures of the 1960s.

Aside from party politics, Pratchett also displays an interest in the politics of sex and race. With the exception of Kin **Arad**, Pratchett's early novels were very male dominated – **Culaina** was Culain in *CP71*, and about the only female character was a rather wet intended wife for Bane. The first **Discworld** novels focused on male characters – the wizards being an all-male society, and **Cohen the Barbarian**'s daughter being an exception, although Pratchett at least parodied the fetishisation of female barbarians (*see* **Sexism**). With *ER* he began to redress the balance, at least raising the issues of sexual equality, and with *WS* introduced more strong female characters. The focus on Tiffany **Aching** in his children's books perhaps obscured the often male world of the City Watch – a job which conflicts with the needs of being a husband and father (*T!*; *see* **Feminism**). In *OYCSM* there is a female space captain – although one who surrenders – and **Kirsty** in *JB* notes her token status.

The different species of the Discworld can be read as different races – and the embracing of **Igors**, dwarfs, trolls, **vampires**, and so forth by the City Watch is an examination of multiculturalism (*see* **Racism**). However, it sometimes smacks of tokenism, and exceptionalism, as this (say) werewolf is fine because of her individual qualities, whereas the others need to be watched with suspicion. Again in the children's fiction, the race issue is confronted more centrally, via **Yo-Less**.

Of course, critics always have to make a distinction between issues that characters raise and opinions that their author shares. *See also* Children's Fiction; Feminism; Johnny Maxwell Trilogy; Kirsty; Power; Racism; Sexism; Stratified Societies *and* War.

Further Reading

Dines, Gail and Jean M. Humez, Eds. 1995. *Gender, Race and Class in Media: A Text-Reader.* Thousand Oaks: Sage.

Newsinger, John. 2003. 'The People's Republic of Treacle Mine Road Betrayed: Terry Pratchett's *Night Watch*'. *Vector: The Critical Journal of the British Science Fiction Association* 232 (November/December). Pp. 15–16.

Andrew M. Butler

Pop Music (*SM*, *LC*)

Pratchett fills his works of **Fantasy** with references to both popular and high culture, partly in an effort to build a convincing secondary world, but mostly to amuse the reader who recognises the references or gets the **parody**. Pop music is one such source for references. Of course, each age has its own music which is popular – **opera**, **musicals** and **music hall** have been popular in various cultures over the last two centuries – but since the early 1950s, popular music has been based around relatively simple guitar chords, a danceable beat and an emotional core to the vocals. It has often derived from black musical culture – blues, soul, gospel and so forth – with the gay community having helped a lot of records get chart success from the 1970s onwards. The musicians – in some cases merely mimers – often become sex symbols and celebrities, role models and figures of desire to children, teenagers and even adults. Pop has divided into various genres over the decades. Pop music is the major target of parody in *SM*, just as **Hollywood films** are in *MP*. It is the outrageous behaviour of pop stars and fans which is first performed by characters possessed by music, and then imitated by **wizards**, Mrs **Whitlow** and others.

Chuck Berry (b.1926) is a blue guitarist, writer and singer, and a pioneer of rock and roll – or what becomes music with rocks in it in *SM*. Playing music from his teens onwards, his breakthrough was in the mid-1950s with songs like 'Roll Over Beethoven' and 'Johnny B. Goode'. He still performs in his eighties. 'Johnny B. Goode' is name-checked and quoted in *SM*, sometimes via the 1950s-set time-travelling **Science Fiction** film *Back to the Future* (1985) where Marty McFly plays the song when he goes back to 1958. Goode can play his guitar like a bell, Imp Y **Celyn**'s playing of his harp is similar; he won it for 'Sioni Bod Da', a 'Welsh' version of the song, presumably. 'Rock and Roll Music', covered by The Beatles, becomes 'Give Me That Music With Rocks In', played by the band.

Elvis Presley during his 1968 comeback.

Elvis Aron Presley (1935–1977) was an American singer of rhythm and blues and hillbilly, well-known for gyrating his hips when he sang and for a quiff. He also appeared in a series of movies, before fading a little from popularity in the 1960s. He made a comeback in 1968, and continued to perform until his early death. His music sounded very like it was sung by a black man, but as a white person in a still segregated country he had huge success. Imp Y Celyn is partially inspired by him, as a little bit Elvish.

Buddy Holly (i.e. Charles Hardin Holley, 1936–1959) was a white, bespectacled rock and roll guitarist from Lubbock, Texas, who died in a plane crash with other musicians – the day the music died, an event which is rather literal in *SM*. He is best known for songs like 'Peggy Sue', 'Not Fade Away', 'That'll Be the Day' and 'Every Day', the latter three of which are quoted in the novel. Imp Y Celyn's name is a translation into Welsh of 'Bud of the Holly'.

Various songs from this period are referenced, such as 'Don't Tread On My New Blue Boots', based on 'Blue Suede Shoes' written in 1955 by Carl Perkins (1932–1998), a hit for Elvis, 'Good Gracious Miss Polly' from 'Good Golly Miss Molly' written by John Marascalco (b.1931) and Robert Blackwell (1922–1989), a hit for Little Richard (b.1932), '**Sto Helit** Lace' was based on 'Chantilly Lace', written and performed by J.P. Richardson (the Big Bopper, 1930–1959) who died in the same plane crash as Holly, and 'There's A Great Deal of Shaking Happening' is Dave 'Curly' Williams and Sunny David's 'Whole Lot of Shakin' Goin' On', a hit for Jerry Lee Lewis (b.1935).

Another singer heavily referenced is Meat Loaf (Michael Lee Aday, b.1947), a rock singer and occasional film actor in movies such as *The*

Rocky Horror Picture Show (1975) as Eddie, *Wayne's World* (1992) as Tiny and *Fight Club* (1999) as Bob Paulsen. His best known song is the rock operatic epic 'Bat Out of Hell' (1977), written by Jim Steinman (b.1947), with a motorcycle sound played on the guitar by Todd Rundgren (b.1948). The British cover of *SM*, by Josh **Kirby**, **Death** on a motorcycle, owes a debt to the album *Bat Out of Hell*'s cover, and the book cover recreates a parodic scene from the book. Death also quotes Jim Steinman's 'Paradise by the Dashboard Light' and 'Love and Death and an American Guitar' about remembering everything. Pratchett chose 'Bat Out of Hell' as one of his ***Desert Island Discs***.

There are also a range of bands which get referenced in the Discworld band names: &U (U2, the highly successful Irish rock group), The Blots (The Inkspots, a black vocal group performing from the 1930s), Dwarfs With Altitude (NWA, also known as Niggaz With Attitude, a west coast American rap group), Insanity (Madness, an English ska band), Lead Balloon (Led Zeppelin the 1960s and 1970s progressive rock band; 'Pathway to Paradise' is 'Stairway to Heaven', from 1971, that has a tune which is still learnt by thousands of aspiring guitar players), Suck (KISS, a 1970s glam rock band from America), The Surreptitious Fabric (The Velvet Underground, an American avant garde rock band, managed at one point by pop artist Andy Warhol (1928–1987)), We're Certainly Dwarfs (They Might Be Giants, an American alternative rock band) and The Whom (The Who, a British mod band from the 1960s and 1970s with punk attitudes). The music written for the adaptation of *SM* featured parodies of various styles of pop music.

Pop music does not only appear in *SM*; in *LC* there is a reference to the hit single 'Down Under', a catalogue of culture associated with **Australia**, as sung by Men at Work.

Pratchett allowed the pop musician Dave **Greenslade** to write and record an album of music inspired by the Discworld. *See also* Dave Greenslade; *Desert Island Discs*; Josh Kirby; Musicals; Music Hall; Opera *and* Parody.

Further Reading

Chambers, Iain. 1985. *Urban Rhythms: Popular Music and Popular Culture*. London: Souvenir Press.

Frith, Simon. 2001. *The Cambridge Companion to Pop and Rock*. Cambridge: Cambridge University Press.

Andrew M. Butler

Power

Many of Pratchett's novels explore the dangers of power, and how it can be as damaging to the person that wields it as to those it is directed against – the old dictum 'power tends to corrupt, and absolute power corrupts absolutely. Great men are almost always bad men', from Lord

John Acton (1834–1902), was never more apt. Power is associated with control over others or oneself, and might be expressed in terms of wealth, status, physical strength, intelligence, **magic** or **narrative**.

Most of the rulers in **Discworld** are Kings – Seriphs and Pharaohs are kings by other names – and plenty of them are disreputable at best and corrupt and evil at worst. Their role is never questioned, as there are no moves from monarchies to republics through the series, although Samuel **Vimes**'s probable ancestor Old Stoneface Vimes of the old **City Watch** killed Lorenzo the Kind the last king of **Ankh-Morpork**. There is the sense that societies, especially **Stratified Societies**, need a leader. However the succession to the throne – often following a coup or an assassination – is not necessarily one which follows a blood line of inheritance by right of birth.

In *WS*, the rightful heir to **Lancre** has been spirited away as a child for his own protection, and grows up as **Tomjon**, the best actor in a travelling troupe. On his return to his kingdom, he has the right to succeed his father **Verence** I and the corrupt deposer, Lord Felmet, but he defers to his half brother who has been the **Fool** in the king's court. Verence I had been a reasonable king, and so is Verence II, although his well-meaning behaviour can lead to disaster, such as an invasion by **vampires** (*CJ*).

Djelibeybi is ruled by a Pharaoh, Teppicymon XXVII at the start of the book, but **Teppic**, his son, succeeds on his death. As pharaoh, he discovers that his actions are limited by the dead weight of tradition, and in particular the high priest Dios, who has strong views about what can be done. Teppic, a trained assassin, is never happy in his role, and realises that Ptraci, as his half-sister, has more right to the position (*P*).

Ankh-Morpork is ruled by a Patrician, currently Havelock **Vetinari**, but was once a monarchy as already noted. Stoneface was later executed for the regicide and the deposition has left the sense that there is a lost heir to the kingdom, who potentially be used as a puppet leader by various power factions in the city. The most probable candidate is Carrot **Ironfoundersson** who has actively rejected the job (*MAA*), but has charisma, is well-liked and gets on with those in power – although not all kings have all three qualities. Nobby **Nobbs** is thought (almost certainly wrongly) to be the descendent of the last Earl of Ankh, and is pushed forward as another candidate (*FOC*). Whilst this is a potential reversal of fool to king, it is actually part of a plot to seize power of the city.

Vetinari is now central to the balance of Ankh-Morpork; in terms of 'one man, one vote', he is the man with the vote. In a city of many competing interests, he has tamed the criminal and antisocial elements – assassins, beggars, seamstresses, thieves and so forth into a series of guilds, which strictly regulate such activities, and stamp out freelance crime. As a balance to this, he has carefully fostered the position of the City Watch by his handling of Vimes, so that no one is above the law, and the guilds are held to their own rules, and the wider laws of justice. Vimes is also able to cut through the pretensions and machinations of the aristocracy, thanks to his background in The **Shades** and his supposed ancestor, and by being married into aristocracy and promoted through the ranks of aristocracy, a limitation is put on Vimes's power. Vetinari may appear to be Machiavellian, but this may be a situation where the ends justify the means. Both Vimes and Carrot are in positions of power, but no one could argue that they did not get there through merit.

Magic is a power which is central to Discworld, and brings with it many dangers, not least the risk that the practitioner will be possessed by a creature from the **Dungeon Dimensions**, or swept away to join them. For all that many of the novels belong in the **Witches** and **Wizards** sequences, actual magic is avoided as often as possible. This is partly because **Fantasy** would be too easy to write if characters could just spell their way out of danger, but also because there is the sense of it needing to have a cost.

The power of witches seems to be drawn from the Earth, but more often they try to use headology – someone is persuaded that something is the case, or a surreptitious spot of chiropractics will fix an ache. Real magic, such as the Borrowing that Granny **Weatherwax** and Tiffany **Aching** engage in, has a physical cost and is not to be entered into lightly.

The powers of wizards lies in words, and some of their actions do endanger the entire Disc. Fortunately most of them are too lazy to pose a frequent threat; magic takes effort, and this is difficult when there is a different hearty meal to enjoy. If they used their magic to gain power over others, then they would have to decide what to do all the time, and that just takes too much effort.

But it is narrative and narrative expectations which wield the most power – whether it is **dragons** which require belief to exist or witch godmothers who have to bear gifts, the power of expectation is very strong. The characters with the real power are the ones that can use their narrative to their own benefit, or, like Johnny **Maxwell**, can manage to form their own narrative and take control of themselves as individuals. This is fine, as long as they do not try to impose their power upon others. *See also* Tiffany Aching; Ankh-Morpork; City Watch; Death; Djelibeybi; Fantasy; Feminism; Lancre; Magic; Johnny Maxwell; Narrative; Politics; Racism; Sexism; Stratified Societies; Patrician Vetinari; Witches *and* Wizards.

Andrew M. Butler

The Pratchett Portfolio see **Kidby, Paul**

Publishers

Within Britain, Terry Pratchett's books have been published by five different publishers, albeit under more imprints. At the start of his career, he was published by a small press Colin **Smythe** Ltd, based in Gerrards Cross, Buckinghamshire. This company published the first editions of *CP*

(1971), *DSS* (1976), *Str* (1981), *COM* (1983) and *LF* (1986) in hardback and in limited numbers. After this, three of the **Discworld** books were published in hardback by Gollancz, but in association with Colin Smythe Ltd: *ER* (1987), *M* (1987) and *S* (1988). After this they were published as by Gollancz alone, and Colin Smythe became Pratchett's agent.

In 1978 New English Library published a paperback of *DSS* with a cover by sf artist Tim White (b.1952), and in 1982 they printed the first paperback edition of *Str*, also with a cover by White. This was remaindered in 1985, with Colin Smythe Ltd buying 300 copies and selling them as published by Colin Smythe Ltd with a new ISBN. NEL publish books in a variety of genres, including **Science Fiction**, **Fantasy**, crime, and in the 1960s and 1970s, various exploitation novels set among biker or skinhead gangs. NEL had been bought by Hodder and Stoughton, and they were perhaps not promoting these books as much as they might have.

Smythe suggested to NEL that they did not want to continue publishing the paperbacks, having already begun negotiating paperback rights with Diane Pearson at Corgi. This is the paperback imprint of Transworld, which had been publishing science fiction and fantasy by authors such as Ray Bradbury (b.1920) and Anne McCaffrey (b.1926), as well as mainstream fiction. They began with *COM* in 1985, and continued with all of the **Discworld** novels apart from the editions of *E* illustrated by Josh **Kirby** and the heavily illustrated (by Paul **Kidby**) *LH*; in addition they reprinted *DSS* and *Str* from 1988 and the paperback edition of the second version of *CP* in 1993. Corgi managed to persuade BBC Radio 4 to broadcast *COM* as a six part serial, which contributed massively to Pratchett's popularity.

By the time of *LF* it was obvious that a bigger hardback operation was needed than Colin Smythe Ltd could offer, and Smythe approached David Burnett at Victor Gollancz Ltd. This company was founded in 1927 by Victor Gollancz (1893–1967), and specialised in literary and popular fiction, often by writers on the leftwing of politics. Many of the Gollancz hardcovers were distinguished by their bright yellow dust wrappers, which signalled science fiction to many readers (although the colour spanned all genres). They turned to David **Langford** for advice and then negotiated a three-book bid for the hardback rights to *ER*, *M* and *S*, initially published in association with Colin Smythe Ltd, as noted above. From *WS* (1988) onwards they were published as by Gollancz alone, usually with a Corgi paperback the following year with a modified version of the hardback cover art. Gollancz, by then perhaps the leading British hardback sf publisher, was sold to Houghton Mifflin in 1989 and then to Cassell in 1992. After *J* (1997) Pratchett moved to the Doubleday imprint of Transworld for his hardcovers, although Gollancz were to publish *LH* (2001) and continued to publish *E* and *UC*, sometimes under a paperback imprint, Vista. Gollancz had been bought from Cassell by Orion in 1998, and was transformed into their specialist science fiction and fantasy imprint. Corgi, a paperback imprint of the same company who owned

Doubleday, continued to publish paperbacks the year after the hardback editions, with modified covers by Kirby and by Paul **Kidby**.

Doubleday published the original hardbacks of the non-Discworld children's books, *T* (1989), *D* (1990), *W* (1990), *OYCSM* (1992), *JD* (1993) and *JB* (1996), the second version of *CP* (1992) and the Discworld novels from *LC* (1998) onwards. Doubleday is an imprint of Transworld, who have also published the Anchor, Bantam, Black Swan, Corgi and Partridge imprints, among others. Doubleday has been merged with Random House since 1999 and its parent company is now the German media giant Bertelsmann AG. They own the book publisher Random House and its American imprints including Ballantine, Bantam, Crown, Del Rey, Doubleday, Knopf, the magazines and newspapers in the Gruner + Jahr group, music labels under the BMG umbrella, including Arista, Jive, RCA and Zomba, and television and radio stations in the RTL group. The ***Science of Discworld*** books are published by Ebury Books, part of Random House.

The situation in America for Pratchett novels is more complex. The first editions of *DSS* (1976) and *Str* (1981) were the hardbacks printed by Colin Smythe Ltd, but with different dust wrappers and ISBNs. *COM* (1985) was also published by St Martin's Press, with a US reprint. The terms offered by them for *LF* were not thought to be acceptable, and so the only US hardback editions of the subsequent Discworld novels until 1994 were Science Fiction Bookclub editions.

The first American paperbacks were published by New American Library or Signet: *Str* (1983), *COM* (1985), *LF* (1988), *ER* (1988), *M* (1989), *S* (1989), *P* (1989), *WS* (1990) (note the order of the last two), *GG* (1990), *MP* (1992), *RM* (1992), *WA* (1992), and *E* (1995) (note the delay in publishing this title).

In the meantime, The **Bromeliad** was sold to Delacorte – *T* (1990), *D* (1991) and *W* (1991) – with some modification of the text for the American market.

The Discworld titles passed to various imprints of HarperCollins, a book publisher which is part of News Corporation owned by Rupert Murdoch (b.1931) and which publishes newspapers, including *The Times* and *The Sun*, owns Twentieth-Century Fox studios and runs various television channels including the Fox Network and BritishSkyBroadcasting. Harper and Brothers had started in 1817 and merged with Row, Peterson & Company in 1962 to Harpers and Row, before being sold to News Corporation in 1987. William Collins had been founded in 1819 in Glasgow, and specialised in religious books. They were taken over by News Corporation in 1989, and merged with Harpers and Row in 1990. HarperCollins published a hardback of *SG* (1994). HarperPrism published *SG* (1994, paperback), *LL* (1995, hardback), *SM* (1995, hardback then paperback), *LL* (1995, paperback), *MAA* (1996, hardback), *FOC* (1996, hardback), *IT* (1997, hardback), *MAA* (1997, paperback), *Msk* (1997, hardback), *FOC* (1997, paperback), *IT* (1998, paperback), *J* (1998, hardback), *Msk* (1998, paperback), *H* (1998, hardback), *J* (1999, paperback), *LC* (1999, hardback),

H (1999, paperback), *CJ* (1999, hardback), *LC* (2000, paperback), *FE* (2000, hardback) and *CJ* (2000, paperback). Hardback editions then were published as by HarperCollins: *TT* (2000), *TOT* (2001), *LH* (2001), *NW* (2002), *WFM* (2003), *MR* (2004), *HFOS* (2004, followed by a paperback for the imprint 2005), *GP* (2004, hardback and paperback), *OYCSM* (2005), WMC (2005), *T!* (2005), *JD* (2006) and *Wint* (2006). Paperbacks of some of the series were published by HarperTorch: a new edition of *ER* (2000, 2005), *FE* (2000), *M* (2001), *S* (2001), *WS* (2001), *P* (2001), *GG* (2001), *TT* (2001), *E* (2002), *MP* (2002), *RM* (2002), *WA* (2002), *NW* (2003), *MR* (2004) and *OYCSM* (2006). A hardback edition of the first Discworld book for children was published by HarperChildren *AMHER* (2001), with HarperTrophy publishing *AMHER* (2003, paperback), *T* (2004), *D* (2004), *W* (2004) and *HFOS* (2005). Eos published the expanded version of *LH* (2001).

Some of the early Discworld novels were reprinted in compact editions by Gollancz: *COM*, *LF*, *ER* and *M* (all 1995), with these editions also issued in a slipcase. There have been a number of omnibi: *The* ***Witches*** *Trilogy* (*ER*, *WS* and *WA*, London: Gollancz, 1994), *The* ***Death*** *Trilogy* (*M*, *RM* and *SM*, London: Gollancz, 1998), *The* ***Bromeliad*** (*T*, *D* and *W*, London: Doubleday, 1998), *The First Discworld Novels* (*COM* and *LF*, Gerrards Cross: Colin Smythe Ltd, 1999), *The* ***City Watch*** *Trilogy* (*GG*, *MAA* and *FOC*, London: Gollancz, 1999), *The* ***Johnny Maxwell Trilogy*** (*OYCSM*, *JD* and *JB*; London: Doubleday, 1999), *The Gods Trilogy* (*P*, *SG* and *H*, London: Gollancz, 2000) and *The* ***Rincewind*** *Trilogy* (*COM*, *LF*, *S* and *E* [sic], London: Gollancz, 2001). In the USA, the Science Fiction Book Club issued omnibi *Rincewind the Wizard* (*COM*, *LF*, *S* and *E*, 1999) and *Tales of Discworld* (*P*, *MP* and *SG*, 2000).

Further bookclub, bookshop reprints and foreign language editions are beyond the scope of this entry, as are repackagings of the books with new covers, although much of this information will be found in the entries for specific titles. *See also* The Bromeliad; The Johnny Maxwell Trilogy; Paul Kidby; Josh Kirby; Merchandising; Plays *and* Colin Smythe.

Andrew M. Butler

Pyramids (The Book of Going Forth) (1989)

An extract appeared in *Gaslight and Ghosts*, edited by Stephen Jones and Jo Fletcher, published by the World Fantasy **Convention** 1988. The first Gollancz edition was 12,300 copies with a cover by Josh **Kirby**; the Corgi paperback (1990) was 151,000 copies in its first edition, with reset text after a 1993 edition, and an alternative black and gold photograph cover available from 2004. In 2000 Gollancz published a hardback with it *SG* and

H as *The Gods Trilogy*, with a print run of about 11,000 copies. *P* won the BSFA Award for best novel (though not the British Fantasy Award as often credited in reference works). It has been translated into Bulgarian, Croatian, Czech, Dutch, Estonian, Finnish, French, German, Greek, Hebrew, Hungarian, Italian, Japanese, Norwegian, Polish, Portuguese, Romanian, Russian, Serbian, Slovakian, Spanish, Swedish and Turkish. The novel is the seventh in the **Discworld** series, a **Coming of Age** narrative subdivided into four books. Its title refers to the pyramids built by the people of **Djelibeybi**. The track 'Pyramids' on *Terry Pratchett's From the Discworld* by Dave **Greenslade** was inspired by this novel. Dave **Langford** reviewed *P* by saying: 'One thinks of Discworld books as being jolly little romps, but they gain comic strength from repeated dealing with final things like death ... not to mention, of course, Death ... Horribly funny and well up to standard' (*Games Magazine*).

'The Book of Going Forth': **Teppic** trains to be an assassin with the Guild at **Ankh-Morpork** until his father Teppicymon XXVII, Pharoah of Djelibeybi, dies. 'The Book of the Dead': Teppic, under pressure from the high priest Dios, commissions the biggest ever pyramid as a monument to his father, risking bankrupting the kingdom. He also saves the life of Ptraci, one of Teppicymon's handmaidens. The pyramid meanwhile transforms reality so that the sun really is pushed through the sky by a beetle. 'The Book of the New Son': Teppicymon, who has already been hanging around as a ghost, comes back to life and helps to save the rest of the not-so-recently departed. Teppic and Ptraci discover that Djelibeybi has vanished off the face of the Disc, leaving rivals **Ephebe** and **Tsort** as neighbours. 'The Book of 101 Things A Boy Can Do': As **war** looms, Teppic solves the riddle of the Sphinx, and helps to defuse the pyramid. The country returns to the Discworld, and he installs Ptraci – apparently his half sister as King of the country. He wants to return to a more adventuresome life, but she will not let him go. Dios, who has managed to be a priest for seven thousand years, is thrown seven millennia back in time by the pyramid's explosion.

Djelibeybi is the Discworld equivalent of **Egypt**, Ephebe of Classical Greece (see **Greek Mythology** *and* **Greek Philosophy**) and Tsort is Troy, so much so that it could be imagined that this is not a Discworld novel at all. The parodic references are much further a field than fantasy now – the assassins' school is modelled on Rugby School for Boys in Tom Brown's Schooldays (1857) by Thomas Hughes (1822–1896), and the assassination looks like a British Driving Test. *See also* Djelibeybi; Egypt; Ephebe; Greek Mythology; Greek Philosophy; History; Power; Religion; Tsort *and* War.

Further Reading

Butler, Andrew M. 1995. 'The BSFA Award Winners: 2, *Pyramids* by Terry Pratchett' *Vector* 186 (December): P. 4.

Andrew M. Butler

Q

Quirm, Leonard of (*WS*, *MAA*, *J*, *FE*, *LH*)

The **Discworld** equivalent of Leonardo da Vinci (1452–1519) who was best known for the *Mona Lisa* (1503–1506) and his notebook full of inventions – such as flying machines and submarines – which seem unlikely to have got off his drawing board. His Vitruvian Man drawing (*c.*1492) of a naked man within a square and a circle is the inspiration for Stephen **Player**'s alternate paperback 'Vitruvian Turtle' cover of *COM* in 1993. The Discworld version has painted the *Mona Ogg* (in *AD*) and several other paintings, and is responsible for various inventions such as the Gonne (*MAA*) and The Going Under the Water Safely Device (*J*), as well as designs for a bicycle, although he's not sure what it does. He is the designer of the *Kite*, a ship designed to fly around the Disc and end up at the **Hub**, slingshot fashion (*LH*). Many of his other designs can be found in *LH*. Naïve as to the potential uses of his inventions, he is kept a permanent guest of Patrician **Vetinari**.

Not to be confused with Ponce da Quirm, who was looking for the Fountain of Youth (*E*) based on Juan Ponce de León (c.1460–1521), a conquistador who in popular myth looked for this in what is now Florida. *See also* Paul Kidby; Stephen Player; Technology *and* Patrician Vetinari.

Andrew M. Butler

Quizbooks

Two official **Discworld** quizbooks have been compiled by David **Langford** with introductions by Pratchett (*see* ***OM* WF***). ***The Unseen University Challenge*** takes its title from the television quiz *University Challenge*, presented by Bamber Gascoigne (b.1935) on ITV (1961–1987) and then by Jeremy Paxman (b.1950) on BBC2 (but still made by Granada) (1994–), which pits groups of university students against each other. Each round begins with a starter for ten points, which is buzzed for, followed by three questions for five marks each which are answered by the team which got the starter question right. This in turn was inspired by its US version, *College Bowl* (1950–1973), although the book is themed questions and has no real connection to its original. The formatting of the book means that sometimes the answers are facing the questions.

The Wyrdest Link takes its title from *The Weakest Link* (2000–), presented by Anne Robinson (b.1944), usually on BBC2 but sometimes (with celebrity contestants playing for charity) on BBC1. Questions are asked for increasing amounts of money, with contestants banking the money or losing it with a wrong answer. At the end of each round a contestant is voted off by the other players, and the next round is shorter. The last two contestants go head to head. The quiz is notorious for the apparent rudeness of the host, the attempts to get even with her by the contestants, and the interviews with the losers. Again, the title is the only real connection to the quizbook.

So You Think You Know Discworld? (London: Hodder Children, 2006) by Clive Gifford is aimed at children, who has written similar volumes on *The Lord of the Rings*, *Doctor Who*, James Bond, Manchester United and many others.

Pratchett was a contestant on *Space Cadets* (1997), a Channel 4 **Science Fiction** quizshow and has featured on *Mastermind* as a specialised subject. *See also* David Langford *and* Merchandising.

Andrew M. Butler

R

Racism

Whilst writing **Fantasy**, Pratchett still tries to deal with real world issues and **politics**, including **sexism** and **feminism** from early in the **Discworld** series. He has also examined issues of race through representation of racism and attempts at multiculturalism and assimilation, both in the Discworld novels and the **Johnny Maxwell Trilogy**.

Race is a term used to describe a group of people who share visible signs such as skin pigmentation, hair types and facial features, as well as self-identification. The term entered the English language in the sixteenth century, at the point when the European population was meeting a whole new set of people from the Americas, Australasian and the interior of Africa. Race became a means of identifying and cataloguing different groups of people. By the nineteenth century, scientists were mistakenly suggesting that race was connected to the actual and potential intelligence and abilities of the individual, and that certain races (namely white Europeans) were superior. Intermarriage with a member of a different race would lead to the diluting of the blood and the degeneration of the race. The categorical differences of appearances became justifications for the inequalities of humanity; 'lesser' races were less human. The science of eugenics led to the holocaust in an attempt to eradicate a perceived lesser race in favour of a master race. A less problematic term might be 'ethnicity', used to designate a group who identify together as sharing a genetic, cultural, linguistic or national heritage – of course, the fact that such factors do not necessarily always coincide or that perception of heritage might be wrong makes this more complicated.

It is clear that there are social, economic and cultural differences between people in specific locations and times which appear to be structured – if not necessarily organised – along lines that seem to demarcate on grounds of a perceived racial identity. Race has a material existence even if it is largely ideological. It is equally important to remember that not all people of a specific race share exactly the same characteristics and that race is not the only defining factor of an individual. At the same time there can be **power** in a self-identification with a specific grouping, especially in a context when that group is being oppressed.

With all that being written, race is not necessarily visible in the Discworld sequence. There is an apparent homogeneity to the humans, **trolls**, golem and werewolves. **Twoflower** is the Discworld equivalent of the Japanese tourist, and it is his gullibility and naïveté that makes him the butt of jokes or target of attacks rather than any difference in skin tone. Any reader is largely free to imagine their own choice of races for each of the characters – and the default assumption is likely to be white. Sometimes racial difference ends up being erased altogether.

The major exception to this comes in the dealings of **Ankh-Morpork** with **Klatch** in *J*. Both Ankh-Morporkians and Klatchians perceive each other as less than human, with distasteful habits, and both sides can use this prejudice to further their own ends. **Colon**, for example, refuses to see any positives in their civilisation and their invention or discovery of alcohol, algebra and the number zero are dismissed as being products of lazy brains or accidents and chance. Nobby **Nobbs** – repeatedly described as subhuman through the sequence – tries to put the opposing view, and finally reminds Colon of how hardworking Goriff is in Mundane Foods in Scandal Alley. Colon is convinced, but Goriff likely remains an exception.

Much **Science Fiction** and Fantasy, in fact, projects racial difference onto other species, so that the encounter with the alien becomes a metaphor for the encounter with the racial other. The positive side of this is the admittance that humans have more in common, irrespective of ethnic or racial background, than they do with whatever the alien is. The downside is the elimination of difference within the species and the tendency of the alien/other to be represented as a threat which has to be destroyed. In *WA* the authorial voice explicitly notes that speciesism has replaced racism, a point repeated in *MAA*.

OYCSM offers a complication of this in its depiction of Johnny **Maxwell**'s encounter with the ScreeWee, and the shift in his mindset which he must go through. The mankind he must save is in fact the ScreeWee, and he must put himself in the place of the other. There are clearly differences between individual ScreeWee in beliefs and actions, and Maxwell realises that ScreeWee is *Homo sapiens*' name for them, rather than their own.

This displacement is continually seen through the **City Watch** novels, where the force grows to admit not only humans and gargoyles, but **dwarfs**, trolls, **werewolves**, **Igors**, **zombies** and eventually even **vampires**. Samuel **Vimes** frequently pairs different species, perhaps in a mute protest at being forced to take them on. **Detritus** and **Cuddy** are paired, despite the historic enmity of trolls and dwarfs. The different characteristics of each species complement the other, so they may form a unit greater than two individuals. Vimes ends up with a utilitarian view of his corps: Sally van Humpeding is useful for her ability to smell blood. On the one hand this is encouraging a kind of multi-culturalism where everyone gets along together, on the other it returns to identifying a race by a special trait. The individual non-human species are homogenous. It is only in the later novels that the distinctions between the dwarfs of Copperhead and Überwald, the high and the low, become clearer, and even then it is perhaps as much cultural as any difference in physical appearance.

Yo-Less in the Johnny Maxwell trilogy becomes defined by his failure to match up with the stereotype of 1990s Black British youth, perhaps in itself underlining assumptions about identity. He wants to be a doctor and is not trying to be cool. In *JD*, the chair of a meeting, Miss Liberty, does not know how to refer to Yo-Less – who she has not previously met – without identifying as the one non-white person in the room. She is clearly trying to avoid racism, but ends up being awkward at best. In *JB* he is the butt of real racism, and even plays along with it, perhaps aware of how attitudes have changed over time. He is more forgiving than **Kirsty**, but resents her defence of him.

Of course, it would be dangerous to deduce the politics of Pratchett from his work – and the fact that he represents an attitude is not the same as endorsing it. The character Carrot **Ironfoundersson** is a human brought up as a dwarf, and so has experience of crossing between cultures. But even he is shown to be racist when it comes to the undead. Even he is fallible as a human being, and Pratchett is entitled to depict racism on the Discworld as much as anything else in human culture. *See also* City Watch; Cuddy; Detritus; Dwarfs; Carrot Ironfoundersson; Johnny Maxwell Trilogy; Kirsty; Politics; Power; Trolls; Samuel Vimes *and* Yo-Less.

Further Reading

Banton, Martin. 1987. *Racial Theories*. Cambridge: Cambridge University Press.
Baldry, Cherith. 'The Children's Books'. *GOL, GOL2*.
Dines, Gail and Jean M. Humez, Eds. 1995. *Gender, Race and Class in Media: A Text-Reader*. Thousand Oaks: Sage.
hooks, Bell. 1992. *Black Looks: Race and Representation*. Boston: South End Press.
James, Edward. 'The City Watch'. *GOL, GOL2*.

Andrew M. Butler

Radio

Radio is a suitable medium for **Fantasy** writers such as Pratchett, because the special effects are better than on film or television, working as they do in the imagination. In fact the early serialisations of *COM* (in 1983) and *ER* (in 1987) on BBC Radio 4 did much to publicise Pratchett's writing beyond the core audience of **Fandom** – and supposedly Pratchett's unisex name helped the sale to *Woman's Hour* of *ER*. *AMHER* (2002), *T* (2004) and *WFM* (2004) were read as serial stories on BBC7.

A number of his books have been broadcast as serials on BBC Radio 4, 5 and 7 – *GG* as a six-parter (1992), *WS* as a four-parter (1995), *OYCSM* as a three-parter (1996), *M* as a four-parter (2004) and *SG* as a four-parter (2006) – and *AMHER* as a single play (2003). The **Ankh-Morpork** National Anthem (see *NDC* and *OM* WF*) was first broadcast on BBC Radio 3 (15 January 1999).

Pratchett has been a guest on ***Desert Island Discs***. *See also* Douglas Adams; Audio Books; *Desert Island Discs and* Plays.

Andrew M. Butler

Ramkin, Lady Sybil (*GG*, *MAA*, *FOC*, *J*, *FE*, *NW*, *WMC?*, *T!*)

Lady Sybil Ramkin first appears in *GG* where she is the remaining scion of a depleted house. Large, very fond of swamp **dragons** (*Draco vulgaris*) and surrounded by Indistinguishable Emmas, her domineering manner disguises a strong sense of noblesse oblige and overpowering shyness.

At the beginning of *MAA*, Lady Sybil has married Sam **Vimes**, and from here on, her main appearances relate to the re-shaping of Sam Vimes. In *FE*, however, Lady Sybil Vimes (as she now is) plays a crucial part. Her rendering of Ironhammer's Ransom aria in a strong amateur colatura secures Vimes's access to the High King at a crucial moment in the drama; Lady Sybil's revenge for many years of school torment against Angua's mother, Lady Serafine von Überwald is a delight; and it is the business and financial acumen of Lady Vimes (and her eye for carpet sizes) that secures for **Ankh-Morpork** the best deal on fats in the region.

At the very end of *FE*, Lady Vimes tells Sam that she is pregnant. Her son, also Sam, creates a centre of calm in Vimes's permanent rage against the world, and it is to read to Sam that Vimes strives to stay alive in *T!*. The children's book *WMC?* doubles both as the book read to Sam, and the book in which we read about Sam. *See also* Ankh-Morpork; Dragons; Opera *and* Samuel Vimes.

Farah Mendlesohn

Reaper Man (1991)

The tenth or eleventh Discworld novel, although the Corgi editions had stopped count by then. It is primarily part of the **Death** sequence, a sequel to *M*, although it does contain **wizards**. The first edition, from Gollancz with a cover by Josh **Kirby**, was 20,200 copies. A Corgi edition in a print run of 175,000 copies appeared in 1992; an alternative black and gold photographic cover was available from 2005. In 1997, Gollancz issued a Collector's Edition in a print run of 5,400 hardbacks and in 1998 published it, along with *M* and *SM*, as *The Death Trilogy*. *RM* has been translated into Bulgarian, Czech, Dutch, Estonian, Finnish, French, German, Hebrew, Hungarian, Japanese, Norwegian, Polish, Portuguese, Russian, Serbian, Spanish, Swedish and Turkish. The title of the novel is a variation on names given to Death, like the Grim Reaper, and has an echo of *Repo Man* (1984), a film directed by Alex Cox (b.1954). The novel includes two mentions of the Amazing Maurice and his Educated Rodents, a narrative Pratchett returned to in *AMHER*. Dominic Wells in *Time Out* wrote: 'Under the guise of a knockabout piss-take of the conventions of Fantasy, this is an oddly touching elegy to a rural England that no longer exists, in this world at least. Death has to seek employment as – what else? – a reaper, and overcome the dreaded combine harvester, supermarkets are living, malevolent entities that threaten life and sanity. The whole recalls Tolkien's Shire, with jokes'.

Thanks to his increasingly human behaviour, Death is made redundant by the Auditors – gods who check on the progress of the universe – and he leaves his domain for his final days. He finds work as an odd job man on the farm run by Miss Renata **Flitworth**, for which he is to be paid sixpence a week. Curiously this is the sort of place he had taken his apprentice Mort **Sto Helit** away from. As Death is absent and not yet replaced, there is a backlog of spirits, including the wizard Windle Poons who had expected to be reincarnated by now. Poons begins to explore **Ankh-Morpork** and meets a variety of other undead beings, including Count and Countess Notfaroutoe, both **vampires**, Schleppel, a bogeyman, Lupine, a wereman (*see* **Werewolves**) and so on. The uncleared life continues to build up, risking havoc. Meanwhile Death faces competition in harvest reaping from the invention of an automatic threshing machine, and has to decide whether to rescue a young girl from a fire or not – a choice he would have scorned Mort for making. In time the new Death appears and they fight, and Death gets his old job back. Windle can die happy, having lived. In the interregnum there had been minor Deaths, for each species, but these are now subsumed into him with the exception of the **Death of Rats**.

The Death novels often include a commentary on the nature of work and personal identity; where work fits into life, how a job can be made superfluous and what happens to those on the scrap heap. *See also* Death; Death of Rats; Renata Flitworth; Vampires; Werewolves *and* Wizards.

Further Reading

Moody, Nickianne. 'Death'. *GOL*.

———. 'Death and Work'. *GOL2*.

Andrew M. Butler

Religion

On **Discworld**, stories are important. Belief/**narrative** imperative is the driving force within this universe, and therefore stories shape people and events and ... gods.

SG and *MR* are the major sources of information on Discworld gods and religions, although there are references here and there throughout most of the books (especially *FOC*). We find out that there are literally billions of small gods on Discworld, most of which are too small to be seen and who will never be worshipped, and who will never have believers to feed them with belief, which is the true life force of the gods. If the god is lucky or manages to pull off a miracle or two, the god gathers enough believers to become a major god with the attendant powers. As seen in *SG*, it is possible for a once major god to lose his or her believers (even though the religion itself is doing well), and become once again a small mote, with only a dim awareness of who it once was.

Anoia Kitchen Hook created by Discworld Merchandising.

The major gods, quarrelsome and bourgeois, live on Cori Celesti, in a palace of marble, alabaster and uncut moquette three-piece suites that they've called Dunmanifestin. (Pratchett mentions that it annoys Discworld citizens that their gods have so little taste. Not only is Dunmanifestin a pun in and of itself, but it is also a play on 'Dunroamin', a stereotypical British house name.) Cori Celesti is a ten mile high spire of grey stone and green ice, and the magic of Discworld earths itself here at the centre of the world in the form of the Aurora Corialis, with great silent sheets of blue, green and octarine light. There are over three thousand major gods living in Dunmanifestin, although it's not certain how many of the deities are using false noses and other disguises to get themselves more believers by operating under different names and appearances.

The gods often amuse themselves by passing their time in various **games** with people as their pawns. Their board is the Discworld. Fate and The Lady often play these games, such as Mad Kings, Star-Crossed Lovers, Floods and Draughts (an easy one) and Mighty Empires (with rules such as The Fall of Great Houses and Destinies of Nations Hanging by a Thread).

There are also demons, whose existence is apparently extent upon belief just as the gods' is. Whether they are 'demons' or 'gods' is essentially the same sort of difference between 'terrorists' or 'freedom fighters', according to Pratchett.

Anthropomorphic personalities might or might not fall into the category of religion: **Death**, War, Time, Chaos, the **Hogfather** (Discworld's equivalent to Santa Claus), Old Man Trouble, the Tooth Fairy, bogeymen of various sorts and so on. These beings have all existed due to belief, with the possible exception of Death, who was there at the beginning, for life always leads to death, whether the concept is believed in or not.

There are also eight beings who are called The Old High Ones. We know very little of them, and neither the Discworld's religions nor the books in **Unseen University**'s **Library** say much about them. We do know that they see the gods as being somewhat more troublesome human beings, and that they control the workings of the multiverse. In prehistory, they reduced the size of humans due to the havoc that sourcerers were causing. It is likely that Death and Time are their servants, as are the Auditors of Reality, and possibly The Creator. Most Discworld citizens do not even know that The Old High Ones exist. It is thought that their role is to observe the universe (in a dynamic way), so that events may continue to happen, much as the History Monks currently do on the Discworld.

We have only seen one of the Old High Ones thus far: Azrael, also known as the Great Attractor or the Death of Universes, who is the beginning and end of time (*RM*). The Death of Discworld is not only his servant but also an aspect of Azrael, much as The **Death of Rats** is an aspect of the Death of Discworld. He is an enormous, rather sad being, so large that a supernova is merely the suggestion of a gleam in his eye. He keeps a clock that is something of the opposite of our clocks, as it goes around once for the entire cycle of the universe, possibly the multiverse. We also know that Azrael is bored.

Some of the gods and demons mentioned in the books are: Alohura (Goddess of lightning in Trob, *COM*), Aniger (Goddess of Squashed Animals, *LH*), Anoia (Goddess of Things that Get Stuck in Drawers, *GP*, *T!*, *Wint*, once the volcano goddess Lela), Astfgl (see *E*), Astoria (Ephebian Goddess of Love), Bibulous (God of Things on Sticks and Wine, *H*, *LH*), Bilious (the Oh God of Hangovers, *H*), Blind Io (Chief of the Gods), Ceno (a liberal god, *FOC*), Czol (ancient goddess of sunken Thut, *GP*), Errata (Goddess of Misunderstandings, *Discworld Noir* (*see* **Games**)), Fate (plays games against the Lady, *COM*, *LF*, *M*, *IT* and *LH*), Fedecks (the Messenger of the Gods, *SG*, *GP* and *Discworld Noir*), Flatulus (Ephebean God of Wind, *SG*, *LH* and *Discworld Noir*), Foorgol (Ephebean God of Avalanches, *SG*), Glipzo (a Goddess of Howandaland, *LH*), God of Evolution (characterised by self-belief and creator of many unique animals, *LC* and *SODIII*), Herne the Hunted (Ramtop's God of Hunted Animals, *WS* and *LL*), Hoki the Jokester (Ramtops trickster God, *ER*, *M* and *LH*), Hyperopia (Goddess of Shoes, *RM* and *Discworld Noir*), The Ice Giants (necessary harbinger of the Apocralypse, S), Ikebana (Goddess of Topiary, *Discworld Noir*), Jimi (God of Beggars, *MAA*), The Lady (a goddess associated with luck, *COM*, *IT* and *LH*), Lamentatio (Goddess of Interminable **Opera**, *Discworld Noir*), Libertina (Goddess of the Sea, Apple Pie and some flavours of ice cream, *SG*), Moon Goddess (Druid Goddess, *LF*), Neoldian (Black Smith of the Gods, *LH* and *Discworld Noir*), Nuggan (God of Paperclips and other office equipment, worshipped in Borogravia, *LH* and *MR*), Offler (crocodile god from **Klatch**), **Om** (the rather indifferent God of **Omnia**, *SG*), Orm (a god resident in hell, *P*), Patina (Epehebian Goddess of Wisdom, *SG* and *LH*), Petulia (Goddess of Prostitutes, *SG*), P'tang P'tang (God from near Omnia with fifty-two believers, *SG*), Quezovercoatl (God of Human Sacrifices, *E*), Reg (God of Club Musicians, *SM*), Skelde, Sweevo (God of Cut Timber, *LH*), Tak (Creator God of the **Dwarfs**, *T!*), Topaxi (God of Mushrooms and forgetfulness, *LF* and *LH*), Ukli (Howandaland god, *LH*), Umcherrel (Soul of the Forest, *LF*), Ur-Gilash (former rival of Om, *SG*), Urika (Goddess of Snow, Saunas and small theatrical audiences, *LH*), Vometia (**Ankh-Morpork** Goddess of Vomit, *LH*), Wilf (God of Astrology, *DA*) and Zephyrus (God of Slight Breezes, *COM*, *SG* and *Discworld Noir*).

Gods, in and of themselves however, are not religion.

It has been observed that 'effort to define religion is as old as the academic study of religion itself' (Arnal 22). There has historically been little consensus as to a firm general definition of religion (either theologically or legally), with no real end to the debate in sight.

Writing in the *Harvard Human Rights Journal*, T. Jeremy Gunn writes about the difficulties of defining the term 'religion'. He writes that there are three approaches that identify what is being defined: '[F]irst, religion in its metaphysical or theological sense (e.g., the underlying truth of the existence of God, the dharma, etc.); second, religion as it is psychologically experienced by people (e.g., the feelings of the religious believer about divinity or ultimate concerns, the holy, etc.); and third, religion as a cultural or social force (e.g., symbolism that binds a community together or separates it from other communities). Definitions of religion typically begin by assuming one of these three different theoretical approaches' Once the primary assumption has been identified, Gunn outlines two main forms of how 'religion' may be defined, either 'essentialist' or 'polythetic'.

An essentialist definition identifies the elements that are necessary for something to be designated as a 'religion'. When a definition of 'religion' is essentialist, it assumes that religion has one or more elements in common with all other religions. The second type of definition, the polythetic, does not require that all religions have specific elements in common. The polythetic approach accepts in the religious believer something 'parallel' to the orthodox belief in God.

If *SG* deals with the nature of God (or gods), *MR* deals at least in part with the nature of faith and religion as moral and behavioural systems and examines how these systems interface with day-to-day lives, choices and decisions. In *MR*, the citizens of Borogravia wrestle with their state religion, even as they struggle in an almost constant state of war: their god Nuggan appears to be weak and insane, so the religion has developed an intermediary in the person of the Duchess, their ruler, who has not been seen for decades. The Nugganites struggle with the nature and practices of a system of belief that cannot address their lives and problems. The Duchess, now deified by the belief of her people, is weak from their suspension of true belief as the consequences of human nature continue to take their toll.

For if a Discworld god is insane or weak, given that belief and narrative causality define all events on the Discworld, it follows that the belief and actions of the believers shaped the god's state. Mind you, Nuggan always was a fussy and rather unpleasant little god. Outside Borogravia, he is known as the God of Paperclips, Correct Things in the Right Place in Small Desk Stationery Sets and Unnecessary Paperwork, who prohibits his followers from eating chocolate, ginger, mushrooms and garlic.

As Pratchett's books have matured from simply amusing parody and satire, he has dealt with much more serious subjects, mainly using a method dubbed 'stealth philosophy', which is to say he hides (sometimes more or less openly) philosophical struggles, questions, and arguments within the scope of his stories – often in the areas of ethics, religion, the mind and science. This is a time-honoured use for the literary forms of **Fantasy** and **Science Fiction**.

Pratchett writes that he sometimes hears from people who know they will soon be meeting Death, and hope that Pratchett has got him right in the Discworld books. *See also* Ankh-Morpork; Brutha; Death; Death of Rats; Ephebe; Greek Mythology; The Hogfather (Character); The Hub; Om; Omnia; Nisodemus; Power *and* Vorbis.

Further Reading
Arnal, William E. 2000. 'Definition'. *Guide to the Study of Religion*. P. 22. Edited by Willi Braun and Russell T. McCutcheon. New York: Cassell.
Gunn, T. Jeremy. 2003. 'The Complexity of Religion and the Definition of "Religion" in International Law'. *Harvard Human Rights Journal* 16 (Spring): http://www.law.harvard.edu/students/orgs/hrj/iss16/gunn.shtml.
Wikipedia, 'Discworld Gods'. http://en.wikipedia.org/wiki/Discworld_gods.

Zina Lee

Ridcully, Mustrum (*MP*, *RM*, *LL*, *SM*, *IT*, *H*, *J*, *LC*, *LH*, *NW*, *GP*, *T!*, 'CCOODD')

One of the more successful (because more long-lived) of the recent **Archchancellors** of the **Unseen University**, **Ankh-Morpork**. His brother, Hughnon, is a High Priest of Blind Io.

Born in the countryside, Ridcully had been absent from the university for sometime when he was elected to the post – during which he had an affair with Granny **Weatherwax** – and presumably nobody else wanted the job. He has maintained his position for a number of years, which has somewhat paralysed the **Stratified Society** of the **Wizards**. He is strong-minded and frequently stubborn, which helps in his every day dealings with underlings such as the bursar and Ponder **Stibbons**, with Patrician **Vetinari** and the **City Watch**. Under his leadership the Unseen University has weathered crazes for music and moving pictures, assassination attempts and attacks by **dragons**. He found himself on a desert island with his colleagues in *LC*, and like his colleagues nurses a certain degree of affection for Mrs **Whitlow**.

His name, Ridcully the Brown, perhaps echoes Radagast the Brown in J.R.R. **Tolkien**'s *The Lord of the Rings* (1954–1955), with Gandalf and Saruman one of the five wizards sent to Middle-earth. However, Radagast is as pliable as Ridcully is fixed in his ways. *See also* Ankh-Morpork; Archchancellors; Rincewind; Ponder Stibbons; Unseen University; Patrician Vetinari; Mrs Whitlow *and* Wizards.

Andrew M. Butler

Rincewind [the Wizzard] (*COM*, *LF*, *S*, *E*, *IT*, *LC*, *LH*, *SOD*, *SODII*, *SODIII*)

Wizards from the **Unseen University** are usually first to eighth level, according to how powerful they are and how far they have mastered **magic**. Rincewind is at level zero, having never scored more than 2% on his exams, and that was for spelling his name right (although he cannot spell wizard, apparently). This lack of magical ability may be down to general incompetence, but it is also connected to his deeply irregular reading of the *Octavo*, a key book in the **Library** containing the eight great spells of the creator, one of which escaped into his head. This seems to have driven out any residual ability to absorb magical techniques; equally the spell's sense of self-preservation suggests that this may be one reason why Rincewind survived all of the perils he faced in *COM* and *LF* – a skill he does retain in later books.

Rincewind puppet created by Discworld Merchandising.

When he first appeared in *COM*, he was down on his luck and saw that he could make a little money from acting as guide to the naïve tourist **Twoflower**, whose thirst to see everything that **Ankh-Morpork** had to offer hardly improved that luck. In an early encounter with **Death**, the first of several, Death is confused given that he'd anticipated meeting Rincewind in distant Psephopololis later that day. Rincewind briefly passes over to our world, as Dr Rjinswand. Rincewind ends the novel going over the edge of the world, but the spell protects him, so that he can appear in the sequel, *LF*, where the need for the speaking of all eight of the great spells means he is required to return to the university. At the end of that novel he is given the **Luggage**, which becomes devoted to him, whether he likes it or not.

In *S* he is forced by the **Archchancellor**'s hat to travel to Al Khali in **Klatch**, in order to prevent it from falling into the hands of **Coin** who, under the control of Ipslore the Red in his staff, is trying to make wizards rule the Discworld. Rincewind returns with **Cohen the Barbarian**'s daughter Conina and Nijel the Destroyer to help prevent this, and to rescue Coin from the **Dungeon Dimensions**. Here he stays until inadvertently summoned by Eric **Thursley**, where he acts as a guide for Eric's three wishes (*E*). In **Tsort** he meets Lavaeolus (literally 'rinser of winds'), possibly an ancestor.

Rincewind is forced by Patrician **Vetinari** to travel to Klatch to fulfil a prophecy, where he is reunited with Twoflower and Cohen (*IT*). His return to Ankh-Morpork is made necessary by the illness of the **Librarian**, who changes form every time he sneezes and his real name is necessary to undo the spell – Rincewind is likely to know it so must be recalled. At the end of the novel he ends up in **XXXX**, the **Australia**-like setting for his narrative in *LC*. In Bugarup he meets a distant relative, Bill Rincewind, Archchancellor of their equivalent of the Unseen University. Rincewind is finally given a chair at the Unseen University, as Egregious Professor of Cruel and Unusual Geography. This makes him perfect to join the crew of the Kite in its flight to the **Hub** (*LH*).

Rincewind was an incredibly popular character among early fans of the sequence, leading to repeated demands to bring him back. There is little character development possible – he is a slapstick figure who does little more than get into danger and run away, or avoid getting into danger by running away. By now he seems to have explored most of Discworld, each location being a **parody** of a real world culture, and there seems little more to do with the role. His recent appearances have been in the *SOD* books, having acquired further jobs along the way – mostly ones the others don't want to do.

The name Rincewind seems to have come from the 'By the Way' society column, written as by Beachcomber in the British newspaper from 1917. The first writer was Major John Arbuthnot (1875–1950), who was succeeded by D.B. Wyndham-Lewis (1891–1969) in 1919, who introduced fictional (comic) characters. From 1924 the column was written by J.B. Morton (1893–1979); from 1965 it become weekly rather than daily, until it was dropped in November 1975. Beachcomber's comic style was an influence upon British **Comedy and Humour**, especially *The Goon Show* (1951–1960), Peter Cook (1937–1995), the magazine *Private Eye*, *Monty Python's Flying Circus* (1969–1974) and Chris Morris (b.1965). Rincewind was one of twelve red-bearded **dwarfs** who often appeared before Mr Justice Cocklecarrot: Amaninter Axling, Sophus Barkayo-Tong, Edel Edeledel, Frums Gillygottle, Guttergorm Guttergormpton, Farjole Merrybody, Badly Oronparser, Churm Rincewind, Scorpion de Rooftrouser, Molonay Tubilderborst, Listenis Youghaupt and Cleveland Zackhouse.

Rincewind was played by Troy Larkin in the short film *Run Rincewind Run* (2007) directed by Daniel Knight and will be played by David Jason (b.1940) in the Sky One version of *COM*. *See also* Cohen the Barbarian; Coin; Comedy and Humour; Counterweight Continent; Death; Dungeon Dimensions; Heroes; The Hub; Klatch; The Librarian; The Luggage; Magic; Narratives; Eric Thursley; Twoflower; Unseen University; Wizards *and* XXXX.

Further Reading

Hill, Penelope. 'Unseen University'. *GOL*, *GOL2*.

Andrew M. Butler

S

Sabalos, Dom[inickdaniel] (*DSS*)

Usually abbreviated to Dom Sabalos. Little more than a child, he is about to succeed to the Chairman of the Board of the planet **Widdershins**. The Sabalos dynasty began with John I, who was lucky enough to discover pilac, a drug which gave longevity without any apparent side effects. John II spent freely, including the purchase of the Cheops pyramid from Earth (compare *P*), and led to the discovery of a strange green mould which allowed organs and limbs to be regrown. He was deposed by Joan who built up the Sabalos family fortune and fathered John III with a cousin. John III was an expert mathematician, particularly in the predictive p-maths, but disappeared, assumed assassinated, just before the birth of his second son, Dom. His godfather is an intelligent planet, the First Syrian Bank.

The rules of p-math do not seem to quite apply to Dom, although it is predicted that he will discover the Jokers' World. As a result, he is the target of a variety of botched assassination attempts, which has led to him being regenerated with the green slime. In fact he is likely being protected by Ig, one of the swamp-igs who are the real power in his universe. As an often hapless, endangered hero he anticipates **Rincewind**. His name perhaps recalls Gaal Dornick, biographer of Hari Seldon the Psychohistorian in the Foundation trilogy, one source for Pratchett's **parody** here (see *DSS*). *See also* Parody *and* Widdershins.

Further Reading

Clute, John. 'Coming of Age'. *GOL*, *GOL2*.

Andrew M. Butler

Science Fiction

A mode of **narrative** which Pratchett wrote in some of his short stories ('**Night Dweller**', '**Hollywood Chickens**', '**# IFDEFDEBUG + "World/Enough" + "Time"** ' and '**Once and Future**') and some of his novels (*DSS*, *Str* and arguably the **Bromeliad** and the **Johnny Maxwell Trilogy**).

The fictional world is usually based upon an extrapolation or imaginative leap taken from the current state of scientific knowledge, such as the impact of a new invention or an encounter with a non-human species or artifact. The British science fiction writer, critic and anthologist Brian Aldiss (b.1925) has written that 'science fiction is the search for a definition of man and his status in the universe which will stand in our advanced but confused state of knowledge (science), and is characteristically cast in the Gothic or post-Gothic mode'. In other words, science fiction may be set in the future or in a distant galaxy, but is always a reflection upon the world contemporary to the writer or the reader.

There has been much argument about what the first true science fiction novel is, and some would nominate *Frankenstein* (1816) by Mary Shelley (1797–1851). Another possible candidate is the work of H.G. Wells (1866–1946), whose *The Time Machine: An Invention* (1895), *The Island of Doctor Moreau* (1896), *The War of the Worlds* (1898) and *The First Men in the Moon* (1901) feature staples of science fiction such as time travel, a mad scientist, alien invasion and space travel, respectively. From 1926 onwards, science fiction became a marketing genre, thanks to the establishment of the magazine Amazing Stories by Luxembourgian émigré Hugo Gernsback (1884–1967). Written science fiction was dominated by **magazines** published in America until the 1960s.

Arthur Dent (Martin Freeman) and Marvin wait in an alien landscape. Still from *The Hitchhikers Guide to the Galaxy* movie (2005), directed by Garth Jennings.

A generation of big names began to write just before the Second World War, championed by John W. Campbell (1910–1971), then the editor of *Astounding*. Isaac Asimov (1920–1992) and Robert A. Heinlein (1907–1988) were perhaps the leading figures, the former to become known for his stories about the fall of the galactic empire which formed the Foundation Trilogy (1942–1951), the latter for a Future History of an ever expanding human society. American science fiction was dominated by resourceful, scientifically educated heroes, with an unironic faith in the American Dream of freedom and individual progress. Arthur C. Clarke (b.1917) from Britain offered a significant challenge, his best known work of the period being *Childhood's End* (1953), although the disaster novels of John Wyndham (1903–1969, real name John Wyndham Parkes Lucas Beynon Harris) had success outside the circle of genre readers.

In the 1960s *New Worlds*, a British magazine edited by Michael Moorcock (b.1939), spearheaded a call for a more literary and experimental fiction – although this had already been coming through in the writings of American authors such as Alfred Bester (1913–1987), Theodore Sturgeon (1918–1985), Philip K. Dick (1928–1982), Robert **Sheckley** (1928–2005) and Ursula Le Guin (b.1929). One of Pratchett's earliest publications was 'Night Dweller' (see *OM* WF*) in the November 1965 issue of *New Worlds*. The age of the magazine was fading and, helped by the cult status of a number of novels – *Stranger in a Strange Land* (1961) by Heinlein and the ecological space opera *Dune* (serial 1963–1965, book 1965) by Frank Herbert (1920–1986) – novels, especially paperback novels, came to shape the genre.

The 1970s has often wrongly been perceived as a doldrums in the genre, although much important work by feminist writers was published; in the British market more writers than ever before earned their living from writing, but the appetite for serious science fiction receded as the decade wore on. One reason for this is the success of blockbuster films such as *Star Wars* (1977). The high budget of sf film and the likelihood of flops meant that they came in and out of favour in Hollywood. A series of sf-tinged horror films had been filmed by Universal Studios in the 1930s and early 1940s, and allegories or satires of communist invasion movies had been filmed in the 1950s. *Star Wars* was the first of a raft of Summer event movies, big budget, blockbuster science fiction films, although it might be argued that this meant that the films needed to be simplified and made more like escapist **Fantasy** to maximise the audience for them. The late 1970s saw an explosion in fantasy trilogies and role playing **games**.

Since the 1980s, the genre has been dominated by cyberpunk, set in near-future gritty locations, featuring computers and other **technology**, with a flavour of noir detective and crime fiction. The leading example of this is *Neuromancer* (1984) written by William Gibson (b.1948). It has also seen a slow re-emergence of British science fiction from the late 1970s doldrums, and an eclipse of the American side of the genre.

Science Fiction

Pratchett's science fiction comes in two distinct phases: the 1970s novels and his 1990s children's trilogies. The 1970s saw a series of novels featuring what became known as Big Dumb Objects – a term coined by British critic Roz Kaveney, in 1981. These were huge artifacts, usually of alien origin, which would be explored by a party of human beings. Key examples of these are *Ringworld* (1970) by Larry Niven (b.1938), with a vast cylindrical planet, *Rendezvous with Rama* (1973) by Arthur C. Clarke, with a huge spaceship, and *Orbitsville* (1975), by Bob Shaw (1931–1996), with a civilisation living on the inside of a huge sphere containing a star. In both *DSS* and *Str*, Pratchett features strange alien artifacts, in the former they are supposedly left behind by a civilisation known as the Jokers, in the later it is a disc-shaped planet, apparently made by the Great Spindle Kings. The strange phenomena encountered in *Str* constantly turn out to have a natural explanation, as machinery or computers underlie events. In both cases a major target of the **parody** is the fiction of Larry Niven.

Another strand of science fiction is the novel of conceptual breakthrough where one or more people come to a new perception about the state of the universe, discovering that there is more to life than what was previously thought. This is again the case in the two early novels, where the Jokers' artifacts turn out to be creations of the Igs, in order to monitor the reactions of human beings and the Spindle Kings were themselves fakes, apparently created by another, even more superior, alien species. *Str* would have been published after the radio broadcast (1978), book publication (1979) and television series of *The Hitch-Hiker's Guide to the Galaxy* (1981) by Douglas **Adams** in which the Earth turns out to be a huge computer, designed to work out the Ultimate Question, which puts a new spin on human history.

Pratchett was to return to science fiction in his two children's series, The **Bromeliad** and the **Johnny Maxwell Trilogy**. At first glance, the nomes living under the floorboards and in odd corners of a department store might be thought of as fantasy, but it is made clear from the start that the nomes are of extraterrestrial origin. In the nomes' encounters with human beings, we have a reverse of the Big Dumb Object narrative; we are sympathising with an alien race who are attempting to comprehend a human artifact of mysterious origin. They are helped in this by The **Thing**, a computer and navigation device. The nomes get to grips with human technology and harness it for their own gain. There is also a sense of conceptual breakthrough as the nomes discover there is more to the world than **Arnold Bros (est. 1905)**.

The first and third Johnny Maxwell novels are science fiction, the ghosts in *JD* being closer to fantasy, although it is just about possible, if misguided, to read all of the books as experiences of Johnny's stressed mind. *OYCSM* features a cliché of science fiction, the computer game in which real aliens are being fought, although here they surrender and demand his help. In *JB* there is time travel back to the Second World **War**, and the alteration of history through an intervention in the past. Johnny certainly sees the world in a new way through his travels, but the time travelling shopping trolley of Mrs **Tachyon** is more of a plot device than a serious scientific development. *See also* Douglas Adams; The Bromeliad; Fantasy; Johnny Maxwell Trilogy, Technology *and* The Thing.

Further Reading

Adams, Douglas. 1979. *The Hitch-Hikers' Guide to the Galaxy*. London: Pan.

Aldiss, Brian with David Wingrove. 1988. *Trillion Year Spree*. London: Grafton.

Clarke, Arthur C. 1973. *Rendezvous with Rama*. New York: Harcourt Brace Jovanovich.

Gibson, William. 1984. *Neuromancer*. New York: Ace.

Heinlein, Robert A. 1961. *Stranger in a Strange Land*. New York: Putnam.

Herbert, Frank. 1965. *Dune*. Philadelphia: Chilton Books.

James, Edward, and Farah Mendlesohn, Eds. 2003. *The Cambridge Companion to Science Fiction*. Cambridge: Cambridge University Press.

Niven, Larry. 1970. *Ringworld*. New York: Ballantine.

Shaw, Bob. 1975. *Orbitsville*. London: Gollancz.

Andrew M. Butler

The Science of Discworld

Initially a book which mixed fiction and scientific explication co-written by Pratchett, Jack **Cohen** and Ian **Stewart**, and now a trilogy of such volumes. The first appeared in an edition of 24,269 hardbacks from Ebury Press (part of Random House) in 1999, with a cover by Paul **Kidby**. A paperback was released in 2000; this was followed by a second edition with two more chapters in a print run of 21,000 copies from Ebury (2002). It was translated into Bulgarian (2nd only), French, German and Polish (1st only). The second volume, *The Globe*, appeared in hardback from Ebury in 2002 with an edition of 33,500 copies and a Kidby cover; the paperback was 2003. This has seen Czech, German and Polish editions. The third volume, *Darwin's Watch*, appeared in 2005 and 2006 from Ebury in hardback and paperback respectively, with a Kidby cover. There have been translations into German and Polish.

The numerous 'Science of . . .' books (like Lawrence Kraus's 1996 *The Physics of Star Trek*) spin-off from popular series to appeal to their fans, but are more than simply fannish apparatus. They describe how the technology of our favourite science fiction worlds might work if the distance between reality and imagination could be bridged; how, for instance, we could extrapolate from current theories of quantum tunnelling to construct Star Trek's transporter. Others aim to teach science by showing, essentially, how science fiction writers get it wrong.

This use of sf as a teaching tool, although (rightly) viewed suspiciously by many of its writers is certainly within the remit claimed by sf's first editor and theorist, Hugo Gernsback (1884–1967), who claimed in the first issue of *Amazing Stories* (April 1926) that its contents were both 'instructive' and 'palatable', and in launching Science Wonder Stories suggested that if children were encouraged to read science fiction there would be a significant gain in the educational standards of the community. *SOD* (1999), with currently two sequels *SODII: The Globe* (2002), and *SODIII: Darwin's Watch* (2005), is neither a sugar-coated attempt to explain physics to fantasy fans, nor the kind of fannish game which imagines that Discworld can be explained by using our scientific vocabulary. **Discworld** operates by story, not science: '**Narrative** causality' instead of Newtonian mechanics. Jack Cohen, Ian Stewart and Terry Pratchett use this supposition to consider how science itself is storied; how much of our favourite explanations of how the world works are in fact 'lies to children' and how science itself is a quest for explanation rather than the explanation itself. In this particularly apt example of 'science fiction' the threads of the 'fiction' and 'science' aspects of the work are there to illuminate and interrogate each other rather than merely be 'entertaining' or 'instructive'.

Cover of *The Science of Discworld* by Terry Pratchett, Ian Stewart and Jack Cohen. Artwork by Paul Kidby. Note the parody of *An Experiment on a Bird in an Air Pump* (1768) by the English artist Joseph Wright (1734–1797).

The structure of all three books is the same. The chapters of a Pratchett-written story are alternated with chapters of commentary by Cohen and Stewart that contrast the reactions of the Discworld wizards to those of scientists and philosophers of science in our world. The first volume describes the creation of 'Roundworld', the pocket-universe formed as a by-product of Ponder **Stibbons**'s attempt to split the thaum (the fundamental unit of magic). It is Discworld's opposite. To the **wizards**' astonishment, it works by means of impersonal laws. It is made up of mundane, non-magical elements: no chelonium, for making world-bearing turtles, no deitium (and therefore no gods), and, above all, no narrativium. On Discworld, things happen because the conventions of story say they must. On Roundworld, metaphor and personification are merely figures of speech and not literal descriptions of the world. Nevertheless, while Roundworld is governed not by personification but by the impersonal rules of science, these rules are themselves constructed, or at least described, and certainly observed by intelligent minds that arise from these rules. We in Roundworld spend much of our time compensating for its lack of narrativium by constructing stories about how the world works and our cultural and moral place in it. We 'paint stories on to the universe'. These stories are called, variously, **Religion**, mythology, **Fairy Tales** or science and they are all true for a given value of 'true'. This does not mean that the authors are not committed to the story of science as an explanation of the universe and our place in it: merely that science is so often a matter of discovering what we do not know and coming up with provisional explanations for it.

The bewildered wizards call **Rincewind** in to investigate and discover a universe operating without the systems they are used to. They are right, Cohen and Stewart say, to be bewildered by the way Roundworld develops without narrativium to shape it, because the universe is bewildering. Time after time, Roundworld develops intelligent minds that are capable of describing and speculating about their environment, but who are wiped out by natural disaster. This process leads to the development of a particularly grubby primate who produces a civilisation which is about to be destroyed by the collision of an asteroid. Thanks to some clever work by the **Librarian**, this fate is avoided.

The second and third volumes of the series, *The Globe* and *Darwin's Watch*, continue to explore our need for story. In *The Globe* humanity is threatened by the **elves** who feed off terror: who exploit our capacity for imagination. We have already learned, from *LL*, that people have used story (see narrative) as a way of insulating themselves from the terror of the Elves. Elves, we tell ourselves, are glamorous. They project glamour. But the root meaning of glamour is illusion, and we are prey to Pratchett's amoral Elves for as long as we accept their illusion. In *The Globe*, the wizards discover that a change has taken place in the history of the human race. They have to make sure that William **Shakespeare** – embodying our desire to impose stories on creation – is born, while the alternate chapters investigate what this means in terms of human culture, or what Cohen and

Stewart call 'extelligence' as opposed to intelligence. Individually we may not be able to understand how aircraft, computers, or the complex series of chemical reactions in biology work. Collectively, we do. Individually, we possess imagination. Imagination is what makes us human – but being able to imagine also allows us to fall for the Elves' glamour until we learn that we can imagine that things we can imagine are imaginary. The wizards can only defeat the Elves when they understand that Elves exploit the stories we tell ourselves about them and we can change those stories to take control. And Shakespeare, the master-storyteller of Western culture, undoes the terrors of the Old Gods by renaming them Mustardseed and Peaseblossom.

In *Darwin's Watch*, not the Elves, but the even more dreadful threat, the bureaucratic Auditors of Reality (*H* and *TOT*) have to be defeated. Charles Darwin (1809–1882) has somehow to be guided to write *The Origin of Species* instead of *The Theology of Species*, the book he has written in all other possible worlds. Cohen and Stewart, in their parallel commentary, bring in Darwin's rival William Paley (1743–1805) and his 'watchmaker' argument for design. As the wizards struggle to get Darwin to write *The Origin of Species*, we realise the nature of his intellectual conflict. In the context of Victorian ideas, the relationship of Darwinist 'natural selection' to theism exists in a vast phase-space of possibilities. It is not so much that Darwinism is 'true' and William Paley's 'Watchmaker' analogy was 'false' but that each is an explanation within the context of a range of other beliefs – more or less true or false – about how the universe works.

Cover of *The Science of Discworld II: The Globe* by Terry Pratchett, Ian Stewart and Jack Cohen. Shakespeare surrounded by wizards. Artwork by Paul Kidby.

Darwin writes *The Origin of Species*, or rather doesn't write it until the wizards manipulate him into the version of reality in which he conceives of the replacement of the 'creationist' model with natural selection. Cohen and Stewart's 'parallel' narrative explores the background to the 'real' Darwin's conception of the theory as well as what we mean by 'theory' and 'evolution'.

Art gives new ways of terrifying people, and the elves take advantage of this but it can also diminish them: stories are the imaginative space where we can imagine that the monsters are dead (*SODII*). In *SODIII* the threat is the opposite: cosmic bureaucrats are not only unimaginative, but without the capacity to imagine what imagination is. They see the defeat of Darwinian ideas as an ideal way to remove that unreliable by-product of the universe called 'Life' from the scene, because however much Darwinism suggested potentially lethal 'survival of the fittest' doctrines, fundamentally it allows us to focus our imaginations upon ourselves and our future. We can experience the stories as stories, complete in themselves, rather than parables composed to illustrate an ideological thesis about science. While Cohen and Stewart comment on them, and it is certainly true that the story of the Roundworld project highlights their arguments more comprehensively and colourfully than their own science fiction inserts in their previous books, they are also authentic Pratchett. He is an equal partner. We read the 'Roundworld' narrative knowing the characters and how they react.

Cover of *The Science of Discworld III: Darwin's Watch* by Terry Pratchett, Ian Stewart and Jack Cohen. Darwin, wizards and a dodo ride a turtle. Artwork by Paul Kidby.

The strength of *SOD* – and why it is in many ways something new in science writing – derives from this multi-voicing of story. By contrasting Discworld with Roundworld, we not only explain science, we also explore it. We look more closely at some of the other stories which might have been: the story of science itself, and how science interrogates itself. As well as being constructed around a story which is entertaining in the same way as any other Discworld story – parodying the scientific method in the same way as *SG* parodies fundamentalist religion – the 'parallel text' method of *The Science of Discworld* allows us to 'look at science from the outside' with fruitful and entertaining results. *See also* Jack Cohen; Fairy Tales; The Librarian; Magic; Narrative; Rincewind; Science Fiction; William Shakespeare; Ian Stewart; Ponder Stibbons; Technology *and* Wizards.

Further Reading

Kraus, Lawrence. 1996. *The Physics of Star Trek*. New York: Harper Perennial.

Andy Sawyer

The Science of Discworld II: The Globe see The Science of Discworld

The Science of Discworld III: Darwin's Watch see The Science of Discworld

'The Sea and Little Fishes' (*OM*WF*)

A **Discworld** novella written for an anthology of tales – *Legends*, edited by Robert Silverberg (New York: Tor, 1998. Pp. 63–97) – set in popular **Fantasy** and borderline **Science Fiction** universes. Other contributors were Stephen King (b.1947) with a Gunslinger story, Terry Goodkind (b.1948) with 'Sword of Truth', Orson Scott Card (b.1951) with 'Alvin Maker', Silverberg himself (b.1935) with 'Majipoor', Ursula Le Guin (b.1929) with 'Earthsea', Tad Williams (b.1957) with 'Memory, Sorrow and Thorn', George R.R. Martin (b.1948) with 'Song of Fire and Ice', Anne McCaffrey (b.1926) with 'Pern', Raymond E. Feist (b.1945) with 'Riftwar' and Robert Jordan (b.1948) with 'The Wheel of Time'. Silverberg also wrote a series of introductions. The publishers issued a sampler of the stories, with Pratchett and Feist's stories printed back to back. Pratchett notes his title comes from ancient wisdom he invented, about how the sea does not care which way the fish swim.

It is the time of the annual witch trials and there is discontent among the **witches** because Granny **Weatherwax** always wins. Letice Earwig, who seems to be appointing herself head of the witches, asks Granny to withdraw to let the others have a chance. Granny starts going around being nice to people, which is very disconcerting to them.

The novella features a cameo from Agnes **Nitt**, apparently before she joined the coven, so it is not entirely clear when the story is set – presumably before *Msk*. The witch trials anticipate *HFOS*. *See also* Agnes Nitt; Granny Weatherwax *and* Witches.

Andrew M. Butler

'The Secret Book of The Dead' (*OM*WF*)

A twenty-nine line poem which first appeared in *Now We Are Sick* (Minneapolis, Minnesota: DreamHaven, 1991; Pp. 29–30), a collection edited by Neil **Gaiman** and anthologist Stephen Jones (b.1953), who usually works in horror. Other contributors to this volume include Brian Aldiss (b.1925), Robert Bloch (1917–1994) the author of *Psycho* (1959) and Alan Moore (b.1953). Some of the items had earlier appeared in *Now We Are Sick Sampler* (Minneapolis, Minnesota: DreamHaven, 1986), but Pratchett's contribution was original. The title of the collection recalls *Now We are Six* (1927), a collection of verse for children by A.A. Milne (1882–1956). DreamHaven is a speciality bookstore in Minneapolis, that occasionally publishes books.

Pratchett's poem is about the death of pets such as dogs, goldfish, tortoises cats and so on, who die in unfortunate circumstances. It rhymes abccb, aside from the last stanza, which is abba, and is nothing like the sentimental tone of Milne. In the opening lines there is a distant echo of 'This Be the Verse' (1971) by Philip Larkin (1922–1985). *See also* Neil Gaiman.

Further Reading

Larkin, Philip. *Collected Poems*. 1988. London: Faber and Faber and Hessle: Marvell Press.
Milne, A.A. 1927. *Now We Are Six*. London: Methuen.

Andrew M. Butler

Sellar, W[alter] C[arruthers] (1898–1951) and Yeatman, R[obert] J[ulian] (1897–1968)

British humorists whose style was an influence on Pratchett. Sellar and Yeatman met at Oriel College, Oxford and wrote together for the magazine *Punch* from 1928, some of the material forming their best known work *1066 and All That* (1931). They also collaborated on *And Now All This* (1932), *Horse Nonsense* (1933) and *Garden Rubbish and other Country Bumps* (1936).

1066 is subtitled *A Memorable History of England, comprising all the parts you can remember, including One Hundred and Three Good Things, Five Bad*

Kings, and Two Genuine Dates and is a spoof history of Britain from the time of the ancient Britons to the end of the First World War in 1918 when America becomes Top Nation and therefore 'History comes to a .' (115). It is based upon the principle that 'History is not what you thought. It is what you can remember. All other history defeats itself' (vii). This results in there being only two truly memorable dates in history, 55 BCE – the invasion of Britain by Rome – which was then the Top Nation – and the invasion of Britain in 1066 by the Normans. It runs through the kings and queens of England, noting when and how they died, noting significant events as Good Things or Bad Things. Originally, the authors noted, there were four dates, but surveys at Eton and Harrow ruled out two of them as being 'not memorable' (vii).

Many of the kings died of surfeits – of palfreys (Henry I), of Sala-dins (Richard I), of peaches and no cider (John), of Barons, Bonifaces (Henry III), of something not recorded as no one admitted to murdering him (Edward II), of Pum-freys (spelt Pontefracts; Richard II) and so on. Malapropisms, conflations and misunderstandings lead to events being mangled, but not entirely beyond recognition: Alfred the Great, who in popular myth burnt some cakes he had been asked to watch, becomes Alfred the Cake. He is described as the first Good King, aside from Good King Wenceslas, and should not be confused with King Arthur, who is memorable but did not exist. Sellar and Yeatman also point out that as the burning was supposed to take place in marshland, the cakes would not have burnt properly because they were damp. The book also includes running jokes, illustrations, anachronisms, footnotes and examination papers.

And Now All This is less focused, claiming to be volume one of the *Hole Pocket Treasury of Absolutely General Knowledge*, focusing on Geography, Woology (Knitting), Ornithology and so on, using much the same format. It was less successful, as indeed have been various attempts to update 1066 to cover the rest of the twentieth century – such as *1966 and All That* (2005) by Craig Brown (b.1957).

The style of comedy, which is to say playing with what is remembered about a particular event or arena rather than what is actually the case, has become a tradition in British comedy, such as the various **Carry-On films** which centre on Cleopatra, Henry VIII, spies, the French Revolution, the National Health Service and so on, and the four series of Blackadder which focus on the medieval period (1983), the Elizabethan age (1986), the Regency period (1987) and the First World War (1989).

Pratchett continues this tradition, his parodies aiming to mangle the memory of the original source. It is most obvious when the novels are focused on **Discworld** versions of real-world countries: *P* is therefore based on everything that is memorable about **Egypt**, *IT* is based on what is memorable about **China**, *J* draws on **Arabic societies**, or at least Western encounters with them and *LC* is based on Australia. The individual confusions of particular characters, and the confused misquotations of other writers, especially of **Shakespeare** but also J.R.R. **Tolkien** and many others, the use of footnotes to add jokes and running gags (hardly original to *1066*) all owe some debt to Sellar and Yeatman. *See also* Carry-On Films; Comedy and Humour; History *and* Parody.

Further Reading
Brown, Craig. 2005. *1966 and All That*. London: Hodder.
Manning, Paul. 1984. *1984 and All That*. London: Futura.
Sellar, W.C. and Yeatman, R.J. 1930. *1066 and All That*. London: Methuen.
———. 1932. *And Now All This*. London: Methuen.
———. 1933. *Horse Nonsense*. London: Methuen.
———. 1936. *Garden Rubbish and other Country Bumps*. London: Methuen.

Andrew M. Butler

Sexism

Terry Pratchett takes a decided interest in issues of sex and gender, so sexism is often openly criticised in his novels (*see* **Feminism**). In general, Pratchett exposes the absurdities of gender determinism by exploring them in cultures parallel to our own, such as **dwarf** culture in the **Discworld** novels, the nome societies in The **Bromeliad**, and the alternate reality of 1941 England of *JB*. However, as satire necessarily addresses stereotypical attitudes and behaviours found in our own cultures, some of his work seems to replicate sexist viewpoints uncritically, especially in its representation of female characters.

One significant example of Pratchett's interrogation of gender norms is the essentially genderless dwarf society. In the Discworld novels, all **dwarfs** are considered 'he' by default; the pronoun 'she' never refers to a dwarf before *FOC*. The one-gender model of dwarf culture merely confuses two-gender species, such as humans (i.e. about the exact relationship of the famous dwarf lovers Bloodaxe and Ironhammer), but it is socially restrictive for those female dwarfs who would like to be openly female. Cheery **Littlebottom**, for instance, does not identify with the masculine endeavours of her fellow dwarfs – fighting, singing about gold, quaffing beer – and yearns instead to wear makeup and lingerie like the human women of the capital city of **Ankh-Morpork**. But when Cheery renames herself 'Cheri' and begins to wear a leather skirt, she shocks even the normally tolerant Captain Carrot **Ironfoundersson**. For though her change makes sense to humans, Cheri's need to express her sexuality challenges traditional dwarf culture; thus, she is treated with contempt by many dwarfs in both *FOC* and *FE*. Interestingly, their derision associates Cheery not only with promiscuous women, but also with homosexual, transgender, and transsexual people who are ill-treated because they exhibit what their societies consider transgressive sexual identities or because they ask that their sexuality be considered as valid as the culturally dominant sexuality. However, in this case, Pratchett is careful to indicate that not all dwarfs are biased, and that, in time, maybe even the Low King of the dwarfs (who is also female) will see it fit to wear a dress.

In *T*, the first book of the Bromeliad, biology seems to be destiny: female Outside Nomes care for the young and the old and do household chores while male Outside Nomes are hunters and leaders. Female Store Nomes cannot join the ranks of the learned Stationeri because it is believed reading would overheat their brains (see **Feminism** for a similar reaction from the **Unseen University Wizards** to the idea of female wizards). These naturalised gender distinctions begin to crumble when the Outside Nomes meet the Store Nomes and realise they must combine forces to move out of the Store before it is demolished. **Grimma**, a strong-headed female Outside Nome learns to read so she can help the Nomes navigate road signs while they drive a Store truck to find a new home. In the second book of the trilogy, *D*, Grimma is a teacher of reading and writing, and her newly acquired knowledge empowers her to disregard Nome rule and refuse marriage to **Masklin**, the Nome leader. She even becomes the organiser of the Nomes (but not their leader) while Masklin is away attempting to find the nome spaceship.

Similarly, sexist attitudes play an important role in *JB*, when Johnny **Maxwell** and his friends travel back in time to **Blackbury**, England during the Second World War. Here, **Kirsty**, an exceptional little girl (*see* **Feminism**) finds herself patronised by the men of the time. When she and Johnny and their friend **Yo-Less** are detained by an army captain for questioning, she shrewdly plays on his chauvinistic conviction that women are weak to catch him off guard and knock him out with a karate chop, proving that sexism is not only illogical, but can be dangerously so.

This is not to say that all of Pratchett's female characters are feminist icons. In fact, many of Pratchett's narratives are firmly entrenched in stereotypical representations of women. Whereas male characters such as Samuel **Vimes**, **Teppic**, **Brutha**, or even **Verence II** could be described as ordinary people whom circumstance has made leaders, Pratchett's female characters tend to exhibit some extraordinary quality that authorises their role as leading figures. For instance, Sergeant Angua von **Überwald** of the **City Watch** novels is respected – even feared – because she is a werewolf, while the semi-mortal Susan **Sto Helit** has inherited her supernatural abilities – such as walking through walls – from her grandfather, **Death**. Even the witch Granny **Weatherwax**, whose harsh personality and unyielding will would make anyone acknowledge her authority, partly derives her **power** from magic. Their exceptional nature makes them de facto abnormal women and, as such, not representative of the great majority of women; their oddity as powerful women is signalled further by their outcast, outsider, or even monstrous status.

Other significant women tend to be presented in the roles of organisers or of saviours of lost men – most notoriously, the formidable Lady Sybil **Ramkin** in the **City Watch** novels, who, though strong and capable, apparently is just the great woman behind her husband, Sam Vimes. Similarly, Grimma in The Bromeliad and Peaches the rat in *AMHER* are interpreters or keepers of knowledge (though some would call them glorified secretaries) but not successful leaders or heroes on their own. Even the resourceful Kirsty of the Johnny Maxwell series is a secondary character, who, unlike her hero, Lt Ripley of the Alien film series, never really gets to be saved Mankind. In fact, Kirsty is a recognisable type of girl in **children's fiction**: the exceptionally talented, occasionally smug, somewhat romantic know-it-all sidekick popularised by the book-smart Hermione Granger from the Harry Potter series. Commonly depicted as bossy, sanctimonious, and generally irritating, the character type seems to have been drawn from the point of view of a boy who does not like gifted girls too much and includes Pratchett's own eccentric Malicia in *AMHER*.

Most notably, Pratchett portrays matrilineal groups, such as the Nac Mac Feegle clans or Nanny **Ogg**'s brood, as rather domineering matriarchies. Indeed, one may read Pratchett's books as giving the distinct impression that the female of the species is the one really in charge. Even in those societies that are nominally patriarchal (as with the Outside Nomes in The Bromeliad), it is plain that the women only pretend not to be in charge. When Grimma instigates a crestfallen Masklin in *T* to 'get out there and lead!' so that the Nomes can move out from the Store, she confirms sexist views that dissatisfied women are the ones who foment civilisation by harassing men to do great deeds. This point is made evident towards the end of *T!*, when Sam Vimes speculates that the 'Ladies Who Organise' – such as his wife Sybil – are already discreetly running the world. However, this view of domestic power as authorising political power is itself an argument often used throughout history to justify woman's role as the supporter of men and of patriarchy. In Pratchett's works, many notable female characters create a niche for themselves in male-dominated societies, but only a few truly challenge the status quo for all women (*see* **Feminism**). *See also* The Bromeliad; Children's Fiction; Dwarfs; Feminism; Grimma; Kirsty; Cheery Littlebottom; Polly Perks; Power; Susan Sto Helit; Angua von Überwald; Unseen University; Granny Weatherwax *and* Wizards.

Further Reading

Connell, R.W. 1987. *Gender and Power: Society, the Person, and Sexual Politics*. Stanford: Stanford University Press.

Gilbert, Sandra M., and Susan Gubar. 1978. *The Madwoman in the Attic: The Woman Writer and the Nineteenth-Century Literary Imagination*. New Haven: Yale University Press.

Moi, Toril. 1985. *Sexual/Textual Politics*. London and New York: Routledge.

Showalter, Elaine. 1982. *A Literature of Their Own: British Novelists from Bronte to Lessing*. London: Virago.

Ximena Gallardo C.

The Shades

An area of **Ankh-Morpork** bounded by the Ankh on the turnward and hubward side, Elm Street on the **widdershins** side and the city wall on the rimward side. It is a network of alleys and streets, and is definitely not a place to wander on your own after dark, or even during the daytime. It is probably the oldest part of the city, which may mean it has been destroyed more than anywhere else. It is home to the Bier and the Troll Tavern, as well as the Seamstresses' Guild, in other words the red light district. Samuel **Vimes** and Nobby **Nobbs** were both born in the area, and grew up on its streets, which might explain their ability to survive. The **City Watch** had a branch in Treacle Mine Road in the Shades (*NW*). There is a folk song 'The Shades of Ankh-Morpork' (*see* Dave **Greenslade**).

A real world equivalent, in architecture if not morality, is The Shambles and surrounding streets in York; any town which has maintained a chaotic medieval street pattern can give some of the flavour.

'Shades of Ankh-Morpork' is a track on the *Terry Pratchett's From the Discworld* CD by Dave **Greenslade**. *See also* Ankh-Morpork; Dave Greenslade; Nobby Nobbs *and* Samuel Vimes.

Andrew M. Butler

Shakespeare, William (1564–1616)

William Shakespeare, poet, dramatist and actor, is also known as the Bard or the Swan of Avon, and he is widely considered to be the greatest dramatist of all time. Pratchett alludes to him in **narrative** elements and quotations throughout the **Discworld** sequence, and even in a specific character.

A large body of tradition, hearsay, and myths have grown up around the figure of the man who wrote thirty-eight plays and other literary works – little of it with proof from primary sources. Conjecture, extrapolation and opinion range from valid to downright outlandish.

In fact, Shakespeare's life is well-documented by the standards of the Elizabethan era. There are over one hundred references to Shakespeare and his immediate family in parish, municipal and commercial documents, and half that many again regarding his plays from contemporaries. (It is Shakespeare's motives, experience, and personal outlook on life that are obscure, but of course it is this information that most want to know.) By evidence of such records we know that Shakespeare was a shrewd businessman and a practical individual who could turn his hand to most things.

There are theories that Shakespeare's identity was used by a nobleman or other person to publish plays (e.g. Edward de Vere, Earl of Oxford

(1550–1604), Sir Francis Bacon (1561–1626), Mary Sidney (1561–1621)). These theories have become less persuasive over time. The current consensus is that Shakespeare may have collaborated with another playwright in at least one instance, and that others may have completed one or two of his plays, but that the works ascribed to him are indeed his.

Parish records show Shakespeare was baptised on 26 April 1564. Counting back three days between birth and baptism, it is assumed that he was born on 23 April 1564. He was buried on 26 April 1616, exactly fifty-two years after his baptism. Tradition says he died of a chill caught while drinking with Ben Jonson (1572–1637) and Michael Drayton (1563–1631), fellow playwrights, on 23 April 1616, but the exact date and cause of his death are unknown.

Shakespeare's mother, Mary Arden, was a member of the gentry of Stratford-on-Avon. She married glover and tenant farmer John Shakespeare, leading citizen of Stratford, who held the positions of high bailiff (mayor) and chief alderman. The family was well-off rather than privileged.

Shakespeare probably attended Stratford Grammar School, where his father's status would have meant a tuition – free education. He would have had the standard Elizabethan curriculum, with Greek and Latin literature, rhetoric and Christian ethics. In 1579, Shakespeare left school, possibly due to financial problems; there are records of his father going into debt, being removed from the town council, missing court and church appearances, and mortgaging his wife's estate to pay his debts. (By the end of his life, John Shakespeare had righted his financial and professional life.) William did not receive further formal education and was not considered a truly learned man by his contemporaries.

From 1578 to 1582 and from 1585 to 1592, we have no primary source materials regarding Shakespeare's life during these so-called 'lost periods'. In 1582, at the age of eighteen, Shakespeare applied for a licence to marry Annan (Ann) Whateley. The next day, he married Anne Hathwey (Hathaway), eight years his senior, who gave birth to a daughter, Susanna, six months later. Speculation has run riot over the different surnames, though it is possible that the clerk simply recorded Anne's name incorrectly on the licence. In 1584 the Shakespeares had twins: Judith and Hamnet (the latter would die at the age of eleven).

Between the early 1590s and 1611, Shakespeare created one of the most extraordinary bodies of work in the history of literature. Leaving London during the plague years of 1592–1594, he set aside playwriting to compose his long epic poems and sonnets, but also found his first major supporter, the third Earl of Southampton (1573–1624). Later, he was to find even greater patronage in the courts of Elizabeth I (1533–1603, ruling from 1558) and James I (1566–1625, ruling England from 1603).

Hamnet died in 1596, and in 1597 Shakespeare purchased a mansion in Stratford known as the New Place. Between 1597 and 1611, Shakespeare was active in London and Stratford, in the latter as an investor in grain dealings. He owned property in the countryside and in London, including Blackfriars Gatehouse, which he purchased in 1613 after he had gone into semi-retirement at the young age of forty-eight.

References to Shakespeare and his works in the Discworld universe are many, especially in *WS*. This includes a reference to Act I, Scene 1 of *Hamlet* (famously, the action starts at midnight and runs for fifteen minutes, yet at the end of the scene dawn is breaking), Magrat **Garlick** makes a **parody** of Ophelia's speech on the meanings of flowers, and there's a theatre called The Dysk, a reference to the Globe, the Burbages' theatre in Southwark built in 1599 where Shakespeare owned a share and acted. The overall narrative of Hamlet is of the grieving son Hamlet attempting to reveal the complicity of his mother, Gertrude, and his uncle, Claudius, in the murder of his father; Hamlet commissions a performance of a play, *The Mouse Trap*, to provoke a confession. *WS* also introduces us to Discworld's version of Shakespeare, a **dwarf** named **Hwel**.

We see a fair amount of Hwel's play *A Night of Kings* in *WS*, which looks and sounds a great deal like *Macbeth*, in which an ambitious wife, Lady Macbeth, encourages her husband, Macbeth, to usurp Duncan the king of Scotland. Macbeth is guided and then haunted by **witches** who prophecy his rise and fall. In *WS*, Pratchett examines the idea that plays and words can manipulate a story to make an audience see the current reality as one wishes the reality to have been, an idea further developed in *LL*, *SODII* and *TT*.

This was not a new idea to Shakespeare, who wrote along politically expedient lines himself; almost all of his 'historical' plays adjusted reality to suit his patrons, the current regime. Failure to do so, of course, could have led to much more severe sanctions than those usually applied to playwrights of today. Part of Shakespeare's genius, though, was that he never let the 'facts' get in the way of a good story.

LL is also full of references to Shakespeare's works, notably some long and enjoyable parodies of the Rude Mechanicals and their play-within-a-play, Pyramus and Thisbe (from *A Midsummer Night's Dream*), and Shawn **Ogg** gives an amusing take on the St. Crispin's Day speech from *King Henry V*.

MR, which is about women dressing as men to fight in an army, contains a reference to *Much Ado About Nothing*, although this is one of the comedies which does not feature a woman disguising herself as a man.

In *SODII*, the **Unseen University Wizards** battle **elves** for the control of Roundworld (our world, or at least what passes for it in that arm of the multiverse). Their main weapon is ensuring the birth and career of one William Shakespeare, because, though in Roundworld there is no narrativium, they have noted that the power of story still works in people's heads. This makes someone like William Shakespeare very important indeed. *See also* Elves; Magrat Garlick; Hwel; Narrative; Nanny Ogg; the Oggs; Parody; Plays; *Science of Discworld II*; Granny Weatherwax *and* Witches.

Further Reading

Shakespeare, William. 2006. Encyclopedia Britannica Premium Service. http://www.britannica.com/eb/article-232308
Mabillard, Amanda. 2000. William Shakespeare of Stratford. http://www.shakespeare-online.com/biography/

Zina Lee

Sheckley, Robert (1928–2005)

American writer of humorous **Science Fiction**, which is a precursor to and possible influence on Pratchett. Sheckley also wrote a series of espionage novels featuring the character Stephen Dain and a trilogy of detective novels featuring Hob Draconian. Born in New York, he began to sell short stories to the American pulp magazines such as *Galaxy*, *If*, *Astounding* and *Fantasy and Science Fiction*. During the period, the genre was undergoing a transition from simplistic adventures written in streamlined prose to something that had more character and depth, and aspired to literary values. Writers who emerged in this period included Alfred Bester (1913–1987), Theodore Sturgeon (1918–1985), Philip K. Dick (1928–1982) and Ursula Le Guin (b.1929). Sheckley produced scores of stories, but began to suffer from writer's block. He also wrote a number of novels. He lived in Ibiza for many years, and was the fiction editor of the magazine *OMNI*. He died in New York, after falling ill on a trip to Russia.

Sheckley's **heroes**, or rather protagonists as they are rarely heroic, constantly find themselves in situations in which they are out of their depth, having been moved from a comfortable, usually Earth-based location, to somewhere entirely alien. They frequently have someone there to advise them, but the advice is not necessarily helpful, or on occasions not even relevant. In *Dimensions of Miracles* (1968), Carmody has somehow won the intergalactic sweepstakes, and whilst he is instantaneously teleported there to pick the Prize up, he will have to make his own way home, and he has no idea where Earth is in the universe, nor even which universe he should be looking in. The Prize can give him advice, but only if it is not sulking. In *Options* (1975), the protagonist Tom Mishkin has crash-landed on a planet with only a robot to advise, only the robot has been programmed for a different planet; this is echoed in Samuel **Vimes**'s use of the wrong organiser in *J.* Often when the protagonists think they have achieved their goal, it is snatched away, or they are mistaken in thinking that they have won. In meantime the characters offer a commentary on philosophy, deal with impeccable if skewed logic, and muse upon what identity is. The amount of invention is astonishing, and this may well explain why Sheckley kept hitting writer's block. However, his pioneering – with others – of a science fiction which was comic and thoughtful, made it possible for Pratchett to have a market.

Sheckley, Robert

The most obvious precursor, aside from similarities to some of the protagonists – **Rincewind** would certainly (not) fit into Sheckley's universe, and Pratchett sometimes uses similarly loose there and back again structures – is a sequence in *Dimension of Miracles* in which Carmody meets people who manufacture planets. This anticipates the idea of Kin **Arad**'s profession in *Str*, although Pratchett puts his own spin on it. Sheckley is also thought to be an influence upon Douglas **Adams**, although Adams claimed he had not read Sheckley at the time of writing *The Hitch-Hiker's Guide to the Galaxy* (1978). *See also* Douglas Adams; Comedy and Humour; Heroes *and* Science Fiction.

Further Reading

Dunn, Thomas P. 1985. 'Existential Pilgrims and Comic Catastrophe in the Fiction of Robert Sheckley'. *Extrapolation* 26 (Spring). Pp. 56–65.
Sheckley, Robert.1968. *Dimension of Miracles*. New York: Dell.
———. 1975. *Options*. New York: Pyramid.
———. 1978. *The Alchemical Marriage of Alistair Crompton*. London: Michael Joseph.
Stephenson, Gregory. 1997. *Comic Inferno: The Satirical Work of Robert Sheckley*. San Bernardino, CA: Borgo Press.

Andrew M. Butler

Small Gods (1992)

The thirteenth book in the **Discworld** series and one that stands relatively alone, possibly being set a century prior to the other novels. The first hardback Gollancz edition consisted of 27,700 copies with a cover by Josh Kirby. The Corgi paperback (1993) had an initial print run of 213,500; since 2004 an alternative black and gold photographic cover has been available. There was a minor textual difference, in order to get a punchline to fall at the top of a page, but this was frustrated by the people doing the layout. In 2000 Gollancz republished *SG*, with *P* and *H*, as *The Gods Trilogy*, in a print run of about 11,000. *SG* has been translated into Bulgarian, Czech, Dutch, Estonian, Finnish, French, German, Hebrew, Hungarian, Japanese, Norwegian, Polish, Russian, Serbian, Spanish, Swedish and Turkish. The title refers to the minor gods that are very localised or very specific – a kind of souped-up saint of, say, teaspoons – and works on the model of small beer. The article 'Thought Progress' (1989, *see OM* WF*), which features Pratchett pondering about tortoises being dropped onto human heads shows how long ideas percolate before publication. John Clute (b.1940), reviewing it in *Interzone* 60, wrote '*Small Gods* is surely the best novel Terry Pratchett has ever written, and the best comedy' (June 1992). The track 'Small Gods' on *Terry Pratchett's From the Discworld* by Dave **Greenslade** was inspired by this novel.

Lu-Tze, one of the history monks, travels to **Omnia** to observe a significant moment in history. **Om**, the deity of Omnia, is fading away fast, as he is down to pretty well his last true believer and so he manifests himself in the form of a tortoise to the novice **Brutha**. Brutha is a little non-plussed to be speaking to his god, but he has other things to worry about as he is roped into **Vorbis**'s plans to dominate their region. Vorbis pretends to be negotiating peace with the people of **Ephebe**, but is in fact planning to invade and convert them. When they return to Omnia, Vorbis proclaims himself the Cenobiarch and Eighth Prophet of Om. Brutha can disprove this, but this puts him into the clutches of the Quisition. Fortunately he is rescued by Om, who arranges to be dropped by an eagle onto Vorbis's head. Brutha is declared leader, as fleets from Ephebe, **Tsort**, **Djelibeybi**, **Klatch** and elsewhere are massing for attack. Brutha tries to negotiate a peaceful way out, and begins to redesign his religion. Lu-Tze returns home, having tweaked history a little.

This novel is obviously an attack on organised **religion**, most obviously monotheistic ones with rigid moral codes. A being who claims to speak for a god obviously has a lot of potential **power**, which may be used for good or ill. Omnian, with its Quisition, desire to burn books and blind spots to compromise, is clearly not a good thing in this moral universe. Brutha, as the new Cenobiarch, has to be careful about what commandments he declaims, because the devil is always in the small print, and they may have unintended consequences. *See also* Brutha; Djelibeybi; Ephebe; Klatch; Lu-Tze; Om; Omnia; Power; Religion; Tsort *and* Vorbis.

Further Reading

Brown, James. 'Believing is Seeing'. *GOL2*.
Mendlesohn, Farah. 'Faith and Ethics'. *GOL*, *GOL2*.

Andrew M. Butler

Smith, Esk[arina] (*ER*)

The first example of a character **Coming of Age** within the **Discworld** series and a daughter rather than eighth son of an eighth son, born to Galdo Smith's wife in **Bad Ass** and delivered by Granny **Weatherwax**. Unfortunately the dying **wizard** Drum Billet assumes she is male and bequeaths his staff to her. As she begins to reveal strange powers, she is looked after by Granny Weatherwax, partly so that the **witch** may keep an eye on her. One of the first spells she learns is Borrowing – that is moving into the head of another creature – and this recalls similar sequences in *A Wizard of Earthsea* (1968) by Ursula Le Guin (b.1929) which of course is about a male rather than female wizard. Aged eight, Esk travels to the **Unseen University** to train to become a wizard but is refused entry as she is female (*see* **Sexism**) and her magic temporarily fails her. However there is a growing sense that the magic is using her rather than vice versa, and this might in time put her and the **Discworld** at risk. She is a formidable presence, albeit no match for Weatherwax. *See also* Bad Ass; Coming of Age; Feminism; Lancre; Magic; Sexism; Unseen University; Granny Weatherwax; Witches *and* Wizards.

Further Reading

Clute, John. 'Coming of Age'. *GOL*, *GOL2*.

Andrew M. Butler

Smythe, Colin (b. 1942)

Former publisher and now agent of Terry Pratchett.

Born in Maidenhead, Berkshire, Smythe was educated at an independent boy's school, Bradfield College, Reading, and then at Trinity College Dublin, from where he graduated in 1963. He set up his own publishing company in 1966, Colin Smythe Ltd, with the proceeds from the sale of his collection of books by the Irish poet W.B. Yeats (1865–1939). He is based in Gerrards Cross, Buckinghamshire, a town just outside the M25 and thus London.

The publisher specialises in books on Irish literature, which remains a particular interest of Smythe. Subjects include AE (G.W. Russell, 1867–1935), Samuel Beckett (1906–1989), Oliver St John Gogarty (1878–1957), Isabella Augusta, Lady Gregory (1852–1932), James Joyce (1882–1941), George Bernard Shaw (1856–1950), J.M. Synge (1871–1909), Oscar Wilde (1854–1900) and Yeats, among many others. It also publishes books on heraldry and medals, folklore and mysticism and parapsychology, many of these overlapping with the interests in Irish mythology and mysticism explored by AE, Lady Gregory and others of their circle. Some fiction has also been published, including works by William Barnwell (b.1943) and Hugh Cook (b.1956). The first of Barnwell's Blessing series, *The Blessing Papers*, had a hardback edition in 1980, but not the other two books of the trilogy. Colin Smythe Ltd published hardcovers of Cook's *The Chronicles of an Age of Darkness* series from *The Wizards and Warriors* (1986) to the fourth volume, *The Walrus and the Warwolf* (paperback 1988, hardback 1992), and distributed Corgi paperbacks with its own ISBNs from Walrus to the ninth, *The Worshippers and the Way* (1992), rather as had been done with *Str*.

But it is his association with Terry Pratchett which is most significant for this volume. The two met in 1968 when Pratchett was still working as a journalist for *The Bucks Free Press*, and had been sent to interview Smythe's co-director Peter Bander-van Duren about *Looking Forward to the Seventies* (1968), edited by Bander-van Duren and published by Colin Smythe Ltd, about the next decade in education. Pratchett told Bander-van Duren that he had been writing a novel in his spare time, and asked if they were interested in publishing it. Pratchett produced some illustrations for the manuscript, and *CP* was eventually published 16 November 1971. Three thousand copies were printed, with about ten hand coloured by Pratchett, and the launch was held at the carpet department in Heales on Tottenham Court Road, London. Over the next decade, Pratchett wrote *DSS* and *Str*, still working as a journalist and writing in the evening, and Colin Smythe Ltd published hardback editions of these. Paperback editions of these two appeared from NEL, but disappointing sales led to Smythe negotiating with Corgi for the paperback edition of *COM*, persuading NEL to forego their option on it. Sales of that and *LF* were such that it became obvious that a bigger publisher was necessary for the hardbacks, so Smythe negotiated a three-book co-publishing deal with Gollancz for *ER*, *M* and *S*. Smythe then moved to acting as Pratchett's agent, negotiating book, film, radio, television and merchandising rights. *See also* Plays *and* Publishers.

Further Reading

Colin Smythe Ltd's homepage: http://www.colinsmythe.co.uk/

Andrew M. Butler

Soul Music (1994)

The sixteenth **Discworld** novel, featuring **Death**'s continued experiences with human beings. The first edition was about 40,000 copies from Gollancz with a cover by Josh **Kirby**. The paperback from Corgi (1995) was 265,000 copies in the first print run; an alternative black and gold photographic cover has been available sine 2005. In 1998 Gollancz published an omnibus of *M*, *RM* and *SM* as *The Death Trilogy* in an edition of 22,000. *SM* has been translated into Bulgarian, Czech, Dutch, Estonian, Finnish, French, German, Hebrew, Japanese, Polish, Russian, Serbian, Spanish and Swedish. Soul music is the music – rock, blues, rap and so on – which possesses characters in much the same way as **Hollywood films** did in *MP*. It is also a genre of music which adds gospel style to rhythm and blues, and emerged in Memphis in the early 1960s. The style is central to the film *The Blues Brothers* (1980). At the start of the book is a note 'The History', giving a story-so-far, largely the events of *M*. It was made into a cartoon by Cosgrove Hall (see ***Soul Music From Terry Pratchett's Discworld***). Mark Thomas in his review observes that: 'Pratchett still occupies a unique place in literature: he manages to be pertinent, funny, original and popular. Even the most debated writer of this century, Bertolt Brecht, described the crucial ingredient for good drama as Spass; translated, it means "play" or "fun". Pratchett has this in abundance' (*The Mail on Sunday* (29 May 1994)).

Mort and Ysabell **Sto Helit** are killed in an accident on Dead Man's Curve and **Death** begins to mourn their passing, turning to drink, the

Klatchian Foreign Legion and then to being a down and out in the streets of **Ankh-Morpork**. In his absence, Susan **Sto Helit** is told the truth about her grandfather and forced to take on the role of Grim Reaper. Imp Y **Celyn** travels from his village of **Llamedos** to the city to become a musician, and finds a strange guitar in a shop which seems to come and go. The guitar music seems to possess people, and, with the aid of C.M.O.T. **Dibbler**, they soon have a huge backing, and the city, including the **wizards**, goes music crazy. Susan knows Imp is being kept alive by the music, but also wants to save him from death – and only the intervention of her grandfather helps her. Imp and his friends leave the city, just ahead of the enraged Musician's Guild.

Llamedos is a village in the **Discworld** equivalent of Wales, complete with rain, bards, harps and Eisteddfods. The game of the book is to recognise the bands which are corrupted: The Whom, &U, We're Certainly Dwarfs, The Surreptitious Fabric, and Lead Balloon, among many others. When Death returns into action, stealing a motorcycle and someone's clothes, he is re-enacting the cover of *Bat Out of Hell* and part of *Terminator 2: Judgment Day* (1991); a later moment of someone emerging from the flames of a crash is also taken from the film. *See also* Ankh-Morpork; Imp Y Celyn; Death; C.M.O.T. Dibbler; Hollywood Films; Llamedos; Pop Music; *Soul Music From Terry Pratchett's Discworld*; Mort Sto Helit; Susan Sto Helit; Ysabell Sto Helit and Wizards.

Further Reading

Hanes, Stacie. 'Death and the Maiden'. *GOL2.*
Moody, Nickianne. 'Death'. *GOL.*
———. 'Death and Work'. *GOL2.*

Andrew M. Butler

Soul Music From Terry Pratchett's Discworld (Television Adaptation) (1997)

Director: Jean Flynn. Producers: Jean Flynn. Executive Producer: Mark Hall. Writer: Martin Jameson. Music: Keith Hopgood and Phil Bush. Cast: Death: Christopher Lee; Imp y Celyn: Andy Hockley; Susan Sto Helit: Debra Gillett; Mustrum Ridcully: Graham Crowden; Mort: Neil Morrissey; Cliff: George Harris; John Jardine; David Holt; Bernard Wrigley; Jimmy Hibbert; Rosalie Scase; Rob Rackstraw; Bryan Pringle; Maggie Fox; Melissa Sinden. Video version: Vision Video, Parte One (four episodes cut together (ASIN: B00004CUEX)), 12 May 1997, Parte Two (three episodes cut together (ASIN: B00004CUF3)), 9 June 1997. Boxset of Parte One and Two, 175 minutes (ASIN: B00004CW4G), 20 October 1997. TV version 7 × 27 minute episodes, 28 December 1998. DVD version: 7 × 27 minute episodes, Region 1: Acorn Media 2001 (ASIN: B00005M0JI); Region 2 and 4: Vision Video 2001 (ASIN: B00005K9MG). Cert. PG. Available with *Wyrd*

Sisters From Terry Pratchett's Discworld as a boxset Region 2, 13 February 2006 (ASIN: B000E99486). Soundtrack CD: Pluto Music: 3 November 1997 (TH 030746).

One of two animated adaptations of the **Discworld** series (see *Wyrd Sisters From Terry Pratchett's Discworld*) commissioned from **Cosgrove Hall** by Channel 4 in the mid-1990s, made in association with ITEL and Ventureworld Films. Although it was a British television production – Channel 4 is a broadcaster funded by advertising with a public service broadcasting remit for reaching minority audiences – it was originally released on video in the UK by Vision Video in two parts. The original release included t-shirts being given away, as well as postcards, and the tapes included an interview with Terry Pratchett and a trailer for Discworld – material from a version of *RM*, done as a pilot. Parte One had three different covers. The series was shown on Australian television in 1998, and on Channel 4 at the end of the year in the middle of the night, December 28 1998. The DVD release includes the episodic version of the adaptation, the interview, the pilot, biographies of Pratchett and the characters and filmographies of the main actors, as well as a Discworld bibliography.

Cover of *Terry Pratchett's Discworld Soul Music, The Illustrated Screenplay.*

Whereas *T* had been a stop motion animation by Cosgrove-Hall, the decision here was to go for cel animation, supplemented at various points by computer animation. A good deal of time in computing processing power has passed since these episodes were made, and what was once cutting-edge risks looking rather dated – this is true of early Disney ventures into CGI, such as their big budget *Aladdin* (1992). Here the computer animation is most visible with the opening credits shot of the

Discworld from space, which is partially repeated in the end credits. Elsewhere it tends to augment the existing animation, and there is much use of an editing programme to make the picture swim and rotate to indicate characters travelling between different states, such as the summoning of **Death**, or rather of Susan **Sto Helit**. At times the rather flat animation suddenly goes three-dimensional, which is rather disconcerting. The animation has a fairly limited range of colours in the depiction of characters, and feels like rather traditional television animation. The pictures remain fairly static, rarely mimicking camera moves. Where the adaptation does score is in a number of background details, such as graffiti on the walls and amusing signposts – 'Ankh-Morpork Welcomes Careful Barbarians' and 'Thank You For Not Invading'. Death's executive toys are also a neat touch.

The director was Jean Flynn, who had earlier directed a version of *Peter and the Wolf* with George Daugherty and had been an animator and assistant director on *Danger Mouse*, among various other productions by Cosgrove Hall. The adaptation was made by Martin Jameson, who had also written episodes of the British ITV soaps *Emmerdale* and *The Bill* and BBC soaps *EastEnders* and *Holby City*. He managed to stay remarkably faithful to the novel, maintaining the four parallel strands of Death mourning Mort and Ysabell **Sto Helit**, Susan taking over for Death, Alberto **Malich** searching for Death and the career of Music With Rocks In.

It was a very smart casting move to have Christopher Lee (b.1922) play Death, his voice was used to great effect in *Dracula* (1958), and since then he has appeared in many horror movies for Hammer and other studios. In contrast, Neil Morrisey (b.1962), in little more than a cameo as Mort, was best known for playing Tony in the British sitcom *Men Behaving Badly* (1992–1999), and Rocky Cassidy in the comedy drama *Boon* (1986–1992). Graham Crowden (b.1922), who plays Mustrum **Ridcully**, also had a sitcom pedigree, *Waiting for God* (1990–1994), and also appeared in *If...* (1968), *Jabberwocky* (1977), *The Company of Wolves* (1984) and many other films, often playing tired, irascible and faintly confused characters. Andy Hockey had played Ox in *Robin Hood: Prince of Thieves* (1991) and had another minor role in *Much Ado About Nothing* (1993). Debra Gillett, who had worked on **Truckers** (1991) as **Grimma**, is good as Susan, although her visual character seems to be modelled on Elsa Lancaster (1902–1986) as the eponymous *Bride of Frankenstein* (1935) – something repeated in **Hogfather (Television Adaptation)**. The character design is usually convincing. The cast list does not specify which actors voiced which characters, so the actors who played the frankly annoying **wizards** cannot be singled out, nor can the actors who play the Klatchian Foreign Legion as if they are Mr Humphries from the BBC sitcom *Are You Being Served?* (1972–1985).

Key to this adaptation has to be the music. Whilst it contains a lot fewer references to bands than the original novel, there is a neat joke in Imp Y **Celyn**'s comment in cheese-making country Quirm 'We're bigger than cheeses now', which echoes a line from John Lennon about the Beatles and Jesus. The adaptation includes a range of performances by Music With Rocks In (and the Socks Pistols) and the music was composed and performed by Keith Hopwood (b.1946) and Phil Bush. Hopwood had been in Herman's Hermits in the 1960s, setting up a Manchester based recording studio in 1973 after he left the band. Cosgrove Hall are also based in Manchester, and had used him to score *The Wind in the Willows* (1983), *Alias the Jester* (1985) and *The BFG* (1989). On the score he plays keyboards and bass guitar. Phil Bush became Hopwood's sound engineer in 1980, and plays much of the guitars on the score. The tracks offer a history of rock music from Buddy Holly and Elvis Presley to Beatles, Traffic-style pyschedelia, Jimi Hendrix, the Blues Brothers and a Sting sound-alike heavy rock number. *See also* Animation; Cosgrove Hall; Death; *Hogfather* (Television Adaptation); Susan Sto Helit; Alberto Malich; Pop Music; Television Adaptations *and Truckers* (Television Adaptation).

Further Reading

Jameson, Martin. 1997. *Soul Music: The Illustrated Screenplay*. London: Corgi.

Andrew M. Butler

Sourcery (1988)

The fifth novel in the **Discworld** sequence, featuring **wizards**. The first edition, published by Gollancz in association with Colin **Smythe** Ltd, was 7,200 copies, with a cover by Josh **Kirby**. The paperback appeared in an edition of 154,500 from Corgi (1989); since 2004 an alternative black and gold photographic cover has been available. In 2001 Gollancz published an omnibus, *The Rincewind Trilogy*, containing *COM*, *LF*, *S* and *E* [sic]. *S* has been translated into Bulgarian, Chinese, Croatian, Czech, Danish, Dutch, Estonian, Finnish, French, German, Greek, Hebrew, Hungarian, Italian, Norwegian, Polish, Portuguese, Romanian, Russian, Serbian, Slovakian, Slovenian, Spanish, Swedish and Turkish. It is dedicated to a woman Pratchett had once seen in Bath with a large suitcase – inspiration for the **Luggage** – and people in towns like (the fictional) Power Cable, Nebraska (which also appears in *GO*). The preface also points out that the book, unlike traditional **Fantasy** novels, does not contain a map. A sourcerer is the eighth son of an eighth son of an eighth son, and a source of sorcery (hence the coinage); Simon (*ER*) is presumably wrongly referred to as a sourcerer. Tom Hutchinson (*c.*1930–2005) raved: 'Let us now praise Terry Pratchett. He has been happily mugging us, in his Discworld books, with that rarest of all SF coshes – laughter. Now he puts in the intellectual boot as well, and the resultant galactic giggle may well be considered his masterpiece. Underneath the archness is a memorable account of how we adapt power before it adapts us' (*The Times*).

Death comes to collect the soul of wizard Ipslore the Red, who seeks refuge in his wizard's staff, which he gives to **Coin** his eighth son. Ten years later Virrid Wayzygoose is getting ready to become **Archchancellor** when he is killed, and Coin takes his place, promising the wizards that they will become more powerful, and rebuilding first the **Unseen University** and then **Ankh-Morpork** with magic. Unfortunately the appearance of a sourcerer is likely to herald battles between wizards and the gods and thus the Apocralypse, so the archchancellor's hat forces **Rincewind**, working in the **Library**, to take it to distant Al Khali. Along the way he encounters **Cohen**'s daughter, Conina, and the hapless barbarian Nijel the Destroyer. Almost out of a sense of guilt, Rincewind returns to Ankh-Morpork and attempts to rescue Coin from the **Dungeon Dimensions** he has fallen into. He succeeds, but remains stuck himself. The battle is won and Ankh-Morpork is restored to its former shabby state.

The potential dark side of magical power is here explored – whilst the wizards are self-indulgent, lazy or in-fighting, they cannot wield much influence, but if they were united under a strong leader, they could threaten the balance and safety of the world. This gives Pratchett the chance to parody the four horseman of the Apocalypse Death, War, Famine and Pestilence (Revelation 6) – which he returned to with Neil **Gaiman** in *GO*. Parts of the novel are set in Al Khali, a parody of western representations of **Arabic society**. *See also* Arabic Societies; Coin; Cohen the Barbarian; Death; Dungeon Dimensions; Neil Gaiman; The Luggage; Libraries; Magic; Rincewind; Unseen University *and* Wizards.

Further Reading

Hill, Penelope. 'Unseen University'. *GOL*, *GOL2*.

Andrew M. Butler

So You Think You Know Discworld? see Quizbooks

Stewart, Ian (b. 1945)

Co-author, with Pratchett and Jack **Cohen**, of the three *SOD* books.

Professor of Mathematics at Warwick University, Director of its Mathematics Awareness Centre, and Fellow of the Royal Society, Ian Stewart is an active research mathematician, involved in popularising maths and other branches of science. His many television appearances include the 1997 Royal Institution Christmas Lectures, devoted to encouraging the love of science among children. He has received a number of prestigious awards, including 2000 Gold Medal of the Institute for Mathematics and Its Applications, and the 2002 Award for Public Understanding of Science and Technology from the American Association for the Advancement of Science. As well as books and research papers on mathematical topics (over 140 published papers according to his Website), he has written articles for general-interest scientific magazines such as Scientific American and New Scientist.

Ian Stewart at the Science Museum.

He is the author of numerous popular-science books including *Nature's Numbers* (1995), *The Magical Maze* (1997) and *Life's Other Secret* (1998). In 1990, he was persuaded by Jack Cohen to attend a **Science Fiction convention** where he was introduced to Terry Pratchett. The result was the collective entity Jack&Ian, whose writings include *The Collapse of Chaos* (1995), *Figments of Reality* (1995), *Evolving the Alien* (2002, also titled *What Does a Martian Look Like?*), and the three *SOD* books in collaboration with Terry Pratchett. Writing on his own, but even more so in his collaboration with Jack Cohen, Ian Stewart's popular-science writing is infused by the way science fiction also tells the story of science, using examples from sf stories to illustrate various points. In their collaborative science writing, Jack&Ian use science fiction as a way of interpreting science not from the 'alien's eye view' of pop-science writing (which assumes an alien viewpoint which rarely goes beyond 'Here is a cute alien: let it explain the world for us') but by using their expertise as scientists, fiction writers, and SF **Fandom**, to play directly with the speculative elements of science fiction. By writing as Jack&Ian, a third, constructed voice arises out of the dialogue between Stewart and Cohen with a different tone to that which they each develop in their own individual books. By adding jokes and other inclusive devices they are able to address their readers directly and help them explore the ways we 'paint stories on the universe'.

Since 1979, Ian Stewart has also published a number of science fiction short stories in British and American sf magazines such as *Analog*, *Omni* and *Interzone*. With Jack Cohen, he has published the novels *Wheelers* (2000) and *Heaven* (2005), which illustrate some of the ideas about possible forms of alien life found in *Evolving the Alien*. *See also* Jack Cohen; Conventions *and Science of Discworld.*

Stewart, Ian

Further Reading [see also entry on Cohen for their collaborations]

Stewart, Ian. 1998. *Life's Other Secret: The New Mathematics of the Living World*. London: Allen Lane.

———. 1997. *The Magical Maze: Seeing the World Through Mathematical Eyes*. London: Weidenfeld & Nicolson.

———. 1995. *Nature's Numbers: Discovering Order and Pattern in the Universe*. London: Weidenfeld & Nicolson.

Andy Sawyer

Stibbons, Ponder (*MP*, *LL*, *H*, *IT*, *LC*, *LH*, *SOD*, *SODII*, *SODIII*, 'CCOODD')

The future career of research wizard Ponder Stibbons in **Unseen University** may have been mapped out in the unusual circumstances in which he sat his final exams, where an accident resulted in his receiving the paper prepared for Victor **Tugelbend** with the single question 'What is your name?' (*MP*). How far this jolts him into the quest for understanding, or whether his first name is a clue to his character all along, is unclear. By *LL* he is introduced as 'Reader in Invisible Writings' (those books not yet in existence that are implied by those which are). Initially lazy and unambitious, he develops a tendency to look for patterns. In *IT* he is the youngest and keenest faculty member investigating the rules of magic by means of HEX, a baroque 'supercomputer'. Frustrated by his colleagues' habit of thinking at cross-purposes, by *H* he is the University's 'token sane person', in charge of the research students in the High Energy Magic Building (first mentioned in an aside in *GG*) where HEX is housed. Offered the chance to assist the God of Evolution (*LC*) he declines when he discovers that the god's perfect, adaptable creature is in fact a cockroach. In *SOD* and its successors he heads an experiment which results in the creation of Roundworld, a world without magic. Stibbons is the embodiment of rational science, whose determination to understand how the universe works is matched by his superiors' inability or unwillingness to understand his explanations. As a result, he uses the word 'quantum' a lot. *See also* Technology; Victor Tugelbend *and* Unseen University.

Andy Sawyer

Sto Helit (*M*, *GG*, *SM*)

A region of **Sto Lat**, in the Sto Plains. The last but one ruler, a Duke, had King Olerve of Sto Lat assassinated and attempted to have Princess Kelirihenna of **Sto Lat** killed, except that Mort **Sto Helit**, then **Death**'s apprentice, refused to take her soul. This caused much confusion among everyone until reality was readjusted. In return for sparing her life, Keli made Mort and his new wife Ysabell **Sto Helit** the Duke and Duchess of

Sto Helit. It has its own version of the **City Watch** (*GG*). However, since Mort and Ysabell die in *SM*, it seems that Susan **Sto Helit** is the current Duchess, assuming the title is a hereditary one, although she seems to have gone into teaching as a governess (*H*) and a teacher (*TOT*). It may be that **power** has reverted to Keli. *See also* Death; Power; Mort Sto Helit; Susan Sto Helit; Ysabella Sto Helit; Sto Lat *and* Keli of Sto Lat.

Andrew M. Butler

Sto Helit, Mort[imer] (*M*, *SM*)

Father of Susan **Sto Helit** and married to Ysabell **Sto Helit**. Mort is tall and has red hair. He is a serious man, and tends to take everything people say at face value. Initially, Mort is a bit spineless and tends to go along with other people so that he doesn't cause friction.

Mort's father, Lezek, deems Mort to be too thoughtful to follow the family business of farming (he is an unsuccessful scarecrow), and sends him off to the local hiring fair where, after being rejected by everybody else, he is eventually chosen to be **Death**'s apprentice.

Once he works his way up, his main duty as Death's apprentice is to learn the craft, and he is allowed to do Death's job on occasion. He takes over full time when Death takes a leave of absence to go on a 'soul searching' journey. During this time, Mort screws up the timeline by saving the life of the princess Keli (*see* Keli of **Sto Lat**), the daughter of the King of Sto Lat, whom Mort had become smitten with. Eventually Death catches wind of Mort's mistake and confronts him in a fiery rage. Mort, having grown up in the role of Death, fights back and, assisted by Ysabell, manages to get Death to concede and allow Mort to live.

Mort goes on to marry Ysabell, and they are given the titles of the Duke and Duchess of Sto Helit by the grateful now-Queen Keli. They are later killed in a freak wagon accident. *See also* Comedy and Humour; Death; Sto Helit; Susan Sto Helit; Ysabella Sto Helit; Sto Lat *and* Keli of Sto Lat.

Further Reading

Butler, Andrew M. 1996. 'Terry Pratchett and the Comedic *Bildungsroman*'. *Foundation* 67 (Summer): Pp. 56–62.
Butler, Andrew M. 'Theories of Comedy'. *GOL GOL2.*

Mark D. Thomas

Sto Helit, Susan (*SM*, *H*, *TOT*)

Daughter of Mort **Sto Helit**, **Death**'s apprentice, and Ysabell Sto Helit, Death's adopted daughter (by then Duke and Duchess of Sto Helit), and thus Death's granddaughter by adoption. Growing up, Susan struggles between her heritage as the granddaughter of an anthropomorphic personality, with the ability to ignore the rules of time and space, and her human heritage, with its attendant desire to accept appearances as truth and live a human-normal life. As a child, she knows her grandfather, who builds her a swing at **Death's Domain**, but her parents decide that too close an association with the ultimate reality is unhealthy for a child and they proceed to raise her to be as 'normal' as possible: to be sensible and to believe that people such as the **Hogfather** and Old Man Trouble are not real. She builds her life around logic, particularly after she is orphaned.

She studied at the Quirm College for Young Ladies, where her only friends were a dwarf and a troll, who also do not entirely fit in with the student body of affluent human girls. During this time, she became reacquainted with her grandfather and his servants, when the **Death of Rats** and Binky, Death's horse, retrieved her from the College to take Death's place. She discovered that her parents' well-meaning upbringing was misguided and took over the family Duty of collecting souls, but breaks with tradition by trying to protect the young man, Imp 'Buddy' Y **Celyn**, from his doom (something which her father had done in *M*). Coming to terms with Death's role as inevitable and, to some extent, desirable, enabled her finally to grieve for her parents' untimely demise.

Susan's strong feeling of superiority, birthed during her boarding school experience and strengthened during her times filling in for Death, contribute to both her problems and successes. After graduation, she worked as a governess for the Gaiter family of **Ankh-Morpork** and used her ability to see and believe in monsters to keep the Gaiter children safe with a monster-killing fireplace poker. On Hogswatch Eve, Death tricked her into helping him save the Hogfather from the assassin Teatime. Unlike Death, she is mostly mortal and therefore can travel to the Tooth Fairy's domain; unlike her companions and foes, she is a stern schoolteacher and can overcome the childlike logic that rules the place. She killed Teatime with the poker and then saved the Hogfather from the Auditors of Reality. From Death, she learnt that humanity's ability to believe in the 'small lies' like the Hogfather and the inevitability of charity and compassion during the darkest time of the year, is simply practice for the ability to believe in the 'larger lies' of justice, duty and mercy.

Later a teacher at Frout Academy, Susan used her ability to ignore the rules of time and space to take her students on fieldtrips across the **Discworld** and throughout history. When the Death of Rats summoned her for Death, she discovered that the Auditors of Reality were again trying to exterminate humanity for their irregularities and that she could help the son of Time, who is, like her, mostly mortal.

She is a striking figure, sharing a facial mark with her father of three fingers, which appears when she is angry, and she has a white streak through her hair – reminiscent of the eponymous *Bride of Frankenstein* (1935) as played by Elsa Lancaster (1902–1986). In theory she is now the Duchess of Sto Helit, but this has not been mentioned.

The similarities between this Susan and the character named Susan Foreman (Carole Ann Ford, b.1940) in early *Doctor Who* episodes (1963–1964), who lives with a time-travelling man she calls grandfather (William Hartnell, 1908–1975), are apparently coincidental. *See also* Imp Y Celyn; Death; Death of Rats; Death's Domain; Hogfather (Character); Mort Sto Helit; Ysabella Sto Helit *and* Sto Lat.

Further Reading

Hanes, Stacie. 'Death and the Maiden'. *GOL2.*

Susan Spilecki

Sto Helit, Ysabell (*LF*, *M*, *SM*)

The adopted daughter of **Death**, wife of Mort **Sto Helit** and mother of Susan **Sto Helit**.

Her parents had died when she was a child and so she was taken into care by Death, for reasons that have not been explained, but may represent an earlier example of Death being curious about human life and relationships, as he especially shows in *M* and *RM*. She then lived with Alberto **Malich** in **Death's Domain**, more or less stuck at the age of sixteen for decades.

When first encountered, in *LF*, she is desperately lonely and is reluctant to let **Rincewind** go; she craves human company – indeed after a lonely adolescence she probably craves male company. Her next appearance sees her as more stand-offish, initially distrustful and resentful of Mort as Death's apprentice – it is clear that Ysabell is able to operate the Duty, so perhaps she had looked to be able take over. Mort and she slowly realise that they are not enemies, and begin to work together, falling in love after some jealousy over Princess Kelirihenna of **Sto Lat**. Death returns them to the **Discworld**, where they become the Duke and Duchess of Sto Helit, and, having had a daughter, are killed in a coach crash.

Her aloof character resembles Estella and her treatment of Pip in *Great Expectations* (1861) by Charles Dickens (1812–1870). *See also* Death; Death of Rats; Death's Domain; Alberto Malich; Rincewind; Mort Sto Helit; Susan Sto Helit; Sto Lat *and* Keli of Sto Lat.

Andrew M. Butler

Sto Lat (*M*, *SM*, *GP*)

A city about twenty miles from **Ankh-Morpork**, on the Sto Plains. Its previous king was Olerve, who was assassinated by a crossbow by an assassin hired by the former Duke of **Sto Helit**. He was succeeded by

Sto Lat

Kelirihenna of **Sto Lat**, also known as Protector of the Eight Protectorates and Empress of the Long Thin Debated Piece Hubwards of Sto Kerrig, who would have been assassinated as well had Mort **Sto Herit** not intervened as **Death**. Keli is very much alive, and is reassured of this by Igneous **Cutwell**, the royal recogniser (*M*). Day to day ruling seems to be done by a mayor (*GP*).

Ankh-Morpork Fifty Pence Green Cabbage stamp created by Discworld Merchandising.

The area is largely flat, aside from a large bolder left behind by the Ice Giants, and is famed for its crops of cabbage, if very little else. It seems likely that Latitian, the **Discworld** equivalent of Dog Latin, derives from this region. It was an early venue for a concert by Imp Y **Celyn**, and Music With Rocks In, but they were quickly banned from the city (*SM*). At some point Moist von **Lipwig** conned Adora Bell Dearheart there (*GP*), a member of the family who invented the Clacks network (*see* **Technology**). The town became the first outside of Ankh-Morpork to join the postal network and get its own stamps.

The name may derive from a Polish song, 'Sto Lat', wishing someone to live for a hundred years. *See also* Imp Y Celyn; Igneous Cutwell; Moist von Lipwig; Sto Helit *and* Kelirihenna of Sto Lat.

Andrew M. Butler

Sto Lat, Princess, later Queen Keli[rihenna] of (*M*, *SM*)

Queen Kelirihenna of **Sto Lat** – more fully Lord of Sto Lat, Protector of the Eight Protectorates and Empress of the Long Thin Debated Piece Hubwards of Sto Kerrig – is the object of assassination plans by the Duke of Sto Helit, but her death is thwarted by the intervention of Mort **Sto Helit** who is filling in for **Death**. Her servants do not seem to recognise that she is not yet dead, and carry on as if she is; the change to the fabric of time threatens the **Discworld**. She seeks the aid of the Wizard Igneous **Cutwell** to try and prove that she is still alive. Eventually he is appointed as the Royal Recogniser, and there are hints of a romantic connection between them. Her other appearance is in *SM*, expelling Imp Y **Celyn** and the Music with Rocks In from Sto Lat.

Keli is to be contrasted with **Fairy Tale** princesses – much play is made of mattresses and peas. Her shorter name, Keli, is an echo of Kelly, which in British popular culture is indicative of a certain dumb blondeness or unrefined but perhaps pretentious working class identity, stereotypically working as a hair dresser or beauty consultant – similar names include Cassandra/Sandra (cf Ksandra, *ER*), Tracey (cf Ptraci, *P*) and Sharon. The association is all the stronger for the success of the BBC sitcom *Birds of a Feather* (1989–1998), with lead characters called Sharon and Tracey (*see* the **Oggs** for more equivalents). *See also* Imp Y Celyn; Igneous Cutwell; Fairy Tales; Sto Helit; Mort Sto Helit; Ysabell Mort Sto Helit *and* Sto Lat.

Andrew M. Butler

Strata (1981)

The last novel by Pratchett to be published before *COM* is one which also features a flat world shaped like a disc, although the genre is here **Science Fiction** rather than **Fantasy**. The first edition was 1001 copies, from Colin **Smythe** Ltd, with a cover by Tim White. The first paperback was published by New English Library (NEL) in 1982 in a print run of about 5,000. There were remaindered in 1985, with 300 copies bought by Colin Smythe Ltd to be sold with their own ISBN. A second paperback edition, with a Josh **Kirby** cover, appeared in an edition of 39,600 from Corgi (1988); this was repaginated in 1991 and had a redesigned Kirby cover in 1998. In 1994 Doubleday printed a new hardback edition of 3,700 copies. *Str* has been translated into Bulgarian, Czech, Dutch, French, German, Polish and Russian. Sue Thomason, reviewing it in *Vector* 176 wrote: 'The unique Pratchett blend of humour and philosophy is well-displayed, and the book's conclusion is both screamingly funny and a serious intellectual challenge. Highly recommended' (June/July 1994).

Kin **Arad**, designer of planets and author of best-seller Continuous Creation, is visited by long-lost astronaut Jago Jalo who tells her of this strange planet. She, along with her companions Marco and Silver, track it down and travel there, crashing into its surface. As they try to make their way to the centre of the planet they have the sense that the place is running down and breaking up. They pass through a series of civilisations which resemble Roman, Viking and **Arabic societies**, although it becomes clear that this is also an alternate history. Eventually Kin discovers the computers that run the planet, and finds out that the planet was made, along with much of the universe, by an extinct species, and not by the Spindle Kings, a different alien race whose wondrous artifacts (and entire existence) had been faked by the universe's manufacturers.

Cover of *Strata*. Artwork by Josh Kirby used on Corgi editions.

The novel takes as its starting point Larry Niven's *Ringworld* (1970), also about the discovery of a vast, planet-sized manufactured object. In this novel an alien called Nessus persuades two humans, the two-hundred-year old Louis Wu and the remarkably lucky Teela Brown, and the samurai-like vicious alien Speaker-to-Aliens. Pratchett would also have been aware of Arthur C. Clarke's *Rendezvous with Rama* (1973) and Bob Shaw's *Orbitsville* (1975), which feature a giant alien spaceship and a Dyson Sphere (a hollow planet containing a star).

Throughout Pratchett's novel, the fantastical turns out to have a scientific explanation, including flying carpets, **dragons** and demons. The Spindle Kings are a cousin of the Jokers from *DSS*, but the novel also anticipates Pratchett's later novels. Kin Arad visits The **Broken Drum** on the planet Kung, and on the alien planet there are a number of figures who appear to be dry-runs for **Death** and who speak in capital letters. It also has the characters exploring a strange land structure of *COM*. *See also* Kin

Arad; Arabic Society; The Broken Drum; Death; Dragons; Science Fiction; Robert Sheckley *and* Technology.

Further Reading
Clute, John. 'Coming of Age'. *GOL*, *GOL2*.

Andrew M. Butler

Stratified Societies

Many societies arrange **power** in pyramid structures, with increasingly few people as the amount of power increases. This leaves a single person in ultimate charge. This is perhaps a patriarchal structure. In some cases the structure is based upon position due to an individual's birth – what family or area they are born into – on others there is a meritocracy, in which individual ability allows someone to rise. There are a number of pyramidic power structures within the **Discworld**.

The first one to be encountered is that of the **wizards** in the **Unseen University** with their eight orders of magic. The higher the level of magic, the higher the order of **Magic**. The eighth level wizard is the **Archchancellor**. It does not strictly branch into eight different wizards at each level – that would quickly get to millions of wizards on the Discworld – and there is the sense that to rise between levels a wizard has to kill off his predecessor. Proof of the hierarchical status of wizards is seen in the positioning of **Rincewind** as a zeroth level wizard, with negative magical abilities. The structure is trumped by the sourcerer (see *S*), the eighth son of an eighth son of an eighth son, who has the ability to create new spells.

Within **Ankh-Morpork** there is a clear power structure, although it is rather shallow. At the head is the Patrician, through most of the novel Havelock **Vetinari**, and he is part of the aristocracy although he maintains power over other lords in the city. Most of the other people in the city seem to be organised into guilds – assassins, thieves, beggars and so forth. These guilds are themselves stratified, with a guild master and their own hierarchies of power. At some points the guilds may challenge the Patrician for power (*GG*), but equally the lords may jockey for position (*J*). Non-guild members may find their freedoms seriously curtailed, especially if they are stupid enough to engage in activities regulated by the guilds – music, as Imp Y **Celyn** discovers, is pretty well a closed shop (*SM*).

Another official body is the **City Watch**, the amalgamated form of the Day and City Watches, currently commanded by Samuel **Vimes**. Vimes himself has moved up the hierarchy of the city, in part through being rewarded by the Patrician for his services to the city, but equally being weighed down with titles to break his spirit. By *GP* he is Duke of Ankh, a high position for someone related to the man who executed the last king of the city. Within the Watch there is also a hierarchy – Lance-Constable,

Constable, Corporal, Sergeant, Sergeant-at-Arms, Captain and Commander. The Watch have also had their moments of acquiring power – the various claims of Carrot **Ironfoundersson** (*GG*) or Nobby **Nobbs** (*MAA*) to rule, the arrest of Vetinari (*TT*) and even taking part in a rebellion on Treacle Mine Road (*NW*).

It is clear from the encounters with other societies, whether in **Klatch**, **Überwald** or Borogravia, whether humans, **vampires** or **dwarfs**, that these are also hierarchical, usually organised around a monarch or patriarch, often both. Discworld is not a place that has embraced democracy.

The **witches**, on the other hand, are an exception to this rule, having a more anarchistic power structure. Whilst she could potentially be defeated, Granny **Weatherwax** is the leader of witches, at least in **Lancre**, and she is taken equally seriously in Ankh-Morpork (*ER*) and **Genua** (*Msk*) once they realise who she is. In the typical coven of the maiden, the mother and the crone, she is the crone, the one with most power, although at any time she may prove to be obsolete and replaced. In the Witch Trials of Lancre she constantly wins ('SALF', *HFOS*), and the other witches compete for second place. This may last only as long as she can maintain both her magical power and her position of respect.

In The **Bromeliad**, the store Nomes are also organised hierarchically, with the **Abbot** as de facto leader of all the nomes in **Arnold Bros (est 1905)**, as well as of the Stationeri. The Stationeri are a clan but not related to each other by birth – they draw upon the other clans of the store who are individual families. Within each family there is also a pecking order, with usually a patriarch at the head of each department – the del Icatessen, the Haberdasheri and so forth. The Abbott maintains his power by refusing to countenance any other world publicly – but he knows enough of **politics** to talk to **Masklin** and take him seriously. The trip outside of the store destroys the pattern of the hierarchy, but there is a sense of a new hierarchy based on drivers and passengers developing, and there is still a Nome leader at the end of the Bromeliad. *See also* Archchancellors; Arnold Bros (est 1905); The Bromeliad; City Watch; Klatch; Magic; Politics; Power; Unseen University; Patrician Vetinari; Überwald *and* Wizards.

Andrew M. Butler

The Streets of Ankh-Morpork (1993)

Subtitled *Being a concise and possibly even accurate Mapp of the Great City of the Discworld: Including Unseen University and environs! Also finest assortment of avenues, lanes, squares and alleys for your walking pleasure.*

This is the first of the four **Discworld** maps, from an idea by Stephen **Briggs**, who at that point had written the plays of *M*, *WS* and *GG*. It is drawn by Stephen **Player**, who was to draw *The Discworld Mapp* two years later. It was published by Corgi in an edition of 80,000 and had been translated into Bulgarian, Czech and German. This item consists of a map of the city of **Ankh-Morpork** and a booklet which contains Pratchett's thoughts on the process of mapping the city, Brigg's account of how he went about doing it, and a smaller map of the city with grid references, followed by the key to where major landmarks are. The line drawings in the booklets are by Briggs.

Cover of *The Streets of Ankh-Morpork* by Stephen Briggs and Terry Pratchett. Artwork by Stephen Player.

Pratchett had not drawn a map of the city when Briggs sent him a copy of his first draft, as he had largely been making the city up as he went along. However there were many references to the geography of the city scattered through the various volumes, which could be pieced together. Briggs describes how initially he began with a real world city that looked the right shape, and tried to adapt that. When it was not satisfactory, he began from scratch and invented all of the geography. A location might have to serve different purposes in different books, and the city put together piecemeal. As Briggs mapped in 1992, *LL* was published, and he had already been told to introduce references to the city which were confirmed as canonical by that novel. The map continued to evolve as *MAA* was written – it came out in 1993 – and this was only set in the city. This was the second of novels to focus on the **City Watch**, and soon novels set largely within the city were also to centre on the Watch, *TT* being an arguable exception.

The Streets of Ankh-Morpork

Like many medieval cities unencumbered by a coastline, Ankh-Morpork is circular in shape, somewhat like an onion in its winding streets. The river Ankh follows a trajectory like the Thames – where the Isle of Dogs would be is the Isle of Gods – but north-south (so to speak – hubwards-rimwards) rather than east-west (turnwards-**widdershins**). Curiously the majority of locations pinpointed on the map are on the east (widdershins/rimwards) bank, with obvious clusters around the **Unseen University** and the Patrician **Vetinari**'s palace. The map also includes various coats of arms of the guilds, that of the thieves being consistent with *FOC*. The Treacle Mine Road area of the map is reproduced with more detail in *NW*, and indeed the map was used to plot one sequence in the novel, a chase by Vimes across the rooftops. *See also* Ankh-Morpork; Stephen Briggs; City Watch; *The Discworld Mapp*; Maps; Merchandising; Stephen Player; Unseen University; Patrician Vetinari *and* Widdershins.

Further Reading

Hills, Matthew. 'Mapping Narrative Spaces'. *GOL, GOL2.*

Andrew M. Butler

T

Tachyon, Mrs (*JD, JB*)

A bag lady resident in **Blackbury**, who appears to have been the same age since the time of the Second World War, or perhaps even earlier. There is no record of her being born, or where she is from, and her existence is only confirmed by people's memories and old photographs. She is rarely seen without her shopping trolley, which contains large bags which somehow can lead to anyone touching the trolley to travel through time to the past or back to the present. Johnny speculates that she is so crazy that she sees things more clearly than anyone else, and she is quite happy in her own way, as long as she is left alone. Her **cat**, Guilty, probably a cousin of **Greebo**, should also be left alone. She is last seen travelling back in time to 1903.

A tachyon is a theoretical atomic particle which travels faster than light, and might be thought of as travelling backwards in time. In **Science Fiction** they are used either for instantaneous communication devices or for travelling through time, which is clearly what is used for here. *See also* Cats; Johnny Maxwell Trilogy; Science Fiction *and* The Trousers of Time.

Andrew M. Butler

Talking Books *see* Audio Books and 'Incubust'

Technology

Science Fiction is frequently about the intersection of humanity with technology, with inventions either made to solve a problem within an imagined society, or causing a new problem. Technology can also be used as part of the background furniture of an imagined world. It was Arthur C. Clarke (b.1917) who argued that any sufficiently advanced technology is indistinguishable from **magic**, and arguably that is the use that Pratchett makes of technology in his few science fiction works.

In *DSS* there are various bits of technology, or artifacts impossible to make without technology, which are relics of an earlier civilisation, apparently the Jokers. In *Str* a whole range of arcane machinery exists to keep its version of the **Discworld** going, although it is seizing up with age. In The **Bromeliad,** the Nomes are aided by the **Thing** in their escape from **Arnold Bros (est 1905)**; it is basically a device that can fill them in on their deep **history**, and gives them a direction to aim in.

Technology is likely to be simply in the Discworld series as they are **Fantasy**, and at the start the world is quasi-medieval, with basic technology such as the sword, the wheel and so on. However, even in *COM* there is the chelysphere, a presumably airtight ship which is launched into space to investigate the sex of the Great **A'Tuin**. **Twoflower**'s iconograph seems a new device as tourism itself is new – it is an imp rather than brownie camera, with a small creature who paints scenes instead of photographs. The imp in a box device is repeated in the personal (dis)organiser that Samuel **Vimes** reluctantly carries from *FOC* onward.

One challenge to this is the ongoing work and invention of Leonard of **Quirm**, a man too dangerous to allow out in public, and who is a permanent 'guest' of Patrician **Vetinari**. He is the inventor of the Gonne which is at the centre of *MAA*, the designer and builder of the submarine in *J* and a flying machine capable of going into the atmosphere in *LH*. He is also the inventor of an espresso machine, various arcade games and a number of weapons. Leonard is unfortunately naïve about the use that may be made of his inventions – they are just exercises in engineering rather than potential weapons of mass destruction.

The High Energy Magic Building of the **Unseen University** is the location of HEX, a Discworld computer. (Note that it is not the Discworld's first computer, that honour going to the Druidic stone circles.) Invented by Skazz (*SM*), it is based around a colony of ants (Anthill inside warns a sign, with a nod towards a silicon chip manufacturer, Intel) and their movements, and a mouse wheel. It has been further developed by Ponder **Stibbons** and apparently by itself. Initially it was used to analyse spells, but perhaps its association with magic has impacted on its very nature. There is now a paternoster to allow ants to shift between levels, and it has clockwork parts. It also seems to be getting interested in electricity (*H*), has a wooden keyboard for data entry – replacing a punch card system – and a mouse – who happily nests in it. It can also control a device for looking at things a long way away – the omniscope (*GP*). Its name may be a nod to HAL 9000 of *2001: A Space Odyssey* (1968) or IBM, to the numerical system hexadecimal, or to the magic spell or hex. It has been involved in the Roundworld project of the *SOD* books, although a new computer at Braseneck College may have now outstripped it (*SODIII*).

Despite objections from **wizards** and the Guild of Engravers, **Ankh-Morpork** has now a working moveable type press, which is owned by Gunilla **Goodmountain** and prints William de **Worde**'s *Ankh-Morpork Times*. This can allow information to be shared between a greater number of people and offers the possibility of a mass media to develop. The wizards objected to the dangers of the same letter blocks being reused in different words (as words have magical properties), whilst the Guild are worried about the loss of jobs in engraving if mass printing becomes possible (*TT*). In the end, however, pragmatism wins out and they rename themselves the Guild of Engravers and Printers – if you cannot beat them, persuade them to join you.

The Clacks is the semaphore system that has been used as a non-magical means of long-distance communication, and one which is more effective than strapping a message to an owl or albatross. Semaphore in the real world was described in detail by Robert Hooke (1635–1703) in 1684, as a system of signalling, but it was the French who put this into action under Claude Chappe (1763–1805), with a network of towers with signalling rods. A variety of similar systems were adopted through Europe before the development of the telegraph began to make it obsolete from the 1830s onwards. The Discworld Clacks was developed by Robert Dearheart (*FE*), linking Ankh-Morpork, **Genua**, **Lancre**, **Sto Lat** and **Überwald**. The Unseen University has its own link to the system, and using HEX has managed to hack the system so that they get their own free messages (but then wizards are rarely charged for public services). It has been run by the Grand Trunk Semaphore Company, which has made a tidy profit from c-mail and c-commerce. However, this was pushed too far, and maintenance was cut to reduce overheads in favour of profits, as a secret consortium took the company over. John Dearheart – Robert's son – attempted to set up a rival trunk, but was killed. Moist von **Lipwig** is manoeuvred into exposing the corruption in *GP*. There appears to be a commentary here on the post-privatisation behaviour of British services such as the railway network.

It is likely that future novels will see more forms of technology and the development of mass production and mass media. There have been occasional mentions of something like an internal combustion engines, although to date cars and trains have not been produced which might supplant horse carriages or broomsticks.

In his non-fiction writings, such as '2001: The Vision and the Reality and High Tech, Why Tech?', Pratchett sings the praises of technology as a tool, especially a word processing programme, and he was an early acquirer of a modem. *See also* The Bromeliad; Gunilla Goodmountain; Magic; Leonard of Quirm; Science Fiction; *Science of Discworld*; Ponder Stibbons; The Thing; Twoflower; Unseen University; Patrician Vetinari; Wizards *and* William de Worde.

Further Reading

Standage, Tom. 1999. *The Victorian Internet: The Remarkable Story of the Telegraph and the Nineteenth Century's Online Pioneers*. London: Phoenix.

Andrew M. Butler

Television Adaptations

There have been six television adaptations of Pratchett's novels to date: see ***Truckers* (Television Adaptation), *Johnny and the Dead* (Television Adaptation)**, ***Wyrd Sisters From Terry Pratchett's Discworld* (Television Adaptation)**, ***Soul Music From Terry Pratchett's Discworld* (Television Adaptation)**, ***Johnny and the Bomb* (Television Adaptation)** and ***Hogfather* (Television Adaptation).** An adaptation of *COM* is (in 2007) in preproduction with Sir David Jason (b.1940) announced as **Rincewind**, Sean Astin (b.1971) as **Twoflower**, Tim Curry (b.1946) as Ymper **Trymon**, Christopher Lee (b.1922) as **Death** and David Bradley (b.1942) as **Cohen the Barbarian**.

Andrew M. Butler

Teppic (*P*)

Son and heir of Teppicymon XXVII, Pharaoh of **Djelibeybi**, and presumably to become Teppicymon XXVIII on his father's demise. Whilst waiting to take up his job, he trains for a trade, that of assassin, with the Guild of Assassins at Ankh-Morpork. The country is being bankrupted by the building of increasingly elaborate burial monuments – in the shape of increasingly large pyramids – and so Teppic figures that he cannot be just a figurehead but ought to learn a trade. He passes with flying colours, and his skills assist him in eluding some of the more onerous duties of being king, and in helping Ptraci. The fact that Ptraci was one of his father's handmaidens was but a bit of a damper on his sense of romance, as does the discovery that they are related to each other. Teppic attempts to rule wisely and dispense justice, but is held back by the conservative ways of Dios, the high priest who has apparently held the job for seven thousand years.

Teppic's awkwardness with people, his interest in architecture, and his sense of a vocation seems to echo Prince Charles's long wait to succeed his mother Elizabeth II, and the awkward conversations which are overheard in news reports of his meeting people, his loathing for modern architecture and so on. *See also* Djelibeybi; Egypt *and* Religion.

Andrew M. Butler

Terry Pratchett's The Colour of Magic: The Graphic Novel (1991)

A **comic** adaptation originally published as a four-shot by the Innovation Corporation and later as a **graphic novel** by Corgi (1992). It has been translated into Polish.

The editor of the comic was David Campiti, who had been and is a comics writer on titles including ***Quantum Leap and Superman***. Campiti acted as a packager of artwork and formed Innovation Publishing in 1988 to publish comics. It was dominated by adaptations of fiction and television, including *Child's Play 2* (1990) and *3* (1991), *Dark Shadows* (1991), *Freddy's Dead: The Final Nightmare* (1991), *Quantum Leap* (1989–1993) and *The Vampire Lestat* (1985), and these were often aimed at an adult female audience rather than a teenaged male one. He left in 1993 to set up another company, Glass House Graphics, which is a comics talent agency. The adaptation was by Scott Rockwell, who at the time was the Submission Editor and Art Director at Innovation, and was approved by Terry Pratchett. It was illustrated by Steven Ross, who was one of about a dozen artists who were considered for the job. Lettering was by Vickie Williams.

Cover of *Terry Pratchett's The Colour of Magic: The Graphic Novel.* Twoflower, Rincewind and The Luggage in front of the Discworld. Artwork by Daerick Gross, Sr.

The four parts of the graphic novel correspond to the four sections of the novel: 'The Colour of Magic', 'The Sending of Eight', 'The Lure of the Wyrm' and 'Close to the Edge': **Twoflower**'s meeting with **Rincewind** in **Ankh-Morpork**, a meeting with Hrun the Barbarian and the summoning of a demon by mention of the number eight, events in Wyrmwood with Hrun and imaginary dragons and finally the encounter with the people at the rim of the Disc, with Rincewind falling off the wall. The first two parts have prologues.

Whilst the adaptation is faithful, it emphasises the lack of plot structure, as Rincewind lurches from one crisis to another rather than trying to achieve a goal or solve a problem. The stage transitions can be awkward, with insufficient scene directions. Rincewind loses his hat at various points (and it is woolly rather than pointed if battered) but finds identical ones to replace it from somewhere. Twoflower, on the other hand, always wears the same clothes despite having his **Luggage**. Usually the glasses are depicted as opaque, but in one frame he is shown as having four eyes – which rather literalises his nickname derived from his wearing glasses. One point where the adaptation does add is in the spread of iconographs taken by his camera.

Most of all, the wit of the prose is lost in the translation between media. It feels more like a work of **Fantasy** rather than a **Parody** of one. Scott Rockwell went on to adapt *LF* (see ***Terry Pratchett's The Light Fantastic: The Graphic Novel***). *See also* Ankh-Morpork; Comics; Graphic Novels; the Luggage; Merchandising; Rincewind; *Terry Pratchett's The Light Fantastic: The Graphic Novel and* Twoflower.

Andrew M. Butler

Terry Pratchett's The Light Fantastic: The Graphic Novel (1992)

A **Comics** adaptation originally published as a four-shot by the Innovation Corporation and later as a **graphic novel** by Corgi in 1993. It has been translated into Polish.

The adaptation was by Scott Rockwell, who had done ***Terry Pratchett's The Colour Of Magic: The Graphic Novel***, the editor was David Campiti (although Campbell is credited for the individual parts), and lettering was by Vickie Williams for parts three and four. The first two parts were illustrated by Steven Ross. (*For biographical details see* ***Terry Pratchett's The Colour of Magic: The Graphic Novel.***) Parts 1 and 2 were lettered by Michelle Beck. Part 1 was painted by Mira Fairchild, part 2 by Doug Nishimura, who has also worked in **Computer Games**. Parts 3 and 4 were illustrated by Joe Bennet, who appears to later be credited as Joe Bennett (b.1968, as Benedito José Nascimento). His first big commissions were for

Marvel in 1994, but he has worked for other companies before signing an exclusive deal with DC Comics.

The first part sees **Rincewind** and **Twoflower**, and the discovery of a red start somewhere ahead of the **Discworld** and the spell that is hiding in Rincewind's head. The second part begins with the rescue, with **Cohen the Barbarian**, of a virgin sacrifice, and detours into **Death's Domain**, where Twoflower teaches the Four Horsemen a game that looks curiously like Bridge. In part 3 Rincewind encounters some **trolls**, whilst his companions are captured by the mercenaries sent after them by the **wizards** to retrieve Rincewind. They escape, thanks to the trolls, and come upon a city gripped by panic about the star. In the last part, Rincewind returns to **Ankh-Morpork**, where **Archchancellor** Galder Weatherwax of the **Unseen University** has retreated into the Tower of Art to read the seven remaining spells of the Octavo. Rincewind saves the day with the eighth spell, and the red sun hatches the eggs which will form new Discworlds.

Cover of *Terry Pratchett's The Light Fantastic: The Graphic Novel.* Death looks over the Discworld. Twoflower and Rincewind. Artwork by Steven Ross.

The presence of an overarching plot, uneven as it may be, makes this adaptation seem less manic than the comic of *COM* – which is of course true of the originals. Joe Bennet's artwork is a vast improvement on the first two parts, and of course he has control over the drawing and colours, making it seem more integrated. But even the early parts has nice touches, for example the zodiac on the floor of one room in the University.

No further comic books were produced in the series until the adaptations of *M* and *GG*, due to disappointing sales in the United States, the primary market for comic books. At this point Pratchett was not a best-selling author in the United States and on a number of occasions switched **publishers**, which militated against promotions of his work. *See also* Ankh-Morpork; Archchancellors; Cohen the Barbarian; Comics; Computer Games; Death's Domain; Games; Graphic Novels; the Luggage; Merchandising; Publishers; Rincewind; *Terry Pratchett's The Colour of Magic: The Graphic Novel*; Trolls; Twoflower; Unseen University *and* Wizards.

Andrew M. Butler

Theatre

Theatre has played a role in *WS*, complete with much **parody** of William **Shakespeare**, and, as **Opera** or **Musicals** in *Msk*. Punch and Judy is played on in '**TOC**'. For discussion of Pratchett's works performed on stage, *see* **Musicals** and **Plays**. *See also* Musicals; Musical Hall; Hwel; Opera; Parody; Plays; Tomjon *and* William Shakespeare.

Andrew M. Butler

'Theatre of Cruelty' (*OM* WF*)

This is a short story set on the **Discworld**, commissioned for a free book magazine (*Bookcase* 45, July/August 1993; Pp. 10–11), which was available in branches of the bookshop and stationers W.H. Smith. A longer version appeared in the programme book for the **convention** OryCon 15, 12–14 November 1993, where Pratchett was guest of honour. A further revision was made for *The Wizards of Odd: Comic Tales of Fantasy* (Edited by Peter Haining. London: Souvenir Press, 1996. Pp. 15–19). The story is available online, most conveniently at http://www.lspace.org/books/toc/. Theatre of cruelty was a concept advanced by Antonin Artaud (1896–1948) in *Theater and Its Double* (1936), where he demanded an extreme physical theatre which would attempt to shatter the illusion of every day reality.

A street entertainer, Charles Slumber, is found dead in **Ankh-Morpork**, his pockets full of pennies. He has been beaten to death by a blunt instrument, strangled with a string of sausages and bitten by two or more sharp-toothed animals. **Colon**, **Nobbs** and even **Vimes** are baffled, whilst Carrot **Ironfoundersson** goes to interrogate **Death**, who he figures was on the scene and so must have witnessed something. Carrot eventually realises that Slumber choked to death, whilst being attacked by the gnomes in the theatre troupe he managed; he used to beat them and has choked on the swozzle, the device that he uses to do their voices in performance.

'Theatre of Cruelty'

This is the Discworld spin on the Punch and Judy Show, a heartening entertainment of spousal abuse, infanticide, homicide and casual violence, and even a triumph over the devil, performed by a puppeteer (a Professor) in a booth, frequently at the seaside or fairgrounds. It dates back to the seventeenth century, and the Italian *Commedia dell'Arte*. *See also* Ankh-Morpork; Frederick Colon; Conventions; Death; Carrot Ironfoundersson; Nobby Nobbs *and* Samuel Vimes.

Further Reading

Artaud, Antonin, 1958. *The Theater and Its Double*. Translated by Mary Caroline Richards. New York: Grove Weidenfeld.

Andrew M. Butler

Thief of Time (2001)

The twenty-sixth **Discworld** novel and loosely a **Death** novel, although Susan **Sto Helit** appears more. It also features the return of **Lu-Tse** from *SG*. The first edition was published by Doubleday, with a Josh **Kirby** cover – some of the proofs had it as *The Thief of Time*. The Corgi paperback was 2002. *TOT* has been translated into Bulgarian, Czech, Dutch, French, German, Polish, Russian and Welsh. The title is a quotation from the English poet Edward Young (1683–1765): 'Procrastination is the thief of time'; in the novel the Procrastinators are prayer-wheel like devices, which stitch together the flow of time, and Lobsang Ludd uses the phrase to refer to himself. The lightning strike towards the end of the novel sends Samuel **Vimes** back in time in *NW*. Peter Ingham wrote in *The Times*: 'perhaps because the theme is so apocalyptic, *Thief of Time* throws into sharp relief the kind of exasperated liberalism that underpins much of Pratchett's humour. Many of his central characters are both resigned to and maddened by an intuitive affection for humankind, with its infuriating ability to dash the highest hopes and to confound the worst fears. A bit like new Labour, really' (12 May 2001).

Over a period of decades, someone appears to Nanny **Ogg**, asking for her help in a birth. Jeremy Clockson, a master of manufacturing clocks, is commissioned by LadyJean to create the most accurate timing device on the Discworld. Death tells Susan – now a teacher – that the world is scheduled to come to an end the following week and that she might want to try and do something to stop it, although he will be busy gathering together the other three Horsemen of the Apocralypse. Lu-Tse is forced to take on orphan Lobsang Ludd as an apprentice. It is the clock which is causing the danger, as the Auditors latest attempt to rationalise the universe. LadyJean, whose name is a version of 'Legion' betrays her fellow Auditor and is reborn as Unity. It turns out that Jeremy and Lobsang are the same person, born of a union between Time and Wen. The clock is destroyed, time restored, and Jeremy and Lobsang unite as one being.

Cover of *Thief of Time*. Artwork by Josh Kirby.

Lu-Tse provides an opportunity to **parody** Buddhism, and the *Kung Fu* (1972) television series, with inscrutable and rather mundane scraps of wisdom. But he also comes across as a version of Morpheus in *The Matrix* (1999), directed by the Wachowski Brothers, and the Auditors as Mr Joneses – although being colour coded links them to *Reservoir Dogs* (1992), directed by Quentin Tarantino (b.1963). Unity is a version of the character Trinity, the beautiful but ultimately tragic female hero. It is suggested that Susan may have feelings for Jeremy – Imp Y **Celyn** seemingly forgotten. *See also* Imp Y Celyn; Death; Hollywood Films; Lu-Tse; Nanny Ogg; Susan Sto Helit *and* Samuel Vimes.

Further Reading

Hanes, Stacie. 'Death and the Maiden'. *GOL2.*

Andrew M. Butler

The Thing (*T*, *D*, *W*)

The flight recorder and navigation computer of the starship Swan, which crash-landed on Earth some fifteen thousand years before the events of The **Bromeliad** trilogy. Its functions are to keep the nomes safe, and to guide them so that they may get home. Unfortunately it needs electricity to function properly, and **Masklin**, **Grimma** and Old Torrit, its guardian, are presumably often too far from electricity for it to be useful. It explains to the old **Abbot** at **Arnold Bros (est. 1905)** that the store is going to be demolished, helps them track down Grandson Richard 39, communicates with the flight deck of the Concorde and eventually communicates with the Swan via a space shuttle and a communications satellite. It can also duplicate itself by downloading a version of itself. Like so many talking computers, it has a fine line in pedantry, sarcasm and being patronising, owing a little, perhaps, to the creations of Robert **Sheckley** or Douglas **Adams**. *See also* The Abbot; Douglas Adams; Arnold Bros (est. 1905); The Bromeliad; Computers; Grimma; Masklin; Robert Sheckley *and* Technology.

Andrew M. Butler

Thud! (2005)

The thirty-fourth **Discworld** novel, and part of the **City Watch** sequence. The first edition was the US HarperCollins hardback, which preceded the UK Doubleday edition (with Paul **Kidby** cover) by ten days. The Corgi paperback appeared in 2006. *T!* was released at the same time as the picture book, *WMC?*, which forms a part of the narrative. Thud is the name of one of the Discworld **Games**, invented by Trevor Truran (b.1942) and often played at **Conventions** (and see **Thud – A Historical Perspective *(OM*WF)***). The novel begins with epigraphs from **dwarf** and **troll** sacred texts. Reflecting on the novel, A.S. Byatt (b.1936) wrote: 'Pratchett writes farcically, and knows blackly' (*The Times* (24 September 2005)).

Trouble is brewing in **Ankh-Morpork**: the painting of the Battle of Koom Valley by Methodia Rascal has been stolen, the dwarf leader Grag Hamcrusher has been murdered, apparently by a troll, and Samuel **Vimes** has been forced to accept an auditor, A.E. Pessimal (*see* also **'CCOODD'**), and Salacia von Humpeding (see **Vampires**), into the City Watch. He tries to investigate the murder, wary that the age-old tensions between the troll and the dwarfs are about to boil over, and slowly becoming aware that something has been discovered by the dwarfs under the city. Hamcrusher has actually been killed by dwarfs, and the murder made to look like it was by a troll (cf the assassination in *J*). An ancient spirit has been disturbed – the Summoning Dark. Vimes realises that the painting is a map to the location of a cube – apiece of ancient **technology** – in the Koom Valley, and travels there with a reproduction of the picture, Sybil **Ramkin**, his son and various members of the watch. Vimes does battle with the Summoning Dark, and is saved by his determination to read *WMC?* to his son. Pessimal is appointed as Vimes's paperwork person.

The **war** echoes any number of conflicts built along **religion** or lifestyle – whether within Northern Ireland or dealing with Muslim culture. The secret of Koom Valley is that it was meant to bring peace between dwarfs and trolls, but in a period of confusion it actually brought millennia of enmity. The novel was perfectly timed for its portrayal of **racism** in an era when multiculturalism was very much under debate –the book anticipated rather than drew on the 7 July 2005 London Bombings. The secret of the painting has some echo of *The Da Vinci Code* (2003) by Dan Brown (b.1964), as does the way that some of the dwarfs died. *See also* Ankh-Morpork; City Watch; Dwarfs; Games; Sybil Ramkin; Racism; Religion; Technology; 'Thud – A Historical Perspective'; Trolls; Vampires; Samuel Vimes *and* War.

Andrew M. Butler

'Thud – A Historical Perspective' (*OM*WF*)

This vignette of fictional history was originally packaged with *Thud! The Discworld Boardgame* (Millennia Marketing, 2003). In the **game**, the two sides are **trolls** and **dwarfs**, who re-enact a version of the Battle of Koom Valley (*T!*, *see* **War**), and the vignette recounts a history of games played by both dwarfs (including *Thud!*) and trolls, as well as more of the history of Koom Valley. The game is intended to replace war, and instead has led to fights between players. *See also* Dwarfs; Games; Racism; Religion; Trolls *and* War.

Andrew M. Butler

Thursley, Eric (*E*)

Like Eskarina **Smith** and **Coin**, Eric Thursley is one of Pratchett's child protagonists (see **Children in the Discworld Series**) who features in a **Coming of Age** narrative and then disappears from the oeuvre. Eric lives at 13 Midden Lane, Pseudopolis, Sto Plains, and is a demonology hacker who has inherited books, **magic** equipment and a parrot from his late grandfather. His parents have given him a pretty free rein, so have not followed his progress. He attempts to summon up a demon from the **Dungeon Dimensions**, but instead retrieves **Rincewind**, last seen at the end of *S*. (It is possible that Eric had some infernal assistance in his conjuring, rather than the demons simply having a bad day.) Rincewind has to grant Eric his three wishes of immortality, omnipotence and meeting the most beautiful woman in the world. As is always the case in three wishes, the devil is in the small print, and they end up first in the Aztec/Inca-like Tezumen in **Klatch**, then **Tsort** and finally a dimension like Hell. Rincewind manages to escape, but Eric's fate is less certain. *See also* Children in the Discworld Series; Coin; Coming of Age; Dungeon Dimensions; Klatch; Magic; Rincewind; Eskarina Smith; Tsort and Wizards.

Andrew M. Butler

Tiffany Aching sequence *see* Aching, Tiffany

Tolkien, J[ohn] R[onald] R[euel] (1892–1973)

A leading **Fantasy** writer. Pratchett first read his three-volume epic *The Lord of the Rings* (1954–1955) on New Year's Eve, 1961, and for a period re-read it every year, much later defending it from the snobbery of critics (see 'Let There Be Dragons', 'Cult Classic', 'Whose Fantasy Are You?' and 'Magic Kingdoms', but compare 'Elves Were Bastards', all reprinted in *OM*WF*).

J.R.R. Tolkien enjoying a pipe in his study at Merton College, Oxford, December 1956.

Tolkien was Professor of English Language and Literature at Merton College, Oxford, between 1945 and 1959 and a novelist, poet and artist, best known for his books set in the Middle-Earth mythos. Through reaching best-seller status, especially from the 1960s, Tolkien perhaps unwittingly set the template for the fantasy boom, especially the financial success of quest fantasy and Sword and Sorcery (*see* Fritz **Leiber**). *The Lord of the Rings* has long since achieved cult status and regularly tops polls such as the Waterstone's Poll of the Century and The BBC Big Read. Some critics dismiss this as the work of organised voting, and see his work as infantile.

Whilst *The Hobbit* (1937) was published as children's fiction, the roots of Middle-earth go back to two decades earlier and Tolkien's work on philology. Having begun to invent a variety of fictional languages which he attributed to the various kinds of **elves**, he needed to find a vehicle in which these tongues could be used, and then a framing narrative to support that. The disarmingly simple narrative – the story of a bourgeois hobbit Bilbo Baggins who is manipulated by the **wizard** Gandalf to pose as a thief for a group of dwarves who are seeking to regain their lost treasure – drops hints of a much bigger world. It also sets up a pattern of a dangerous incident followed by feasting, which also underlies the belated follow-up, *The Lord of the Rings*. Here the ring which Bilbo found in his encounter with the creature Gollum is found to be a thing of great power, needing to be destroyed by being cast into the Crack of Doom by his nephew Frodo Baggins lest it be the means of the evil Sauron taking over Middle-earth. The underlying mythos is much richer here, leading to the posthumous publishing of most of this material beginning with *The Silmarillion* (1977). Tolkien's depictions of elves, **dwarves**, **trolls** and **dragons**, his writing style, his use of **maps** and his **narrative** structures has done much to set a pattern of fantasy as a genre, and has provided a template to be subverted.

At first Pratchett was more content to follow in Tolkien's footsteps than to **parody** them; the first version of *CP* is a quest in the Tolkien tradition, with Bane for example being a version of Aragorn, the lost king in waiting and Pismire being a version of Gandalf. *COM* was much more parodic of the tropes of fantasy, and the Tolkien tradition underlies much of it, along with references to Leiber, Robert E. Howard (1906–1936), H.P. Lovecraft (1890–1937) and Anne McCaffrey (b.1926).

The less competent side of Gandalf is the prototype which is being parodied in the depiction and reference to wizards in the **Discworld**. Tolkien created five wizards: Gandalf the Grey, reincarnated as Gandalf the White after dying in a battle with the monstrous Balrog, Saruman the White, Radagast the Brown and two blue wizards who vanished into the east. These colours are echoed in a reference to wizard laundry turning whites into grey (*ER*) and in the nickname of Archchancellor Mustrum **Ridcully** being Ridcully the Brown. The Balrog appears, as the Balgrog fought by Victor **Tugelbend**. The **dwarf** Gildor Inglorion advises Frodo in *The Fellowship of the Ring*: 'Do not meddle in the affairs of Wizards ... for they are subtle and quick to anger', and Ysabell **Sto Helit** mangles this in conversation with Mort **Sto Helit**. There is a variation on the same phrase in *LL*, after an attack on a character who disrespected the **Librarian**.

Tolkien's elves are rather more fey and shining than those depicted by Pratchett (he compares their cruelty to **cats** – *see* 'Elves Were Bastards'), particularly in *LL* and *WFM* and its sequels, although the butt here is more likely to be the fairies in *A Midsummer's Night Dream* by William **Shakespeare** and some of its camper derivatives, such as productions of the ballet composed by Felix Mendelssohn (1809–1847). Magrat, having alluded to a line by Titania, Queen of the Elves, is cut off before she can echo the Elvish greeting 'A star shines on the hour of our meeting' (*WS*).

The naming, language and depiction of dwarfs as gold-loving creatures who live under mountains and are suspicious of other species is something inspired by Tolkien's dwarves; in The Hobbit they are prepared to sacrifice anything in order to get their hands on gold. Dwarf dwellings, such as the mines of Moria, are guarded by invisible runes and the same is true in *WA*, with Granny **Weatherwax** and Nanny **Ogg** riffing on how you can see a wizard has written you invisible runes. At the end of their trip through the mines, they even encounter a version of Gollum.

Tolkien, J.R.R.

Dwarf sex is set up in *WA* as an area of mystery, with the difference between male and females difficult to ascertain. This derives from a reference in Appendix A, Section 3 of *The Return of the King* where Dís is the only female named in the account of the dwarves, and the rarity of marriages is noted, as dwarves are more interested in money than romance. Dwarf sex differences become a plot issue for the **City Watch** and Cheery **Littlebottom** from *FOC* onwards. Cheery makes herself some earrings, and it is noted that dwarfs are famous for their (often magical) rings.

The ring central to *The Lord of the Rings* is joked about in *WS* as Nanny Ogg notes the tendency of magic rings to find their way home after being thrown somewhere inaccessible; there is certainly the sense that Bilbo's ring decides when it has had enough of a particular bearer, and moves to a new owner.

Tolkien's largely male world, where sex is almost entirely absent, is reflected in the maleness of the early **Discworld** novels, but this is redressed by the introduction of the Witches from *ER* onwards (although **Twoflower** and **Rincewind** clearly visit some fleshpots on their travels). There is a recurring coyness about sex and sexuality, albeit sometimes Pratchett is clearly playing with that naïveté, which perhaps reflects some anxieties about the mixed age range of his readership. *See also* Cats; Dragons; Dwarfs; Elephants; Elves; Fantasy; Fritz Leiber; Cheery Littlebottom; Maps; Narrative; Parody; William Shakespeare; 'TB'; Trolls *and* Wizards.

Further Reading

Carpenter, Humphrey. 1977. *J.R.R. Tolkien: A Biography.* London: George Allen and Unwin.

———. 1978. *The Inklings: J.R.R. Tolkien, C.S. Lewis, Charles Williams and their Friends.* London: George Allen and Unwin.

Garth, John. 2003. *Tolkien and the Great War: The Threshold of Middle-earth.* London: HarperCollins.

Shippey, T.A. 1982. *The Road to Middle-Earth.* London: George Allen and Unwin.

———. 2000. *Tolkien: Author of the Century.* London: HarperCollins.

Tolkien, J.R.R. 1954. *The Fellowship of the Ring* London: George Allen and Unwin.

———.1937. *The Hobbit, Or There and Back Again.* London: George Allen and Unwin.

———. 1955. *The Return of the King.* London: George Allen and Unwin.

———. 1977. *The Silmarillion.* London Allen and Unwin.

———.1954. *The Two Towers.* London: George Allen and Unwin.

Andrew M. Butler

Tomjon (*WS*)

The rightful heir of the throne of **Lancre**, who was spirited away as a child for his own safety at the time of the deposition of **Verence** I. He is initially brought up by the **witches**, whose inability to get a straight cover story lead to his unlikely name. They give him three gifts; to get on with people, to remember the words and to be who he thinks he is. He is adopted by a travelling troupe of actors, run by Olwyn Vitoller and becomes a great actor in **plays**, especially those written by **Hwel**. On his return to Lancre he is involved with a play which is meant to discredit the witches and make Felmet into a hero, but the plan simply succeeds in outing Felmet's villainy. Tomjon has the option to succeed to the throne, but defers to his half brother – who has been the court **Fool**. It seems as if they share a mother, Verence I being not the only unfaithful one in the marriage. *See also* The Fool; Heroes; Hwel; Lancre; Narrative; Plays; Verence I *and* Witches.

Andrew M. Butler

A Tourist Guide To Lancre (1998)

Subtitled *A Discworld Mapp Including a Pyctorial Guide to the Lancre Fells and a description of a picturefque and charming walk in thys charming and hospitable country.* It was originally published by Corgi in an edition of 75,000 and has been translated into Czech.

It was devised by Terry Pratchett and Stephen **Briggs**, with a view of **Lancre** painted by Paul **Kidby**. The third **Discworld** map, this time depicting Lancre, an area in the Ramtops which is notable for its **Witches**. As usual the pattern is an illustrated booklet relating to the area in question, and the map itself. This time there is no explanation as to the process of mapping, but then unlike **Ankh-Morpork** and the **Discworld** there was less evidence to reconcile.

Much of the booklet is given over to an account of and by Eric Wheelbrace, an inveterate hiker now presumed dead thanks to trying to walk across the dancers, a stone circle wrapped in local superstition. Wheelbrace's 'Lancre: Gateway to the Ramtops' is an account of the kingdom and its population. The extract from 'A Pictorial Guide to the Lancre Fells' by Wheelbrace gives advice for walkers, on planning a route and one walk, from Lancre Town to the Dancers, complete with line drawings, the Briggs. The inspiration for this is the fell walker Alfred Wainwright (1907–1991), who published a series of guides to the Lake District, the Pennine Way and a coast to coast walk from Robin Hood's Bay in Yorkshire to St Bees, Cumbria. As well as describing the routes and the terrain, he illustrated them with his own sketches.

It also contains 'An additional Vue of Lankre' by Nanny **Ogg** which offers further description of Lancre and its witches, and reads as if it were dictated to a scribe – as no doubt it was, for the sum of a dollar. This is supplemented with her account of Lancre folk lore, such as the Lancre Oozer, A Mummers Play and the Witch Trials.

The booklet concludes with the key to the map – the wider area of Lancre, and the enlarged views of Lancre Town and Lancre Castle. The map depicts Lancre as a vertiginous land, built of towers of chalk cliffs, and appears to be numbered almost at random in tune with the key. In the four corners of the map there is the coat of arms of **Verence II**, pictures of

Nanny Ogg, Granny **Weatherwax**, the Queen of the Elves and a horned figure, Herne the Hunted (*WS*, *LL*). *See also* Stephen Briggs; Discworld; Magrat Garlick; Paul Kidby; Lancre; Maps; Nanny Ogg; Verence; Granny Weatherwax *and* Witches.

Andrew M. Butler

'Troll Bridge' (*OM*WF*)

A short story, possibly set on the **Discworld**, first published in *After the King*, edited by Martin H. Greenberg (New York: Tor, 1992; Pp. 46–56). Its title is a pun on toll bridges, and in the Discworld, **trolls** sometimes make a living by charging a fee for crossing a bridge; among Norwegian **Fairy Tales** there is the story of the Three Billy Goats Gruff. *After the King* was an anthology in honour of J.R.R. **Tolkien**, with contributions from **Fantasy** writers Charles de Lint (b.1951), Stephen R. Donaldson (b.1947) and Jane Yolen (b.1939), who also wrote the introduction (and see '**Once and Future**'). The story has been filmed by Snowgum Films – *see* ***Troll Bridge*** **(Film Adaptation)**.

Pratchett picks up on the sense of the world changing and developing at the end of *The Lord of the Rings* (1954–1955), and how perhaps it no longer has room for heroes – a similar impulse is partly explored in '**Final Reward**' in the character of Erdan. Here the elderly **Cohen the Barbarian** sets out in order to kill a troll, to fulfil a life-long ambition. He meets Mica the troll, and the two get to talking about the old days, when every bridge had its own troll, and woods were full of giant spiders rather than logging operations. Civilisation makes a land unfit for heroes.

The presence of Cohen suggests that this is a Discworld story, and a line that Cohen has spent all his booty because he did not expect to live into his old age would explain why he so often appears as penniless. However Mica's thoughts are suppressed by the cold when usually the opposite is true – unless the point here is that for this troll it needed to be even colder. *See also* Fairy Tales; Fantasy; 'Final Reward'; Heroes; 'Once and Future'; J.R.R. Tolkien; *Troll Bridge* (Film Adaptation) *and* Trolls.

Andrew M. Butler

Troll Bridge (Film Adaptation)

Director and Producer: Daniel Knight. Writer: Daniel Knight and Terry Pratchett. Cinematography: Nick Hallam. Sepsis Leech: John Jenkins, Young Cohen: Ange Galati, Cohen the Barbarian: Bob Wood, Mica: Daniel Knight. 20 minutes.

A live action version of the short story (see **'Troll Bridge'**) filmed over a five day period in October 2004 – and one day in late 2006 – by Snowgum Films, based in Melbourne, Australia. The rights were acquired in May 2003, and since production the project has been in post-production, including a delay to avoid competing with the television adaptation of **Hogfather**. It begins with an invented scene not in the story, Young Cohen rescuing a virgin sacrifice, to add action to the film.

Still from *Run Rincewind, Run* by Snowgum Films.

Daniel Knight had appeared on stage in *M* and directed *WS* and his adaptation of *S*, the latter of which he had also adapted. Knight filmed *Ordinary Americans* (2005) – to be screened during stage productions of Ben Elton's *Popcorn – The Morning After* (2006) and *Undead Ted* (2007). Other films are in post-production. His *Run Rincewind Run* was used at the opening of Nullas Anxietas, the 2007 Australian Discworld **Convention**. (Director, Producer and Writer: Daniel Knight. Cast: Rincewind: Troy Larkin. Terry Pratchett: Terry Pratchett.) *See also* Cohen the Barbarian; Conventions; *Hogfather* (Television Adaptation); Plays; Rincewind *and* 'TB'.

Further Reading

Snowgum Films homepage: http://www.snowgumfilms.com/

Andrew M. Butler

Trolls

One of the major species of the **Discworld**. They are sentient rock (metamorphorical rock), in humanoid form, generally hailing from the Ramtop mountains or **Überwald**. Their silicon brains work much more efficiently in cooler weather, and a troll in the midday sun may be confused for a piece of rock, possibly with rich mineral deposits. This may be the source of their ancient dispute with the **Dwarfs**, although this is crystallised over the Battle of Koom Valley (*T!*, *see* **War**). Trolls are tough and pretty well indestructible.

Trolls are named after kinds of stone and mineral, and notable ones include **Detritus** of the **City Watch**, the gangster Chrysoprase (*LF*, *WS*, *MAA* and *SM*) who owns the Cavern Club and musician Lias Bluestone (*SM*). Thethis, a sea-troll (*COM*), Mr Chert, owner of a sawmill (*WA*, *see* **'TB'**) actors and later City Watch members Flint and Morraine (*MP* and *MAA*), the actress Ruby (*MP*), Bauxite, Bluejohn and Zorgo, a Retro-phrenologist (*MAA*), Igneous the Potter (*FOC*), the boxing troll Rocky (*TT*) and the drug addict Brick (*T!*). Troll gods include Chondrodite, the god of love, Gigalith, who makes trolls wiser and Silicarous who brings good fortune (*MP*). Monolith appears to be a folk hero, but is worshipped like a god (*MAA*, *FOC*).

In the **Fairy Tale** of the Three Billy Goats Gruff, a troll is used as the guardian of a bridge. This inspired 'TB', in which **Cohen the Barbarian** and Mica the troll reminisce about the old days and how things have changed. (Note that Mica's brain appears to work differently form other trolls.) From guarding bridges, it is not far to using them as doormen, bouncers and (literally) heavies. *See also* Cohen the Barbarian; Detritus; Dwarfs; Fairy Tales; 'Thud! – A Historical Perspective'; 'TB'; Überwald *and* War.

Andrew M. Butler

The Trousers of Time

Pratchett's unique contribution to the possible-world theory (analogous to the many-worlds theory within quantum physics) is the Trousers of Time. This visual aid (rendered artistically in *SODIII*) expresses the belief that in critical moments in **history** time can split. Pratchett's characters are frequently aware of the existence of the other worlds, and in one or two cases that they are in the wrong leg of the pair of trousers. We first see a hint of the Trousers of Time in *M*, where the titular character tries to change history, only to see it spring back like a rubber band, but it is *J*, *LL* and *NW* which make best use of the idea.

In *LL*, **elves** invade **Lancre**. Granny **Weatherwax**'s ability to see them off is hampered by intruding visions of other Granny Weatherwaxes. **Witches** are used to knowing that they will know when they are due to die, but for each 'self' the outcome is different; the result is a strobe effect in her foresight. Meanwhile Archchancellor Mustrum **Ridcully** has been listening to his junior faculty member Ponder **Stibbons**, and spends much of the crisis nostalgic over the girl he left behind, and the Mustrum Ridcully who married an Esme Weatherwax. It is Ponder Stibbons who provides the memorable visualisation.

In *J* Samuel **Vimes** makes the decision to chase 71-hour Ahmed into the deserts of **Klatch**. As he leaves **Ankh-Morpork** he snatches up his personal organiser. In a split second his hand goes into the wrong leg of time, and what he carries with him is the organiser of the other Sam Vimes, the one who chose to stay home and defend the city. For the rest of the novel Sam is haunted by the voice of the organiser, which has previously been instructed to tell him what is going to happen – for the other world. In *NW* Sam slips into the past and accidentally sends Ankh-Morpork down a new leg of the trouser. He spends most of the book trying to 'right' history (partially with the aid of **Lu-Tse**).

Beyond **Discworld**, the Trousers of Time turn up again in *JB*. Johnny **Maxwell** and his friends are taken into the past by the time in Mrs **Tachyon**'s shopping trolley (stored in black plastic bags). Wobbler is stranded when he accidentally encourages a runaway (his grandfather) and the future is changed to one in which burgers are sold by blue and white franchises.

The most extensive discussion of possible worlds is in *SODII* and *SODIII* which posit an infinite number of possible worlds. In the first, elves trap humanity in fear and they fail to leave the world in time to avoid the asteroid. In the second, there are many worlds in only one of which Charles Darwin (1809–1882) wrote *The Origin of the Species*. In all others, he wrote *The Theology of the Species* and humanity died out. *See also* Elves; History; Johnny Maxwell Trilogy; Lu-Tse; Johnny Maxwell; Mustrum Ridcully; *Science of Discworld*; Ponder Stibbons; Mrs Tachyon; Samuel Vimes; Granny Weatherwax *and* Witches.

Farah Mendlesohn

Truckers **(1989)**

The first book in The **Bromeliad**, Nomes or Truckers trilogy. The first edition was 11,300 copies, from Doubleday, with a cover by Josh **Kirby**. The paperback appeared from Corgi in 1990, in a print run of 86,000, with a modification to the cover in 1999 and two new formats appearing in 2004 with covers by David **Wyatt**. The trilogy was collected into one volume as *The Bromeliad* (1998) by Doubleday, in a print run of about 10,000 copies; a Corgi paperback followed in 2007. *T* has been translated into Bulgarian, Czech, Danish, Finnish, French, German, Greek, Hebrew, Hungarian, Icelandic, Italian, Japanese, Polish, Romanian, Russian, Serbian, Slovakian, Slovenian, Spanish and Swedish. Truckers are the drivers of long-distance lorries – like the nomes. The book is dedicated to Pratchett's daughter, Rhianna. It begins with a note on nomes, and is divided into chapters, each preceded by an extract from *The Book of Nome*. It was adapted as *Truckers* by **Cosgrove Hall** in 1992, with an illustrated and abridged tie-in book published by Ladybird (1992) (*see* ***Truckers* (Television Adaptation)**). This has been performed as an amateur and professional play, with Pratchett's programme book article 'The Big Store' revealing his inspiration in a real store he visited as a child (see *OM*WF*). Andy Sawyer, reviewing it in *Vector* 155, wrote: 'Pratchett's humour, relying on the reader seeing the larger pattern the characters miss in favour of misunderstandings and perfectly constructed illogic, is ideally suited for children. Adults too, for that matter' (April 1990).

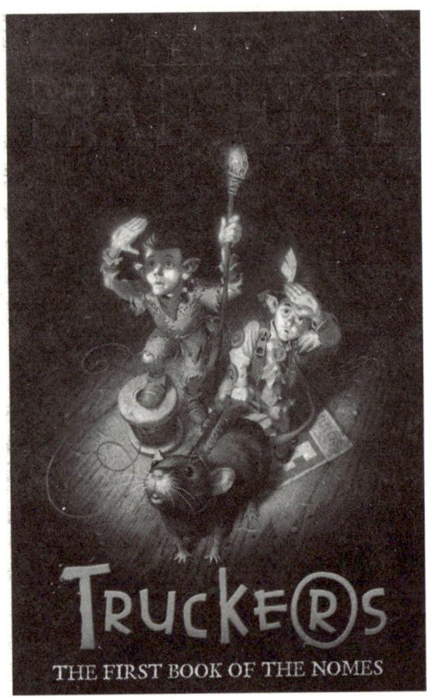

Cover of *Truckers*. Artwork by David Wyatt.

Masklin, **Grimma** and Granny Morkie are among a small group of nomes who discover **Arnold Bros (est. 1905)**, a departmental store in Grimethorpe (*see* **Blackbury**). The nomes that live in the department store do not believe in an outside world, and have set up rigid clans, which are frequently rivals, under the overall charge of The **Abbot**. Masklin carries with him The **Thing**, a metal device which turns out to be a flight computer of some kind, from the spaceship that carried the nomes to Earth. The Thing informs them that the store will be demolished in twenty-one days, but many of the department nomes do not believe this or do not think that there is anywhere that they can go instead. However, the Abbot dies, with his last wish being that the nomes travel to safety, with Gurder as their new Abbot. Angalo de **Haberdasheri** stows away on a truck, and realises they can steal one of these and use it to escape in. As the nomes begin to learn how to drive a lorry, the demolition of the store begins. The nomes escape, and find a quarry that will be a temporary home.

The book is a children's narrative, with some meditation on the nature of power and control. Angalo's father, the Duke, is set in his ways and cannot believe that there is an Outside, so denies its existence. The Abbot is cannier – he cannot be publicly seen to believe in it, but will do so off the record. *See also* The Abbot; Arnold Bros (est. 1905); Blackbury; The Bromeliad; Children's Fiction; Cosgrove Hall; Grimma; Angalo de Haberdasheri; Masklin; The Thing *and Truckers* (Television Adaptation).

Further Reading

Baldry, Cherith. 'The Children's Books'. *GOL, GOL2.*
Hunt, Peter. 2001. 'Terry Pratchett'. Pp. 86–121. In Peter Hunt and Millicent Lenz, *Alternative Worlds in Fantasy Fiction*. London: Continuum.

Andrew M. Butler

Truckers (Television Adaptation) (1991)

Directors: Jackie Cockle, Chris Taylor and Francis Vose. Producers: Brian Cosgrove and Mark Hall. Executive Producer: John Hambley. Writer: Brian Trueman. Cinematography: Jerry Andrews. Cast: Masklin: Joe McGann; Grimma: Debra Gillet; Granny Morkie/Baroness of Delicacy: Rosalie Williams; Torrit and Count of Hardware: John Jardine; The Thing: Edward Kelsey; Angelo de Haberdasheri: Nigel Carrington; Duke de Haberdasheri: David Scase; Dorcas: Brian Trueman; The Abbot: Michael Hordern; Gurder: Brian Southwood and Vinto Pimmie: Jimmy Hibbert. TV version: 13 × 11 minute episodes broadcast 10 January–3 April 1992. Video version: P.T. Video, 110 minutes (ASIN: B00004CM0K), 1 May 2000. Certificate U.

Still from the Cosgrove Hall television adaptation of *Truckers*, 1991. The attempt to drive the truck.

Truckers (Television Adaptation)

A stop motion animation of the novel *T* with live action filmed inserts, produced by **Cosgrove Hall** Productions Ltd for Thames Television. This was a faithful adaptation of the original book – see that entry for a plot summary – beginning with the voice of The **Thing** as a narrator explaining the background of the story, and beginning the action with the truck escaping from the store, pursued by a police car. The rest of the story is told in flashback, with further nested flashbacks for memories of the Outside nomes and Angalo de **Haberdasheri**'s adventures when he takes a journey on another truck. The story ends with the nomes at the quarry, and **Masklin** thinking that this is only a temporary stop, as the quarry is owned by humans. The Thing suggests that they may have to fly, and shows a picture of Concorde.

The cartoon was made on a low budget, and the camerawork feels very static when compared to later productions by, say, Aardman Animations, especially the Wallace and Gromit cartoons. The faces do change expression and the hands move, and characters ascend on escalators or descend on ropes. It is certainly possible to forget that it is animated and invest in the story. A lot of attention is paid to detail, and there are plenty of found or stolen objects as the props or sets for the narrative.

Some of the actors had been involved in other Cosgrove Hall productions. Edward Kelsey – whose most famous role is of the permanently ill and complaining but seemingly immortal Joe Grundy in the BBC Radio 4 soap *The Archers* – played Colonel K. who gave Danger Mouse his orders in the cartoon of the same name (1981–1992), as well as the rodent's archnemesis Baron Silas Greenback. He also plays a part in their version of *The Wind in the Willows* (1983). It is a curiously flat performance, as the Thing in the book has a drier sense of wit. Jimmy Hibbert had provided vocal work on *The BFG* (1989) and was to go on to work on their two **Discworld** cartoons, as well as writing scripts for episodes of *Danger Mouse* and its spin-off *Count Duckula* (1988–1993).

Brian Trueman gives dual service as writer and voice artist – he had previously done both on episodes of *Jamie and the Magic Torch* (1976–1979), *Cockleshell Bay* (1980–1986) and *Danger Mouse*, where he played Stiletto, the Baron's sidekick. He would go on to write and play Nanny, among other characters, for *Count Duckula*. He seems to be very respectful of the source material, not deviating significantly from it, and distributes the Book of Nome material between the Thing as narrator and the **Abbott** and Gurder.

Joe McGann (b.1958) is one of a number of acting brothers, with Paul (b.1959), Mark (b.1961) and Stephen (b.1963), born in Liverpool, but his accent is toned down for the role of Masklin. At the time he was best known for playing Charlie Burrows in the Central Television/ITV situation comedy, *The Upper Hand* (1990–1995). Sir Michael Hordern (1911–1995) was a respected actor of stage and screen, and seems perfectly cast as the Abbot, as he tended to play befuddled and confused characters, often not quite at one with their surroundings. He had already done voice work in the cartoon adaptations of *Paddington* (1975–1984), where he narrated and did the other voices, and played Frith in *Watership Down* (1978). He played Gandalf in the 1979 BBC *Jackanory* adaptation of *The Hobbit* (1937) by J.R.R. **Tolkien**, and reprised the role in the 1981 BBC Radio 4 adaptation of *The Lord of the Rings* (1954–1955).

Besides knowing quotations perhaps aimed at keeping the adult audience's interest, there is an in-joke referring to Cosgrove Hall productions. As the nomes search the **Arnold Bros (est. 1905)** store for a bottle labelled 'drink me' as seen in *Alice's Adventures in Wonderland* (1865) by Lewis Carroll (1832–1898): one of the nomes retunes the close circuit televisions and briefly sees an extract of first *Danger Mouse* and then *The Wind in the Willows* on the screen.

Whilst the exterior of the Arnold Bros store is clearly a model, complete with model trucks, many of the shots involving humans and the outside are filmed on location. The store is Lewis's, in Manchester, and both sequences of humans walking, and blown up photographs of the location are used to place the nomes in a human world. The human policeman, trucker and security guards are all played by uncredited actors, with the footage slowed down to simulate the difference in life speeds of the humans and the nome. A real interior of a truck seems to be used when a human is driving.

Pratchett was pleased with the adaptation, and Cosgrove Hall got as far as story-boarding the sequels, *D* and *W*, before Thames's loss of their ITV regional broadcasting franchise during 1992 pulled the rug from under the process. There was no one at ITV to champion the programme, and it was therefore stuck in development hell despite the relaunch of Cosgrove Hall. Corgi released a picture book to tie in with the series and Ladybird produced a limited vocabulary storybook. The rights to the trilogy now seem to belong with DreamWorks SKG, with the possibility that Andrew Adamson (b.1966) and Joe Stilman, creators of *Shrek* (2001), might film it. *See also* The Abbot; Arnold Bros (est. 1905); Blackbury; The Bromeliad; Children's Fiction; Cosgrove Hall; Grimma; Angalo de Haberdasheri; Masklin; *Soul Music From Terry Pratchett's Discworld*; Television Adaptations; The Thing *and Wyrd Sisters From Terry Pratchett's Discworld.*

Further Reading

Terry Pratchett's Truckers. Loughborough: Ladybird, 1992.

Andrew M. Butler

The Truth (2000)

The twenty-fifth **Discworld** novel, not part of any series but featuring the **City Watch** seen from the outside. The first edition, from Doubleday with a cover by Josh **Kirby**, was published in 2000, the Corgi paperback in 2001.

It has been translated into Bulgarian, Czech, Dutch, French, German, Polish and Russian. The title is a reference to Jesus speaking to Jews in John 8, 32: 'And ye shall know the truth, and the truth shall make you free', the last part of which forms the frequently misspelt motto of *The Ankh-Morpork Times*. The famous Soviet newspaper, *Pravda*, translates as *The Truth*. The novel has an epigraph comparing the sewers of **Ankh-Morpork** to those of Seattle. Peter Ingham wrote: 'though Discworld novels do not carry anything so crass as a message, they often have a point ... This novel asks questions about the tricky nature of truth, a slippery beast at the best of times but especially so in journalism. As the masthead of William's paper has it: "The truth shall make ye fret"' (*The Times* (4 November 2000)).

Cover of *The Truth*. Artwork by Josh Kirby.

William de **Worde**, estranged son of Lord de Worde, writes a monthly newsletter to various wealthy patrons (including **Verence II**) about interesting things in Ankh-Morpork. Dwarfs Gunilla **Goodmountain** and Caslong have developed the first movable type printing press in Ankh-Morpork and de Worde immediately sees that this could lead to a more frequent newsletter. He sets this up with Sacharissa Cripslock as a reporter and the vampire Otto **Chriek** as iconographer, but meets opposition from the monopolist Guild of Engravers and the trouble fearing Samuel **Vimes**. There is soon a big story for him to report: gangsters

Mr Pin and Mr Tulip have been engaged to remove **Vetinari**. Their plan is to replace him with a double, but the Patrician's **dog** Wuffles attacks them and they improvise by stabbing a clerk and pinning the crime on their Döppelgänger before kidnapping the Patrician. De Worde wonders where the dog has gone, and is led to him by Gaspode, acting as Deep Throat. Pin and Tulip pay the newspaper a visit and the offices burn down, killing Tulip. The conspiracy is revealed, and William discovers his father is behind the plot.

Newspapers and journalism are obviously behind the parody here – Pratchett was a journalist prior to becoming a novelist and no doubt draws on his own experiences here. The team of Bob Woodward (b.1943) and Carl Bernstein (b.1944), who with the aid of their informer Deep Throat unravelled the Richard Nixon backed burglary of the Watergate building, is another source, and Water Gate is a street mentioned in the novel. William de Worde's name is a juxtaposition of William Caxton (c.1420-c.1492) and Wynkyn de Worde (d.1534) and Goodmountain is an Anglicisation of Johannes Gutenberg (1398–1468), the inventor of movable type printing in Europe. Caslong is a respelling of Caslon, a font. Mr Pin and Mr Tulip seem to have modelled their dialogue on *Pulp Fiction* (1994). *See also* Ankh-Morpork; Otto Chriek; City Watch; Dogs; Gunilla Goodmountain; Technology; Verence; Patrician Vetinari; Samuel Vimes *and* William de Worde.

Andrew M. Butler

Trymon, Ymper (*LF*)

Briefly **Archchancellor** of the **Unseen University**, and the 305th holder of the role.

Under the rule of Galder Weatherwax (a distant cousin of Granny **Weatherwax**) he rises to second in command of one of the orders of **wizards**, and very much keeps his eye on his chance of succession to the leadership. Weatherwax has probably got to his position by the death of his predecessor, so he is on his guard for much of the time, but he is finally killed during the completion of a summoning spell which conjures up **Twoflower**'s luggage. Trymon determines that he wants the power of the eight great spells for himself, seven of which are contained in the spell book Octavo and one of which is in **Rincewind**'s head. Even the seven are too much for him, and he is possessed by beings from the **Dungeon Dimensions**.

It should be made clear that Trymon is not evil, he is merely bureaucratic and ambitious, a stickler for administration, and driven by ruthless logic. He has no sense of imagination, let alone of style. The character is absent from the middle section of the book, returning briefly in a climactic battle with Rincewind. *See also* Archchancellors; Dungeon Dimensions; the Luggage; Rincewind; Twoflower; Unseen University; Granny Weatherwax *and* Wizards.

Andrew M. Butler

Tsort (*P*, *E*)

Tsort is the **Discworld**'s answer to Troy (*see* **Greek Mythology**). Apparently, however, in Pratchett's world, there was no definitive ending to the Trojan War, for the Tsorteans in *P* make war on the certainly fifth century Athenians of **Ephebe**. Instead, the two city-states, separated only by **Djelibeybi**, have been hereditary enemies since the Tsortean Wars. Nor have they learned anything much over the centuries; their tactics are the traditional ones they have learned from epic: multiple Trojan horses (one on rockers, for the officers) are *de rigeur* for warfare between these two states. In addition, they are foolishly fond of one of the worst military ideas of the ancient world: the battle elephant that Hannibal (247–183 BCE) took over the Alps. This exploitation of the comic potential of **elephants** is in the tradition of Will Cuppy's portrait of Hannibal in *The Decline and Fall of Practically Everybody* (1950). Tsortean and Ephebean elephants, however, seem to be used only to cart the wood necessary to built Trojan horses in the desert.

The Iliad and *The Odyssey* tell the stories of the war at Troy (present-day Turkey) and the events surrounding it. Composed by illiterate bards, these epics took shape over centuries, and were orally transmitted by professional performers and composers. These Homeridai (children of Homer), or rhapsodes, learned the roughly sixteen thousand lines of *The Iliad* and some twelve thousand lines of *The Odyssey* by heart.

Orally transmitted stories, however, are only as good as the bards who perform them. No poet of Homeric stature has hewn the story of Tsort into shape. Copolymer's account of the Tsortean Wars is ludicrously full of gaps, memory slips, and pointless repetitions. Nevertheless, his listeners, Xeno and Ibid weep with pleasure to hear the tale. **Teppic** has more sense.

This is a pointed dig at Athenians' reverence for and love of Homeric epic. By the fifth century in Athens, rhapsodes performed at the yearly Panatheneia festival. So popular were these epics that seven different cities claimed to be the birthplace of Homer. *The Iliad* and *The Odyssey* were the core of an Athenian child's education, and many major texts of the fifth century are studded with quotations from these epics. *See also* Djelibeybi; Elephants; Ephebe; Greek Mythology; Greek Philosophy *and* Teppic.

Further Reading
Schein, Seth L. 1985. *The Mortal Hero: An Introduction to Homer's Iliad*. Berkeley, Ca.: University of California Press.
Stubbings, Frank H. and Alan J. Wace. 1963. *Companion to Homer*. London:Macmillan.

Amy Vail

Tugelbend, Victor (*MP*)

Formally a perpetual student, although also incredibly lazy. He has a thin moustache, and does not particularly mind what he does, as long as it is romantic. He did not particularly want to be a **wizard**, but the hours were good, there was a certain amount of prestige with even being a student wizard, and it left plenty of time for drinking alcohol (*see* **Drink**). His uncle had left him a legacy that meant he would be funded indefinitely as long as he did not pass, but at the same time he needed to score above 80%. However, he is called away by Holy Wood, **Discworld**'s version of Hollywood, and with the assistance of Gaspode the Wonder **Dog**, he breaks into moving pictures. His audition recalls the apocryphal story about Fred Astaire (1899–1987) being commented on by RKO Pictures: 'Can't sing. Can't act. Balding. Can dance a little', but later he is cast in the Clark Gable (1901–1960) role in *Blown Away*. His wizard training recalls that of Richard Grimsdyke in *Doctor in the House* (1952) by Richard Gordon (b.1921), who was also funded through his education and therefore tried to prolong the process for as long as he could. *See also* Dogs; Drink; Unseen University *and* Wizards.

Andrew M. Butler

'Turntables of the Night' (*OM* WF*)

This story was written for a Young Adult anthology of original fiction, *Hidden Turnings*, edited by Diana Wynne Jones (London: Methuen, 1989; Pp. 169–180). Jones (b.1934) is more usually a writer of **Fantasy** for children and young adults.

An unnamed narrator is telling a police officer about the disappearance of his friend Wayne. Wayne is an obsessive collector of music, having filled several rooms of his home with records. He and Wayne have got together to run a business providing discos, and at the last one of these a stranger had arrived, asking for Wayne. He is seven foot tall, skeletally thin and wears a skull mask. Wayne has a long conversation with the visitor about collecting musicians, including composers of the seventeenth, eighteenth and nineteenth centuries. The power amp explodes, presumably killing Wayne, although not a trace of his body has been found.

Reading between the lines, the visitor is clearly **Death**, later to be associated with music in *SM*, and of course all the musicians that he names are indeed dead. Death here wears a black silk suit with rhinestones and flares, as well as a big silver medallion, a nod towards Elvis Presley (1935–1977). *See also* Children's Fiction; Death; Fantasy *and* Pop Music.

Andrew M. Butler

Twoflower (*COM*, *LF*, *IT*)

The **Discworld**'s first tourist, who arrives in **Ankh-Morpork** with The **Luggage**, a large amount of money and an invisible mug me sign on his back. Curiously, however, he is the sort of wise fool that survives everything the city and all the main continent of Discworld has to throw at him, which is typical of **Comedy** narratives.

In **Bes Pelargic** in the **Agatean Empire** on the **Counterweight Continent** he works in insurance, and his home country is so wealthy with gold, that his domestically average savings look like a vast sum of money in the rest of the world. The Patrician, presumably but not definitely **Vetinari**, needs to ensure that he survives his visit to the city for reasons of international **politics**. Meanwhile, by a stroke of luck for the Patrician, **Rincewind** has nobly stepped into the breach as native guide to keep him out of trouble, in return for a few gold coins. This is only moderately successful, as Twoflower's explanation of insurance (say that the gamble that a particular building won't burn down within the next year) leads to an arson attack on The **Broken Drum** (later The **Mended Drum**) which takes a fair amount of the city with it. The two of them travel between dimensions and across the planet, and finally to Krull, which is located right on the edge of the Discworld. Whereas it is largely bad luck (and **narrative** convenience) which sees Rincewind falling off the edge of the world, it is the stubborn enthusiasm and naïveté of Twoflower which leads to him sailing in a submarine-like device, the chelysphere (*see* **Technology**), into space to try and ascertain the sex of the Great **A'Tuin**.

The two are reunited in *LF*, where the **wizards** of the **Unseen University** want Rincewind back for the spell lodged in his head, and the two of them begin heading back to Ankh-Morpork, unaware of the encounter with Ymper **Trymon** that awaits the inept wizard. Along the way they encounter **Cohen the Barbarian**. At the end of the novel, Twoflower decides it is time to go home, and bequeaths the Luggage to Rincewind, although the latter is not sure that this is really an act of generosity.

It is not until Rincewind ends up in the Agatean Empire that the two are reunited. Twoflower has written and published *What I Did On My Holidays*, which sparked a revolution. Twoflower's wife has been killed, Twoflower has been thrown into prison and their daughters, Pretty Butterfly and Lotus Blossom, help lead the Red Army. At the end of *IT*, Cohen makes Twoflower the Grand Vizier of the Empire.

With his iconography box and endless enthusiasm, Twoflower is the stereotypical image of the Japanese tourist with cameras clicking all the time. He has glasses, long shorts, a loud shirt and an unending grin. His structural role is to be the stranger in the strange land, the visitor to utopia, who can have the ways of the world explained to him for the sake of the readers. *See also* Agatean Empire; Ankh-Morpork; Great A'Tuin; Bes Pelargic; The Broken Drum; China; Cohen the Barbarian; Comedy and Humour; Counterweight Continent; The Luggage; Narrative; Politics; Rincewind; Technology *and* Ymper Trymon.

Andrew M. Butler

U

Überwald (*CJ*, *FE*, *AMHER*)

Überwald is a region in the **Discworld** near the Ramtop Mountains, whose name is an alternate version of Transylvania or 'Beyond the Forest'. If **Lancre** is an area with elements of the **Fairy Tale**, then this zone is associated with horror – Transylvania was an area of Romania where eastern Europe met the expanded Asian world and thanks to *Dracula* (1897) by Bram Stoker became associated with **vampires** in the popular imagination, an association further cemented by **Hollywood Films** such as the Universal horror cycles and the films made by Hammer.

Überwald (sometimes Uberwald) has been ruled over by both vampires and werewolves. Although **Dwarfs** are increasingly dominant, they are locked in rivalry with the **Trolls**. Its wealth derives from the mining of the fatty deposits left by the fifth **elephant** which crashed into the Discworld (*FE*). In *CJ*, the Magpyr family of vampires journey to Lancre at the invitation of King **Verence** II, and it is only with some difficulty that a full-scale invasion is averted. Some vampires are trying to move with more modern attitudes, forming a temperance society (the Black Ribboners – see **Diaries**) and Otto **Chriek** is one such immigrant into **Ankh-Morpork**

(*FOC*). Angua Delphine von **Überwald** is another incomer, but a werewolf, who has joined the **City Watch** and become a useful citizen of the city. She returns there briefly in *FE*, having gone missing. Another member of the Watch, Cheery **Littlebottom**, hails from Überwald, and is the member of a more traditional clan of **dwarfs** than Carrot **Ironfoundersson** came from. The various **Igors** also hail from this region.

In *AMHER*, the **narrative** is set in Bad Blintz, where Maurice, his orphan, Keith, and a number of rats attempt to pull their 'The Pied Piper of Hamelin' (1849) style heist. However, they realise that there is a much deeper corruption to the town than this. Keith settles down in the town, helping to make it a tourist attraction – there presumably now being tourists other than just **Twoflower**. *See also* Otto Chriek; Diaries; Dwarfs; Elephants; Hollywood Films; Igors Cheery Littlebottom; Trolls; Angua von Überwald *and* Vampires.

Andrew M. Butler

Überwald, Angua Delphine von (*MAA*, *FOC*, *J*, *FE*, *TT*, *NW*, *MR*, *T!*)

Angua is the daughter of Baron Guye and Serafine Soxe-Bloonberg von Überwald, the oldest and most prestigious of **werewolf** families in **Überwald**. She left Überwald due to the actions of her brother Wolfgang, who likes to run roughshod over those he feels are beneath him, including their siblings Elsa and Andrei, who are yennorks (i.e. non-changing werewolves).

After leaving Überwald, Angua moved to **Ankh-Morpork** and joined the **City Watch**, where she has risen to the rank of sergeant. Her werewolf abilities give her a heightened sense of smell and tremendous fighting abilities, which aid her in her job as a member of the Watch. Despite these benefits, Angua would prefer the life of a regular human. Both humans and wolves hold a hatred for werewolves, and although Angua can control her transformations (except during 'that time of the month': i.e. full-moon), she cannot truly fit in with either society.

Very soon after joining the Watch, Angua and Captain Carrot **Ironfoundersson** fall in love. This causes a great deal of consternation for Angua, who believes that she will have to leave him some day because humans and werewolves cannot co-exist. Carrot does not agree with this sentiment, and for now, she accepts his decision. *See also* Ankh-Morpork; City Watch; Carrot Ironfoundersson; Racism; Überwald; Vampires *and* Werewolves.

Further Reading

James, Edward. 'The City Watch'. *GOL*, *GOL2*.

Mark D. Thomas

The Unadulterated Cat: A Campaign For Real Cats (1989)

Illustrated by Gray **Jolliffe**, this is a humorous 'non-fiction' volume which discusses the true nature of **cats**, how they behave and how human beings interact with them, complete with cartoons complementing the text. It was originally published in a large paperback format by Gollancz in an edition of 50,250. A standard paperback followed in 1992, running to 42,750 copies. In 1995 Gollancz printed a version with a new cover – releasing 10,000 copies. Gollancz released it under their Vista imprint in 1996, with another 5,000 copies. In 1999 a version was put out by Orion – an imprint connected to the same company that owned Gollancz – and a hardback finally appeared in 2002, with some additional illustrations. The book has been translated into Czech, Dutch, Finnish, French, German, Hungarian, Italian Korean, Polish, Russian, Serbian, and Swedish, and follows in the tradition of such cartoon books as Simon Bond's *One Hundred and One Uses of a Dead Cat* (1981) and Charles Platt's *How to Be a Happy Cat* (1987), the latter also illustrated by Jolliffe. These often serve as stocking fillers, especially for cat lovers, at Christmas.

As Pratchett has given us the malevolent, violent and scarred **Greebo** and Guilty, Mrs **Tachyon**'s cat, it should be no surprise that he dismisses the sleek, groomed and well-behaved pedigree cat which would win best of show. The real cat is a hunter-killer, prefers to eat food off the kitchen floor rather than a personalised food bowl, has a mysterious or unknown parentage and has the ability to hear fridge doors being opened from two rooms away. Pratchett explains that he first got a cat in order to dissuade other cats from trespassing on his land; this of course is nonsense, as many people acquire additional cats that simply turn up and eat from the bowl and never get around to leaving.

Pratchett outlines the various types of cats – farm cats, black cats with white paws, neighbour's cats, boot-faced cats, factory cats and so forth – gives advice on feeding and disciplining them, describes historical cats and discusses sex and hygiene. Perhaps the most useful piece of advice – although plainly if something practical is wanted, this is the wrong book – is that any name given to a cat has to be something that can be yelled out the backdoor without causing too much embarrassment. He also explains the Schrödinger's Cat thought experiment, which is used in quantum mechanics. A cat is placed in a box with a poison phial, rigged up so it has an even chance of breaking if a radioactive atom, also in the box, decays. The cat is said to be both dead and alive until the box is opened to observe the result – although the amount of protesting that the cat does might be a give away. Pratchett goes on to point out that most cats are quite capable of getting out of (or into) boxes, locked houses, garages and sheds, seemingly passing through the wall. The experiment is also referenced in *LL*, where the states are living, dead and absolutely livid and *LH*, where Alberto **Malich** explains it to **Death** (*see also* **The Trousers of Time** *and*

'**DWCN**'). *See also* Cats; Death; Greebo; Gray Jolliffe; Mrs Tachyon *and* The Trousers of Time.

Andrew M. Butler

Unseen University (*COM*, *LF*, *ER*, *S*, *GG*, *E*, *MP*, *RM*, *LL*, *MAA*, *SM*, *IT*, *H*, *J*, *LC*, *TT*, *AMHER*, *LH*, *SOD*, *SODII*, *SODIII* and 'CCOODD')

The major centre of tertiary education on the **Discworld**, and featured in all of the novels which include the **Wizards**. Pratchett did not attend university, preferring to go into journalism during his A Levels, and so his knowledge of the institution is mediated through fictional, televisual and filmic representations of dons, fellows, bursars, librarians and support staff.

Model of the Unseen University Organ created by Discworld Merchandising.

The first few Discworld novels did not maintain continuity as strongly as later volumes, so in *COM* and *LF* there are other faculties beyond those devoted to magic – Astropsychology, Astrozoology, Cosmochelonian Studies, a Faculty of Medicine and so on – with no mention of these until *LC*. In *COM* there is a fifth level female wizard, Marchesa, in Krull, when much is made of Eskaranda Smith's femaleness in *ER*; indeed Esk vanishes from the canon in future books. According to the DC, Marchesa was educated at a magical college in Krull, which might be a co-educational establishment, unlike the strictly male Unseen University that likely looks down upon a junior institution. There was also a changing cast between the early novels – **Archchancellors** had a low life expectancy until the appointment of Mustrum Ridcully in *MP*. Equally it seems to have been the same bursar in different novels, although jobs title of some characters are not consistent.

The University was established roughly 2000 years before *COM*, by Alberto **Malich** in *c*.AM1282 and is situated on Sator Square, not far from the palace of the Patrician **Vetinari**. Much of the wealth of the University derives from rents from building in the area, and the hiring out of some of the University rooms for outside events – Samuel **Vimes** held his wedding there. The University does not tend to be taxed – as refusal often offends – and they have an uneasy relationship with the Guilds which represent one of the other power bases in the city, along with the aristocracy and the Patrician himself. The wizards tend to acquiesce to his requests because it would be impolite not to.

The precise dimensions of the University are impossible to ascertain, but it is certainly bigger on the inside. It includes one of the largest **Libraries** in history, which exists largely in **L-Space** thanks to the amount of magic contained in its shelved volumes. One recent building is the High Energy Magic Building, the domain of Ponder **Stibbons** and home of HEX, one of the few computers on Discworld. This is where experimental magic is carried out. A central feature of the University is the Tower of Art, some 800 feet tall with 8,888 steps to its summit in a spiral. The residual magic in this largely disused feature has led to some odd kinks in the local evolution of fauna, equally the waste left around the back of the University has boosted the intelligence of Gaspode (*see* **Dogs**), and Maurice (*see* **Cats**) and his educated rodents. The University has been destroyed at least once, most notably during *S*, but it was recreated from scratch – and as this was too disturbing it was immediately recreated again as the scruffier place people were acquainted with.

Students are rare, mostly seen hanging out in the High Energy Magic Building. Victor **Tugelband** was a perpetual student until the events of *MP*; since he would be funded as long as he studied, he figured he would study as long as possible. There are occasional classes, in the virtual room 3b, and lectures, in the transdimensional 5b, and there are examinations. Most of the time, the students are free to study whatever their interests take them, or to **drink** copious amounts of alcohol. On graduation, students are free to leave, although few seem to do, with Igneous **Cutwell** (*M*) being a notable exception. **Rincewind**, on the other hand, is free to leave whilst having failed to graduate.

Most wizards seem to hang around at University, occasionally teaching the next generation of wizards, but mostly eating good meals and enjoying indoor plumbing. They are occasionally troubled by the dead man's shoes principle of promotion, and do have to watch their backs as a result, and there is a sign that the Patrician is beginning to take a look at what they actually do (*see* **'CCOODD'**), to which they have responded to with aggressive apathy by putting it on the agenda to discuss setting up a subcommittee over.

Below stairs is run by Mrs **Whitlow**, one of the few visible females in the organisation, and an object of fascination for a number of the wizards. (There are likely other females there, but the help tends to be invisible.) The garden is looked after Modo, a **dwarf**. The college porters or Bledlows form a sort of police force, and indeed include former members of the **City Watch** among their number. They are led by McArbre.

It might be worth noting that Bledlows is a village in Buckinghamshire, to the north of where Pratchett grew up. The inspiration for the Unseen University itself is likely to include *Lucky Jim* (1954) by Kingsley Amis (1922–1995), with its incompetent and reluctant central character surrounded by pompous fools, various novels by David Lodge (b.1935) including *Changing Places* (1975) where an American and British academic switch places and the American finds himself in a hotbed of amateurism, *The History Man* (1975) by Malcolm Bradbury (1932–2000), with its reference to not trusting anyone over thirty-five (sixty-five in *LC*) and *Decline and Fall* (1928) by Evelyn Waugh (1903–1966) for student high jinks. The schoolmasters of **Gormenghast** also seem to be a precursor.

Pratchett also draws on the Invisible College, referenced by Mary Gentle (b.1956) in *Rats & Gargoyles* (1990) and sequels, which is inspired by the story of the loose grouping of seventeenth century scholars, including Robert Boyle (1627–1691), Robert Hooke (1635–1703) and Christopher Wren (1632–1723). Boyle set up the Royal Society in 1660, devoted to science, but also having some roots in esoteric mystical organisations such as the Rosicrucians and the Freemasons. The Invisible College has since come to cover the sharing of knowledge by Independent Scholars outside of the university sector.

The University has tended to be depicted in counterpoint with another narrative – most notably that of Rincewind (for example *LC*) but also to Susan **Sto Helit** and **Death** (*RM* and *H*). More recently it has appeared in tandem with Roundworld in the *SOD* books.

The track 'Unseen University/The Librarian' on *Terry Pratchett's From the Discworld* by Dave **Greenslade** was inspired by the location and the character. *See also* Archchancellors; Coin; Igneous Cutwell; Death; Diaries; Gormenghast; The Librarian; Libraries; L-Space; Magic; Alberto Malich; Pop Music; Rincewind; *The Science of Discworld*; Sexism; Eskarina Smith; Ponder Stibbons; Susan Sto Helit; Victor Tugelbund; *The Unseen University Cut-Out Book*; Patrician Vetinari; Samuel Vimes; Granny Weatherwax; Mrs Whitlow *and* Wizards.

Further Reading

Amis, Kingsley. 1953. *Lucky Jim: A Novel*. London: Gollancz.

Bradbury, Malcolm. 1975. *The History Man*. London: Secker & Warburg.

Gentle, Mary. 1990. *Rats & Gargoyles*. London and New York: Bantam.
Hill, Penelope. 'Unseen University'. *GOL, GOL2.*
Lodge, David. 1975. *Changing Places: A Tale of Two Campuses*. London: Secker and Warburg.
Waugh, Evelyn. 1928. *Decline and Fall: An Illustrated Novelette*. London, Chapman & Hall.

Andrew M. Butler

The Unseen University Challenge (1996) *see* Langford, David and Quizbooks

The Unseen University Cut-Out Book (2006)

Co-produced with Bernard **Pearson** and Alan Batley, who is an illustrator and model-maker living in Norwich. It was published by Doubleday.

Based on Pearson's model of the **Unseen University**, Alan Batley created seven origami and cut-out buildings that recreate it in paper, including the clock tower, the Great Hall, the High Energy Magic Building, the **Library**, Modo's Garden Shed, the Observatory and the Tower of Art. Pratchett contributes a foreword, 'Everything Under One Roof', as does Pearson, 'It's All in the Mind'. It is aimed at modellers from ten upwards. *See also* Libraries; Merchandising; Bernard Pearson *and* Unseen University.

Andrew M. Butler

Cover of *The Unseen University Cut-Out Book* by Terry Pratchett, Alan Batley & Bernard Pearson.

Vampires

Discworld vampires, like **Igors** and werewolves, are all descendants of the Gothic tradition which emerges in literature in the eighteenth century and continues in a variety of narrative and cultural forms to the present day. *CJ* was the first **Discworld** novel to feature vampires as major characters and also displays traits of the vampire story in its narrative. In the novel the Magpyrs, a family of vampires, echo the Gothic archetype popularised by Bram Stoker (1847–1912), the aristocratic, blood-sucking *Dracula* (1897), in his journey from Transylvania to England as they leave their home in **Überwald** to travel to **Lancre**. However, following the tradition that a vampire can only enter your abode if you invite them in, the Magpyrs are only able to invade Lancre because they are invited to the Christening of Magrat **Garlick** and King **Verence II**'s baby. The traditional vampire narrative also includes the possession of a young woman, in *CJ* this is demonstrated by the abduction of Agnes **Nitt**. There is also the frantic race back to the castle for a final showdown, although the showdown in *CJ* is unlike that of any other vampire story, with the lust for blood evolving into a need for a nice cup of tea.

Model of the Vampire's Castle created by Discworld Merchandising.

Much of the humour in *CJ* arises from the ways in which the Magpyr family and their entourage differ from the traditional notion of the vampire. Although the story of the vampire emerges from the traditions of the nineteenth century gothic novel, it is twentieth century cinema that defines how the vampire should appear. In *Nosferatu* (1921), directed by F.W. Murnau (1888–1931), the vampire follows Stoker's description of a tall man dressed all in black, feral and predatory with his long finger nails and pointed teeth. However, the image changes in *Dracula* (1931), directed by Tod Browning (1882–1962), which sees the charismatic Bela Lugosi (1882–1956) dressed in aristocratic evening dress complete with silk lined opera cloak. Acknowledging the accusation in *Grundrisse* (written by 1857) by Karl Marx (1818–1883) that capital had a vampire-like effect on the working classes, the film situates 1930s European aristocrats as parasites living in luxury on the toil and suffering of others. Proving an influential and popular cinematic critique of capitalism, the vampire since Lugosi has been portrayed as a dualistic character with the outward appearance of elegance and sophistication hiding the monster within.

Although Pratchett draws on the popular notion of vampire to create the Magpyrs he adds his customary twist to their characters. So although they sleep in coffins and have the traditional need to feast on the blood of their victims, the Magpyrs reject the full evening dress of their ancestors in favour of elegant little waistcoats. Count Magpyr trains his family to endure small doses of sunlight, holy water and various religious icons in order to build up a tolerance. The entourage includes a group of female vampires reminiscent of the brides of Dracula and the vampires of both sexes are depicted as physically attractive representing the sexuality traditionally associated with vampirism. In an inversion of contemporary gothic fashions the young vampires reject the traditional names and pretending to be an accountant is considered the height of fashion.

Lacrimosa's reluctance to drink wine poses the question of whether the vampires are really evil or simply different. The reinstatement of the old count at the end of the book suggests that the vampires are not inherently evil but that it is their actions and their treatment of others that make them so. This is demonstrated in the Escrow stopover. The Magpyrs treat the people of Escrow as cattle, at the signal of a bell the inhabitants line up in order for the vampires to feed on them and are told they are good citizens for doing so. This scenario may be seen as a reflection of any hegemonic submission, be it to capitalist notions of democracy or to the media espoused notion of the body beautiful. Therefore Pratchett implies that the drinking of blood is nothing compared to making people complicit in the sacrifice of their family and friends.

The Magpyrs are not the only vampires to feature in the Discworld and a variety of solitary vampire characters in other stories represent other character types. In *FOC*, the master of **Ankh-Morpork** heraldry, Dragon King of Arms, is a vampire. He represents all **Vimes**'s prejudices about his species as he is cunning, manipulative, power hungry and murderous. In contrast, *FOC* also shows a suicidal vampire that is repeatedly killed due to his various dangerous (for a vampire) occupations. This character later emerges as the Ankh-Morpork Times's intrepid photographer Otto **Chriek**. Otto is a black ribboner, a member of the Überwald league of temperance, an organisation which forswears blood in the same way that earthly temperance leagues abstain from drinking alcohol. By negating the threatening aspect of the vampire, Pratchett presents Otto as an eccentric outsider, initially tolerated as ridiculous, and by *GP* he is accepted as an individual in the melting pot of Ankh-Morpork.

Lady Margolotta in *FE* is another black ribboner, but unlike Otto she is never portrayed as ridiculous. Her abstinence, like Vimes's, could be broken at any moment. An old friend and lover of **Vetinari**, Lady Margolotta is not a tame vampire. She has simply transcended the thirst for blood into a more pure lust for power, mirroring the variations of vampirism in contemporary vampire novels such as *Lost Souls* (1992) by Poppy Z. Brite (b.1967).

This variety is further expanded when two younger female vampires step out of the traditional formality of evening dress and into the alternative formality of a uniform. Maladict in *MR* enlists in the Ins and Outs and Salacia Deloresista Amanita Trigestatra Zeldana Malifee ... von Humpeding (Sally) in *T!* joins the Ankh-Morpork **City Watch**. Both retain the virtues of vampirism: physical strength, heightened sensory abilities, poise, impeccable dress sense and the ability to transform, without either the thirst for blood of the Magpyrs or Lady Margolotta's lust for power. Using the power of the vampire in the service of the state, they represent a fundamental shift in the power structure of the species; a taming of the monster, a democratisation of the despot, a domestication of the wild.
See also Cats; Otto Chriek; Diaries; Fantasy; Magrat Garlick; Hollywood Films; Igors; Agnes Nitt; Überwald; Verence II, Patrician Vetinari *and* Samuel Vimes.

Further Reading

Brite, Poppy Z. 1992. *Lost Souls*. London: Penguin.
Gelder, Ken. 1994. *Reading the Vampire*. London: Routledge.
Stoker, Bram. 1897. *Dracula*, London.

Eve Smith

Verence I (*WS*)

A king of **Lancre**, who had been known to burn down cottages, but always paid compensation and showed some consideration to his subjects. He was also fond of exercising his *Droit de seigneur* (lord's right), which is coyly unexplained in the novel – a number of characters assuming it is some kind of **dog** – but is the supposed right in some medieval societies for the feudal lord to have sex with a woman on her wedding night, or indeed with any virgin he chooses. It seems likely that Verence has at least one child born out of wedlock – the **Fool**, who bears a physical resemblance to him and **Tomjon**. He was murdered by his brother, Felmet, by being pushed down the stairs and stabbed with his own dagger. Unable to have eternal rest, he will haunt the castle of Lancre – or, thanks to the wisdom of Nanny **Ogg** – any stone from the castle. In particular he whispers in Felmet's ear and puts extra salt in his food, trying to drive him mad. He also manages to kidnap **Greebo** as a means of attracting the attention of the **Witches**. His usurper was in turn succeeded by the Fool as **Verence II**. *See also* Dogs; The Fool; Lancre; Nanny Ogg; William Shakespeare; Tomjon; Verence II *and* Witches.

Andrew M. Butler

Verence II (*WS, LL, CJ*) *see* The Fool, later King Verence II

Vetinari, Patrician Havelock (*COM, M, S, GG, MP, RM, MAA, SM, IT, MSK, FOC, J, FE, TT, LH, NW, GP, T!*, 'CCOODD')

Vetinari is the Patrician (i.e. ruler) of **Ankh-Morpork**. Vetinari is a rail thin man with a piercing stare and tends to dress all in black. During the struggle with Dr Cruces and the Gonne, Vetinari was shot in the leg, and now, in public, walks with a limp and a cane. However, in private, he tends to move about without any problems. He has a steady, calm demeanour, which tends to make other people nervous because they can never tell what he is really thinking or where he might be taking a conversation. He also rarely issues commands, just suggestions, yet they are always followed because nobody wants to consider the consequences.

He works in the Oblong Office at the Patrician's Palace, formerly the Royal Winter Palace. At official functions, Vetinari sits on a plain wooden chair below the Royal Golden Throne, though part of this is because the Golden Throne is no longer Golden (thanks to thieves) and is instead some rotting wood covered in gold foil.

Vetinari is generally disliked by all of the city's leaders because his ability to always know what is going on, and his secretive nature, tends to make everybody else look stupid. However, he manages to maintain his position (where so many before him have failed), because the city is obviously running better now than ever before (it also helps that while everybody dislikes him, he has managed to make them dislike one another even more). Besides, any attempt to remove him from office has seen him come right back to it. Vetinari has survived being turned into a lizard, being removed from office by a dragon, getting shot, being continually poisoned with arsenic (the latter he allowed to continue, despite solving how it was being done, just so that **Vimes** would have something to do), and being framed for assault and embezzlement from the city treasury.

His most recent removal from office involves his unconditional surrender to **Klatch** during the war over Leshp and his subsequent arrest by Commander Vimes and the Watch at the command of Lord Rust, who had taken charge of Ankh-Morpork in Vetinari's absence. Vetinari, however, was one step ahead of everybody else, and tricked Klatch into thinking they were gaining Leshp when he (Vetinari, with the help of Fred **Colon**, Nobby **Nobbs**, and Leonard of **Quirm**) really sunk it to the bottom of the ocean again. However, there was no proof that Vetinari was involved with this plot, and he was released to resume his position as Patrician. Despite all of these attempts on his life and position, Vetinari seems to have come through none the worse for wear and completely unfazed by it all, and because of his skill at avoiding death and deposition, Vetinari is the only person, besides Samuel Vimes, to be taken off the Assassin's Guild's register (i.e. the Assassins refuse to accept any contracts on his life).

As a young man, Vetinari attended the school at the Assassin's Guild, and passed with high marks, especially in attention-to-detail. The only class he failed was stealth, and only because he was so good at it, his teacher thought he had to be using magic, and therefore was cheating. Vetinari uses this skill to this day, tending to show up unannounced leaving everybody worried about how long he might have been there listening in (the answer, of course, is always: long enough).

Although pragmatic, Vetinari can be swayed by emotion, albeit rarely. For example, upon viewing the 'death' of the man he thinks is John Keel (actually Vimes gone back in time), he is moved to join in the battle during the Glorious 25th of May and fight for the future that 'Keel' was hoping to create (Vetinari eventually figures out that the Keel he was fighting for was really Vimes). It is possible that this is what set him on the path to eventually become Patrician.

Vetinari only truly initiates change in Ankh-Morpork when it is absolutely necessary. As an example, initially Vetinari sees the **City Watch** as being necessary to the make-up of the city, but not necessary for being useful. One of Vetinari's first moves as Patrician was to legalise the Thieves' and Seamstresses' Guilds, not necessarily legalising their actions, but making them more organised. Having a functional Watch would only mess this arrangement up. However, with the resurgence of then Captain Vimes, the Watch proves useful is breaking up the coup of the dragon, which had deposed Vetinari. Vetinari then realised how useful the watch could be, and allowed them to grow into a fairly large police force.

Yet, despite all of his tendencies, Vetinari has no real desire to rule. He is moved to what he does out of pride for the city of Ankh-Morpork. He is well aware of (and accepts as truth) Carrot **Ironfoundersson**'s potential claim to the throne of Ankh-Morpork, and seems more than willing to step aside should Carrot ever decide to make that claim. However, for now, he is content with running the city. *See also* Ankh-Morpork; City Watch; Frederick Colon; Dogs; Carrot Ironfoundersson; Nobby Nobbs; Leonard of Quirm; Power and Samuel Vimes.

Further Reading

Brown, James. 'Believing is Seeing'. *GOL2*.
James, Edward. 'The City Watch'. *GOL*, *GOL2*.
Mendlesohn, Farah. 'Faith and Ethics'. *GOL*, *GOL2*.

Mark D. Thomas

Vimes, His Grace, the Duke of Ankh, Commander Sir Samuel (*GG*, 'TOC', *MAA*, *FOC*, *J*, *FE*, *TT*, *NW*, *MR*, *GP*, *T!*, *WMC?*)

Samuel Vimes is the head of the **Ankh-Morpork City Watch**. He was born in extreme poverty on Cockbill Street in the Ankh-Morpork slums, and enlisted in the Watch as a youth. His rise through the ranks was accompanied by increased cynicism and frustration; by mature manhood, he is a wretched, bitter alcoholic (*see* **Drink**). He is Captain of the Watch, but the Night Watch consists of a motley group of three men: stolid career-sergeant, a scoundrel, and a raw recruit. Begotten in the poorest neighbourhood in the city, by adulthood Vimes has only managed to reach the gutter – but after being hauled literally from the gutter to his feet by Fred **Colon**, Nobby **Nobbs**, and Carrot **Ironfoundersson**, Vimes catches a second chance. Through a combination of merit, circumstance, and the Patrician **Vetinari**'s Machiavellian patronage, rises to become His Grace, the Duke of Ankh, Commander Sir Samuel Vimes.

Samuel Vimes lights a cigarette with a convenient dragon. Artwork by Paul Kidby.

Vimes, Sir Samuel

Vimes is the ranking member of the Night Watch from the beginning, and advances as the force expands to include a wide variety of complementary talents; Vimes's own strength is an innate ability to see through preconceived notions, which is better characterised as a refusal to privilege received ideas over what is actually in front of him, regardless of how counterintuitive the facts may seem. He has a sort of immunity to illusion, composed of idealistic stubbornness; his early life almost certainly held no false hopes, so he never assumes anything at all. Vimes does not regard himself as terribly intelligent, but he uses his abilities to their uttermost limits. Where faster thinkers leap readily from a premise to a final conclusion without support in between, Vimes reasons painfully and steadily toward the next conclusion, however small, until he arrives at an answer or runs out of questions, maintaining an unbroken line of empirical thought. Whatever he may lack in speed, he recoups in reliability, and for a police officer it is better to be right slowly than wrong quickly. His simple, step-by-step logic leaves no openings for political machinations by the aristocrats in Ankh-Morpork – his methodology is not vulnerable to other players whose motives are something other than eventually arriving at the truth. Vimes hardly considers himself an intellectual, but he is extremely observant and has an excellent memory; he is able to take in and store information until connections become possible. He is also smart enough to seek out expert help when necessary. When a dragon terrorises Ankh-Morpork, he notices the oddities about it and seeks the advice of the local dragon authority, Lady Sybil **Ramkin**. Vimes does not know a lot about **dragons**, but he takes in the evidence and never assumes that he is qualified to draw a conclusion from incomplete information.

Model of The Old Watch House in Treacle Mine Road created by Discworld Merchandising.

Although he is resistant to the idea of opening the Watch to members of other species, once he accepts the necessity of (or is forced into) doing so, Vimes grudgingly acquires a team of subordinates whose skills and natural abilities he is able to deploy as if they were his own: Angua von **Überwald**, Carrot and **Detritus** each bring more to the table than average human beings would do. All of them are immensely strong and capable fighters, which suffices until the Watch develops depth in later novels. Angua is not only a woman, which aids somewhat with gender relations, but also has common sense and the sensory abilities of her kind (*see* **Feminism**); Carrot is not only a more than capable fighter, he is preternaturally charismatic, and his acculturation as a **dwarf** adds considerable diplomatic talent and tact, something that Vimes himself is particularly in wanting; Detritus is, almost literally, a foundation stone for an organisation that must necessarily rely at times on physical force, and is a way in to the large **troll** population of the city. Until the Watch recovers from falling so low as to be almost nothing, Vimes's subordinates complete him; they are, in effect, one policeman. Vimes comes into his own as a leader through effectively directing others as extensions of himself, and bringing them along the same path. Vimes never stops struggling against injustice. Despite human weaknesses, he is an ethical man. His plain refusal to go outside the rule of law eventually has a marked effect on Ankh-Morpork; the Night Watch become a respectable force, and veterans are tellingly called 'Sammies' due to his influence. In large measure, Vimes's character revolves around his ability to make connections between facts and between people, although he loathes mysteries and could be called a misanthrope.

Vimes hates all things political, but he is from the outset a political figure. He is a former member of the urban underclass, who has been made a member of the nobility, and is aware that the nobles and guild leaders regard him as a commoner. Vimes is descended from Suffer-Not-Injustice Vimes, a Watch Commander who deposed and executed a tyrannical king; for the same unyielding resistance to the aristocrats of Ankh-Morpork, Samuel Vimes has inherited his ancestor's nickname 'Old Stoneface'. Ostensibly as a reward, but in reality to gain a more powerful agent, Lord Vetinari revives the title of Watch Commander, elevating Vimes to the post and to the traditional rank of knight that goes along with it – drawing Vimes deeper into the political workings of Ankh-Morpork and giving him better footing to deal with the city nobles. When Vetinari revives the Vimes family arms and creates Samuel Dux Vimes, his evolution is complete.

Over time, Vimes grows into his Dukedom, becoming more sophisticated and successful in each book. At first, Lady Ramkin, whom he marries at the end of *MAA*, was a helpful presence, lending him her lifetime of experience with the nobility; in *MR*, she is back in Ankh-Morpork with their infant son. Vimes is no longer dependent on anyone's help to navigate the political sphere. *See also* Ankh-Morpork; City Watch;

Vimes, Sir Samuel

Frederick Colon; Coming of Age; Cuddy; Detective and Noir Fiction; Detritus; Dragons; Drink; Feminism; Igor; Carrot Ironfoundersson; Cheery Littlebottom; Nobby Nobbs; Racism; Lady Sibyl Ramkin; Sexism; Angua van Überwald *and* Patrician Vetinari.

Further Reading

Brown, James. 'Believing is Seeing'. *GOL2.*
James, Edward. 'The City Watch'. *GOL, GOL2.*
Mendlesohn, Farah. 'Faith and Ethics'. *GOL, GOL2.*

Stacie L. Hanes

Vorbis (*SG*)

A leading member of the Church of **Omnia**, and a mainstay in their Quisition. He has no compunction in ordering pain to be given to others if he thinks that they are not following the true way. Very capable of using what surrounds him to his advantage, he takes up **Brutha** as someone who can help his conquest of **Ephebe**, and on his return after wandering through a desert, claims that **Om** has spoken to him, and declares himself the Cenobiarch – ruler of Omnia – and the Eighth Prophet of Om. In an attempt to bribe Brutha, he makes the novice a bishop, but when this does not buy his silence, Vorbis turns to the Quisition. He is killed by Om being dropped on his bald head, and hangs around in an afterlife desert for a century until Brutha dies.

His behaviour recalls some of the worst excesses of the various Inquisitions and incarnations of the Congregation for the Doctrine of the Faith, of the Catholic Church, aimed at routing out blasphemers, witches and false converts to Christianity. His name has been given to the Ogg Vorbis sound compressing code designed as a free alternative to MP3 (the Ogg part being nothing to do with Nanny). *See also* Brutha; Ephebe; Om; Omnia *and* Religion.

Further Reading

Brown, James. 'Believing is Seeing'. *GOL2.*
Mendlesohn, Farah. 'Faith and Ethics'. *GOL, GOL2.*

Andrew M. Butler

W

War

Carl von Clauswitz (1780–1831) said that 'War is a continuation of **politics** by other means', and the threat of war gives Pratchett a variety of contexts where he is able to write about politics. In each book in the **Johnny Maxwell Trilogy**, a specific war is invoked, but in the **Discworld** series actually warfare is arguably avoided until *MR*; war is perhaps too serious a subject for **Comedy** to deal with although satires like *Catch-22* (1961) by Joseph Heller (1923–1999) and sitcoms like *Blackadder Goes Forth* (1989) provoke much laughter whilst not shirking away from the bloodshed.

In *OYCSM*, Johnny **Maxwell** is playing a **computer game** in which he shoots aliens, but he somehow enters into the game space when the alien ScreeWee surrender and he has to help them find their way home, defending them from other aliens (presumably other human players of the game). The book offers the reader the opportunity to read this as a symptom of the stresses in Johnny's life; his parents are arguing and the Gulf War (1991) plays out on television every night. Norman Schwarzkopf (b.1934), the Commander in Chief of the US and Commandant of the coalition forces against Iraq, is presented as the choreographer of the war, and the machismo of his nickname 'Stormin' Norman' comes in for particular satire. The spectacle of the virtual war is indistinguishable from the graphics of computer games, a point repeated in the provocative *The Gulf War Did Not Take Place* (1991; translated 1995) by Jean Baudrillard (b.1929). (Another work of **Children's Fiction** which explores the war is *Gulf* (1992) by Robert Westall (1929–1993).)

In *JD* the horrors of World War One lie behind the story of trying to save the graveyard in **Blackbury**. Johnny and his friends attempt to find out if any famous people were buried there, and stumble across the story of the Blackbury Old Pals Regiment, a group of solders all from the same area who were killed in one battle aside from one survivor, Tommy Atkins, who dies during the course of the novel. It seems to have been a senseless sacrifice, and underlines the anti-war theme.

It seems inevitable that *JB* sees the characters transported back in time to World War Two, and the day of a bombing raid on the town. Again there is the sense of how insignificant people are put into terrible situations over which they have little control, but it is as much the contrast between the past and present which is important as the war itself.

It seems unlikely that a pro-war children's book could be published now, but the same could be said for adult fiction. There seems to be no sense of the notion of a just war in the Discworld sequence, just various degrees of stupidity. With the temporary disappearance of **Djelebeybi** in *P*, **Tsort** and **Ephebe** find themselves to be direct neighbours, and prepare the battle over their new border. The return of the lost country prevents real bloodshed, in a last minute retreat from the depiction of warfare.

It is the appearance of land in *J* that leads to conflict, in a novel whose very title suggests Pratchett's attitude to war, and especially warmongers. The island of Leshp appears in the Circle Sea, leading to rival claims for it from **Ankh-Morpork** and **Klatch** and both powers going to a war footing. Again the **narrative** convenience of the island sinking out of sight avoids the need for blood to shed. Lord Ronnie Rust is the latest in a long line of daft military men in his family, and is an arms dealer whose interests would have been served by war. He is opposed by Samuel **Vimes**, who uses the full force of the law to arrest both armies for criminal acts – although in doing so he does realise that he has been expertly manipulated by Patrician **Vetinari**.

LH also offers an aborted war in the Silver Horde's attack on the **Hub** and the Gods; this is less successful than their earlier coup in the **Agatean Empire**, which established **Cohen the Barbarian** as a new ruler. Again it is narrative that defeats them – Carrot **Ironfoundersson's hero** status would ensure their defeat so they stop fighting.

The centuries of fighting between **dwarfs** and **trolls** is played out through a number of books, notably those focusing on the **City Watch**. The relationship between **Detritus** and **Cuddy** shows how hatred and rivalry can turn into respect and comradeship in the right circumstances (*GG* and *MAA*). The politics of the dwarfs impinges on Ankh-Morpork in the lead up to the coronation of the Low King in *FE* and in feelings about the Battle of Koom valley in *T!*

But it is in *MR* that war is central as a theme to a novel, and William de **Worde** appears as a war correspondent and Samuel **Vimes** is a special ambassador, despairing of the stupidity of the fighting parties. The difficult conditions that soldiers face, and the nonsenses of propaganda and patriotism are explored through the novel. The cross-dressing of individuals at various levels in the army hierarchy, and Polly **Perks**'s willingness to return to war (*see* **Feminism**), suggest that here the war is not the result of the stupidity of men – as it appears to be throughout the rest of the oeuvre – but of the stupidity of women. Women can perform as aggressively and ruthlessly as men, which is equality of a sorts but not a reassuring one. Whilst we are made to care for the characters in the regiment, we are never made to care for one of them who has fallen in battle – it remains a curiously bloodless war after all.

See also Agatean Empire; Ankh-Morpork; Blackbury; Children's Fiction; Cohen the Barbarian; Comedy and Humour; Computers; Djelebeybi; Dwarfs; Ephebe; Feminism; Games; Heroes; the Hub; Johnny Maxwell Trilogy; Klatch; Johnny Maxwell; Narrative; Polly Perks; Politics; Trolls; Tsort; Patrician Vetinari; Samuel Vimes *and* William de Worde.

Further Reading
Agnew, Kate and Geoff Fox. 2001. *Children at War: From the First World War to the Gulf.* London: Continuum.
Baudrillard, Jean. 1995. *The Gulf War Did Not Take Place.* Translated and edited by Paul Patton. Sydney: Power.
Mendlesohn, Farah. 'Faith and Ethics'. *GOL*, *GOL2.*
Westall, Robert. 1992. *Gulf.* London: Methuen.

Andrew M. Butler

Weatherwax, Granny Esmerelda (*ER*, *WS*, *WA*, *LL*, 'SALF', *Msk*, *CJ*, *WFM*, *HFOS*, *SODII*, *Wint*)

Esmerelda (Granny) Weatherwax is the dominant member of the **Lancre** coven, possibly the most potent witch the **Discworld** has ever produced – her nearest rival is the legendary Black Aliss, who may have been evil but at the least was ambivalent due to her access to **power** (*CJ*). According to the Discworld canon, Granny has achieved almost mythical status in her own lifetime; she has surpassed Black Aliss's **Fairy Tale** exploits by a considerable margin, although in concert with Nanny **Ogg** and Magrat **Garlick**. The author's views are clearly expressed by the title of the short story 'The Sea and Little Fishes', in which Granny is likened to a force so vast that the other Ramtops witches cannot see that it is there. The **dwarfs** and **trolls** of the Ramtops give her a wide berth, considering her trouble on a scale far better avoided than engaged.

Model of Granny's cottage created by Discworld Merchandising.

Weatherwax, Granny

Granny is the most feared and respected of the witches; she is consequently their leader, although witches have no formal organisation. Through much of the canon, the Lancre coven is composed of Granny, Nanny, and Magrat; Granny leads the coven as she leads the rest of the witches, by virtue of age and skill, but their talents complement hers. Granny is competent in all areas of witchcraft, but is not the best at everything: Magrat is a better doctor, and Nanny is a better midwife. Granny excels in borrowing, headology and brewing potions. She is able to borrow the bodies of animals, travelling with them for a short time and using their senses and natural attributes; she always repays them for their unwitting assistance with food or shelter. Headology is a deep knowledge of how people think – psychology infused by a touch of magic. Although her jam is inedible, Granny's hair-restoring potion and aphrodisiac elixir are famous.

The Ramtops, particularly in the Weatherwax line, have borne a number of powerful witches and wizards over the generations, some good, some less so: no one knows much about Esme Weatherwax's grandmother, Alison Weatherwax; her sister Lily **Weatherwax** left home as a young woman, eventually to rule the city of **Genua** as a despotic fairy godmother; a distant relative, Galder Weatherwax, became an **Archchancellor** of **Unseen University**.

The Lancre Witches novels are a modern exploration of story of the triune goddess, known for centuries as the Maiden, Mother and Crone; on the Discworld, they are more cautiously referred to as 'the Maiden, the mother, and the … Other One' because Granny is not flattered by her designation as the crone. Later books develop the theme, expanding the coven to include Agnes **Nitt**, moving Magrat beyond maidenhood, and blurring the boundaries between roles to show how each is connected to the others. Granny is a particularly sensitive study in characterisation – she never surrendered her maidenhood, she merely grew beyond it; she has never given birth to a child of her own, but has fostered and protected countless lives over the years; and she has always been the one to whom the villagers come with the hard choices and the deaths. In her primary role as the Crone, she stands between her people and the worst scourges of mortality, shielding them from unnecessary pain and easing their deaths. She is the witch who most often administers palliative herbs to the terminally ill, and it is she who washes and shrouds the bodies of the dead in preparation for the grave.

Granny's cottage is the definitive, classic witch's cottage, located in the forests of the Ramtops, on a narrow track above the village of **Bad Ass**, in the kingdom of Lancre. It is a small dwelling with slanted walls, a thatched roof, a perpetually stuck front door, and an irregularly shaped stone chimney; the building is an unobtrusive part of the glade in which it sits, less a disturbance of nature than an example of nature rearranged slightly to permit human habitation. Nearby are the goat shed, the outhouse, an exotic and dangerous herb garden, a well and Granny's beehives.

Studies of Granny Weatherwax. Artwork by Paul Kidby.

Weatherwax, Granny

Over the course of the Discworld series, as her power and knowledge have grown, Granny has overcome Drum Billet and his staff (*ER*), the Duchess and Duke Felmet (*WS*), Erzulie Gogol and Lady Lilith (*WA*), Diamanda Tockley and the Elf Queen (*LL*), the Opera Ghost (*Msk*), the Magpyr **vampire** clan (*CJ*) and her own inclinations toward darkness. The tendency toward magical talent that runs in Granny's family comes with a curse of sorts, in the form of the ever-present knowledge that the possessor of power can use it however she wills, with no one to stand in her way. Perhaps Granny's greatest achievement has been prevailing over her own mind.

Persistent themes of Granny's **narrative** are the distinctions between power, darkness, and evil. She has enough power to enforce her will on just about anyone, and she must live with the instinctive temptation to do so – but her belief that it would be wrong checks her impulses. Granny has everything it takes to be the perfect wicked witch, but chose long ago to reject a scripted life. Granny's story is almost entirely about choice: she chooses what she will be. When her choices must affect other lives, she disturbs those lives as little as possible, even when her abilities mean that wrenching them into alignment with her wishes would be simple. Her power is fuelled by the constant tension between the allure of what is easy and the will to do what is right. However, the choice to be good and do right is not the same as choosing to be a sweet little old lady. *See also* Tiffany Aching; Archchancellors; Bad Ass; Fairy Tales; Magic; Magrat Garlick; Genua; Lancre; Agnes Nitt; Nanny Ogg; Power; Eskarina Smith; Lily Weatherwax *and* Wizards.

Further Reading

Mendlesohn, Farah. 'Faith and Ethics'. *GOL*, *GOL2*.
Sayer, Karen. 'The Witches'. *GOL*, *GOL2*.

Stacie L. Hanes

Weatherwax, Lily (*WA*)

Lily Weatherwax is a witch, a fairy godmother, *éminence grise* in the city of **Genua**, and Granny **Weatherwax**'s elder sister. She appears only in *WA*, as the manipulative, pitiless advisor to the ruler of Genua, whom she set on the throne; she conspired to murder the old duke, exile his mistress and their heir, and install her created puppet in his place.

Lily ran away from **Lancre** at a young age, driven by conflict with her family and the desire for **power**. In her role as a powerful lady in Genua, her exercise of authority is absolute; she controls every aspect of life in the city, using magic to direct the lives of the people who live there, casting them in **Fairy Tale** and enforcing 'happy' endings.

Fairy godmothers always come in pairs, one good and one evil; despite the harm she does, executing citizens for minor offences, jailing others in the duke's dungeons, and having originally usurped power by murder, Lily sees herself as 'the good one' because she gives people what they want. Lily is certainly more willing to use her power, and the godmother's wand, but whether she or Esmerelda Weatherwax is the more powerful witch remains arguable. *See also* Fairy Tales; Genua; Lancre; Magic; Narrative; Power *and* Granny Weatherwax.

Further Reading
Sayer, Karen. 'The Witches'. *GOL*, *GOL2*

Stacie L. Hanes

Websites

The **Discworld** has a thriving internet presence, ranging from the publishers' official Websites, and those of licensed merchants, to the mailing lists, sites and other efforts of **fandom**.

Discworld **merchandising** remains tightly controlled, and is largely internet-based for sales. Long-time Discworld business ventures include Paul **Kidby's** art, the Cunning Artificer Bernard **Pearson's** stamps and jewellery, and C.M.O.T. [Stephen] **Briggs's** badges and miscellaneous products. **Clarecraft** have gone out of business, but for some time produced a range of figures and other items, and sponsored the Clarecraft Discworld Event, or CCDE.

The most prominent fan organisations are the Klatchian Foreign Legion, a US-based club which produces a free electronic newsletter called the *WOSSNAME*, and the UK-based Guild of Fans and Disciples, or GOFAD, which produces a print newsletter (their motto is Totus In Reticulus Non Possibilis Est, or Not Everyone Can Be On The Net) called *Ramtop to Rimfall*. GOFAD is known as the 'Official Unofficial' Terry Pratchett fan club, because neither Terry Pratchett nor his agent Colin **Smythe** has anything to do with running it, but do nevertheless support the club by contributing information, such as current book tour dates.

Discworld Monthly has been online and available by email since May 1997. A substantial source of news and articles, with large readership, its editors are Jason Anthony, William Barnett and Richard Massey.

There is also a Discworld MUD, an online, multiplayer, text-based game.

One of the most vociferous fan groups is not an official organisation at all: alt.books.pratchett (abp) and alt.fan.pratchett (afp) are Usenet groups populated by an extremely diverse community of Discworld fans. The former is restricted to on-topic discussion of the books themselves, while the latter is a forum where fans may discuss anything at all, which sometimes includes the Discworld novels; Terry Pratchett has occasionally posted on both groups. The core members of the Usenet Discworld groups collectively maintain one of the largest, best organised Websites dedicated to Discworld fandom and information, called the L-Space Web, after the concept of **L-Space** in the novels. The L-Space Web features some pages of interest only to newsgroup regulars (afpers), such as an extensive FAQ section, articles on the history of afp, a collection of photos of regular contributors to the newsgroups, and a recipe archive, but also archives information which might be useful to any Pratchett fan or researcher: a biography, official contact information, press clippings, photographs, information about **conventions**, links to on- and offline fan activity, professional and fan art, links to merchandise sites, Discworld **games**, an exhaustive primary bibliography, some literary criticism, and a vast collection of annotations for Discworld publications. Lspace.org maintains a reliable list of resources updated with reasonable frequency. It also now hosts a Wiki.

The most prominent Website with a specific purpose is that of the Discworld Convention, or DWCon; it is primarily devoted to convention-specific information such as guest biographies, registration information, travel directions, hotel accommodations, the convention programme, the convention organisers' contact information, volunteer opportunities, photo galleries, the Chronicle, and convention policies. *See also* Stephen Briggs; Clarecraft; Computers; Conventions; Fandom; Games; Paul Kidby; Bernard Pearson *and* Colin Smythe.

Further Reading

Internet-based enterprises are ephemeral; the addresses may change, but any of them should be easy to locate via search engine. The following were accurate at the time of writing:

Briggs, Stephen. http://www.cmotdibbler.com/
Colin Smythe Ltd. http://www.colinsmythe.co.uk/
Cunning Artificer. http://www.artificer.co.uk/
Discworld Convention. http://www.dwcon.org/
Discworld Monthly. http://www.discworldmonthly.co.uk/
Discworld MUD. http://discworld.atuin.net/lpc/
Guild of Fans and Disciples. http://www.geocities.com/Area51/1777//
HarperCollins Pratchett Pages.
http://www.harpercollins.com/authors/7848/Terry_Pratchett/index.aspx
Kidby, Paul: official http://www.paulkidby.com/
Kidby, Paul: personal http://www.paulkidby.net/
Klatchian Foreign Legion. http://groups.yahoo.com/group/WOSSNAME/
L-Space. http://www.lspace.org/
Transworld Pratchett Pages. http://www.booksattransworld.co.uk/terrypratchett/home.htm

Stacie L. Hanes

The Wee Free Men: A Story of Discworld (2003)

The thirtieth **Discworld** novel, aimed at children, and the first of the Tiffany **Aching** novels – it is a **Coming of Age** narrative which features **witches**. The first edition, with a cover by Paul **Kidby**, was published by

Doubleday. Corgi released B Format and mass-market editions in 2004. It has been translated into Catalan, Chinese, Czech, Danish, Dutch, Estonian, Finnish, French, German, Greek, Indonesian, Italian, Japanese, Korean, Latvian, Lithuanian, Norwegian, Polish, Romanian, Russian, Spanish, Swedish and Turkish. It was the winner of the Teen Choice W.H. Smith Book Award (2004). The Wee Free Men are the Nac Mac Feegles, a group of fighting and drinking pictsies like those depicted in *CJ*, although the name derives from the Wee Frees, a nickname for the Free Church of Scotland. The book is divided into named chapters, headed with pictures by Kidby. An author's afterword acknowledges the inspiration of *The Fairy Feller's Master-Stroke* (1855–1864), a painting of fairies by Richard Dadd (1817–1886). An illustrated edition has been announced, with art by Stephen **Player**. Sam Raimi (b.1959) has been announced as director of a **Hollywood film** adaptation. Michael Dirda (b.1948) wrote: 'Pratchett's second children's "story of Discworld," displays his usual virtues – a mimic's ear for speech patterns and accents, perfect timing and balance to his sentences, a fast-moving plot that grows increasingly frenetic, monitory portraits of the self-important, narrow-minded and spiritually dry, a plea for kindness to animals and respect for the natural world and, not least, an exuberant and irresistible cleverness' (*Washington Post* (8 May 2003)).

Tiffany is nine-years-old and lives on the Aching Farm in the Chalk, and is aware of a mysterious spirit Jenny Green-Teeth being in a nearby river, so uses her brother, Wentworth, as bait to try and catch her. Later she visits the travelling teachers, and meets Miss Tick, a witch, and a talking toad. Tick warns her that something awful is going to happen – indeed it does, when the Queen of the Fairies (from *LL*) kidnaps Wentworth. Tiffany is found by the Nac Mac Feebles, the blue-skinned, red-haired pictsies exiled from the fairy kingdom, and they help her on her quest. Their leader, the queen bee-like Kelda, dies, and they appoint Tiffany as her successor. Tiffany will have to marry one of them and provide hundreds of children; she avoids this by suggesting a wedding date many years in the future. Tiffany rescues Roland, son of the Baron of Chalk, and confronts the Queen of the Fairies, who retaliates with lawyers. Fortunately the toad was a lawyer before an argument with a fairy godmother and saves the day. She is able to retrieve her brother, but Roland takes all the credit. Tick, Granny **Weatherwax** and Nanny **Ogg** show up, and advise Tiffany on what being a witch entails – although in a sense she has learned this from memories of her granny who was also a witch.

The fairy kidnap is a staple of **Fairy Tales** and **Fantasy**, although *Labyrinth* (1986) directed by Jim Henson (1936–1990) seems to be a likely precursor. An earlier source is a Scottish folktale about seeking for a child kidnapped by **elves**, 'Childe Rowland', which was the inspiration for versions by Robert Browning (1812–1889) – 'Childe Rowland to the Dark Tower Came' (1855) – and Joseph Jacobs (1854–1916) in *English Folk and Fairy Tales* (1892). The Nac Mac Feebles resemble the Smurfs, but are parodies of Scottish culture, especially as represented in quasi-historical films. *See also* Tiffany Aching; Coming of Age; Elves; Fairy Tales; Fantasy; Paul Kidby; Nanny Ogg; Stephen Player; Granny Weatherwax *and* Witches.

Further Reading

Baldry, Cherith. 'The Children's Books'. *GOL2.*
Sayer, Karen. 'The Witches'. *GOL2.*

Andrew M. Butler

Werewolves

Relatively rare in accounts of the **Discworld**, the being which transforms between human and wolf, in tradition at the full moon, and can be killed with a silver bullet. A werewolf stuck in one form – either always human or wolf – is known as Yennorks. There are also weremen, wolves who turn into men at the full moon (see Lupine who fell in love with a werewolf, Ludmilla Cake, *RM*).

Angua von **Überwald** is the most notable werewolf, a member of the **City Watch** and lover of Carrot **Ironfoundersson**. She is the daughter of Baron Guye von Überwald and Lady Serafine, rulers of Bonk, **Überwald**, and brother to Wolfgang von Überwald. Wolfgang is violent and cruel, and thirsty for power, so takes part in the attempts to destroy the **Dwarf** Low King (*FE*). Werewolves are enemies of and rivals to **vampires**.

Pratchett is drawing on millennia of folklore, with stories about transformations between human and wolf dating back at least as far as **Greek Mythology** and Norse folktales. Folk and **Fairy Tales** vary as to whether the transformation only takes place at the full moon, whether the condition is inheritable or whether it is contagious, through a bite. The plant wolfsbane is also either a charm against lycanthropy or a cause of it. The key popular version of the legend is *The Wolf Man* (1941), directed by George Waggner (1894–1984) and starring Lon Chaney Jr (1906–1973). This emphasised the roles of wolfsbane and silver, with sequels using the full moon as the key to transformation. There has been a steady trickle of **Hollywood Films** since 1981, which saw both *The Howling*, directed by Joe Dante (b.1946), and *An American Werewolf in London*, directed by John Landis (b.1950), both of which border on **parody**, and which seem to be referenced in *MAA*. *See also* City Watch; Dogs; Fairy Tales; Greek Mythology; Hollywood Films; Parody; Überwald; Angua von Überwald *and* Vampires.

Further Reading

Baring-Gould, Sabine. 1865. *The Book of Were-Wolves: Being an Account of a Terrible Superstition.* London: Smith, Elder.

Andrew M. Butler

Where's My Cow? A Discworld Picture Book For People of All Sizes (2005)

An illustrated **Discworld** novel which coincides with *T!*, and is a story within a story (within a story). The illustrator is Melvyn Grant, who has produced covers for **Science Fiction** and **Fantasy** novels, among others, and lives on the south east coast of England. He used to work in oils on canvas but now uses a computer. It was originally published by Doubleday; there is a Czech translation.

Every day Commander Samuel **Vimes** of the **City Watch** returns home at six o'clock to read a story to his son, Sam. The story is *Where's My Cow?*, and is about someone who is looking for their cow, and instead locates several different animals – a sheep, a horse, a chicken, a hippopotamus – in the hunt. Young Sam does the animals' noises. However, Vimes objects that his son is growing up in an urban environment not a rural one, so he changes the story to *Where's My Daddy?*, with the hunter finding Foul Ole Ron, Coffin' Henry, C.M.O.T. **Dibbler**, **Detritus** and **Vetinari** rather than his father. The story is interrupted by the arrival of Lady Sybil **Ramkin**, and he returns to the original tale.

The illustrations are in three main styles, gentle, largely pink, green and blue shades for the nursery, with well-lit rooms and a three dimensional feel, a much flatter, less varied use of pink, green and blue for the story Vimes tells, and a darker, murkier, foggy palette for the **Ankh-Morpork** scenes. Sometimes the two or three styles co-exist on the same page. Grant seems to have used actors as his model for many of the characters – Vimes is Pete Postlethwaite (b.1945), Dibbler is Eric Idle (b.1943), Vetinari looks like Gary Oldman (b.1958), although there is now a tradition of depicting him as looking like Stephen **Briggs**. The cover of the book that Vimes reads is almost identical to the real world one – the Discworld not having bar codes. The story recalls any number of children's stories or poems in which a character does something or looks for something repeatedly, sometimes with the chance for audience participation. Children's metafiction is not new – *The Stinky Cheese Man and Other Stories* (1992) by writer Jon Scieszka (b.1954) and illustrator Lane Smith (b.1959) has tales interrupted or postponed and the characters interacting with the copyright page; other works by the same authors also play with **Fairy Tales**. *See also* Ankh-Morpork; Stephen Briggs; City Watch; Children's Fiction; C.M.O.T. Dibbler; Detritus; Fairy Tales; Lady Sybil Ramkin; Patrician Vetinari *and* Samuel Vimes.

Further Reading

Doonen, Jane. 1993. *Looking at Pictures in Picture Books*. Stroud: Thimble Press.

Mendlesohn, Farah. 2003. 'Catching 'em Young: Picture Book Science Fiction for the Under Sevens'. *Vector: The Critical Journal of the British Science Fiction Association* 227 (January/February): P. 47.

Nodelman, Perry. 2000. 'Inside Picture Books'. *Lion and the Unicorn* 24.1 (January). Pp. 150–156.

Sipe, Lawrence R. 1998. 'How Picture Books Work: A Semiotically Framed Theory of Text-Picture Relationships'. *Children's Literature in Education* 29.2 (June). Pp. 97–108.

Andrew M. Butler

Whitlow, Mrs (*ER, MP, SM, LC, SOD, SODII, SODIII*)

The sturdy, dependable house-keeper of the **Wizards** of the **Unseen University** of **Ankh-Morpork**, and – aside presumably from Eskarina **Smith** – the only female presence in a world of bachelors, although presumably there is a large female cleaning staff that is invisible to the wizards. She is responsible for keeping things clean, neat and tidy, aside from when the University or the **Discworld** is threatened with some new nemesis. In *SM* she somewhat lets her hair down, becoming a fan of Music with Rocks in It. In *LC* it is she who accidentally closes the window, cutting them off from returning to the University. The wizards begin looking after her, reversing the usual practice, and several of them conceive a crush on her. There may have been a Mr Whitlow, but – as with Granny **Weatherwax** – sometimes it's safer not to ask.

The character perhaps owes something to Mrs Kate Bridges of the ITV drama *Upstairs Downstairs* (1971–1975) and Mrs Pearce from *Pygmalion* (1913)/*My Fair Lady* (1964). *See also* Ankh-Morpork; Eskarina Smith; Unseen University *and* Wizards.

Andrew M. Butler

Widdershins (*DSS*)

The planet at the heart of *DSS*, indeed, as home to the swamp-igs, centre to the universe in which the novel is set, but it is apparently run by a human-like species called sinistrals. It is a largely liquid world, with oceans, swamps and marshes, and has at least two moons. The attempted purchase of the smaller of which led to the deposing of John Sabalos III. The Sabalos dynasty, based on the wealth from the longevity drug pilac extracted from crustaceans, rules the planet as a business. At the time of the novel's setting, Dom **Sabalos** is about to take over from his missing father, the company having largely been dominated by Joan I his grand-mother in the intervening period. It seems likely that much of the history of the planet has been arranged by the telepathic and powerful swamp-igs, who have faked the Jokers' artifacts and have evolved the various other intelligent species in the universe.

Widdershins means counter clockwise, or against the path of the sun, and is the opposite of deiseal, clockwise. This fits the novel into the history of utopian fiction – utopia (outopia) literally meaning no-place, Samuel Butler (1835–1902) almost reverses the spelling of nowhere in his *Erewhon* (1872) and William Morris (1834–1896) wrote *News from Nowhere* (1890) (and note also Ecalpon (*COM*)). In the Discworld series the word is opposed to turnwards, the direction of rotation of the disc – to be contrasted with hubwards-rimwards. In superstition, the word has negative connotations, being associated with bad luck and the risk of being transported to fairy realms. It is also associated with left-handedness, and most sinistrals, including Dom, are left-handed. *See also* Dom Sabalos.

Andrew M. Butler

Wings (1989)

Subtitled *The Third Book of the Nomes*, this is the third book in The **Bromeliad**, Nomes or Truckers trilogy. The first edition was 13,900 copies, from Doubleday with a Josh **Kirby** cover. The Corgi 1991 paperback was a print run of 107,000, with a modification to the cover design possibly happening in 1999's reprint. Corgi issued B Format and mass market editions in 2004 with new artwork by David **Wyatt**. It was collected with *T* and *D* into *The Bromeliad* (Doubleday, 1998, *c.*10,000 copies and Corgi, 2007). *W* has been translated into Bulgarian, Czech, Danish, Finnish, French, German, Greek, Hebrew, Hungarian, Italian, Japanese, Polish, Romanian, Russian, Serbian, Slovakian, Slovenian, Spanish and Swedish. Wings here refer to aeroplanes, geese and spaceships. The book is dedicated to Pratchett's wife, Lyn, his daughter, Rhianna and an alligator seen in Florida. It begins with a summary of the story so far, 'In the beginning. . .', and is divided into chapters, each preceded by an extract from *A Scientific Encyclopedia for the Enquiring Young Nome* by Angalo de **Haberdasheri**. The *Junior Bookshelf* review notes: 'Now that the trilogy is complete it is possible to see its proportions justly. It is indeed more than the sum of its parts. The fun is still there, much of it of a farcical knockabout kind, but the story has several layers of meaning. The irony is more penetrating, the social comment sharper. Perhaps the effect might have been greater if the author had exercised his powers of self-censorship. The force of some of its message is dissipated over three volumes'.

Masklin, Gurder and Angalo Angalo de **Haberdasheri**; are waiting at an airport, trying to locate Grandson Richard 39, descendent of **Arnold Bros (est. 1905)**, and find him with the aid of The **Thing**. The three nomes sneak onto a Concorde headed for Florida, and narrowly avoid being discovered by the flight crew. Once in Florida they discover another tribe of nomes, who speak a language closer to the original nomish and realise that there must be nomes all over the planet. They use a goose to fly to Kennedy

Space Center, and Masklin contrives to be found by humans to get him and the Thing closer to the space shuttle. Eventually they manage to contact their ship, hidden in a crater on the moon, and call it back to Earth. They return to **Blackbury**, via South America, where they pick up a Bromeliad. Most of the nomes leave on the ship, but Gurder stays behind, trying to track down other nomes to tell them about the ship.

The frogs in the Bromeliad are an allegory for the nomes, living most of their lives in one world, not aware of what else is going on in the universe. Meanwhile Gurder's belief system takes a beating on seeing the deity Richard, especially when he realises that He has a hole in one of his socks; Gurder copies the style as an act of homage, and is later shocked to believe that not only does he believe in Arnold Bros, but Richard believes in him. Angalo also wants deities such as Arnold Bros to exist, so he can refuse to believe in him. *See also* Arnold Bros (est. 1905); Blackbury; The Bromeliad; Children's Fiction; Angalo de Haberdasheri; Masklin *and* The Thing.

Further Reading

Baldry, Cherith. 'The Children's Books'. *GOL*, *GOL2*.

Hunt, Peter. 2001. 'Terry Pratchett'. Pp. 86–121. Peter Hunt and Millicent Lenz. *Alternative Worlds in Fantasy Fiction*. London: Continuum.

Andrew M. Butler

Wintersmith (2006)

The thirty-fifth **Discworld** novel, aimed at children, and the third of the Tiffany **Aching** novels. A hardback and large format paperback appeared from Doubleday, with a cover by Paul **Kidby**, and mass market and B Format paperbacks appeared in 2007. It has been translated into Finnish, German and Romanian. *Wint* has a prologue of definitions of Nac Mac Feegle words and an author's afterword, on Morris Dancing, and is divided into chapters. The title is the name of a character within the novel, the personification of winter (cf the **Hogfather (Character)**). Jonathan Wright called it: 'A wise, witty and warm novel that's both serious and, as ever with Pratchett, very, very, funny. And a book with a grand heroine. Really, you've got to love Tiffany: who else would dare to give Granny Weatherwax a fluffy kitten? Greebo's life will never be the same again' (*SFX* (November 2006)).

Tiffany is now sent to live with Miss Treason, a witch who has filled her cottage with novelty skulls and other witchly accoutrements. On a visit to the Dark Morris, Tiffany joins in and inadvertently dances with wintersmith, who falls in love with her and can track her down through her lost white horse bracelet. Miss Treason plans her funeral and then dies the day after the party; Annagramma Hawkin is offered the place and can only work as a real witch with help from the others. Tiffany lives with Nanny **Ogg**, and has taken on some of the powers of Lady Summer; plants grow from any wood she steps on, and she receives the cornucopia which produces endless food. Meanwhile wintersmith is getting more persistent in his wooing, sending Tiffany-shaped snowflakes to cover the Chalk, killing sheep and putting Tiffany's brother Wentworth at risk. Granny **Weatherwax** persuades the Nac Mac Feegles to go with Roland into the Underworld to retrieve Lady Summer. Tiffany kisses wintersmith and melts him with her magical heat. The cycle of the seasons begins again.

The book is a variation on the Orpheus in the Underworld and the various other underworld kidnap myths, such as the one in which Persephone spends part of the world in the underworld with Hades – in fact a Discworld parallel is even cited. Much folk ritual is about the cycle of life, which maps onto the cycle of the seasons and even the cycle of the day, so it is hardly surprising that there are Discworld rituals and personifications glimpsed here – the Hogfather draws on the same kind of mythos. Morris dancing has been alluded to in *RM*, *GG* and *LL*, as well as in *Str*, and is usually about the coming of Spring; the Dark Morris brings on winter. *See also* Tiffany Aching; Children's Fiction; Coming of Age; Greek Mythology; The Hogfather (Character); Magic; Nanny Ogg; Power; Granny Weatherwax *and* Witches.

Andrew M. Butler

Witches

Witches are the female practitioners of magic on the **Discworld**; stories of the **Lancre** Witches form one of the major story arcs in the canon. The Lancre Witches stories include the novels *WS*, *WA*, *LL*, *Msk* and *CJ*, as well as the short story '**SALF**'; *WFM* marks a split in the Witches arc and begins the story of a young witch, Tiffany **Aching**, of the Chalk, continued in *HFOS* and *Wint*.

Thematically, the witch stories are about life, in the organic sense: they deal with power, community, and life, from a number of overlapping angles. They are based on a blend of British folklore, benign satire of modern Wicca, and a reinterpretation of the Triple Goddess myth.

The element that makes witches what they are is mystical power, in which they are like **wizards**. However, witches differ from wizards in their methodology, source of power, and organisation (wizards are hierarchical and witches technically are not), but alike at the most basic level of practice, where rules are perhaps only guidelines. Although they have no chain of command, witches are extremely competitive; they tend to sort themselves by shows of power at the yearly Witch Trials, whereas the wizards move up in rank by destroying their rivals. Seniority among witches is reckoned by age and ability.

'The Salem Witch', *c.* 1925.

Witches derive power in a sense through the land of the Discworld; they use herbs and their own influence, both mystical and purely conventional. Their power is more subtle and flexible than wizardly magic, used mainly to nudge stalled events into their appropriate natural motions with as little trauma as possible, whereas wizards rely more on raw power. Both use what should be termed spellcraft, but witches embrace formal structure far less than do wizards; in most cases, witches persuade their power to come forth from animals, plants, and the Disc itself, while wizards compel theirs by means of staffs and arcane formulae. Witch magic is to a great extent organic, and their practices rarely attempt to force nature to take a contrary course. Witches appear to be far more aware of wizardly power than the reverse; the showier character of wizard magic makes it seem more potent than witch magic, but applied carefully and in line with the natural forces, witchcraft can even turn away Death as long as the act does not pervert the natural order.

Respect for the land itself is very important for witches, to the point that the Kingdom of Lancre cries to them for help. Witches are fundamentally rural; they usually live in small, individual cottages that blend with the natural environment, looking as if they have sprung up from local materials. Wizards, on the other hand, tend toward towers and other structures with architecture, such as the buildings of **Unseen University**. When a witch senses **Death** approaching, she will try to leave the cottage much as she found it, ready for its next occupant, in contrast to the wizardly tendency to drink as much wine and spend as much money as possible before dying – witches own little, regarding most things as being theirs only for a time.

Witches are bound intimately to the communities they serve, in contrast to the 'town and gown' antagonism that is always just below the surface of interactions between wizards and non-wizards. The witches come from the land and from among the people who live there; witches are deeply enmeshed in the lives of the villages under their care, knowing and caring for individuals from the cradle to the grave – much of their power is a direct result of their deep understanding of the people and the land. They provide the practical help remote rural villages need on a constant basis, whereas wizards tend to spend more time on study and theory. The very basic nature of a witch's knowledge and understanding of her people is at the bottom of her power, and is in large measure the reason witches are both respected and feared – they have arcane knowledge of a very humane kind, that comes quite literally from the lifelong study of people.

The gifts which underlie aptitude for the craft – such as the capacity to observe closely and understand clearly – are rare enough, and rarer still in combination with real magical talent. Witches are comparatively rare people, and becoming more so. In principle, every village has a resident witch, but in the Century of the Fruitbat, fewer girls have been called to the craft; many witches are kept very busy aiding the people of several villages, so that the broomstick hardly has time to cool off between house calls. Witch magic is taught on a one-to-one basis by older witches to apprentices, in pairings that seem to happen naturally. Life as a witch is never forced on young girls, at least by other witches; however, girls with a great deal of talent often find that choosing, and being chosen by, a compatible mentor is in some sense inevitable. The tradition of letting likeminded witches find one another is a matter of letting nature do what nature will do; the custom of individual apprenticeship is the root of a vital continuity, which reflects the bond between witches, the Disc, their power and their people, allowing the village to continue as an unbroken, healthy body.

The endless circle of village life is at the heart of witchcraft, and the Witches stories. Witches are present for all of the natural events of villagers' lives, from childbirth to laying out the dead, and everything in between. Life is the focus of the Witches arc – how it begins, how it works, and how it ends. As herbalists, midwives, and doctors, they brew aphrodisiac potions, nurture new lives, care for the sick, and comfort the dying. Magrat **Garlick** is one of the better herbalists of the Ramtops; Nanny **Ogg**, according to the canon, is the best midwife on the Disc with no exception from any time or place; Granny **Weatherwax** cannot be classified as clearly, but it is she the people seek out to ease the passage of the dying.

The witches' involvement in the intimate ebb and flow of community life lends itself to the exploration of the ancient myth of the triple goddess, referred to in the Discworld novels as the Maiden, the Mother, and the … Other One. At one time, Magrat Garlick was clearly the maiden, Nanny Ogg the mother, and Granny the crone; however, as the characters develop and change, the lines have shifted and blurred.

The Witches arc is given continuity after the divergence by the presence of Granny Weatherwax, dominant witch of the Lancre coven and possible mentor to Tiffany Aching. The witch stories now incorporate the Lancre Witches, who include Esmerelda (Granny) Weatherwax, Gytha (Nanny) Ogg, Magrat Garlick, and Agnes **Nitt**, as well as a good many other Ramtops witches who appear in minor roles, and the Chalk Witches, although Tiffany Aching is so far the only witch from the Chalk to be a major character. Her story continues through *HFOS* and *Wint*, with *When I Am Old I Shall Wear Midnight* (projected); Granny and other familiar characters are present at least up to *Wint*. *ER*, the third Discworld novel, introduced Granny Weatherwax and was the first to feature a witch as a main character. *ER* features only Granny, in a form critics have suggested is significantly different from later novels; *WS* brings Granny, Nanny, and Magrat together; Agnes is introduced in *LL*, and promoted to a major character in *Msk*. *See also* Tiffany Aching; Death; Feminism; Magrat Garlick; Desiderata Hollow; Lancre; Magic; Agnes Nitt; Nanny Ogg; Power; Eskarina Smith; Granny Weatherwax; Lily Weatherwax *and* Wizards.

Further Reading

Eliade, Mircea. 1976. *Occultism, Witchcraft and Cultural Fashions: Essays in Comparative Religion*. University of Chicago Press: Chicago.
Fry, Carrol L. 1990. '"What God Doth the Wizard Pray To": Neo-Pagan Witchcraft and Fantasy Fiction'. *Extrapolation* 31.4: Pp. 333–346.
Sayer, Karen. 'The Witches'. *GOL, GOL2*.

Stacie L. Hanes

Witches Abroad (1991)

The twelfth book in the Discworld series, featuring **witches**. The first edition of the novel, from Gollancz with a cover by Josh **Kirby**, was 25,000 copies. The Corgi edition (1992) initially had 190,000 copies; since 2005 there has been an alternative black and gold photographic cover available. In 1994, Gollancz collected it with *ER* and *WS* as *The Witches Trilogy*, in an edition of 21,250 copies. *WA* has been translated into Bulgarian, Czech, Dutch, Estonian, Finnish, French, German, Hebrew, Hungarian, Norwegian, Polish, Portuguese, Russian, Serbian, Spanish, Swedish and Turkish. The title is fairly literal – the witches travel to **Genua** during the course of the book – but it has related connotations of being at large or around (as in 'Witches are abroad') or being wide of the mark. The novel is dedicated to those who wanted to know the words to the Hedgehog Song, as sung by Nanny **Ogg**. (Heather Wood provided one answer – see http://members.aol.com/hwood50/hw/hedgehog.html.) Tom Hutchinson (*c*.1930–2005) suggested in his review: 'This is all a bit more self-conscious than we're used to from Pratchett and, while his jokes are still the best thing since Wodehouse, his intent has a very definite serious undertow' (*The Times*).

The witch Desiderata **Hollow** is dying, but has one more task she needs to complete: to prevent Esmerelda from marrying a prince in distant Genua. She fixes on Magrat **Garlick** to leave the task to, knowing that if she expressly forbids Granny **Weatherwax** and Nanny Ogg from going along, they will inevitably turn up. True to form, it is all three witches from the *WS* coven who travel to Genua, with **Greebo** in tow. En route they find themselves in a number of **Fairy Tales**, such as *Sleeping Beauty, Little Red Riding Hood and The Three Little Pigs*, and they realise that someone appears to be controlling stories. In fact their progress is being watched, and hampered, by Lily **Weatherwax**, long-lost evil sister of Granny, who is ruling Genua. The witches reach the city and substitute Magrat for Esmerelda at the ball, and also have to deal with the voodoo-tinged plans for revenge of Mrs Erzulie Gogol. Twelve years earlier the rightful ruler of Genua had been deposed by a Duc and Lily, but Gogol has resurrected him as Baron Saturday. Granny and Lily go head to head, with a climax in a hall of mirrors.

The novel's themes are related to power – magical and narrative. The witches very rarely perform any magic, preferring to rely instead on Headology (or psychology), so the voodoo witch Gogol needs to be viewed with suspicion. Narratives seem to behave like ideologies – the oppressed daughter has to marry the prince, the sister of an evil sister has to be good, and so on. The trick is for people to make their own story, rather than be enslaved by another's. *See also* Fairy Tales; Feminism; Magrat Garlick; Genua; Greebo; Desiderata Hollow; Lancre; Narrative; Magic; Nanny Ogg; Power; Granny Weatherwax *and* Lily Weatherwax.

Further Reading

Sayer, Karen. 'The Witches'. *GOL, GOL2.*

Andrew M. Butler

Wizards

Wizards are the male practitioners of magic on the **Discworld**; stories of the **Unseen University** wizards or **Rincewind** form one of the major story arcs in the canon and a sidebar trilogy. The wizards stories include the novels *COM, LF, ER, S, IT, LC, LH, SOD, SODII, SODIII* and 'CCOODD', with minor appearances in other novels such as *E*, those in the **City Watch** sequence and *MP, SM, H, J* and *CJ.*

The element that makes wizards what they are is mystical power, in which they are like **witches**. However, witches differ from wizards in their methodology, source of power, and organisation. Wizard knowledge is in language, and in particular language which is stored in books – which means they are particularly suspicious of the use of words by lay people (see, say, William de **Worde**). Symbolically at least their power is channelled through their staff (in the sense of a long wooden stick rather than the people they employ, although see Mrs **Whitlow**) and their hats. Wizards are essentially hierarchical, at the Unseen University being based around a **Stratified Society** beneath eight eighth level wizards. A wizard usually moves up a level by killing his predecessor. This repetition of objects which thrust into the sky – mirrored in the architecture of the Unseen University – and the wizard's staff which (in the words of a Discworld folk song) has a knob on its end (*see* Dave **Greenslade**) have obvious phallic connotations; with the exception of Eskarina **Smith** all wizards are male (although Granny **Weatherwax** was offered a chair). Witches tend to avoid doing Magic unless absolutely necessary, generally preferring to rely on headology; wizards are much the same, but more often for reasons of laziness.

Wizards are not new to Pratchett, of course, being a staple of **Children's Fiction**. *The Wonderful Wizard of Oz* (1900) by L. Frank Baum (1856–1919) features a wizard who is a fraud; the stage magician Oscar Zoroaster Phadrig Isaac Norman Henkel Emmannuel Ambroise Diggs accidentally ended up in Oz and was worshipped as a great sorcerer, a notion he did nothing to disabuse them of. In J.R.R. **Tolkien's** Middle-earth stories five wizards were sent to intervene in the affairs of men, **dwarves**, **elves** and so forth, and the most famous of these is Gandalf the Grey, later Gandalf the White. Pratchett's wizards are notable by their differences from Tolkien's – they lack competence.

Discworld fan dressed as a wizard.

Of course it is impossible to ignore the highly successful novels about the training of wizards – the Earthsea novels by Ursula Le Guin (b.1929). In *A Wizard of Earthsea* (1968), the young boy Duny, known as Sparrowhawk, is damaged by an attempt to use magic to defend his home village. A local wizard, Ogion, heals him, gives him the name of Ged and send him to the wizard school on the isle of Roke.

The wizards of Discworld are mostly associated with universities, in particular the Unseen University of **Ankh-Morpork**, but also the equivalent in Bugarup, **XXXX**, Krull and Pseudopolis. There are exceptions – Rincewind was a wizard at large through general incompetence, although at various points he has been welcomed back into the fold as the Egregious Professor of Cruel and Unusual Geography and Igneous **Cutwell** operates on a freelance basis. On the whole, however, the eighth son of an eighth son (Esk notwithstanding) is automatically admitted to the designation of wizard, and entitled to be educated at the Unseen University. This seems to be such a cushy number that relatively few of them want to leave the campus once they have graduated – it must be the meals, the facilities and the indoor plumbing. Mustrum **Ridcully**, the most successful **Archchancellor** of the university of recent years, was unusual in having spent a number of decades in the countryside, and Ipslore the Red has been driven away from the place (*S*). Ipslore in turn breaks the rule by having sex and reproducing – the eighth son of an eighth son of an eighth son is a sourcerer, someone able to create magic without spells, and **Coin** was such a figure. Esk's friend Simon is also a sourcerer, although apparently without the complex family tree.

The Wizards are sometimes called upon by Ankh-Morpork in times of trouble, which can be when the trouble really starts. When the music tries to take over the city in *SM*, some of the wizards throw away their stuffy image and start behaving like teenaged rock fans, quiffs and all. The **Librarian** even becomes a member of the Band With Rocks In. In *J*, Prince Khufurah receives an honorary degree from the university for political reasons, which becomes part of a larger **War** between the city and **Klatch**. In *LH* Patrician **Vetinari** involves the wizards in the attempt to send a vessel to the **Hub** to defeat the Silver Horde (*see* **Cohen the Barbarian**).

They are also used in international **politics** between the **Agatean Empire** and **Ankh-Morpork**, in terms of giving support to Rincewind and **Twoflower**, or removing them from the city if the situation changed. In *E* the Unseen University is being haunted, and the Wizards summon **Death** in order to investigate, learning that Rincewind is somehow behind it. In *IT* it is necessary for the **Counterweight Continent** to be visited by the Great Wizzard, who they assume is Rincewind. His help is needed again when the Librarian falls magically ill, and they realise that Rincewind is probably the only person to remember his true name; true names have magical power over an individual's identity. In an attempt to locate him, the Wizards find themselves stranded on a desert island without the requisite eight gramophone records.

Wizards

As Pratchett has shifted to investigating the politics of Ankh-Morpork, its **City Watch** and other organisations and businesses, as well as following a new witch in the shape of Tiffany **Aching**, the wizards have been sidelined to some extent from the main sequence of novels into a series of science books, *SOD*, *SODII* and *SODIII*. The High Energy Magic building is a centre for serious research and **technology**, where young wizards have discovered that they can dispense with all those mumbo jumbo words in favour of a few simple ingredients. They are also trying to split the thaum, the basic magical atom. Two projects which have emerged from this building are HEX and Roundworld. The former is an ant-based computer, first built by Skazz (*SM*), but which has seemed to take on a life of its own in later novels. HEX enables the Unseen University to hack into the clacks network and send free messages. Roundworld is an artificial world created from the need to dispense with a large amount of magical energy – it is poured into a new, non-magical space that is a separate universe. Roundworld is used by Pratchett as a parallel to Earth and this enables his co-writers, Jack **Cohen** and Ian **Stewart** to explain various bits of science to the readers.

It is not impossible that a wizards novel will be part of the main sequence again, but there would seem to be few more places that Rincewind can be sent to. *See also* Ankh-Morpork; Archchancellors; Children's Fiction; Jack Cohen; Coin; Igneous Cutwell; Death; Diaries; Gormenghast; Dave Greenslade; The Librarian; Libraries; L-Space; Magic; Alberto Malich; Politics; Pop Music; Mustrum Ridcully; Rincewind; *The Science of Discworld*; Sexism; Eskarina Smith; Ian Stewart; Ponder Stibbons; Stratified Societies; Technology; J.R.R. Tolkien; Victor Tugelbund; *The Unseen University Cut-Out Book*; Patrician Vetinari; War; Granny Weatherwax; Mrs Whitlow *and* XXXX.

Further Reading

Aires, Nick. 2005. 'Wizards'. *The Greenwood Encyclopedia of Science Fiction and Fantasy Themes, Works, and Wonders*. Pp. 896–898. Edited by Gary Westfahl. Westport, Ct.: Greenwood.

Le Guin, Ursula. 1968. *A Wizard of Earthsea*. New York: Parnassus.

Andrew M. Butler

Wodehouse, P[elham] G[renville] (1881–1975)

Prolific English comic novelist, playwright, lyricist and screenplay writer, to whom Pratchett has frequently been compared – by Neil **Gaiman**, by Brendan Wignall in *The Oxford Times* (alongside Evelyn Waugh (1903–1966) and Tom Sharpe (b.1928)), by Tom Hutchinson (*c.*1930–2005) in *The Times* and so on. The touchstones are their use of ensemble humour, the formal rules which structure their novels, their rate of output, their creation of the sense of a real world, peopled with vivid characters, and the good spirits in which the authors seem to operate.

P.G. Wodehouse on a 1930s cigarette card.

Wodehouse was born in Guildford to parents who were usually resident in Hong Kong, as his father was a civil servant there. Brought up more by aunts than his mother, he was sent to various boarding schools and was largely educated at Dulwich College, leaving in 1900 just before Raymond Chandler (1888–1959) attended. His father retired through ill-health, scuppering any plans to go to Oxford University, and Wodehouse worked for the Hong Kong and Shanghai Bank in London. At first he wrote in his spare time, selling stories and other pieces to *The Public School Magazine*, *St James's Gazette* and *Tit-Bits* and eventually managed to get some work filling in on the 'By the Way' column on the London newspaper *The Globe* when its usual writer, William Beach Thomas (1868–1957), was on holiday. taking it on entirely when he retired. He also began to write novels that were serialised in the magazines.

In 1904 he was commissioned to write a lyric for a show *Sergeant Brut* to be performed at the Strand Theatre, London, and in 1906 actor-manager Seymour Hicks (1871–1949) hired him to write topical encores and lyrics for musicals at the Aldwych, pairing him with the American composer Jerome Kern (1885–1945). Wodehouse was later to work with Kern on 'Bill' (1918), a song reworked for *Show Boat* (1927), as well as with Ivor Novello (1893–1951) on *The Golden Moth, a Musical Play* (1921) and Cole Porter (1891–1964) on the musical *Anything Goes* (1934).

Having already been to America, Wodehouse returned in pursuit of a potential literary agent, A.E. Baerman, who had sold serial rights to *Love Among the Chickens* (1906) for a thousand dollars, but had not been forthcoming with the money. In 1909, resident in New York, he sold stories to *Cosmopolitan* and *Collier's Weekly*, but soon returned to London and *The Globe*, although he now had an honest American agent. For the next few years he moved between London, New York and France, meeting Ethel Newton Rowley, a widow with a daughter Leonora, in New York and marrying her in September 1914. The First World War had broken out but Wodehouse was unable to enlist due to poor eyesight.

Having already worked on screenplays, Wodehouse went to Hollywood in 1929 and had lunch at a reception given for Winston Churchill at the studio Metro-Goldwyn-Mayer, meeting producer Louis B. Mayer (1882–1957). Ethel started negotiating terms for Wodehouse to start writing for MGM, but in the meantime he was approached by Samuel Goldwyn (1882–1974) to write a film for him. In the end he was engaged for six months by MGM, doing little more than adding a bit of dialogue to *Those Three French Girls* (1930). The option was renewed, with little more produced; due to an interview in which Wodehouse joked about how overpaid he'd been, it was not renewed a second time. Paramount were to make an offer in 1934, and in 1936 he returned to MGM, again unproductively, and he also wrote the screenplay (for RKO) of *A Damsel in Distress* (1937), based on his 1919 novel.

At the outbreak of the Second World War, he remained at his French house in Le Touquet, and in 1940, he was interned by the Nazis in a lunatic asylum at Tost, Upper Silesia, then in Germany. About six months before his sixtieth birthday he was released and went to Berlin, were he began to deliver radio broadcasts to America. To the USA, which was not yet at war, these were little more than amusing talks about his treatment in the camp, but in Britain it led to accusations of treason, bracketed at times alongside Lord Haw-Haw (William Joyce, 1906–1946). Wodehouse was arrested, but faced no charges. He returned to America in 1947 and in 1955 became an American citizen. In January 1975 he was knighted, dying a month later in Long Island, New York.

He is best known for his novels and stories set in a number of distinct sequences. *The Jeeves and Wooster* stories, which began with 'Extricating Young Gussie' in the *Saturday Evening Post* (September 15 1915) and feature the butler Jeeves and his dim-witted master Bertie Wooster. In the stories, Wooster or his friends get into a variety of scrapes and difficulties, such as getting engaged, from which Jeeves then has to rescue them. Wooster is a member of the Drones Club, which is also frequented by Clarence Threepwood, Lord Emsworth of Blandings Castle. The Blandings stories feature Emsworth, who wants to retreat from his family life to spend time with his pigs; the first comprise *Something Fresh* (1915). One visitor to Blandings is Rupert Psmith, who was expelled from Eton and goes though a series of misadventures with his old school friend, Mike Jackson.

Wodehouse is therefore a writer of series fiction, rather like Pratchett, although there is the sense that the novels are all set in the same universe, essentially a **Fantasy** version of upper class England which probably never existed. The stories and books can stand alone, but more would be gained by reading several of the sequences. The ineffectual characters in Pratchett perhaps owe something to Wodehouse's characters.

One criticism levelled at Wodehouse is his difficulties in dealing with women in his fiction and especially in depicting romantic interludes, as John Clute has written, 'the comedy writer Pratchett most resembles, P.G. Wodehouse, also had profound difficulties in handling sexual material in his work'. In the early Discworld novels, Pratchett tends to ignore this issue, then begins to make jokes about the coyness of characters such as Magrat **Garlick**. Even in the lengthy marriage of Samuel **Vimes** to Lady Sybil **Ramkin** the two spend relatively little time together, Vimes being more focused on his job. Finally both Wodehouse and Pratchett have received great public adulation, but have received insufficient critical attention, Wodehouse being dismissed by the Irish playwright Sean O'Casey (1880–1964) as 'English literature's performing flea'. Neil **Gaiman** has repeatedly suggested that Pratchett has more range than Wodehouse, in plots, characters, subject matter and themes. *See also* Comedy and Humour.

Further Reading

Green, Benny. 1981. *P.G. Wodehouse: A Literary Biography*. Oxford: Oxford University Press.

Connolly, Joseph. 1979. *P.G. Wodehouse: An Illustrated Biography*. London: Eel Pie.

Andrew M. Butler

Worde, William de (*CJ*, *TT*, *MR*, *GP*, *T!*)

The editor of **Ankh-Morpork**'s first newspaper, and a brave man in his opposition to the Guild of Engravers (who dislike movable type as it makes their skills obsolete), **wizards** (who worry about letters being reused in inappropriate words) and Samuel **Vimes** and the Patrician **Vetinari** who worry about the stories he prints. He employs Otto **Chriek** as an iconographer and Sacharissa Cripslock as a reporter and writer of headlines. She is able to work around de Worde's fanatical honesty – and in *GP* the two appear to be married. His paper is printed by Mr **Goodmountain**'s presses. He becomes a **war** correspondent in the Borogravia vs Zlobenia campaign (*MR*).

De Worde's father is Lord de Worde, an influence he is trying to escape from, which is just as well given his attempt to depose the Patrician. De Worde's elder brother, Rupert, trained at the Guild of Assassins, and was one of the rare casualties of the brief war against **Klatch** (*J*).

William de Worde's first appearance in the oeuvre was in an entry in the *DC*, some years before the appearance of *TT*, and he seems likely to remains as a minor cameo role, recalling Pratchett's experiences in newspapers. His name is a juxtaposition of William Caxton (*c*.1420–*c*.1492) and Wynkyn de Worde (d.1534), who popularised the printing press in England in the late fifteenth century. It must not be forgotten that Pratchett worked as a journalist when he left school. *See also* Ankh-Morpork; Otto Chriek; Gunilla Goodmountain; Klatch; Technology; Patrician Vetinari; Samuel Vimes; War *and* Wizards.

Andrew M. Butler

Wyatt, David (b.1968)

British born artist, who grew up in Sussex and was fascinated by the books of Alan Garner (b.1934) and comics. After art college, his first job was on 'Tharg's Future Shock' for *2000AD*. After a failed attempt to become a musician in a band, he moved to Dartmoor, Devon, to become an artist. He has worked in a number of techniques, including acrylics, thick paint, collage and scanning. He has produced the cover of *Contagion* (2003) for the band prog rock band Arena, artwork for Danbury Mint mugs inspired by J.R.R. Tolkien and covers for novels by writers such as Garner, John M. Ford (1957–2006), Sara Douglass (b.1957) and Sean Russell (b.1952). He has produced artwork for Terry Pratchett **calendars**, as well as covers for *AMHER*, *CP92 T*, *D*, *W* and The **Bromeliad**. *See also* Calendars.

Andrew M. Butler

The Wyrdest Link (2002) *see* Langford, David and Quizbooks

Wyrd Sisters (1988)

An extract from the sixth **Discworld** novel appeared in the British **Science Fiction** magazine *Interzone* 26 (November/December 1988) prior to publication. The first edition from Gollancz was 6,700 copies, with a cover by Josh **Kirby**. The paperback from Corgi (1989) was initially 110,000 copies; this was reset in 1997. From 2004 an alternative black and gold photographic cover has been available. In 1994 Gollancz issued an omnibus of *ER*, *WS* and *WA* as *The Witches Trilogy*. *WS* has been translated into Bulgarian, Croatian, Czech, Dutch, Estonian, Finnish, French, German, Greek, Hebrew, Hungarian, Icelandic, Italian, Japanese, Norwegian, Polish, Portuguese, Romanian, Russian, Serbian, Slovakian, Slovenian, Spanish, Swedish and Turkish. Whilst Granny **Weatherwax** had previously appeared (*ER*), the featuring of her coven marks this as the first of the **Witches** sequence. The Weird Sisters are the Three Witches from *Macbeth* by William **Shakespeare**, drawing partly on **Greek Mythology** of the Three Fates, but more on the three Norns of Germanic folklore. Wyrd is the Anglo-Saxon for Fate. The novel's subtitle is 'Starring Three Witches, also kings, daggers, crowns, storms, dwarfs, cats, ghost, spectres, apes, bandits, demons, forests, heirs, jester, tortures, trolls, turntables, general rejoicing and diverse alarums'. It was animated by **Cosgrove Hall** (*see* ***Wyrd Sisters From Terry Pratchett's Discworld*** **(Television Adaptation)**). The track 'Wyrd Sisters' on *Terry Pratchett's From the Discworld* by Dave **Greenslade** was inspired by this novel.

King **Verence I** has been murdered by his brother Lord Felmet, and now haunts the royal castle of **Lancre**. His son has been spirited away, named **Tomjon** by a newly formed witch's coven and placed in the care of a troupe of travelling thespians. Felmet, increasingly wracked with guilt and a despot, starts trying to crack down on witches and fifteen years later decides that commissioning a play about evil witches will turn the people of Lancre against them. Felmet is killed, but the court **Fool** rather than Tomjon succeeds to the throne.

The most obvious sources are plays by Shakespeare – Macbeth for the scheming wife and ambitious but guilty murder and Hamlet for murder by brother, a ghost and the use of a play to expose the truth. The **dwarf Hwel** is the Discworld counterpart of the Bard, who also writes plays or speeches with echoes of Richard III, Henry V and Henry IV Part Two. He is also inspired to write comedy sequences reminiscent of classic Hollywood comedy, and shares a **musical** muse with Andrew Lloyd Webber. The Fool who becomes a king is a familiar device, as is the wise fool, and the person who refuses **power** is a common theme within the sequence. *See also* Cosgrove Hall; The Fool; Magrat Garlick; Greek Mythology; Hollywood Comedies; Hwel; Lancre; Musicals; Narrative; Nanny Ogg; Plays; Politics; Power; William Shakespeare; Theatre; Tomjon; Verence; Granny Weatherwax; Witches; *Wyrd Sisters From Terry Pratchett's Discworld* (Television Adaptation).

Further Reading

Sayer, Karen. 'The Witches'. *GOL, GOL2.*

Andrew M. Butler

Wyrd Sisters From Terry Pratchett's Discworld (Television Adaptation) (1997)

Director: Jean Flynn. Producers: Jean Flynn. Executive Producer: Mark Hall. Writer: Martin Jameson. Music: Keith Hopgood and Phil Bush. Cast: Death: Christopher Lee; Magrat: Jane Horrocks; Nanny Ogg: June Whitfield; Granny Weatherwax: Annette Crosbie; Duchess Felmet: Eleanor Bron; The Fool/Tomjon: Les Dennis; Duke Felmet: Rob Rackstraw; and Andy Hockley, David Holt, Jimmy Hibbert, Melissa

Sinden and Taff Girdlestone. TV version: 6 x 25 minute episodes, broadcast Channel 4, 18 May-22 June 1998. Video version: 147 minutes, UK: Vision Video, 20 October 1997, three tapes (ASIN: B00004CV82), US: Acorn Media, 11 August 1999, three tapes (ASIN: B00000INBZ). DVD version: 140 minutes, Region 1/All regions/NTSC: Acorn Media, 31 July 2001 (ASIN: 156938374X); Regions 2 and 4: Universal Pictures Video, 6 November 2000 (ASIN: B000050GPB). Certificate PG. Available with *Soul Music From Terry Pratchett's Discworld* as a boxset Region 2, 13 February 2006 (ASIN: B000E99486).

Cover of *Terry Pratchett's Discworld, Wyrd Sisters, The Illustrated Screenplay.*

One of two animated adaptations of the Discworld series (*see* ***Soul Music From Terry Pratchett's Discworld***) commissioned from **Cosgrove Hall** by Channel 4 in the mid-1990s, made in association with ITEL and Ventureworld Films. This was broadcast on Channel 4 at 6pm on Sundays, and later released on video and DVD. The DVD release includes an edited version of the adaptation rather than individual episodes (although it shows an episode one screen, and evidence of the editing), the pilot, biographies of Pratchett and the characters and filmographies of the main actors, as well as a Discworld bibliography.

This was cel animation with some computer animation – notably the credits which were also used on the *SM* adaptation. The animation is perhaps flatter but feels more consistent than the other adaptation – this slightly predates it and was certainly shown first. The adaptation is tauter than the seven episodes of *SM*, being written here by Jimmy Hibbert who was a regular writer, script-editor and voice-over artist on Cosgrove Hall productions – he had been a voice on *Danger Mouse* (1981–1992), script editor and writer on *Count Duckula* (1988–1993), Vinto Pimmie in their version of *T*, played some roles in their version of *SM* and went on to be Ben in the new version of *Bill and Ben* (2001). Hibbert maintains much of Pratchett's dialogue, and sometimes incorporates description into dialogue.

The casting feels more even than that for *SM*, without the annoying voices that the **wizards** had, although playing the demon WxrtHltl-jwlpklz as camp misfires a little. The sonorous voice of Christopher Lee (b.1922) is perfect as **Death**, although he is largely confined to the first and last episodes, with the death of **Verence** and the performance of the play for Duke Felmet; his role is much bigger in *SM*.

The three witches are played by actresses best known for their work on sitcoms. Magrat **Garlick** is played by Jane Horrocks (b.1964), who came to prominence in the play *Road* (1986) and its film version (1987) written by Jim Cartwright (b.1958), which eventually led to him writing *The Rise and Fall of Little Voice* (1992) filmed as *Little Voice* (1998) for her. She remains best known for the part of the ditzy P.A., Bubble, in the BBC sitcom *Absolutely Fabulous* (1992–). She seems to alternate between dumb blondes and victims. June Whitfield (b.1925) played the sensible elderly mother figure, June Monsoon, in *Absolutely Fabulous*, but appeared on television and radio since the 1950s with comedy stars such as Tony Hancock (1924–1968), Stanley Baxter (b.1926), Frankie Howerd (1917–1992) and Terry Scott (1927–1994), appearing as the latter's husband in the BBC sitcom *Happy Ever After* (1974–1978) and the near copy *Terry and June* (1979–1987). She also appeared in several **Carry-On films**. She is often cast in sensible, maternal roles. Scottish actress Annette Crosbie (b.1934) is best known for playing the long-suffering and occasionally tragic figure Margaret Meldrew in the BBC sitcom *One Foot in the Grave* (1990–2000), but also played the voice of Galadriel in the cartoon version of *The Lord of the Rings* (1978) and the house-keeper Janet MacPherson in the ITV revival of *Doctor Finlay* (1993–1996).

Eleanor Bron (b.1934) has also appeared in *Absolutely Fabulous*, as Edina's mother, but began as a satirist in the Cambridge Footlight revue *The Last Laugh* (1959) with Peter Cook (1937–1995). She was part of the 1960s satire boom, including the BBC *Not So Much a Programme, More a Way of Life* (1964–1965), *My Father Knew Lord George* (1965), *The Late Show* (1966–1967) and had a cameo in *City of Death* (1979), a Douglas **Adams** co-scripted story for *Doctor Who*. She is in full Lady Macbeth mode as Duchess Felmet.

Rob Rackstraw (b.1965) plays Duke Felmet with a voice partway between Vincent Price (1911–1993) and Lawrence Olivier (1907–1989) as the eponymous Richard III (1955), or perhaps as Peter Sellers (1925–1980) doing a Shakespearean actor performing *Hard Day's Night* (1965). Rackstraw is mostly a voice actor, who worked on *Avenger Penguins* (1993), *Bob the Builder* (1993-) and the adaptation of *SM*. To balance his Olivier, the uncredited part of Davey the actor playing Death is played as a doddering and forgetful Sir John Gielgud (1904–2000).

In the double role of **Tomjon**/Verence the **Fool** was Les Dennis (b.1954), a Liverpudlian comedian, television presenter and actor. He came to fame as part of the ITV (LWT) sketch show *Russ Abbott's Madhouse* (1980–1985) and then the sketch show *The Russ Abbott Show* on BBC (1986–1991) and the second series on ITV (Granada) (1995–1996). He was often paired in a double act with Dustin Gee (1942–1986), on LWT's impressions show *Who Do You Do?* (1972–1976), in Abbott's shows and in BBC's *The Laughter Show* (1984–1985, as *Les and Dustin's Laughter Show* (1985–1986). After Gee's early death from a heart attack, it was renamed *The Les Dennis Laughter Show* (1987–1988). Dennis hosted the ITV quiz show *Family Fortunes* (1987–2002), and acted in occasional roles, especially in soaps. The doubled role requires him to show much versatility, in terms of parodying the classical actor, treading a fine line between chewing the carpet and being inspiring, and in being both the foolish and wise version of the Fool, with a romantic subplot with Magrat.

A neat touch is having **Hwel** the **dwarf** look like William **Shakespeare** and sound as if he is from Birmingham (close enough to Stratford-upon-Avon). His unexplained inspirations from **Musicals** and **Hollywood Comedy** are either described or appear in black and white or sepia thought bubbles. *See also* Animation; Carry-On Films; Cosgrove Hall; The Fool; Hollywood Comedies; Magrat Garlick; Hwel; Lancre; Musicals; Narrative; Nanny Ogg; Plays; Politics; Power; William Shakespeare; *Soul Music From Terry Pratchett's Discworld* (Television Adaptation); Television Adaptations; Theatre; Tomjon; Verence; Granny Weatherwax *and* Witches.

Further Reading

Jameson, Martin. 1996. *Wyrd Sisters: The Illustrated Screenplay*. London: Corgi.

Andrew M. Butler

X

XXXX (*RM, LC*)

A fabled lost continent, in fact the newest (latest built) continent. In *RM* we hear that there is a lost colony of **wizards** there, wearing hats fringed with corks hanging off strings, and that it is somewhere near the rim. In *LC* we meet them, at Bugarup University, under the leadership of Bill Rincewind, a distant relation of **Rincewind the Wizzard**. The continent includes a whole range of exotic fauna, flora, food, drink, customs and architecture, which Rincewind discovers when he ends up there, including an antipodean version of C.M.O.T. **Dibbler**.

XXXX in part refers to X the unknown (the unknown number in equations), with earlier names for an imagined southern continent in the real world being Terra Incognita – unknown land, a variant on the fictional Nowhere/Erewhon, No Place (outopia) and so forth. More obviously, with XXXX being a **parody** of **Australia**, the reference is being made to a brand of lager brewed, exported or brewed under license by Castlemaine Perkins since 1924. The brewery is based in Milton, Brisbane, and the Xs refer to the lager's strength: XXXX is four per cent. The lager was popularised by a series of adverts with the slogan, 'Australians wouldn't give a XXXX for anything else', the XXXX standing as a euphemism for a four letter word. *See also* Australia; Counterweight Continent; C.M.O.T. Dibbler; Rincewind *and* Wizards.

Andrew M. Butler

Y

Yo-Less (*OYCSM*, *JD*, *JB*)

A friend of Johnny **Maxwell**, his nickname deriving from the fact that he does not say 'Yo', which is perceived to be part of black British slang. Previously he had been known as Nearly Crucial and MC Spanner. His real name is not given. His interests and hobbies are typically English – train spotting, morris dancing, brass bands and *Star Trek* – which exposes people's unthinking **racism** as there is nothing ethnically defined about them. His grandparents came to Britain from the West Indies in the 1950s. His mother works at the local hospital, and he wants to be a doctor, or possibly a lawyer, when he grows up; he can already suggest that Johnny's experiences with the game are simply projections caused by the stresses in their lives. When he travels in town back to 1941 in *JB*, he is called 'Sambo' by a shopkeeper, and he initially plays along with this, although his real anger comes when **Kirsty** tries to soothe his feelings. She further puts her foot in it by stereotyping him about his fitness and athleticism. He presumably forgets about this, as he does the rest of the events in the novel. *See also* Children's Fiction; Coming of Age; Johnny Maxwell Trilogy; Kirsty; Johnny Maxwell *and* Racism.

Andrew M. Butler

Young, Adam (*GO*)

An apparently ordinary eleven year old child, but is in fact the Antichrist, having been swapped by mistake at birth. (The purported Antichrist, Warlock, the son of an American ambassador, is in fact a normal child.) His first name is presumably a pointer to the Adam of Genesis, the first man and one who, with Eve, fell when tempted. This Adam turns out to be made of sterner stuff and when the offer to rule the world comes, he turns it down. Adam's climactic rebellion may only mark a temporary postponement of the Final Days, but then of course his biological father, Lucifer, was not particularly obedient.

Adam is a member of a gang, currently called the Them, with Wensleydale, Brian, token girl Pepper and his **dog**. This resembles the Outlaws in the William stories produced from 1919 by Richmal Compton (1890–1969) and the Famous Five in the books written 1942–1963 by Enid Blyton (1897–1968) in its imaginary adventures. (Kirsty ironically notes her tokenism in *JB*.) The nostalgia of the endless summer of childhood which envelops the gang is an effect of his aura, which protects the Oxfordshire village of Tadfield. The gang serves as a counter to the Four Horsemen of the Apocalypse, **Death**, Famine, **War** and Pollution (and compare the foursome with *S*). *See also* Coming of Age; Death; Dogs *and* War.

Andrew M. Butler

Abbreviations of Terry Pratchett's Works

AD	*The Art of Discworld*
AMHER	*The Amazing Maurice and His Educated Rodents*
'CCOODD'	'A Collegiate Casting-Out of Devilish Devices'
CJ	*Carpe Jugulum*
COM	*The Colour of Magic*
CP	*The Carpet People*
CP71	*The Carpet People* (1971 version)
CP92	*The Carpet People* (1992 version)
D	*Diggers*
DA	*Discworld Almanak*
'DWCN'	'Death and What Comes Next'
DC	*Discworld Companion*
DD	*Death's Domain*
DSS	*The Dark Side of the Sun*
E	*Eric*
ER	*Equal Rites*
FE	*The Fifth Elephant*
FOC	*Feet of Clay*
GG	*Guards! Guards!*
GO	*Good Omens*
GP	*Going Postal*
H	*Hogfather*
HFOS	*A Hat Full of Sky*
IT	*Interesting Times*
J	*Jingo*
JB	*Johnny and the Bomb*
JD	*Johnny and the Dead*
LC	*The Last Continent*
LF	*The Light Fantastic*
LH	*The Last Hero*
LL	*Lords and Ladies*
M	*Mort*
MAA	*Men at Arms*
MP	*Moving Pictures*
Msk	*Maskerade*
MR	*Monstrous Regiment*
NDC	*New Discworld Companion*
NW	*Night Watch*
OYCSM	*Only You Can Save Mankind*
P	*Pyramids*
RM	*Reaper Man*
S	*Sourcery*
SA	*The Streets of Ankh-Morpork*
'SALF'	'The Sea and Little Fishes'
SG	*Small Gods*
SM	*Soul Music*
SOD	*The Science of Discworld*
SODII	*The Science of Discworld II*
SOD III	*The Science of Discworld III*
Str	*Strata*
T	*Truckers*
T!	*Thud!*
'TB'	'Troll Bridge'
TGL	*A Tourist's Guide to Lancre*
'TOC'	'Theatre of Cruelty'
TT	*The Truth*
TOT	*Thief of Time*
W	*Wings*
WA	*Witches Abroad*
WFM	*The Wee Free Men*
Wint	*Wintersmith*
WMC?	*Where's My Cow?*
WS	*Wyrd Sisters*

Note

GOL is Butler, Andrew M., Edward James and Farah Mendlesohn, eds. *Terry Pratchett: Guilty of Literature*. Reading: Science Fiction Foundation, 2000.

GOL2 Butler, Andrew M., Edward James and Farah Mendlesohn, eds. *Terry Pratchett: Guilty of Literature*. Baltimore, Maryland: Old Earth Books. 2004.

List of Illustrations

45. Ten Pence Stamp. Discworld Merchandising. The Cunning Artificer.

46. Model of The Mended Drum. Discworld Merchandising. The Cunning Artificer.

47. Cover of *Monstrous Regiment.* Random House.

48. Cast of *Les Miserables.* Jonathan Drake/Reuters. Corbis UK Ltd.

49. Cover of *Nanny Ogg's Cookbook.* Random House.

50. Cover of *Night Watch.* Random House.

51. Cover of *Only You Can Save Mankind.* Random House.

52. Twinning ceremony, Wincanton. The Cunning Artificer.

53. Cover of *Terry Pratchett's Wyrd Sisters, The Play.* Random House.

54. First professional stage presentation of *Guards! Guards!*, 1998. Starstock. Photoshot.

55. Cover of *Terry Pratchett's Mort, The Play.* Random House

56. Elvis Presley. Frank Carroll/Sygma. Corbis UK Ltd.

57. Anoia Kitchen Hook. Discworld Merchandising. The Cunning Artificer.

58. Rincewind puppet. Discworld Merchandising. The Cunning Artificer.

59. Still from *The Hitchhikers Guide to the Galaxy* movie. Content Mine International. Alamy.

60. Cover of *The Science of Discworld.* Random House.

61. Cover of *The Science of Discworld II: The Globe.* Random House.

62. Cover of *The Science of Discworld III: Darwin's Watch.* Random House.

63. Cover of *Terry Pratchett's Discworld Soul Music, The Illustrated Screenplay.* Random House.

64. Ian Stewart. University of Warwick.

65. Ankh-Morpork Fifty Pence Green Cabbage stamp. Discworld Merchandising. The Cunning Artificer.

66. Cover of *Strata.* Random House.

67. Cover of *The Streets of Ankh-Morpork.* Random House.

68. Cover of *Terry Pratchett's The Colour of Magic: The Graphic Novel.* Random House.

69. Cover of *Terry Pratchett's The Light Fantastic: The Graphic Novel.* Random House.

70. Cover of *Thief of Time.* Random House.

71. J.R.R. Tolkien. Haywood Magee/Picture Post. Getty Images.

72. Still from *Run Rincewind, Run.* Snowgum Films.

73. Cover of *Truckers.* Random House.

74. Still from the Cosgrove Hall television adaptation of *Truckers*, 1991. The attempt to drive the truck. Fremantle Archive Stills.

75. Cover of *The Truth.* Random House.

76. Model of the Unseen University Organ. Discworld Merchandising. The Cunning Artificer.

77. Cover of *The Unseen University Cut-Out Book.* Random House.

78. Model of the Vampire's Castle. Discworld Merchandising. The Cunning Artificer.

79. 'Samuel Vimes' by Paul Kidby. Courtesy of Paul Kidby.

80. Model of The Old Watch House in Treacle Mine Road. Discworld Merchandising. The Cunning Artificer.

81. 'Studies of Granny Weatherwax' by Paul Kidby. Courtesy of Paul Kidby.

82. 'The Salem Witch', *c.*1925. Lake County Museum. Corbis UK Ltd.

83. Model of Granny's cottage. Discworld Merchandising. The Cunning Artificer.

84. Discworld fan dressed as a wizard. The Cunning Artificer.

85. P.G. Wodehouse on a 1930s cigarette card. Pictorial Press Ltd. Alamy.

86. Cover of *Terry Pratchett's Discworld, Wyrd Sisters, The Illustrated Screenplay.* Random House.

Select Bibliography

Primary

Short Works

Pratchett, Terry. 1963. 'The Hades Business'. *Science Fantasy* 60: Pp. 66–76.

———.1965. 'The Hades Business'. Pp. 119–130 in *The Unfriendly Future*. Edited by Tom Boardman Jr. London: NEL.

———. 1965. 'Night Dweller'. *New Worlds* 156 (November): 83–88.

———. 1983. 'And Mind the Monoliths'. *Bath & West Evening Chronicle* (3 April 1983).

———. 1987. 'Alien Christmas'. *Ansible* 50 (August/September 1987).

———. 1987. 'Twenty Pence with Envelope and Seasonal Greetings'. *Time Out* (16–30 December 1987).

———. 1988. 'Incubust'. P. 53 in *The Drabble Project*. Edited by Rob Meades and David B. Wake. Birmingham: Beacon Publications.

———. 1989. 'Roots'. Pp. 73–75 in *The Roots of Fantasy*. Edited by Shelley Dutton Berry. Seattle: 15th World Fantasy Convention.

———. 1989. 'Thought Progress'. *20/20* (May): P. 143.

———.1989. 'Turntables of the Night'. Pp. 169–180 in *Hidden Turnings*. Edited by Diana Wynne Jones. London: Methuen.

———. 1990. 'Hollywood Chickens'. Pp. 2–10 in *More Tales from the Forbidden Planet*. Edited by Roz Kaveney. London: Titan Books.

———. 1990. '#ifdefDEBUG + 'World/Enough' + 'Time''. Pp. 79–93 in *Digital Dreams*. Edited by David V. Barrett. London: NEL.

———. 1991. 'The Secret Book of the Dead'. Pp. 29–30 in *Now We Are Sick*. Edited by Neil Gaiman and Stephen Jones. Minneapolis, Minnesota: DreamHaven.

———.1991. 'Whose Fantasy Are You?' *Bookcase* (17 September 1991): 19.

———. 1992. 'Elves Were Bastards'. *Programme Book*. Rotterdam, Holland: Hillcon III (Beneluxcon 18).

———. 1992. 'Troll Bridge'. Pp. 46–56 in *After the King*. Edited by Martin H. Greenberg. New York: Tor.

———. 1993. 'High Tech, Why Tech?' *The Electronic Author* (Summer): P. 2.

———. 1993. 'Let There Be Dragons'. *The Bookseller* (11 June 1993): Pp. 60, 62.

———. 1993. 'Theatre of Cruelty'. *Bookcase* 45 (July/August): Pp. 10–11.

———. 1995. 'Once and Future'. Pp. 41–60 in *Camelot*. Edited by Jane Yolen. New York: Philomel.

———. 1996. 'FTB'. *Western Daily Press* (24 December 1996).

———. 1996. 'Introduction'. David Langford. *The Unseen University Challenge: Terry Pratchett's Discworld Quizbook*. London: Gollancz. Pp. 5–7.

———. 1996. 'On Writing'. *The Faces of Fantasy: Photographs by Patti Perret*. New York: Tor.

———. 1996. 'Sheer Delight'. *SFX Magazine* (April): 31.

———. 1998. 'Introduction'. P. 6 in *The Ultimate Encyclopedia of Fantasy*. Edited by David Pringle. London: Carlton.

———. 1998. 'Terry on Tour'. *SFX Magazine* (June): Pp. 64–68.

———. 1998. 'The Sea and Little Fishes'. Pp. 63–97 in *Legends*. Edited by Robert Silverberg. New York: Tor.

———. 1999. 'Fantasy Kingdom'. *The Sunday Times Review* (4 July 1999): P. 4.

———. 1999. 'Foreword'. P. vii in *Brewer's Dictionary of Phrase and Fable*. Edited by Adrian Room. London: Cassell.

———. 2000. '2001: The Vision and the Reality'. *The Sunday Times* (24 December 2000): Pp. 5, 17.

———. 2000. 'Imaginary Worlds, Real Stories'. *Folklore*: Pp. 159–168.

———. 2000. 'The Orangutans are Dying'. *The Mail on Sunday Review* (2000): P. 63.

———. 2001. 'The Choice Word'. *The Book of Favourite Words*. Edited by Gordon Kerr. London: Bloomsbury.

———. 2001. 'Cult Classic'. Pp. 78–80, 82–83 in *Meditations on Middle-Earth*. Edited by Karen Haber. New York: St Martin's Press.

———. 2001. 'Introduction'. David Langford. *The Leaky Establishment*. Abingdon, Oxon: Big Engine. Pp. vii–viii.

———. 2001. 'A Word About Hats'. *Sunday Telegraph* (2001): P. 4.

———. 2002. 'Death and What Comes Next'. *TimeHunt.*

———. 2002. 'Introduction'. David Langford. *The Wyrdest Link: The Second Discworld Quizbook.* London: Gollancz, Pp. ix–x.

———. 2002. 'Nac Mac'. *Programme Book.* Hinckley: Discworld Convention, Pp. 16–17.

———. 2002. 'Neil Gaiman: Amazing Master Conjurer'. *Programme Book.* Boston: Boskone. P. 39.

———. 2003. 'Paperback Writer'. *The Guardian* (6 December 2003).

———. 2003. 'Thud – A Historical Perspective'. *Thud! The Discworld Boardgame.*

———. 2004. '2001: The Vision and the Reality'. Pp. 85–88 in *Once More * With Footnotes.* Edited by Priscilla Olson and Sheila M. Perry. Framingham, MA: The NESFA Press.

———. 2004. 'Alien Christmas'. Pp. 193–197 in *Once More * With Footnotes.* Edited by Priscilla Olson and Sheila M. Perry. Framingham, MA: The NESFA Press.

———. 2004. 'And Mind the Monoliths'. Pp. 71–73 in *Once More * With Footnotes.* Edited by Priscilla Olson and Sheila M. Perry. Framingham, MA: The NESFA Press.

———. 2004. 'The Ankh-Morpork National Anthem'. Pp. 191–192 in *Once More * With Footnotes.* Edited by Priscilla Olson and Sheila M. Perry. Framingham, MA: The NESFA Press.

———. 2004. 'Apology'. Pp. 15–16 in *Once More * With Footnotes.* Edited by Priscilla Olson and Sheila M. Perry. Framingham, MA: The NESFA Press.

———. 2004. 'The Big Store'. Pp. 43–44 in *Once More * With Footnotes.* Edited by Priscilla Olson and Sheila M. Perry. Framingham, MA: The NESFA Press.

———. 2004. 'The Choice Word'. Pp. 215 in *Once More * With Footnotes.* Edited by Priscilla Olson and Sheila M. Perry. Framingham, MA: The NESFA Press.

———. 2004. 'Cult Classic'. Pp. 209–213 in *Once More * With Footnotes.* Edited by Priscilla Olson and Sheila M. Perry. Framingham, MA: The NESFA Press.

———. 2004. 'Death and What Comes Next'. Pp. 167–169 in *Once More * With Footnotes.* Edited by Priscilla Olson and Sheila M. Perry. Framingham, MA: The NESFA Press.

———. 2004. 'Doctor Who?' Pp. 27–29 in *Once More * With Footnotes.* Edited by Priscilla Olson and Sheila M. Perry. Framingham, MA: The NESFA Press.

———. 2004. 'Elves Were Bastards'. Pp. 177–179 in *Once More * With Footnotes.* Edited by Priscilla Olson and Sheila M. Perry. Framingham, MA: The NESFA Press.

———. 2004. 'Faces of Fantasy/On Writing'. Pp. 237–238 in *Once More * With Footnotes.* Edited by Priscilla Olson and Sheila M. Perry. Framingham, MA: The NESFA Press.

———. 2004. 'Final Reward'. Pp. 59–69 in *Once More * With Footnotes.* Edited by Priscilla Olson and Sheila M. Perry. Framingham, MA: The NESFA Press.

———. 2004. 'Foreword, *Brewer's Dictionary of Phrase and Fable'.* Pp. 161–162 in *Once More * With Footnotes.* Edited by Priscilla Olson and Sheila M. Perry. Framingham, MA: The NESFA Press.

———. 2004. 'FTB'. Pp. 75–78 in *Once More * With Footnotes.* Edited by Priscilla Olson and Sheila M. Perry. Framingham, MA: The NESFA Press.

———. 2004. 'The Hades Business'. Pp. 31–41 in *Once More * With Footnotes.* Edited by Priscilla Olson and Sheila M. Perry. Framingham, MA: The NESFA Press.

———. 2004. 'High Tech, Why Tech?' Pp. 89–91 in *Once More * With Footnotes.* Edited by Priscilla Olson and Sheila M. Perry. Framingham, MA: The NESFA Press.

———. 2004. 'Hollywood Chickens'. Pp. 19–25 in *Once More * With Footnotes.* Edited by Priscilla Olson and Sheila M. Perry. Framingham, MA: The NESFA Press.

———. 2004. "# ifdefDEBUG + 'World/Enough' + 'Time'". Pp. 149–159 in *Once More * With Footnotes.* Edited by Priscilla Olson and Sheila M. Perry. Framingham, MA: The NESFA Press.

———. 2004. 'Imaginary Worlds, Real Stories'. Pp. 239–251 in *Once More * With Footnotes.* Edited by Priscilla Olson and Sheila M. Perry. Framingham, MA: The NESFA Press.

———. 2004. 'Incubust'. P. 57 in *Once More * With Footnotes.* Edited by Priscilla Olson and Sheila M. Perry. Framingham, MA: The NESFA Press.

———. 2004. 'Introduction: *The Leaky Establishment*'. Pp. 139–141 in *Once More * With Footnotes.* Edited by Priscilla

Olson and Sheila M. Perry. Framingham, MA: The NESFA Press.
———. 2004. 'Introduction: *The Ultimate Encyclopedia of Fantasy*'. Pp. 175–176 in *Once More * With Footnotes.* Edited by Priscilla Olson and Sheila M. Perry. Framingham, MA: The NESFA Press.
———. 2004. 'Introduction: *The Unseen University Challenge*'. Pp. 83–84 in *Once More * With Footnotes.* Edited by Priscilla Olson and Sheila M. Perry. Framingham, MA: The NESFA Press.
———. 2004. 'Introduction: *The Wyrdest Link*'. Pp. 97–98 in *Once More * With Footnotes.* Edited by Priscilla Olson and Sheila M. Perry. Framingham, MA: The NESFA Press.
———. 2004. 'Let There Be Dragons'. Pp. 143–147 in *Once More * With Footnotes.* Edited by Priscilla Olson and Sheila M. Perry. Framingham, MA: The NESFA Press.
———. 2004. 'Magic Kingdoms'. Pp. 255–259 in *Once More * With Footnotes.* Edited by Priscilla Olson and Sheila M. Perry. Framingham, MA: The NESFA Press.
———. 2004. 'Medical Notes'. Pp. 181–183 in *Once More * With Footnotes.* Edited by Priscilla Olson and Sheila M. Perry. Framingham, MA: The NESFA Press.
———. 2004. 'Neil Gaiman: Amazing Master Conjurer'. Pp. 171–174 in *Once More * With Footnotes.* Edited by Priscilla Olson and Sheila M. Perry. Framingham, MA: The NESFA Press.
———. 2004. 'No Worries'. Pp. 219–226 in *Once More * With Footnotes.* Edited by Priscilla Olson and Sheila M. Perry. Framingham, MA: The NESFA Press.
———. 2004. 'Once and Future'. Pp. 261–273 in *Once More * With Footnotes.* Edited by Priscilla Olson and Sheila M. Perry. Framingham, MA: The NESFA Press.
———. 2004. 'The Orangutans are Dying'. Pp. 187–190 in *Once More * With Footnotes.* Edited by Priscilla Olson and Sheila M. Perry. Framingham, MA: The NESFA Press.
———. 2004. 'Paperback Writer'. Pp. 53–55 in *Once More * With Footnotes.* Edited by Priscilla Olson and Sheila M. Perry. Framingham, MA: The NESFA Press.
———. 2004. 'Roots of Fantasy'. Pp. 93–96 in *Once More * With Footnotes.* Edited by Priscilla Olson and Sheila M. Perry. Framingham, MA: The NESFA Press.
———. 2004. 'The Sea and Little Fishes'. Pp. 103–137 in *Once More * With Footnotes.* Edited by Priscilla Olson and Sheila M. Perry. Framingham, MA: The NESFA Press.
———. 2004. 'The Secret Book of the Dead'. Pp. 253–254 in *Once More * With Footnotes.* Edited by Priscilla Olson and Sheila M. Perry. Framingham, MA: The NESFA Press.
———. 2004. 'Sheer Delight'. P. 185 in Once *More * With Footnotes.* Edited by Priscilla Olson and Sheila M. Perry. Framingham, MA: The NESFA Press.
———. 2004. 'Theatre of Cruelty'. Pp. 79–82 in *Once More * With Footnotes.* Edited by Priscilla Olson and Sheila M. Perry. Framingham, MA: The NESFA Press.
———. 2004. 'Thought Progress'. Pp. 99–101 in *Once More * With Footnotes.* Edited by Priscilla Olson and Sheila M. Perry. Framingham, MA: The NESFA Press.
———. 2004. 'Thud – A Historical Perspective'. Pp. 163–165 in *Once More * With Footnotes.* Edited by Priscilla Olson and Sheila M. Perry. Framingham, MA: The NESFA Press.
———. 2004. 'Troll Bridge'. Pp. 227–235 in *Once More * With Footnotes.* Edited by Priscilla Olson and Sheila M. Perry. Framingham, MA: The NESFA Press.
———. 2004. 'Turntables of the Night'. Pp. 199–200 in *Once More * With Footnotes.* Edited by Priscilla Olson and Sheila M. Perry. Framingham, MA: The NESFA Press.
———. 2004. 'Twenty Pence with Envelope and Seasonal Greetings'. Pp. 45–51 in *Once More * With Footnotes.* Edited by Priscilla Olson and Sheila M. Perry. Framingham, MA: The NESFA Press.
———. 2004. 'Whose Fantasy Are You?' Pp. 217–218 in *Once More * With Footnotes.* Edited by Priscilla Olson and Sheila M. Perry. Framingham, MA: The NESFA Press.
———. 2004. 'A Word About Hats'. Pp. 275–277 in *Once More * With Footnotes.* Edited by Priscilla Olson and Sheila M. Perry. Framingham, MA: The NESFA Press.
———. 2005. 'A Collegiate Casting-Out of Devilish Devices' (*Times Higher Educational Supplement* (13 May 2005).

———. 2006. 'Terry on Neil'. *Good Omens Anniversary Edition*. New York: William Morrow.

Novels

Pratchett, Terry. *The Carpet People*. Gerrards Cross: Colin Smythe Ltd, 1971.
———. 1976. *The Dark Side of the Sun*. Gerrards Cross: Colin Smythe Ltd.
———. 1981. *Strata*. Gerrards Cross: Colin Smythe Ltd.
———. 1982. *Strata*. London: NEL.
———. 1983. *The Colour of Magic*. Gerrards Cross: Colin Smythe Ltd.
———. 1985. *The Colour of Magic*. London: Corgi.
———. 1985. *The Light Fantastic*. Gerrards Cross: Colin Smythe Ltd.
———. 1986. *The Light Fantastic*. London: Corgi.
———. 1987. *Equal Rites*. London: Gollancz in association with Colin Smythe Ltd.
———. 1987. *Equal Rites*. London: Corgi.
———. 1987. *Mort*. London: Gollancz in association with Colin Smythe Ltd.
———. 1988. *Mort*. London: Corgi.
———. 1988. *Sourcery*. London: Gollancz in association with Colin Smythe Ltd.
———. 1988. *Strata*. London: Corgi.
———. 1988. *The Dark Side of the Sun*. London: Corgi.
———. 1988. *Wyrd Sisters*. London: Gollancz.
———. 1989. *Pyramids: The Book of Going Forth*. London: Gollancz.
———. 1989. *Guards! Guards!* London: Gollancz.
———. 1989. *Sourcery*. London: Corgi.
———. 1989. *The Colour of Magic*. Introduction by Terry Pratchett. London: Colin Smythe Ltd.
———. 1989. *The Unadulterated Cat*. London: Gollancz.
———. 1989. *Truckers: The First Book of the Nomes*. London: Doubleday.
———. 1989. *Wyrd Sisters*. London: Corgi.
———. 1990. *Diggers: The Second Book of the Nomes*. London: Doubleday.
———. 1990. *~~Faust~~ Eric*. London: Gollancz.
———. 1990. *Guards! Guards!* London: Corgi.
———. 1990. *Moving Pictures*. London: Gollancz.
———. 1990. *Pyramids: The Book of Going Forth*. London: Corgi.
———. 1990. *Truckers: The First Book of the Nomes*. London: Corgi.
———. 1990. *Wings: The Third Book of the Nomes*. London: Doubleday.
———. 1991. *Diggers: The Second Book of the Nomes*. London: Corgi.
———. 1991. *~~Faust~~ Eric*. London: Gollancz.
———. 1991. *Moving Pictures*. London: Corgi.
———. 1991. *Reaper Man*. London: Gollancz.
———. 1991. *Wings: The Third Book of the Nomes*. London: Corgi.
———. 1991. *Witches Abroad*. London: Gollancz.
———. 1992. *Lords and Ladies*. London: Gollancz.
———. 1992. *Only You Can Save Mankind*. London: Doubleday.
———. 1992. *Reaper Man*. London: Corgi.
———. 1992. *Small Gods*. London: Gollancz.
———. 1992. *The Carpet People* (second version). London: Doubleday.
———. 1992. *Witches Abroad*. London: Corgi.
———. 1993. *Johnny and the Dead*. London: Doubleday.
———. 1993. *Lords and Ladies*. London: Corgi.
———. 1993. *Men at Arms*. London: Gollancz.
———. 1993. *Only You Can Save Mankind*. London: Corgi.
———. 1993. *Small Gods*. London: Corgi.
———. 1993. *The Carpet People* (second version). London: Corgi.
———. 1994. *Interesting Times*. London: Gollancz.
———. 1994. *Johnny and the Dead*. London: Corgi.
———. 1994. *Men at Arms*. London: Corgi.
———. 1994. *Soul Music*. London: Gollancz.
———. 1995. *Interesting Times* London: Corgi.
———. 1995. *Maskerade*. London: Gollancz.
———. 1995. *Soul Music*. London: Corgi.
———. 1996. *~~Faust~~ Eric*. London: Vista.
———. 1996. *Feet of Clay*. London: Gollancz.
———. 1996. *Hogfather*. London: Gollancz.
———. 1996. *Johnny and the Bomb*. London: Doubleday.
———. 1996. *Maskerade*. London: Corgi.
———. 1997. *Feet of Clay*. London: Corgi.
———. 1997. *Hogfather*. London: Corgi.
———. 1997. *Jingo*. London: Gollancz.
———. 1997. *Johnny and the Bomb*. London: Corgi.

———. 1998. *Jingo*. London: Corgi.
———. 1998. *The Last Continent*. London: Doubleday.
———. 1999. *Carpe Jugulum*. London: Doubleday.
———. 1999. *The Last Continent*. London: Corgi.
———. 1999. *The Fifth Elephant*. London: Doubleday.
———. 1999. *Carpe Jugulum*. London: Corgi.
———. 2000. *The Fifth Elephant*. London: Corgi.
———. 2000. *The Truth*. London: Doubleday.
———. 2001. *Thief of Time*. London: Doubleday.
———. 2001. *The Truth*. London: Corgi.
———. 2001. *The Last Hero*. London: Doubleday.
———. 2001. *The Amazing Maurice and His Educated Rodents*. London: Doubleday.
———. 2002. *Thief of Time*. London: Corgi.
———. 2002. *Night Watch*. London: Doubleday.
———. 2002. *The Amazing Maurice and His Educated Rodents*. London: Corgi.
———. 2003. *The Wee Free Men*. London: Doubleday.
———. 2003. *Night Watch*. London: Corgi.
———. 2003. *Monstrous Regiment*. London: Doubleday.
———. 2004. *The Wee Free Men*. London: Corgi.
———. 2004. *Monstrous Regiment*. London: Corgi.
———. 2004. *Going Postal*. London: Doubleday.
———. 2004. *A Hat Full of Sky*. London: Doubleday.
———. 2005. *Thud!* London: Doubleday.
———. 2005. *A Hat Full of Sky*. London: Corgi.
———. 2005. *Going Postal*. London: Corgi.
———. 2005. *Where's My Cow?* London: Doubleday.
———. 2006. *Wintersmith*. London: Doubleday.
———. 2006. *Thud!* London: Corgi.
———. 2007. *Wintersmith*. London: Corgi.

Plays, Screenplays, Maps, Diaries and Other Collaborations

Briggs, Stephen. 1996. *Johnny and the Dead*. Oxford: Oxford University Press.
———. 1996.*Mort: The Play*. London: Corgi.
———. 1996. *Wyrd Sisters, The Play*. London: Corgi.
———. 1997. *Guards! Guards! The Play*. London: Corgi.
———. 1997. *Men At Arms, The Play*. London: Corgi.
———. 1998. *Maskerade, The Play*. London: Samuel French.
———. 1999. *Carpe Jugulum, The Play*. London: Samuel French.
———. 2002. *The Fifth Elephant, The Play*. London: Methuen.
———. 2002. *Interesting Times, The Play*. London: Methuen.
———. 2002. *The Truth, The Play*. London: Methuen.
———. 2003. *The Amazing Maurice and His Educated Rodents*. Activity section by Jenny Roberts. Oxford: Oxford University Press.
———. 2004. *Monstrous Regiment, The Play*. London: Methuen.
———. 2004. *Night Watch, The Play*. London: Methuen.
———. 2005. *Going Postal*. London: Methuen.
———. 2005. *Jingo, The Play*. London: Methuen,
Briggs, Stephen and Terry Pratchett. 1993. *The Streets of Ankh-Morpork*. London: Corgi.
Brown, Irana. 2001. *Lords and Ladies, The Play*. London: Samuel French.
Jameson, Martin. 1996. *Wyrd Sisters: The Illustrated Screenplay*. London: Corgi.
———. 1997. *Soul Music: The Illustrated Screenplay*. London: Corgi.
Jean, Vadim and Terry Pratchett. 2006. *Hogfather: The Illustrated Screenplay*. London: Gollancz.
Kidby, Paul and Terry Pratchett. 2004. *The Art of Discworld*. London: Victor Gollancz.
Pratchett, Terry. 1992. *Terry Pratchett's Truckers*. Loughborough: Ladybird.
Pratchett, Terry, Alan Batley and Bernard Pearson. 2006. *The Unseen University Cut-Out Book*. London: Doubleday.
Pratchett, Terry and Stephen Briggs. 1994. *The Discworld Companion*. London: Gollancz.
———. 1995. *The Discworld Mapp*. Painted by Stephen Player. London: Corgi.
———. 1997. *The Discworld Companion – Updated Edition*. London: Vista.

———. 1997. *Discworld's Unseen University Diary*. Illustrated by Paul Kidby. London: Victor Gollancz.

———. 1998. *Discworld's Ankh-Morpork City Watch Diary 1999*. Illustrated by Paul Kidby. London: Victor Gollancz.

———. 1999. *Discworld Assassin's Guild Yearbook and Diary 2000*. Illustrated by Paul Kidby. London: Victor Gollancz.

———. 2000. *Discworld Fools' Guild Yearbook and Diary 2001*. Illustrated by Paul Kidby. London: Victor Gollancz.

———. 2001. *Discworld Thieves' Guild Yearbook and Diary 2002*. Illustrated by Paul Kidby. London: Victor Gollancz.

———. 2002. *Discworld (Reformed) Vampyre's Diary 2003 Sponsored by the Uberwald League of Temperance*. Illustrated by Paul Kidby. London: Victor Gollancz.

———. 2003. *The New Discworld Companion*. London: Gollancz.

———. 2006. *Ankh-Morpork Post Office Handbook and Discworld Diary 2007*. Illustrated by Paul Kidby. London: Victor Gollancz.

Pratchett, Terry, Stephen Briggs and Tina Hannan. 1999. *Nanny Ogg's Cookbook Including recipes, items of Antiquarian Lore, Improving Observations of Life, Good Advice for Young People on the Threshold of the Adventure That is Marriage, Notes on Etiquette & Many Other Helpful Observations that will Not Offend the Most Delicate Sensibilities*. Illustrated by Paul Kidby. London: Doubleday.

———. 2001. *Nanny Ogg's Cookbook Including recipes, items of Antiquarian Lore, Improving Observations of Life, Good Advice for Young People on the Threshold of the Adventure That is Marriage, Notes on Etiquette & Many Other Helpful Observations that will Not Offend the Most Delicate Sensibilities*. Illustrated by Paul Kidby. London: Corgi.

Pratchett, Terry, Stephen Briggs and Paul Kidby. 1998. *A Tourist Guide to Lancre*. London: Corgi.

Pratchett, Terry and Neil Gaiman. 1990. *Good Omens: The Nice and Accurate Prophecies of Agnes Nutter. Witch: A Novel*. London: Doubleday.

———. 1991. *Good Omens: The Nice and Accurate Prophecies of Agnes Nutter. Witch: A Novel*. London: Corgi.

Pratchett, Terry and Paul Kidby. 1999. *Death's Domain*. London: Corgi.

Pratchett, Terry and Bernard Pearson. 2004. *Discworld Almanak*. London: Corgi.

Pratchett, Terry, Ian Stewart and Jack Cohen. 1999. *The Science of Discworld*. London: Ebury Press.

———. 2002. *The Science of Discworld*. 2nd ed. London: Ebury Press.

———. 2002. *The Science of Discworld II: The Globe*. London: Ebury Press.

———. 2003. *The Science of Discworld II: The Globe*. London: Ebury Press.

———. 2005. *The Science of Discworld III: Darwin's Watch*. London: Ebury Press.

———. 2006. *The Science of Discworld III: Darwin's Watch*. London: Ebury Press.

Secondary

Adams, Douglas. 1979. *The Hitch-Hiker's Guide to the Galaxy*. London: Pan.

Adams, Douglas and Mark Cawardine. 1990. *Last Chance To See...* London: William Heinemann.

Adams, Rachel and David Savran Eds. 2002. *The Masculinity Studies Reader*. London: Blackwell.

Agnew, Kate and Geoff Fox. 2001. *Children at War: From the First World War to the Gulf*. London: Continuum.

Aires, Nick. 2005. 'Wizards'. Pp. 896–898 in *The Greenwood Encyclopedia of Science Fiction and Fantasy Themes, Works, and Wonders*. Edited by Gary Westfahl. Westport, CT: Greenwood.

Aldiss, Brian with David Wingrove. *Trillion Year Spree: The History of Science Fiction*. London: Gollancz, 1986.

Alexander, Caroline. 'Echoes of the Heroic Age: Ancient Greece Part 1'. *National Geographic* 166. 6 (1999): P. 58.

Amis, Kingsley. *Lucky Jim: A Novel*. London: Gollancz, 1953.

Aristotle, Horace and Longinus. *Classical Literary Criticism*. Harmondsworth, Middlesex: Penguin, 1965.

Armitt, Lucie. *Theorizing the Fantastic*. London: Edward Arnold, 1996.

Arnal, William E. 'Definition'. *Guide to the Study of Religion*. Edited by Willi Braun and Russell T. McCutcheon. New York: Cassell, 2000. 6.

Artaud, Antonin. *The Theater and Its Double*. Translated by Mary Caroline Richards. New York: Grove Weidenfeld, 1958.

Attebery, Brian. *Strategies of Fantasy*. Bloomington and Indianapolis: Indiana University Press, 1992.

Bacon-Smith, Camille. *Science Fiction Culture*. Philadelphia: University of Pennsylvania Press, 1999.

Bakhtin, Mikhail. *Rabelais and His World*. Translated by Helene Iswolksy. Chicago, MA. and London: MIT Press, 1968.

———. *Speech Genres and Other Late Essays*. Translated by Verne W. McGee. Edited by Carol Emerson and Michael Holquist. Austin: University of Texas Press, 1986.

Baldry, Cherith. 'The Children's Books'. *Terry Pratchett: Guilty of Literature*. Foreword by David Langford. Edited by Andrew M. Butler, Edward James and Farah Mendlesohn. Reading: SFF, 2000. Pp. 20–34.

———. 'The Children's Books'. *Terry Pratchett: Guilty of Literature*. Edited by Andrew M. Butler, Edward James and Farah Mendlesohn. 2nd ed. Baltimore, Maryland: Old Earth Books, 2004. Pp. 41–65.

Banton, Martin. *Racial Theories*. Cambridge: Cambridge University Press, 1987.

Baring-Gould, Sabine. *The Book of Were-Wolves: Being an Account of a Terrible Superstition*. London: Smith, Elder, 1865.

Baudrillard, Jean. *The Gulf War Did Not Take Place*. Translated and edited by Paul Patton. Sydney: Power, 1995.

Beresford, Elisabeth. *The Wombles*. London: Benn, 1968.

Bergson, Henri. *Laughter: An Essay on the Meaning of the Comic*. London: Macmillan and Co, Limited, 1921.

Blake, Andrew. *The Land Without Music: Music, Culture and Society in Twentieth-Century Britain*. Manchester: Manchester University Press, 1997.

Bleiler, Richard, ed. *Supernatural Fiction Writers: Contemporary Fantasy and Horror*. Detroit: Gale, 2003.

Bradbury, Malcolm. 1975. *The History Man*. London: Secker & Warburg.

Brite, Poppy Z. *Lost Souls*. London: Penguin, 1992.

Brown, Craig. *1966 and All That*. London: Hodder, 2005.

Brown, James. 'Believing is Seeing: Silas Tomkyn Comberbanche and Terry Pratchett'. *Terry Pratchett: Guilty of Literature*. Edited by Andrew M. Butler, Edward James and Farah Mendlesohn. 2nd ed. Baltimore, Maryland: Old Earth Books, 2004. Pp. 238–260.

Brown, Martin. 'Imaginary Places, Real Monuments: Field Monuments of Lancre'. *Digging Holes in Popular Culture: Archaeology and Science Fiction*. Edited by Miles Russell. Oxford: Oxbow Books, 2002. Pp. 67–76.

Bulfinch, Thomas. *Bulfinch's Greek and Roman Mythology*. New York: Collier Books, 1971.

Burton, Maurice. *Universal Dictionary of Mammals of the World*. New York: Thomas Crowell Company, 1968.

Butler, Andrew M. 'The BSFA Award Winners: 2, *Pyramids* by Terry Pratchett'. *Vector: The Critical Journal of the British Science Fiction Association* 186 (December 1995): P. 4.

———. 'Terry Pratchett and the Comedic *Bildungsroman*'. *Foundation* 67 (Summer 1996): Pp. 56–62.

———. 'Review of Terry Pratchett, *Jingo*'. *Vector: The Critical Journal of the British Science Fiction Association* 198 (March/April 1998): Pp. 27–28.

———. 'Theories of Humour'. *Terry Pratchett: Guilty of Literature*. Edited by Andrew M. Butler, Edward James and Farah Mendlesohn. Reading: SFF, 2000. Pp. 35–50.

———. 'Review of Terry Pratchett, *Thief of Time*'. *Vector: The Critical Journal of the British Science Fiction Association* 218 (July/August 2001): P. 30.

———. *Terry Pratchett*. Harpenden: Pocket Essentials, 2001.

———. 'A Story About Stories: Terry Pratchett's *The Amazing Maurice and His Educated Rodents*'. *Vector: The Critical Journal of the British Science Fiction Association* 227 (January/February 2003): Pp. 10–11.

———. 'Theories of Humour'. *Terry Pratchett: Guilty of Literature*. Edited by Andrew M. Butler, Edward James and Farah Mendlesohn. 2nd ed. Baltimore, Maryland: Old Earth Books, 2004. Pp. 67–88.

———. '"We has found the enemy and they is us': Virtual War and Empathy in Four Children's Science Fiction Novels'. *Lion and the Unicorn* 28.2 (April 2004): Pp. 171–185.

Butler, Andrew M., Edward James and Farah Mendlesohn, eds. *Terry Pratchett: Guilty of Literature*. Foreword by David Langford. Reading: Science Fiction Foundation, 2000.

———. 'Preface'. *Terry Pratchett: Guilty of Literature*. Edited by Andrew M. Butler, Edward James and Farah Mendlesohn. Reading: Science Fiction Foundation, 2000. Pp. v–viii.

———, eds. *Terry Pratchett: Guilty of Literature*. 2nd ed. Baltimore, Maryland: Old Earth Books, 2004.

———. 'Preface'. *Terry Pratchett: Guilty of Literature*. Edited by Andrew M. Butler, Edward James and Farah Mendlesohn. 2nd ed. Baltimore, Maryland: Old Earth Books, 2004. Pp. vii–xiii.

Campbell, Mark. *Carry On Films*. Harpenden: Pocket Essentials, 2005.

Carlyle, Thomas. *On Heroes and Hero-worship and the Heroic in History*. Lincoln, Nebraska: University of Nebraska Press, 1966.

Carpenter, Humphrey. *J.R.R. Tolkien: A Biography*. London: George Allen and Unwin, 1977.

———. *The Inklings: J.R.R. Tolkien, C.S. Lewis, Charles Williams and their Friends*. London: George Allen and Unwin, 1978.

Chambers, Aidan. *The Reluctant Reader*. Oxford: Pergamon, 1969.

Chambers, Iain. *Urban Rhythms: Popular Music and Popular Culture*. London: Souvenir Press, 1985.

Clarke, Arthur C. *Rendezvous with Rama*. New York: Harcourt, Brace, Jovanovich, 1973.

Clute, John. 'The Big Sellers, 3: Terry Pratchett'. *Interzone* 33 (1990): Pp. 24–27.

———. 'Coming of Age'. *Terry Pratchett: Guilty of Literature*. Edited by Andrew M. Butler, Edward James and Farah Mendlesohn. Reading: SFF, 2000. Pp. 7–19.

———. 'Coming of Age'. *Terry Pratchett: Guilty of Literature*. Edited by Andrew M. Butler, Edward James and Farah Mendlesohn. 2nd ed. Baltimore, Maryland: Old Earth Books, 2004. Pp. 15–30.

Clute, John and John Grant, eds. *The Encyclopedia of Fantasy*. London: Orbit, 1997.

Cohen, Jack and Ian Stewart. *The Collapse of Chaos*. London: Viking, 1994.

———. *Figments of Reality*. Cambridge: Cambridge University Press, 1995.

———. *Wheelers*. London: Warner Aspect, 2000.

———. *Evolving the Alien*. London: Ebury, 2002.

———. *Heaven*. London: Warner Aspect, 2005.

Cohen, S. Marc, Patricia Curd and C.D.C. Reeve, eds. *Readings in Ancient Greek Philosophy: From Thales to Aristotle*. Indianapolis, IN: Hackett, 2005.

Connell, R.W. *Gender and Power: Society, the Person, and Sexual Politics*. Stanford: Stanford University Press, 1987.

Connolly, John. *P.G. Wodehouse: An Illustrated Biography*. London: Eel Pie Press, 1979.

Contemporary Literary Criticism. Volume 197: Louis Begley, Terry Pratchett, Christina Hoff Summers and Lanford Wilson. Detroit: Thomson Gale, 2005.

Cormier, Robert. *The Chocolate War*. New York: Pantheon, 1974.

Dentith, Simon. *Parody*. London: Routledge, 2000.

Dines, Gail and Jean M. Humez, eds. *Gender, Race and Class in Media: A Text-Reader*. Thousand Oaks: Sage, 1995.

Doherty, Brian, ed. *American Crime Fiction: Studies in the Genre*. London: Macmillan, 1988.

Doonen, Jane. *Looking at Pictures in Picture Books*. Stroud: Thimble Press, 1993.

Doyle, Sir Arthur Conan. *The Penguin Complete Adventures of Sherlock Holmes*. Harmondsworth, Middlesex: Penguin, 1984.

Dunn, Thomas P. 'Existential Pilgrims and Comic Catastrophe in the Fiction of Robert Sheckley'. *Extrapolation* 26.1 (Spring 1985): Pp. 56–65.

Ebrey, Patricia Buckley. *The Cambridge Illustrated History of China*. Cambridge: Cambridge University Press, 1999.

Eliade, Mircea. *Occultism, Witchcraft and Cultural Fashions: Essays in Comparative Religion*. University of Chicago Press: Chicago, 1976.

Eliot, T.S. 'London Letter'. *The Dial* 73 (December 1922): Pp. 659–663.

English, George. 'Tripping the Light Fantastic: Terry Pratchett'. *Language and Learning* (September/October 1994): Pp. 33–35.

Findlay, Allan M. *The Arab World*. London: Routledge, 1994.

Fiske, John, Bob Hodge and Graeme Turner. *Myths of Oz: Reading Australian Popular Culture*. Sydney: Allen and Unwin, 1987.

Freud, Sigmund. *Jokes and their Relation to the Unconscious*. London: Routledge, 1966.

———. 'Humour'. *Art and Literature*. Harmondsworth, Middlesex: Penguin, 1990. Pp. 425–433.

Frith, Simon. *The Cambridge Companion to Pop and Rock*. Cambridge: Cambridge University Press, 2001.

Fry, Carrol L. "What God Doth the Wizard Pray To': Neo-Pagan Witchcraft and Fantasy Fiction'. *Extrapolation* 31.4 (1990): Pp. 333–346.

Gaiman, Neil. *Don't Panic: The Official Hitch-Hikers Guide to the Galaxy Companion*. London: Titan Books, 1988.

———. *The Sandman*. London: Titan, 1990.

———. 'Webs'. *More Tales from the Forbidden Planet*. Edited by Roz Kaveney. London: Titan Books, 1990. Pp. 136–144.

———. *Death: The High Cost of Living*. London: Titan Books, 1994.

———. *Neverwhere*. London: Penguin, 1997.

———. *Stardust: Being a Romance Within the Realms of Faerie*. London: Titan, 1998.

———. *Coraline*. London: Bloomsbury, 2002.

———. *Anansi Boys*. London: Bloomsbury, 2005.

———. Email to AJP, June 2006.

Gaiman, Neil and David K. Dickson. *Don't Panic: The Official Hitch-Hikers Guide to the Galaxy Companion*. London: Titan Books, 1993.

Gaiman, Neil, David K. Dickson and M.J. Simpson. *Don't Panic: The Official Hitch-Hikers Guide to the Galaxy Companion*. London: Titan Books, 2003.

Gaiman, Neil and M.J. Simpson. *Don't Panic: The Official Hitch-Hikers Guide to the Galaxy Companion*. London: Titan Books, 2002.

Gaiman, Neil and Alex Stewart, Eds. *Temps: Volume One*. London: ROC, 1991.

Galbreath, Robert. 'Taoist Magic in the Earthsea Trilogy'. *Extrapolation* 21.3 (Fall 1980): Pp. 262–268.

Gardiner-Scott, Tanya J. *Mervyn Peake: The Evolution of a Dark Romantic*. New York: Peter Lang, 1989.

Garth, John. *Tolkien and the Great War: The Threshold of Middle-earth*. London: HarperCollins, 2003.

Gelder, Ken. *Reading the Vampire*. London: Routledge, 1994.

Gentle, Mary. *Rats & Gargoyles*. London and New York: Bantam, 1990.

Gentle, Mary and Roz Kaveney, eds. *The Weerde: Book 1*. London: ROC, 1992.

Gibson, William. *Neuromancer*. New York: Ace, 1984.

Gilbert, Sandra M. and Susan Gubar. *The Madwoman in the Attic: The Woman Writer and the Nineteenth-Century Literary Imagination*. New Haven: Yale University Press, 1978.

Gottlieb, Anthony. *The Dream of Reason: A History of Western Philosophy*. London: Penguin, 2001.

Gray, Frances. *Women and Laughter*. London: Macmillan, 1994.

Green, Benny. *P.G. Wodehouse: A Literary Biography*. Oxford: Oxford University Press, 1981.

Greenland, Colin. 'Death and the Modem'. *Fear* 19 (July 1990): Pp. 23–26.

Grout, Donald J. and Hermine Williams Weigel. *A Short History of Opera*. 4th ed. New York: Columbia University Press, 2003.

Gunn, T. Jeremy. 'The Complexity of Religion and the Definition of "Religion" in International Law'. *Harvard Human Rights Journal* 16 (Spring 2003).

Hanes, Stacie. 'Death and the Maiden'. *Terry Pratchett: Guilty of Literature*. Edited by Andrew M. Butler, Edward James and Farah Mendlesohn. 2nd ed. Baltimore, Maryland: Old Earth Books, 2004. Pp. 171–191.

———. 'A Pussy in Black Leather: Greebo & the Queer Aesthetic; OR, Someone Had to Do It'. *Vector: The Critical Journal of the British Science Fiction Association* 241 (May/June 2005): Pp. 10–13.

Hargreaves, Stella. 'The SF Kick: Terry Pratchett Interviewed'. *Interzone* 81 (March 1994): Pp. 25–28.

Haut, Woody. *Neon Noir: Contemporary American Crime Fiction*. London: Serpent's Tail, 1999.

Hayward, Susan. *Key Concepts in Cinema Studies*. London: Routledge, 1996.

Heinlein, Robert A. *Stranger in a Strange Land*. New York: Putnam, 1961.

———. *Orphans of the Sky: A Novel*. New York: Putnam, 1964.

Herbert, Frank. *Dune*. Philadelphia: Chilton Books, 1965.

Herodotus of Halicarnassus. *Histories*. Translated by Aubrey de Selincourt. London: Penguin Classics, 2003.

Higgins, Graham. 'The String Man'. *Temps Volume 1*. Edited by Neil Gaiman and Alex Stewart. London: Roc, 1991. Pp. 189–204.

———. 'Jabberwockish'. *Villains!* Edited by Mary Gentle and Roz Kaveney. London: Roc, 1992. Pp. 251–282.

———. 'Sounds and Sweet Airs'. *The Weerde: Book 2.* Edited by Mary Gentle and Roz Kaveney. London: Roc, 1993. Pp. 151–178.

Hill, Penelope. 'Unseen University'. *Terry Pratchett: Guilty of Literature.* Edited by Andrew M. Butler, Edward James and Farah Mendlesohn. Reading: SFF, 2000. Pp. 51–65.

———. 'Unseen University'. *Terry Pratchett: Guilty of Literature.* Edited by Andrew M. Butler, Edward James and Farah Mendlesohn. 2nd ed. Baltimore, Maryland: Old Earth Books, 2004. Pp. 89–107.

Hills, Matt. *Fan Cultures.* London: Routledge, 2002.

Hills, Matthew. 'Mapping Narrative Space'. *Terry Pratchett: Guilty of Literature.* Edited by Andrew M. Butler, Edward James and Farah Mendlesohn. Reading: SFF, 2000. Pp. 129–144.

———. 'Mapping Narrative Spaces'. *Terry Pratchett: Guilty of Literature.* Edited by Andrew M. Butler, Edward James and Farah Mendlesohn. 2nd ed. Baltimore, Maryland: Old Earth Books, 2004. Pp. 217–237.

Holliday, Liz. 'SFC Interviews: Terry Pratchett'. *Science Fiction Chronicle* 13.7 (April 1992): Pp. 5, 26–27.

hooks, bell. *Black Looks: Race and Representation.* Boston: South End Press, 1992.

Hornung, Erik. *The One and the Many: Conceptions of God in Ancient Egypt.* Translated by John Baines. Ithaca: Cornell University Press, 1996.

Hume, Kathryn. *Fantasy and Mimesis: Responses to Reality in Western Literature.* New York and London: Methuen, 1984.

Hunt, Peter, Ed. *Children's Literature: The Development of Criticism.* London: Routledge, 1990.

———. *An Introduction to Children's Literature.* Oxford: Opus, 1994.

———. 'Terry Pratchett'. Peter Hunt and Millicent Lenz. *Alternative Worlds in Fantasy Fiction.* London: Continuum, 2001. Pp. 86–121.

Hunt, Peter and Millicent Lenz. *Alternative Worlds in Fantasy Fiction.* London and New York: Continuum, 2001.

James, Edward. 'The City Watch'. *Terry Pratchett: Guilty of Literature.* Edited by Andrew M. Butler, Edward James and Farah Mendlesohn. Reading: SFF, 2000. Pp. 112–128.

———. 'The City Watch'. *Terry Pratchett: Guilty of Literature.* Edited by Andrew M. Butler, Edward James and Farah Mendlesohn. 2nd ed. Baltimore, Maryland: Old Earth Books, 2004. Pp. 193–216.

———. 'Weaving the Carpet'. *Terry Pratchett: Guilty of Literature.* Edited by Andrew M. Butler, Edward James and Farah Mendlesohn. 2nd ed. Baltimore, Maryland: Old Earth Books, 2004. Pp. 31–40.

James, Edward and Farah Mendlesohn, eds. *The Cambridge Companion to Science Fiction.* Cambridge: Cambridge University Press, 2003.

Jolliffe, Gray. *Man's Best Friend Introducing Wicked Willie in the Title Role.* With text by Peter Mayle. London: Pan, 1984.

———. *Wicked Willie's Low-Down on Men: The Essential Guide to Male Misbehaviour.* London: Pan, 1987.

———. *Willie's Away!* London: Pan, 1988.

Katz, Wendy R. 'Some Uses of Food in Children's Literature'. *Children's Literature in Education* 11.4 (Winter 1980): Pp. 192–199.

Kaveney, Roz, Ed. *Tales from the Forbidden Planet.* London: Titan, 1987.

———. *More Tales from the Forbidden Planet.* London: Titan, 1990.

Kidby, Paul. *The Pratchett Portfolio.* London: Gollancz, 1996.

———. *The Art of Discworld.* London: Gollancz, 2005.

Kincaid, Paul. 'Terry Pratchett Interview'. *Interzone* 25 (September/October 1988): Pp. 17–19, 39.

———. *A Very British Genre: A Short History of British Fantasy and Science Fiction.* Folkestone: BSFA, 1995.

King, Geoff. *Film Comedy.* London: Wallflower Press, 2002.

Kirby, Josh. *The Josh Kirby Poster Book.* London: Corgi, 1990.

———. *In the Garden of Unearthly Delights.* With text by Nigel Suckling. Limpsfield, Surrey, UK: Paper Tiger, 1991.

———. *The Josh Kirby Discworld Portfolio.* Limpsfield, Surrey, UK: Paper Tiger, 1993.

———. *A Cosmic Cornucopia.* With text by David Langford. London: Paper Tiger, 1999.

Kitto, H.D.F. *The Greeks*. London: Penguin, 1991.
Knox, John. *The First Blast of the Trumpet Against the Monstrous Regiment of Women*. Edited by Edward Arbur. AMS Press: New York, 1967.
Kraus, Lawrence. *The Physics of Star Trek*. New York: Harper Perennial, 1996.
Kropf, Carl R. 'Douglas Adams's Hitchhiker Novels as Mock Science Fiction'. *Science Fiction Studies* 15.1 (March 1988): Pp. 61–70.
Kutzer, M.D. 'Thatchers and Thatcheries: Lost and Found Empires in Three British Fantasies'. *Lion and the Unicorn* 22.2 (1998): Pp. 196–210.
Langford, David. *The Unseen University Challenge: Terry Pratchett's Discworld Quizbook*. London: Gollancz/Vista, 1996.
———. *A Cosmic Cornucopia*. With art by Josh Kirby. London: Paper Tiger, 1999.
———. 'Foreword'. *Terry Pratchett: Guilty of Literature*. Edited by Andrew M. Butler, Edward James and Farah Mendlesohn. Reading: SFF, 2000. Pp. 1–6.
———. *The Complete Critical Assembly*. Gillette, NJ: Cosmos Books, 2001.
———. *The Wyrdest Link: The Second Discworld Quizbook*. London: Gollancz, 2002.
———. *Up Through an Empty House of Stars: Reviews and Essays 1980–2002*. Holicong, PA: Cosmos Books, 2003.
———. 'Introduction'. *Terry Pratchett: Guilty of Literature*. Edited by Andrew M. Butler, Edward James and Farah Mendlesohn. 2nd ed. Baltimore, Maryland: Old Earth Books, 2004. Pp. 3–14.
———. '*The Colour of Magic* by Terry Pratchett (1983)'. *The Greenwood Encyclopedia of Science Fiction and Fantasy: Themes, Works, and Wonders*. Edited by Gary Westfahl. Westport, Connecticut: Greenwood Press, 2005. Pp. 973–975.
Larkin, Philip. 1988. *Collected Poems*. Faber & Faber and Marvell Press: London and Hessle.
Leiber, Fritz. 1968. *Swords Against Wizardry*. New York: Ace.
———. 1968. *Swords in the Mist*. New York: Ace.
———. 1968. *The Swords of Lankhmar*. New York: Ace.
———. 1970. *Swords Against Death*. New York: Ace.
———. 1970. *Swords and Deviltry*. New York: Ace.
———. 1977. *Swords & Ice Magic*. New York: Ace.
———. 1988. *The Knight and Knave of Swords*. New York: Morrow.
Lodge, David. 1975. *Changing Places: A Tale of Two Campuses*. London: Secker and Warburg.
Macintyre, Stuart. 1999. *A Concise History of Australia*. Cambridge: Cambridge University Press.
Manlove, Colin. 1999. *The Fantasy Literature of England*. London: Macmillan.
Manning, Paul. 1984. *1984 and All That*. London: Futura.
Mansfield, Peter. 1973. *The Ottoman Empire and its Successors*. London: Macmillan.
Martin, Thomas R. 2000. *Ancient Greece: From Prehistoric to Hellenistic Times*. New Haven: Yale University Press.
Marvell, Andrew. 2005. *The Complete Poems*. Edited by Elizabeth Story Donno. Introduction by Jonathan Bate. London: Penguin.
Mayle, Peter. 1989. *A Year in Provence*. London: Hamish Hamilton.
McAleavy, Henry. 1967. *The Modern History of China*. London: Weidenfeld and Nicolson.
Meades, Robert and David B. Wake, Eds. 1988. *The Drabble Project*. Birmingham: Beccon Publications.
———. 1990. *Drabble II: Double Century*. Birmingham: Beccon Publications.
Mendlesohn, Farah. 2000. 'Faith and Ethics'. Pp. 145–161 in *Terry Pratchett: Guilty of Literature*. Foreword by David Langford. Edited by Andrew M. Butler, Edward James and Farah Mendlesohn. Reading: SFF.
———. 2003. 'Catching 'em Young: Picture Book Science Fiction for the Under Sevens'. *Vector: The Critical Journal of the British Science Fiction Association* 227 (January/February): P. 47.
———. 2004. 'Faith and Ethics'. Pp. 238–260 in *Terry Pratchett: Guilty of Literature*. Edited by Andrew M. Butler, Edward James and Farah Mendlesohn. 2nd ed. Baltimore, Maryland: Old Earth Books.
———. 2004. 'Toward a Taxonomy of Fantasy'. *Journal of the Fantastic in the Arts* 13.2: Pp. 169–183.
Milne, A.A. 1927. *Now We Are Six*. London: Methuen.
Moers, Walter. 2001. *The 13 1/2 Lives of Captain Bluebear: A Novel*. Translated by Alan Brownjohn. London: Vintage.

Moi, Toril. 1985. *Sexual/Textual Politics*. London and New York: Routledge.
Moody, Nickianne. 2000. 'Death'. Pp. 99–111 in *Terry Pratchett: Guilty of Literature*. Edited by Andrew M. Butler, Edward James and Farah Mendlesohn. Reading: SFF.
———. 2004. 'Death and Work'. Pp. 153–170 in *Terry Pratchett: Guilty of Literature*. Edited by Andrew M. Butler, Edward James and Farah Mendlesohn. 2nd ed. Baltimore, Maryland: Old Earth Books.
Moorcock, Michael. 1987. *Wizardry and Wild Romance: A Study of Epic Fantasy*. London: Gollancz.
Newsinger, John. 2003. 'The People's Republic of Treacle Mine Road Betrayed: Terry Pratchett's *Night Watch*'. *Vector: The Critical Journal of the British Science Fiction Association* 232 (November/December): Pp. 15–16.
Nicholls, Stan. 1993. 'Terry Pratchett Leaves the Furniture Alone'. Pp. 340–347 in *Wordsmiths of Wonder: Fifty Interviews with Writers of the Fantastic*. London: Orbit.
Niven, Larry. 1970. *Ringworld*. New York: Ballantine.
Nobel Foundation, The. 1965. *Nobel Lectures, Physics 1922–1941*. Amsterdam: Elsevier.
Nodelman, Perry. 2000. 'Inside Picture Books'. *Lion and the Unicorn* 24.1 (January): Pp. 150–156.
Norton, Mary. 1952. *The Borrowers*. London: Dent.
O'Brien, Robert C. 1975. *Z for Zachariah*. New York: Atheneum.
Parker, Vic. 2006. *Terry Pratchett*. London: Heinemann.
Peake, Mervyn. 1946. *Titus Groan*. London: Eyre & Spottiswoode.
———. 1950. *Gormenghast*. London: Eyre & Spottiswoode.
———. 1959. *Titus Alone*. London: Eyre & Spottiswoode.
———. 1968. *Titus Alone*. Revised edition by New York: Ballantine.
Platt, Charles. 1986. *How to be a Happy Cat*. London: Gollancz.
Pringle, David, Ed. 1997. *St James' Guide to Fantasy Writers*. New York: St Martin's Press.
———. 1998. *The Ultimate Encyclopedia of Fantasy*. London: Carlton.
Rickman, Gregg, Ed. 2001. *The Film Comedy Reader*. New York: Limelight.
Robb, Brian J. 2001. *Laurel & Hardy*. Harpenden: Pocket Essentials.
Rose, Margaret A. 1993. *Parody: Ancient, Modern, and Post-Modern*. Cambridge: Cambridge University Press.
Rubinstein, Gillian. 1986. *Space Demons*. Norwood, SA: Omnibus Books.
Said, Edward. 1978. *Orientalism: Western Conceptions of the Orient*. Harmondsworth, Middlesex: Penguin.
Sawyer, Andy. 2000. 'The Librarian and His Domain'. Pp. 66–82 in *Terry Pratchett: Guilty of Literature*. Edited by Andrew M. Butler, Edward James and Farah Mendlesohn. Reading: SFF.
———. 2000. 'Narrativium and Lies-to-Children: Palatable Instruction in *The Science of Discworld*'. *HJEAS-Hungarian Journal of English and American Studies* 6: Pp. 155–178.
———.2002. 'Narrativium and Lies-to-Children: Palatable Instruction in *The Science of Discworld*'. *Journal of the Fantastic in the Arts* 13.1: Pp. 62–81.
———. 2004. 'The Librarian and His Domain'. Pp. 108–130 in *Terry Pratchett: Guilty of Literature*. Edited by Andrew M. Butler, Edward James and Farah Mendlesohn. 2nd ed. Baltimore, Maryland: Old Earth Books.
Sayer, Karen. 2000. 'Witches'. Pp. 83–98 in *Terry Pratchett: Guilty of Literature*. Edited by Andrew M. Butler, Edward James and Farah Mendlesohn. Reading: SFF.
———. 2004. 'The Witches'. Pp. 131–152 in *Terry Pratchett: Guilty of Literature*. Edited by Andrew M. Butler, Edward James and Farah Mendlesohn. 2nd ed. Baltimore, Maryland: Old Earth Books.
Schein, Seth L. 1985. *The Mortal Hero: An Introduction to Homer's Iliad*. Berkeley, California: University of California Press.
Sellar, W.C. and R.J. Yeatman. 1930. *1066 and All That*. London: Methuen.
———. 1932. *And Now All This*. London: Methuen.
———. 1933. *Horse Nonsense*. London: Methuen.
———. 1936. *Garden Rubbish and other Country Bumps*. London: Methuen.
Shakespeare, William. 2003. *Twelfth Night*. Edited by Elizabeth Story Donno. Introduced by Penny Gay. Cambridge: Cambridge University Press.
Shaw, Bob. 1975. *Orbitsville*. London: Gollancz.

Shaw, Ian, Ed. 2000. *Oxford History of Ancient Egypt*. Oxford: Oxford University Press.

Sheckley, Robert. 1955. 'The Accountant'. *Citizen in Space*. New York: Ballantine. Pp. 17–26.

———. 1958. *Immortality Delivered*. New York: Avalon.

———. 1966. *Mindswap*. New York: Delacorte.

———. 1968. *Dimension of Miracles*. New York: Dell.

———. 1975. *Options*. New York: Pyramid.

———. 1978. *The Alchemical Marriage of Alistair Crompton*. London: Michael Joseph.

———. 1993. *The Alternative Detective*. New York: Forge.

Shippey, T.A. 1982. *The Road to Middle-Earth*. London: George Allen and Unwin.

———. 2000. *Tolkien: Author of the Century*. London: HarperCollins.

Showalter, Elaine. 1982. *A Literature of Their Own: British Novelists from Brontë to Lessing*. London: Virago.

Sievker, Phyllis. 1997. *Santa Claus, Last of the Wild Men: The Origins and Evolution of Saint Nicholas, Spanning 50,000 Years*. Jefferson, North Carolina: McFarland.

Simpson, M.J. 2003. *Hitchhiker: A Biography of Douglas Adams*. London: Hodder and Stoughton.

Sipe, Lawrence R. 1998. 'How Picture Books Work: A Semiotically Framed Theory of Text-Picture Relationships'. *Children's Literature in Education* 29.2 (June): Pp. 97–108.

Slusser, George E. and Eric S. Rabkin, eds. 1987. *Intersections: Fantasy and Science Fiction*. Carbondale and Edwardsville: Southern Illinois Press.

Stableford, Brian. 1987. *The Sociology of Science Fiction*. San Bernadino: Borgo Press.

Stephenson, Gregory. 1997. *Comic Inferno: The Satirical Work of Robert Sheckley*. San Bernardino, California: Borgo Press.

Stewart, Ian. 1995. *Nature's Numbers: Discovering Order and Pattern in the Universe*. London: Weidenfeld & Nicolson.

———. 1997. *The Magical Maze: Seeing the World Through Mathematical Eyes*. London: Weidenfeld & Nicolson.

———. 1998. *Life's Other Secret: The New Mathematics of the Living World*. London: Allen Lane.

Stoker, Bram. 1897. *Dracula*. London: Constable.

Stubbings, Frank H. and Alan J. Wace. 1963. *Companion to Homer*. London: Macmillan.

Stump, Paul. 1977. *The Music's All That Matters: History of Progressive Rock*. London: Quartet.

Swindells, Robert. 1984. *Brother in the Land*. Oxford: Oxford University Press.

Tatar, Maria. 1999. *The Classic Fairy Tales: Texts, Criticism*. New York: Norton.

Thomas, Dylan. 1954. *Under Milk Wood: A Play For Voices*. London: J.M. Dent.

Todorov, Tzvetan. 1975. *The Fantastic: A Structural Approach to a Literary Genre*. Translated by Richard Howard. Cleveland and London: The Press of Case Western Reserve University.

Tolkien, J.R.R. 1937. *The Hobbit, or There and Back Again*. London: George Allen and Unwin.

———. 1954. *The Fellowship of the Ring*. London: George Allen and Unwin.

———. 1954. *The Two Towers*. London: George Allen and Unwin.

———. 1955. *The Return of the King*. London: George Allen and Unwin.

———. 1964. 'On Fairy-Stories'. *Tree and Leaf*. London: Unwin.

———. 1977. *The Silmarillion*. London: Allen and Unwin.

Tulloch, John and Henry Jenkins. 1995. *Science Fiction Audiences: Watching Dr Who and Star Trek*. London: Routledge.

Wake, David B. and David J. Howe, Eds. 1993. *Drabble Who*. Birmingham: Beccon Publications.

Waugh, Evelyn. 1928. *Decline and Fall: An Illustrated Novelette*. London, Chapman & Hall.

Webber, Richard. 2003. *The Complete A-Z of Everything Carry On*. London: HarperCollins.

Westall, Robert. 1992. *Gulf*. London: Methuen.

Westfahl, Gary W., Ed. 2005. *The Greenwood Encyclopedia of Science Fiction and Fantasy: Themes, Works and Wonders*. Westport, Connecticut: Greenwood.

White, T.H. 1946. *Mistress Masham's Repose*. London: Cape.

———. 1958. *The Once and Future King*. London: Methuen.

Whitman, C.H. 1964. *Aristophanes and the Comic Hero*. Cambridge, Massachusetts: Harvard.

Wignall, Brendan. 1991. 'Throwing People to Stories'. *Interzone* 51: Pp. 6–12.
Winnington, G. Peter. 2000. *Vast Alchemies: The Life and Work of Mervyn Peake*. London: Peter Owen.
Wolfe, Gary K. 1986. *Critical Terms for Science Fiction and Fantasy: A Glossary and Guide to Scholarship*. Westport, Connecticut: Greenwood.
Woodroffe, Patrick. 1987. *The Second Earth: The Pentateuch Re-told*. London: Paper Tiger.
Young, Elizabeth. 1993. 'Funny Old World: From the Mind of Terry Pratchett'. *The Guardian Weekend* (23 October 1993): Pp. 6, 9–10.
Zipes, Jack. 1987. *Victorian Fairy Tales*. London: Methuen.
———. 2000. *Sticks and Stones: The Troublesome Success of Children's Literature from Slovenly Peter to Harry Potter*. New York: Routledge.

Web Pages

Adams, Douglas. http://www.douglasadams.com/
Apple computers page on Graham Higgins: http://www.apple.com/za/creative/digitalimaging/grahamhiggins/index.html
Briggs, Stephen. http://www.cmotdibbler.com/
'Carry On Line'. http://www.carryonline.com/
Colin Smythe Ltd. http://www.colinsmythe.co.uk/
'Cosgrove Hall Ate My Brain'. http://www.nyanko.pwp.blueyonder.co.uk/chamb/
Cosgrove-Hall Films. http://www.chf.co.uk/
Discworld Convention. http://www.dwcon.org/
Discworld Monthly. http://www.discworldmonthly.co.uk/
Discworld MUD. http://discworld.atuin.net/lpc/
Encyclopedia Britannica. 'Schroedinger, Erwin'. http://www.britannica.com/eb/article-9066219
———. 'Shakespeare, William'. http://www.britannica.com/eb/article-232308
English Music Hall. http://www.amaranthdesign.ca/musichall/past/lloyd.htm
Gaiman, Neil. http://www.neilgaiman.com/
Gaiman, Neil and Terry Pratchett (n.d.) 'Crowley and Aziraphale's New Year's Resolutions'. *HarperCollins*, http://www.harpercollins.com/author/AuthorExtra.aspx?displayType=essay&authorID=3417.
The Guardian. 'Author Profiles'. http://books.guardian.co.uk/authors/author/0,,-187,00.html
Guild of Fans and Disciples. http://www.geocities.com/Area51/1777//
Gunn, T. Jeremy. 'The Complexity of Religion and the Definition of 'Religion' in International Law'. *Harvard Human Rights Journal* 16 (Spring 2003): http://www.law.harvard.edu/students/orgs/hrj/iss16/gunn.shtml.
Hackney Empire. http://www.hackneyempire.co.uk/.
Hannan, Tina. http://web.onetel.com/~wulf1/index.htm
HarperCollins. Pratchett Pages. http://www.harpercollins.com/authors/7848/Terry_Pratchett/index.aspx
Higgins, Graham. http://www.pokkettz.demon.co.uk/
Hinckley, Paul. *A Dictionary of Great War Slang*. http://sir.cyivs.cy.edu.tw/~hchung/warslang.htm.
ISIS. http://www.isis-publishing.co.uk/
Kidby, Paul. http://www.paulkidby.com/
Klatchian Foreign Legion. http://groups.yahoo.com/group/WOSSNAME/
Langford, David. 'Book Covers by Josh Kirby'. [checklist prepared with Kirby]: http://ansible.co.uk/misc/joshlist.html
L-Space. http://www.lspace.org/
Mabillard, Amanda. 2000. 'William Shakespeare of Stratford'. http://www.shakespeare-online.com/biography/
Pearson, Bernard. http://www.artificer.co.uk/
Player, Stephen. http://www.playergallery.com
Pratchett, Terry. Carnegie Medal Acceptance Speech, 2001. http://www.carnegiegreenaway.org.uk/press/pres_terspeach.htm
———. 'Paperback Writer'. *The Guardian* (6 December 2003) http://books.guardian.co.uk/review/story/0,12084,1100081,00.html
———. 'Theatre of Cruelty'. http://www.lspace.org/books/toc/
Quantum Technology Centre, University of Southampton. http://www.qtc.ecs.soton.ac.uk/cat.html

Robinson, Tony. http://www.unofficialtonyrobinsonwebsite.co.uk/pages/audio_books/audio_books_pratchett.html
Rules for Cripple Mr Onion: http://cripplemronion.info/
Silver, Steven H. 'A Conversation with Terry Pratchett – Part 1'. *SF Site*. http://www.sfsite.com/04b/tp79.htm
Snowgum Films homepage: http://www.snowgumfilms.com/
'Thud!' http://www.thudgame.com/
Transworld Pratchett Pages. http://www.booksattransworld.co.uk/terrypratchett/home.htm
'Whippit Inn'. http://www.thewhippitinn.com/
Wikipedia. 'Discworld Gods'. http://en.wikipedia.org/wiki/Discworld_gods.
———. 'Sweet Polly Oliver'. http://en.wikipedia.org/wiki/Sweet_Polly_Oliver
Windyridge CDs. Music Hall and Variety Songs on CD. http://www.musichallcds.com/index.html.

About the Editor and Contributors

Editor

Andrew M. Butler teaches Media and Cultural Studies at Canterbury Christ Church University in the UK. He has written widely on science fiction and fantasy, including on Terry Pratchett. For *Vector: The Critical Journal of the British Science Fiction Association*, he was features editor 1995–2005, and he has been a guest editor for *Foundation: The International Review of Science Fiction* and *Science Fiction Studies*. He is also a member of the board of editorial consultants for the latter and has become an editor of *Extrapolation*. His article 'Thirteen Ways of Looking at the British Boom' (*Science Fiction Studies* 30.3, 2003) won the 2004 Pioneer Award for Excellence in Science Fiction Criticism. With Farah Mendlesohn and Edward James, he co-edited *Terry Pratchett: Guilty of Literature* (2000; 2nd edn. 2004), which was nominated for a Hugo award, and, with Farah Mendlesohn, *The True Knowledge of Ken MacLeod* (2003). He is the editor of *Christopher Priest: The Interaction* (2005).

Contributors

Alex Bussey works in the Research Office of Thames Valley University.

Juliana Froggatt has written about Terry Pratchett for *Strange Horizons*, where she is a reviews editor. She has also met him twice and made him sign things both times.

Ximena Gallardo C. is an Assistant Professor at the City University of New York-LaGuardia and co-author of *Alien Woman: The Making of Lt. Ellen Ripley* (Continuum 2004).

David Langford is an author and editor who has won many awards and published some thirty books. For further details, see his entry in this volume.

Zina Lee, a writer, journalist and reviewer, has an entire bookcase devoted just to Terry Pratchett books – not simply the hardcovers, but also the books picked up here and there as a lending library for friends. These days, she considers herself to live more online than in a specific geographical location ... except for that bookcase, of course.

Farah Mendlesohn was co-editor with Andrew M. Butler and Edward James of *Terry Pratchett: Guilty of Literature* and won a Hugo with Edward James for their editing of *The Cambridge Companion to Science Fiction* (2003). She is also the author of *Diana Wynne Jones: Children's Literature and the Fantastic Tradition* (Routledge 2005).

Alan J. Porter is a regular writer on pop culture with a couple of books to his credit plus articles in various magazines.

Andy Sawyer is the Librarian of the Science Fiction Foundation Collection at the Sydney Jones Library, University of Liverpool and is reviews editor of *Foundation: The International Review of Science Fiction.*

Susan Spilecki has published poems in *White Knuckles*, *Star*Line*, *Pirate Writings* and elsewhere and has taught writing.

Mark D. Thomas is a writer living in the north-east United States and has been a Terry Pratchett fan for as long as he can remember.

Amy Vail is Assistant Professor of Classics in the Honors College at Baylor University. Her interests include ancient warfare, Homeric epic and singing opera.

Index

Page numbers in **bold** indicate the location of the main entry.